Math+

2nd Edition

Lesson Guide

Book Staff and Contributors

Sarah Bruce, Tony Freedman   *Content Specialists*
Jennifer Marrewa   *Senior Instructional Designer*
Jill Tunick   *Senior Text Editor*
Debra Foulks   *Text Editor*
Suzanne Montazer   *Creative Director, Print and ePublishing*
Julie Jankowski   *Senior Print Visual Designer, Cover Designer*
Steve Mawyer   *Media Editor*
David Stienecker   *Writer*
Amy Eward   *Senior Manager, Writers*
Susan Raley   *Senior Manager, Editors*
Luz Long   *Senior Project Manager*
Nols Myers   *Director K–8, Program Management*

Lynda Cloud   *Executive Vice President, Product Development*
David Pelizzari   *Vice President, K^{12} Content*
Kim Barcas   *Vice President, Creative*
Christopher Frescholtz   *Senior Director, Program Management*

Lisa Dimaio Iekel   *Director, Print Production and Manufacturing*

Ilustrations Credits
All illustrations © K12 Inc. unless otherwise noted
Cover: Snowboarder. © Ipatov/Shutterstock.com

About K12 Inc.
K12 Inc. (NYSE: LRN) is K12 Inc. (NYSE: LRN) drives innovation and advances the quality of education by delivering state-of-the-art digital learning platforms and technology to students and school districts around the world. K12 is a company of educators offering its online and blended curriculum to charter schools, public school districts, private schools, and directly to families. More information can be found at K12.com.

ISBN: 978-1-60153-437-8   (online book)
ISBN: 978-1-60153-449-1   (printed book)

Printed by Walsworth, Marceline, MO, July 2019.

Contents

Whole Number Multiplication

Whole Number Division Sense

Algebra Thinking

Geometry

Semester Review and Checkpoint

Whole Numbers and Multiple Operations

Fractions and Probability

Measurement: Length and Time

Measurement: Capacity and Weight

Mathematical Reasoning

Perimeter and Area

Semester Review and Checkpoint

Glossary

Program Overview

Lesson Overview

The table at the beginning of each lesson tells you what activities are in the lesson and whether students are on the computer (**ONLINE**) or at a table or desk (**OFFLINE**). The expected time for each activity is given.

Content Background

The Content Background tells you what students will learn in the lesson, and it explains any complex math concepts, putting the lesson into perspective with wider math knowledge.

Advance Preparation

Some lessons require preparation that extends beyond gathering materials. In these cases, the lesson includes an Advance Preparation section.

Lesson Objectives and Prerequisite Skills

Each lesson teaches the Lesson Objectives. The lesson assumes that students know the Prerequisite Skills from their previous math experience. The Get Ready activity is designed to remind students of the Prerequisite Skills and to prepare them for the lesson.

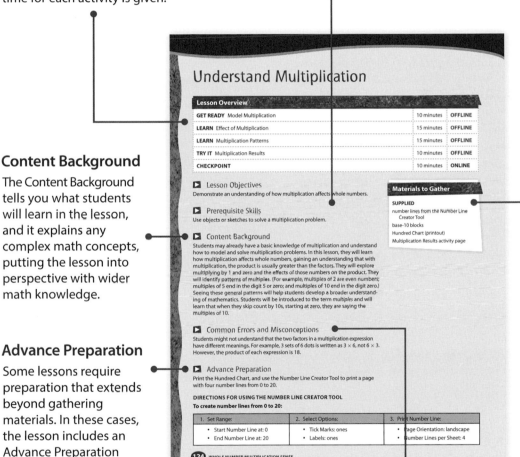

Materials

This box tells you what materials students will need in the lesson. More information about the materials is included on the next page of this overview.

Common Errors and Misconceptions

Research shows that students might misunderstand certain concepts, which then leads to misunderstanding of more advanced concepts. When certain research applies to a lesson, the lesson has a Common Errors and Misconceptions section.

Materials

K[12] supplies math materials, including this Lesson Guide and the Activity Book, the student book.

The **block set** includes various counters as well as 2-D and 3-D shapes. Note that the blocks are labeled with letters. The materials lists in each lesson refer to these blocks by their letter (for instance, B blocks or BB blocks or C blocks). The O blocks refer to the cubes. These blocks aren't labeled with the letter O, but the hole in each block resembles this letter. Within the lesson, you might see a more descriptive term, such as "circles" for the B blocks. A set of base-10 blocks contains blocks representing ones, tens, and hundreds.

Printouts, Plastic Sheet Cover, and Dry-Erase Markers

A lesson may ask you to print a document showing a number line, place-value chart, or other math tool. These documents will be reused throughout the course. We recommend that you obtain a plastic sheet cover and dry-erase markers so students can place the sheet over the printout and write answers on the sheet. They can then erase the answers and reuse the printout multiple times.

Important: Some printouts, including graded Checkpoints, require students to measure shapes or angles. By default, many printers scale documents to fit to a printable area. Be sure to turn off page scaling so that documents print at 100% of their intended size.

Number and Symbol Cards

Index cards labeled with numbers or symbols are frequently called for in the lessons. We recommend that you create a set of index cards numbered 0–100 and use them throughout the course. You can also write on index cards the symbols that will be used most frequently: − (minus), + (plus), = (equals), > (greater than), < (less than).

Math Notebook, Paper, and Pencil

Obtain a binder or spiral notebook to serve as the Math Notebook in which students will work problems, make sketches, and write answers to the problems in the Activity Book. Students should always have notebook paper and a pencil handy. These materials are not listed in each lesson.

Also Needed

Other common items are called for in lessons, designated in the materials list as "Also Needed." Gather or purchase these materials, such as a ruler, scissors, and index cards.

Working Through a Lesson

When you go online with students to do a math lesson, you will see a list of the activities that are included in the lesson.

The Lesson Guide also gives an overview of lesson activities. Instructions for online activities are online. Students may complete these activities independently, or you may sit at the computer with them, reading text to them as necessary. The Lesson Guide may include a teaching tip or other information. In some cases, such as when an open-ended Learning Tool is used, there will be instructions to follow in the Lesson Guide. The online screen will guide you to follow these instructions.

Instructions for offline activities are in the Lesson Guide. These activities may use supplied or common materials, and some include pages from the Activity Book.

Types of Activities

Skills Update Some lessons contain a short problem set covering previously learned math skills taught in previous units or a game to build fluency, or speed, with math facts. Skills Updates appear online only. Students should complete them independently.

Get Ready Review of previous math knowledge that will be needed for this lesson. The Get Ready activities can be online or offline.

Learn Presentation of math concepts, or guided practice. The Learn activities can be online or offline.

Try It Practice problems on the concepts taught in the lesson. Students should complete these problems independently. The Try It activities can be online or in the Activity Book.

Checkpoint Assessments of whether students have learned the objectives taught in the lesson or lessons. Not every lesson has a Checkpoint. In some Checkpoints, students show or explain their answers, and you record their performance.

In addition to the regular Checkpoints, **Unit Reviews** and **Unit Checkpoints** are lessons at the end of each unit. Each semester ends with a **Semester Review** and **Semester Checkpoint**.

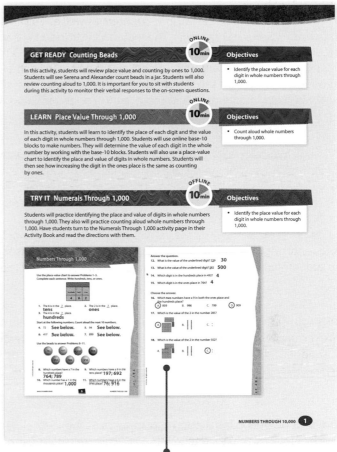

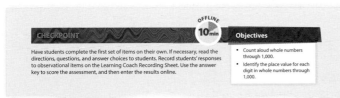

Answer Keys

The Lesson Guide includes the answers, shown in magenta, to the Activity Book pages. The answer keys for offline Checkpoints and Use What You Know activities are provided online. Online Checkpoints are scored by the computer, so no answer key is provided.

Extended Problems An opportunity at the end of each unit to solve problems by integrating the mathematical concepts and skills students have learned from previous units and within the current unit. These lessons contain real-world problems and other problems requiring more complex reasoning. Students submit their completed work.

Online Activities

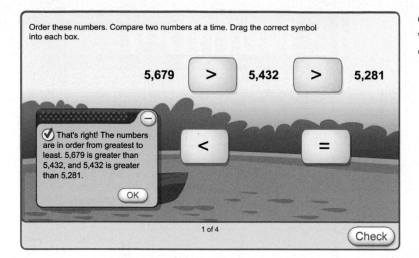

Online activities show whether students answered correctly.

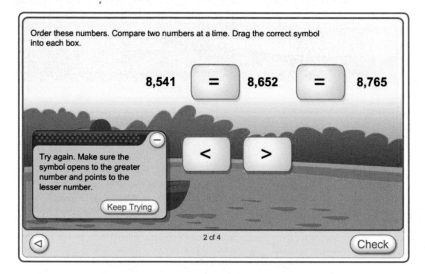

If students answer incorrectly, they see feedback. They should select Keep Trying to try again. If they answer incorrectly a second time, they can select Show Me to see the correct answer.

Learning Tools are online activities that you set up to give students math exercises that apply to what they are learning in a specific lesson.

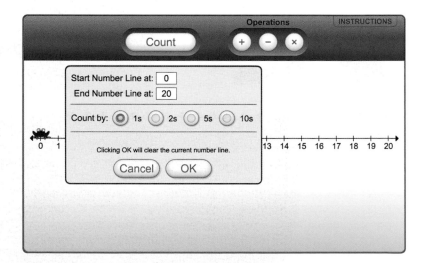

Whole Number Sense

▶ Unit Objectives

- Identify the place value for each digit in whole numbers through 1,000.
- Count aloud whole numbers through 1,000.
- Compare whole numbers through 1,000.
- Order three or more whole numbers through 1,000.
- Round numbers through 1,000.
- Round whole numbers through 1,000 to the nearest ten.
- Round whole numbers through 1,000 to the nearest hundred.

▶ Big Ideas

Place-value notation makes it easier to write and operate on large numbers.

▶ Unit Introduction

In this unit, students will continue their journey through numbers all the way up to 1,000. They will start with place value and counting, and then they will learn to see place values as cumulative multiples of 10. They will round out this unit with rounding. Students will use place-value understanding to round whole numbers to the nearest ten or hundred.

▶ Keywords

boundary number
compare
digit
divide
even numbers
expanded form

greater-than symbol (>)
less-than symbol (<)
multiple
odd numbers
place value

place-value chart
place-value mat
place-value period
round (v.)
standard form

Numbers Through 1,000

Lesson Overview

LEARN Counting Beads	10 minutes	**ONLINE**
LEARN Place Value Through 1,000	20 minutes	**ONLINE**
LEARN Count to 1,000	10 minutes	**OFFLINE**
TRY IT Numerals Through 1,000	10 minutes	**OFFLINE**
CHECKPOINT	5 minutes	**ONLINE**
CHECKPOINT	5 minutes	**OFFLINE**

▶ Lesson Objectives

- Identify the place value for each digit in whole numbers through 1,000.
- Count aloud whole numbers through 1,000.

▶ Content Background

Students will learn to identify the place and value of digits in numbers through 1,000. Students will also learn to count aloud numbers through 1,000, starting at any number less than 1,000.

The smallest base-10 block is a ones cube. It has a value of 1. Ten ones cubes combine to make a tens rod. It has a value of 10. Ten tens rods combine to make a hundreds flat. It has a value of 100. Ten hundreds flats combine to make a thousands cube. It has a value of 1,000. Students can use these blocks to model and represent numbers.

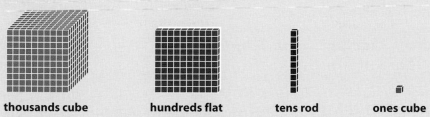

| thousands cube | hundreds flat | tens rod | ones cube |

Students often struggle to understand the value of each digit in a number. They may incorrectly say that the greatest digit in a number has the greatest value. First, students must understand that the numbers 0 through 9 are called *digits*. The digits 0 through 9 can be used to write any number in the base-10 system. The math term *digit* refers to a specific number within another number.

Example: In the number 462, there are three digits: 4, 6, and 2.

hundreds	tens	ones
4	6	2

Materials to Gather

SUPPLIED

Count to 1,000 activity page

Numerals Through 1,000 activity page

Checkpoint (printout)

Checkpoint Answer Key (printout)

place-value mat

base-10 blocks

The place where a digit is located is its *place value*. Once students are able to identify the place value of each digit in whole numbers to 1,000, they can then use the place value to determine the digit's value. For example, in the number 462, the 4 is in the hundreds place and has a value of 400.

Starting from right to left, each group of three digits (or place-value positions) in a whole number is called a *place-value period*. Commas separate each period and are useful when reading greater whole numbers correctly.

▶ Common Errors and Misconceptions

- Students might not realize that a digit's place-value position determines its value. For example, students might think the digits in 14 have values of 1 and 4, not 10 and 4.

- Students might not think of numbers as groups of tens, hundreds, and so on. For example, students might think of 24 only as 24 single units, not 2 tens and 4 ones.

- Students might have difficulty thinking of numbers as groups of tens, hundreds, and so on because some English number words do not emphasize place value. For example, the number word *twelve* does not suggest 1 ten and 2 ones.

- Students might have difficulty thinking of numbers as groups of tens, hundreds, and so on because the teaching of place-value concepts often moves too quickly to the use of abstract symbols.

▶ Safety

Be sure students have ample space to work with the base-10 blocks.

ONLINE

10min

LEARN Counting Beads

Students will review counting by ones to 1,000. They will see Serena and Alexander count beads in a jar. As the beads appear, have students count aloud. 0rst students will start at 1 and count forward to 10. Then they'll jump to 297 and count forward to 300. After that, they'll go to 995 and count forward to 1,000. Students will then review place value and see why 3 and 300 are so different. Finally they will identify the place value of the digits in a three-digit number.

It is important for you to sit with students during this activity to monitor their counting and responses to on-screen questions.

If students are having difficulty counting numbers in the hundreds, have them practice counting two-digit numbers. Remind students that counting by ones follows a pattern. The digit in the ones place increases by 1 each time you count forward.

Objectives

- Identify the place value for each digit in whole numbers through 1,000.

- Count aloud whole numbers through 1,000.

LEARN Place Value Through 1,000

ONLINE 20 min

Objectives

Students will learn to identify the place and value of each digit in whole numbers through 1,000. They will use online base-10 blocks to make numbers. They will determine the value of each digit in the whole number by working with the base-10 blocks. Students will also use a place-value chart to identify the place and value of digits in whole numbers. They will then see how increasing the digit in the ones place is the same as counting by ones.

- Identify the place value for each digit in whole numbers through 1,000.

LEARN Count to 1,000

OFFLINE 10 min

Objectives

Students will learn to count whole numbers through 1,000. They will use base-10 blocks and a place-value chart to model numbers and show counting by ones.
Gather the base-10 blocks and place-value mat.

- Count aloud whole numbers through 1,000.

1. Begin by practicing counting aloud by ones from 0 to 50. Explain the pattern for counting by ones.

   Say: The digit in the ones place increases by 1 for 0 through 9. Then we regroup the ones to make a 10, and the digit in the ones place becomes 0.

   Emphasize that counting by ones will always produce this pattern, even when counting greater numbers.

2. Have students use base-10 blocks to model the number 836 on their place-value mat. Tell students the number is eight hundred thirty-six.

3. Ask students to identify the ones place and the digit in the ones place. Tell students that when we count by ones, the digit in the ones place increases by one.

4. Have students add ones cubes, one at a time, to the ones place. Count aloud with students each time a ones cube is added to the place-value mat. Continue counting forward to 850. Remember to regroup 10 ones to make 1 ten each time there are 10 ones in the ones place.

5. Next make the number 196, using base-10 blocks, on the place-value mat. Continue counting forward to 212, adding ones cubes to the place-value mat and regrouping when needed. Have students use 10 of their tens rods to make a second hundreds flat.

6. When students are comfortable using the base-10 blocks to count by ones, practice counting aloud without the blocks. Start at the following numbers: 500, 538, 850, 875, and 898. Count forward 15 to 20 numbers each time. Students should identify when they go across place values.

7. Have students turn to the Count to 1,000 activity page in their Activity Book and read the directions with them. Students should copy the problems from the Activity Book into their Math Notebook as necessary and solve them there.

Tips

If students are having difficulty counting greater numbers, have them practice counting two- and three-digit numbers by ones. Recognizing the pattern in the ones place when counting by ones is an important skill. Students can continue to model numbers using a place-value mat and base-10 blocks until they understand and can explain the pattern.

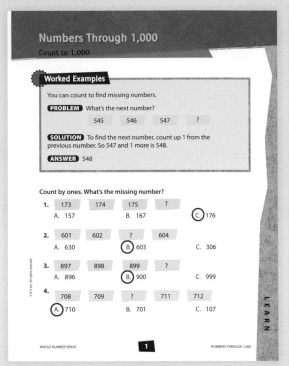

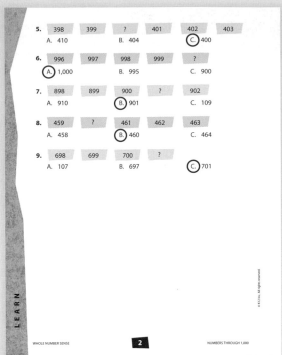

Numbers Through 1,000
Count to 1,000

Worked Examples

You can count to find missing numbers.

PROBLEM What's the next number?

| 545 | 546 | 547 | ? |

SOLUTION To find the next number, count up 1 from the previous number. So 547 and 1 more is 548.

ANSWER 548

Count by ones. What's the missing number?

1.
| 173 | 174 | 175 | ? |
A. 157   B. 167   C. 176

2.
| 601 | 602 | ? | 604 |
A. 630   B. 603   C. 306

3.
| 897 | 898 | 899 | ? |
A. 896   B. 900   C. 999

4.
| 708 | 709 | ? | 711 | 712 |
A. 710   B. 701   C. 107

5.
| 398 | 399 | ? | 401 | 402 | 403 |
A. 410   B. 404   C. 400

6.
| 996 | 997 | 998 | 999 | ? |
A. 1,000   B. 995   C. 900

7.
| 898 | 899 | 900 | ? | 902 |
A. 910   B. 901   C. 109

8.
| 459 | ? | 461 | 462 | 463 |
A. 458   B. 460   C. 464

9.
| 698 | 699 | 700 | ? |
A. 107   B. 697   C. 701

WHOLE NUMBER SENSE — 1 — NUMBERS THROUGH 1,000

WHOLE NUMBER SENSE — 2 — NUMBERS THROUGH 1,000

TRY IT Numerals Through 1,000

OFFLINE 10 min

Objectives

Students will practice identifying the place and value of digits in whole numbers through 1,000. They also will practice counting aloud whole numbers through 1,000. Have students turn to the Numerals Through 1,000 activity page in their Activity Book and read the directions with them.

Students should copy the problems from the Activity Book into their Math Notebook as necessary and solve them there.

- Identify the place value for each digit in whole numbers through 1,000.
- Count aloud whole numbers through 1,000.

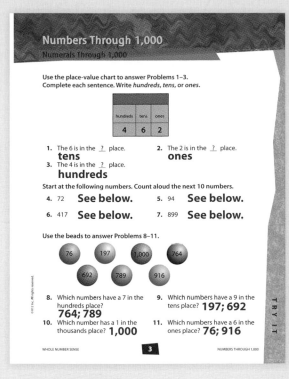

Numbers Through 1,000
Numerals Through 1,000

Use the place-value chart to answer Problems 1–3.
Complete each sentence. Write *hundreds, tens,* or *ones.*

hundreds	tens	ones
4	6	2

1. The 6 is in the ? place. **tens**
2. The 2 is in the ? place. **ones**
3. The 4 is in the ? place. **hundreds**

Start at the following numbers. Count aloud the next 10 numbers.

4. 72 **See below.**
5. 94 **See below.**
6. 417 **See below.**
7. 899 **See below.**

Use the beads to answer Problems 8–11.

76   197   1,000   764
692   789   916

8. Which numbers have a 7 in the hundreds place? **764; 789**
9. Which numbers have a 9 in the tens place? **197; 692**
10. Which number has a 1 in the thousands place? **1,000**
11. Which numbers have a 6 in the ones place? **76; 916**

WHOLE NUMBER SENSE   **3**   NUMBERS THROUGH 1,000

T R Y   I T

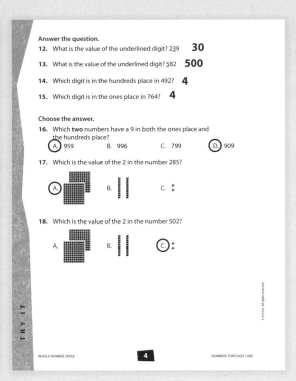

Answer the question.
12. What is the value of the underlined digit? 2<u>3</u>9 **30**
13. What is the value of the underlined digit? <u>5</u>82 **500**
14. Which digit is in the hundreds place in 492? **4**
15. Which digit is in the ones place in 764? **4**

Choose the answer.
16. Which **two** numbers have a 9 in both the ones place and the hundreds place?
(A.) 959   B. 996   C. 799   (D.) 909

17. Which is the value of the 2 in the number 285?
(A.)   B.   C.

18. Which is the value of the 2 in the number 502?
A.   B.   (C.)

T R Y   I T

WHOLE NUMBER SENSE   **4**   NUMBERS THROUGH 1,000

Additional Answers

4. 73; 74; 75; 76; 77; 78; 79; 80; 81; 82
5. 95; 96; 97; 98; 99; 100; 101; 102; 103; 104
6. 418; 419; 420; 421; 422; 423; 424; 425; 426; 427
7. 900; 901; 902; 903; 904; 905; 906; 907; 908; 909

ONLINE
5min

CHECKPOINT

Objectives

Students will complete this part of the Checkpoint online. If necessary, read the directions, problems, and answer choices to students and help students with keyboard or mouse operations.

- Identify the place value for each digit in whole numbers through 1,000.

OFFLINE
5min

CHECKPOINT

Objectives

The Checkpoint and its answer key are located in the Resources section of *Math+ Purple Lesson Guide.* Open the Checkpoint. Record students' responses on the Learning Coach Recording Sheet. Use the answer key to score the Checkpoint, and then enter the results online.

- Count aloud whole numbers through 1,000.

Compare and Order Numbers Through 1,000

Lesson Overview

GET READY Compare Numbers Through 100	5 minutes	ONLINE
LEARN Compare Numbers Through 1,000	15 minutes	ONLINE
LEARN Order Numbers Through 1,000	15 minutes	ONLINE
TRY IT Compare and Order Numbers	5 minutes	ONLINE
CHECKPOINT	10 minutes	ONLINE

▶ ## Lesson Objectives

- Compare whole numbers through 1,000.
- Order three or more whole numbers through 1,000.

▶ ## Prerequisite Skills

Compare whole numbers through 100 by using the symbols $<$, $=$, or $>$.

▶ ## Content Background

The terms *sign* and *symbol* are often used interchangeably. Although *sign* may be used to refer to greater than ($>$), less than ($<$), and equals ($=$), *symbol* will be used in this lesson as it is a more accurate mathematical term. In math, *sign* specifically refers to the positive signs and negative signs of numbers.

▶ ## Common Errors and Misconceptions

- Students might compare numbers based on the ones digits as opposed to the digits in the greatest place-value position. For example, students might think 69 is greater than 71 because 9 is greater than 1.
- Students might have more difficulty using the word *less* to compare numbers than using the word *more*.
- Students might misinterpret the equals symbol ($=$) as a signal they should "do" something. For example, in the number sentence $5 + 3 =$ ___, students might think the equals symbol means "adds up to" or "produces." So they might view $8 = 5 + 3$ or $8 = 8$ as unacceptable or wrong because they believe the equals symbol must be followed by the answer to a problem.

Materials to Gather

SUPPLIED

base-10 blocks (optional)

place-value mat (optional)

GET READY Compare Numbers Through 100

ONLINE 5min

Students will use <, >, and = to compare two numbers through 100.
As students complete the activity, ask the following questions:

- Which is the greater number?
- Which is the lesser number?
- How can you say the comparison a different way? (Note: One set of numbers is equal. The comparison for those numbers cannot be said a different way.)

Objectives

- Compare whole numbers through 100 by using the symbols <, =, or >.

Tips

Students can build the numbers in each pair with base-10 blocks, and then compare the blocks.

LEARN Compare Numbers Through 1,000

ONLINE 15min

Students will use <, >, and = to compare whole numbers through 1,000. First, students will identify the place-value position that is used to compare two numbers. For instance, if the numbers were 643 and 651, students would see that the digits in the hundreds places were the same. They would then look at the digits in the tens places. They would determine that 643 is less than (<) 651.

Then students will identify the symbol that correctly compares two numbers. Finally, students will order the digits in three-digit numbers to make the greatest numbers possible. They'll use the numbers they ordered in comparison statements.

Objectives

- Compare whole numbers through 1,000.

Tips

Students can write numbers in place-value charts to help make comparisons.

LEARN Order Numbers Through 1,000

ONLINE 15min

Students will use the <, >, and = symbols to order three or more numbers through 1,000 from greatest to least or least to greatest.
As students complete the activity, ask the following questions:

- Which is the greatest number?
- Which is the least number?
- How can you order the numbers a different way? (Note: One set of numbers is equal. Those numbers cannot be ordered in a different way.)

Objectives

- Order three or more whole numbers through 1,000.

Tips

Students can use a number line to help order numbers from greatest to least or least to greatest.

TRY IT Compare and Order Numbers

Objectives

- Compare whole numbers through 1,000.
- Order three or more whole numbers through 1,000.

Students will practice comparing and ordering numbers through 1,000.

CHECKPOINT

Objectives

- Compare whole numbers through 1,000.
- Order three or more whole numbers through 1,000.

Students will complete an online Checkpoint. If necessary, read the directions, problems, and answer choices to students and help them with keyboard or mouse operations.

Round Numbers Through 1,000

Lesson Overview

GET READY Compare Numbers	5 minutes	ONLINE
LEARN Round to the Nearest Ten	15 minutes	ONLINE
LEARN Round to the Nearest Hundred	15 minutes	OFFLINE
TRY IT Round to Tens and Hundreds	15 minutes	OFFLINE
CHECKPOINT	10 minutes	ONLINE

▶ Lesson Objectives

- Round whole numbers through 1,000 to the nearest ten.
- Round whole numbers through 1,000 to the nearest hundred.
- Round numbers through 1,000.

▶ Prerequisite Skills

- Identify the place value for each digit in whole numbers through 1,000.
- Compare whole numbers through 1,000.

Materials to Gather

SUPPLIED

Round to the Nearest Hundred (printout)

Round to Tens and Hundreds activity page

▶ Content Background

Students will learn how to round whole numbers through 1,000. They will use a number line to visualize the position of a target number between two boundary numbers. Boundary numbers are the numbers less than and greater than the target number. For example, if the target number 845 is to be rounded to the nearest hundred, the boundary numbers are 800 and 900. Students decide whether 845 is closer to 800 or to 900. The answer is that 845 rounded to the nearest hundred is 800. The selection of boundary numbers depends on whether the problem asks for rounding to the nearest ten or hundred. Then students identify the boundary number that is closest to the target number.

This lesson provides students with their first experience rounding numbers. Numbers are rounded to the nearest ten or hundred.

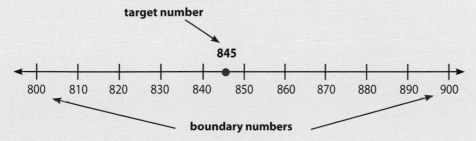

▶ Advance Preparation

Print one copy of Round to the Nearest Hundred.

GET READY Compare Numbers

Students will review place value through 1,000. Then they will use place value to compare whole numbers through 1,000. Students will determine if comparisons are true or false.

As students complete the activity, have them say each comparison correctly. For example, "Four hundred thirty-two is greater than two hundred eighty-nine."

Objectives

- Identify the place value for each digit in whole numbers through 1,000.
- Compare whole numbers through 1,000.

Tips

Students can use a place-value chart to compare numbers.

LEARN Round to the Nearest Ten

Students will learn that rounding is useful when they don't need to know an exact amount. They will help Serena and Alexander round amounts of jelly beans to the nearest hundred.

Students will then use number lines to round numbers to the nearest ten. They will learn that the target number is the number that they are asked to round (in this activity, to the nearest ten). They will learn that when they round to the nearest ten, boundary numbers are the multiples of ten that are before and after the target number. After finding the boundary numbers, students will identify which boundary number is closer to the target number.

As students complete the activity, ask the following questions:

- What is the target number?
- What place are you rounding to? tens
- What are the boundary numbers?
- Which boundary number is closer to the target number?

Objectives

- Round whole numbers through 1,000 to the nearest ten.

LEARN Round to the Nearest Hundred

Students will use number lines on the Round to the Nearest Hundred printout to round numbers. First, students will identify the boundary numbers. Boundary numbers are the tens or hundreds that are before and after the target number. Then students will identify which boundary number is closer to the target number. If the target number is exactly halfway between the boundary numbers, students should round to the greater number.

Gather the Round to the Nearest Hundred printout.

Objectives

- Round whole numbers through 1,000 to the nearest hundred.

Tell students that they can round numbers to the nearest hundred. Explain that when they round to the nearest hundred, they look for the hundreds before and after the target number. Then they choose the hundred that the target number is closest to.

1. Give students the Round to the Nearest Hundred printout. Point to the number line to 1,000. Have students count by hundreds.

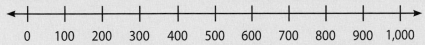

2. Mark a dot on the number line where 838 would go, and label it **838**.

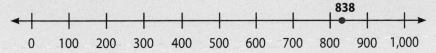

3. **Ask:** Look at the number line, and underline the two boundary numbers for rounding 838 to the nearest hundred. 800 and 900

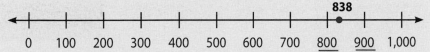

4. **Ask:** Is 838 closer to 800 or 900? Circle the closer number. 800

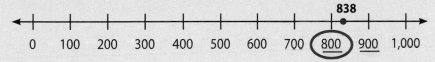

5. Repeat Steps 2–4 for the target numbers that follow, having students round to the nearest hundred. Remind students that if the target number is exactly halfway between the boundary numbers, they should round to the greater number.

   - 862
   - 250
   - 671
   - 845
   - 431

   Have students write the boundary numbers in their Math Notebook and circle the one that the target number is closer to.

Target number	Boundary numbers
862	800, (900)
250	200, (300)
671	600, (700)
845	(800,) 900
431	(400,) 500

TRY IT Round to Tens and Hundreds

Objectives

- Round numbers through 1,000.

Students will practice rounding numbers through 1,000. Have students turn to the Round to Tens and Hundreds activity page in their Activity Book and read the directions with them.

Students should copy the problems from the Activity Book into their Math Notebook as necessary and solve them there.

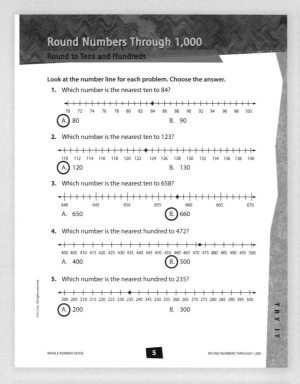

Round Numbers Through 1,000
Round to Tens and Hundreds

Look at the number line for each problem. Choose the answer.

1. Which number is the nearest ten to 84?
   (A.) 80   B. 90

2. Which number is the nearest ten to 123?
   (A.) 120   B. 130

3. Which number is the nearest ten to 658?
   A. 650   (B.) 660

4. Which number is the nearest hundred to 472?
   A. 400   (B.) 500

5. Which number is the nearest hundred to 235?
   (A.) 200   B. 300

Write the answer.

6. If you want to round 348 to the nearest hundred, what are the boundary numbers? **300 and 400**

7. Round 343 to the nearest ten. **340**

8. Round 465 to the nearest hundred. **500**

Choose the answer.

9. Michael wants to round 809 to the nearest hundred. Which boundary numbers should he use?
   A. 800 and 810   (B.) 800 and 900
   C. 800 and 1,000   D. 700 and 800

10. Dawn says 14 rounded to the nearest ten is 10. Eddie says 14 rounded to the nearest ten is 0. Who is correct? Why?
    (A.) Dawn is correct because the ten nearest to 14 is 10.
    B. Eddie is correct because 14 is closer to 0 than to 20.

11. Which shows 408 rounded to the nearest hundred?
    A. 401   B. 410   (C.) 400   D. 500

12. Which shows 132 rounded to the nearest ten?
    A. 100   (B.) 130   C. 140   D. 200

13. Which shows 678 rounded to the nearest hundred?
    A. 600   B. 670   C. 680   (D.) 700

14. Which shows 765 rounded to the nearest ten?
    A. 700   B. 760   (C.) 770   D. 800

Write the answer.

15. Gina wants to round 672 to the nearest ten. Explain how she should do it. **See right.**

16. Explain how to round 452 to the nearest hundred. **See right.**

17. Lila says that 772 rounded to the nearest hundred is 700. Is Lila correct? Explain why or why not. **See right.**

18. Calvin rounded the numbers 122 and 237 to the nearest ten before adding. Marsha rounded the same numbers to the nearest hundred before adding. Which method gave the closer estimate?

    Calvin's method

Additional Answers

15. 670; Answers will vary.
    Sample explanation: 672 is closer to 670 than to 680.

16. 500; Answers will vary.
    Sample explanation: 452 is closer to 500 than to 400.

17. No.
    Sample explanation: 772 rounded to the nearest hundred is 800, not 700. 772 is closer to 800 than it is to 900.

ONLINE
10 min

Objectives

Students will complete an online Checkpoint. If necessary, read the directions, problems, and answer choices to students and help them with keyboard or mouse operations.

- Round whole numbers through 1,000 to the nearest ten.
- Round whole numbers through 1,000 to the nearest hundred.

Core Focus
Rounding

▶ ## Lesson Objectives

- Round whole numbers through 1,000 to the nearest ten.
- Round whole numbers through 1,000 to the nearest hundred.

▶ ## Prerequisite Skills

- Identify the place value for each digit in whole numbers through 1,000.
- Compare whole numbers through 1,000.

▶ ## Content Background

Students will review how to round whole numbers through 1,000 to the nearest ten and nearest hundred. They will use a number line to visualize the position of a target number between two boundary numbers.

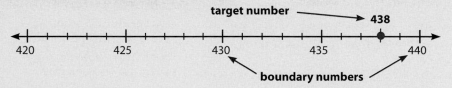

Students will use their knowledge of rounding numbers to solve real-world problems.

Materials to Gather

SUPPLIED

Round to Solve activity page

GET READY Order Numbers Through 1,000

ONLINE
5min

Students will review using the $<$, $>$, and $=$ symbols to order three or more numbers through 1,000 from greatest to least and from least to greatest.
As students complete the activity, ask the following questions:

- Which is the greatest number? How do you know?
- Which is the least number? How do you know?
- How can you order the numbers a different way? (Note: If numbers are ordered from least to greatest, they can be ordered from greatest to least. If they are ordered from greatest to least, they can be ordered from least to greatest.)

Objectives

- Order three or more whole numbers through 1,000.

Tips

Students can use a number line to help order numbers from greatest to least and from least to greatest.

LEARN Round to the Nearest Ten and Hundred

Objectives

- Round whole numbers through 1,000 to the nearest ten.
- Round whole numbers through 1,000 to the nearest hundred.

Students will learn that rounding is useful when they don't need to know an exact amount or want to make an estimate. They will help Alexander round the number of baseball cards in his collection to the nearest ten and to the nearest hundred.

Students will then use number lines to round three-digit numbers to the nearest ten and nearest hundred to solve problems. As they solve problems, students will need to recall that a target number is the number that they are asked to round (in this activity, first to the nearest ten and then to the nearest hundred). They will recall that when they round to the nearest ten, boundary numbers are the multiples of 10 that are before and after the target number. When they round to the nearest hundred, boundary numbers are the multiples of 100 that are before and after the target number.

After finding the boundary numbers, students will identify which boundary number is closer to the target number. If the target number is exactly halfway between the boundary numbers, students should round to the greater number.

As students complete the activity, ask the following questions:

- What is the target number?
- What place are you rounding to? (tens or hundreds)
- What are the boundary numbers?
- Which boundary number is closer to the target number?

TRY IT Round to Solve

Objectives

- Round whole numbers through 1,000 to the nearest ten.
- Round whole numbers through 1,000 to the nearest hundred.

Students will practice rounding whole numbers through 1,000 to the nearest ten and nearest hundred. Have students turn to the Round to Solve activity page in their Activity Book and read the directions with them.

Students should copy the problems from the Activity Book into their Math Notebook as necessary and solve them there.

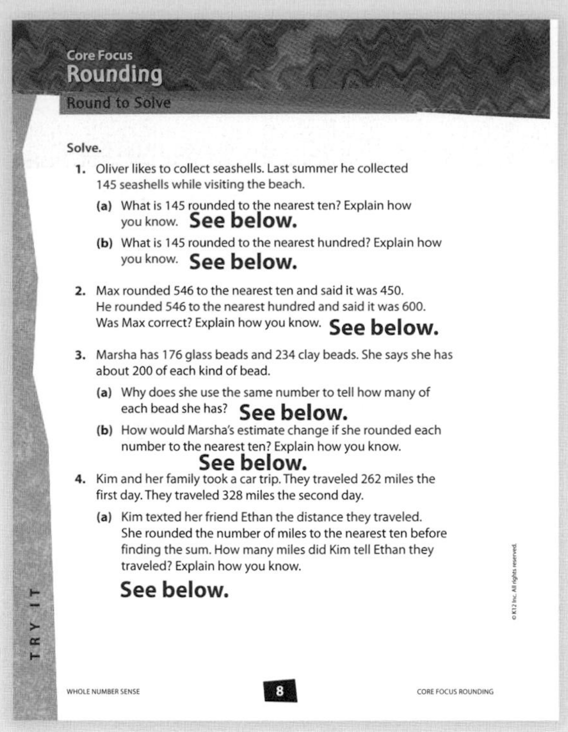
Core Focus
Rounding
Round to Solve

Solve.

1. Oliver likes to collect seashells. Last summer he collected 145 seashells while visiting the beach.
   (a) What is 145 rounded to the nearest ten? Explain how you know. **See below.**
   (b) What is 145 rounded to the nearest hundred? Explain how you know. **See below.**
2. Max rounded 546 to the nearest ten and said it was 450. He rounded 546 to the nearest hundred and said it was 600. Was Max correct? Explain how you know. **See below.**
3. Marsha has 176 glass beads and 234 clay beads. She says she has about 200 of each kind of bead.
   (a) Why does she use the same number to tell how many of each bead she has? **See below.**
   (b) How would Marsha's estimate change if she rounded each number to the nearest ten? Explain how you know. **See below.**
4. Kim and her family took a car trip. They traveled 262 miles the first day. They traveled 328 miles the second day.
   (a) Kim texted her friend Ethan the distance they traveled. She rounded the number of miles to the nearest ten before finding the sum. How many miles did Kim tell Ethan they traveled? Explain how you know.
   See below.

TRY IT

© K12 Inc. All rights reserved.

WHOLE NUMBER SENSE 8 CORE FOCUS ROUNDING

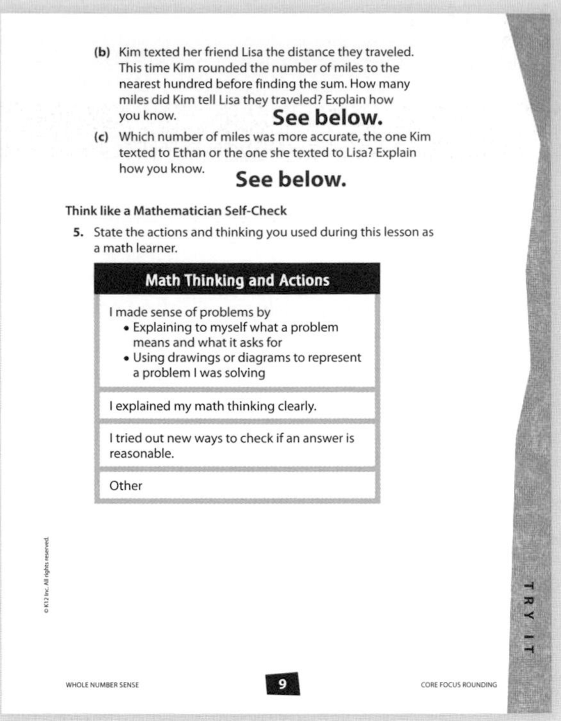
   (b) Kim texted her friend Lisa the distance they traveled. This time Kim rounded the number of miles to the nearest hundred before finding the sum. How many miles did Kim tell Lisa they traveled? Explain how you know. **See below.**
   (c) Which number of miles was more accurate, the one Kim texted to Ethan or the one she texted to Lisa? Explain how you know. **See below.**

Think like a Mathematician Self-Check

5. State the actions and thinking you used during this lesson as a math learner.

Math Thinking and Actions
I made sense of problems by • Explaining to myself what a problem means and what it asks for • Using drawings or diagrams to represent a problem I was solving
I explained my math thinking clearly.
I tried out new ways to check if an answer is reasonable.
Other

© K12 Inc. All rights reserved.

TRY IT

WHOLE NUMBER SENSE 9 CORE FOCUS ROUNDING

Additional Answers

1. **(a)** 150; **Possible explanation:** 145 is exactly halfway between 140 and 150, so 145 rounds to 150.

   (b) 100; **Possible explanation:** 145 is closer to 100 than 200, so 145 rounds to 100.

2. Max was not correct. **Possible explanation:** 546 rounds to 550 because it is closer to 550 than 540 on a number line. 550 rounds to 600, but 546 rounds to 500 because 546 is closer to 500 than 600.

3. **(a) Possible answer:** Marsha rounded each number to the nearest hundred. 175 rounds to 200 and 225 rounds to 200.

   (b) 180 and 230; **Possible explanation:** 176 is closer to 180 than 170. 234 is closer to 230 than 240.

4. **(a)** about 590 miles; **Possible explanation:** 262 rounded to the nearest ten is 260. 328 rounded to the nearest ten is 330. $260 + 330 = 590$.

   (b) about 600 miles; **Possible explanation:** 262 rounded to the nearest hundred is 300. 328 rounded to the nearest hundred is 300. $300 + 300 = 600$.

   (c) The number of miles Kim texted to Ethan is more accurate. **Possible explanation:** Rounding to the nearest ten is closer to the actual number of miles than rounding to the nearest hundred.

CHECKPOINT

ONLINE 10min

Students will complete an online Checkpoint. If necessary, read the directions, problems, and answer choices to students and help them with keyboard or mouse operations.

Objectives

- Round whole numbers through 1,000.

Unit Review

Lesson Overview

UNIT REVIEW Look Back	10 minutes	**ONLINE**
UNIT REVIEW Checkpoint Practice	50 minutes	**ONLINE**
▶ **UNIT REVIEW** Prepare for the Checkpoint		

▶ Unit Objectives

- Identify the place value for each digit in whole numbers through 1,000.
- Count aloud whole numbers through 1,000.
- Compare whole numbers through 1,000.
- Order three or more whole numbers through 1,000.
- Round numbers through 1,000.
- Round whole numbers through 1,000 to the nearest ten.
- Round whole numbers through 1,000 to the nearest hundred.

▶ Advance Preparation

In this lesson, students will have an opportunity to review previous activities in the Whole Number Sense unit. Look at the suggested activities in Unit Review: Prepare for the Checkpoint online and gather any needed materials.

> **Materials to Gather**
>
> There are no materials to gather for this lesson.

UNIT REVIEW Look Back

 10 min ONLINE

Students will review key concepts from the unit to prepare for the Unit Checkpoint.

Objectives

- Review unit objectives.

UNIT REVIEW Checkpoint Practice

50 min ONLINE

Students will complete an online Checkpoint Practice to prepare for the Unit Checkpoint. If necessary, read the directions, problems, and answer choices to students. Have students answer the problems on their own. Review any missed problems with students.

Objectives

- Review unit objectives.

▶ UNIT REVIEW Prepare for the Checkpoint

What you do next depends on how students performed in the previous activity, Unit Review: Checkpoint Practice. If students had difficulty with any of the problems, complete the appropriate review activity listed in the table online.

Unit Checkpoint

▶ Unit Objectives

- Identify the place value for each digit in whole numbers through 1,000.
- Count aloud whole numbers through 1,000.
- Compare whole numbers through 1,000.
- Order three or more whole numbers through 1,000.
- Round numbers through 1,000.
- Round whole numbers through 1,000 to the nearest ten.
- Round whole numbers through 1,000 to the nearest hundred.

Materials to Gather

There are no materials to gather for this lesson.

UNIT CHECKPOINT Online

Objectives

- Assess unit objectives.

Students will complete the Unit Checkpoint online. Read the directions, problems, and answer choices to students. If necessary, help students with keyboard or mouse operations.

Extended Problems: Reasoning

Lesson Overview

USE WHAT YOU KNOW Offline   60 minutes   **OFFLINE**

▶ Lesson Objectives

This lesson assesses the following objectives:

- Round whole numbers through 1,000 to the nearest ten.
- Round whole numbers through 1,000 to the nearest hundred.
- Identify the place value for each digit in whole numbers through 1,000.
- Compare whole numbers through 1,000.

Materials to Gather

SUPPLIED

Extended Problems: Reasoning (printout)

Extended Problems: Reasoning Answer Key (printout)

USE WHAT YOU KNOW Offline

OFFLINE 60 min

Objectives

- Apply lesson objectives.

The Extended Problems: Reasoning and its answer key are located online in the Resources section of *Math+ Purple Lesson Guide*. Give students the Extended Problems: Reasoning. Read the directions, problems, and answer choices to students, if necessary.

You will grade this assignment.

- Students should complete the assignment on their own.
- Students should submit the completed assignment to you.

Whole Number Addition and Subtraction

▶ Unit Objectives

- Recognize and solve a story problem in which two quantities are combined.
- Recognize and solve a story problem in which a quantity changes by addition or subtraction.
- Recognize and solve a story problem in which two quantities are compared by the use of addition or subtraction.
- Recognize and solve a story problem in which one quantity must be changed to equal another quantity.
- Identify odd and even numbers and describe their characteristics.
- Find the sum or difference of whole numbers with sums and minuends up through 1,000.
- Assess the reasonableness of answers using mental computation and estimation strategies including rounding.

▶ Big Ideas

- Inverses undo each other. Addition and subtraction are inverse operations, and multiplication and division are inverse operations.
- The use of letters, numbers, and mathematical symbols makes possible the translation of complex situations or long word statements into concise mathematical sentences or expressions.

▶ Unit Introduction

In this unit, students will review and extend their understanding of addition and subtraction. They will look at addition and subtraction in a general way to notice the effects that adding and subtracting have on whole numbers. For instance, when whole numbers greater than zero are added the sum is greater than either of the numbers being added. This and other insights about addition and subtraction will help students' basic understanding of how our number system works. Students will also add numbers with sums through 1,000 and they will subtract from numbers through 1,000. They will use place value to understand how addition and subtraction work, and they will review and expand their skill with the traditional algorithm (the traditional steps for adding or subtracting greater numbers). Students will then put their skills to work in context, solving a variety of story problems in which quantities are combined, or one quantity is changed by addition or subtraction, or quantities are compared, or one quantity is made equal to another. By the end of this unit, students will have greater skill with addition and subtraction calculations as well as story problems.

▶ Keywords

addends	difference	sum
algorithm	regrouping	whole numbers

Odd and Even Number Patterns

▶ Lesson Objectives

Identify odd and even numbers and describe their characteristics.

▶ Prerequisite Skills

Count by 2s though 100.

▶ Content Background

Students will learn to identify numbers as odd or even by looking at the last digit in the number. They will also use B blocks to see that even numbers can be divided evenly into two groups while odd numbers cannot. Students will make conclusions about the sums and differences of even and odd numbers.

Recognizing patterns in the number system, such as odd and even numbers, helps students solve a variety of problems more easily. An even number of objects can be divided into two equal groups. An even number always ends with one of the even digits: 0, 2, 4, 6, or 8. An odd number of objects cannot be divided into two equal groups. There will always be one object left over. An odd number always ends with one of the odd digits: 1, 3, 5, 7, or 9.

▶ Advance Preparation

Label index cards with the following numbers, one per card: 5, 6, 6, 8, 9, 9. Label 5 more index cards **even** and 4 cards **odd**.

Materials to Gather

SUPPLIED

blocks – B (all colors)

Odd or Even? activity page

ALSO NEEDED

index cards – 15, labeled

Hundred Chart (printout, optional)

GET READY Numbers to 100

- Count by 2s through 100.

Students will use the Number Line Learning Tool to review skip counting odd and even numbers. The learning tool has audio for numbers being counted.

DIRECTIONS FOR USING THE NUMBER LINE LEARNING TOOL

1. Click Count and choose the following:
   - Start Number Line at: 0
   - End Number Line at: 30
   - Count by: 2s

   Click OK.

2. Have students click each number to count by 2s. As they click each number, the frog will hop to the number and it will be said aloud. The number line will slide over automatically when necessary to display more numbers. When they reach 30, students should click Count Again and repeat.

3. Repeat Steps 1 and 2 with the following selections. (Students will count by 2s again, but this time they'll count by odd numbers for two of the number lines.) Click Count to change the number line.
   - 1–21
   - 74–100
   - 51–75

LEARN Sort Odd and Even Numbers

- Identify odd and even numbers and describe their characteristics.

Tips

Students can also use the Hundred Chart printout to color odd and even numbers.

Students will explore odd and even numbers. They will use the online Hundred Chart Learning Tool. By shading odd and even numbers on a hundred chart, they will begin to recognize that for even numbers the digit in the ones place is alway 0, 2, 4, 6, or 8, and for odd numbers the digit in the ones place is always 1, 3, 5, 7, or 9. Students will then do an activity in which they will try to make even groups of objects. They'll see that an even number of objects can always be separated into two equal groups, but an odd number of objects can never be separated into equal groups. They'll learn that if you try to show an odd number of objects in two equal groups, there is always one left over.

DIRECTIONS FOR USING THE HUNDRED CHART LEARNING TOOL

1. Have students identify the even numbers on the chart. Have them click the pink paint choice and count by 2s on the chart, starting at 0 and clicking every other number as they count aloud. When they click, the number will be highlighted in pink and will be said aloud. If an incorrect number is clicked, simply have them click it again to remove the color. When they marked all the even numbers, have them click the speaker icon to hear the numbers counted aloud.

2. Have students identify the odd numbers on the chart. Have them click the blue paint choice and count by 2s on the chart, starting with 1. Have them count aloud as they click every second number. When they have marked all the odd numbers, have them click the speaker icon to hear the numbers counted aloud.

3. Have students look for patterns on the chart.
   Examples: the numbers appear in columns on the chart; even numbers end in 0, 2, 4, 6, or 8 and odd numbers end in 1, 3, 5, 7, or 9

LEARN Sums of Odd and Even Numbers

Objectives

- Identify odd and even numbers and describe their characteristics.

Students will continue to explore even and odd numbers. They have seen that you can separate an even number of objects into two equal groups, but if you try to separate an odd number of objects into two equal groups, there is always one left over. Students will use circle blocks to recognize the following:

- If two even numbers are added, the sum is even.
- If two odd numbers are added, the sum is even.
- If an even number and an odd number are added, the sum is odd.

Gather the circle blocks and the index cards you prepared.

Tips

You can extend this activity by allowing students to add greater numbers. Ask students to find the sum of $34 + 38$, $51 + 29$, and $42 + 37$ and predict whether the sum will be even or odd.

ADDING EVEN NUMBERS

1. Tell students they will explore the sums of even and odd numbers. Remind them that a sum is the answer to an addition problem and is found by combining two groups.

2. Place the 6 card on a desk or table. Ask students if this number even or odd, then place an even card to the right, leaving room for the circles.

   Have student show that 6 is even by counting 6 yellow circles and placing them in pairs as shown.

   Remind students that even numbers can be shown in two equal groups. Ask students to point out the two equal groups. (Each column is a group.)

3. Place the index card with the 8 on the desk or table as shown. Ask students if 8 is even or odd. Have students place an even card across from the 8. Have students count 8 yellow circles and place them in pairs to show 8 as two equal groups.

4. Ask students to look at the circles. Explain that if you combine the 6 circles and the 8 circles, they form a total that can be shown as two equal groups. (Slide the circles closer to each other.) This shows the total must be an even number. Point out that you don't have to count how many there are to see that it's an even amount because you can see two equal groups.

5. Have students count the total to verify that it is an even number. 14 Tell students we know that any time you combine two even numbers, you get an even number, because the two columns always form two equal groups.

6. Test the rule that whenever you add two even numbers, you get an even number. Choose numbers that are easy to add with mental arithmetic and see if the sum is always an even number. Try $10 + 8$, $20 + 30$, and $100 + 44$. Students should become convinced that whenever two even numbers are added, the sum is even.

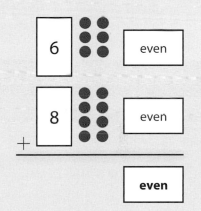

ADDING ODD NUMBERS

7. Repeat Steps 2 and 3 with two odd numbers, 5 and 9, as shown. Place the 5 card and ask if it is even or odd. Have students place the appropriate cards.

    Have students place 5 blue circles, arranging them in pairs. The fifth circle will not be part of a matching pair. This unmatched circle is what makes the number odd. Replace that fifth circle with a red circle, placing it as shown.

8. Place the 9 card and have students count out 9 blue circles, arranging them in pairs. The ninth circle will not have a match. Have students replace the ninth circle with a red circle, placing it as shown.

9. Have students observe what happens when you combine the two odd numbers. Slide the circles from the two numbers closer so that the unmatched circles for each number come together to form a pair. Tell students that the total forms two equal groups and is therefore an even number. This is true whenever two odd numbers are added together.

ADDING AN EVEN NUMBER AND AN ODD NUMBER

10. Repeat Steps 2 and 3 with an even number, 6, and an odd number, 9. Work through the problem as before. Have students notice that when they combine the two sets of circles, the total will have a circle with no match. This makes the sum odd.

11. Have students repeat Step 10 using other pairs of even and odd numbers. Pick numbers that are easy to add with mental arithmetic. Students should recognize that if an even number and an odd number are shown with circles, there will always be one circle without a match. So the sum will always be odd.

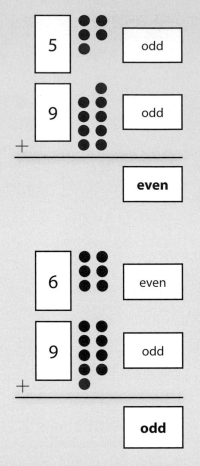

TRY IT Odd or Even?

OFFLINE **15**min

Objectives

Students will practice identifying numbers and sums as odd or even. Have students turn to the Odd or Even? activity page in their Activity Book and read the directions with them.

Students should copy the problems from the Activity Book into their Math Notebook as necessary and solve them there.

- Identify odd and even numbers and describe their characteristics.

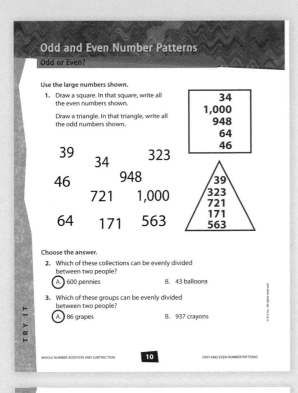

Odd and Even Number Patterns
Odd or Even?

Use the large numbers shown.

1. Draw a square. In that square, write all the even numbers shown.

   Draw a triangle. In that triangle, write all the odd numbers shown.

```
39        34        323
  46        948
    721    1,000
  64      171    563
```

```
┌──────────┐
│   34     │
│  1,000   │
│   948    │
│   64     │
│   46     │
└──────────┘
```

```
    △
   /39\
  /323 \
 /721   \
/ 171    \
/563      \
```

Choose the answer.

2. Which of these collections can be evenly divided between two people?

   (A.) 600 pennies   B. 43 balloons

3. Which of these groups can be evenly divided between two people?

   (A.) 86 grapes   B. 937 crayons

TRY IT

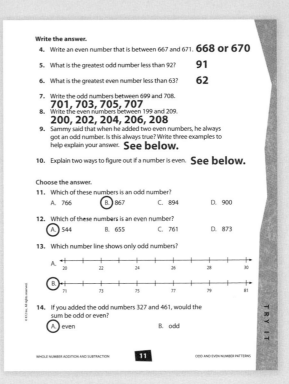

Write the answer.

4. Write an even number that is between 667 and 671. **668 or 670**

5. What is the greatest odd number less than 92? **91**

6. What is the greatest even number less than 63? **62**

7. Write the odd numbers between 699 and 708.
   701, 703, 705, 707

8. Write the even numbers between 199 and 209.
   200, 202, 204, 206, 208

9. Sammy said that when he added two even numbers, he always got an odd number. Is this always true? Write three examples to help explain your answer. **See below.**

10. Explain two ways to figure out if a number is even. **See below.**

Choose the answer.

11. Which of these numbers is an odd number?

    A. 766   (B.) 867   C. 894   D. 900

12. Which of these numbers is an even number?

    (A.) 544   B. 655   C. 761   D. 873

13. Which number line shows only odd numbers?

    A. ┤────┼────┼────┼────┼────┼────├
        20   22   24   26   28   30

    (B.) ┤────┼────┼────┼────┼────┼────├
        71   73   75   77   79   81

14. If you added the odd numbers 327 and 461, would the sum be odd or even?

    (A.) even   B. odd

TRY IT

Challenge Question

Choose the answer.

15. Andre and Ben both have an odd number of baseballs. Andre buys 2 more baseballs and Ben buys 5 more baseballs. Which statement is true?

    A. Andre now has an even number of baseballs and Ben now has an even number of baseballs.

    B. Andre now has an odd number of baseballs and Ben now has an odd number of baseballs.

    C. Andre now has an even number of baseballs and Ben now has an odd number of baseballs.

    (D.) Andre now has an odd number of baseballs and Ben now has an even number of baseballs.

TRY IT

Additional Answers

9. This is not true. **Examples:** $8 + 8 = 16$; $2 + 4 = 6$; $12 + 6 = 18$

10. If the number is shown using pairs of circle blocks and there are no circles left over, the number is even. If a number ends in 0, 2, 4, 6, or 8, the number is even.

ONLINE
10min

CHECKPOINT   **Objectives**

Students will complete an online Checkpoint. If necessary, read the directions, problems, and answer choices to students and help them with keyboard or mouse operations.

- Identify odd and even numbers and describe their characteristics.

Addition and Subtraction Answers

GET READY Add Numbers Through 100	10 minutes	ONLINE
LEARN Addition to 1,000	10 minutes	ONLINE
TRY IT Add Numbers Through 1,000	15 minutes	OFFLINE
LEARN Subtraction to 1,000	10 minutes	ONLINE
TRY IT Subtract Numbers Through 1,000	15 minutes	OFFLINE

▶ ## Lesson Objectives

Find the sum or difference of whole numbers with sums and minuends up through 1,000.

▶ ## Prerequisite Skills

Find the sum or difference of whole numbers with sums and minuends up through 100.

▶ ## Content Background

Addition is combining, or putting together, groups of objects. The total number of objects is the sum. Subtraction is taking a lesser amount away from a greater amount. The amount left over is the difference. Students should be able to use the terms *addends*, *sum*, and *difference* within the context of addition and subtraction.

 Algorithm is a mathematical term for a repeated step-by-step mathematical procedure, such as adding or subtracting numbers. Regrouping is a critical component of the traditional addition and subtraction algorithms. The term *regrouping* has replaced the old terms *carrying* and *borrowing*. Many algorithms exist for performing any given operation.

 Students will see the step-by-step process of the algorithm on the screen. They will do problems first with on-screen base-10 blocks and then with numbers in a place-value chart. Students will then see how they can break apart numbers as an additional strategy for adding and subtracting whole numbers. This should help students move from concrete to abstract representations and provide them with different computational strategies for solving addition and subtraction problems.

Materials to Gather

SUPPLIED

Add Numbers Through 1,000
  activity page

Subtract Numbers Through 1,000
  activity page

Place-Value Chart Through Thousands
  (printout, optional)

base-10 blocks (optional)

ONLINE
10min

GET READY Add Numbers Through 100

Students will solve online addition problems by using the Place-Value Addition Learning Tool.

Objectives

- Find the sum or difference of whole numbers with sums and minuends up through 100.

DIRECTIONS FOR USING THE PLACE-VALUE ADDITION LEARNING TOOL

1. Click Begin Setup and choose the following:
   - Present addition problems with SUMS up to: 99
   - Allow REGROUPING in problems: YES

2. Have students complete the problems given. Continue as time allows. Students can reset a problem by clicking the Menu button, then clicking Restart. They can click Cancel if they decide they no longer want to change the problem.

LEARN Addition to 1,000

Students will see a three-digit addition problem solved using the traditional step-by-step procedures. The problem will be shown in a place-value chart to help students see that they are adding ones, tens, and hundreds and regrouping as they move to each place-value position. Students will then see an alternative strategy that shows how to break apart numbers to add the hundreds, tens, and ones.

Objectives

- Find the sum or difference of whole numbers with sums and minuends up through 1,000.

TRY IT Add Numbers Through 1,000

Students will add two or more numbers with and without regrouping. Have students turn to the Add Numbers Through 1,000 activity page in their Activity Book and read the directions with them.

Students should copy the problems from the Activity Book into their Math Notebook as necessary and solve them there.

Objectives

- Find the sum or difference of whole numbers with sums and minuends up through 1,000.

Tips

Allow students to use base-10 blocks or the Place-Value Chart Through Thousands to solve the problems.

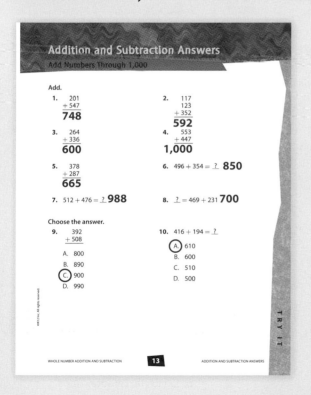

Addition and Subtraction Answers
Add Numbers Through 1,000

Add.

1. 201
   + 547
   748

2. 117
    123
   + 352
   592

3. 264
   + 336
   600

4. 553
   + 447
   1,000

5. 378
   + 287
   665

6. 496 + 354 = ? **850**

7. 512 + 476 = ? **988**

8. ? = 469 + 231 **700**

Choose the answer.

9. 392
   + 508
   A. 800
   B. 890
   (C.) 900
   D. 990

10. 416 + 194 = ?
   (A.) 610
   B. 600
   C. 510
   D. 500

WHOLE NUMBER ADDITION AND SUBTRACTION   **13**   ADDITION AND SUBTRACTION ANSWERS

TRY IT

LEARN Subtraction to 1,000

Students will solve subtraction problems with on-screen base-10 blocks by using the Place-Value Subtraction Learning Tool. They will then see a three-digit subtraction problem solved using the traditional step-by-step procedures. The problem will be shown in a place-value chart to help students see that they are subtracting ones, tens, hundreds, and thousands and regrouping as necessary to solve the problem. Students will then see an alternative strategy that shows how to break apart numbers to subtract the hundreds, tens, and ones.

- Find the sum or difference of whole numbers with sums and minuends up through 1,000.

DIRECTIONS FOR USING THE PLACE-VALUE SUBTRACTION LEARNING TOOL

1. Click Begin Setup and choose the following:
   - Present subtraction problems with MINUENDS up to: 999
   - Allow REGROUPING in problems: YES
2. Have students complete the problems given. Continue as time allows. Students can reset a problem by clicking the Menu button, then clicking Restart. They can click Cancel if they decide they no longer want to change the problem.

TRY IT Subtract Numbers Through 1,000

Students will subtract greater numbers. Have students turn to the Subtract Numbers Through 1,000 activity page in their Activity Book and read the directions with them.

Students should copy the problems from the Activity Book into their Math Notebook as necessary and solve them there.

- Find the sum or difference of whole numbers with sums and minuends up through 1,000.

Tips

Allow students to use base-10 blocks or the Place-Value Chart Through Thousands to solve the problems.

Addition and Subtraction Answers
Subtract Numbers Through 1,000

Subtract.

1. 714
   −337
   377

2. 502
   −261
   241

3. 863
   − 530
   333

4. 1,000
   − 836
   164

5. 144
   − 88
   56

6. 599 − 157 = ?   **442**

7. 521 − 304 = ?   **217**

8. 925 − 475 = ?   **450**

Choose the answer.

9. 762 − 156 = ?
   A. 706
   B. 616
   C. 606
   D. 506

10. 856
    − 563
    A. 213
    B. 293
    C. 313
    D. 393

TRY IT

WHOLE NUMBER ADDITION AND SUBTRACTION   **14**   ADDITION AND SUBTRACTION ANSWERS

Combine and Change Problems

Lesson Overview

GET READY Number Sentences and Story Problems	5 minutes	**ONLINE**
LEARN Combine Problems	10 minutes	**ONLINE**
TRY IT Solve Combine Problems	10 minutes	**ONLINE**
LEARN Change Problems	15 minutes	**ONLINE**
TRY IT Solve Change Problems	10 minutes	**ONLINE**
CHECKPOINT	10 minutes	**ONLINE**

▶ Lesson Objectives

- Recognize and solve a story problem in which two quantities are combined.
- Recognize and solve a story problem in which a quantity changes by addition or subtraction.

▶ Prerequisite Skills

- Recognize and solve word problems involving sums up through 100 in which two quantities are combined.
- Recognize and solve word problems involving sums or minuends up through 100 in which one quantity changes by addition or subtraction.

Materials to Gather

There are no materials to gather for this lesson.

▶ Content Background

Researchers have classified addition and subtraction story problems into different categories.

Many addition problems are categorized as *combine problems*. In these problems, students combine two or more groups to get a sum or total. In some combine problems, they need to find the sum. In others, they need to find one of the addends. Students can write an addition number sentence with a missing addend, such as $3 + ? = 7$. They can use subtraction to find the missing addend or they can ask themselves, "3 plus what number equals 7?" When students encounter combine problems, they may find that using a part-part-total chart will help them understand how to find the missing quantity and write the number sentence that represents the problem. The chart can also help students understand the opposite or *inverse* relationship between addition and subtraction.

Some story problems are categorized as *change problems* because they describe situations in which a starting quantity changes by having more added to it or having some taken away. When students encounter change problems, they may find that using a start-change-result chart will help them understand how to write the number sentence that represents the problem. The start-change-result chart is very similar to the part-part-total chart. While these charts can be used interchangeably in story problems involving a change of an amount, the start-change-result chart suggests the action of a change problem more clearly. Therefore, this chart helps students more easily recognize a problem involving change versus one where two parts are simply combined.

Students do not need to memorize the types of problems. Instead, they should gain the experience and confidence necessary to read a problem, create a mental image, and figure out which quantities within the problem to add or subtract to find the solution.

GET READY Number Sentences and Story Problems

Students will match number sentences to stories. The problems illustrate two kinds of story problems—combine problems (in which amounts are combined using addition) and change problems (in which an amount changes because something is added to or taken away from it).

Tips	Encourage students to make a sketch to model the problems.

Objectives

- Recognize and solve word problems involving sums up through 100 in which two quantities are combined.
- Recognize and solve word problems involving sums or minuends up through 100 in which one quantity changes by addition or subtraction.

LEARN Combine Problems

Students will learn about combine problems, or story problems in which two quantities are combined.

In combine story problems, students will be finding the sum or total.
Example: $30 + 70 = ?$
Other times students will be finding one of the numbers being added (a missing addend).
Example: $30 + ? = 100$ or $? + 70 = 100$
Combine problems can be put in a part-part-total chart to see the relationship of the numbers. Whenever you combine two numbers, each number is part of the total. The problem $30 + 70 = ?$ can be shown like this. Students add $30 + 70$ to get the total.

The key to the chart is that once you put numbers in it, you can see four relationships. It shows the sum in two ways, and it shows that the total minus a part equals the other part.

Objectives

- Recognize and solve a story problem in which two quantities are combined.

Total	
?	
30	70
Part	Part

Total	
100	
30	70
Part	Part

$30 + 70 = 100$
$70 + 30 = 100$
$100 - 30 = 70$
$100 - 70 = 30$

When students encounter combine story problem, they can put the numbers in a part-part-total chart to help them write the number sentence. When there is a missing addend, students often count up to find the missing number. However, if the numbers are difficult, it's easiest to find the missing part by subtracting the part that's known. The following charts show the three kinds of problems that can be solved with the chart previously filled in.

Combine Problems	Missing Total		Missing Addend		Missing Addend	
	Total		**Total**		**Total**	
	?		100		100	
	30	70	?	70	30	?
	Part	Part	Part	Part	Part	Part
Number Sentence	$30 + 70 = ?$		$? + 70 = 100$		$30 + ? = 100$	
Solution	$30 + 70 = 100$		$100 - 70 = 30$		$100 - 30 = 70$	

As students do the problems in this lesson, have them make a part-part-total chart for any problem they find difficult.

TRY IT Solve Combine Problems

10 min ONLINE

Objectives

Students will practice solving story problems where two quantities are combined. They will identify the number sentence that can be used to solve a problem and then find the solution.

- Recognize and solve a story problem in which two quantities are combined.

Tips Students may wish to use a part-part-total chart to determine whether they need to find a part or a total to solve the problem.

LEARN Change Problems

15 min ONLINE

Objectives

Students will learn how to solve change problems, or story problems where one quantity changes by addition or subtraction. They will use a start-change-result chart to help them solve the problems. Let's say that students are asked to solve the following change problem:

- Recognize and solve a story problem in which a quantity changes by addition or subtraction.

- Alexander had 30 apples. He picked 60 more. How many apples does he have altogether?

Students can use a start-change-result chart to help them solve this problem. Alexander started with one amount, 30. Students should put 30 in the start section of the chart. Then Alexander's amount changed, because he picked 60 more apples. Since Alexander got more apples, students should put a plus symbol ($+$) after the 30 in the chart. Next they should put 60 in the change section of the chart to show how much Alexander's amount changed. They can then solve the problem by adding the amounts. Students would put the answer, 90, in the result box.

Start	$+$ or $-$	Change	$=$	Result
30	$+$	60	$=$	?

Students would use the chart to solve.

$30 + 60 = 90$

Some problems, however, are not as straightforward. Look at this one.

- Alexander had 45 apples. He picked some more apples. He then had 120 apples. How many apples did he pick?

This is a missing-addend problem. Some students will count up from 45 to 120, but they should also know that they can subtract 120 − 45 to get 75.

Start	+ or −	Change	=	Result
45	+	?	=	120

Students would use the chart to solve.

45 + ? = 120
120 − 45 = 75

Sometimes story problems are worded in such a way that they begin with the result. In problems like this, it may help to rearrange the boxes in the chart, as follows:

- At the end of the day, Alexander had 120 apples. He started with a wagon full of apples in the morning and then picked 75 more. How many were in the wagon when he started?

If students put the result box first, their chart might look like the one that follows. Students would solve this problem using subtraction.

Result	=	Start	+ or −	Change
120	=	?	+	75

As students do problems in this online activity, have them make start-change-result charts. Ask them to think about the change and choose either addition or subtraction depending on whether the change increases the start number or decreases it.

ONLINE

10 min

TRY IT Solve Change Problems

Objectives

Students will answer questions online to solve story problems where one quantity changes by addition or subtraction. They will identify the number sentence that can be used to solve a problem and then solve some problems.
Be sure that students have paper and pencil available to find solutions.

- Recognize and solve a story problem in which a quantity changes by addition or subtraction.

Tips Encourage students to put the numbers from the story problems into start-change-result charts to help them determine the number sentence.

ONLINE

10 min

CHECKPOINT

Objectives

Students will complete an online Checkpoint. If necessary, read the directions, problems, and answer choices to students and help them with keyboard or mouse operations.

- Recognize and solve a story problem in which two quantities are combined.
- Recognize and solve a story problem in which a quantity changes by addition or subtraction.

Compare and Equalize Story Problems

Lesson Overview

GET READY Compare Numbers to 1,000	10 minutes	**ONLINE**
LEARN Compare Problems	10 minutes	**ONLINE**
TRY IT Compare and Solve	10 minutes	**OFFLINE**
LEARN Equalize Problems	10 minutes	**ONLINE**
TRY IT Make Equal Amounts	10 minutes	**OFFLINE**
CHECKPOINT	10 minutes	**ONLINE**

▶ Lesson Objectives

- Recognize and solve a story problem in which two quantities are compared by the use of addition or subtraction.
- Recognize and solve a story problem in which one quantity must be changed to equal another quantity.

▶ Prerequisite Skills

- Recognize and solve word problems involving numbers up to 100 in which two quantities are compared by the use of addition or subtraction.
- Recognize and solve word problems involving numbers up to 100 in which one quantity must be changed to equal another quantity.
- Find the sum or difference of whole numbers with sums and minuends up through 1,000.

▶ Content Background

Students will solve *compare problems* and *equalize problems*. They will write number sentences in which two quantities are compared or one quantity is changed to match another.

Compare problems are story problems in which two quantities are compared. In compare problems, students must compare two groups to find how many more or fewer are in one group. Here's a compare problem:

- Ron has 12 marbles. Alexander has 18. How many more marbles does Alexander have than Ron?

To solve this problem, students can make a row of 12 objects and a row of 18 objects. Using one-to-one correspondence, they can count how many objects do not have a match to find the difference.

As students move to greater numbers where counting isn't practical, they can model the problems with a diagram showing bars for each number.

- Andre collected 712 pennies and Kelly collected 540 pennies. How many more pennies did Andre collect than Kelly? (or: How many fewer pennies did Kelly collect than Andre?)

Materials to Gather

SUPPLIED

Compare and Solve activity page

Make Equal Amounts activity page

blocks – B (19 of any color, optional)

712	
540	?

The bars of the diagram help students see the relationship between the numbers. They should recognize that they can subtract to find the difference.

Equalize problems are story problems that require students to compare two quantities or make two quantities equal. Here's an example of an equalize problem:

- Andre collected 712 pennies and Kelly collected 540 pennies. How many more pennies must Kelly collect to have the same number of pennies as Andre?

Students should come to realize that *how many more one quantity is than another* is the same as *how many fewer the second quantity is than the first*.

Once they understand this concept, they will be ready to learn how to *equalize* quantities, or determine how many more should be added to one quantity to make it equal to another quantity. As they practice solving equalize problems, students should make the connection that the difference between two amounts is the same as the number needed to make the two amounts equal.

GET READY Compare Numbers to 1,000

ONLINE 10 min

Students will complete online story problems in which two quantities are compared to find the difference.

Objectives

- Find the sum or difference of whole numbers with sums and minuends up through 1,000.

Tips If students have trouble with the idea of comparing numbers, have them use B blocks to compare 7 and 12. Have them make a row of 7 circles and a row of 12 circles and match up pairs of circles in the two rows. Circles that do not have a match represent the difference between the two numbers.

LEARN Compare Problems

ONLINE 10 min

Students will solve story problems in which they compare two amounts by adding or subtracting. Have paper and pencil available for them to use to solve the problems. Encourage students to draw comparison bars to compare the numbers concretely.

Objectives

- Recognize and solve a story problem in which two quantities are compared by the use of addition or subtraction.

TRY IT Compare and Solve

Students will practice solving story problems in which two quantities are compared. They will identify the number sentence that can be used to solve a problem and then find the solution. Have students turn to the Compare and Solve activity page in their Activity Book and read the directions with them.

Students should copy the problems from the Activity Book into their Math Notebook as necessary and solve them there. Encourage them to draw a diagram to compare the numbers.

- Recognize and solve a story problem in which two quantities are compared by the use of addition or subtraction.

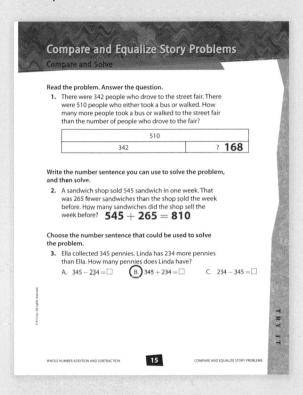

ONLINE
10min

LEARN Equalize Problems

Objectives

Students will solve story problems in which they will compare amounts and then add or subtract to make one amount equal to the other. Encourage students to draw a diagram with bars to compare the amounts.

- Recognize and solve a story problem in which one quantity must be changed to equal another quantity.

TRY IT Make Equal Amounts

Objectives

- Recognize and solve a story problem in which one quantity must be changed to equal another quantity.

Students will practice solving story problems where one quantity changes to equal another quantity. They will identify the number sentence that can be used to solve a problem and then find the solution. Have students turn to the Make Equal Amounts activity page in their Activity Book and read the directions with them.

Students should copy the problems from the Activity Book into their Math Notebook as necessary and solve them there. Students may want to draw a diagram to help them solve the problem.

Compare and Equalize Story Problems
Make Equal Amounts

Read the problem. Write the number sentence and the solution to the problem.

1. There are 192 pumpkin seeds. There are 399 watermelon seeds. How many more pumpkin seeds do you need if you want to have the same amount as the watermelon seeds?

   number sentence: _?_ **192 + ? = 399**

   solution: _?_ **207 pumpkin seeds**

2. Farmer Li has 245 pounds of green beans. He has 103 pounds of peas. How many pounds of green beans would he have to sell to have the same amount of green beans and peas?

   number sentence: _?_ **245 − ? = 103**

   solution: _?_ **142 pounds of green beans**

Choose the number sentence that could be used to solve this problem.

3. The City Art Gallery has 458 paintings in its collection. If it buys 257 more paintings, it will have as many paintings as the State Art Gallery. How many paintings does the State Art Gallery have?

   A. 257 − 458 = □

   B. 458 − 257 = □

   C. 458 + 257 = □

TRY IT

WHOLE NUMBER ADDITION AND SUBTRACTION **16** COMPARE AND EQUALIZE STORY PROBLEMS

CHECKPOINT

Objectives

- Recognize and solve a story problem in which two quantities are compared by the use of addition or subtraction.
- Recognize and solve a story problem in which one quantity must be changed to equal another quantity.

Students will complete an online Checkpoint. If necessary, read the directions, problems, and answer choices to students and help them with keyboard or mouse operations.

Core Focus
Check for Reasonable Answers

▶ Lesson Objectives

Assess the reasonableness of answers using mental computation and estimation strategies including rounding.

▶ Prerequisite Skills

Use models or drawings to show how addition and subtraction are inversely related.

▶ Content Background

Students will represent a problem using equations and diagrams to make sense of a problem. They will learn and apply strategies that help them solve one- and two-step addition and subtraction problems. Previously, students have used the four-step problem-solving plan to solve problems:

Step 1: Understand the problem.

Step 2: Make a plan.

Step 3: Carry out the plan.

Step 4: Look back.

Students often think they are finished solving a problem when they have an answer. In this lesson, emphasis is put on Step 4, Look back to check whether an answer is reasonable or whether students need to return to the problem to rethink what they have done and make a new plan for solving it. Students will learn mental computation and estimation strategies for quickly checking for reasonableness of the problem's answer.

Materials to Gather

SUPPLIED

Apply Checking Strategies activity page

Prove It: Reasonable or Not? activity page

GET READY Number Sentence Matchup

ONLINE
5min

Students will think about possible addition and subtraction relationships represented on a number line. They choose number sentences that could represent those relationships.

Objectives

- Use models or drawings to show how addition and subtraction are inversely related.

LEARN Strategies to Check Answers

Objectives

- Assess the reasonableness of answers using mental computation and estimation strategies including rounding.

Students will use mental math and estimation strategies to check whether their answer to an addition or subtraction problem is reasonable. They will practice breaking apart numbers in a problem in ways that make the numbers easier to add or subtract mentally.

Students will find compatible numbers, or numbers close to the numbers in the problem, that make answers easier to estimate and assess for reasonableness. They will also use number lines and diagrams as tools to help them check for reasonableness.

Encourage students to try out the strategies in their Math Notebook as they work through the problems online.

Tips

Remind students that a common mistake is to try to answer the second part of the problem before they find the answer to the first part.

Point out that students need to clearly show both steps of a two-step problem.

LEARN Apply Checking Strategies

Objectives

- Assess the reasonableness of answers using mental computation and estimation strategies including rounding.

Students will put together what they've learned about fluently adding and subtracting to solve two-step problems using the four-step problem-solving plan. They will focus on choosing a strategy to check for reasonableness of their answer. For example, they could find compatible numbers to estimate, round numbers, or use a drawing or number line to quickly assess if the answer is reasonable. Let students know that they will practice using all four problem-solving steps as they solve the one- and two-step problems. Tell them that they will use the strategies they've just learned to check if the answers are reasonable.

Gather the Applying Checking Strategies activity page.

1. Look at the Apply Checking Strategies activity page. Read each step of Problem 1 of the Worked Examples with students.

   Ask: What is another way to check if this answer is reasonable? You could round each number (220 and 120) and subtract in your head, or you could make both numbers compatible (220, and 125 or 120) and subtract in your head or on paper.

2. Read each step of Problem 2 of the Worked Examples with students. Make sure students understand that there are two parts, or steps, to this problem and that they need to find the answers to the first part before they can find the answer to the second part. The answer to the second part is the actual answer to the problem.

3. Have students complete Problem 1 of the problem set on their own. Guide students to follow the four-step problem-solving plan modeled in the Worked Examples to solve and explain the problem.

Worked Examples

You can use the four problem-solving steps to solve the problems. Don't forget the last step to check if your answer is reasonable or if you need to rethink or redo your answer. Be sure to look back.

- Understand the problem.
- Make a plan.
- Carry out the plan.
- Look back.

PROBLEM 1 Risa read about the new exhibit at the city aquarium. The largest tank used to have 123 fish. More fish were added to the tank for the exhibit. Now the tank has 219 fish. How many fish were added to the tank for the exhibit?

SOLUTION

UNDERSTAND THE PROBLEM
I need to know how many fish were added.

MAKE A PLAN
I will make a chart to figure out what equation to write. I will write an equation to find the missing value.

CARRY OUT THE PLAN

❶ Make a chart.

Start	+ or −	Change	=	Result
123	+	?	=	219

❷ Write an equation: $123 + ? = 219$.

---

❸ Subtract to solve the equation: $219 - 123 = 96$.

LOOK BACK

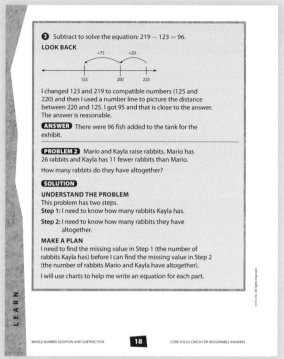

I changed 123 and 219 to compatible numbers (125 and 220) and then I used a number line to picture the distance between 220 and 125. I got 95 and that is close to the answer. The answer is reasonable.

ANSWER There were 96 fish added to the tank for the exhibit.

PROBLEM 2 Mario and Kayla raise rabbits. Mario has 26 rabbits and Kayla has 11 fewer rabbits than Mario. How many rabbits do they have altogether?

SOLUTION

UNDERSTAND THE PROBLEM
This problem has two steps.
Step 1: I need to know how many rabbits Kayla has.

Step 2: I need to know how many rabbits they have altogether.

MAKE A PLAN
I need to find the missing value in Step 1 (the number of rabbits Kayla has) before I can find the missing value in Step 2 (the number of rabbits Mario and Kayla have altogether).

I will use charts to help me write an equation for each part.

CARRY OUT THE PLAN

❶ Make a chart to represent Step 1:

26	
?	11

❷ Write and solve an equation: $26 - 11 = ?$
Kayla has 15 rabbits.

❸ Use your answer to Step 1 (Kayla has 15 rabbits) to make a chart to represent Step 2.

?	
26	15

❹ Write and solve an equation: $26 + 15 = ?$
Mario and Kayla have 41 rabbits altogether.

LOOK BACK
Step 1: I changed 11 and 26 to compatible numbers (about 10 and 25) and estimated. $25 - 10$ is about 15, so my answer is reasonable.

Step 2: I added 25 to 15 and got 40. That is very close to 41, so the answer is reasonable.

ANSWER Mario and Kayla have 41 rabbits altogether.

Solve.

1. Jake's club collected 273 cans, 87 bottles, and 62 plastic jugs to be recycled. How many more cans did the club collect than bottles and jugs combined?

   (a) Solve the problem. Explain how you got your answer. **See right.**

   (b) Explain how you checked whether your answer was reasonable. **See right.**

Answers

1. **(a) Sample answer:** The club collected 124 cans.

   Step 1: I combined 87 and 62 to find the total number of bottles and jugs. $87 + 62 = 149$

   Step 2: I subtracted 149 to compare the number of bottles and jugs combined with the number of cans. $273 - 149 = 124$

   (b) Sample answer: Students might make a drawing to show that 87 and 62 are combined. Then they might make another drawing to show that amount (149) compared with 273.

Step 1

87	62

Step 2

87	62

273

OFFLINE
15 min

Objectives

Students will represent and solve one- and two-step problems. They will use estimation and mental computation strategies to prove whether an answer is reasonable. Encourage students to use drawings and number sentences as they solve the problems themselves. Have students turn to the Prove It: Reasonable or Not? activity page in their Activity Book and read the directions with them.

   Students should copy the problems from the Activity Book into their Math Notebook as necessary and solve them there.

- Assess the reasonableness of answers using mental computation and estimation strategies including rounding.

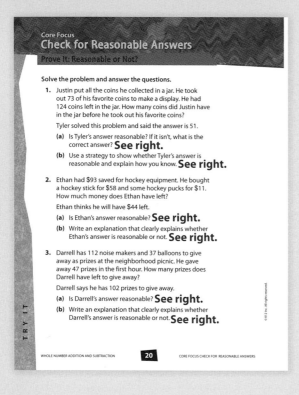

Additional Answers

1. **(a)** No, Tyler's answer is not reasonable. He had 197 coins.

   (b) Students might use compatible numbers of $125 + 75$ to estimate that the answer should be about 200, or they might use compatible numbers on an open number line to show that they added about $125 + 75$ to get 200 for an answer.

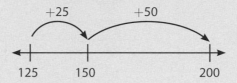

   +25   +50

   125   150   200

2. **(a)** Ethan's answer is not reasonable.

   (b) He paid about $60 for the hockey stick and about $10 for the pucks, so he spent about $60 + 10$, or about $70. He had about $90 saved, so $90 - $70 is about $20 left.

3. **(a)** Darrell's answer is reasonable. He has 102 prizes left to give away.

   (b) Darrell's had about 110 noisemakers and about 40 balloons, so he had about $110 + 40$, or 150 prizes in all. He gave away about 50 prizes, so $150 - 50$ is about 100 prizes left. The first drawing should show that 110 and 40 is combined. The second drawing should show 150 compared to about 50.

   Step 1

150	
110	40

   Step 2

150

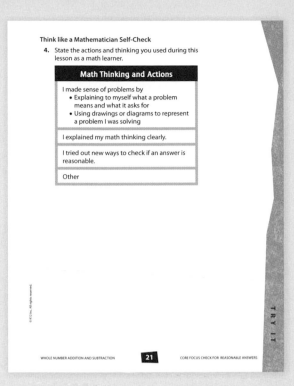

Think like a Mathematician Self-Check

4. State the actions and thinking you used during this lesson as a math learner.

Math Thinking and Actions
I made sense of problems by • Explaining to myself what a problem means and what it asks for • Using drawings or diagrams to represent a problem I was solving
I explained my math thinking clearly.
I tried out new ways to check if an answer is reasonable.
Other

TRY IT

CHECKPOINT

ONLINE 15 min

Students will complete an online Checkpoint. If necessary, read the directions, problems, and answer choices to students and help them with keyboard or mouse operations.

Objectives

- Assess the reasonableness of answers using mental computation and estimation strategies including rounding.

Unit Review

Lesson Overview

UNIT REVIEW Look Back	10 minutes	**ONLINE**
UNIT REVIEW Checkpoint Practice	50 minutes	**ONLINE**
⇥ **UNIT REVIEW** Prepare for the Checkpoint		

▶ Unit Objectives

- Recognize and solve a story problem in which two quantities are combined.
- Recognize and solve a story problem in which a quantity changes by addition or subtraction.
- Recognize and solve a story problem in which two quantities are compared by the use of addition or subtraction.
- Recognize and solve a story problem in which one quantity must be changed to equal another quantity.
- Identify odd and even numbers and describe their characteristics.
- Find the sum or difference of whole numbers with sums and minuends up through 1,000.
- Assess the reasonableness of answers using mental computation and estimation strategies including rounding.

Materials to Gather

There are no materials to gather for this lesson.

▶ Advance Preparation

In this lesson, students will have an opportunity to review previous activities in the Whole Number Addition and Subtraction unit. Look at the suggested activities in Unit Review: Prepare for the Checkpoint online and gather any needed materials.

UNIT REVIEW Look Back

ONLINE **10**min

Objectives

- Review unit objectives.

Students will review key concepts from the unit to prepare for the Unit Checkpoint.

UNIT REVIEW Checkpoint Practice

ONLINE **50**min

Objectives

- Review unit objectives.

Students will complete an online Checkpoint Practice to prepare for the Unit Checkpoint. If necessary, read the directions, problems, and answer choices to students. Have students answer the problems on their own. Review any missed problems with students.

⇥ UNIT REVIEW Prepare for the Checkpoint

What you do next depends on how students performed in the previous activity, Unit Review: Checkpoint Practice. If students had difficulty with any of the problems, complete the appropriate review activity listed in the table online.

Unit Checkpoint

| **UNIT CHECKPOINT** Online | 60 minutes | **ONLINE** |

▶ Unit Objectives

- Recognize and solve a story problem in which two quantities are combined.
- Recognize and solve a story problem in which a quantity changes by addition or subtraction.
- Recognize and solve a story problem in which two quantities are compared by the use of addition or subtraction.
- Recognize and solve a story problem in which one quantity must be changed to equal another quantity.
- Identify odd and even numbers and describe their characteristics.
- Find the sum or difference of whole numbers with sums and minuends up through 1,000.
- Assess the reasonableness of answers using mental computation and estimation strategies including rounding.

Materials to Gather

There are no materials to gather for this lesson.

UNIT CHECKPOINT Online

Students will complete the Unit Checkpoint online. Read the directions, problems, and answer choices to students. If necessary, help students with keyboard or mouse operations.

Objectives

- Assess unit objectives.

Extended Problems: Real-World Application

USE WHAT YOU KNOW Offline   60 minutes : **OFFLINE**

▶ Lesson Objectives

This lesson assesses the following objectives:

- Assess the reasonableness of answers using mental computation and estimation strategies including rounding.
- Solve two-step word problems using addition and subtraction.
- Add up to 4 two-digit numbers using strategies based on place value and properties of operations.
- Fluently add and subtract within 1,000 using strategies and algorithms based on place value, properties of operations, and/or the relationship between addition and subtraction.
- Draw a scaled bar graph to represent a data set with several categories. Solve two-step "how many" and "how many less" problems using information presented in scaled bar graphs.
- Add and subtract 1,000 using concrete models or drawings and strategies based on place value, properties of operations, and/or the relationship between addition and subtraction.
- Apply mathematical knowledge and skills to evaluate and analyze real-world situations.

Materials to Gather

SUPPLIED

Extended Problems: Real-World Application (printout)

Extended Problems: Real-World Application Answer Key (printout)

USE WHAT YOU KNOW Offline

OFFLINE 60min

Objectives

- Apply mathematical knowledge and skills to evaluate and analyze real-world situations.

The Extended Problems: Real-World Application and its answer key are located online in the Resources section for this unit in the Online Book Menu of *Math+ Purple Lesson Guide*. Give students the Extended Problems: Real-World Application. Read the directions, problems, and answer choices to students, if necessary.

You will grade this assignment.

- Students should complete the assignment on their own.
- Students should submit the completed assignment to you.

Whole Number Multiplication Sense

▶ Unit Objectives

- Use objects or sketches to solve a multiplication problem.
- Use a model to explain multiplication as repeated addition of the same quantity.
- Use an area model to explain multiplication.
- Demonstrate an understanding of how multiplication affects whole numbers.
- Explain and apply the commutative property of multiplication.

- Explain and apply the zero property of multiplication.
- Explain and apply the multiplication property of 1.
- Demonstrate automatic recall of multiplication facts.
- Explain and apply the associative property of multiplication.
- Explain and apply the distributive property of multiplication.

▶ Big Ideas

- Multiplication and division can be represented by models and by using math symbols.
- Multiplication can be understood as repeated addition or can be represented through area models.
- Inverses undo each other. Addition and subtraction are inverses, and multiplication and division are inverses.
- The commutative and associative properties can be used to simplify expressions.
- Multiplying any number by 1, the multiplicative identity, results in a product that is the given number.

▶ Unit Introduction

In this unit, students will focus on multiplication. They will become familiar with factors (the numbers that are multiplied) and products (answers). Students know their 2s, 5s, and 10s multiplication facts and have shown multiplication as arrays and repeated addition. They will work in this unit with area models to explain multiplication. They will explain the effects of multiplication on numbers and notice that multiplying generally results in numbers greater than they started with. They will revisit the commutative property, which says that the order in which two numbers are multiplied doesn't affect the result, and they'll investigate what happens when numbers are multiplied by zero and 1. Students will work on their multiplication facts through 10 × 10. They will track the facts they've covered on a multiplication facts chart, and they will post the facts they've fully memorized on a multiplication facts poster on the wall.

▶ Keywords

area model	factor	multiplication symbol
array	grid	multiply
associative property of multiplication	identity property of multiplication	operation
commutative property of multiplication	linear pattern	product
expression	multiple	repeated addition
	multiplication	skip count
	multiplication facts	zero property of multiplication

Model and Explain Multiplication

GET READY Model with Arrays	5 minutes	ONLINE
LEARN Model with Equal Groups	15 minutes	ONLINE
LEARN Model with Base-10 Blocks	15 minutes	OFFLINE
TRY IT Model Multiplication	15 minutes	OFFLINE
CHECKPOINT	10 minutes	ONLINE

▶ Lesson Objectives

- Use objects or sketches to solve a multiplication problem.
- Use a model to explain multiplication as repeated addition of the same quantity.

▶ Prerequisite Skills

- Use concrete objects or sketches of arrays to model multiplication problems.
- Use concrete objects or sketches to model and explain multiplication as repeated addition.

▶ Content Background

Students have used arrays and repeated addition to solve multiplication problems. They may already know their multiplication facts for 2s, 5s, and 10s. In this lesson, students will use objects and sketches to model and explain multiplication problems for other factors.

Multiplication is an operation used when there are equal groups. The multiplication symbol is used to say "groups of" or "rows of." For example, 3 groups of 5 objects would be shown with the expression 3×5. The expression is read "3 times 5." On the other hand, 5 groups of 3 objects would be shown with the expression 5×3 and read "5 times 3."

A multiplication number sentence is composed of two numbers, called factors, that are multiplied to produce the solution, or product. An array is a rectangular arrangement of objects in rows and columns. The number of rows is the first factor in a multiplication number sentence, and the number of columns is the second factor. The total number of objects in the entire array is the product.

Materials to Gather

SUPPLIED

base-10 blocks

blocks – B (40 of any color)

Model Multiplication activity page

GET READY Model with Arrays

ONLINE 5 min

Students will represent multiplication as arrays for the 2s, 5s, and 10s facts. They will review the concepts that multiplication is about equal groups and that a multiplication fact can be shown as an array or as groups of objects. For example, 5 ×2 can be shown with 5 rows of 2 objects or 5 groups of 2 objects.

Objectives

- Use concrete objects or sketches of arrays to model multiplication problems.
- Use concrete objects or sketches to model and explain multiplication as repeated addition.

LEARN Model with Equal Groups

ONLINE 15 min

Students will use online objects and sketches to solve multiplication problems. They will model multiplication problems as equal groups and explain multiplication as repeated addition of the same quantity on a number line.

Objectives

- Use objects or sketches to solve a multiplication problem.
- Use a model to explain multiplication as repeated addition of the same quantity.

LEARN Model with Base-10 Blocks

OFFLINE 15 min

Students will use objects to solve multiplication problems that have one factor greater than 10. They will use base-10 blocks to model the equal groups and then combine all the tens and all the ones to find the total.
   Gather the base-10 blocks.

Objectives

- Use objects or sketches to solve a multiplication problem.
- Use a model to explain multiplication as repeated addition of the same quantity.

Tips

Have students write the addition sentence vertically so they can add all the ones and then add the tens.

1. Write 8 × 11 in the Math Notebook. Explain that it would take a long time to draw a sketch to show this multiplication problem. Tell students that they can use base-10 blocks to model the problem.
2. Ask students how many groups of 11 should be shown and how they can show the problem with the fewest blocks. Eight groups of 11 should be shown; having 1 tens rod and 1 ones cube in each group uses the fewest blocks.
3. **Ask:** How can we find the total? Count by tens and then add on by ones.
4. Repeat Steps 1–3 using the problem 6 × 10. Guide students to determine that they should use tens rods to model the problem.
5. Write 4 × 8.

   Ask: How many groups should we show? 4

   Ask: How many should be shown in each group? 8

   Guide students to show 8 ones cubes in each of 4 groups.
6. **Ask:** How can we group the blocks to find the total? Discussion should include grouping the tens and the ones to find the total.
7. Have students combine any groups of 10 ones cubes into 1 tens rod. Then have students count the tens and the ones to find the total.

   Ask: What is 4 × 8? 32

   Have students explain how they found their answer.
8. Have students write a repeated addition problem to check their answer.
   8 + 8 + 8 + 8 = 32

9. Repeat Steps 5–8 with the following problems:
   - 3×13 Three groups of 13 should be shown; 13 should be shown in each group; $3 \times 13 = 39$; $13 + 13 + 13 = 39$.
   - 3×15 Three groups of 15 should be shown; 15 should be shown in each group; $3 \times 15 = 45$; $15 + 15 + 15 = 45$.

10. **Say:** Peter has 4 bags of pennies. Each bag has 15 pennies. How can you use base-10 blocks to show this problem? Answers should include showing 4 groups, each consisting of 1 tens rod and 5 ones cubes.

11. Have students model the problem. Then have them tell the multiplication problem that describes what they have shown. 4×15

    Finally have students tell the addition sentence they can use to solve the problem. $15 + 15 + 15 + 15 = 60$

OFFLINE
15 min

TRY IT Model Multiplication

Students will practice using objects or sketches to solve multiplication problems and will explain multiplication as repeated addition. Gather the B blocks for students to use as counting objects. Have students turn to the Model Multiplication activity page in their Activity Book and read the directions with them.

Students should copy the problems from the Activity Book into their Math Notebook as necessary and solve them there.

Objectives

- Use objects or sketches to solve a multiplication problem.
- Use a model to explain multiplication as repeated addition of the same quantity.

Tips

Allow students to use models to help them answer the problems.

Model and Explain Multiplication
Model Multiplication

Use the picture of circle blocks to answer Problems 1–5.

●●●●   ●●●●   ●●●●

1. How many groups are there?
   3
2. How many objects are in each group?
   4
3. What multiplication sentence is shown?
   $3 \times 4 = 12$
4. What addition sentence can you use to find the total?
   $4 + 4 + 4 = 12$
5. How can you use a number line to find the total?
   See below.

Use the picture of base-10 blocks to answer Problems 6 and 7.

6. How can you show 4×12 with addition?
   $12 + 12 + 12 + 12$
7. What is the product or total?
   48

Use circle blocks to explain how to solve, and give the answer.
8. $4 \times 9 = \square$ **Show 4 groups of 9 blocks.**
   $4 \times 9 = 36$

Draw a sketch to show the answer, and give the answer.
9. $6 \times 2 = \square$ **Sketch 6 groups of 2 objects.**
   $6 \times 2 = 12$

TRY IT

WHOLE NUMBER MULTIPLICATION SENSE   **22**   MODEL AND EXPLAIN MULTIPLICATION

Additional Answers

5.
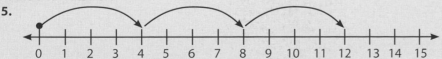

Use the pictures of frogs to answer the question.

10. Adrianna wants to know the total number of frogs in the ponds. Write one number sentence using addition and one number sentence using multiplication that she could use to solve the problem. **See below.**

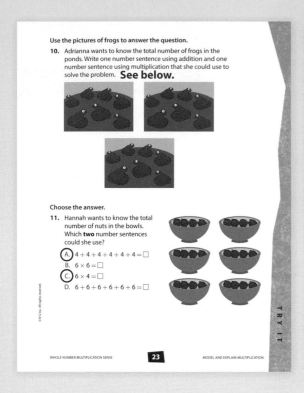

Choose the answer.

11. Hannah wants to know the total number of nuts in the bowls. Which **two** number sentences could she use?

Ⓐ $4 + 4 + 4 + 4 + 4 + 4 = \square$
B. $6 \times 6 = \square$
Ⓒ $6 \times 4 = \square$
D. $6 + 6 + 6 + 6 + 6 + 6 = \square$

Choose the answer.

12. Which is another way to write $8 \times 2 = \square$?
A. $2 + 2 = \square$
Ⓑ $2 + 2 + 2 + 2 + 2 + 2 + 2 + 2 = \square$
C. $8 + 8 + 8 + 8 = \square$
D. $8 + 8 + 8 + 8 + 8 + 8 + 8 + 8 = \square$

13. Which shows $5 \times 6 = \square$?

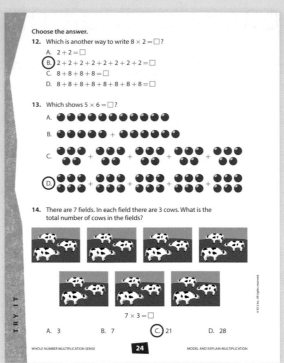

14. There are 7 fields. In each field there are 3 cows. What is the total number of cows in the fields?

$7 \times 3 = \square$

A. 3   B. 7   Ⓒ 21   D. 28

Additional Answers

10. $7 + 7 + 7 = \square$
      $3 \times 7 = \square$
      Both answers are 21.

ONLINE

10 min

CHECKPOINT

Students will complete an online Checkpoint. If necessary, read the directions, problems, and answer choices to students and help them with keyboard or mouse operations.

Objectives

- Use objects or sketches to solve a multiplication problem.
- Use a model to explain multiplication as repeated addition of the same quantity.

Area Models for Multiplication (A)

Lesson Overview

GET READY Arrays and Multiplication	10 minutes	**ONLINE**
LEARN Show Multiplication with Area Models	25 minutes	**ONLINE**
TRY IT Area Models	25 minutes	**OFFLINE**

▶ ## Lesson Objectives

Use an area model to explain multiplication.

▶ ## Prerequisite Skills

Use concrete objects or sketches of arrays to model multiplication problems.

▶ ## Content Background

Students have used objects arranged in arrays to model and explain multiplication as repeated addition. In this lesson, students will learn what area models are and will use them to explain multiplication.

Multiplication is an operation used when there are equal groups. The multiplication symbol is used to say "groups of" or "rows of." For example, 3 groups of 5 objects would be shown as 3×5 and read as "3 times 5." On the other hand, 5 groups of 3 objects would be shown as 5×3 and read "5 times 3."

A multiplication number sentence is composed of two numbers, called factors, that are multiplied to produce the solution, or product. An array is a rectangular arrangement of objects in rows and columns. The number of rows is the first factor in a multiplication number sentence, and the number of columns is the second factor. The total number of objects in the entire array is the product.

The area model for multiplication is shown as the area of a rectangle in a grid showing the square units. An area model can also be a rectangle made of base-10 blocks that are in rows of tens rods and ones cubes lying end to end.

▶ ## Common Errors and Misconceptions

- Students might add the second factor too many or too few times. For example, for 4×5, students might add $4 + 4 + 4 + 4$.
- Students might undercount or overcount when using the count-by-n strategy.

▶ ## Advance Preparation

Print two copies of the Centimeter Grid Paper.

Materials to Gather

SUPPLIED

blocks – E (40 of any color)

Centimeter Grid Paper (printout)

Area Models activity page

GET READY Arrays and Multiplication

Objectives

Students will review representing multiplication as arrays for the 2s and 5s facts. They will review using skip counting and repeated addition to find the product, or answer.

- Use concrete objects or sketches of arrays to model multiplication problems.

ONLINE

LEARN Show Multiplication with Area Models

Objectives

Students will learn what an area model is. They will use area models to represent and explain multiplication. They'll learn that an array of squares can be pushed together to translate into an area model of equal rows on a grid. And they'll see that the equal rows form a rectangle.
Gather one copy of the Centimeter Grid Paper.

- Use an area model to explain multiplication.

DIRECTIONS FOR USING THE GRID LEARNING TOOL

1. Tell students that they can make an area model by shading squares on the tool.

2. Have students choose a color. Then have them shade squares to show 2×4. Tell them that they will shade 2 rows of 4 squares.

3. Guide students to shade the squares in one corner of their grid paper to make a picture that resembles their online model.

   Ask: What is the product of 2 times 4? 8

4. Have students count the shaded squares. Then have them say the addition sentence they can use to find the value of 2×4. $4 + 4 = 8$

5. Have students clear the grid.

6. Have students shade squares to show 4×6. Check that they have shaded adjacent squares to form a rectangle made up of 4 rows of 6 squares.

7. Have students tell you the multiplication sentence and the addition sentence shown by the area model. $4 \times 6 = 24$; $6 + 6 + 6 + 6 = 24$

8. Repeat Steps 2–5 with the following problems:
   - 7×4 28; $4 + 4 + 4 + 4 + 4 + 4 + 4 = 28$
   - 3×7 21; $7 + 7 + 7 = 21$

9. Have students use their grid paper to copy a 3×7 grid like the one they made on the screen. Have them label the grid with the multiplication sentence and the addition problem they can use to find the value. Students should shade 3 rows of 7 squares on the grid paper and write $3 \times 7 = 21$ and $7 + 7 + 7 = 21$.

10. Have students shade the grid to show 3×4. Then have them say the multiplication fact. Students should shade 3 rows of 4 squares and say $3 \times 4 = 12$.

11. Near the 3 rows of 4, have students shade the grid to show 4×3 and say the multiplication fact. Students should shade 4 rows of 3 squares and say $4 \times 3 = 12$.

12. Have students compare the two models they just shaded. Discuss how the models are alike, including the fact that the product is the same.

Ask: Is multiplication still repeated addition when it is represented as an area model? Yes, because you see 3 rows of 4 or 3 groups of 4 and you can add $4 + 4 + 4$ to find the total of 12.

13. Have students shade 3×4 and 4×3 on their grid paper. Have them write the multiplication fact and the repeated addition fact next to each area model.

TRY IT Area Models

OFFLINE

25min

Objectives

- Use an area model to explain multiplication.

Students will practice using area models to explain and solve multiplication problems. Gather the E blocks and one copy of the Centimeter Grid Paper; students will use these to solve some problems. Have students turn to the Area Models activity page in their Activity Book and read the directions with them.

Students should copy the problems from the Activity Book into their Math Notebook as necessary and solve them there.

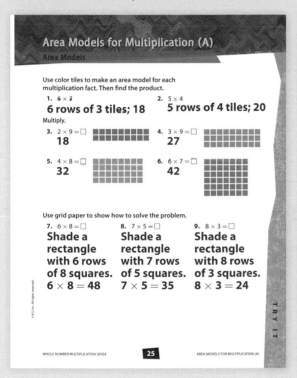

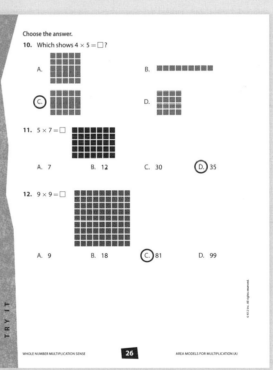

Area Models for Multiplication (B)

Lesson Overview

LEARN Blocks and Grids	20 minutes	**ONLINE**
LEARN Model and Add	20 minutes	**OFFLINE**
TRY IT Solve with Area Models	10 minutes	**OFFLINE**
CHECKPOINT	10 minutes	**ONLINE**

▶ Lesson Objectives

Use an area model to explain multiplication.

▶ Prerequisite Skills

Use concrete objects or sketches of arrays to model multiplication problems.

▶ Content Background

Students will learn more about factors and multiplication. This lesson uses Base-10 Grid Paper. The Base-10 Grid Paper has smaller and more numerous squares than Centimeter Grid Paper. The Base-10 Grid Paper is marked with a darker line every 10 squares, thus the name referring to base-10. The purpose of the Base-10 Grid Paper is to allow students to multiply greater numbers and to count by 10 for quicker calculation.

▶ Common Errors and Misconceptions

- Students might add the second factor too many or too few times. For example, for 4×5, students might add $4 + 4 + 4 + 4$.
- Students might undercount or overcount when using the count-by-*n* strategy.

▶ Advance Preparation

Print two copies of the Base-10 Grid Paper.

Materials to Gather

SUPPLIED

Base-10 Grid Paper (printout)

Solve with Area Models activity page

LEARN Blocks and Grids

ONLINE **20**min

Objectives

- Use an area model to explain multiplication.

Students will use area models to show multiplication problems with factors of 10 or greater. They will use online base-10 blocks to represent the problem and then use the online Grid Learning Tool to shade the area represented by a multiplication problem. The purpose of this activity is to guide students toward a faster and easier way to multiply. For instance, when 5×23 is shaded on a grid, it clearly shows the product. Students can look at the shaded area and can easily count the tens and ones. This builds students' conceptual understanding of multiplication and prepares them for learning to do multiplication without the aid of models in the future.

DIRECTIONS FOR USING THE GRID LEARNING TOOL

1. Tell students that they can represent multiplication problems on the grid. Have them choose a color. Then have them show 5 × 7 by shading 5 rows of 7 squares.

   Ask: How many squares are shaded? 35

   Ask: What is the product of 5 × 7? 35

   Have students record the problem in their Math Notebook. 5 × 7 = 35

2. Have students click the down arrow at the bottom of the screen to show two grids. Ask students to show 4 × 13 by shading 4 rows of 13. To shade a row of 13, students should shade a row of 10 in the grid on the left and shade 3 squares in the same row in the grid on the right.

   Ask: How many squares are shaded? 52

   Ask: What is the product of 4 × 13? 52

   Have students record the problem in their Math Notebook. 4 × 13 = 52

   Observe how students figure out how many squares there are. Most will count rows of 10 and then count the rest of the squares. If they do not use this method, suggest it to them.

3. Have students click the down arrow at the bottom of the screen to show three grids. Ask students to show 4 × 23 by shading 4 rows of 23. Have students use the grid to determine the product. Have them record the problem in their Math Notebook. 4 × 23 = 92

4. Have students do the following problems in the same way:
   - 8 × 12 96
   - 3 × 25 75

   As time permits, have students make up problems, show them on the grid, and record the problems and answers in the Math Notebook.

LEARN Model and Add

OFFLINE

20min

Objectives

- Use an area model to explain multiplication.

Students will use area models to represent and solve multiplication problems. They will use Base-10 Grid Paper to make area models. The models represent multiplication problems where one factor is greater than 10. Then students will find products in a variety of ways, including using repeated addition expressed vertically.

Gather one copy of the Base-10 Grid Paper.

Tips

Encourage students to try a variety of methods to find each product.

1. Write the problem 4 × 23. Then have students shade squares on grid paper to show the problem. Encourage students to explain how they can use the markings on the grid paper to help them quickly count 10s. Count the rows of tens first and then count the ones.

2. Have students write 4 × 23 next to the area model and write the product.
   4 × 23 = 92

3. Have students draw lines on the grid paper separating the rectangle into a 4 × 10 rectangle, a second 4 × 10 rectangle, and a 4 × 3 rectangle. Have students write the product for each area model on the divided rectangles. They should write 40 on each 4 × 10 rectangle and 12 on the 4 ×3 rectangle.

4. **Ask:** What is 40 + 40 + 12? 92

   Say: We can multiply 4 × 23, or we can break apart 23 and multiply 4 × 10, 4 × 10, and 4 × 3, and then add the products. The answer is the same.

5. Write the problem 6 × 11. Have students shade squares on the grid paper to show the problem.

6. **Ask:** How can you use the sketch to find the product of 6 times 11? I can count the number of shaded squares.

7. Have students find the product by counting the squares on the grid paper. Have them write the multiplication problem. 6 × 11 = 66

8. Have students draw a line on the grid paper to separate the rectangle into one 6 × 10 rectangle and one 6 × 1 rectangle. Students should find each partial product and write the partial products in the rectangles on the grid paper.

   Ask: What is 6 × 10 plus 6 × 1? 66

9. Discuss with students which method they prefer to use to find the product.

10. Have students sketch area models on grid paper for the following multiplication problems. Have them find each product two different ways, recording their solutions on the grid paper.

    • 2 × 24 48

    • 4 × 24 96

11. **Ask:** How could you use what you know about 2 × 24 to find the product of 4 × 24? Four is the double of 2, so I could just double the product of 2 × 24 to find the product of 4 × 24.

12. Have students sketch an area model on grid paper to show 6 ×16. Have them draw lines on the grid paper to separate the rectangle into a 6 × 10, 6 × 5, and 6 × 1 rectangle. Point out that 10, 5, and 1 are all multiplication facts that they know.

13. Have students fill in the partial products in each smaller rectangle.

    Ask: What is 60 + 30 + 6? 96

    Ask: So what is 6 × 16? 96

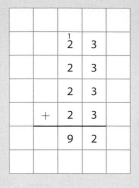

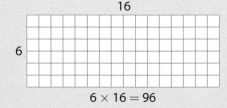

6 × 16 = 96

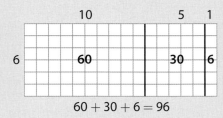

60 + 30 + 6 = 96

OFFLINE

10min

TRY IT Solve with Area Models

Objectives

Students will work with area models to show multiplication. Gather one copy of the Base-10 Grid Paper. Have students turn to the Solve with Area Models activity page in their Activity Book and read the directions with them.

   Students should copy the problems from the Activity Book into their Math Notebook as necessary and solve them there.

• Use an area model to explain multiplication.

Answer the question.

1. Which model shows $17 \times 4 = \square$? Choose the answer.

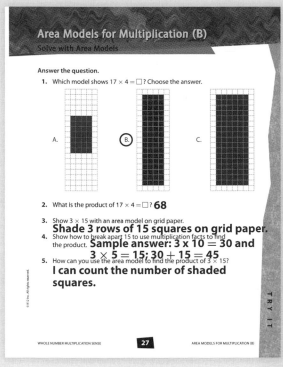

A.   (B.)   C.

2. What is the product of $17 \times 4 = \square$? **68**

3. Show 3×15 with an area model on grid paper.
Shade 3 rows of 15 squares on grid paper.

4. Show how to break apart 15 to use multiplication facts to find the product. **Sample answer: 3 x 10 = 30 and 3 × 5 = 15; 30 + 15 = 45**

5. How can you use the area model to find the product of 3×15?
I can count the number of shaded squares.

T R Y   I T

Multiply.

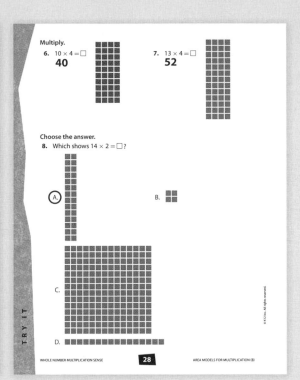

6. $10 \times 4 = \square$
40

7. $13 \times 4 = \square$
52

Choose the answer.

8. Which shows $14 \times 2 = \square$?

(A.)   B.

C.

D.

T R Y   I T

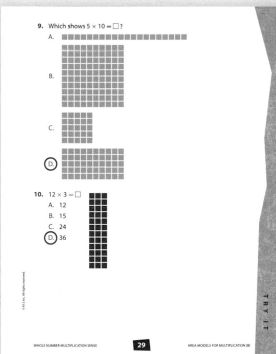

9. Which shows $5 \times 10 = \square$?

A.

B.

C.

(D.)

10. $12 \times 3 = \square$
A. 12
B. 15
C. 24
(D.) 36

T R Y   I T

CHECKPOINT

ONLINE
10min

Students will complete an online Checkpoint. If necessary, read the directions, problems, and answer choices to students and help them with keyboard or mouse operations.

Objectives

- Use an area model to explain multiplication.

Understand Multiplication

Lesson Overview

GET READY Model Multiplication	10 minutes	**OFFLINE**
LEARN Effect of Multiplication	15 minutes	**OFFLINE**
LEARN Multiplication Patterns	15 minutes	**OFFLINE**
TRY IT Multiplication Results	10 minutes	**OFFLINE**
CHECKPOINT	10 minutes	**ONLINE**

▶ Lesson Objectives

Demonstrate an understanding of how multiplication affects whole numbers.

▶ Prerequisite Skills

Use objects or sketches to solve a multiplication problem.

▶ Content Background

Students may already have a basic knowledge of multiplication and understand how to model and solve multiplication problems. In this lesson, they will learn how multiplication affects whole numbers, gaining an understanding that with multiplication, the product is usually greater than the factors. They will explore multiplying by 1 and zero and the effects of those numbers on the product. They will identify patterns of multiples. (For example, multiples of 2 are even numbers; multiples of 5 end in the digit 5 or zero; and multiples of 10 end in the digit zero.) Seeing these general patterns will help students develop a broader understanding of mathematics. Students will be introduced to the term *multiples* and will learn that when they skip count by 10s, starting at zero, they are saying the multiples of 10.

▶ Common Errors and Misconceptions

Students might not understand that the two factors in a multiplication problem have different meanings. For example, 3 sets of 6 dots is written as 3×6, not 6×3. However, the product of each expression is 18.

▶ Advance Preparation

Print the Hundred Chart, and use the Number Line Creator Tool to print a page with four number lines from 0 to 20.

DIRECTIONS FOR USING THE NUMBER LINE CREATOR TOOL

To create number lines from 0 to 20:

1. Set Range:	2. Select Options:	3. Print Number Line:
• Start Number Line at: 0 • End Number Line at: 20	• Tick Marks: ones • Labels: ones	• Page Orientation: landscape • Number Lines per Sheet: 4

Materials to Gather

SUPPLIED

number lines from the Number Line Creator Tool

base-10 blocks

Hundred Chart (printout)

Multiplication Results activity page

GET READY Model Multiplication

Objectives

- Use objects or sketches to solve a multiplication problem.

Students will make a sketch to model a multiplication problem. They will then write a related addition problem and skip count to solve.

1. Have students write 4×5. Ask them to sketch 4×5 in any way they like. Options include:
   - an array with 4 rows of 5 circles (or dots, stars, or other objects)
   - a drawing of 4 groups of 5 circles
   - a grid showing 4 rows of 5 squares shaded
   - a number line starting at zero and showing 4 jumps of 5

2. Near their drawing, have students write the problem as repeated addition. $5 + 5 + 5 + 5 = 20$

3. Have students skip count by 5s to find the total. Have them record the answer. 5, 10, 15, 20

4. Remind students of the different ways they could have represented the problem so that they are familiar with various ways to show multiplication.

Tips

Reinforce that the first factor is the number of groups and the second factor is the number in each group.

LEARN Effect of Multiplication

Objectives

- Demonstrate an understanding of how multiplication affects whole numbers.

Students will explore how multiplication affects whole numbers. They will learn the following patterns.

When both factors are greater than 1,
- The product is greater than either factor.
- The product will be to the right of both factors on the number line.

When a factor is zero,
- The product is zero.

When a factor is 1 (and there are only two factors),
- The product is the other factor.

Gather the number lines you printed from the Number Line Creator Tool.

1. **Say:** In an addition problem where two numbers greater than zero are added, the sum is greater than either of the addends.

   To illustrate this, show the problem $8 + 7$ on a number line.

   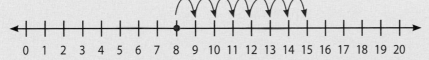

   Have students notice that the sum is to the right of each number being added, so it's greater than either number being added.

2. Remind students that multiplication is repeated addition.

   Ask: If you multiply two numbers greater than 1, do you think the product will always be greater than or less than the factors? The product will always be greater than the factors.

Have students work the problem 3 × 5 on a number line as an example.

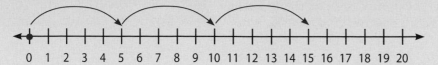

Point out that the product (15) is greater than either of the factors (3 and 5).

Ask: When you multiply two numbers greater than 1, will the answer always be greater than either of the numbers? Yes

Have students make up some problems, such as 2 × 10 and 3 × 100, to verify that this seems to be true.

3. **Say:** When both numbers in a problem are greater than 1, you can think of the problem on a number line and see that there's more than one jump. So the product is definitely greater than the number you started with. For example, if the problem is 3 × 5, there's more than one jump of 5. The product will definitely be greater than 5. The same is true if the factors in the problem are reversed. In our example, if you change the problem to 5 × 3, there's more than one jump of 3.

4. Tell students that as long as both factors are greater than 1, the product is always greater than either factor. On the number line, the product will always be to the right of either factor. The answer to 3 × 5 is 15; this product is to the right of both 3 and 5.

5. **Ask:** When is the product not greater than both factors? when a factor is zero or 1

   Ask: What happens when you multiply by zero? When you multiply by 1? When I multiply by zero, I get zero. When I multiply by 1, I get the other factor.

6. Summarize for students.

   Say: When multiplying two whole numbers, the product is usually greater than the factors. The only times this is not true are when multiplying by zero or 1. When zero is a factor, the product is always zero, and when 1 is a factor, the product is the other factor.

LEARN Multiplication Patterns

OFFLINE 15 min

Objectives

- Demonstrate an understanding of how multiplication affects whole numbers.

Students will learn the term *multiple* and will identify patterns that result when multiplying two factors.

Gather the base-10 blocks and the Hundred Chart.

1. Have students model 1 × 10 using base-10 blocks. Students should show 1 tens rod.

   Ask students to say and write the number sentence and the product.
   1 × 10 = 10

   Repeat for 2 × 10, 3 × 10, and 4 × 10.

   Ask students why no ones cubes are needed. Since we're showing 1 ten, 2 tens, 3 tens, and so on, we can show them with just tens rods.

   Have students notice that each product has a zero in the ones place, showing that there are no ones.

2. Have students circle each product. Explain that these are all multiples of 10.

   Have students skip count by 10 (10, 20, 30, and so on). Explain that when they skip count by 10, they are saying the multiples of 10. Have students notice that all multiples of 10 end with the digit zero in the ones place.

3. Have students skip count by 5s on the Hundred Chart. Have them shade each multiple of 5 and then look for a pattern.

   Ask: What do you notice about multiples of 5? Multiples of 5 always end in the digit 5 or zero.

4. Write the following in two columns as shown:

1×5	2×5
3×5	4×5
5×5	6×5
7×5	8×5
9×5	10×5

   Have students use base-10 blocks to show the products of 1×5, 2×5, 3×5, and 4×5. Have them record the products. Ask them to explain why there are always either 5 ones cubes or zero ones cubes when making multiples of 5. Guide students to see that when multiplying by an odd number, the product will have 5 ones and when multiplying by an even number, the product will have only tens rods and zero ones because two 5s equal one 10.

5. Have students solve the following problems and look for a pattern:

$4 \times 10 = 40$	$6 \times 10 = 60$	$8 \times 10 = 80$	$5 \times 10 = 50$
$4 \times 5 = 20$	$6 \times 5 = 30$	$8 \times 5 = 40$	$5 \times 5 = 25$

   Discuss the pattern. Help students recognize that multiplying 5 times a number is the same as half of 10 times the same number—in other words, the product of 10 and a number is twice the product of 5 and that same number.

6. Explore multiples of 2 by having students count by 2s and write the following for multiples of 2:

1×2	2×2	3×2	4×2	5×2
6×2	7×2	8×2	9×2	10×2

   Ask students to identify each product as an even or odd number. All products are even numbers.

   Explain that all multiples of 2 are even numbers because when you multiply by 2, you make groups of 2, and every multiple of 2 is an even number.

TRY IT Multiplication Results

OFFLINE
10 min

Objectives

Students will practice determining the result of multiplication on whole numbers. Have students turn to the Multiplication Results activity page in their Activity Book and read the directions with them.

   Students should copy the problems from the Activity Book into their Math Notebook as necessary and solve them there.

- Demonstrate an understanding of how multiplication affects whole numbers.

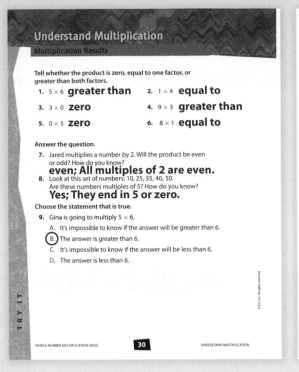

Understand Multiplication
Multiplication Results

Tell whether the product is zero, equal to one factor, or greater than both factors.

1. 5×6 **greater than**
2. 1×4 **equal to**
3. 3×0 **zero**
4. 9×3 **greater than**
5. 0×5 **zero**
6. 8×1 **equal to**

Answer the question.

7. Jared multiplies a number by 2. Will the product be even or odd? How do you know?
even; All multiples of 2 are even.

8. Look at this set of numbers: 10, 25, 35, 40, 50. Are these numbers multiples of 5? How do you know?
Yes; They end in 5 or zero.

Choose the statement that is true.

9. Gina is going to multiply 5×6.
   A. It's impossible to know if the answer will be greater than 6.
   B. The answer is greater than 6.
   C. It's impossible to know if the answer will be less than 6.
   D. The answer is less than 6.

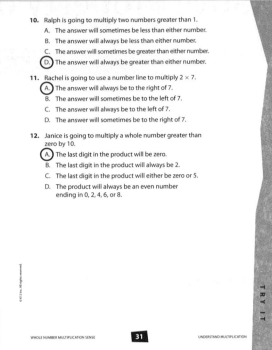

10. Ralph is going to multiply two numbers greater than 1.
    A. The answer will sometimes be less than either number.
    B. The answer will always be less than either number.
    C. The answer will sometimes be greater than either number.
    D. The answer will always be greater than either number.

11. Rachel is going to use a number line to multiply 2×7.
    A. The answer will always be to the right of 7.
    B. The answer will sometimes be to the left of 7.
    C. The answer will always be to the left of 7.
    D. The answer will sometimes be to the right of 7.

12. Janice is going to multiply a whole number greater than zero by 10.
    A. The last digit in the product will be zero.
    B. The last digit in the product will always be 2.
    C. The last digit in the product will either be zero or 5.
    D. The product will always be an even number ending in 0, 2, 4, 6, or 8.

CHECKPOINT

ONLINE 10 min

Students will complete an online Checkpoint. If necessary, read the directions, problems, and answer choices to students and help them with keyboard or mouse operations.

Objectives

- Demonstrate an understanding of how multiplication affects whole numbers.

Commutative Property of Multiplication

Lesson Overview

GET READY Area Models	5 minutes	**ONLINE**
LEARN Change the Order	10 minutes	**ONLINE**
LEARN Factor Switch	15 minutes	**ONLINE**
LEARN Three Factors	15 minutes	**ONLINE**
TRY IT Apply the Commutative Property	10 minutes	**OFFLINE**

▶ Lesson Objectives

Explain and apply the commutative property of multiplication.

▶ Prerequisite Skills

Demonstrate understanding that the order in which numbers are multiplied does not affect the product.

▶ Content Background

Students now have a basic knowledge of multiplication, and they understand how to model and solve multiplication problems by skip counting or using repeated addition. In this lesson, they will be reminded that a multiplication problem can be represented by rows and squares. For instance, 7 × 10 is represented by 7 rows of 10 squares and can be solved easily by skip counting by 10s. In contrast, 10 × 7 is represented with 10 rows of 7 squares. Since it's more difficult to skip count by 7s, students will use the commutative property of multiplication to change the order of the factors and will multiply 7 × 10 to get the product. They will learn about the commutative property of multiplication.

The commutative property of multiplication states that two or more factors can be multiplied in any order and the product does not change. For example, 5 × 3 = 15 and 3 × 5 = 15, so 5 × 3 = 3 × 5.

▶ Common Errors and Misconceptions

Students might not realize that the two factors in a multiplication problem have different meanings. For example, 3 sets of 6 dots is written as 3 × 6, not 6 × 3. However, the product of each is 18.

GET READY Area Models

ONLINE
5 min

Students will see multiplication represented using an area model. They will see 5 × 8 represented as 5 rows of 8 squares. Then they'll see that when the model is turned sideways, it shows 8 × 5 or 8 rows of 5 squares. In each case, although the problem is different, the product or total number of squares is the same.

Objectives

- Demonstrate understanding that the order in which numbers are multiplied does not affect the product.

LEARN Change the Order

ONLINE
10min

Objectives

- Explain and apply the commutative property of multiplication.

Students will explore the commutative property of multiplication. They will see multiplication problems shown using an area model with squares on a grid. They'll see that the order of the factors does not affect the product.

Remind students that the first factor is the number of rows and the second factor is the number of squares in each row, or the number of columns. If necessary, help students solve the the problem by writing it as repeated addition. For example, $10 \times 7 = 7 + 7 + 7 + 7 + 7 + 7 + 7 + 7 + 7 + 7$, and $7 \times 10 = 10 + 10 + 10 + 10 + 10 + 10 + 10$. Repeated addition will help students see how the order of the factors affects how the problem is solved but doesn't affect the product.

LEARN Factor Switch

ONLINE
15min

Objectives

- Explain and apply the commutative property of multiplication.

Students will practice using the commutative property of multiplication to solve problems. They will see that $7 \times 5 = 35$ and will use that information to solve 5×7.

LEARN Three Factors

ONLINE
15min

Objectives

- Explain and apply the commutative property of multiplication.

Students have been using the commutative property of multiplication to solve problems that have only two factors. The commutative property always deals with only two factors at a time, but it can be used in problems with more than two factors to make the problems easier to solve.

In multiplication, any of the factors can be switched with another factor and the product will be the same. In this activity, students will first review how they commonly use the commutative property of addition in problems with three or more numbers, making those problems easier to solve. They will then use the commutative property of multiplication to make multiplication problems easier when there are three factors. For instance, $5 \times 7 \times 2$ is easily solved when reordered as $5 \times 2 \times 7$.

TRY IT Apply the Commutative Property

OFFLINE
10min

Objectives

- Explain and apply the commutative property of multiplication.

Students will practice applying the commutative property of multiplication. Have students turn to the Apply the Commutative Property activity page in their Activity Book and read the directions with them.

Students should copy the problems from the Activity Book into their Math Notebook as necessary and solve them there.

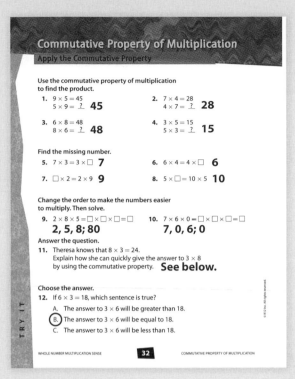

Commutative Property of Multiplication

Apply the Commutative Property

Use the commutative property of multiplication to find the product.

1. $9 \times 5 = 45$
   $5 \times 9 = \underline{?}$ **45**

2. $7 \times 4 = 28$
   $4 \times 7 = \underline{?}$ **28**

3. $6 \times 8 = 48$
   $8 \times 6 = \underline{?}$ **48**

4. $3 \times 5 = 15$
   $5 \times 3 = \underline{?}$ **15**

Find the missing number.

5. $7 \times 3 = 3 \times \square$ **7**

6. $6 \times 4 = 4 \times \square$ **6**

7. $\square \times 2 = 2 \times 9$ **9**

8. $5 \times \square = 10 \times 5$ **10**

Change the order to make the numbers easier to multiply. Then solve.

9. $2 \times 8 \times 5 = \square \times \square \times \square = \square$
   2, 5, 8; 80

10. $7 \times 6 \times 0 = \square \times \square \times \square = \square$
    7, 0, 6; 0

Answer the question.

11. Theresa knows that $8 \times 3 = 24$.
    Explain how she can quickly give the answer to 3×8 by using the commutative property. **See below.**

Choose the answer.

12. If $6 \times 3 = 18$, which sentence is true?

    A. The answer to 3×6 will be greater than 18.

    B. The answer to 3×6 will be equal to 18.

    C. The answer to 3×6 will be less than 18.

TRY IT

WHOLE NUMBER MULTIPLICATION SENSE   **32**   COMMUTATIVE PROPERTY OF MULTIPLICATION

Additional Answers

11. **Example:** She knows that changing the order of the numbers that are multiplied doesn't change the product, so 3×8 will also equal 24. (Other correct answers are acceptable.)

Multiplication Facts (A)

Lesson Overview

GET READY Groups of Objects	5 minutes	ONLINE
LEARN Factors of Zero and 1	10 minutes	OFFLINE
LEARN Multiplication Facts Chart	20 minutes	OFFLINE
LEARN Multiply 3s	15 minutes	OFFLINE
TRY IT Multiplication Practice	10 minutes	ONLINE

▶ Lesson Objectives

- Explain and apply the zero property of multiplication.
- Explain and apply the multiplication property of 1.
- Demonstrate automatic recall of multiplication facts.

▶ Prerequisite Skills

- Demonstrate understanding of the rule for multiplying by zero.
- Demonstrate understanding that any number multiplied by 1 results in the same number ($n \times 1 = n$).

▶ Content Background

Students have a basic understanding of multiplication. They will expand on this knowledge by learning about the zero property of multiplication and the multiplication property of 1. They will focus on fact memorization with the goal of automatically recalling the 3s multiplication facts. Students have already learned the multiplication facts for 2s, 5s, and 10s, and they should continue to practice those.

As students study math, they will learn that both zero and 1 are special numbers. In multiplication, the result of multiplying any number by 1 is that same number, but multiplying any number by zero always results in the answer of zero. These two facts are very important for students to remember.

Skip counting provides a firm foundation for multiplication. However, students must memorize and automatically recall their multiplication facts to truly succeed in math.

The commutative property of multiplication states that two numbers can be multiplied in any order and the product does not change. Even if the property is still not completely understood by students, they should recognize that once they know the product of 8×2 is 16, they also know the product of 2×8.

▶ Advance Preparation

Print the Multiplication Facts Chart, the Multiplication Facts Poster, and the Centimeter Grid Paper. Tape together the pieces of the Multiplication Facts Poster.

Materials to Gather

SUPPLIED

blocks – B (7 of any color)
Multiplication Facts Chart (printout)
Multiplication Facts Poster (printout)
Centimeter Grid Paper (printout)

ALSO NEEDED

coloring pencils or crayons
tape, clear

GET READY Groups of Objects

Students will practice representing multiplication expressions with the factors zero and 1. Remind students that the numbers that are multiplied are called *factors* and the answer is called the *product*.

Students will see that a number multiplied by 1 equals the number itself. They will see that a number multiplied by zero equals zero. They will see that 4×0 can be shown as 4 groups of zero objects. Remind students that 0×4 would be shown by zero groups of 4 objects.

- Demonstrate understanding of the rule for multiplying by zero.
- Demonstrate understanding that any number multiplied by 1 results in the same number ($n \times 1 = n$).

OFFLINE

10 min

LEARN Factors of Zero and 1

Objectives

Students will model multiplication by zero and 1. Then they will practice solving problems with factors of zero and 1.

Gather the B blocks.

1. Make one pile of 7 B blocks.

   Say: Here is one group of 7 circles. What multiplication problem does it represent? 1×7

   Ask: What is the product? 7

   Have the students use the same 7 blocks to show the problem 7×1. Students should spread the 7 blocks out to show 7 groups of 1.

   Ask: What is the product? 7

   Ask students what the rule is for multiplying by 1. One times any number is just that number, and any number times 1 is just the number you started with.

2. Ask students to show you zero groups of 7, and then 7 groups of zero. Ask what the product is in each case. zero

   Ask students to show you zero groups of 10,000 and tell you the product. zero

   Have students explain the rule for multiplying by zero. Any number times zero is zero, or zero times any number is zero.

3. Tell students that since they know the rules for multiplying by zero and 1, they can do any problem with a factor of zero or 1 quickly. Say each of these problems. Ask students to tell you the product.

- Explain and apply the zero property of multiplication.
- Explain and apply the multiplication property of 1.

Tips

Write the multiplication problems in the Math Notebook, if you wish, and have students write each product.

• 7×0 0	• 35×1 35	• $0 \times 2,000$ 0
• 10×1 10	• 1×17 17	• 450×1 450
• 0×9 0	• 245×0 0	• 1×42 42

4. Present the following simple story problems, which apply the zero property of multiplication. Ask students to give each answer.

   - There are zero paintbrushes in each box of art supplies. There are 24 boxes of art supplies. How many paintbrushes are there? $24 \times 0 = 0$; zero paintbrushes

   - There are 562 boxes in the warehouse. Each box has zero items. How many items are in all the boxes together? $562 \times 0 = 0$; zero items

5. If students answer either of the above story problems incorrectly, show them the expression for that problem and explain how the story problem is an example of the zero property of multiplication. Remind students that multiplying any number by zero results in an answer of zero.

OFFLINE 20min

LEARN Multiplication Facts Chart

Objectives

- Demonstrate automatic recall of multiplication facts.

Tips

Make a set of multiplication flash cards for problems with factors of 0, 1, 2, 5, and 10. Show students the cards and ask them to say the product. If they have the fact memorized, they can record the product on the chart.

Students will use a Multiplication Facts Chart to record the multiplication facts they have learned. They will also use the Multiplication Facts Poster that was assembled to hang on the wall. On the poster, students will record only the products of facts they have memorized. Those are the products they can say without pausing to do a mental calculation. In multiplication, the order in which factors are multiplied doesn't affect the product (multiplication is commutative). Thus, when students learn 3 × 4, they will also know 4 × 3 and can record both products on the Multiplication Facts Chart.

Gather the Multiplication Facts Poster and Multiplication Facts Chart.

1. Show students the Multiplication Facts Chart and the Multiplication Facts Poster. Explain that the small chart will be used to record which multiplication facts they've learned, and the poster will record those that are truly memorized. Explain that the goal is to memorize all the multiplication facts. Remind them that they already know many of the facts.

2. Guide students in how to use the chart to record products. Explain that the numbers on the bottom and on the left of the chart are factors, and each number on the bottom will pair with a number on the left to create a multiplication fact. Students will write each fact's product in the square where the column and row meet. (Be sure students go along the bottom to get the first factor and up for the second factor. Doing this will help them later when they do graphing, using the same routine to find points on a graph.)

3. Begin at the bottom and work from left to right: 0 × 0, 1 × 0, 2 × 0, 3 × 0, to 10 × 0. Have students match each factor along the bottom to zero on the left and record the product in the 0s and 1s chart.

4. Explain that since they know the products when the second factor is zero, they also know the products when the first factor is zero. Guide students to fill in the column that corresponds to multiplying by zero.

5. Repeat Steps 3 and 4 for the 1s multiplication facts. The highlighted area of the 0s and 1s chart shows the products of the 0s and 1s facts that students should write.

6. Check students' recall of the 2s, 5s, and 10s facts before recording those products in the chart. Remind students that they can skip count by 2s, 5s, or 10s to solve these facts.

7. At the end of the activity, have students record the product for any 0s, 1s, 2s, 5s, or 10s facts they have memorized on the Multiplication Facts Poster. The highlighted areas on the charts show the products that students should write.

8. Have students write the facts on the Multiplication Facts Chart and write the products in pencil on the Multiplication Facts Poster. (In several days, if students have truly memorized the facts and can recall them quickly, they can write them on the poster with a colored marker.)

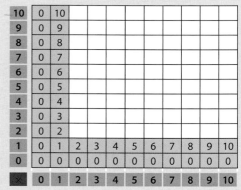

Multiplication Facts Chart Completed for 0s and 1s

10	0	10									
9	0	9									
8	0	8									
7	0	7									
6	0	6									
5	0	5									
4	0	4									
3	0	3									
2	0	2									
1	0	1	2	3	4	5	6	7	8	9	10
0	0	0	0	0	0	0	0	0	0	0	0
✖	0	1	2	3	4	5	6	7	8	9	10

Multiplication Facts Chart Completed for 2s, 5s, and 10s

10	0	10	20	30	40	50	60	70	80	90	100
9	0	9	18			45					90
8	0	8	16			40					80
7	0	7	14			35					70
6	0	6	12			30					60
5	0	5	10	15	20	25	30	35	40	45	50
4	0	4	8			20					40
3	0	3	6			15					30
2	0	2	4	6	8	10	12	14	16	18	20
1	0	1	2	3	4	5	6	7	8	9	10
0	0	0	0	0	0	0	0	0	0	0	0
✖	0	1	2	3	4	5	6	7	8	9	10

LEARN Multiply 3s

Objectives

- Demonstrate automatic recall of multiplication facts.

Students will model and solve the 3s multiplication facts. Because students know 0 × 3, 1 × 3, and 2 × 3, they will start at 3 × 3. There are only six facts to memorize. With the commutative facts, students will fill in 11 new facts in the Multiplication Facts Chart.

Gather the Multiplication Facts Chart, Centimeter Grid Paper, and coloring pencils or crayons.

1. Have students draw and color an area model to show 7 × 3 (7 rows of 3) on the grid paper.
2. Ask students to skip count by 3s to find the product. 3, 6, 9, 12, 15, 18, 21
3. Have students record the multiplication sentence below the area model. 7 × 3 = 21
4. Repeat Steps 1–3 for these facts: 3 × 3, 4 × 3, 5 × 3, 6 × 3, 7 × 3, 8 × 3, and 9 × 3. Examples of area models on grid paper are shown.

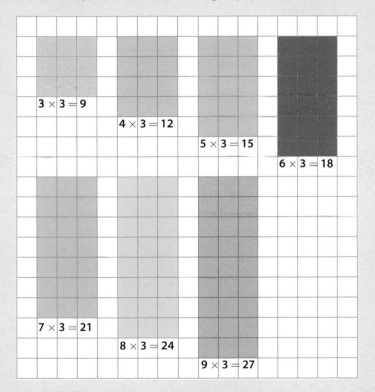

3 × 3 = 9
4 × 3 = 12
5 × 3 = 15
6 × 3 = 18
7 × 3 = 21
8 × 3 = 24
9 × 3 = 27

5. Remind students that changing the order of the factors in a multiplication problem does not change the product. Point out they also know the following facts because of the commutative property: 3 × 4, 3 × 5, 3 × 6, 3 × 7, 3 × 8, and 3 × 9.

6. Have students write the new 3s facts on the Multiplication Facts Chart and write the products in pencil on the Multiplication Facts Poster. (In several days, if students have truly memorized the facts and can recall them quickly, they can write them on the poster with a colored marker.)

Note: The highlighted area on the Multiplication Facts Chart shows the 3s multiplication facts that students should have filled in during this activity. The other, nonhighlighted products in the chart are the ones that they previously learned.

Multiplication Facts Chart
Completed for 3s

	0	1	2	3	4	5	6	7	8	9	10
10	0	10	20	30	40	50	60	70	80	90	100
9	0	9	18	27		45					90
8	0	8	16	24		40					80
7	0	7	14	21		35					70
6	0	6	12	18		30					60
5	0	5	10	15	20	25	30	35	40	45	50
4	0	4	8	12		20					40
3	0	3	6	9	12	15	18	21	24	27	30
2	0	2	4	6	8	10	12	14	16	18	20
1	0	1	2	3	4	5	6	7	8	9	10
0	0	0	0	0	0	0	0	0	0	0	0
	0	1	2	3	4	5	6	7	8	9	10

TRY IT   Multiplication Practice

Objectives

Students will use online flash cards to practice their 3s multiplication facts. They should say each answer aloud. They can flip the card to check their answer or they can go on to the next card if they know their answer is correct. If students have difficulty memorizing the 3s, have them count by 3s to 30 to get familiar with the numbers that are multiples of 3.

- Explain and apply the zero property of multiplication.
- Explain and apply the multiplication property of 1.
- Demonstrate automatic recall of multiplication facts.

Multiplication Facts (B)

Lesson Overview

GET READY Multiplication Review	10 minutes	**ONLINE**
LEARN Use 2s Facts to Solve Multiplication	20 minutes	**OFFLINE**
LEARN Recall 4s Facts	20 minutes	**ONLINE**
TRY IT Practice Multiplication	10 minutes	**OFFLINE**

▶ ## Lesson Objectives

Demonstrate automatic recall of multiplication facts.

▶ ## Prerequisite Skills

- Demonstrate automatic recall of multiplication facts for 2 through 10×2.
- Demonstrate automatic recall of multiplication facts for 5 through 10×5.
- Demonstrate understanding that the order in which numbers are multiplied does not affect the product.

Materials to Gather

SUPPLIED

Centimeter Grid Paper (printout)

Multiplication Facts Chart (printout)

Multiplication Facts Poster (printout)

Practice Multiplication activity page

▶ ## Content Background

Students will practice previously learned multiplication facts and will also learn the 4s facts. They will learn a strategy that will help them memorize their 4s facts.

Skip counting provides a foundation for multiplication. However, students must memorize and automatically recall their multiplication facts to truly succeed in math. They should begin to realize that changing the order in which numbers are multiplied does not affect the product. (For example, if they know $8 \times 2 = 16$, they will also know the product of 2×8.)

▶ ## Advance Preparation

Print the Centimeter Grid Paper. Have the Multiplication Facts Chart and Multiplication Facts Poster ready or print new ones if needed.

GET READY Multiplication Review

Objectives

Students will continue to practice multiplication facts. They will use online flash cards to practice these facts. Have students say or write the answers.

- Demonstrate automatic recall of multiplication facts for 2 through 10×2.
- Demonstrate automatic recall of multiplication facts for 5 through 10×5.
- Demonstrate understanding that the order in which numbers are multiplied does not affect the product.

LEARN Use 2s Facts to Solve Multiplication

Objectives

Students will use their knowledge of the 2s multiplication facts to learn multiplication facts for 4s.

Gather the Centimeter Grid Paper, Multiplication Facts Chart, and Multiplication Facts Poster.

1. Ask students to create an area model on the grid paper to show 3×4. Remind students that the first factor, 3, names the number of rows and the second factor, 4, names the number in each row.

2. Have students count by 4s to find the product. 4, 8, 12

3. Write the multiplication fact $3 \times 4 = 12$.

4. Explain to students that skip counting by 4s is not necessarily as easy as skip counting by 2s and that they can use their 2s facts to solve facts for 4.

5. **Say:** Since $2 \times 2 = 4$, or double 2 is 4, you can double the 2s facts to find the facts for 4.

6. Ask students to find the product of 6×2. 12

   Explain that they can double that product to find the product of 6×4.

   Ask: What is the double of 12? 24

   Explain that to find the product of 6×4, they can use $6 \times 2 = 12$, double the 12, and identify 24 as the product of 6×4.

7. Ask students to find the product of 9×4. 36

   Point out that they can break apart the factor 9 to find the product of 9×4.

   Say: Since 5 plus 4 equals 9, you can multiply both addends by 4 and add the sums to find 9×4. For example, $5 \times 4 = 20$ and $4 \times 4 = 16$; $20 + 16 = 36$.

   Explain that you can break apart 9 into any two addends with the sum of 9 and arrive at the same product. Break apart 9 into $2 + 7$ as another example: $2 \times 4 = 8$; $7 \times 4 = 28$; $8 + 28 = 36$.

8. Have students find the products for the following problems using whatever strategy is easiest for them: $1 \times 4, 2 \times 4, 3 \times 4, 4 \times 4, 5 \times 4, 6 \times 4$, $7 \times 4, 8 \times 4, 9 \times 4$, and 10×4.

   For some problems, students may choose to find the 2s fact and double the product. For example, to solve 8×4, students would think of $8 \times 2 = 16$. The answer to 8×4 would be the double of 16. Thus, $8 \times 4 = 32$.

Tips

If students have difficulty seeing that 4 times a number is the double of 2 times a number, have them use the grid paper to shade 6×4 (6 rows of 4). Then draw a line under the second row to show students how the grid can be seen as two sets of 6 rows of 2.

Multiplication Facts Chart
Completed for 4s

×	0	1	2	3	4	5	6	7	8	9	10
10	0	10	20	30	40	50	60	70	80	90	100
9	0	9	18	27	36	45					90
8	0	8	16	24	32	40					80
7	0	7	14	21	28	35					70
6	0	6	12	18	24	30					60
5	0	5	10	15	20	25	30	35	40	45	50
4	0	4	8	12	16	20	24	28	32	36	40
3	0	3	6	9	12	15	18	21	24	27	30
2	0	2	4	6	8	10	12	14	16	18	20
1	0	1	2	3	4	5	6	7	8	9	10
0	0	0	0	0	0	0	0	0	0	0	0

For other problems, students may choose to reverse the order of the factors to turn the problem into one they know. For example, 5×4 could be turned into 4×5, which students will know equals 20. Or students may wish to substitute a similar problem and then add to or subtract from the product as needed. For 9×4, a student might think of $10 \times 4 = 40$ and then take away 4 to find that $9 \times 4 = 36$. Other students may decide to use the distributive property that they learned earlier. For example, 7×4 could be turned into $2 \times 4 + 5 \times 4 = 8 + 20 = 28$. Any strategy that students use is okay. But remind them that ultimately they need to memorize the facts so that there is no mental calculation.

9. Have students write the 4s facts in pencil on the Multiplication Facts Chart and write the products on the Multiplication Facts Poster. (In several days, if students have truly memorized the facts and can recall them quickly, they can write them on the poster with a colored marker.)

LEARN Recall 4s Facts

ONLINE 20 min

Students will practice recalling the multiplication facts for 4. They will enter the answer to a problem and check their answer. Then they'll use online flash cards to further reinforce their knowledge of 4s facts.

Objectives

- Demonstrate automatic recall of multiplication facts.

TRY IT Practice Multiplication

OFFLINE 10 min

Students will practice solving multiplication problems. Have students turn to the Practice Multiplication activity page in their Activity Book and read the directions with them.

Students should copy the problems from the Activity Book into their Math Notebook as necessary and solve them there.

Objectives

- Demonstrate automatic recall of multiplication facts.

Multiplication Facts (B)
Practice Multiplication

Multiply.

1. $2 \times 3 = \underline{?}$ **6**
2. $8 \times 4 = \underline{?}$ **32**
3. $\begin{array}{r} 4 \\ \times 4 \\ \hline \end{array}$ **16**
4. $\begin{array}{r} 3 \\ \times 5 \\ \hline \end{array}$ **15**
5. $\begin{array}{r} 3 \\ \times 0 \\ \hline \end{array}$ **0**
6. $\begin{array}{r} 4 \\ \times 2 \\ \hline \end{array}$ **8**
7. $8 \times 3 = \underline{?}$ **24**
8. $4 \times 6 = \underline{?}$ **24**
9. $3 \times 4 = \underline{?}$ **12**
10. $4 \times 10 = \underline{?}$ **40**
11. $3 \times 1 = \underline{?}$ **3**
12. $3 \times 10 = \underline{?}$ **30**
13. $\begin{array}{r} 4 \\ \times 3 \\ \hline \end{array}$ **12**
14. $\begin{array}{r} 7 \\ \times 3 \\ \hline \end{array}$ **21**
15. $\begin{array}{r} 4 \\ \times 5 \\ \hline \end{array}$ **20**
16. $\begin{array}{r} 4 \\ \times 9 \\ \hline \end{array}$ **36**
17. $7 \times 4 = \underline{?}$ **28**
18. $6 \times \underline{?} = 18$ **3**
19. $\underline{?} \times 1 = 4$ **4**
20. $3 \times 3 = \underline{?}$ **9**
21. $1 \times 4 = \underline{?}$ **4**
22. $\underline{?} \times 4 = 24$ **6**
23. $4 \times \underline{?} = 32$ **8**
24. $9 \times 4 = \underline{?}$ **36**
25. $\begin{array}{r} 10 \\ \times 4 \\ \hline \end{array}$ **40**
26. $\begin{array}{r} 0 \\ \times 10 \\ \hline \end{array}$ **0**
27. $4 \times 7 = 28$
    $7 \times 4 = \underline{?}$ **28**
28. $3 \times 9 = 27$
    $9 \times 3 = \underline{?}$ **27**
29. $2 \times 10 = 20$
    $10 \times 2 = \underline{?}$ **20**
30. $4 \times 3 = 12$
    $3 \times 4 = \underline{?}$ **12**

WHOLE NUMBER MULTIPLICATION SENSE   **33**   MULTIPLICATION FACTS (B)

T R Y   I T

Multiplication Facts (C)

Lesson Overview

GET READY Multiplication Blimp Review	10 minutes	**ONLINE**
LEARN Multiplication Facts for 6	10 minutes	**ONLINE**
LEARN Multiplication Facts for 7	15 minutes	**ONLINE**
LEARN Multiplication Fact Match	15 minutes	**OFFLINE**
TRY IT Facts for 6 and 7	10 minutes	**OFFLINE**

▶ Lesson Objectives

Demonstrate automatic recall of multiplication facts.

▶ Prerequisite Skills

- Demonstrate automatic recall of multiplication facts for 2 through 10 × 2.
- Demonstrate automatic recall of multiplication facts for 5 through 10 × 5.
- Demonstrate understanding that the order in which numbers are multiplied does not affect the product.

▶ Content Background

Students will practice previously learned multiplication facts and will also learn the facts for 6 and 7. They will learn a strategy that will help them memorize their facts for 6 and 7.

Skip counting provides a foundation for multiplication. However, students must memorize and automatically recall their multiplication facts to truly succeed in math. They should begin to realize that changing the order in which numbers are multiplied does not affect the product. (For example, if they know 8 × 2 = 16, they will also know the product of 2 × 8.)

▶ Advance Preparation

Have the Multiplication Facts Chart and Multiplication Facts Poster ready or print new ones if needed.

Prepare a set of index cards for the new multiplication facts. Each card should have the fact on one side and the answer on the other.

- 6 × 6 36
- 7 × 6 42
- 8 × 6 48
- 9 × 6 54
- 6 × 7 42
- 7 × 7 49
- 8 × 7 56
- 9 × 7 63

Materials to Gather

SUPPLIED

Multiplication Facts Chart (printout)

Multiplication Facts Poster (printout)

index cards – labeled with multiplication facts

Facts for 6 and 7 activity page

GET READY Multiplication Blimp Review

Students will continue to practice previously learned multiplication facts. They will play an online review game.

Objectives

- Demonstrate automatic recall of multiplication facts for 2 through 10 × 2.
- Demonstrate automatic recall of multiplication facts for 5 through 10 × 5.
- Demonstrate understanding that the order in which numbers are multiplied does not affect the product.

LEARN Multiplication Facts for 6

Students will use their knowledge of the multiplication facts for 3 to learn the multiplication facts for 6. Students will also use the commutative property, which states that the order in which two numbers are multiplied does not affect the product.

In general, students should use whatever strategy works for them to learn and memorize the multiplication facts. The strategies explained can help students get an answer until they have the facts memorized, but there is no substitute for memorizing the facts eventually. Memorization is essential for doing multiplication of greater numbers.

Objectives

- Demonstrate automatic recall of multiplication facts.

LEARN Multiplication Facts for 7

Students will learn and practice their multiplication facts for 7. Encourage students to use whatever strategy seems easiest to find the products for these multiplication facts. Emphasize that the goal is to memorize the facts so that students don't have to spend time making mental calculations.

Objectives

- Demonstrate automatic recall of multiplication facts.

LEARN Multiplication Fact Match

Students will review the multiplication facts for 6 and 7 by adding the facts to the Multiplication Facts Chart. They will continue to practice these facts by playing a memory game in which they provide either the answer for a multiplication fact or the fact that goes with the answer. This game will help students get familiar with the multiples of 6 and 7 so they can start to memorize these eight facts.

Gather the Multiplication Facts Chart, Multiplication Facts Poster, and labeled index cards.

1. Have students write the products of the new multiplication facts for 6 and 7 on the Multiplication Facts Chart. They should write the products for 6×6, 7×6, 8×6, 9×6, 6×7, 7×7, 8×7, and 9×7.

Objectives

- Demonstrate automatic recall of multiplication facts.

2. Sort the index cards into two piles: the facts for 6 and the facts for 7. Take one pile at a time and turn the cards answer-side up. Have students flip through the four cards for the 6s, looking at the answer and saying the matching problem. (For example, if students see 54, they should say 9 × 6.) Do this for several rounds, shuffling the cards after each round. Then turn the cards problem-side up and have students say the matching answers. Repeat for several rounds, shuffling the cards after each round.

3. Repeat Step 2 with the four cards for the 7s facts.

4. Shuffle the two stacks together and continue to practice. Note that there will be two cards with 42 as an answer, 7 × 6 and 6 × 7. Either problem is acceptable when this answer card comes up.

5. Have students write the products for the 6s and 7s in pencil on the Multiplication Facts Poster. (In several days, if students have truly memorized the facts and can recall them quickly, they can write them on the poster with a colored marker.)

	0	1	2	3	4	5	6	7	8	9	10
10	0	10	20	30	40	50	60	70	80	90	100
9	0	9	18	27	36	45	54	63			90
8	0	8	16	24	32	40	48	56			80
7	0	7	14	21	28	35	42	49	56	63	70
6	0	6	12	18	24	30	36	42	48	54	60
5	0	5	10	15	20	25	30	35	40	45	50
4	0	4	8	12	16	20	24	28	32	36	40
3	0	3	6	9	12	15	18	21	24	27	30
2	0	2	4	6	8	10	12	14	16	18	20
1	0	1	2	3	4	5	6	7	8	9	10
0	0	0	0	0	0	0	0	0	0	0	0
×	0	1	2	3	4	5	6	7	8	9	10

OFFLINE

10 min

TRY IT Facts for 6 and 7

Objectives

- Demonstrate automatic recall of multiplication facts.

Students will practice multiplication facts by solving problems. Have students turn to the Facts for 6 and 7 activity page in their Activity Book and read the directions with them.

Students should copy the problems from the Activity Book into their Math Notebook as necessary and solve them there.

Before students do the problems on the activity page, have them practice any facts they have not yet memorized. They should complete all the problems on the activity page that they can do quickly, then go back and complete the rest.

Multiplication Facts (C)
Facts for 6 and 7

Multiply.

1. 6 × 3 = **18**   2. 7 × 9 = **63**   3. 7 × 7 = **49**   4. 6 × 8 = **48**
5. 6 × 5 = **30**   6. 6 × 1 = **6**   7. 7 × 4 = **28**   8. 7 × 3 = **21**
9. 9 × 7 = **63**   10. 2 × 6 = **12**   11. 6 × 7 = **42**   12. 4 × 5 = **20**
13. 7 × 6 = ? **42**   14. 4 × 5 = ? **20**
15. 8 × 6 = ? **48**   16. 3 × 7 = ? **21**
17. 6 × 10 = ? **60**   18. 0 × 3 = ? **0**
19. 7 × 1 = ? **7**   20. 9 × 7 = ? **63**
21. ? × 2 = 14 **7**   22. 7 × ? = 42 **6**
23. 2 × 7 = ? **14**   24. 3 × 6 = ? **18**
25. 5 × ? = 35 **7**   26. 7 × ? = 28 **4**
27. 9 × ? = 54 **6**   28. 10 × ? = 70 **7**
29. 7 × 9 = 63
    9 × 7 = ? **63**   30. 6 × 8 = 48
    8 × 6 = ? **48**
31. 6 × 10 = 60
    10 × 6 = ? **60**   32. 7 × 8 = 56
    8 × 7 = ? **56**

TRY IT

WHOLE NUMBER MULTIPLICATION SENSE   **34**   MULTIPLICATION FACTS (C)

Multiplication Facts (D)

Lesson Overview

GET READY Multiplication Fact Recall	5 minutes	**ONLINE**
LEARN Multiply by 8	15 minutes	**OFFLINE**
LEARN Multiply by 9	15 minutes	**OFFLINE**
LEARN Fact Practice for 8s and 9s	15 minutes	**ONLINE**
TRY IT Multiplication Minutes	10 minutes	**OFFLINE**

▶ ## Lesson Objectives

Demonstrate automatic recall of multiplication facts.

▶ ## Content Background

Students will practice previously learned multiplication facts and will also learn the 8s and 9s facts. They will learn strategies that will help them memorize their 8s and 9s facts.

Multiplication facts provide the foundation for learning to multiply greater numbers and for eventually doing long division. While the many strategies students have learned help them find answers, students need to memorize and automatically recall their multiplication facts to truly succeed in math. They should realize that changing the order in which numbers are multiplied does not affect the product. (For example, if they know $8 \times 6 = 48$, they will also know the product of 6×8.)

▶ ## Advance Preparation

Have the Multiplication Facts Chart ready or print a new one if needed. Have the Multiplication Facts Poster available.

Materials to Gather

SUPPLIED

Multiplication Facts Chart (printout)

Multiplication Facts Poster (printout)

blocks – B (optional)

Multiplication Minutes activity page

GET READY Multiplication Fact Recall

Objectives

- Demonstrate automatic recall of multiplication facts.
- Demonstrate understanding that the order in which numbers are multiplied does not affect the product.

Students will play a game in which they practice previously learned multiplication facts.

Remind students that they can switch the order of the factors to solve a multiplication problem.

LEARN Multiply by 8

Objectives

- Demonstrate automatic recall of multiplication facts.

Students will use their knowledge of doubling multiplication facts to learn the 8s multiplication facts. They will also use the commutative property, which states that the order in which two numbers are multiplied does not affect the product.

Gather the Multiplication Facts Chart.

Tips

Have students try to count by 8s to help them become familiar with the multiples of 8.

1. Explain to students that they are now ready to learn their 8s facts and that since they already know 0 × 8 through 7 × 8, they only have to learn two new facts: 8 × 8 and 9 × 8. Emphasize that the goal is to memorize the facts so they don't have to pause and calculate to get a product.

2. Tell students that they can use their knowledge of other facts to solve the 8s multiplication facts.

    Say: Since 8 is the double of 4, you can double the 4s facts to find the facts for 8. For instance, to find 3 × 8, you could think of 3 × 4 = 12 and double it to get 3 × 8 = 24.

    For 6 × 8, you could think of 6 × 4 = 24 and double it to get 6 × 8 = 48.

    For 8 × 8, you could think of 8 × 4 = 32 and double it to get 8 × 8 = 64.

    For 9 × 8, it's easier to just think of 10 × 8 = 80 and take away one 8 to get 9 × 8 = 72.

3. Explain to students that, if needed, they could think of the commutative fact. For example, instead of 7 × 8, they could think of 8 × 7. Then they could think "2 × 7 is 14, double that to get 4 × 7 is 28, and double that to get 8 × 7 is 56." Remind students that these are only ways to get the answer until they have the facts memorized.

4. Have students write the two new facts for 8 (8 × 8 and 8 × 9) on the Multiplication Facts Chart. When these facts have been filled in, the only space left will be for the fact 9 × 9.

Multiplication Facts Chart
Completed for 8s

×	0	1	2	3	4	5	6	7	8	9	10
10	0	10	20	30	40	50	60	70	80	90	100
9	0	9	18	27	36	45	54	63	72		90
8	0	8	16	24	32	40	48	56	64	72	80
7	0	7	14	21	28	35	42	49	56	63	70
6	0	6	12	18	24	30	36	42	48	54	60
5	0	5	10	15	20	25	30	35	40	45	50
4	0	4	8	12	16	20	24	28	32	36	40
3	0	3	6	9	12	15	18	21	24	27	30
2	0	2	4	6	8	10	12	14	16	18	20
1	0	1	2	3	4	5	6	7	8	9	10
0	0	0	0	0	0	0	0	0	0	0	0

LEARN Multiply by 9

Objectives

- Demonstrate automatic recall of multiplication facts.

Students will learn strategies to memorize the 9s multiplication facts. They will record the new 9s fact on the Multiplication Facts Chart.

Gather the Multiplication Facts Chart and Multiplication Facts Poster.

Tips

Provide B blocks for students to use to complete the multiplication and determine the products, if you wish.

1. Show students the following hands-on method for learning 9s facts:

   - Hold out both hands in front of you with your thumbs close together and touching, fingers spread apart.

   - Number the fingers from left to right 1–10.

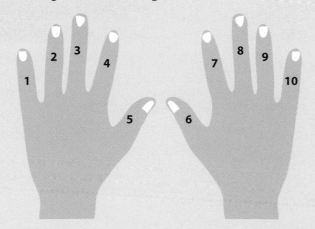

   - Have students bend one finger at a time and count to say the number that this finger represents. For practice, call out numbers and have students bend the correct finger. For example, if you call out "4," students should bend the index finger on their left hand.

   - Tell students that their fingers are a special calculator they can use for the 9s multiplication facts.

   - Explain that to find any product from 1 × 9 through 10 × 9, they can bend the finger representing the first factor and count the number of fingers to the left of the bent finger. That number tells how many tens are in the product. The number of fingers to the right of the bent finger tells the number of ones in the product. For example, to find 4 × 9, students can bend the index finger on the left hand (the finger marked 4). There are 3 fingers to the left of the bent finger, so there are 3 tens, or 30, and 6 fingers to the right of the bent finger, so there are 6 ones. So 4 × 9 = 36. For 7 × 9, bend the seventh finger (index finger on the right hand). There are 6 fingers, or 6 tens, to the left of the bent finger and 3 fingers, or 3 ones, to the right of the bent finger, so 7 × 9 = 63. Remind students that they must count all the fingers to the left and right of the bent finger, including the thumbs. After doing this process just a few times, students will become adept at quickly seeing the answer.

   - Point out to students that when they drop a finger, the number of fingers to the left will always be one less than the finger they dropped. If they drop finger number 8 to do 8 × 9, there will be 7 fingers to the left, so 8 × 9 will start with 7 in the tens place. But since there are 9 fingers up altogether, if there are 7 fingers to the left there must be 2 fingers to the right. So 8 × 9 = 72. For 7 × 9 they drop finger number 7, so there are 6 fingers to the left and there must be 3 to the right; thus, 7 × 9 = 63.

2. Tell students that they can see this pattern if they look at the 9s facts. The sum of the digits in the product always equals 9.

$1 \times 9 = 9;$ 9

$2 \times 9 = 18;$ $1 + 8 = 9$

$3 \times 9 = 27;$ $2 + 7 = 9$

$4 \times 9 = 36;$ $3 + 6 = 9$

$5 \times 9 = 45;$ $4 + 5 = 9$

$6 \times 9 = 54;$ $5 + 4 = 9$

$7 \times 9 = 63;$ $6 + 3 = 9$

$8 \times 9 = 72;$ $7 + 2 = 9$

$9 \times 9 = 81;$ $8 + 1 = 9$

$10 \times 9 = 90;$ $9 + 0 = 9$

3. Have students use a strategy to complete the facts for 9: $1 \times 9, 2 \times 9, 3 \times 9, 4 \times 9, 5 \times 9, 6 \times 9, 7 \times 9, 8 \times 9, 9 \times 9$, and 10×9. Students should write the facts in their Math Notebook.

4. Have students write the product for 9×9 on the Multiplication Facts Chart.

5. Explain that since students know their multiplication facts, they also are beginning to learn division facts. Point to the Multiplication Facts Poster. Select a product and have students identify the corresponding multiplication facts. For example, point to 28. Students should identify the facts 4×7 and 7×4. Tell students that 28 divided by 7 is 4, and 28 divided by 4 is 7. Complete several examples but do not push this concept too hard. Encourage students to see the relationship between multiplication and division.

LEARN Fact Practice for 8s and 9s

ONLINE 15 min

Objectives

Students will practice the 8s and 9s multiplication facts. At the end of the activity, have students write the 8s and 9s facts in pencil on their Multiplication Facts Poster. (In several days, if students have truly memorized the facts and can recall them quickly, they can write them on the poster with a colored marker.)

- Demonstrate automatic recall of multiplication facts.

TRY IT Multiplication Minutes

OFFLINE 10 min

Objectives

Students will practice the multiplication facts for 8 and 9. Have students turn to the Multiplication Minutes activity page in their Activity Book and read the directions with them.

Students should copy the problems from the Activity Book into their Math Notebook as necessary and solve them there.

- Demonstrate automatic recall of multiplication facts.

Before students do the problems on the activity page, have them practice any facts they have not yet memorized. They should complete all the problems on the activity page that they can do quickly, then go back and complete the rest.

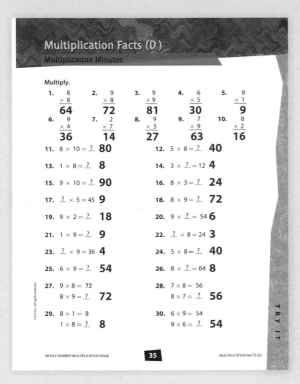

Multiplication Facts (D)
Multiplication Minutes

Multiply.

1. 8 × 8 = **64**	2. 9 × 8 = **72**	3. 9 × 9 = **81**	4. 6 × 5 = **30**	5. 9 × 1 = **9**
6. 9 × 4 = **36**	7. 2 × 7 = **14**	8. 9 × 3 = **27**	9. 7 × 9 = **63**	10. 8 × 2 = **16**

11. 8 × 10 = ? **80**   12. 5 × 8 = ? **40**

13. 1 × 8 = ? **8**   14. 3 × ? = 12 **4**

15. 9 × 10 = ? **90**   16. 8 × 3 = ? **24**

17. ? × 5 = 45 **9**   18. 8 × 9 = ? **72**

19. 9 × 2 = ? **18**   20. 9 × ? = 54 **6**

21. 1 × 9 = ? **9**   22. ? × 8 = 24 **3**

23. ? × 9 = 36 **4**   24. 5 × 8 = ? **40**

25. 6 × 9 = ? **54**   26. 8 × ? = 64 **8**

27. 9 × 8 = 72
    8 × 9 = ? **72**   28. 7 × 8 = 56
    8 × 7 = ? **56**

29. 8 × 1 = 8
    1 × 8 = ? **8**   30. 6 × 9 = 54
    9 × 6 = ? **54**

T R Y   I T

WHOLE NUMBER MULTIPLICATION SENSE   **35**   MULTIPLICATION FACTS (D)

Multiplication Facts (E)

LEARN Strategy Review	20 minutes	**ONLINE**
LEARN Multiplication Facts 0–10	15 minutes	**ONLINE**
TRY IT Fast Facts	15 minutes	**ONLINE**
CHECKPOINT	10 minutes	**ONLINE**

▶ Lesson Objectives

Demonstrate automatic recall of multiplication facts.

▶ Prerequisite Skills

- Demonstrate automatic recall of multiplication facts for 2 through 10×2.
- Demonstrate automatic recall of multiplication facts for 5 through 10×5.
- Demonstrate understanding that the order in which numbers are multiplied does not affect the product.

▶ Content Background

Students will practice previously learned multiplication facts and will focus on memorizing the facts.

Multiplication facts provide the foundation for learning to multiply greater numbers and for eventually doing long division. Although the many strategies students have learned help them find answers, students need to memorize and automatically recall their multiplication facts to truly succeed in math. They should realize that changing the order in which numbers are multiplied does not affect the product. (For example, if they know $8 \times 6 = 48$, they will also know the product of 6×8.)

▶ Advance Preparation

Have the Multiplication Facts Poster available.

Materials to Gather

SUPPLIED

Multiplication Facts Poster (printout)

LEARN Strategy Review

ONLINE 20min

Students will use online flash cards to practice multiplication facts and strategies. They will start with the 9s facts so they can focus on the most challenging facts first.

Emphasize that the strategies for getting the product of a multiplication fact are only for use until the fact is memorized. Ultimately, students should know the products without doing any calculating.

Students will be using all the multiplication strategies they have learned. Keep this list handy for reference; you may also want to write it in the Math Notebook.

- Any number times zero equals zero.
- Any number times 1 equals that number.

Objectives

- Demonstrate automatic recall of multiplication facts.

- To multiply a number by 2, just add the number to itself, or double it. For example, $6 \times 2 = 6 + 6$.

- When solving facts for 3, skip count by 3s or switch the factors and use repeated addition. For 7×3, think 3×7 and add $7 + 7 + 7 = 21$.

- When solving facts for 4, double the 2s fact to find the product. 4×7 is the same as 2×7 doubled.

- When solving facts for 5, skip count by 5s. Or multiply by 10 and figure out what half of that answer is—that number will be the 5s fact.

- When solving for 6, double the 3s fact to find the product. 6×7 is the same as 3×7 doubled.

- When solving facts for 7, memorize 7×7. For all the other 7s facts, reverse the order of the factors and use a rule for the other factor. For 7×3, think of 3×7, which you can solve by adding $7 + 7 + 7$.

- When solving facts for 8, double the 4s facts to find the product. 8×7 is the same as 4×7 doubled.

- When solving facts for 9, use finger multiplication, or multiply the number by 10 and subtract the number. For 9×8, think 10×8 and then take away one 8 to get $9 \times 8 = 72$.

LEARN Multiplication Facts 0–10

ONLINE **15**min

Objectives

- Demonstrate automatic recall of multiplication facts.

Students will complete online activities to review multiplication facts. When they have finished, have students add any additional facts they have mastered to the Multiplication Facts Poster. Students should write the facts in pencil. (In several days, if students have truly memorized the facts and can recall them quickly, they can write them on the poster with a colored marker.)

TRY IT Fast Facts

ONLINE **15**min

Objectives

- Demonstrate automatic recall of multiplication facts.

Students will practice multiplication facts with factors 0 through 10 with the Fast Facts Learning Tool.

DIRECTIONS FOR USING THE FAST FACTS LEARNING TOOL

1. Have students enter their name and car number as well as choose the color of the car.

2. Choose the following options:
   - Choose the facts you want to practice: Multiplication
   - Choose multiples: Click a gray number in column 1 to choose all the multiples of that number. (For example, clicking the 8 in column 1 will select all the 8s facts.) You can also choose any individual facts with which students need additional practice.
   - Mode: Race Mode

3. Have students type the answer to each problem as it appears on the screen. After students finish, review the results. Note problems students answered incorrectly. Also note their time.

4. Repeat the activity. Have students try to beat their time and improve their accuracy.

5. If time remains, customize the "Choose multiples" screen and have students review the facts with which they had difficulty.

ONLINE

10min

CHECKPOINT

Objectives

Students will complete an online Checkpoint. If necessary, read the directions, problems, and answer choices to students and help them with keyboard or mouse operations.

- Demonstrate automatic recall of multiplication facts.

Associative Property of Multiplication

Lesson Overview

GET READY Group to Add and Multiply	10 minutes	OFFLINE
LEARN Different Ways to Group Factors	30 minutes	OFFLINE
TRY IT Group and Multiply	10 minutes	OFFLINE
CHECKPOINT	10 minutes	ONLINE

▶ Lesson Objectives

Explain and apply the associative property of multiplication.

▶ Prerequisite Skills

Demonstrate understanding of the associative properties of addition and multiplication.

▶ Content Background

Students may already have a basic understanding that in addition, the addends can be grouped in any order to make the addition easier. This is called the associative property of addition. In this lesson, students will focus on a similar idea in multiplication that says when multiplying three or more numbers, they can be grouped in any way, which is called the associative property of multiplication.

The associative property of multiplication, sometimes known as the grouping property of multiplication, states that changing the way factors are grouped does not change the product. You can use parentheses to group factors to show which numbers are to be multiplied first. Students will learn about parentheses and will use them to group factors.

The order of operations principle states that factors in a horizontal row must be multiplied from left to right. However, if there are parentheses around a subgroup of these factors, always multiply the grouped factors first. For example, if students want to multiply $7 \times 5 \times 2$, they could multiply 7×5 to get 35 and then multiply 35×2 to get 70. However, if students use the associative property of multiplication to group 5 and 2 first, the problem becomes easier: $7 \times (5 \times 2)$. By multiplying within the parentheses to get 10, they then multiply 7 and 10 to get 70.

▶ Advance Preparation

Gather or label index cards to make number and symbol cards. You will need the following:

- 2 sets of cards with numerals 0 through 9
- 2 cards with multiplication symbols $\times$
- 1 card with an opening parenthesis symbol (
- 1 card with a closing parenthesis symbol)

Materials to Gather

SUPPLIED

Group and Multiply activity page

ALSO NEEDED

index cards – labeled with numbers and symbols

GET READY Group to Add and Multiply

Objectives

- Demonstrate understanding of the associative properties of addition and multiplication.

Students will review the associative properties of addition and multiplication. The associative properties of addition and multiplication state that changing the grouping of addends or factors does not affect the sum or product, respectively.

There are no materials to gather for this activity. Use the Math Notebook for writing the examples and problems.

1. Write $(8 + 5) + 5$. Point to the parentheses and explain that the parentheses tell which two numbers to add first.

2. **Say:** The associative property of addition says that changing the grouping of addends does not change the sum. Therefore, we can move the parentheses when adding three addends.

   Write $8 + (5 + 5)$.

3. Have students find each sum.

4. **Ask:** Which addition problem is easier to solve? Students may say $8 + (5 + 5)$ is easier to solve because 5 plus 5 is 10, and adding to 10 is easier than adding to 13.

5. Write $(3 + 7) + 2$. Discuss the benefits of solving the problem as written or grouping the addends differently. Help students see that 3 plus 7 is 10, and making 10 is a good strategy to use when adding three or more numbers.

6. Repeat Step 5 with $(5 + 6) + 4$. Guide students to see that $6 + 4$ makes 10, so they might want to move the parentheses on this problem.

7. Write $(6 \times 7) \times 0$. Point out that this is a multiplication problem, not an addition problem.

8. **Say:** The associative property of multiplication is like the associative property of addition. You can change the grouping of factors without changing the product.

9. Write $6 \times (7 \times 0)$.

   Say: Sometimes moving the parentheses makes it easier to multiply.

   Discuss with students how they would solve each problem and which problem was easier to simplify.

10. Write the following problems. Have students determine whether they would like to solve the problem as written or group the factors differently.

    - $5 \times (2 \times 3)$
    - $(2 \times 5) \times 5$

    Help students see that the product of 2 and 5 is 10, and it is easy to multiply by 10.

Tips

Have students find sums or products in different groupings to help determine which grouping is easier to solve.

LEARN Different Ways to Group Factors

Objectives

- Explain and apply the associative property of multiplication.

Students will explain and apply the associative property of multiplication. They will use parentheses to group factors in a multiplication problem. Students will find the product of three factors.

Gather the number and symbol cards. Use the Math Notebook for writing the examples and problems.

1. Arrange the number and symbol cards to show $(2 \times 3) \times 4$. Remind students that the parentheses tell which two numbers to multiply first.

2. **Ask:** How will you solve this problem? First, I will multiply 2 and 3. Then I will multiply the product by 4.

   Have students solve the problem.

3. Move the parentheses cards to show $2 \times (3 \times 4)$. Have students solve the problem.

4. **Ask:** What do you notice about the product of both problems? They are the same—24.

5. Repeat Steps 1–4 using $2 \times 4 \times 5$, positioning the parentheses cards to group 2×4 first and 4×5 next.

6. **Say:** The associative property of multiplication says that changing the grouping of factors does not change the product. Therefore, when multiplying three factors, you can change the grouping to find the product.

7. Arrange the number and symbol cards to show $(7 \times 5) \times 2$. Have students solve the problem by adding $35 + 35$.

   Move the parentheses cards to show $7 \times (5 \times 2)$. Have students solve the problem.

   Review that $5 \times 2 = 10$, making the problem 7×10. Discuss that multiplying 5 and 2 first makes it easier to solve $7 \times 5 \times 2$ because students are confident about multiplying any number by 10. Then review that $7 \times 5 = 35$, making the problem 35×2. Conclude that 7×10 is easier to solve than 35×2.

8. Arrange the number and symbol cards to show $(3 \times 4) \times 5$. Have students solve the problem any way they can. The problem 12×5 can be seen as ten 5s, which is 50, and two more 5s to get 60.

   Move the parentheses cards to show $3 \times (4 \times 5)$. Have students solve the problem.

   Ask: Which grouping was easier to solve? Students may say that multiplying 4 and 5 first makes it easier to solve $3 \times 4 \times 5$ because multiplying 3 times 20 is easier than 12 times 5.

9. Repeat Step 8 using $2 \times 5 \times 6$.

10. Arrange the number cards face down on the table. Have students choose three cards and place them in a row.

11. Have students place the multiplication symbol cards between the number cards to form a multiplication problem. Then have students use the parentheses cards to group the factors in a way that makes the problem easiest to solve.

12. Have students explain why they chose to position the parentheses cards as they did.

13. Repeat Steps 10–12 several times. Have students find the products of the simpler problems—ones that use lesser numbers.

14. Write the following statement:

    If $(5 \times 7) \times 3 = 105$, then what is $5 \times (7 \times 3)$?

    Help students see that the same three factors are used in both problems, but the grouping is different. Guide students to determine that the product is the same. Remind students that the associative property of multiplication says that changing the grouping of factors does not change the product.

15. Write the following statement:

    If $6 \times (3 \times 5) = 90$, then what is $(6 \times 3) \times 5$?

    Students should determine the product is 90.

Make the number cards one color, the multiplication symbol cards a second color, and the parentheses symbol cards a third color for visual distinction.

TRY IT   Group and Multiply

OFFLINE 10 min

Objectives

- Explain and apply the associative property of multiplication.

Students will practice applying the associative property of multiplication. Have students turn to the Group and Multiply activity page in their Activity Book and read the directions with them.

Students should copy the problems from the Activity Book into their Math Notebook as necessary and solve them there. Note that for Problems 1 and 2, students do not find the value of the problems but instead show another way to regroup the factors. For Problems 1–5, the answers shown are sample answers. Answers will vary.

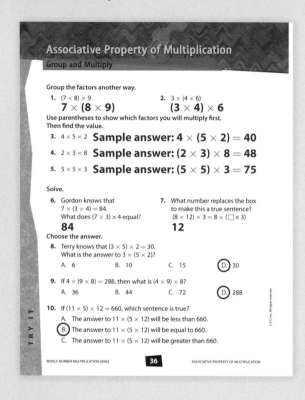

Associative Property of Multiplication
Group and Multiply

Group the factors another way.

1. $(7 \times 8) \times 9$

    $7 \times (8 \times 9)$

2. $3 \times (4 \times 6)$

    $(3 \times 4) \times 6$

Use parentheses to show which factors you will multiply first. Then find the value.

3. $4 \times 5 \times 2$ **Sample answer: $4 \times (5 \times 2) = 40$**

4. $2 \times 3 \times 8$ **Sample answer: $(2 \times 3) \times 8 = 48$**

5. $5 \times 5 \times 3$ **Sample answer: $(5 \times 5) \times 3 = 75$**

Solve.

6. Gordon knows that $7 \times (3 \times 4) = 84$. What does $(7 \times 3) \times 4$ equal?

    84

7. What number replaces the box to make this a true sentence? $(8 \times 12) \times 3 = 8 \times (\square \times 3)$

    12

Choose the answer.

8. Terry knows that $(3 \times 5) \times 2 = 30$. What is the answer to $3 \times (5 \times 2)$?

    A. 6   B. 10   C. 15   **D.** 30

9. If $4 \times (9 \times 8) = 288$, then what is $(4 \times 9) \times 8$?

    A. 36   B. 44   C. 72   **D.** 288

10. If $(11 \times 5) \times 12 = 660$, which sentence is true?

    A. The answer to $11 \times (5 \times 12)$ will be less than 660.

    B. The answer to $11 \times (5 \times 12)$ will be equal to 660.

    C. The answer to $11 \times (5 \times 12)$ will be greater than 660.

WHOLE NUMBER MULTIPLICATION SENSE   **36**   ASSOCIATIVE PROPERTY OF MULTIPLICATION

TRY IT

CHECKPOINT

ONLINE 10 min

Objectives

- Explain and apply the associative property of multiplication.

Students will complete an online Checkpoint. If necessary, read the directions, problems, and answer choices to students and help them with keyboard or mouse operations.

Core Focus
Properties of Multiplication

Lesson Overview

GET READY Multiplication Facts Review	10 minutes	**ONLINE**
LEARN Using Properties of Multiplication	30 minutes	**ONLINE**
TRY IT Applying Properties of Multiplication	10 minutes	**OFFLINE**
CHECKPOINT	10 minutes	**ONLINE**

▶ Lesson Objectives

- Explain and apply the commutative property of multiplication.
- Explain and apply the associative property of multiplication.
- Explain and apply the distributive property of multiplication.

▶ Prerequisite Skills

- Use concrete objects or sketches of arrays to model multiplication problems.
- Demonstrate automatic recall of multiplication facts.

▶ Content Background

Students will review the commutative, associative, and distributive properties of multiplication and will use the properties as strategies for solving multiplication problems.

The commutative property of multiplication states that changing the order of factors doesn't affect the product. For example $8 \times 9 = 9 \times 8$.

The associative property of multiplication, sometimes known as the grouping property of multiplication, states that changing the way factors are grouped does not change the product. You can use parentheses to group factors to show which numbers are to be multiplied first. For example, $(4 \times 5) \times 7 = 4 \times (5 \times 7)$.

The distributive property of multiplication states that multiplying a number by a sum gives the same answer as multiplying the number by each addend of the sum and adding the products, For example, $6 \times 9 = 6 \times (5 + 4) = (6 \times 5) + (6 \times 4) = 30 + 24 = 54$

▶ Common Errors and Misconceptions

- Students might not realize that the two factors in a multiplication problem have different meanings. For example, 4 rows of 9 is written as 4×9, not 9×4. However, the product of each phrase is 36.
- Students may not understand how the associative and commutative properties differ. Point out that the commutative property is about the order of factors. The associative property is about the way factors are grouped when there are more than two factors involved.

Materials to Gather

SUPPLIED

Applying Properties of Multiplication activity page

GET READY Multiplication Facts Review

Students will practice reviewing previously learned multiplication facts and will focus on memorizing the facts.

Multiplication facts provide the foundation for learning to multiply greater numbers and for eventually doing long division. Although the students have learned many strategies that can help them find answers, they need to memorize and automatically recall their multiplication facts to truly succeed in math. Students should recognize that changing the order in which numbers are multiplied does not affect the product.

- Demonstrate automatic recall of multiplication facts.

LEARN Using Properties of Multiplication

ONLINE
30min

Objectives

As students review and explore the commutative property of multiplication, they will see multiplication problems shown with an area model consisting of squares on a grid. Using area models helps students visualize the concept. Remind students that the first factor is the number of rows and the second factor is the number of squares in each row, or the number of columns.

Students will review and apply the associative property of multiplication as it applies to solving multiplication problems with three factors. They will use parentheses to group the factors of a single problem in different ways, noting that the product does not change. Students will also recognize that how factors are grouped can affect how easy or difficult a problem is to solve.

Students will review and explore the distributive property of multiplication by using area models to observe how one factor can be broken apart into two addends. Each of the addends is then multiplied by the other factor. The product is found by adding the two products. Students will recognize that the distributive property can help them multiply larger numbers.

- Explain and apply the commutative property of multiplication.
- Explain and apply the associative property of multiplication.
- Explain and apply the distributive property of multiplication.

TRY IT Applying Properties of Multiplication

OFFLINE
10min

Objectives

Students will apply and explain how they can use the commutative, associative, and distributive properties of multiplication to solve problems. Have students turn to the Applying Properties of Multiplication activity page in their Activity Book and read the directions with them.

Students should copy the problems from the Activity Book into their Math Notebook as necessary and solve them there.

- Explain and apply the commutative property of multiplication.
- Explain and apply the associative property of multiplication.
- Explain and apply the distributive property of multiplication.

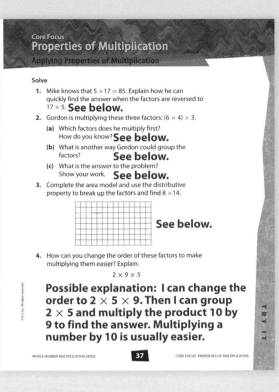

Core Focus
Properties of Multiplication
Applying Properties of Multiplication

Solve

1. Mike knows that $5 \times 17 = 85$. Explain how he can quickly find the answer when the factors are reversed to 17×5. **See below.**

2. Gordon is multiplying these three factors: $(6 \times 4) \times 3$.

    (a) Which factors does he multiply first? How do you know? **See below.**

    (b) What is another way Gordon could group the factors? **See below.**

    (c) What is the answer to the problem? Show your work. **See below.**

3. Complete the area model and use the distributive property to break up the factors and find 8×14.

    See below.

4. How can you change the order of these factors to make multiplying them easier? Explain.

    $2 \times 9 \times 5$

    Possible explanation: I can change the order to $2 \times 5 \times 9$. Then I can group 2×5 and multiply the product 10 by 9 to find the answer. Multiplying a number by 10 is usually easier.

WHOLE NUMBER MULTIPLICATION SENSE   37   CORE FOCUS PROPERTIES OF MULTIPLICATION

Think like a Mathematician Self-Check

5. State the actions and thinking you used during this lesson as a math learner.

Math Thinking and Actions

I made sense of problems by
- Explaining to myself what a problem means and what it asks for
- Using drawings or diagrams to represent a problem I was solving

I explained my math thinking clearly.

I tried out new ways to check if an answer is reasonable.

Other

WHOLE NUMBER MULTIPLICATION SENSE   38   CORE FOCUS PROPERTIES OF MULTIPLICATION

Answers

1. **Possible explanation:** Mike knows that changing the order of the factors doesn't change the product, so 17×5 will also equal 85. Other correct answers are acceptable.

3. Answer may vary. **Possible answer:**

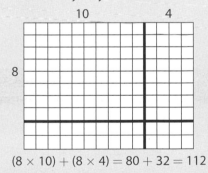

$(8 \times 10) + (8 \times 4) = 80 + 32 = 112$

2. **(a)** Gordon multiplies 6×4 first because the factors are in parentheses.

    (b) Possible answer: $6 \times (4 \times 3)$; Some students may recognize that the factors can be grouped in any way, such as $(3 \times 6) \times 4$.

    (c) Possible answer: $6 \times 4 = 24$; $24 \times 3 = 72$.

ONLINE
10 min

CHECKPOINT

Students will complete an online Checkpoint. If necessary, read the directions, problems, and answer choices to students and help them with keyboard or mouse operations.

Objectives

- Explain and apply the commutative property of multiplication.

- Explain and apply the associative property of multiplication.

- Explain and apply the distributive property of multiplication.

Unit Review

▶ Unit Objectives

This lesson reviews the following objectives:

- Use objects or sketches to solve a multiplication problem.
- Use a model to explain multiplication as repeated addition of the same quantity.
- Use an area model to explain multiplication.
- Demonstrate an understanding of how multiplication affects whole numbers.
- Explain and apply the commutative property of multiplication.
- Explain and apply the zero property of multiplication.
- Explain and apply the multiplication property of 1.
- Demonstrate automatic recall of multiplication facts.
- Explain and apply the associative property of multiplication.
- Explain and apply the distributive property of multiplication.

Materials to Gather

There are no materials to gather for this lesson.

▶ Advance Preparation

In this lesson, students will have an opportunity to review previous activities in the Whole Number Multiplication Sense unit. Look at the suggested activities in Unit Review: Prepare for the Checkpoint online and gather any needed materials.

UNIT REVIEW Look Back

ONLINE 10min

Students will review key concepts from the unit to prepare for the Unit Checkpoint.

Objectives

- Review unit objectives.

UNIT REVIEW Checkpoint Practice

ONLINE 50min

Students will complete an online Checkpoint Practice to prepare for the Unit Checkpoint. If necessary, read the directions, problems, and answer choices to students. Have students answer the problems on their own. Review any missed problems with students.

Objectives

- Review unit objectives.

⇥ UNIT REVIEW Prepare for the Checkpoint

What you do next depends on how students performed in the previous activity, Unit Review: Checkpoint Practice. If students had difficulty with any of the problems, complete the appropriate review activity listed in the table online.

Unit Checkpoint

UNIT CHECKPOINT Online · 60 minutes · **ONLINE**

▶ **Unit Objectives**

This lesson assesses the following objectives:

- Use objects or sketches to solve a multiplication problem.
- Use a model to explain multiplication as repeated addition of the same quantity.
- Use an area model to explain multiplication.
- Demonstrate an understanding of how multiplication affects whole numbers.
- Explain and apply the commutative property of multiplication.
- Explain and apply the zero property of multiplication.
- Explain and apply the multiplication property of 1.
- Demonstrate automatic recall of multiplication facts.
- Explain and apply the associative property of multiplication.
- Explain and apply the distributive property of multiplication.

Materials to Gather

There are no materials to gather for this lesson.

ONLINE
60min

UNIT CHECKPOINT Online

Students will complete the online Unit Checkpoint. If necessary, read the directions, problems, and answer choices to students and help them with keyboard or mouse operations.

Objectives

- Assess unit objectives.

Extended Problems: Real-World Application

USE WHAT YOU KNOW Offline   60 minutes   **OFFLINE**

▶ Lesson Objectives

This lesson assesses the following objectives:

- Explain the meaning of a multiplication equation with a product within 100.
- Use objects or sketches to solve a multiplication problem.
- Solve word problems involving measurements and arrays using multiplication or division within 100.
- Explain and apply the commutative property of multiplication within 100.
- Explain and apply the associative property of multiplication within 100.
- Explain and apply the distributive property of multiplication within 100.
- Solve two-step word problems limited to whole numbers.
- Represent a data set with up to four categories on a bar graph (with single-unit scale).
- Represent a data set with up to four categories on a picture graph (with single-unit scale).
- Solve simple compare problems using information from a bar graph.
- Solve simple put-together problems using information from a bar graph.
- Solve word problems involving dollar bills, quarters, dimes, nickels, and pennies, using $ (dollars) and ¢ (cents) symbols appropriately.
- Apply mathematical knowledge and skills to evaluate and analyze real-world situations.

Materials to Gather

SUPPLIED

Extended Problems: Real-World
     Application (printout)

USE WHAT YOU KNOW Offline   **OFFLINE 60min**

Open the Extended Problems: Real-World Application. Read the directions, problems, and answer choices to students, if necessary.
    The teacher will grade this assignment.

- Students should save the graded assignment to their computer. In the filename, they should replace "studentname" with their last name followed by their first initial.
- Students should complete the assignment on their own.
- Students should submit the completed assignment according to the teacher's instructions.

Objectives

- Apply mathematical knowledge and skills to evaluate and analyze real-world situations.

Whole Number Multiplication

▶ Unit Objectives

- Use objects or sketches to solve a multiplication story problem.
- Solve a multiplication problem involving a multidigit factor and a one-digit factor.
- Use multiplication to solve a story problem that involves equal groups.
- Use multiplication to solve a story problem that involves equal measures.
- Create a story problem that can be represented by a multiplication number sentence.

▶ Big Ideas

- Multiplication and division can be represented by models and by using math symbols.
- The use of letters, numbers, and mathematical symbols makes possible the translation of complex situations or long word statements into concise mathematical sentences or expressions.

▶ Unit Introduction

In this unit, students will learn the step-by-step process, the algorithm, to solve multiplication computation problems in which a one-digit factor is multiplied by a multidigit factor. They will model story problems and then use their multiplication computation skills to solve multiplication story problems involving equal groups or equal measures. Finally they will create their own story problems and show how their problems can be represented by number sentences. Overall students will move from solving both computation and story problems with concrete objects to being able to solve them with numbers and symbols by using number sentences and the multiplication algorithm.

▶ Keywords

division
equal groups
equal measures

factor
grid

partial product
product

Multiplication Story Problems

Lesson Overview

GET READY Represent Multiplication with Symbols	5 minutes	**ONLINE**
LEARN Model Multiplication Story Problems	25 minutes	**OFFLINE**
TRY IT Model and Solve Problems	20 minutes	**OFFLINE**
CHECKPOINT	10 minutes	**ONLINE**

▶ **Lesson Objectives**

Use objects or sketches to solve a multiplication story problem.

▶ **Prerequisite Skills**

Use models and math symbols to represent multiplication.

▶ **Content Background**

Students will learn to solve story problems involving multiplication. They will review the concept that multiplication involves combining equal groups. The multiplication symbol ($\times$) represents the phrase "groups of." For example, the expression 5×8 represents 5 groups of 8 objects. As students move toward more difficult problems, it is important for them to model problems with objects and sketches to see the connection between the meaning of multiplication and the way to calculate problems.

A multiplication number sentence has at least two numbers, called factors, that are multiplied to produce the solution, or product.

An array is a rectangular arrangement of objects in rows and columns. The number of rows in the array is the first factor in a multiplication number sentence, and the number of columns in the array is the second factor. The expression 5×8 would be shown as 5 rows of 8. The total number of objects in the entire array is the product.

▶ **Common Errors and Misconceptions**

- Students might need exposure to a variety of models (such as rectangular array or area) when learning multiplication as a conceptual operation. Using only repeated addition models and the term *times* can lead to a basic misunderstanding of multiplication. This misunderstanding will complicate future use of multiplication when working with decimals and fractions.

- Students might view multiplication and division algorithms as rules to be followed. This leads to a misunderstanding that the numbers involved are separate digits rather than grouped amounts representing place values. The result is often an incorrect answer because of students' misunderstanding of estimation, place value, and reasonableness of results.

Materials to Gather

SUPPLIED

blocks – B (all)

base-10 blocks

Model Multiplication Story Problems activity page

Model and Solve Problems activity page

GET READY Represent Multiplication with Symbols

ONLINE 5min

Objectives

- Use models and math symbols to represent multiplication.

Students will practice representing multiplication. They will write the factors shown in a multiplication model and then write the product.

OFFLINE 25min

LEARN Model Multiplication Story Problems

Objectives

- Use objects or sketches to solve a multiplication story problem.

Students will use objects and sketches to model and solve multiplication story problems. They will learn to match the words and phrases in a story problem to the numbers in a multiplication sentence.

Gather the B blocks and base-10 blocks. View or print the Model Multiplication Story Problems activity page.

Students should copy the problems from the Activity Book to their Math Notebook as necessary and solve them there.

1. Read Worked Example 1 with students. Explain how the model represents the rows of tomato plants.

2. Look at the multiplication number sentence. Show students how each number in the multiplication sentence matches a statement in the story problem.

3. Remind students that the first factor in a multiplication number sentence tells the number of groups, or rows, and the second factor tells the number in each group, or row.

4. Have students use skip counting or repeated addition to check the product.

5. Read Worked Example 2 with students.

6. Discuss the sketch with students. Explain that each rectangle represents a vase and the tulips represent the flowers Ted put in each vase. Explain how the objects in the sketch match the information in the story problem.

7. Have students use skip counting or repeated addition to check the product. Discuss with students how they can use the sketch to check the product.

8. Read Worked Example 3 with students.

9. Explain how the groups of base-10 blocks represent the number of weeks and dollar amount in the story problem.

10. Point out that grouping all the tens rods together and all the ones cubes together makes it easier to count them. Have students use skip counting or repeated addition to check the product.

11. Have students complete Problems 1–6 on their own. Then have students share their models and sketches. Ask them to identify the phrases in the problems that match the numbers in each multiplication number sentence.

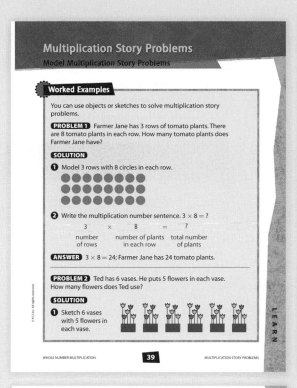

Multiplication Story Problems
Model Multiplication Story Problems

Worked Examples

You can use objects or sketches to solve multiplication story problems.

PROBLEM 1 Farmer Jane has 3 rows of tomato plants. There are 8 tomato plants in each row. How many tomato plants does Farmer Jane have?

SOLUTION

❶ Model 3 rows with 8 circles in each row.

❷ Write the multiplication number sentence. $3 \times 8 = ?$

$$3 \times 8 = ?$$
number of rows · number of plants in each row · total number of plants

ANSWER $3 \times 8 = 24$; Farmer Jane has 24 tomato plants.

PROBLEM 2 Ted has 6 vases. He puts 5 flowers in each vase. How many flowers does Ted use?

SOLUTION

❶ Sketch 6 vases with 5 flowers in each vase.

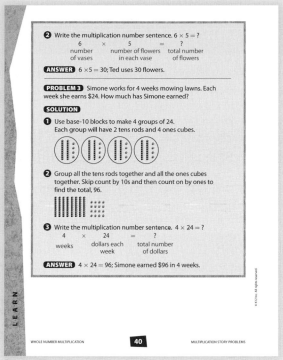

❷ Write the multiplication number sentence. $6 \times 5 = ?$

$$6 \times 5 = ?$$
number of vases · number of flowers in each vase · total number of flowers

ANSWER $6 \times 5 = 30$; Ted uses 30 flowers.

PROBLEM 3 Simone works for 4 weeks mowing lawns. Each week she earns $24. How much has Simone earned?

SOLUTION

❶ Use base-10 blocks to make 4 groups of 24. Each group will have 2 tens rods and 4 ones cubes.

❷ Group all the tens rods together and all the ones cubes together. Skip count by 10s and then count on by ones to find the total, 96.

❸ Write the multiplication number sentence. $4 \times 24 = ?$

$$4 \times 24 = ?$$
weeks · dollars each week · total number of dollars

ANSWER $4 \times 24 = 96$; Simone earned $96 in 4 weeks.

Use circle blocks to model the problem. **Models will vary.**
Write the multiplication number sentence and solve.

1. Farmer Ted has 8 containers. He puts 2 tomato plants in each container. How many tomato plants does he use? **See below.**

2. There are 7 baskets of peppers. There are 5 peppers in each basket. How many peppers are there altogether? **See below.**

Make a sketch to model the problem. **Sketches will vary.**
Write the multiplication number sentence and solve.

3. Jane buys 2 bags of onions. There are 10 small onions in each bag. How many onions are there in all? **See below.**

4. There are 9 shelves. There are 3 pumpkins on each shelf. How many pumpkins are on the shelves altogether? **See below.**

Use base-10 blocks to model the problem. **Models will vary.**
Write the multiplication number sentence and solve.

5. Andre has 4 packs of seeds. Each pack has 22 seeds. How many seeds does Andre have? **See below.**

6. Mark works for 5 weekends picking berries. He earns $15 each weekend. How much does Mark earn? **See below.**

Additional Answers

1. **Sample answer:** Students make 8 groups of 2 circles. $8 \times 2 = ?$; $8 \times 2 = 16$

2. **Sample model:** Students make 7 groups of 5 circles. $7 \times 5 = ?$; $7 \times 5 = 35$

3. **Sample sketch:** Students make a sketch of 2 groups of 10 circles. $2 \times 10 = ?$; $2 \times 10 = 20$

4. **Sample answer:** Students make a sketch of 9 groups of 3 circles. $9 \times 3 = ?$; $9 \times 3 = 27$

5. **Sample answer:** Students make 4 groups of blocks; each group has 2 tens rods and 2 ones cubes. $4 \times 22 = ?$; $4 \times 22 = 88$.

6. **Sample answer:** Students make 5 groups of blocks; each group has 1 tens rod and 5 ones cubes. $5 \times \$15 = ?$; $5 \times \$15 = \$75$.

OFFLINE
20min

Objectives

- Use objects or sketches to solve a multiplication story problem.

Students will practice modeling and solving multiplication problems. Gather the B blocks and base-10 blocks. View or print the Model and Solve Problems activity page and read the directions with students.

Students should copy the problems from the Activity Book into their Math Notebook as necessary and solve them there.

Tips

Encourage students to find each product in different ways to check their answers.

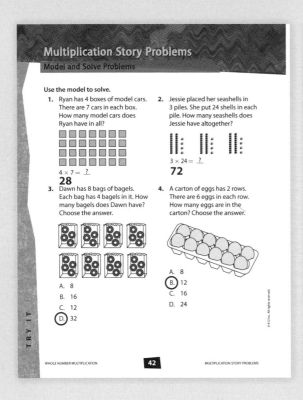

Multiplication Story Problems
Model and Solve Problems

Use the model to solve.

1. Ryan has 4 boxes of model cars. There are 7 cars in each box. How many model cars does Ryan have in all?

   $4 \times 7 =$?
   28

2. Jessie placed her seashells in 3 piles. She put 24 shells in each pile. How many seashells does Jessie have altogether?

   $3 \times 24 =$?
   72

3. Dawn has 8 bags of bagels. Each bag has 4 bagels in it. How many bagels does Dawn have? Choose the answer.

   A. 8
   B. 16
   C. 12
   D. 32

4. A carton of eggs has 2 rows. There are 6 eggs in each row. How many eggs are in the carton? Choose the answer.

   A. 8
   B. 12
   C. 16
   D. 24

Use circles blocks or make a sketch.

5. Cole has a bookshelf with 5 shelves. He places 4 books on each shelf. How many books are on the bookshelf?
   $5 \times 4 =$? **See below.**

6. There are 7 picnic benches at the park. There are 6 children on each bench. How many children are sitting on the benches in all?
   $7 \times 6 =$? **See below.**

Use circles blocks or make a sketch.
Write the multiplication number sentence and solve.

7. Theo has 5 bags of peaches. There are 5 peaches in each bag. How many peaches does Theo have altogether? **See below.**

8. There are 8 baskets of strawberries. There are 10 strawberries in each basket. How many strawberries are there in all? **See below.**

Use circle blocks to model and solve.

9. Alyssa has 3 boxes of crayons. Each box has 8 crayons. How many crayons does Alyssa have? **24**

10. Tom has 3 fields on his farm. Each field has 7 cows. How many cows are on Tom's farm? **21**

11. Rachel has 4 boxes of buttons. Each box has 7 buttons. How many buttons does Rachel have? **28**

Additional Answers

5. 20; Models will vary. **Sample model:** Students make an array of 5 rows of 4 circles.

6. 42; Models will vary. **Sample answer:** Students make a sketch of 7 groups of 6 circles.

7. $5 \times 5 =$?; $5 \times 5 = 25$; Models will vary. **Sample model:** Students make an array of 5 rows of 5 circles.

8. $8 \times 10 =$?; $8 \times 10 = 80$; Models will vary. **Sample model:** Students make a sketch of 8 groups of 10 circles.

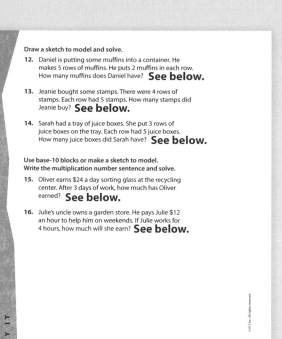

Draw a sketch to model and solve.

12. Daniel is putting some muffins into a container. He makes 5 rows of muffins. He puts 2 muffins in each row. How many muffins does Daniel have? **See below.**

13. Jeanie bought some stamps. There were 4 rows of stamps. Each row had 5 stamps. How many stamps did Jeanie buy? **See below.**

14. Sarah had a tray of juice boxes. She put 3 rows of juice boxes on the tray. Each row had 5 juice boxes. How many juice boxes did Sarah have? **See below.**

Use base-10 blocks or make a sketch to model.
Write the multiplication number sentence and solve.

15. Oliver earns $24 a day sorting glass at the recycling center. After 3 days of work, how much has Oliver earned? **See below.**

16. Julie's uncle owns a garden store. He pays Julie $12 an hour to help him on weekends. If Julie works for 4 hours, how much will she earn? **See below.**

TRY IT

WHOLE NUMBER MULTIPLICATION | 44 | MULTIPLICATION STORY PROBLEMS

Additional Answers

12. Daniel has 10 muffins.

13. Jeanie bought 20 stamps.

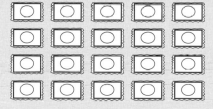

14. Sarah had 15 juice boxes.

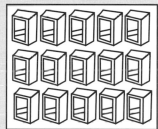

15. $3 \times \$24 = ?$; $3 \times \$24 = \$72$; Models will vary. **Sample model:** Students use base-10 blocks to show 3 groups of 24 with 2 tens rod and 4 ones cubes in each group.

16. $4 \times \$12 = ?$; $4 \times \$12 = \$48$; Models will vary. **Sample model:** Students use base-10 blocks to show 4 groups of 12 with 1 tens rod and 2 ones cubes in each group.

ONLINE

10min

CHECKPOINT

Students will complete an online Checkpoint. If necessary, read the directions, problems, and answer choices to students and help them with keyboard or mouse operations.

Objectives

- Use objects or sketches to solve a multiplication story problem.

Multiply Multidigit by 1-Digit Numbers

Lesson Overview

GET READY Multiplication Fast Facts	5 minutes	**ONLINE**
LEARN Multiply with Partial Products	15 minutes	**ONLINE**
LEARN Standard Multiplication Algorithm	10 minutes	**ONLINE**
TRY IT Multiply Two Ways	20 minutes	**OFFLINE**
CHECKPOINT	10 minutes	**ONLINE**

▶ Lesson Objectives

Solve a multiplication problem involving a multidigit factor and a one-digit factor.

▶ Prerequisite Skills

Demonstrate automatic recall of multiplication facts.

▶ Content Background

Students know how to multiply a one-digit number by another one-digit number. In this lesson, students will learn to solve problems by multiplying a one-digit number by a multidigit number, a number that has more than one digit.

In many problems, students will have equal groups and will be asked for the total. Until they learn to multiply using a standard step-by-step process, they will have a greater risk of error when they add large groups. Suppose they were asked to find the total of 9 groups of 52 objects. They would be forced to find the sum of 9 addends of 52. The potential for error is great. Multiplication simplifies the entire process, and students should understand this benefit of knowing how to multiply.

Students need to understand why the standard process adults use to multiply actually works. Therefore, rather than moving into a step-by-step process (called an algorithm) that has no meaning, students will begin to learn multiplication by using what they know about place value and simple multiplication facts, recording that information as they work through the problems.

Learning to multiply in this way accomplishes two things:

- Students will understand the meaning behind the multiplication process. They will eventually use it as a shortcut.

- Students will also learn strategies for mentally multiplying some problems they would otherwise think they had to write down.

Materials to Gather

SUPPLIED

Multiply Two Ways activity page

▶ Common Errors and Misconceptions

- Students might add the second factor too many or too few times when using repeated addition. For example, for 5×4, students might add $4 + 4 + 4 + 4$.

- Students might undercount or overcount when using the count-by-n strategy.

- Students might view multiplication and division algorithms as rules to be followed. This leads to a misunderstanding that the numbers involved are separate digits rather than grouped amounts representing place values. The result is often an incorrect answer because of students' misunderstanding of estimation, place value, and reasonableness of results.

GET READY Multiplication Fast Facts

ONLINE **5**min

Objectives

- Demonstrate automatic recall of multiplication facts.

Students will continue to practice automatic recall of multiplication facts by playing a timed game. Note which facts are difficult for students and practice them with flash cards, such as the 6s or 7s facts.

LEARN Multiply with Partial Products

 ONLINE **15**min

Objectives

- Solve a multiplication problem involving a multidigit factor and a one-digit factor.

Students will learn how to use partial products to multiply a multidigit factor by a one-digit factor. It is important to participate with students during this activity to help them understand the partial-product method of multiplication.

Students will use place value to break the greater number up and show it in expanded form. They will multiply each number in the expanded form by the one-digit factor to get part of the product. These parts are called partial products. Then students will add the partial products to find the product of the original problem.

Tips

Review place value and expanded form with students. This review will help them use partial products to multiply.

LEARN Standard Multiplication Algorithm

 ONLINE **10**min

Objectives

- Solve a multiplication problem involving a multidigit factor and a one-digit factor.

Students will learn how to multiply a multidigit factor and a one-digit factor, using a step-by-step procedure, or algorithm. Emphasize that students can always solve a problem with partial products to check their solutions.

TRY IT   Multiply Two Ways

Objectives

- Solve a multiplication problem involving a multidigit factor and a one-digit factor.

Students will practice finding the product of a multidigit factor and a one-digit factor by using partial products and the standard algorithm. They should use the method they're most comfortable with for a given problem. When students use the standard algorithm, make sure they keep each digit of the answer in the proper place-value position. View or print the Multiply Two Ways activity page and read the directions with students.

Students should copy the problems from the Activity Book into their Math Notebook as necessary and solve them there.

Tips

To help students align the digits in the standard algorithm, use a pencil to draw light, vertical lines separating the digits in the ones, tens, and hundreds places.

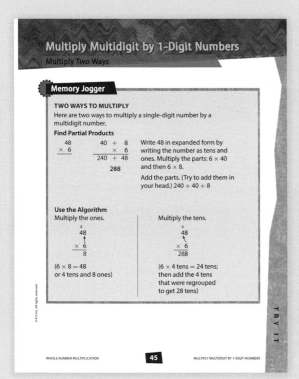

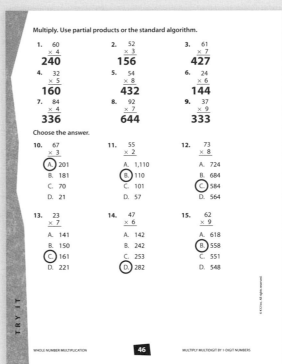

CHECKPOINT

Objectives

- Solve a multiplication problem involving a multidigit factor and a one-digit factor.

Students will complete an online Checkpoint. If necessary, read the directions, problems, and answer choices to students and help them with keyboard or mouse operations.

Multiply Equal Groups (A)

Lesson Overview

GET READY Model and Solve	5 minutes	**ONLINE**
LEARN Multiply with Equal Groups	15 minutes	**ONLINE**
LEARN Multiplication Story Problems	20 minutes	**OFFLINE**
TRY IT Multiply Groups and Objects	20 minutes	**OFFLINE**

▶ Lesson Objectives

Use multiplication to solve a story problem that involves equal groups.

▶ Prerequisite Skills

- Use grouping to solve simple multiplication problems.
- Use objects or sketches to solve a multiplication story problem.

▶ Content Background

Students will solve multiplication story problems involving equal groups of objects. They will multiply multidigit numbers by one-digit numbers.

Multiplication is an operation used when there are equal groups. The multiplication symbol ($\times$) represents the phrase "groups of." For example, 5×8 represents 5 groups of 8 objects. As students move toward more difficult problems, they will move away from models and sketches. They will solve problems using the partial-product method or the standard algorithm (the traditional steps for muliplication). The partial-product method involves writing a multidigit number in expanded form (for example, $58 = 50 + 8$) and then multiplying each part by a single-digit factor. Using this method helps students make a connection between the meaning of multiplication and the steps to calculate problems.

▶ Common Errors and Misconceptions

- Students might add the second factor too many or too few times when using repeated addition. For example, for 5×4, students might add $4 + 4 + 4 + 4$.
- Students might undercount or overcount when using the count-by-n strategy.
- Students might view multiplication and division algorithms as rules to be followed. This leads to a misunderstanding that the numbers involved are separate digits rather than grouped amounts representing place values. The result is often an incorrect answer because of students' misunderstanding of estimation, place value, and reasonableness of results.

Materials to Gather

SUPPLIED

Multiplication Story Problems activity page

Multiply Groups and Objects activity page

base-10 blocks (optional)

GET READY Model and Solve

ONLINE
5min

Objectives

- Use grouping to solve simple multiplication problems.
- Use objects or sketches to solve a multiplication story problem.

Students will use models to solve a multiplication story problem that involves equal groups. They will see that the answer is the same whether they solve the problem with repeated addition or with multiplication.

LEARN Multiply with Equal Groups

ONLINE
15min

Objectives

- Use multiplication to solve a story problem that involves equal groups.

Students will learn to solve story problems involving equal groups. Encourage students to use whatever method they are most comfortable with to solve the problems.

LEARN Multiplication Story Problems

OFFLINE
20min

Objectives

- Use multiplication to solve a story problem that involves equal groups.

Students will use multiplication to solve story problems that involve equal groups. View or print the Multiplication Story Problems activity page and read the directions with students.

Students should copy the problems from the Activity Book into their Math Notebook as necessary and solve them there.

Tips

Provide base-10 blocks for students to model and solve the multiplication problems.

1. Tell students that they will multiply to solve the story problems on the activity page.

2. Read the Worked Example together. Emphasize that each phrase in the problem represents a part of the multiplication sentence. Guide students to see that the 99 ants represent the number of groups, and the 6 legs per ant represent the number in each group. Point out that it would be difficult to draw 99 groups of 6, so students can just use numbers to solve the problem.

3. Point out the multiplication number sentence used to solve the problem. Tell students there are two ways to find the answer to this sentence: partial products and the standard algorithm.

4. Go over the two ways to solve the problem. Point out that both ways lead to the same answer: 594 legs.

5. Have students complete Problems 1–5. Encourage them to use the multiplication method that works best for each problem. Encourage them to use the standard steps for multiplying (the algorithm) when the numbers are too difficult to work with in their head. When students use the algorithm, help them line up the numbers and multiply the one-digit number by the ones, tens, and hundreds, regrouping where necessary. Remind them to show how they solved each problem.

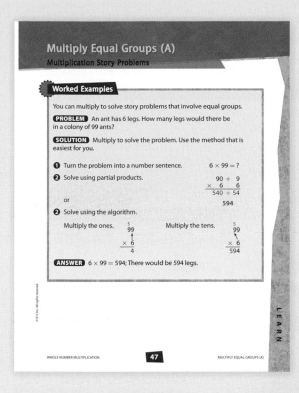

Multiply Equal Groups (A)
Multiplication Story Problems

Worked Examples

You can multiply to solve story problems that involve equal groups.

PROBLEM An ant has 6 legs. How many legs would there be in a colony of 99 ants?

SOLUTION Multiply to solve the problem. Use the method that is easiest for you.

❶ Turn the problem into a number sentence. $6 \times 99 = ?$

❷ Solve using partial products.

$$\begin{array}{r} 90 + 9 \\ \times \quad 6 \quad 6 \\ \hline 540 + 54 \end{array}$$

or

$$594$$

❷ Solve using the algorithm.

Multiply the ones.
$$\begin{array}{r} {}^{5}\ \\ 99 \\ \times \ 6 \\ \hline 4 \end{array}$$

Multiply the tens.
$$\begin{array}{r} {}^{5}\ \\ 99 \\ \times \ 6 \\ \hline 594 \end{array}$$

ANSWER $6 \times 99 = 594$; There would be 594 legs.

Multiply to solve.

1. A sheep has 4 feet.
   There are 80 sheep in the herd.
   How many feet are there altogether?
   ? feet **320**

2. A chicken has 2 legs.
   There are 67 chickens in the coop.
   How many legs are there altogether?
   ? legs **134**

3. An octopus has 8 arms.
   If there are 64 octopuses in the ocean, how many arms are there altogether?
   ? arms **512**

4. A starfish has 5 arms.
   There are 83 starfish at the aquarium.
   How many arms are there altogether?
   ? arms **415**

5. Spiders have 8 legs.
   If the zoo has 70 spiders, how many spider legs are there altogether?
   ? legs **560**

OFFLINE

20 min

TRY IT Multiply Groups and Objects

Students will practice using multiplication to solve story problems. View or print the Multiply Groups and Objects activity page and read the directions with students.

Students should copy the problems from the Activity Book into their Math Notebook as necessary and solve them there.

Objectives

- Use multiplication to solve a story problem that involves equal groups.

Multiply Equal Groups (A)
Multiply Groups and Objects

Solve.

1. Sally bought 4 apples for each person in her family. There are 3 people in Sally's family. How many apples did Sally buy?
   12

2. Oliver has a box of avocados. There are 6 rows of avocados. Each row has 7 avocados. How many avocados are in the box?
   42

3. A baker bought 3 large cartons of eggs. There were 18 eggs in each carton. How many eggs did the baker buy?
   54

4. A store has 7 large fish tanks. There are 30 fish in each tank. How many fish are in the fish tanks?
   210

5. Kelly just got a new bookcase. It has 6 shelves. Kelly puts 54 books on each shelf. How many books are in the bookcase?
   324

6. Mr. Carter ordered 6 stacks of bricks. Each stack has 80 bricks. How many bricks did Mr. Carter order in all?
   480

Choose the answer.

7. Shirley is putting new tile on the wall behind her sink. She is putting 8 rows of tiles on the wall. There will be 40 tiles in each row. How many tiles does Shirley need?
   A. 32   B. 48   (C.) 320   D. 32,000

8. Frida has 14 baskets. Each basket has 8 apples. What is the total number of apples in the baskets?
   (A.) 112   B. 82   C. 56   D. 22

9. The cafeteria had a display of milk bottles. There were 6 rows of milk bottles. Each row had 12 milk bottles. How many milk bottles were in the display?
   A. 12   B. 18   C. 66   (D.) 72

Multiply Equal Groups (B)

Lesson Overview

LEARN Train Station Multiplication	20 minutes	**ONLINE**
LEARN Multiplication Computation	20 minutes	**OFFLINE**
TRY IT Multiply to Solve	20 minutes	**OFFLINE**

▶ Lesson Objectives

Use multiplication to solve a story problem that involves equal groups.

▶ Prerequisite Skills

- Use grouping to solve simple multiplication problems.
- Use objects or sketches to solve a multiplication story problem.

▶ Content Background

Students will continue to solve multiplication story problems involving equal groups of objects. They will multiply multidigit numbers by one-digit numbers.

Multiplication is an operation used when there are equal groups. The multiplication symbol ($\times$) represents the phrase "groups of." For example, 5×8 represents 5 groups of 8 objects. As students move toward more difficult problems, they will move away from models and sketches. They will solve problems using the partial-product method, or the standard algorithm (the traditional steps for muliplication). The partial-product method involves writing a multidigit number in expanded form (for example, $324 = 300 + 20 + 4$) and then multiplying each part by a single-digit factor. Using this method helps students make a connection between the meaning of multiplication and the steps to calculate problems.

▶ Common Errors and Misconceptions

- Students might add the second factor too many or too few times when using repeated addition. For example, for 5×4, students might add $4 + 4 + 4 + 4$.
- Students might undercount or overcount when using the count-by-n strategy.
- Students might view multiplication and division algorithms as rules to be followed. This leads to a misunderstanding that the numbers involved are separate digits rather than grouped amounts representing place values. The result is often an incorrect answer because of students' misunderstanding of estimation, place value, and reasonableness of results.

Materials to Gather

SUPPLIED

Multiplication Computation activity page

Multiply to Solve activity page

LEARN Train Station Multiplication

ONLINE 20min

Students will use multiplication to solve story problems. They may use different methods to solve the problems. When solving 4×24, some students will use the partial-product method, where they multiply 4×20 and 4×4 and add the products together. Others will use the standard algorithm (the traditional steps for multiplying) to solve the problem.

Objectives

- Use multiplication to solve a story problem that involves equal groups.

Tips

Encourage students to use the multiplication method they are most comfortable with to solve each problem. Have paper and pencil available.

LEARN Multiplication Computation

OFFLINE 20min

Students will use computation to solve story problems involving equal groups. View or print the Multiplication Computation activity page

Students should copy the problems from the Activity Book to their Math Notebook as necessary and solve them there.

1. Tell students they will multiply to solve the story problems on the activity page.

2. Read the Worked Example together. Emphasize that each phrase in the problem represents a part of the multiplication number sentence. Guide students to see that the 96 mini boxes represent the number of equal groups and the 8 crayons represent the number in each group. They should use the sentence 96×8 to solve the problem.

3. Encourage students to use the multiplication method with which they are most comfortable to solve the problem.

4. Have students complete Problems 1 and 2 on their own. They may use either the partial-product method or the standard algorithm.

5. Remind students to show how they solved each problem.

Objectives

- Use multiplication to solve a story problem that involves equal groups.

Tips

Review the partial-product method and the standard algorithm with students.

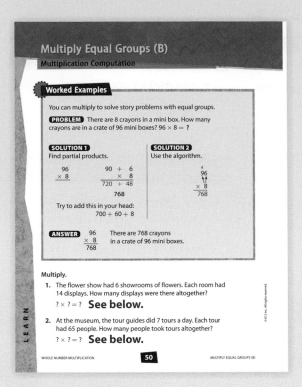

Additional Answers

1. $6 \times 14 = 84$

Partial Products

$$
\begin{array}{r}
10 \;+\; 4 \\
\times \;\; 6 \\
\hline
60 \;+\; 24 \\
84
\end{array}
$$

Algorithm

$$
\begin{array}{r}
2 \\
14 \\
\times \;\; 6 \\
\hline
84
\end{array}
$$

2. $7 \times 65 = 455$

Partial Products

$$
\begin{array}{r}
60 \;+\; 5 \\
\times \;\; 7 \\
\hline
420 \;+\; 35 \\
455
\end{array}
$$

Algorithm

$$
\begin{array}{r}
3 \\
65 \\
\times \;\; 7 \\
\hline
455
\end{array}
$$

TRY IT Multiply to Solve

Students will practice solving story problems using multiplication. View or print the Multiply to Solve activity page and read the directions with students.

   Students should copy the problems from the Activity Book into their Math Notebook as necessary and solve them there.

- Use multiplication to solve a story problem that involves equal groups.

Multiply Equal Groups (B)
Multiply to Solve

Solve.

1. Janelle bought 6 large boxes of mangoes. There were 14 mangoes in each box. How many mangoes did Janelle buy?
84

2. The camp counselor gave 3 plums to each camper. There were 26 campers. How many plums did the counselor give out?
78

3. Kelly knit 9 rows in her sweater. Each row had 85 stitches. How many stitches did Kelly knit?
765

4. A nut factory had 98 pounds of almonds in each crate. If there were 4 crates, how many pounds of almonds did the factory have?
392

Choose the answer.

5. Simone was paving a pathway in her yard. She had 9 rows of small paving stones. Each row had 46 stones. How many paving stones did she use?
   A. 314   B. 364
   C. 414   D. 514

6. The caterer has 23 plates. He wants to put 4 potatoes on each plate. How many potatoes does the caterer need?
   A. 27   B. 82
   C. 90   D. 92

7. Cindy drew some squares on her paper. She drew 15 rows of squares. Each row had 6 squares. How many squares did Cindy draw?
   A. 105   B. 90
   C. 75   D. 21

8. A grocery store had 5 crates of **toothpaste**. Each crate had 82 tubes of toothpaste. How many tubes of toothpaste did the grocery store have?
   A. 410   B. 400
   C. 310   D. 87

TRY IT

WHOLE NUMBER MULTIPLICATION **51** MULTIPLY EQUAL GROUPS (B)

Multiplication with Equal Measures

Lesson Overview

GET READY Multidigit Multiplication	10 minutes	OFFLINE
LEARN Multiply Equal Measures	15 minutes	ONLINE
LEARN Equal-Measures Story Problems	15 minutes	OFFLINE
TRY IT Solve Equal-Measures Story Problems	15 minutes	OFFLINE
CHECKPOINT	5 minutes	ONLINE

▶ Lesson Objectives

Use multiplication to solve a story problem that involves equal measures.

▶ Prerequisite Skills

Solve a multiplication problem involving a multidigit factor and a one-digit factor.

▶ Content Background

Students have learned how to solve multiplication story problems. In this lesson, they will solve story problems involving equal measures.

Multiplication is usually associated with combining equal groups of objects. The equal groups can also be groups of equal measures like distances, amounts of time, or amounts of money. For example, if students line up 6 toothpicks end to end and each toothpick is 2 inches long, they have 6 equal groups of 2. They can use multiplication to find the total length of the line of toothpicks.

▶ Common Errors and Misconceptions

- Students might add the second factor too many or too few times when using repeated addition. For example, for 5×4, students might add $4 + 4 + 4 + 4$.
- Students might undercount or overcount when using the count-by-n strategy.
- Students might view multiplication and division algorithms as rules to be followed. This leads to a misunderstanding that the numbers involved are separate digits rather than grouped amounts representing place values. The result is often an incorrect answer because of students' misunderstanding of estimation, place value, and reasonableness of results.

Materials to Gather

SUPPLIED

Equal-Measures Story Problems
   activity page

Solve Equal-Measures Story Problems
   activity page

GET READY Multidigit Multiplication

OFFLINE
10 min

Students will solve multiplication problems involving a two-digit factor and a one-digit factor. They will see how using known multiplication facts can help them solve related facts.

1. Have students solve 8 × 100 (write the problem vertically) using the traditional steps in which they multiply 8 times each digit.

2. Explain to students that solving a problem like this is very easy when they understand place value. They can just multiply 8 times the 1 in the hundreds place to get 8 in the hundreds place and all the other places will just have zeros. So It's like multiplying 8 × 1 and putting 2 zeros at the end of that number to get 800. Encourage students to make a connection between this concept and the problem 8 × 100.

3. Have students solve 8 × 100.

4. Give students the problem 8 × 99. Before students solve the problem, discuss how the numbers are close to the problem 8 × 100. See if students can use the problem 8 × 100 to solve 8 × 99.

5. Have students solve the problem and discuss their solutions. Guide students to say that the product of 8 × 99 can be seen as 99 × 8, or 99 groups of 8. Since they know that 100 groups of 8 would be 800, they could surmise that 99 groups of 8 would be 800 − 8, or 792.

LEARN Multiply Equal Measures

ONLINE
15 min

Objectives

Students will learn to solve multiplication story problems involving equal measures such as time, money, length, and capacity. Have them work the problems on paper and enter the answers on the screen to check their work. Students should solve problems using whatever method they are most comfortable with.

- Use multiplication to solve a story problem that involves equal measures.

LEARN Equal-Measures Story Problems

OFFLINE
15 min

Objectives

Students will practice solving multiplication story problems involving equal measures such as time, capacity, length, and height. View or print the Equal-Measures Story Problems activity page and read the directions with students.
   Students should copy the problems from the Activity Book into their Math Notebook as necessary and solve them there.

- Use multiplication to solve a story problem that involves equal measures.

1. Ask students to explain when they can use multiplication to solve a story problem. Students should explain that they can use multiplication when the story problem is about combining equal groups.

2. Discuss several examples of different measurements that can be thought of as equal groups, such as distance, height, length, time, weight, or capacity. Explain that students can multiply these equal measures just as they would multiply equal groups.

3. Read the Worked Example with students. Point out that 14 inches is the amount that gets added over and over. Tell them that this amount gets added 6 times. Explain that since multiplication is repeated addition, they can multiply 6 times 14 to solve the problem. Make sure students understand how the multiplication number sentence was determined.

4. Read each problem with students. Ask them which amount gets added over and over, and how many times it gets added. Have students tell you the multiplication number sentence that can be used to solve each problem, and then solve it.

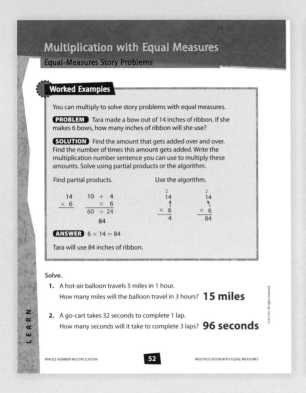

Multiplication with Equal Measures
Equal-Measures Story Problems

Worked Examples

You can multiply to solve story problems with equal measures.

PROBLEM Tara made a bow out of 14 inches of ribbon. If she makes 6 bows, how many inches of ribbon will she use?

SOLUTION Find the amount that gets added over and over. Find the number of times this amount gets added. Write the multiplication number sentence you can use to multiply these amounts. Solve using partial products or the algorithm.

Find partial products.

$$\begin{array}{r} 14 \\ \times\ 6 \end{array} \quad \begin{array}{r} 10\ +\ 4 \\ \times\ 6 \\ \hline 60\ +\ 24 \\ 84 \end{array}$$

Use the algorithm.

$$\begin{array}{r} \overset{2}{14} \\ \times\ 6 \\ \hline 4 \end{array} \quad \begin{array}{r} \overset{2}{14} \\ \times\ 6 \\ \hline 84 \end{array}$$

ANSWER $6 \times 14 = 84$

Tara will use 84 inches of ribbon.

Solve.

1. A hot-air balloon travels 5 miles in 1 hour.
How many miles will the balloon travel in 3 hours? **15 miles**

2. A go-cart takes 32 seconds to complete 1 lap.
How many seconds will it take to complete 3 laps? **96 seconds**

LEARN

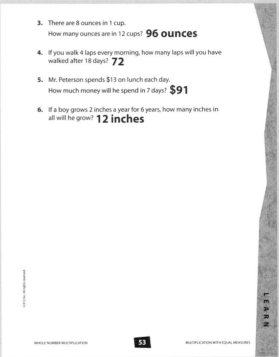

3. There are 8 ounces in 1 cup.
How many ounces are in 12 cups? **96 ounces**

4. If you walk 4 laps every morning, how many laps will you have walked after 18 days? **72**

5. Mr. Peterson spends $13 on lunch each day.
How much money will he spend in 7 days? **$91**

6. If a boy grows 2 inches a year for 6 years, how many inches in all will he grow? **12 inches**

LEARN

TRY IT Solve Equal-Measures Story Problems

OFFLINE **15**min

Objectives

- Use multiplication to solve a story problem that involves equal measures.

Students will practice solving multiplication story problems involving equal measures. View or print the Solve Equal-Measures Story Problems activity page and read the directions with students.

Students should copy the problems from the Activity Book into their Math Notebook as necessary and solve them there.

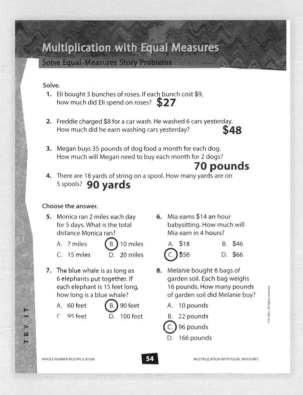

Multiplication with Equal Measures

Solve Equal-Measures Story Problems

Solve.

1. Eli bought 3 bunches of roses. If each bunch cost $9, how much did Eli spend on roses? **$27**

2. Freddie charged $8 for a car wash. He washed 6 cars yesterday. How much did he earn washing cars yesterday? **$48**

3. Megan buys 35 pounds of dog food a month for each dog. How much will Megan need to buy each month for 2 dogs? **70 pounds**

4. There are 18 yards of string on a spool. How many yards are on 5 spools? **90 yards**

Choose the answer.

5. Monica ran 2 miles each day for 5 days. What is the total distance Monica ran?
   - A. 7 miles
   - B. 10 miles
   - C. 15 miles
   - D. 20 miles

6. Mia earns $14 an hour babysitting. How much will Mia earn in 4 hours?
   - A. $18
   - B. $46
   - C. $56
   - D. $66

7. The blue whale is as long as 6 elephants put together. If each elephant is 15 feet long, how long is a blue whale?
   - A. 60 feet
   - B. 90 feet
   - C. 95 feet
   - D. 100 feet

8. Melanie bought 6 bags of garden soil. Each bag weighs 16 pounds. How many pounds of garden soil did Melanie buy?
   - A. 10 pounds
   - B. 22 pounds
   - C. 96 pounds
   - D. 166 pounds

WHOLE NUMBER MULTIPLICATION **54** MULTIPLICATION WITH EQUAL MEASURES

ONLINE **5**min

CHECKPOINT

Objectives

- Use multiplication to solve a story problem that involves equal measures.

Students will complete an online Checkpoint. If necessary, read the directions, problems, and answer choices to students and help them with keyboard or mouse operations.

Write Multiplication Stories (A)

Lesson Overview

GET READY Solve Multiplication Story Problems	10 minutes	**ONLINE**
LEARN Types of Multiplication Story Problems	20 minutes	**OFFLINE**
LEARN Write Your Own Story Problems	20 minutes	**OFFLINE**
TRY IT Match a Number Sentence to a Problem	10 minutes	**ONLINE**

▶ ## Lesson Objectives

Create a story problem that can be represented by a multiplication number sentence.

▶ ## Prerequisite Skills

- Use multiplication to solve a story problem that involves equal groups.
- Solve a multiplication problem involving a multidigit factor and a one-digit factor.

▶ ## Content Background

Students have a basic understanding of multiplication and how to solve multiplication story problems. In this lesson, they will create their own multiplication story problems.

Usually students solve problems written by others. However, one of the best ways to learn and practice a new skill is to teach it to someone else. By writing problems of their own, students become the teacher. They must think about all the parts needed to write a good multiplication story problem.

As students study and work through the variety of multiplication story problems and also create some of their own, they may notice many different types of problems. Some of the different types of problems are those with arrays and area models and those involving equal groups and equal measures. Students are not expected to memorize or explain these types of problems. However, encouraging them to use variety in the types of problems they write will help them better understand multiplication story problems.

Materials to Gather

SUPPLIED

Types of Multiplication Story Problems activity page

GET READY Solve Multiplication Story Problems

Objectives

Students will solve a multiplication story problem using partial products.

- Use multiplication to solve a story problem that involves equal groups.
- Solve a multiplication problem involving a multidigit factor and a one-digit factor.

LEARN Types of Multiplication Story Problems

Objectives

Students will review what they know about story problems, multiplication, and ways of showing multiplication. They will learn the steps to write story problems. They will use this information to write their own multiplication story problems.

First follow the directions in Steps 1–5 with students. Then view or print the Types of Multiplication Story Problems activity page.

- Create a story problem that can be represented by a multiplication number sentence.

Tips

Allow students to sketch each problem to determine if it is an array, area-model, equal-groups, or equal-measures problem.

1. Review different types of multiplication story problems. Present each situation below and ask students to give an example, either verbally or with a drawing.
   - array **Example:** 5 rows of 10 seats; $5 \times 10 = 50$
   - area model **Example:** squares on a grid that is 3 squares by 4 squares; $3 \times 4 = 12$
   - equal groups **Example:** 6 packs of 14, $6 \times 14 = 84$
   - equal measures **Example:** running 20 meters 5 times; $5 \times 20 = 100$

2. Discuss how to get ideas for story problems and present examples. Guide students in picking a general theme, getting specific, and then thinking of what to include in the problem.

   Say: If you want to write a story problem, first you need a good story. Start by picking a theme.

   Present an example about hamsters.

   Say: Let's pick animals, more specifically, hamsters. Now we have to think about what hamsters do that can be included in a problem.

   Ask: What are some things hamsters do? Hamsters eat, sleep, run on the hamster wheel, put food in their cheek pouches, and build nests.

   Say: Now let's start thinking of problems. If we want problems with greater numbers, we might need many hamsters. So let's say we have a hamster farm with more than 10 but fewer than 30 hamsters.

   Ask: How many hamsters should we have on the farm? Accept any number between 10 and 30.

3. Explain that the next step is thinking of problems that involve multiplying. Point out that for each problem, students need to write a multiplication number sentence.

4. Together, write a problem about the hamsters on the farm. Identify the multiplication number sentence for that problem. **Example:** There are 21 hamsters on the farm. Each hamster eats 2 pounds of food each month. How many pounds of food do the hamsters eat in 1 month altogether? The number sentence is $21 \times 2 = ?$

5. Brainstorm with students other themes they could use to write multiplication stories. Have students move from general theme to specific topic to items to include in the problem. Use the following questions:

   - What is your theme? **Example:** circus, zoo, party, library, weather
   - What specifically would your problem be about? **Example:** clowns, lions, balloons, books, snowfall
   - Give an example of something you would multiply. **Example:** price of a ticket to the show, amount of food the lions eat each day, number of balloons each guest gets, number of books in piles, amount of snow in 4 weeks

6. Have students turn to the Types of Multiplication Story Problems activity page in their Activity Book and read the directions with them. Students should copy the problems from the Activity Book into their Math Notebook as necessary and solve them there. (Note: Students only need to identify the types of story problems; they do not need to solve the multiplication problems presented.)

7. Read the Worked Example with students. To make sure they understand why an area model is the best model for the problem, ask how they would make the area model that shows the details in the problem. Students should say that they would make a grid with 9 rows, each with 10 squares.

8. Read Problem 1 with students. Ask them which type of story problem best matches this particular problem. Guide them to see that this is an equal-groups problem. There are the same number of objects in each group. 3 hamster pellets; 32 hamsters

9. Read Problem 2 with students. Ask them which type of story problem best matches this particular problem. Guide them to see that this is an equal-measures problem. Ask them what amount gets added over and over. the number of yards Hamie Hamster runs

10. Read Problem 3 with students. Ask them which type of story problem best matches this particular problem. Guide them to see that this is an area-model problem because the pictures form a grid of squares. Ask them how many rows there are and how many pictures in each row. 24 rows; 3 pictures in each row

    Remind students that in an area model, the objects are touching, and point out that this problem says that the photos will be side by side, with edges touching.

11. Read Problem 4 with students. Ask them which type of story problem best matches this particular problem. Guide them to see that this is an array problem. Ask them how many rows there are, and how many cages are in each row. 5 rows; 18 cages in each row

12. Have students solve Problems 5 and 6 on their own. Read the problems to them if needed. Allow time to discuss their answers.

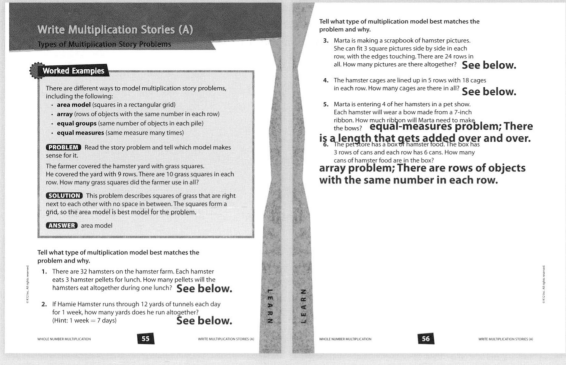

Write Multiplication Stories (A)
Types of Multiplication Story Problems

Worked Examples

There are different ways to model multiplication story problems, including the following:
- **area model** (squares in a rectangular grid)
- **array** (rows of objects with the same number in each row)
- **equal groups** (same number of objects in each pile)
- **equal measures** (same measure many times)

PROBLEM Read the story problem and tell which model makes sense for it.

The farmer covered the hamster yard with grass squares. He covered the yard with 9 rows. There are 10 grass squares in each row. How many grass squares did the farmer use in all?

SOLUTION This problem describes squares of grass that are right next to each other with no space in between. The squares form a grid, so the area model is best model for the problem.

ANSWER area model

Tell what type of multiplication model best matches the problem and why.

1. There are 32 hamsters on the hamster farm. Each hamster eats 3 hamster pellets for lunch. How many pellets will the hamsters eat altogether during one lunch? **See below.**

2. If Hamie Hamster runs through 12 yards of tunnels each day for 1 week, how many yards does he run altogether? (Hint: 1 week = 7 days) **See below.**

Tell what type of multiplication model best matches the problem and why.

3. Marta is making a scrapbook of hamster pictures. She can fit 3 square pictures side by side in each row, with the edges touching. There are 24 rows in all. How many pictures are there altogether? **See below.**

4. The hamster cages are lined up in 5 rows with 18 cages in each row. How many cages are there in all? **See below.**

5. Marta is entering 4 of her hamsters in a pet show. Each hamster will wear a bow made from a 7-inch ribbon. How much ribbon will Marta need to make the bows? **equal-measures problem; There is a length that gets added over and over.**

6. The pet store has a box of hamster food. The box has 3 rows of cans and each row has 6 cans. How many cans of hamster food are in the box? **array problem; There are rows of objects with the same number in each row.**

WHOLE NUMBER MULTIPLICATION — 55 — WRITE MULTIPLICATION STORIES (A)

WHOLE NUMBER MULTIPLICATION — 56 — WRITE MULTIPLICATION STORIES (A)

Additional Answers

1. equal-groups problem; There are groups with the same number of objects in each group.

2. equal-measures problem; The same amount gets added over and over.

3. area-model problem; There are squares in a rectangular grid.

4. array problem; There are rows of objects with the same number in each row.

OFFLINE

20min

LEARN Write Your Own Story Problems

Objectives

- Create a story problem that can be represented by a multiplication number sentence.

Students will write story problems for a given multiplication sentence. Have students turn to the Types of Multiplication Story Problems activity page in their Activity Book. Students will refer to this page in this activity.

1. Explain to students that they will write their own multiplication story problem.

2. Write the multiplication number sentence 6×16 on a sheet of paper. Have students make up an equal-groups story problem about hamsters by using this number sentence. Encourage students to use their imagination. Share this example with students:
   - The 6 oldest hamsters collected seeds. They each collected 16 seeds in their pouches. How many seeds did they collect altogether?

3. Ask students to share their story problem. Check that their story problem matches the multiplication number sentence.

4. Have students look at the Types of Multiplication Story Problems activity page. Review the different ways that multiplication can be shown—by an array, by an area model, by equal groups, and by equal measures.

5. Have students write another story problem that uses the same number sentence as the earlier problem (6 × 16). This problem should use an array. **Example:** The hamsters were given 6 rows of 16 pellets to play a game.

6. Repeat Step 5 to write another story problem that uses an area model. **Example:** The hamsters were given squares of tissue to use for their nests. There were 6 rows of tissue squares with 16 tissue squares in each row. How many tissue squares were there in all?

7. Repeat Step 5 to write another story problem involving equal measures. **Example:** A hamster ran through 6 tunnels. Each tunnel was 16 feet long. How many feet did the hamster run?

8. Discuss with students how the different story problems are alike and how they are different.

TRY IT Match a Number Sentence to a Problem

ONLINE
10min

Students will complete an online Try It. If necessary, read the directions, problems, and answer choices to students and help them with keyboard or mouse operations.

Objectives

- Create a story problem that can be represented by a multiplication number sentence.

Write Multiplication Stories (B)

Lesson Overview

LEARN Multiplication Story Problem Book	40 minutes	OFFLINE
TRY IT Story Writing	10 minutes	ONLINE
CHECKPOINT	10 minutes	ONLINE

▶ Lesson Objectives

Create a story problem that can be represented by a multiplication number sentence.

▶ Prerequisite Skills

- Use multiplication to solve a story problem that involves equal groups.
- Use multiplication to solve a story problem that involves equal measures.
- Solve a multiplication problem involving a multidigit factor and a one-digit factor.

▶ Content Background

Students have a basic understanding of multiplication and how to solve multiplication story problems. In this lesson, they will continue to create their own multiplication story problems.

Usually, students solve problems written by others. However, one of the best ways to learn and practice a new skill is to teach it to someone else. By writing problems of their own, students become the teacher. They must think about all the parts needed to write a good multiplication story problem.

As students study and work through the variety of multiplication story problems, and also create some of their own, they may notice many different types of problems. Some of the different types of problems are those with arrays and area models and those involving equal groups and equal measures. Students are not expected to memorize or explain these types of problems. However, encouraging them to use variety in the types of problems they write will help them better understand multiplication story problems.

▶ Advance Preparation

Cut each sheet of wide-line handwriting paper into halves, as shown.

▶ Safety

Make sure students handle the scissors carefully and be sure to store them in a safe place. Supervise students as they work with the stapler.

Materials to Gather

SUPPLIED

Types of Multiplication Story Problems activity page

ALSO NEEDED

scissors, adult

scissors, pointed-end safety

household objects – stapler

glue stick

markers

paper, construction – 2 sheets

paper, wide-line handwriting – 2 sheets

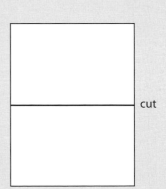

cut

Objectives

- Create a story problem that can be represented by a multiplication number sentence.

Students will use what they know about story problems, multiplication, and ways of showing multiplication to create a book of multiplication story problems. Their book will have four problems. The directions say that students should use a different model for multiplication for each problem—array, area model, equal groups, and equal measures. If students wish, they may use the same model for all the problems or they may use any combination of models.

The examples in this activity all use the same numbers (4 and 23) so students can see the same numbers used with the four types of models. Students may use different numbers in each problem if they wish.

Encourage students to create problems that are challenging enough to show off their multiplication skills. They may choose to show the worked solutions on the individual pages in their book, or they may prefer to show the answers to all problems on the book's last page.

Gather the construction paper, stapler, glue stick, markers, and the four half-sheets of lined paper. View or print the Types of Multiplication Story Problems activity page. Students will refer to this page in Step 6.

1. Review with students how to write their own multiplication story problem. Suggest that they begin with an amusement park theme.

2. Write the number sentence $4 \times 23 = ?$ on a sheet of paper. Tell students that they will be using this multiplication number sentence to write story problems.

3. Share this example with students:

   - Each log of the Raging Rapids Water Slide seats 4 people. If 23 logs went down the slide in 1 hour, how many people rode the water slide?

   Point out how the number sentence was used in the example.

4. Have students create their own amusement park problem using the number sentence $4 \times 23 = ?$ Encourage them to use their imagination.

5. Ask students to read their story problem aloud. Check that their story problem matches the number sentence.

6. Have students look at the Types of Multiplication Story Problems activity page. Review the different ways that multiplication can be shown—by an array, by an area model, by equal groups, and by equal measures.

7. Have students write another problem using the same number sentence. This problem should be one that can be modeled with an array. **Example:** In the parking lot, there are 4 rows of cars. There are 23 cars in each row. How many cars are there in all?

8. Repeat Step 7 for a problem that can use an area model. **Example:** People are having lunch in the picnic area of the amusement park. There are 4 rows of square blankets. There are 23 blankets in each row. How many picnic blankets are there in all?

9. Repeat Step 7 for a problem involving equal measures. **Example:** Each roller coaster car is 4 feet long. If 23 roller coaster cars are placed end to end, how long would the coaster be?

10. Discuss with students how their story problems are alike and how their problems are different.

11. Distribute the four half-sheets of lined paper.

12. Explain to students that they will make their own multiplication story problem book. Encourage them to choose a theme for their problems. If they are having difficulty coming up with ideas, have them look through magazines or newspapers to help them think of a theme.

13. Have students write four multiplication story problems. Tell them to write one problem of each type (array, area model, equal groups, and equal measures) and to write each problem on a separate piece of lined paper.

14. Have students assemble a multiplication story problem book. Give students the sheets of construction paper. Fold the sheets of construction paper in half and staple on the fold as shown.

15. Use the front page as the cover. Have students glue each story problem onto a page in their book.

16. Suggest that students title their book and create an illustration for each problem. They can use pictures from magazines, clip art, or their own drawings.

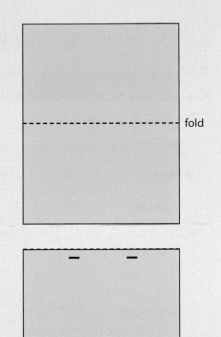

Tips Instead of stapling along the fold, use a hole punch and string to secure the pages. Students may add more pages to their book.

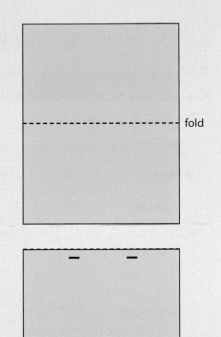

TRY IT Story Writing

ONLINE 10 min

Students will complete an online Try It. If necessary, read the directions, problems, and answer choices to students and help them with keyboard or mouse operations.

Objectives

- Create a story problem that can be represented by a multiplication number sentence.

CHECKPOINT

ONLINE 10 min

Students will complete an online Checkpoint. If necessary, read the directions, problems, and answer choices to students and help them with keyboard or mouse operations.

Objectives

- Create a story problem that can be represented by a multiplication number sentence.

Core Focus
Solve Multiplication Story Problems

Lesson Overview

GET READY Represent Multiplication	5 minutes	ONLINE
LEARN Use Multiplication Strategies	30 minutes	ONLINE
TRY IT Use Multiplication Strategies for Problems	15 minutes	OFFLINE
CHECKPOINT	10 minutes	ONLINE

▶ Lesson Objectives

- Use objects or sketches to solve a multiplication story problem.
- Solve a multiplication problem involving a multidigit factor and a one-digit factor.
- Use multiplication to solve a story problem that involves equal groups.
- Use multiplication to solve a story problem that involves equal measures.

▶ Prerequisite Skills

Use models and math symbols to represent multiplication.

▶ Content Background

In this lesson, students will model story problems and use their multiplication computation skills to solve story problems involving equal groups or equal measures. Students will move from solving both computation and story problems with concrete objects and various strategies to being able to solve them with numbers and symbols by using number sentences and the multiplication algorithm. Students will review the step-by-step process, the standard algorithm, to solve multiplication computation problems in which a one-digit factor is multiplied by a multidigit factor.

▶ Common Errors and Misconceptions

- Students might need exposure to a variety of models (such as rectangular arrays or areas) when learning multiplication as a conceptual operation. Using only repeated addition models and the term *times* can lead to a basic misunderstanding of multiplication. This misunderstanding will complicate future use of multiplication when working with decimals and fractions.
- Students might view the standard multiplication algorithm as rules to be followed. This leads to a misunderstanding that the numbers involved are separate digits rather than grouped amounts representing place values. The result is often an incorrect answer because of students' misunderstanding of estimation, place value, and reasonableness of results.

▶ Advance Preparation

Print one copy of the Grid Paper for Area Models.

Materials to Gather

SUPPLIED

Use Multiplication Strategies for Problems activity page
Grid Paper for Area Models (printout)

ALSO NEEDED

ruler, dual-scale

GET READY Represent Multiplication

ONLINE
5min

Objectives

- Use models and math symbols to represent multiplication.

Students will practice representing multiplication. They will write the factors shown in a multiplication model and then write the product.

LEARN Use Multiplication Strategies

ONLINE
30min

Objectives

- Use objects or sketches to solve a multiplication story problem.
- Solve a multiplication problem involving a multidigit factor and a one-digit factor.
- Use multiplication to solve a story problem that involves equal groups.
- Use multiplication to solve a story problem that involves equal measures.

Students will review what they know about multiplication and ways of showing multiplication in the context of real-world story problems. Students will use objects and sketches to model and solve multiplication story problems. They will also review how to use arrays, area models, partial products, and the standard algorithm to solve multiplication problems that involve multiplying a two-digit factor by a one-digit factor

Students may use different methods to solve story problems. For example, when solving 7 × 14, some students may use an area model, while others may use the partial-product method, in which they multiply 7 × 10 and 7 × 4 and add the products. Other students may use the standard algorithm (the traditional steps for multiplying) to solve the problem.

As students work with various multiplication strategies, they will apply those strategies to solving multiplication problems that involve equal groups and equal measures. Have them work the problems on paper and enter the answers on the screen to check their work. Encourage students to use whatever method or strategy they are most comfortable with when solving these problems.

TRY IT Use Multiplication Strategies for Problems

OFFLINE
15min

Objectives

- Use objects or sketches to solve a multiplication story problem.
- Solve a multiplication problem involving a multidigit factor and a one-digit factor.
- Use multiplication to solve a story problem that involves equal groups.
- Use multiplication to solve a story problem that involves equal measures.

Students will practice using modeling strategies and the standard algorithm to solve multiplication story problems. Gather the Grid Paper for Area Models and the ruler. View or print the Use Multiplication Strategies for Problems activity page. Students should copy the problems from the Activity Book into their Math Notebook as necessary and solve them there.

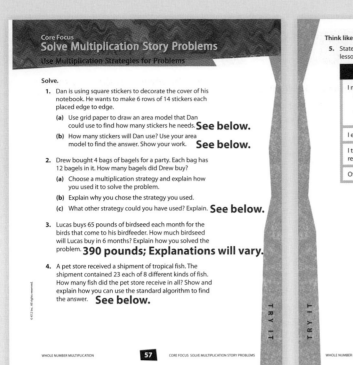

Solve.

1. Dan is using square stickers to decorate the cover of his notebook. He wants to make 6 rows of 14 stickers each placed edge to edge.

   (a) Use grid paper to draw an area model that Dan could use to find how many stickers he needs. **See below.**

   (b) How many stickers will Dan use? Use your area model to find the answer. Show your work. **See below.**

2. Drew bought 4 bags of bagels for a party. Each bag has 12 bagels in it. How many bagels did Drew buy?

   (a) Choose a multiplication strategy and explain how you used it to solve the problem.

   (b) Explain why you chose the strategy you used.

   (c) What other strategy could you have used? Explain. **See below.**

3. Lucas buys 65 pounds of birdseed each month for the birds that come to his birdfeeder. How much birdseed will Lucas buy in 6 months? Explain how you solved the problem. **390 pounds; Explanations will vary.**

4. A pet store received a shipment of tropical fish. The shipment contained 23 each of 8 different kinds of fish. How many fish did the pet store receive in all? Show and explain how you can use the standard algorithm to find the answer. **See below.**

T R Y I T

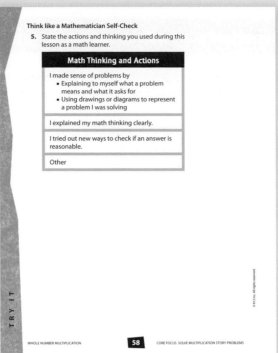

Think like a Mathematician Self-Check

5. State the actions and thinking you used during this lesson as a math learner.

Math Thinking and Actions
I made sense of problems by • Explaining to myself what a problem means and what it asks for • Using drawings or diagrams to represent a problem I was solving
I explained my math thinking clearly.
I tried out new ways to check if an answer is reasonable.
Other

T R Y I T

Answers

1. **(a)** Answer may vary. **Possible answer:**

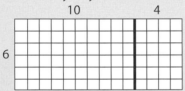

   (b) Dan will use 84 stickers.
   $(6 \times 10) + (6 \times 4) = 84$

2. **(a) (b) (c)** Drew bought 48 bagels. Strategies will vary. Students might draw a picture or use an array, partial products, or the standard algorithm. Check students' work and explanations.

4.
$$\begin{array}{r} 2 \\ 23 \\ \times\ 8 \\ \hline 184 \end{array}$$

   The store received 184 tropical fish. **Possible explanation:** First, multiply the ones: $3 \times 8 = 24$. Put the 2 tens above the tens place and the 4 in the ones place in the answer. Next, multiply the tens: $2 \times 8 = 16$. Add the 2 regrouped tens: $16 + 2 = 18$ tens, or 180. Write the 1 for the hundreds place and the 8 for the tens place in the answer.

CHECKPOINT

Objectives

Students will complete an online Checkpoint. If necessary, read the directions, problems, and answer choices to students and help them with keyboard or mouse operations.

- Use objects or sketches to solve a multiplication story problem.
- Solve a multiplication problem involving a multidigit factor and a one-digit factor.
- Use multiplication to solve a story problem that involves equal groups.
- Use multiplication to solve a story problem that involves equal measures.

Unit Review

▶ Unit Objectives

This lesson reviews the following objectives:

- Use objects or sketches to solve a multiplication story problem.
- Solve a multiplication problem involving a multidigit factor and a one-digit factor.
- Use multiplication to solve a story problem that involves equal groups.
- Use multiplication to solve a story problem that involves equal measures.
- Create a story problem that can be represented by a multiplication number sentence.

Materials to Gather

There are no materials to gather for this lesson.

▶ Advance Preparation

In this lesson, students will have an opportunity to review previous activities in the Whole Number Multiplication unit. Look at the suggested activities in Unit Review: Prepare for the Checkpoint online and gather any needed materials.

UNIT REVIEW Look Back

ONLINE **10** min

Students will review key concepts from the unit to prepare for the Unit Checkpoint.

Objectives

- Review unit objectives.

UNIT REVIEW Checkpoint Practice

ONLINE **50** min

Students will complete an online Checkpoint Practice to prepare for the Unit Checkpoint. If necessary, read the directions, problems, and answer choices to students. Have students answer the problems on their own. Review any missed problems with students.

Objectives

- Review unit objectives.

⊵ UNIT REVIEW Prepare for the Checkpoint

What you do next depends on how students performed in the previous activity, Unit Review: Checkpoint Practice. If students had difficulty with any of the problems, complete the appropriate review activity listed in the table online.

Unit Checkpoint

UNIT CHECKPOINT Online   60 minutes | **ONLINE**

▶ Unit Objectives

This lesson assesses the following objectives:

- Use objects or sketches to solve a multiplication story problem.
- Solve a multiplication problem involving a multidigit factor and a one-digit factor.
- Use multiplication to solve a story problem that involves equal groups.
- Use multiplication to solve a story problem that involves equal measures.
- Create a story problem that can be represented by a multiplication number sentence.

Materials to Gather

There are no materials to gather for this lesson.

ONLINE

UNIT CHECKPOINT Online   **60**min

Students will complete the Unit Checkpoint online. If necessary, read the directions, problems, and answer choices to students and help them with keyboard or mouse operations.

Objectives

- Assess unit objectives.

Extended Problems: Reasoning

Lesson Overview

USE WHAT YOU KNOW Offline ⋮ 60 minutes ⋮ **OFFLINE**

▶ Lesson Objectives

This lesson assesses the following objectives:

- Multiply within 100.
- Solve word problems involving equal groups using multiplication or division within 100.
- Solve word problems involving measurements and equal groups using multiplication or division within 100.
- Determine the unknown whole number in a multiplication or division equation, within 100.
- Multiply one-digit whole numbers by multiples of 10 in the range 10 to 90.
- Solve two-step word problems, limited to whole numbers.
- Analyze complex problems using mathematical knowledge and skills.

Materials to Gather

SUPPLIED

Extended Problems: Reasoning (printout)

Extended Problems: Reasoning Answer Key (printout)

USE WHAT YOU KNOW Offline

OFFLINE

60min

The Extended Problems: Reasoning and its answer key are located in the Resources section for this unit in the Online Book Menu of *Math+ Purple Lesson Guide*. Give students the Extended Problems: Reasoning. Read the directions, problems, and answer choices to students, if necessary.

You will grade this assignment.

- Students should complete the assignment on their own.
- Students should submit the completed assignment to you.

Objectives

- Analyze complex problems using mathematical knowledge and skills.

Whole Number Division Sense

▶ Unit Objectives

- Use objects or sketches to solve a division problem.
- Explain division as repeated subtraction.
- Explain the meaning of the ÷ symbol.
- Explain and apply the division property of 1.
- Demonstrate understanding that division by zero is undefined.
- Recognize the meaning of the three symbols for division.
- Explain division as the sharing of a quantity into equal groups.
- Demonstrate an understanding of the inverse relationship between multiplication and division.
- Use the inverse relationship of multiplication and division to compute and check results.
- Demonstrate an understanding of the effects of division on whole numbers.
- Use division to solve a story problem that involves equal groups.
- Use division to solve a story problem that involves equal measures.
- Create a story problem that can be represented by a division number sentence.
- Solve a story problem involving two or more operations.

▶ Big Ideas

- Multiplication and division can be represented by models and by using math symbols.
- Division can be understood as repeated subtraction or as division of a quantity into equal groups.
- Addition, subtraction, multiplication, and division can be represented by models and by using math symbols.
- Inverses undo each other. Addition and subtraction are inverse operations, and multiplication and division are inverse operations.

▶ Unit Introduction

In this unit, students will develop a further understanding of division. They will practice using the terms *dividend*, *divisor*, and *quotient*. Students will model division problems with concrete objects and sketches. They will explain division as repeated subtraction and explain the meaning of the division symbol. They will explain that division by 1 leaves a number unchanged, and they will demonstrate an understanding that division by zero has no answer. They will learn the three symbols for division: the standard division symbol, the fraction bar, and the long-division symbol. It is important for students to understand that these symbols have the same meaning even though they're used in different situations. Students will explain division as sharing a quantity into equal groups. They will see the inverse relationship between multiplication and division. Finally students will take a step back and generalize to see that when numbers are divided, the answer, or quotient, is less than the number being divided, the dividend. The exception is when dividing by 1 or zero.

▶ Keywords

dividend	equal groups	inverse relationship
division	equal sharing	multiplication fact family
division by 1	fraction bar	quotient
division symbol (÷)	inverse operations	repeated subtraction
divisor		

Model and Explain Division

Lesson Overview

GET READY Explore Division	10 minutes	OFFLINE
LEARN Model Equal Groups	10 minutes	OFFLINE
LEARN Use Repeated Subtraction	15 minutes	OFFLINE
TRY IT Represent Division Problems	15 minutes	OFFLINE
CHECKPOINT	10 minutes	ONLINE

▶ Lesson Objectives
- Use objects or sketches to solve a division problem.
- Explain division as repeated subtraction.
- Explain the meaning of the ÷ symbol.

▶ Prerequisite Skills
- Use models and math symbols to represent division.
- Use repeated subtraction to do division problems.
- Recognize that the ÷ sign refers to division.
- Correctly use the ÷ symbol.

▶ Content Background

Students will learn to explain division as sharing. They will be introduced to division modeled as equal groups, repeated subtraction, and equal measures. Finally they will explain the meaning of the division symbol (÷) and recognize the three different symbolic representations of division.

Division is an operation involving distributing an amount equally. Students can use division to find the number of equal groups or equal measures when they know both the total number and the number that shows how the total will be shared. They can also find the number being shared when they know both the total number and the number of groups or units of measure.

Since students understand fair sharing from an early age, use that idea to begin discussing division. Students need to say "divided by" when stating division problems and writing division symbols. Do not use the phrase *divided into*. Likewise, do not ask how many times a number *goes into* another number.

When writing a division number sentence, the first number tells the total number and is called the *dividend*. The next number tells the number students are dividing by and is called the *divisor*. The answer tells how many groups or objects or units have been shared and is called the *quotient*.

This format will be used with students throughout this lesson.

24	÷	4	=	6
dividend	divided by	divisor	equals	quotient

> **Materials to Gather**
>
> **SUPPLIED**
>
> blocks – B (all colors)
>
> number lines from the Number Line Creator Tool
>
> Represent Division Problems activity page
>
> **ALSO NEEDED**
>
> index cards – 5

▶ Common Errors and Misconceptions

Students might view multiplication and division algorithms as rules to be followed. This leads to a misunderstanding that the numbers involved are separate digits rather than grouped amounts representing place values. The result is often an incorrect answer because of students' misunderstanding of estimation, place value, and reasonableness of results.

▶ Advance Preparation

DIRECTIONS FOR USING THE NUMBER LINE CREATOR TOOL

To create number lines from 0 to 35:

1. Set Range:	2. Select Options:	3. Print Number Line:
• Start Number Line at: 0 • End Number Line at: 35	• Tick Marks: ones	• Page Orientation: landscape • Number Lines per Sheet: 2

GET READY Explore Division

OFFLINE 10 min

Students will explore multiplication and division with models and objects. They will use multiplication to find the total number of objects in equal groups. Then they will divide a number of objects into equal groups, and use repeated subtraction to model division.

Gather the blocks and the index cards.

1. Display 5 groups of circles with 4 circles in each group.

2. **Ask:** How many groups are there? 5

3. **Ask:** How many circles are in each group? 4

4. Explain that multiplication is used to find the total amount by combining equal groups.

5. **Ask:** How many circles are there in all? 20

6. Write $5 \times 4 = 20$. Explain that the multiplication sentence is read as "5 groups of 4 equals 20 in all."

7. **Say:** You have 20 pretzels and you want to share them equally among 5 people.

   Explain that 20 divided by 5, or 20 objects placed into 5 equal groups, describes this situation. Write $20 \div 5 = ?$ Point out the division symbol and identify it as such.

8. Repeat the sharing situation. Tell students that they will use the circles to represent pretzels and the index cards to represent the groups. Have students count out 20 circles and lay the 5 index cards on a flat surface.

Objectives

- Use models and math symbols to represent division.
- Use repeated subtraction to do division problems.
- Recognize that the $\div$ sign refers to division.
- Correctly use the $\div$ symbol.

9. Have students place one circle in each of the 5 groups until all the circles have been distributed. This is an example of what the students' completed answer should look like.

10. **Ask:** How many circles are in each group? 4

    Refer back to the division sentence and write the answer. $20 \div 5 = 4$

11. **Ask:** How many pretzels does each person get? 4

12. **Say:** This time, you have 25 pretzels that you want to divide by making equal groups of 5.

    Have students write the division problem to represent 25 divided by 5. Be sure students use the division symbol correctly. $25 \div 5$

13. Explain that students will use repeated subtraction to solve this problem.

14. Have students show 25 circles. Then have them take away a group of 5 circles.

    Say: This is one group of 5.

    Then have students take away another group of 5.

    Say: This is another group of 5.

    Explain that by repeatedly taking away groups of 5, students are modeling repeated subtraction.

15. Continue having students take away groups of 5 until there are no more groups of 5.

16. **Ask:** How many groups of 5 did you subtract? 5

17. **Ask:** How many are left over? 0

LEARN Model Equal Groups

OFFLINE 10 min

Objectives

Students will use objects and sketches to solve division problems. They will model equal sharing by divvying up totals and dividing amounts to make equal groups.
 Gather the blocks.

1. **Say:** Winnie has 18 flowers. She wants to put an equal number of flowers into 3 vases. How many flowers will be in each vase?

2. Draw 3 large ovals on paper and explain to students that the ovals represent the vases. Make the ovals large enough so that 6 circles will fit inside each one.

- Use objects or sketches to solve a division problem.
- Explain division as repeated subtraction.
- Explain the meaning of the ÷ symbol.

3. Display 18 circles.

   Say: These are 18 little round flowers. To solve the problem, put the same number of flowers in each of the 3 vases.

4. Have students solve the problem by placing the circles into the vases. They will find that there are 6 flowers in each vase. Here is an example of how the circles could be arranged in groups.

Tips

Connect each number in the division sentence to the words in the story problem.

5. Write 18 ÷ 3 = 6.

Say: This problem is read as "18 divided by 3 equals 6."

Point to the expression. Tell students that in this problem, there are a total of 18 objects (flowers), placed into 3 equal groups, with 6 in each group.

6. **Say:** In this problem we had objects to divide into equal groups and wanted to find out how many objects would be in each group. We can represent this type of problem by showing the total divided by the number of groups using a division symbol.

7. Point to 18 ÷ 3 = 6. Write "number in all" below the 18, "number of groups" below the 3, and "number in each group" below the 6.

18	÷	3	=	6
number in all		number of groups		number in each group

8. **Say:** Alexander has 24 seeds. He plants 4 seeds in each pot. How many pots does he use?

9. Have students count out 24 circles and separate them into groups of 4 circles.

Ask: How many groups did you make? 6

Here is an example of how the circles could be arranged.

10. Write 24 ÷ 4 = 6. Be sure to leave space between this number sentence and the previous one. Have students read the problem as "24 divided by 4 equals 6."

Ask: What does the division symbol show? It shows that 24 objects (seeds) placed into equal groups of 4 makes 6 groups.

11. **Say:** In this problem, we had 24 seeds that we divided into groups with a certain number in each group, and we had to find how many groups there were. We can represent this type of problem by showing the total divided by the number in each group using a division symbol.

12. Point to 24 ÷ 4 = 6. Write "number in all" below the 24, "number in each group" below the 4, and "number of groups" below the 6.

24	÷	4	=	6
number in all		number in each group		number of groups

13. Have students use sketches to solve the following problems. After they solve each problem, write the accompanying division sentence. Have students state each division sentence, saying "divided by" as they read the division symbol.

- Serena has 16 mystery books. She puts 8 books on each shelf. How many shelves does she use? 2
  Here is a sample sketch.

   16 ÷ 8 = 2

- Ron has 20 stickers and wants to put an equal number on 5 rockets. How many stickers will be on each rocket? 4
Here is a sample sketch.

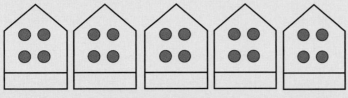

$$20 \div 5 = 4$$

LEARN Use Repeated Subtraction

OFFLINE 15 min

Students will use repeated subtraction to solve division problems. They will take away groups of circles, make backward jumps on a number line, and write subtraction sentences to show repeated subtraction.

Gather the blocks and the number lines you printed from the Number Line Creator Tool.

1. **Say:** We can use division to separate a total amount into a given number of equal groups. We can also use division to make equal groups of a given amount. We can use repeated subtraction to determine the number of equal groups.

2. **Ask:** Winnie has 35 painted eggs and wants to put 5 eggs in each basket. How many baskets does she need?

3. Have students count out a total of 35 circles. Guide students to repeatedly take away groups of 5 to see how many groups of 5 are in 35. Students should make 7 groups of 5.

4. **Ask:** What division number sentence means "35 objects placed into equal groups of 5"? 35 divided by 5 equals 7.

5. Write $35 \div 5 = 7$. Ask students what each number represents. They should explain that 35 is the number in all (total amount), 5 is the number in each group, and 7 is the number of groups.

35	÷	5	=	7
number in all		number in each group		number of groups

6. Point to the 7, and tell students that the answer to a division problem is called a quotient.

7. Remind students that when they solved $35 \div 5$, they repeatedly took away 5. Explain to students that this can also be done with a number line.

8. Display the labeled number line. Have students start at 35 and make backward jumps of 5 to zero. Have student show their jumps with a curved arrow and label them with −5.

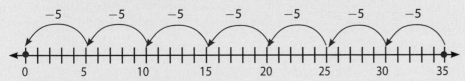

$35 - 5 = 30$
$30 - 5 = 25$
$25 - 5 = 20$
$20 - 5 = 15$
$15 - 5 = 10$
$10 - 5 = 5$
$5 - 5 = 0$

9. **Ask:** How many jumps did you make? 7

Say: You have shown 35 divided by 5 equals 7

Point to the number sentence.

Objectives

- Use objects or sketches to solve a division problem.
- Explain division as repeated subtraction.
- Explain the meaning of the ÷ symbol.

Tips

Have students use circles or a number line to solve $63 \div 9$ and $40 \div 8$. Compare solutions to the repeated subtraction solutions.

10. Review the subtraction shown on the number line.

11. Summarize the activity with students. They can model division with objects and sketches. They can explain the meaning of the division symbol and can solve division problems by using repeated subtraction with numbers and on a number line. They know that a division problem can ask how many groups with a certain number of objects they can make from a given number of objects. Or it can ask how many would be in each group if they divided a given number of objects into a given number of groups. Students have seen that the problem $35 \div 5 = ?$ can ask how many groups of 5 they can make with 35 objects, or how many would be in each group if they divided 35 into 5 equal groups.

TRY IT Represent Division Problems

OFFLINE
15 min

Objectives

Students will practice using objects, sketches, and repeated subtraction to solve division problems. Have students turn to the Represent Division Problems activity page in their Activity Book and read the directions with them.

Students should copy the problems from the Activity Book into their Math Notebook as necessary and solve them there.

- Use objects or sketches to solve a division problem.
- Explain division as repeated subtraction.
- Explain the meaning of the $\div$ symbol.

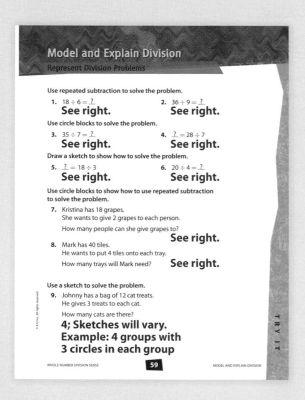

Additional Answers

1. $18 - 6 = 12$
   $12 - 6 = 6$
   $6 - 6 = 0$
   6 was subtracted 3 times, so $18 \div 6 = 3$.

2. $36 - 9 = 27$
   $27 - 9 = 18$
   $18 - 9 = 9$
   $9 - 9 = 0$
   9 was subtracted 4 times, so $36 \div 9 = 4$.

3. 5; Students should divide the 35 circle blocks into 7 equal groups with 5 circle blocks in each group.

4. 4; Students should divide the 28 circle blocks into 7 equal groups with 4 circle blocks in each group.

5. 6; Students should draw 3 groups of 6 or 6 groups of 3.
   $18 \div 3 = 6$

6. 5; Students should draw 4 groups of 5 or 5 groups of 4.
   $20 \div 4 = 5$

7. 9; **Example:** Start with 18 circle blocks. Move 2 circle blocks to another pile. Move another 2 circle blocks to a new pile. Keep moving 2 circle blocks to new piles until the 18 circle blocks are divided into piles of 2. Count the number of piles.

8. 10; **Example:** Start with 40 circle blocks. Move 4 circle blocks to another pile. Move another 4 circle blocks to a new pile. Keep moving 4 circle blocks to new piles until the 40 circle blocks are divided into piles of 4. Count the number of piles.

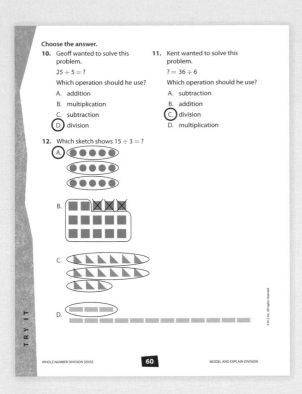

Choose the answer.

10. Geoff wanted to solve this problem.

   $25 \div 5 = ?$

   Which operation should he use?

   A. addition
   B. multiplication
   C. subtraction
   D. division

11. Kent wanted to solve this problem.

   $? = 36 \div 6$

   Which operation should he use?

   A. subtraction
   B. addition
   C. division
   D. multiplication

12. Which sketch shows $15 \div 3 = ?$

   A.

   B.

   C.

   D.

ONLINE

10 min

CHECKPOINT

Students will complete an online Checkpoint. If necessary, read the directions, problems, and answer choices to students and help them with keyboard or mouse operations.

Objectives

- Explain division as repeated subtraction.

Applying Division Symbols and Rules

Lesson Overview

LEARN Division Three Ways	15 minutes	**ONLINE**
LEARN Dividing with 1 and Zero	15 minutes	**OFFLINE**
LEARN Practice with Flash Cards	10 minutes	**ONLINE**
TRY IT Division Symbols and Properties	10 minutes	**OFFLINE**
CHECKPOINT	10 minutes	**ONLINE**

▶ Lesson Objectives

- Explain and apply the division property of 1.
- Demonstrate understanding that division by zero is undefined.
- Recognize the meaning of the three symbols for division.

▶ Prerequisite Skills

- Use models and math symbols to represent division.
- Demonstrate understanding that any number multiplied by 1 results in the same number ($n \times 1 = n$).
- Use repeated subtraction to do division problems.
- Use equal sharing to do division problems.
- Recognize that the $\div$ sign refers to division.
- Correctly use the $\div$ symbol.

▶ Content Background

Students have a basic understanding of division. They will apply their understanding to explore division properties and different representations of division. Students will learn three different ways to represent a division problem. They will also learn the result of dividing a number by 1 or zero and dividing zero by a number. When dividing a number by 1, the quotient is always the original number. When dividing a number by zero, the answer is undefined. It is acceptable for students to say there is no answer.

There are three different symbols to show division. These are the standard division symbol, as in $6 \div 2$; the fraction bar, as in $\frac{6}{2}$; and the long-division symbol, as in $2\overline{)6}$. In each of these examples, the division problem should be read as "6 divided by 2." Becoming familiar with the different representations of division will help students with division and assist them in the future study of fractions. Use the following chart to guide students to say and write fractions properly.

Materials to Gather

SUPPLIED

Division Symbols and Properties activity page

Division Sentence	Say	Write
$12 \div 4 = 3$	12 divided by 4 equals 3	12 and say "divided by" as you write the standard division symbol
$\frac{12}{4} = 3$	12 divided by 4 equals 3	12 and say "divided by" as you write the fraction bar
$4\overline{)12}^{\,3}$	12 divided by 4 equals 3	12 and say "divided by" as you draw the long-division symbol, $\overline{)}$

Avoid using the phrase *4 goes into 12* with students. Say "12 divided by 4," or "4 divides 12." Although students may be splitting 12 "into" 4 groups, it makes no sense to say that 4 goes into 12. Students should consistently relate what they are doing to division. The expression *goes into* becomes a rote phrase that can lead to misconceptions for students.

▶ Common Errors and Misconceptions

- Students might view multiplication and division algorithms as rules to be followed. This leads to a misunderstanding that the numbers involved are separate digits rather than grouped amounts representing place values. The result is often an incorrect answer because of students' misunderstanding of estimation, place value, and reasonableness of results.

- Students might not relate their knowledge of division (its symbols, procedures, and facts) to what they already know in order to make meaningful, everyday connections.

ONLINE
15min

LEARN Division Three Ways

Objectives

- Recognize the meaning of the three symbols for division.

Students will learn the three symbols to show division. They will complete division problems using these symbols. They will see division written in the following three ways: $6 \div 2$; $\frac{6}{2}$, and $2\overline{)6}$. Help students say each division problem properly. In all cases, they should read the problem as "[dividend] divided by [divisor]." For example, all three examples here would be read as "6 divided by 2."

OFFLINE
15min

LEARN Dividing with 1 and Zero

Objectives

- Explain and apply the division property of 1.
- Demonstrate understanding that division by zero is undefined.
- Recognize the meaning of the three symbols for division.

Students will investigate division by 1 and zero. They will also explore dividing zero by any number. They will see why dividing by zero has no possible answer. There are no materials to gather for this activity.

DIVIDING BY 1

1. Tell students that when you divide a number by 1, the answer is the same as the number you are dividing. To help students understand this concept, begin by reviewing multiplication by 1. Explain to students that any number multiplied by 1 is the original number because there is only one group. Give an example: If you have 1 group of 5 grapes, you have 5 grapes altogether.

2. Tell students that if you divide the 5 grapes into 1 group there would be 5 grapes in the group because $5 \div 1 = 5$. Point to each number in the division sentence and explain its meaning.

$$5 \qquad \div \qquad 1 \qquad = \qquad 5$$

number in all   number of groups   number in each group

3. Tell students that, similar to multiplication, any number divided by 1 is the original number.

4. Have students practice this concept by finding the quotient in each of the following problems:

- $27 \div 1 = ?$ 27

- $1\overline{)35}$? 35

- $\dfrac{6,367}{1} = ?$ 6,367

- $87 \div 1 = ?$ 87

- $\dfrac{259}{1} = ?$ 259

- $2,345,657,765 \div 1 = ?$ 2,345,657,765

Point out that the last problem may seem challenging but students can still find the quotient following the rule for dividing by 1.

DIVIDING BY ZERO

5. Explain to students that unlike division by 1, division by zero has no possible answer. Use the idea of repeated subtraction to explain this concept to students.

   Say: It doesn't make sense to ask how many times you can subtract zero from a quantity of objects to get to zero. You could subtract zero forever and you would never get to zero.

6. Explain that when dividing by zero, there is no answer. Write $63 \div 9 = ?$ Explain that students could find the answer by solving this problem: $? \times 9 = 63$. They would get an answer of 7. Write 7 as the quotient.

7. Write $6 \div 0 = ?$ Again, explain that students could find the answer by solving $? \times 0 = 6$, but no number would work because $? \times 0$ would always be 0, not 6 or any other number. (*Note:* $0 \div 0 = ?$ is a different case, which is reserved for later courses.)

8. Show students the following problems. Ask students to solve them and to explain their answers.

- $35 \div 0 = ?$

- $0\overline{)87}$?

- $\dfrac{6,367}{0} = ?$

- $87 \div 0 = ?$

- $\dfrac{259}{0} = ?$

- $2,345,657,765 \div 0 = ?$

These problems have no possible answer.

DIVIDING ZERO BY A NUMBER

9. Explain to students that while there is no answer when a number is divided by zero, they can divide zero by a number. Discuss with students the example $0 \div 3 = 0$. If 0 objects are placed into 3 groups, there are 0 objects in each group.

10. Have students answer the following problems and explain their answers:

    - $0 \div 5 = ?$ 0
    - $0 \div 37 = ?$ 0

    - $7\overline{)0}$ $\overset{?\ 0}{}$
    - $9\overline{)0}$ $\overset{?\ 0}{}$

    - $\dfrac{0}{8} = ?$ 0
    - $0 \div 3,300,486 = ?$ 0

    Students should explain that the answer is always zero because 0 objects placed into any number of groups always results in 0 objects in each group. Also, any number times zero is zero.

11. Review with students the following division rules:

    - Any number divided by 1 is the original number.
    - There is no possible answer when a number is divided by zero.
    - Zero divided by any number is always zero.

12. Give students the following problems and have them answer aloud:

    - $64 \div 1 = ?$ 64
    - $81 \div 0 = ?$ no possible answer
    - $0 \div 55 = ?$ 0

LEARN Practice with Flash Cards

ONLINE 10 min

Students will use online flash cards to practice dividing with 1 and zero. They will practice doing division problems that use the three representations for division. Students should call out the problems as well as the answers and then click to see if they are correct. They should become accustomed to the fact that any number divided by 1 is the same number, and that zero divided by a number is zero, but a number divided by zero has no answer.

Objectives

- Explain and apply the division property of 1.
- Demonstrate understanding that division by zero is undefined.
- Recognize the meaning of the three symbols for division.

TRY IT Division Symbols and Properties

OFFLINE 10 min

Students will practice writing the different ways to show a division problem. Have students say the problem as they write it. Students will also practice dividing with 1 and zero. Have students turn to the Division Symbols and Properties activity page in their Activity Book and read the directions with them.

Students should copy the problems from the Activity Book into their Math Notebook as necessary and solve them there.

Objectives

- Explain and apply the division property of 1.
- Demonstrate understanding that division by zero is undefined.
- Recognize the meaning of the three symbols for division.

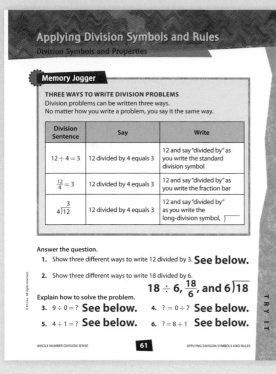

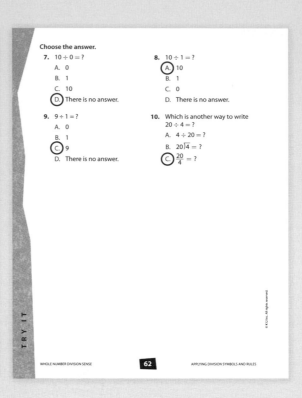

Additional Answers

1. $12 \div 3$, $\frac{12}{3}$, and $3\overline{)12}$

3. There is no answer when you try to divide by zero.

4. Zero divided into 7 groups would be zero in each group, or zero divided into groups of 7 would be zero groups. Zero divided by any number is zero.

5. Four objects divided into 1 group will give 4 objects in the group. If you divide any number by 1, the answer is always the same as the given number.

6. Eight objects divided into 1 group will give 8 objects in the group. If you divide any number by 1, the answer is always the same as the given number.

CHECKPOINT

ONLINE 10min

Students will complete an online Checkpoint. If necessary, read the directions, problems, and answer choices to students and help them with keyboard or mouse operations.

Objectives

- Explain and apply the division property of 1.
- Demonstrate understanding that division by zero is undefined.
- Recognize the meaning of the three symbols for division.

Division as Sharing

Lesson Overview

LEARN Division Fact Practice	10 minutes	**ONLINE**
LEARN Division and Equal Sharing	25 minutes	**OFFLINE**
TRY IT Explain Division	15 minutes	**OFFLINE**
CHECKPOINT	10 minutes	**ONLINE**

▶ Lesson Objectives

Explain division as the sharing of a quantity into equal groups.

▶ Prerequisite Skills

- Use equal sharing to do division problems.
- Use objects or sketches to solve a division problem.

▶ Content Background

Students will use models and sketches to explain division as a way to share a quantity equally.

One way to divide is to separate objects into "fair shares" or equal groups. For example, $16 \div 8 = 2$ means students place 16 objects into groups of 8 to make 2 equal groups, or they separate 16 objects into 8 equal groups with 2 objects in each group. In either case, 16 is the dividend, 8 is the divisor, and the answer, or quotient, is 2. When dividing to form equal groups, students are given the total and the number of groups, and they have to find the number in each group. For example, if they have 21 divided by 3 and they want to find out how many would be in each group, they would "deal out" the objects, one by one, into three groups until they had no objects left. Then they would count the number in each group. There are 7 in each group, so $21 \div 3 = 7$.

▶ Common Errors and Misconceptions

Students might not relate their knowledge of division (its symbols, procedures, and facts) to what they already know in order to make meaningful, everyday connections.

Materials to Gather

SUPPLIED

blocks – B (all colors)

Explain Division activity page

ONLINE
10min

LEARN Division Fact Practice

Students will play a game to practice division facts. Have students say each problem aloud. For the first few problems, ask them to explain what the problem means. For example, for the problem $21 \div 7$, students should say either "How many groups of 7 can you make with 21 objects?" or "If you shared 21 objects among 7 people, how many objects would each person get?" In either case, the correct answer is 3.

Objectives

- Explain division as the sharing of a quantity into equal groups.

OFFLINE
25min

- Explain division as the sharing of a quantity into equal groups.

Students know how to model division problems to explain division as repeated subtraction. Now they will learn how to model division problems to explain division as equal sharing.

With repeated subtraction, students show the number of groups they can make with a given number. With equal sharing, they imagine the total amount shared among a given number of people. For example, say students want to model the problem $21 \div 3 = ?$ With repeated subtraction, they would show this as the number of groups of 3 they can make with 21. But with equal sharing, they would show it as the total, 21, shared among 3 people. They would distribute the 21 objects into 3 equal groups. With either method, the answer is the same, 7.

Gather the blocks.

1. **Say:** Suppose we have 21 fish to separate evenly into 3 bowls.

2. Have students use 21 circles to represent the fish and draw 3 large ovals to represent the fishbowls to model the story.

3. **Ask:** How could we write the story as a division problem?

   Guide students to write the division problem three different ways. In each case, students should write and say the "21," then say "divided by" as they write the division symbol, and then write and say "3." Be sure they write "$= ?$" for the first two ways and that they put a question mark above the long-division symbol.

   $21 \div 3 = ?, \frac{21}{3} = ?$, and $3\overline{)21}^{?}$

4. Have students say the problem: "21 divided by 3 equals ?"

5. Point to the division symbol, and ask students what it means in this problem. Students should say it means separating 21 fish into 3 equal groups.

6. Have students act out the problem. Tell them to place 1 fish (1 circle) in each fishbowl (oval) and repeat this until all the circles have been used and there is an equal number in each fishbowl.

   Ask: How many fish are in each bowl? 7

7. Have students write the quotient in each division problem they wrote. Have them read each problem aloud as "21 divided by 3 equals 7."

   $21 \div 3 = 7; \frac{21}{3} = 7$; and $3\overline{)21}^{7}$

8. Present the following problem: There are 45 raffle tickets to sell for the club fundraiser. There are 9 people in the club. How many tickets does each person have to sell so that everyone sells an equal amount?

9. Ask students to solve the problem. Allow them to solve this problem in the way that is easiest for them. Have them explain division as equal sharing as they do the problem. Some students may wish to use a sketch or circles, while other will just want to use a number sentence and work it out on paper.

10. Have students write the division sentence three ways and explain the meaning. Students should explain that 45 shared equally in 9 groups is 5 in each group, so each member has to sell 5 tickets.

11. Have students make up a division problem that involves equal sharing, and have them write it in their Math Notebook. Suggest a theme of interest to the students. Have them model the problem and show how to write the division three ways.

TRY IT Explain Division

Objectives

- Explain division as the sharing of a quantity into equal groups.

Students will practice explaining division as equal sharing. Gather the blocks. Have students turn to the Explain Division activity page in their Activity Book and read the directions with them.

Students should copy the problems from the Activity Book into their Math Notebook as necessary and solve them there.

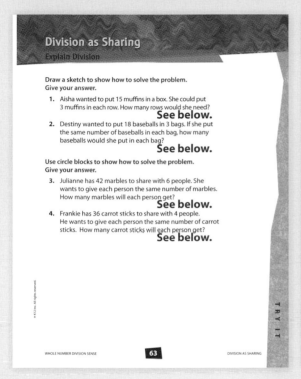

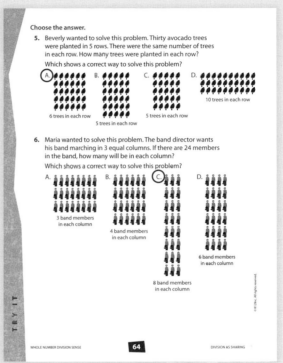

Additional Answers

1. Students should draw 5 rows with 3 muffins in each row. Aisha would need 5 rows for the muffins.

2. Students should draw 3 bags with 6 baseballs in each bag. Destiny would put 6 baseballs in each bag.

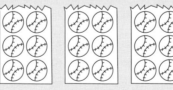

3. Students should divide 42 circles into 6 equal groups. Each person will get 7 marbles.

4. Students should divide 36 circles into 4 equal groups. Each person will get 9 carrot sticks.

ONLINE

10min

CHECKPOINT

Objectives

- Explain division as the sharing of a quantity into equal groups.

Students will complete an online Checkpoint. If necessary, read the directions, problems, and answer choices to students and help them with keyboard or mouse operations.

Relating Multiplication and Division

Lesson Overview

GET READY Number Relationships	5 minutes	OFFLINE
LEARN Repeated Addition and Subtraction	10 minutes	ONLINE
LEARN Related Division Facts	15 minutes	ONLINE
LEARN Related Multiplication Facts	10 minutes	ONLINE
TRY IT Inverse Operations	15 minutes	OFFLINE
CHECKPOINT	5 minutes	ONLINE

▶ ## Lesson Objectives

Demonstrate an understanding of the inverse relationship between multiplication and division.

▶ ## Prerequisite Skills

- Use models or drawings to show how addition and subtraction are inversely related.
- Use objects or sketches to solve a multiplication problem.
- Use objects or sketches to solve a division problem.

▶ ## Content Background

Students have an understanding of the relationship between addition and subtraction and the concept that one operation can undo the other. Students also understand that multiplication is the same as using repeated addition, and division is the same as using repeated subtraction. In this lesson, they will learn about the inverse relationship between multiplication and division. They will be able to identify related multiplication and division facts and complete fact families.

Inverse operations undo each other. For example, in the problem $3 \times 4 = 12$, the operation that would undo multiplying by 4 is dividing by 4. So the inverse of $3 \times 4 = 12$ is $12 \div 4 = 3$. When studying inverses, or opposite operations, students also use the related facts in a fact family. The facts related to $3 \times 4 = 12$ and $12 \div 4 = 3$ are $4 \times 3 = 12$ and its inverse, $12 \div 3 = 4$.

In multiplication and division, an array can be a helpful visual tool. An array is a drawing of objects in rows and columns. An array for $3 \times 4 = 12$ would have 3 rows with 4 objects in each row.

Materials to Gather

SUPPLIED

blocks – B (all colors)

Inverse Operations activity page

array for $3 \times 4 = 12$

▶ ## Common Errors and Misconceptions

Students might view multiplication and division algorithms as rules to be followed. This leads to a misunderstanding that the numbers involved are separate digits rather than grouped amounts representing place values. The result is often an incorrect answer because of students' misunderstanding of estimation, place value, and reasonableness of results.

GET READY Number Relationships

Objectives

- Use models or drawings to show how addition and subtraction are inversely related.
- Use objects or sketches to solve a multiplication problem.
- Use objects or sketches to solve a division problem.

Students will demonstrate the relationship between addition and subtraction. They will use models and sketches to solve related multiplication and division problems. Gather the blocks.

1. Write $3 + 2 = 5$. Have students use circle blocks to model the problem by showing a group of 3 circles and a group of 2 circles, then putting them together to show the total, 5.

2. Ask students how they can use subtraction to check the sum of $3 + 2$. Students should explain that they can use either $5 - 2 = 3$ (the inverse of $3 + 2$) or the related fact, $5 - 3 = 2$, to check the sum.

   Have students use circles to model the subtraction.

3. Discuss with students how addition and subtraction are related. Be sure students understand that addition and subtraction are opposite, or inverse, operations and that addition and subtraction undo each other.

4. Tell students that they can look at multiplication and division as opposites as well. Have them draw an array to model the problem $3 \times 6 = 18$. Students should show 3 rows of 6. Explain that the array represents the problem $3 \times 6 = 18$.

5. Have students label their array $3 \times 6 = 18$.

6. Have students use their array to show that 18 divided by 6 is 3. They can circle the rows to show the division. Have students write $18 \div 6 = 3$ under the multiplication sentence.

7. Summarize by explaining to students that just as addition and subtraction are opposites, multiplication and division are opposites. The opposite of $3 + 2 = 5$ is $5 - 2 = 3$, and the opposite of $3 \times 6 = 18$ is $18 \div 6 = 3$.

LEARN Repeated Addition and Subtraction

Objectives

- Demonstrate an understanding of the inverse relationship between multiplication and division.

Students will learn about the inverse relationship between multiplication and division. They will use their understanding of repeated addition for multiplication and repeated subtraction for division to see that multiplication and division are opposite, or inverse, operations.

LEARN Related Division Facts

Objectives

- Demonstrate an understanding of the Inverse relationship between multiplication and division.

Students will identify the inverse division fact for a given multiplication fact. They'll also identify the inverse multiplication fact for a given division fact, and they'll use their understanding of inverse operations to identify an unknown quantity in a multiplication or division problem. Students will also learn about fact families.

10 min

LEARN Related Multiplication Facts

Objectives

Students will use online flash cards to practice identifying inverse multiplication and division facts. Have students say each fact aloud and then say the inverse fact and check their answer.

- Demonstrate an understanding of the inverse relationship between multiplication and division.

OFFLINE

15 min

TRY IT Inverse Operations

Objectives

Students will practice identifying related multiplication and division problems. They will use their understanding of inverse operations to identify an unknown quantity in a multiplication or division problem. View or print the Inverse Operations activity page.

- Demonstrate an understanding of the inverse relationship between multiplication and division.

Tips   Draw an array to model the given division or multiplication fact to help students identify the inverse fact.

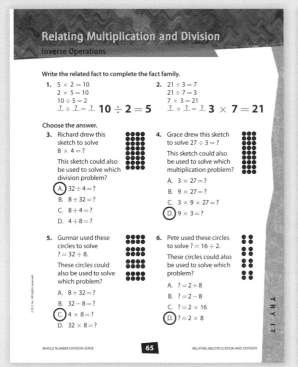

Relating Multiplication and Division
Inverse Operations

Write the related fact to complete the fact family.

1. $5 \times 2 = 10$
    $2 \times 5 = 10$
    $10 \div 5 = 2$
    $? \div ? = ?$ **10 ÷ 2 = 5**

2. $21 \div 3 = 7$
    $21 \div 7 = 3$
    $7 \times 3 = 21$
    $? \times ? = ?$ **3 × 7 = 21**

Choose the answer.

3. Richard drew this sketch to solve
    $8 \times 4 = ?$
    This sketch could also be used to solve which division problem?
    Ⓐ $32 \div 4 = ?$
    B. $8 \div 32 = ?$
    C. $8 \div 4 = ?$
    D. $4 \div 8 = ?$

4. Grace drew this sketch to solve $27 \div 3 = ?$
    This sketch could also be used to solve which multiplication problem?
    A. $3 \times 27 = ?$
    B. $9 \times 27 = ?$
    C. $3 \times 9 \times 27 = ?$
    Ⓓ $9 \times 3 = ?$

5. Gunnar used these circles to solve
    $? = 32 \div 8$.
    These circles could also be used to solve which problem?
    A. $8 + 32 = ?$
    B. $32 - 8 = ?$
    Ⓒ $4 \times 8 = ?$
    D. $32 \times 8 = ?$

6. Pete used these circles to solve $? = 16 \div 2$.
    These circles could also be used to solve which problem?
    A. $? = 2 + 8$
    B. $? = 2 - 8$
    C. $? = 2 \times 16$
    Ⓓ $? = 2 \times 8$

WHOLE NUMBER DIVISION SENSE   **65**   RELATING MULTIPLICATION AND DIVISION

TRY IT

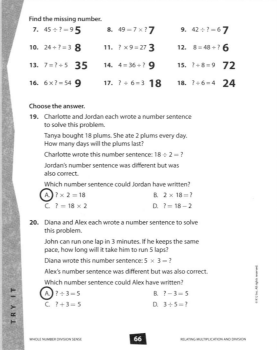

Find the missing number.

7. $45 \div ? = 9$ **5**
8. $49 = 7 \times ?$ **7**
9. $42 \div ? = 6$ **7**
10. $24 \div ? = 3$ **8**
11. $? \times 9 = 27$ **3**
12. $8 = 48 \div ?$ **6**
13. $7 = ? \div 5$ **35**
14. $4 = 36 \div ?$ **9**
15. $? \div 8 = 9$ **72**
16. $6 \times ? = 54$ **9**
17. $? \div 6 = 3$ **18**
18. $? \div 6 = 4$ **24**

Choose the answer.

19. Charlotte and Jordan each wrote a number sentence to solve this problem.
    Tanya bought 18 plums. She ate 2 plums every day. How many days will the plums last?
    Charlotte wrote this number sentence: $18 \div 2 = ?$
    Jordan's number sentence was different but was also correct.
    Which number sentence could Jordan have written?
    Ⓐ $? \times 2 = 18$
    B. $2 \times 18 = ?$
    C. $? = 18 \times 2$
    D. $? = 18 - 2$

20. Diana and Alex each wrote a number sentence to solve this problem.
    John can run one lap in 3 minutes. If he keeps the same pace, how long will it take him to run 5 laps?
    Diana wrote this number sentence: $5 \times 3 = ?$
    Alex's number sentence was different but was also correct.
    Which number sentence could Alex have written?
    Ⓐ $? \div 3 = 5$
    B. $? - 3 = 5$
    C. $? + 3 = 5$
    D. $3 \div 5 = ?$

WHOLE NUMBER DIVISION SENSE   **66**   RELATING MULTIPLICATION AND DIVISION

TRY IT

ONLINE

5 min

CHECKPOINT

Objectives

Students will complete an online Checkpoint. If necessary, read the directions, problems, and answer choices to students and help them with keyboard or mouse operations.

- Demonstrate an understanding of the inverse relationship between multiplication and division.

Use Inverse Relationships

Lesson Overview

GET READY Complete the Fact Family	5 minutes	**OFFLINE**
LEARN Check with Multiplication	20 minutes	**OFFLINE**
LEARN Use Multiplication to Divide	15 minutes	**ONLINE**
TRY IT Multiply or Divide and Check	10 minutes	**OFFLINE**
CHECKPOINT	10 minutes	**ONLINE**

▶ Lesson Objectives

Use the inverse relationship of multiplication and division to compute and check results.

▶ Prerequisite Skills

Demonstrate an understanding of the inverse relationship between multiplication and division.

▶ Content Background

Students have an understanding of the inverse relationship between multiplication and division. In this lesson, they will learn to use the inverse relationship to solve division problems and check results.

Inverse operations undo each other. For example, in the problem $3 \times 4 = 12$, the operation that would undo multiplying by 4 is dividing by 4. So the inverse of $3 \times 4 = 12$ is $12 \div 4 = 3$. When studying inverses, or opposite operations, students also use the related facts in a fact family. The facts related to $3 \times 4 = 12$ and $12 \div 4 = 3$ are $4 \times 3 = 12$ and the inverse, $12 \div 3 = 4$.

Understanding the relationship between multiplication and division allows students to use multiplication to solve division problems and helps them check their work.

Materials to Gather

SUPPLIED

Check with Multiplication activity page

Multiply or Divide and Check activity page

GET READY Complete the Fact Family

5min OFFLINE

Objectives

- Demonstrate an understanding of the inverse relationship between multiplication and division.

Students will review the multiplication and division facts that make up a multiplication fact family. They will see that a multiplication fact and its related fact make up two parts of a fact family. (For example, $5 \times 8 = 40$ and $8 \times 5 = 40$ are two parts of the same fact family.) Two multiplication facts and their inverses make up the four facts in a multiplication fact family.

There are no materials to gather for this activity.

1. Write the following facts with missing parts as indicated.

- $5 \times 8 = 40$
- $8 \times \underline{?} = 40$ 5

- $40 \div 8 = 5$
- $40 \div \underline{?} = 8$ 5

Tips

Remind students that the value on each side of the equals symbol should be the same.

2. Have students fill in the missing parts, and ask what patterns they see. **Sample answers:** The multiplication problems have the same factors in reverse order. Both multiplication problems have the answer 40. The division problems both have a dividend of 40. All problems use the same three numbers.

   Remind students that these four facts make up a multiplication fact family.

3. Point to the two multiplication facts and explain that these are related facts because they are both multiplication facts and they both use the same numbers.

4. Point to the two division facts and explain that these are related facts because they are both division facts and they both use the same numbers.

5. Point from each multiplication fact to its corresponding division fact and tell students that each division fact is the inverse of its corresponding multiplication fact. Point from the division facts back to the multiplication facts and tell students that each multiplication fact is the inverse of its corresponding division fact. Have students notice that when we say the inverse to a fact, the numbers are in reverse order.

LEARN Check with Multiplication

20min OFFLINE

Objectives

- Use the inverse relationship of multiplication and division to compute and check results.

Students will review multiplication fact families. They will solve division story problems and use multiplication to check division problems.

View or print the Check with Multiplication activity page. Students should copy the problems from the Activity Book to their Math Notebook as necessary and solve them there.

Tips

Write each story problem on a sheet of paper. Have students identify the numbers and key words that indicate how to solve the problem.

1. Read the first Worked Example with students. Remind students that the four facts in a multiplication fact family use the same three numbers. After going over the Worked Example, have students say the four facts aloud to hear the pattern of the numbers.

2. Have students complete Problems 1–3 on their own. Point out that in Problem 3, the fact given is a division fact and that students' first step should be to find the inverse multiplication fact. Then they should find the related division fact that uses the same numbers as the first one, and write that fact. Finally they should write the inverse multiplication fact for the division fact they just wrote. Check students' answers.

3. Read the second Worked Example with students.

4. Have students complete Problems 4–6 on their own. Check students' answers. If students have difficulty with these problems, help them see that division can be used to solve all three problems.

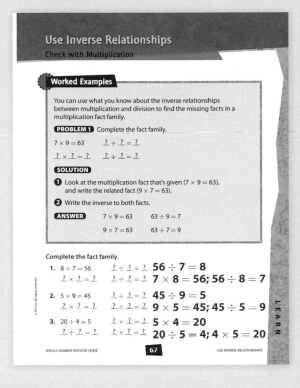

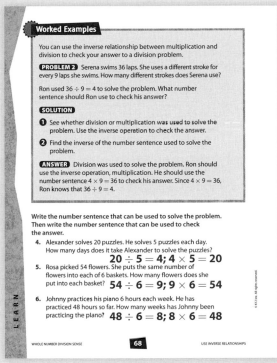

LEARN Use Multiplication to Divide

ONLINE 15 min

Students will practice their division facts using online activities.

Tips Encourage students to use the inverse multiplication facts to solve the division problems.

Objectives

- Use the inverse relationship of multiplication and division to compute and check results.

TRY IT Multiply or Divide and Check

Students will practice using the inverse relationship of multiplication and division to compute and check results. View or print the Multiply or Divide and Check activity page and read the directions with students.

Students should copy the problems from the Activity Book into their Math Notebook as necessary and solve them there.

Tips Help students identify phrases in the story problems that indicate whether a total is being divided into equal parts, or equal parts are being combined.

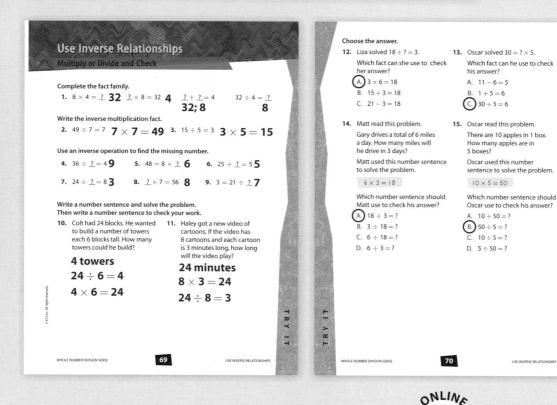

Use Inverse Relationships
Multiply or Divide and Check

Complete the fact family.

1. $8 \times 4 = ?$ **32** $? \times 8 = 32$ **4** $? \div ? = 4$ **32; 8** $32 \div 4 = ?$ **8**

Write the inverse multiplication fact.

2. $49 \div 7 = 7$ $\mathbf{7 \times 7 = 49}$ 3. $15 \div 5 = 3$ $\mathbf{3 \times 5 = 15}$

Use an inverse operation to find the missing number.

4. $36 \div ? = 4$ **9**   5. $48 = 8 \times ?$ **6**   6. $25 \div ? = 5$ **5**

7. $24 \div ? = 8$ **3**   8. $? \times 7 = 56$ **8**   9. $3 = 21 \div ?$ **7**

Write a number sentence and solve the problem.
Then write a number sentence to check your work.

10. Colt had 24 blocks. He wanted to build a number of towers each 6 blocks tall. How many towers could he build?

4 towers
$24 \div 6 = 4$
$4 \times 6 = 24$

11. Haley got a new video of cartoons. If the video has 8 cartoons and each cartoon is 3 minutes long, how long will the video play?

24 minutes
$8 \times 3 = 24$
$24 \div 8 = 3$

TRY IT

Choose the answer.

12. Liza solved $18 \div ? = 3$.
Which fact can she use to check her answer?
(A.) $3 \times 6 = 18$
B. $15 + 3 = 18$
C. $21 - 3 = 18$

13. Oscar solved $30 = ? \times 5$.
Which fact can he use to check his answer?
A. $11 - 6 = 5$
B. $1 + 5 = 6$
(C.) $30 \div 5 = 6$

14. Matt read this problem.
Gary drives a total of 6 miles a day. How many miles will he drive in 3 days?
Matt used this number sentence to solve the problem.
$6 \times 3 = 18$
Which number sentence should Matt use to check his answer?
(A.) $18 \div 3 = ?$
B. $3 \div 18 = ?$
C. $6 \div 18 = ?$
D. $6 \div 3 = ?$

15. Oscar read this problem.
There are 10 apples in 1 box. How many apples are in 5 boxes?
Oscar used this number sentence to solve the problem.
$10 \times 5 = 50$
Which number sentence should Oscar use to check his answer?
A. $10 \div 50 = ?$
(B.) $50 \div 5 = ?$
C. $10 \div 5 = ?$
D. $5 \div 50 = ?$

CHECKPOINT

Students will complete an online Checkpoint. If necessary, read the directions, problems, and answer choices to students and help them with keyboard or mouse operations.

Effects of Division

Lesson Overview

LEARN Compare the Quotient and Dividend	15 minutes	**OFFLINE**
LEARN Parts of a Division Sentence	10 minutes	**ONLINE**
LEARN Dividend, Divisor, and Quotient	15 minutes	**ONLINE**
TRY IT Division Results	10 minutes	**ONLINE**
CHECKPOINT	10 minutes	**ONLINE**

▶ ## Lesson Objectives

Demonstrate an understanding of the effects of division on whole numbers.

▶ ## Prerequisite Skills

Use objects or sketches to solve a division problem.

▶ ## Content Background

Students will examine the effects of division on whole numbers. They will learn that when they divide a whole number by another whole number less than the dividend and greater than 1, the quotient is a lesser number than the original dividend. Also, when they divide by 1, they get the same number as the dividend.

Every division sentence has a dividend, a divisor, and a quotient. The dividend is the number being divided, the divisor is the number students are dividing by, and the quotient is the answer.

$$30 \div 6 = 5$$
dividend   divisor   quotient

An important note to emphasize now and remember for students' future work with division: They only get an answer that is less than the dividend when they divide by a whole number that is greater than 1 and also less than the dividend. When a whole number is divided by a number less than 1, the answer will actually be greater than the dividend. Students will realize this fact when they study division by fractions and decimals less than 1.

▶ ## Common Errors and Misconceptions

Students might view multiplication and division algorithms as rules to be followed. This leads to a misunderstanding that the numbers involved are separate digits rather than grouped amounts representing place values. The result is often an incorrect answer because of students' misunderstanding of estimation, place value, and reasonableness of results.

Materials to Gather

SUPPLIED

There are no supplied materials to gather for this lesson.

ALSO NEEDED

Index cards – 3 (optional)

OFFLINE
15 min

- Demonstrate an understanding of the effects of division on whole numbers.

Students will use logic, patterns, and what they know about multiplication and division to understand the effects of division on whole numbers.

Gather the index cards, if using.

1. Write $3 \times 4 = 12$.

   Say: When you multiply two whole numbers greater than 1, the product is greater than either number.

   Have students give another example to show this.

2. **Ask:** What happens when you multiply a number by 1? The number stays the same.

   Have students give an example of multiplying a number by 1.

3. **Ask:** What happens when you multiply a number by 0? The product is zero.

   Have students give an example of multiplying a number by 0.

4. Tell students they will explore division and how the answer, or quotient, compares to the starting amount, or dividend.

5. Write the following division problem and corresponding term for each number.

12	÷	3	=	4
dividend		divisor		quotient

6. Give the definition of each term. Have students write the definitions in their Math Notebook or on index cards.

   dividend: the total number being divided

   divisor: the number you are dividing by

   quotient: the answer

7. Present the following problem:

   - The dividend is 30 and the divisor is 6. What is the quotient?

8. Have students write the fact all three ways, identify the dividend and the divisor, and show the quotient.

   $$30 \div 6 = 5 \qquad \frac{30}{6} = 5 \qquad 6 \overline{)\,30\,}^{\;5}$$

   30 is the dividend, 6 is the divisor, and 5 is the quotient.

9. Repeat Step 8 for each of the following problems:

   - The dividend is 21 and the divisor is 3. What is the quotient? 21 is the dividend, 6 is the divisor, and 7 is the quotient.

   - The dividend is 15 and the divisor is 5. What is the quotient? 15 is the dividend, 5 is the divisor, and 3 is the quotient.

   - The dividend is 20 and the divisor is 4. What is the quotient? 20 is the dividend, 4 is the divisor, and 5 is the quotient.

10. Ask students to underline the dividend and circle the quotient in each problem. Ask them what they notice about the value of the quotient compared to the dividend. The quotient is less than the dividend in each case.

11. Ask students if they think this will always happen. Ask them if they can think of a case where it isn't true.

    Have students explore this by dividing 12 by 6, 4, 3, 2, and 1. Guide students to see that when the divisor is 1, the dividend and the quotient are equal, so this is an exception to the rule.

Have students make a poster showing a division problem with the dividend, divisor, and quotient labeled and defined.

LEARN Parts of a Division Sentence

Objectives

- Demonstrate an understanding of the effects of division on whole numbers.

Students will practice division vocabulary terms. They will identify the highlighted number in a division number sentence as the dividend, divisor, or quotient.

LEARN Dividend, Divisor, and Quotient

Objectives

- Demonstrate an understanding of the effects of division on whole numbers.

Students will observe what happens when certain parts of a division problem remain the same while other parts change. They will see the dividend stay the same and the divisor increase. And they will see the dividend Increase while the divisor stays the same. Remind students that the dividend is the total amount that is being divided up and the divisor can be seen as the number of people sharing the total. So if the total stays the same and the number of people sharing increases, each person's share decreases. The mathematical way to say this is

- If the dividend stays the same and the divisor increases, the quotient decreases.

On the other hand, if the total amount increases and the number of people sharing stays the same, each person's share increases. The mathematical way to say this is

- If the dividend increases and the divisor stays the same, the quotient increases.

TRY IT Division Results

Objectives

- Demonstrate an understanding of the effects of division on whole numbers.

Students will complete an online Try It. If necessary, read the directions, problems, and answer choices to students and help them with keyboard or mouse operations.

CHECKPOINT

Objectives

- Demonstrate an understanding of the effects of division on whole numbers.

Students will complete an online Checkpoint. If necessary, read the directions, problems, and answer choices to students and help them with keyboard or mouse operations.

Solve Division Story Problems

Lesson Overview

GET READY Division Fact Practice	5 minutes	ONLINE
LEARN Divide a Collection of Marbles	15 minutes	ONLINE
LEARN Yard Sale Math	10 minutes	OFFLINE
LEARN Division at the Zoo	10 minutes	OFFLINE
TRY IT Solve Story Problems with Division	10 minutes	ONLINE
CHECKPOINT	10 minutes	ONLINE

▶ Lesson Objectives

- Use division to solve a story problem that involves equal groups.
- Use division to solve a story problem that involves equal measures.

▶ Prerequisite Skills

Demonstrate automatic recall of division facts.

▶ Content Background

Students should be comfortable dividing with two-digit dividends involving basic division and multiplication facts. In this lesson, they will solve division story problems involving equal groups and equal measures.

Division is an operation that involves equal sharing. Students can use division to find the number of equal groups when they know the number of objects and the number in each group. They can also find the number in each group when they know the total and the number of groups. Since students understand "fair sharing" from an early age, this idea is a great place to begin discussing division.

When working with division story problems involving equal measures, avoid using phrases that lead students to think the problem is about measurement. However, students should report their answers using the appropriate unit that is given in the problem.

When students know the total measurement and the measure of one part, they divide to find the number of parts. For example, Amy bought 63 inches of ribbon. She cut it into 7-inch pieces. How many pieces of ribbon did she have? To find the number of 7-inch pieces (the measure of each part), students divide 63 by 7: $63 \div 7 = 9$. Amy has 9 pieces of ribbon. When students know the total measurement and the number of parts, they can use division to find the measure of each part. For example, John bought 63 inches of wire. He cut it into 9 equal pieces. How long was each piece? To find the length of each piece, divide 63 by 9 (the number of equal pieces): $63 \div 9 = 7$. Each piece is 7 inches long.

Students should be encouraged to use proper division language. The total amount is the dividend. The number that the dividend is divided by is the divisor. The answer, or solution, is the quotient.

▶ Common Errors and Misconceptions

Students might not relate their knowledge of division (its symbols, procedures, and facts) to what they already know in order to make meaningful, everyday connections.

GET READY Division Fact Practice

ONLINE **5**min

Students will play a game to practice division facts. Have students say each problem aloud. For the first few problems, ask them to explain what the problem means. For example, for the problem $21 \div 3 = 7$, students should say either "How many groups of 7 can you make with 21 objects?" or "If you shared 21 objects among 7 people, how many objects would each person get?" In either case, the correct answer is 3.

Objectives

• Demonstrate automatic recall of division facts.

LEARN Divide a Collection of Marbles

ONLINE **15**min

Students will watch an online demonstration of how to use division to solve a story problem. They will see how to check division with multiplication.

They will also see how to use a related multiplication fact to find an unknown quantity other than the quotient in a division sentence

Objectives

• Use division to solve a story problem that involves equal groups.

Tips

After students watch the demonstration, have them solve the problems on their own to reinforce the procedure.

LEARN Yard Sale Math

OFFLINE **10**min

Students will learn to find the cost of an item by dividing the total cost by the total number of items.

View or print the Yard Sale Math activity page and read the directions with students. They should copy the problems from the Activity Book into their Math Notebook as necessary and solve them there.

1. Read the Worked Examples with students.

2. Read the directions with students and have them complete Problems 1–6. Make sure they have completed each problem correctly before they move on to the next problem.

3. Assist students as needed with the problems. If students have difficulty, first encourage them to look at the Worked Examples and follow the process shown. If they still have difficulty, help them apply the process shown in the Worked Examples.

Objectives

• Use division to solve a story problem that involves equal measures.

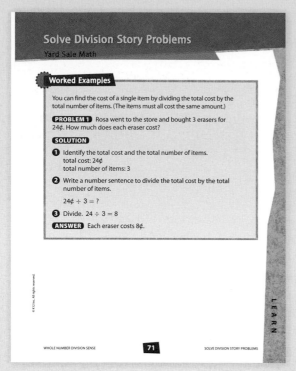

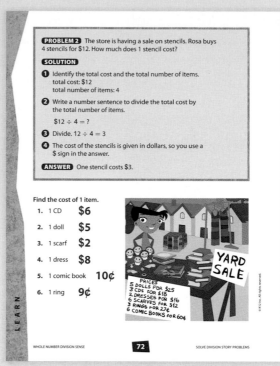

LEARN Division at the Zoo

Students will solve division story problems involving equal measures. The questions deal with objects, time, and measurement.

View or print the Division at the Zoo activity page and read the directions with students. They should copy the problems from the Activity Book into their Math Notebook as necessary and solve them there.

1. **Say:** Some story problems have an amount that is used over and over to make a total. For example, the amount could be a number of miles or a number of hours. Those amounts are equal measures. You can often solve equal-measures problem with division.

2. Read the problem in the Worked Example. Tell students they know the total amount, $27, and they know the price of one ticket, $9. They want to know how many $9 tickets Mr. Marshall can buy with $27.

3. Read the solution with students.

4. Have students complete Problems 1–8 on their own.

5. Problems 9–12 use a problem that has an unknown total. Help students write a division number sentence with a question mark first as the unknown. If students write a multiplication sentence, guide them to think about the problem as the total divided by the number of children, which will equal the number of ounces that each child received.

Objectives

- Use division to solve a story problem that involves equal measures.

Solve Division Story Problems
Division at the Zoo

Worked Example

Equal-measure problems have an amount that is used over and over to make a total. It could be a total distance; a total amount of money; a total amount of time; or a total amount of water, sand, or other material.

You can use division to solve many story problems involving equal measures.

PROBLEM Mr. Marshall has $27 to spend on tickets to the zoo. Tickets cost $9 each. How many tickets can Mr. Marshall buy?

SOLUTION

❶ Figure out what you're being asked to find. The question asks how many $9 tickets Mr. Marshall can buy with $27.

❷ Write the number sentence you can use to solve the problem.
$27 ÷ $9 = ?

❸ Divide. 27 ÷ 9 = 3

ANSWER Mr. Marshall can buy 3 tickets.

Use this story problem to solve Problems 1–4.

A penguin swims 42 miles in a day. If the penguin swims 7 miles per hour, how many hours does it swim in a day?

1. What are you being asked to find?
number of hours the penguin swims in a day

2. What division number sentence can you use to solve the problem?
42 ÷ 7 = ?

3. What is the answer to the division number sentence?
6

4. What is the answer to the story problem?
A penguin swims 6 hours in a day.

Use this story problem to solve Problems 5–8.

The zoo feeds one of its reptiles 63 pounds of food in 7 days. If the same amount of food is used each day, how many pounds of food are used in a day?

5. What are you being asked to find?
number of pounds of food used in a day

6. What division number sentence can you use to solve the problem?
63 ÷ 7 = ?

7. What is the answer to the division number sentence?
9

8. What is the answer to the story problem?
The zoo uses 9 pounds of food in a day.

Use this story problem to solve Problems 9–12.

The petting zoo had a jar of grain for visiting children to feed the goats. The grain was divided into 8-ounce cups. The jar was empty after 9 children fed the goats. How many ounces of grain were in the jar at the start?

9. What are you being asked to find?
number of ounces of grain in the jar at the start

10. What division number sentence can you use to solve the problem?
? ÷ 9 = 8

11. What is the answer to the division number sentence?
72

12. What is the answer to the story problem?
There were 72 ounces of grain in the jar at the start.

TRY IT Solve Story Problems with Division

ONLINE 10min

Objectives

- Use division to solve a story problem that involves equal groups.
- Use division to solve a story problem that involves equal measures.

Students will complete an online Try It. If necessary, read the directions, problems, and answer choices to students and help them with keyboard or mouse operations.

CHECKPOINT

ONLINE 10min

Objectives

- Use division to solve a story problem that involves equal groups.
- Use division to solve a story problem that involves equal measures.

Students will complete an online Checkpoint. If necessary, read the directions, problems, and answer choices to students and help them with keyboard or mouse operations.

Write Division Story Problems

Lesson Overview

GET READY Division Fast Facts	5 minutes	ONLINE
LEARN Creating Division Story Problems	10 minutes	ONLINE
LEARN Division Story Examples	10 minutes	OFFLINE
LEARN Write Your Own Division Story Problems	15 minutes	OFFLINE
TRY IT Identify Matching Story Problems	10 minutes	ONLINE
CHECKPOINT	10 minutes	ONLINE

▶ **Lesson Objectives**

Create a story problem that can be represented by a division number sentence.

▶ **Prerequisite Skills**

- Use the inverse relationship of multiplication and division to compute and check results.
- Demonstrate automatic recall of multiplication facts.

▶ **Content Background**

Students will learn how to create their own story problems that can be solved by writing number sentences using basic division facts.

Most often students solve problems others present to them. However, one of the best ways to learn is to teach something yourself. By writing problems of their own, students are placed into the role of teacher and must think about all the parts needed to write a good problem.

When students divide, they separate objects into "fair shares," or equal groups. For example, $16 \div 8 = 2$ means they separate 16 objects into 2 groups with 8 objects in each group. Sixteen is the dividend, 8 is the divisor, and the answer, 2, is the quotient.

As students study and work through the variety of division story problems, and also create some of their own, they may notice different types of problems that can be solved by dividing. Some of the different types are sharing an amount, making equal groups from an amount, figuring out equal measures, and finding the cost of one item when they know the cost of many. While students are not expected to learn to identify or explain these types of problems, they should be encouraged to use variety in the types of problems they write.

▶ **Common Errors and Misconceptions**

Students might not relate their knowledge of division (its symbols, procedures, and facts) to what they already know in order to make meaningful, everyday connections.

Materials to Gather

SUPPLIED

Division Story Examples activity page

GET READY Division Fast Facts

Students will use the Fast Facts Learning Tool to solve basic division facts.

DIRECTIONS FOR USING THE FAST FACTS LEARNING TOOL

1. Have students enter their name and car number as well as choose the color of the car.

2. Choose the following options:
   - Choose the facts you want to practice: Division
   - Choose quotients: Click the Problems button, then choose facts to either challenge or build confidence, depending on the student.
   - Mode: Race Mode

3. As each problem appears on the screen, have students type the answer and then press Enter. After students finish, review the results on the Fast Facts Results screen. Note how many problems students answered incorrectly. Also record their time for future reference. You can click under the Lap tables on this screen to see exactly which problems students answered correctly (shown in white) and which ones they missed (shown in red).

4. Repeat the activity. Have students try to beat their time and improve their accuracy.

5. If time remains, customize the Choose quotients screen and specifically choose the facts with which students had difficulty. Then have them run another race.

Objectives

- Demonstrate automatic recall of multiplication facts.
- Use the inverse relationship of multiplication and division to compute and check results.

Tips

If you want to have students get used to the game first, go to Test Drive Mode and enter 5 for the number of problems. Then move to Race Mode.

LEARN Creating Division Story Problems

Students will view examples of equal groups, equal measures, and equal sharing story problems.

Objectives

- Create a story problem that can be represented by a division number sentence.

LEARN Division Story Examples

Students will learn how to write different types of division story problems. View or print the Division Story Examples activity page and read the directions with students. Students should copy the problems from the Activity Book into their Math Notebook as necessary and solve them there.

Objectives

- Create a story problem that can be represented by a division number sentence.

1. Read the Worked Example with students. Then have them describe, in their own words, the process for writing a division story problem.

2. Have students complete Problems 1–4. You may have students respond verbally, by writing, or by sketching.
   - If students have difficulty thinking of ideas for problems, refer them to the steps described in the Worked Example.
   - If students have difficulty coming up with a particular type of problem, such as a problem about sharing, read them the sample answer. Students can then base their problem on the sample.

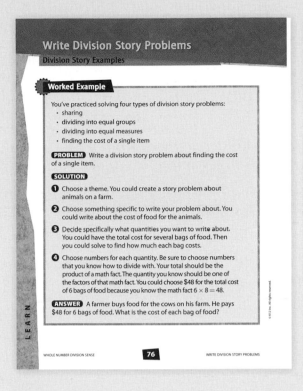

Write Division Story Problems
Division Story Examples

Worked Example

You've practiced solving four types of division story problems:
- sharing
- dividing into equal groups
- dividing into equal measures
- finding the cost of a single item

PROBLEM Write a division story problem about finding the cost of a single item.

SOLUTION

① Choose a theme. You could create a story problem about animals on a farm.

② Choose something specific to write your problem about. You could write about the cost of food for the animals.

③ Decide specifically what quantities you want to write about. You could have the total cost for several bags of food. Then you could solve to find how much each bag costs.

④ Choose numbers for each quantity. Be sure to choose numbers that you know how to divide with. Your total should be the product of a math fact. The quantity you know should be one of the factors of that math fact. You could choose $48 for the total cost of 6 bags of food because you know the math fact $6 \times 8 = 48$.

ANSWER A farmer buys food for the cows on his farm. He pays $48 for 6 bags of food. What is the cost of each bag of food?

WHOLE NUMBER DIVISION SENSE · 76 · WRITE DIVISION STORY PROBLEMS

Write the given type of division story problem. Then solve the problem.

1. Write a story problem about dividing into equal shares. Choose something specific to write about. For example, you could write about sharing an equal number of apples or cookies with some of your friends. Decide what the total number of items is. Then decide how many ways you are going to share it equally.

2. Write a story problem about dividing into equal groups. For example, you could write about dividing something you've collected into equal groups. Decide on the total number of the objects you are dividing. Then decide on the number of groups or the number of items in each group.

3. Write a story problem about dividing into equal measures. Remember, equal-measure problems have an amount that is used over and over to make a total. It could be a total distance or length; a total amount of money; or a total amount of water, flour, sand, or some other material. Choose the total amount. Then decide how you want to divide it.

4. Write a story problem about finding the cost of a single item. You might think about something you've seen for sale in a store. Decide how much several items cost and how many items there are.

WHOLE NUMBER DIVISION SENSE · 77 · WRITE DIVISION STORY PROBLEMS

Additional Answers

1. **Sample answer:** There are 4 friends. The friends share 12 cookies equally. How many cookies does each friend get? $12 \div 4 = 3$; Each friend gets 3 cookies.

2. **Sample answer:** There are 42 cups in 6 packages. Each package has the same number of cups. How many cups are in each package? $42 \div 6 = 7$; There are 7 cups in each package.

3. **Sample answer:** Mike has 18 feet of rope. He cuts the rope into 3 equal pieces. How long is each piece? $18 \div 3 = 6$; Each piece of rope is 6 feet long.

4. **Sample answer:** A store is selling a package of 3 T-shirts for $24. What is the cost of each T-shirt? $24 \div 3 = 8$; Each T-shirt costs $8.

OFFLINE 15 min

LEARN Write Your Own Division Story Problems

Objectives

- Create a story problem that can be represented by a division number sentence.

Students will write story problems for a given division sentence.

View or print the Division Story Examples activity page. Students will use the page as a reference in this activity.

1. Have students look at the Worked Example on the Division Story Examples activity page. Review the different ways division can be shown—sharing, dividing into equal groups, dividing into equal measures, and finding the cost of a single item.

2. Write the number sentence $48 \div 6 = ?$. Tell students that they will use that number sentence to write their own story problem that involves sharing. Encourage students to use their imagination.

   Say: The story problem can be serious. Or it can be silly, like this one:

   - The guinea pigs harvested 48 extra-large pumpkins. They want to share them equally among the 6 guinea pig houses. How many pumpkins will each house get?

3. Ask students to read their story aloud. Check that their story matches the number sentence.

4. Have students write another problem using the same number sentence. This problem should involve finding the cost of a single item. **Sample answer:** The art store sells small canvases at a price of 6 for $48. How much does each canvas cost?

5. Discuss with students how the two stories they wrote are alike and how they are different. Answers will vary. Students should note that the same number sentence was used in both problems. They should also note that the problems were different types—one was a sharing problem and the other was a problem that required finding the cost of a single item.

6. You may wish to have students write story problems for the other types (dividing into equal groups and equal measures).

TRY IT Identify Matching Story Problems

ONLINE **10**min

Students will complete an online Try It. If necessary, read the directions, problems, and answer choices to students and help them with keyboard or mouse operations.

Objectives

- Create a story problem that can be represented by a division number sentence.

CHECKPOINT

ONLINE **10**min

Students will complete an online Checkpoint. If necessary, read the directions, problems, and answer choices to students and help them with keyboard or mouse operations.

Objectives

- Create a story problem that can be represented by a division number sentence.

Core Focus
Two-Step Division Problems

▶ Lesson Objectives

Solve a story problem involving two or more operations.

▶ Prerequisite Skills

- Use the inverse relationship of multiplication and division to compute and check results.
- Use division to solve a story problem that involves equal groups.

Materials to Gather

SUPPLIED

Solve Two-Step Story Problems
    activity page

▶ Content Background

Students should be comfortable dividing. In this lesson, students will identify and solve the operations in multistep, real-world story problems, using the operations addition, subtraction, multiplication, and division.

As students study and work through the variety of two-step division story problems, they may notice different types of problems that can be solved by dividing. Some of the different types are sharing an amount, making equal groups from an amount, figuring out equal measures, and finding the cost of one item when the know the cost of many items. Although students are not expected to learn to identify or explain these types of problem, they should be encouraged to recognize the variety of story problems that can be solved with division or with division in combination with other operations.

▶ Common Errors and Misconceptions

Students might quickly read through a problem and immediately begin to compute with the numbers, often choosing the wrong operation because they did not take time to read through and understand the context of the problem. Students need to learn to use "slow-down" mechanisms that can help them concentrate on thoroughly understanding a problem before they solve it.

GET READY Food Bank Math

Students will use a story problem about a community food bank to review dividing objects into equal groups. In completing several related story problems, students will be given a chance to review using division facts to solve division number sentences. If necessary, encourage students to work with paper and pencil offline before entering their answers online. Encourage students to solve each problem with whatever method or strategy works best for them.

Objectives

- Use the inverse relationship of multiplication and division to compute and check results.
- Use division to solve a story problem that involves equal groups.

LEARN Solve Two-Step Division Problems

ONLINE 20min

Students will use a step-by-step chart to help them solve story problems that involve more than one step and more than one operation. They will follow a problem-solving strategy to help them identify what they are asked to find, what facts are given in the problem, what steps they need to take, and what operations they need to use to solve the problem.

Objectives

- Solve a story problem involving two or more operations.

TRY IT Solve Two-Step Story Problems

OFFLINE 20min

Students will interpret multistep story problems and explain the strategies and operations they used to solve them. View or print the Solve Two-Step Story Problems activity page and read the directions with students.

Students should copy the problems from the Activity Book into their Math Notebook as necessary and solve them there.

Objectives

- Solve a story problem involving two or more operations.

Tips

Encourage students to use the problem-solving steps from the Learn activity to help them solve the story problems.

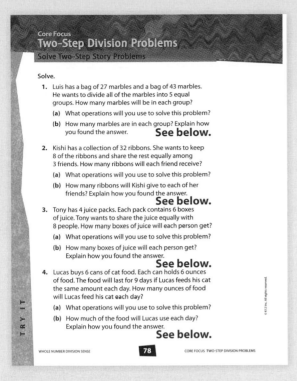

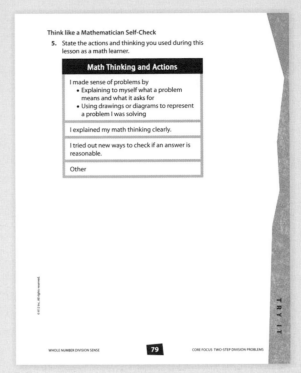

Answers

1. (a) I will add and then I will divide.

(b) 14; **Possible explanation:** First I added the number of marbles in each bag to find the total number of marbles. Then I divided the total number of marbles by 5, the number of groups.

3. (a) I will multiply and then I will divide.

(b) 3; **Possible explanation:** First I multiplied the number of packs by the number of boxes in each pack to find the total number of boxes of juice. Then I divided the product by 8, the number of people sharing the juice.

2. (a) I will subtract and then I will divide.

(b) 8; **Possible explanation:** First I subtracted the number of ribbons Kishi wants to keep from the number of ribbons in her collection. Then I divided the difference by 3, the number of friends Kishi wants to give the remaining ribbons to.

4. (a) I will multiply and then I will divide.

(b) 4 ounces; **Possible explanation:** First I multiplied the number of cans by the number of ounces in each can. Then I divided the product by 9 to find how much food Lucas will use each day.

ONLINE

10 min

CHECKPOINT

Objectives

Students will complete an online Checkpoint. If necessary, read the directions, problems, and answer choices to students and help them with keyboard or mouse operations.

- Solve a story problem involving two or more operations.

Unit Review

Lesson Overview

UNIT REVIEW Look Back	10 minutes	**ONLINE**
UNIT REVIEW Checkpoint Practice	50 minutes	**ONLINE**
⏩ **UNIT REVIEW** Prepare for the Checkpoint		

▶ Unit Objectives

This lesson reviews the following objectives:

- Use objects or sketches to solve a division problem.
- Explain division as repeated subtraction.
- Explain the meaning of the ÷ symbol.
- Explain and apply the division property of 1.
- Demonstrate understanding that division by zero is undefined.
- Recognize the meaning of the three symbols for division.
- Explain division as the sharing of a quantity into equal groups.
- Demonstrate an understanding of the inverse relationship between multiplication and division.
- Use the inverse relationship of multiplication and division to compute and check results.
- Demonstrate an understanding of the effects of division on whole numbers.
- Use division to solve a story problem that involves equal groups.
- Use division to solve a story problem that involves equal measures.
- Create a story problem that can be represented by a division number sentence.
- Solve a story problem involving two or more operations.

Materials to Gather

There are no materials to gather for this lesson.

▶ Advance Preparation

In this lesson, students will have an opportunity to review previous activities in the Whole Number Division Sense unit. Look at the suggested activities in Unit Review: Prepare for the Checkpoint online and gather any needed materials.

ONLINE
10min

UNIT REVIEW Look Back

Students will review key concepts from the unit to prepare for the Unit Checkpoint.

Objectives

- Review unit objectives.

ONLINE
50min

Objectives

- Review unit objectives.

Students will complete an online Checkpoint Practice to prepare for the Unit Checkpoint. If necessary, read the directions, problems, and answer choices to students. Have students answer the problems on their own. Review any missed problems with students.

⇥ UNIT REVIEW Prepare for the Checkpoint

What you do next depends on how students performed in the previous activity, Unit Review: Checkpoint Practice. If students had difficulty with any of the problems, complete the appropriate review activity listed in the table online.

Unit Checkpoint

UNIT CHECKPOINT Online   60 minutes   **ONLINE**

▶ Unit Objectives

This lesson assesses the following objectives:

- Use objects or sketches to solve a division problem.
- Explain division as repeated subtraction.
- Explain the meaning of the ÷ symbol.
- Explain and apply the division property of 1.
- Demonstrate understanding that division by zero is undefined.
- Recognize the meaning of the three symbols for division.
- Explain division as the sharing of a quantity into equal groups.
- Demonstrate an understanding of the inverse relationship between multiplication and division.
- Use the inverse relationship of multiplication and division to compute and check results.
- Demonstrate an understanding of the effects of division on whole numbers.
- Use division to solve a story problem that involves equal groups.
- Use division to solve a story problem that involves equal measures.
- Create a story problem that can be represented by a division number sentence.
- Solve a story problem involving two or more operations.

Materials to Gather

There are no materials to gather for this lesson.

ONLINE

60min

UNIT CHECKPOINT Online

Students will complete the Unit Checkpoint online. If necessary, read the directions, problems, and answer choices to students and help them with keyboard or mouse operations.

Objectives

- Assess unit objectives.

Extended Problems: Real-World Application

USE WHAT YOU KNOW Offline | 60 minutes | **OFFLINE**

▶ Lesson Objectives

This lesson assesses the following objectives:

- Explain the meaning of a division equation that includes dividends within 100.
- Solve word problems involving arrays using multiplication or division within 100.
- Solve word problems involving equal groups using multiplication or division within 100.
- Apply the distributive property of multiplication within 100.
- Explain division as an unknown-factor problem.
- Determine the unknown whole number in a multiplication or division equation, within 100.
- Divide within 100.
- Multiply within 100.
- Represent a data set with up to four categories on a picture graph (with a single-unit scale).
- Represent a data set with up to four categories on a bar graph (with a single-unit scale).
- Record length measurements on a line plot in which the horizontal scale is marked off in whole-number units.
- Apply mathematical knowledge and skills to evaluate and analyze real-world situations.

Materials to Gather

SUPPLIED

Extended Problems: Real-World Application (printout)

OFFLINE

60min

USE WHAT YOU KNOW Offline

Open the Extended Problems: Real-World Application. Read the directions, problems, and answer choices to students, if necessary.

The teacher will grade this assignment

- Students should save the graded assignment to their computer. In the filename, they should replace "studentname" with their last name followed by their first initial.
- Students should complete the assignment on their own.
- Students should submit the completed assignment according to the teacher's instructions.

Objectives

- Apply mathematical knowledge and skills to evaluate and analyze real-world situations.

Algebra Thinking

▶ Unit Objectives

- Use a mathematical expression to represent a relationship between quantities.
- Use an equation to represent a relationship between quantities.
- Use an inequality to represent a relationship between quantities.
- Select the appropriate symbol to show an operation or a relationship that makes a number sentence true.
- Determine a missing number in an equation or an inequality.

- Extend a linear pattern, such as stating what number comes next in a series.
- Recognize and describe a linear pattern, such as counting by 5s or multiplying 5 times a number to reach 100, by its rule.
- Identify patterns in addition or multiplication facts.
- Solve a simple story problem that involves a function.
- Identify odd and even numbers and describe their characteristics.
- Use a variable to represent an unknown number in an equation.

▶ Big Ideas

- Addition, subtraction, multiplication, and division can be represented by models and by using math symbols.
- The equals symbol denotes an equivalent relationship.
- An expression represents a value that can be a number, a variable, or a group of numbers, variables, and operation symbols. Some examples of expressions are $10 - 4 + 1$, $3 + x$, $5y + 2$, b, and 5.
- Rules can be used to generate number patterns.

▶ Unit Introduction

In this unit, students will begin thinking algebraically. Algebra is a branch of mathematics focused on representing real-world relationships as equations, or number sentences, and then solving for unknowns in these number sentences.

Students will learn that expressions show quantities (for example, $9 + 2$) and that number sentences show the relationship between quantities (for example, $9 + 2 = 11$ or $9 + 2 < 15$). They will learn that the same expression can be shown in many ways: $8 + 2$, 10, and $6 + 4$ are equal expressions. Building on the idea of equal and unequal expressions, students will compare quantities using the symbols $<$, $>$, and $=$. They will learn that number sentences are like balances. For example, if a number sentence uses the equals symbol, the expressions on either side of the symbol must be balanced, or equal.

Students will also learn about patterns in which the same number is added to or subtracted from each term. They will find the next term in patterns, solve story problems with patterns, and determine rules for patterns.

▶ Keywords

array	function	linear pattern
equals symbol ($=$)	greater-than symbol ($>$)	number sentence
expression	less-than symbol ($<$)	simplify

Mathematical Expressions

Lesson Overview

GET READY Problem Solving Through 1,000	5 minutes	ONLINE
LEARN Match Expressions	20 minutes	ONLINE
LEARN Story Expressions	20 minutes	OFFLINE
TRY IT Identify and Write Expressions	15 minutes	OFFLINE

▶ **Lesson Objectives**

Use a mathematical expression to represent a relationship between quantities.

▶ **Prerequisite Skills**

Write and solve addition or subtraction number sentences to represent problem-solving situations with sums and minuends up through 1,000.

▶ **Content Background**

A mathematical expression is a combination of numbers and symbols that represents a given value. For example, $2 + 3$ and $4 - 3$ are expressions. An expression can also be a single number. The number 5 alone is an expression.

An expression does not include the symbols $=$, $<$, and $>$. When two or more expressions are put together with an equals symbol ($=$), this creates an equation. For example, $2 + 3$ is an expression, but $2 + 3 = 5$ is an equation.

When two or more expressions are put together with a less-than ($<$), greater-than ($>$), or not-equal-to ($\neq$) symbol, this creates an inequality. While $2 + 3$ and 6 are each expressions, $2 + 3 < 6$ is an inequality. (We will not introduce the terms *equation* and *inequality* to students at this level; we will refer to both as number sentences.)

In this lesson, students will learn about expressions. They will see that many word phrases can be written as expressions. For instance, "3 more than 4" can be written as $3 + 4$. And "3 less than 7" can be written as $7 - 3$.

Materials to Gather

SUPPLIED

blocks – B (any color, optional)

Story Expressions activity page

Identify and Write Expressions activity page

GET READY Problem Solving Through 1,000

ONLINE

5min

Objectives

Students will read addition and subtraction story problems and choose the correct expression that matches the problem. They will determine the correct sum or difference to solve the problem. Point out to students that expressions are used to make number sentences, but expressions do not include an equals symbol.

- Write and solve addition or subtraction number sentences to represent problem-solving situations with sums and minuends up through 1,000.

LEARN Match Expressions

Objectives

- Use a mathematical expression to represent a relationship between quantities.

Students will learn that math expressions are numbers or numbers and operation symbols $(+, -, \times, \div)$ combined to show a value. An expression can even be a missing value, such as the question mark in $? = 2 + 3$. Students will also learn that expressions make up number sentences but are not themselves number sentences. Expressions never have an equals symbol $(=)$.

In this activity, students will learn that number phrases (for example, 3 more than 4) can be written as expressions. Here are a few examples:

- 3 more than 4 $4 + 3$
- 3 less than 7 $7 - 3$
- twice as many as 5 5×2
- 8 divided into 2 equal groups $8 \div 2$

LEARN Story Expressions

Objectives

- Use a mathematical expression to represent a relationship between quantities.

In this activity, students will create mathematical expressions to match stories.

View or print the Story Expressions activity page. Students should copy the problems from the Activity Book into their Math Notebook as necessary and solve them there.

1. Before working on the activity page, introduce the idea that when students write number sentences to solve story problems, they use expressions on each side of the equals symbol. (Be careful not to use the terms *number sentence* and *expression* interchangeably.)

2. Remind students that an expression can be just a number, such as 5, or a missing value shown by just a question mark. And it can have operation symbols, such as $+, -, \times, \div$. These are all expressions: $5 + 3$, $8 - ?$, 14, $? \div 2$, and even just $?$ by itself. But expressions never have an equals symbol. Only number sentences, which are made up of expressions, have an equals symbol. These are number sentences: $? + 5 = 10$, $10 - ? = 5$, $8 \div ? = 4$.

3. Tell students they will create expressions to match stories from the Activity Book.

4. Go over the Worked Examples and the sample problems. Guide students to do Problems 1–8.

5. Direct students' attention to Problem 9.

   Say: Sara has 24 tickets. Then she buys or sells 6 more. Which word—*buys* or *sells*—completes the story so that it matches the expression shown?

   Students should realize that since 6 is added to 24, Sara buys more tickets. When she buys more tickets, she is adding to the amount she already has.

6. Have students complete the rest of the activity page in their Math Notebook.

Tips

If students have difficulty, have them act out the story situations using B blocks for the objects.

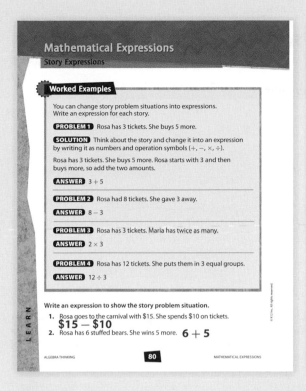

Mathematical Expressions
Story Expressions

Worked Examples

You can change story problem situations into expressions. Write an expression for each story.

PROBLEM 1 Rosa has 3 tickets. She buys 5 more.

SOLUTION Think about the story and change it into an expression by writing it as numbers and operation symbols (+, −, ×, ÷).

Rosa has 3 tickets. She buys 5 more. Rosa starts with 3 and then buys more, so add the two amounts.

ANSWER 3 + 5

PROBLEM 2 Rosa had 8 tickets. She gave 3 away.

ANSWER 8 − 3

PROBLEM 3 Rosa has 3 tickets. Maria has twice as many.

ANSWER 2 × 3

PROBLEM 4 Rosa has 12 tickets. She puts them in 3 equal groups.

ANSWER 12 ÷ 3

Write an expression to show the story problem situation.

1. Rosa goes to the carnival with $15. She spends $10 on tickets.
   $15 − $10
2. Rosa has 6 stuffed bears. She wins 5 more. **6 + 5**

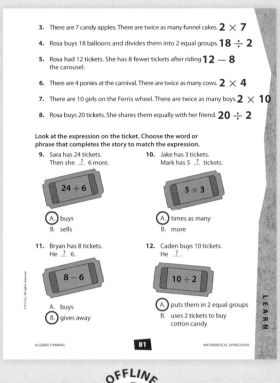

3. There are 7 candy apples. There are twice as many funnel cakes. **2 × 7**
4. Rosa buys 18 balloons and divides them into 2 equal groups. **18 ÷ 2**
5. Rosa had 12 tickets. She has 8 fewer tickets after riding the carousel. **12 − 8**
6. There are 4 ponies at the carnival. There are twice as many cows. **2 × 4**
7. There are 10 girls on the Ferris wheel. There are twice as many boys. **2 × 10**
8. Rosa buys 20 tickets. She shares them equally with her friend. **20 ÷ 2**

Look at the expression on the ticket. Choose the word or phrase that completes the story to match the expression.

9. Sara has 24 tickets. Then she _?_ 6 more.

   24 + 6

   Ⓐ buys
   B. sells

10. Jake has 3 tickets. Mark has 5 _?_ tickets.

    5 × 3

    Ⓐ times as many
    B. more

11. Bryan has 8 tickets. He _?_ 6.

    8 − 6

    A. buys
    Ⓑ gives away

12. Caden buys 10 tickets. He _?_ .

    10 ÷ 2

    Ⓐ puts them in 2 equal groups
    B. uses 2 tickets to buy cotton candy

TRY IT Identify and Write Expressions

OFFLINE 15 min

Students will practice identifying and writing expressions that match given values and stories. View or print the Identify and Write Expressions activity page and read the directions with students.

Students should copy the problems from the Activity Book into their Math Notebook as necessary and solve them there.

Objectives

- Use a mathematical expression to represent a relationship between quantities.

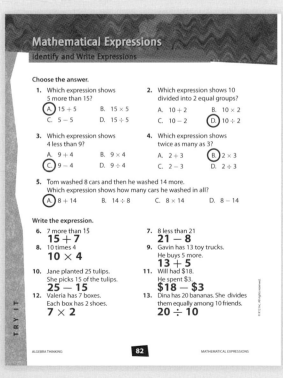

Mathematical Expressions
Identify and Write Expressions

Choose the answer.

1. Which expression shows 5 more than 15?
   Ⓐ 15 + 5   B. 15 × 5
   C. 5 − 5   D. 15 ÷ 5

2. Which expression shows 10 divided into 2 equal groups?
   A. 10 + 2   B. 10 × 2
   C. 10 − 2   Ⓓ 10 ÷ 2

3. Which expression shows 4 less than 9?
   A. 9 + 4   B. 9 × 4
   Ⓒ 9 − 4   D. 9 ÷ 4

4. Which expression shows twice as many as 3?
   A. 2 + 3   Ⓑ 2 × 3
   C. 2 − 3   D. 2 ÷ 3

5. Tom washed 8 cars and then he washed 14 more. Which expression shows how many cars he washed in all?
   Ⓐ 8 + 14   B. 14 ÷ 8   C. 8 × 14   D. 8 − 14

Write the expression.

6. 7 more than 15
   15 + 7
7. 8 less than 21
   21 − 8
8. 10 times 4
   10 × 4
9. Gavin has 13 toy trucks. He buys 5 more.
   13 + 5
10. Jane planted 25 tulips. She picks 15 of the tulips.
    25 − 15
11. Will had $18. He spent $3.
    $18 − $3
12. Valeria has 7 boxes. Each box has 2 shoes.
    7 × 2
13. Dina has 20 bananas. She divides them equally among 10 friends.
    20 ÷ 10

Expressions and Number Sentences (A)

Lesson Overview

GET READY Expression Matchup	10 minutes	**ONLINE**
LEARN Is It Equal?	20 minutes	**ONLINE**
LEARN Same Value	15 minutes	**OFFLINE**
TRY IT Equal Expressions	15 minutes	**OFFLINE**

▶ Lesson Objectives

Use an equation to represent a relationship between quantities.

▶ Prerequisite Skills

Write and solve addition or subtraction number sentences to represent problem-solving situations with sums and minuends up through 1,000.

▶ Content Background

A mathematical expression is a combination of numbers and symbols that represents a given value. For example, $2 + 3$ and $4 - 3$ are expressions. An expression can also be a single number. The number 5 alone is an expression.

An expression does not include the symbols $=$, $<$, and $>$. When two or more expressions are put together with an equals symbol ($=$), this creates an equation. For example, $2 + 3$ is an expression, but $2 + 3 = 5$ is an equation.

When two or more expressions are put together with a less-than ($<$), greater-than ($>$), or not-equal-to ($\neq$) symbol, this creates an inequality. While $2 + 3$ and 6 are each expressions, $2 + 3 < 6$ is an inequality. (We will not introduce the terms *equation* and *inequality* to students at this level; we will refer to both as number sentences.)

In this lesson, students will learn about number sentences that have an equals symbol (equations). The equals symbol shows that two expressions have the same value. It is important that students begin to view the equals symbol as a way to show a relationship and not as a symbol that tells one to find the answer.

▶ Advance Preparation

Label 2 sets of index cards with numbers 0 through 9. Label 4 other cards with the $+$, $-$, $\times$, and $\div$ symbols. On 5 additional cards, write one each of the following expressions:

- $8 + 2$
- $15 - 3$
- $7 + 0$
- 5×1
- $4 + 4$

GET READY Expression Matchup

ONLINE 10min

Students will read addition and subtraction story problems and choose the correct expression that represents the problem. They will then determine the correct sum or difference to solve the problem.

Objectives

- Write and solve addition or subtraction number sentences to represent problem-solving situations with sums and minuends up through 1,000.

LEARN Is It Equal?

ONLINE 20min

Students will explore the equals symbol and learn that number sentences show two equal expressions. They will see that a number sentence is like a balance where expressions on both sides have the same value. Students will practice finding different expressions with the same value. Understanding that the equals symbol is used to show a relationship between two expressions is emphasized throughout the activity.

Objectives

- Use an equation to represent a relationship between quantities.

LEARN Same Value

OFFLINE 15min

Students will learn about the equals symbol (=) and writing number sentences. An equals symbol shows that two expressions have the same value. A number sentence can show that two expressions are equal. Here are some examples of number sentences:

$4 + 1 = 5$ $6 = 6$ $9 = 10 - 1$ $3 + 4 = 9 - 2$

Understanding that the equals symbol is used to show a relationship between two expressions is emphasized throughout the activity. Gather the labeled index cards.

1. Show students the $8 + 2$ expression card. Have students record the expression in their Math Notebook and determine its value. 10

2. Ask students to use the number cards and symbol cards to make an expression that is equal to the expression on the $8 + 2$ card. (For example, $8 + 2$ has the same value as $6 + 4$.) Have students record this expression and several others. **Sample answers:** $5 + 5, 2 \times 5, 1 + 9, 12 - 2, 90 - 80$

3. Have students continue to find other expressions that are equal. Ask them to use more than one operation symbol in each expression. Have students record their expression. **Sample answer:** $3 + 5 + 2$

4. Discuss with students the number of different expressions that have the same value as the expression on the card. Guide students to see that there is an endless number of expressions with the same value.

5. Place the other expression cards face down in front of students. Ask students to select an expression card and use the number cards and symbol cards to create an expression that's equal to the expression on the card they chose. Have students write the two expressions (the one they selected and the one they came up with) as a number sentence. Repeat this step.

6. Repeat Step 5 two or three times, using different expression cards.

Objectives

- Use an equation to represent a relationship between quantities.

Tips

Point out that when students solve a story problem, they write a number sentence with an expression on each side of an equals symbol. Present a few simple story problems, and have students write the number sentence. **Example:** Sam has 16 flowers. He gives 4 flowers to his sister. How many flowers does he have left? **Number sentence:** $16 - 4 = 12$

7. Place the equals symbol card in front of students. Ask students to explain what the symbol means and how it is used. Remind students that the equals symbol is used in number sentences and shows that two expressions have the same value or are equal.

8. Have students look at their lists of number sentences.

   Ask: Where did you place the equals symbol? between two equal expressions
   Ask: How do you know that you wrote a number sentence? I have two expressions that have the same value separated by an equals symbol.

9. Have students read their number sentences aloud. **Sample answer:** $8 + 2 = 10 - 0$ is read "Eight plus two is equal to ten minus zero."

TRY IT Equal Expressions

OFFLINE
15min

Objectives

Students will practice writing equal expressions and number sentences. For Problem 1, they will write five expressions equal to the given expression. Encourage them to use different operations and even more than one operation in an expression. Remember that the number of equivalent expressions is limitless. For Problems 2–6, students will match equal expressions and then place an equals symbol between the expressions to form a number sentence. Check students' placement of the equals symbol.

View or print the Equal Expressions activity page and read the directions with students. They should copy the problems into their Math Notebook as necessary and solve them there.

- Use an equation to represent a relationship between quantities.

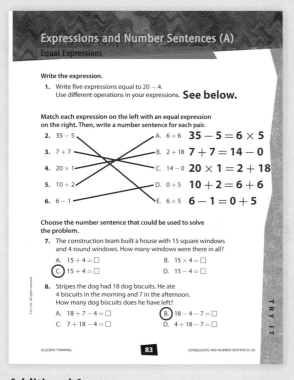

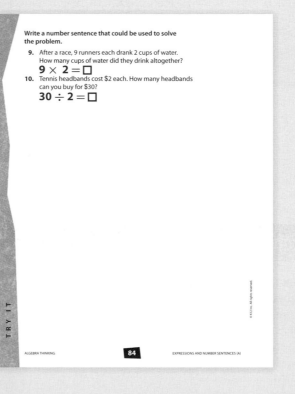

Additional Answer
1. Answers will vary. **Sample answers:** $8 + 8$; 2×8; $12 + 4$; $32 \div 2$; $4 + 4 + 4 + 4$; $16 - 0$

Expressions and Number Sentences (B)

Lesson Overview

LEARN Carnival Game	30 minutes	**ONLINE**
TRY IT Choose the Number Sentence	15 minutes	**OFFLINE**
CHECKPOINT	15 minutes	**ONLINE**

▶ Lesson Objectives

Use an equation to represent a relationship between quantities.

▶ Prerequisite Skills

Write and solve addition or subtraction number sentences to represent problem-solving situations with sums and minuends up through 1,000.

▶ Content Background

A mathematical expression is a combination of numbers and symbols that represents a given value. For example, $2 + 3$ and $4 - 3$ are expressions. An expression can also be a single number. The number 5 alone is an expression.

An expression does not include the symbols $=$, $<$, and $>$. When two or more expressions are put together with an equals symbol ($=$), this creates an equation. For example, $2 + 3$ is an expression, but $2 + 3 = 5$ is an equation.

When two or more expressions are put together with a less-than ($<$), greater-than ($>$), or not-equal-to ($\neq$) symbol, this creates an inequality. While $2 + 3$ and 6 are each expressions, $2 + 3 < 6$ is an inequality. (We will not introduce the terms *equation* and *inequality* to students at this level; we will refer to both as number sentences.)

In this lesson, students will continue to learn about number sentences that have an equals symbol (equations). The equals symbol shows that two expressions have the same value. It is important that students begin to view the equals symbol as a way to show a relationship and not as a symbol that tells one to find the answer.

Materials to Gather

SUPPLIED

blocks – B (any color, optional)

Choose the Number Sentence activity page

LEARN Carnival Game

ONLINE 30min

Students will review the meaning and use of multiplication and division. Then they will explore choosing a number sentence that matches a story problem. Remind students that number sentences are made up of expressions. The equals symbol in a number sentence shows that the expressions on each side have the same value.

Also remind students that multiplication is a way of adding equal groups quickly and that division is taking a number of objects and dividing those objects into equal groups.

Objectives

- Use an equation to represent a relationship between quantities.

Tips

If students have difficulty with a problem, have them model it with B blocks or other objects.

TRY IT Choose the Number Sentence

OFFLINE
15 min

Objectives

- Use an equation to represent a relationship between quantities.

Students will choose the number sentence that matches a given story problem. They will then write number sentences to match story problems. They do not need to solve the story problems; rather, they should stay focused on practicing turning the words into number sentences.

View or print the Choose the Number Sentence activity page and read the directions with students. They should copy the problems from the Activity Book into their Math Notebook as necessary and solve them there.

Expressions and Number Sentences (B)
Choose the Number Sentence

Choose the number sentence that represents the problem.

1. Candy Apple Café sells candy apples at the carnival. On Friday, 120 candy apples were sold. On Saturday, 60 candy apples were sold. How many candy apples in all were sold on those 2 days?

   (A) □ = 120 + 60   B. □ = 120 − 60
   C. 120 ÷ 60 = □

2. The clowns are putting on a show at the carnival. There are 50 people watching the show. Before the show is over, 12 people leave and 9 people arrive. How many people are watching the show now?

   A. □ = 50 + 12 + 9   B. □ = 50 − 12 − 9
   (C) □ = 50 − 12 + 9

3. Candy apples cost $4 each. Jerome and his friends want to buy 8 candy apples. How much money do they need?

   A. □ = 4 + 8   (B) □ = 4 × 8
   C. □ = 8 ÷ 4

4. There are 20 people riding the roller coaster. They are in 5 cars, and an equal number of people are in each car. How many people are in each car?

   (A) 20 ÷ 5 = □   B. 20 × 5 = □
   C. 20 + 5 = □   D. 20 − 5 = □

ALGEBRA THINKING **85** EXPRESSIONS AND NUMBER SENTENCES (B)

Choose the number sentence that represents the problem.

5. Paula read 5 pages of her book each hour for 3 hours. How many pages did she read in all?

   A. 5 + 3 = □   (B) 5 × 3 = □
   C. 5 ÷ 3 = □   D. 5 − 3 = □

6. Dario had $30. He spent $12 at the toy store and $10 at the paper store. How much money does he have left?

   A. $30 + $12 + $10 = □   B. $30 + $12 − $10 = □
   C. $12 + $30 − $10 = □   (D) $30 − $12 − $10 = □

7. Sasha had 43 table tennis balls. She lost 22 of them and then found 12. How many balls does she have now?

   A. 43 + 22 + 12 = □   B. 43 − 22 − 12 = □
   C. 43 + 22 − 12 = □   (D) 43 − 22 + 12 = □

Write a number sentence that could be used to solve the problem.

8. Kelly read 250 pages on Saturday and 50 pages on Sunday. How many pages did Kelly read on these 2 days?
   250 + 50 = □

9. The bakery baked 35 loaves of bread. Of the loaves, 18 were white. The rest were wheat. How many loaves were wheat?
   35 − 18 = □ or 35 = 18 + □

10. The gazelle spends 12 hours a day grazing for food. How many hours would the gazelle spend grazing in 5 days?
   5 × 12 = □ or 12 × 5 = □

ALGEBRA THINKING **86** EXPRESSIONS AND NUMBER SENTENCES (B)

CHECKPOINT

ONLINE
15 min

Objectives

- Use an equation to represent a relationship between quantities.

Students will complete an online Checkpoint. If necessary, read the directions, problems, and answer choices to students and help them with keyboard or mouse operations.

Expression Comparison (A)

Lesson Overview

GET READY Compare Numbers and Expressions	15 minutes	ONLINE
LEARN Show Expressions	15 minutes	ONLINE
LEARN Compare Expressions	20 minutes	OFFLINE
TRY IT Represent Situations	10 minutes	OFFLINE

▶ Lesson Objectives

Use an inequality to represent a relationship between quantities.

▶ Prerequisite Skills

- Use an equation to represent a relationship between quantities.
- Compare whole numbers through 10,000.

▶ Content Background

Students will use the greater-than (>) and less-than (<) symbols to compare expressions. The greater-than symbol points to the right, and the less-than symbol points to the left. However, it is easier for students to remember that these two comparison symbols point to the lesser number and open to the greater number.

The terms *sign* and *symbol* are often used interchangeably. Although *sign* may be used to refer to greater than (>), less than (<), and equals (=), the term *symbol* will be used in this lesson because it is a more accurate mathematical term. In math, *sign* specifically refers to the positive signs and negative signs of numbers.

▶ Advance Preparation

Label 3 index cards with words and symbols for greater than (>), less than (<), and equals (=). On 10 index cards, write one each of the following math expressions:

- 3×5
- 9×2
- 2×5
- 6×2
- 3×6
- $9 + 6$
- $5 + 5$
- $4 + 12$
- $8 + 8$
- $9 + 3$

Materials to Gather

SUPPLIED

Represent Situations activity page

ALSO NEEDED

index cards – labeled with words and symbols

index cards – labeled with expressions

GET READY Compare Numbers and Expressions **15min** ONLINE

Objectives

Students will use a greater-than symbol (>) or a less-than symbol (<) to compare numbers and expressions.

- Use an equation to represent a relationship between quantities.
- Compare whole numbers through 10,000.

LEARN Show Expressions   **15min** ONLINE

Objectives

Students will match expressions to story problem situations, which is an important skill in learning to solve story problems. Remind students that expressions by themselves do not include an equals symbol. However, numbers sentences, which compare expressions, can include a less-than, greater-than, or equals symbol.

- Use an inequality to represent a relationship between quantities.

LEARN Compare Expressions   **20min** OFFLINE

Objectives

Students will use an equals symbol to show equivalent expressions. Then they will use greater-than and less-than symbols to compare expressions. Gather the labeled index cards.

- Use an inequality to represent a relationship between quantities.

Tips

Have students write the sum or product on the back of each number-expression card. Then have them flip over the cards to check their number sentences.

1. Display the 10 prepared number-expression cards. Set the 3 symbol cards aside.

2. Choose an expression, such as $9 + 6$, and display the equals symbol ($=$) card after it. Read the expression displayed: "nine plus six equals." Point out that the equals symbol is read as "equals" in a number sentence. Ask students to name the sum. 15

3. Tell students they need to identify another expression that has a value of 15 to make a true number sentence. 3×5

   Have students read the completed number sentence, emphasizing the equivalent quantities.

4. Return the expressions to the group of number expression cards.

5. Repeat Steps 2–4 three more times.

6. Put the equals symbol aside and display the greater-than (>) and less-than (<) symbols.

7. Choose two expressions that are not equal, such as $4 + 12$ and 6×2. Explain to students that when expressions are not equal, they should use the greater-than or less-than symbol to make a number sentence.

8. Ask students which symbol should be placed between the two expressions to make a true number sentence. Remind students that the symbol points to the lesser quantity and opens to the greater quantity.

9. Have students read the number sentence and check that it is true. Have them say the product or sum of each expression.

10. Repeat Steps 7–9 three more times.

TRY IT Represent Situations

Objectives

- Use an inequality to represent a relationship between quantities.

Students will practice using the greater-than (>), less-than (<), and equals (=) symbols to compare expressions. Then they will practice choosing an expression that matches a given situation. View or print the Represent Situations activity page and read the directions with students.

Students should copy the problems from their Activity Book into their Math Notebook as necessary and solve them there.

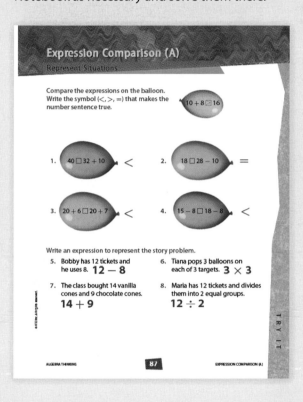

Expression Comparison (A)
Represent Situations

Compare the expressions on the balloon. Write the symbol (<, >, =) that makes the number sentence true.

$10 + 8 \boxtimes 16$

1. $40 \square 32 + 10$ <
2. $18 \square 28 - 10$ =
3. $20 + 6 \square 20 + 7$ <
4. $15 - 8 \square 18 - 8$ <

Write an expression to represent the story problem.

5. Bobby has 12 tickets and he uses 8. $12 - 8$

6. Tiana pops 3 balloons on each of 3 targets. 3×3

7. The class bought 14 vanilla cones and 9 chocolate cones. $14 + 9$

8. Maria has 12 tickets and divides them into 2 equal groups. $12 \div 2$

ALGEBRA THINKING 87 EXPRESSION COMPARISON (A)

TRY IT

Expression Comparison (B)

Lesson Overview

LEARN Situation Expressions	20 minutes	**ONLINE**
LEARN Compare Quantities	20 minutes	**OFFLINE**
TRY IT Write Expressions	10 minutes	**OFFLINE**
CHECKPOINT	10 minutes	**ONLINE**

▶ Lesson Objectives

Use an inequality to represent a relationship between quantities.

▶ Prerequisite Skills

- Use an equation to represent a relationship between quantities.
- Compare whole numbers through 10,000.

▶ Content Background

Students will continue to use the greater-than ($>$) and less-than ($<$) symbols to compare expressions. The greater-than symbol points to the right, and the less-than symbol points to the left. However, it is easier for students to remember that these two comparison symbols point to the lesser number and open to the greater number.

The terms *sign* and *symbol* are often used interchangeably. Although *sign* may be used to refer to greater than ($>$), less than ($<$), and equals ($=$), the term *symbol* will be used in this lesson because it is a more accurate mathematical term. In math, *sign* specifically refers to the positive signs and negative signs of numbers.

Materials to Gather

SUPPLIED

Compare Quantities activity page

Write Expressions activity page

LEARN Situation Expressions

ONLINE
20min

Students will match math expressions with everyday situations. Then they will learn how to break apart a situation and write the two expressions as a comparison number sentence. Allow them to calculate problems with paper and pencil.

Objectives

- Use an inequality to represent a relationship between quantities.

LEARN Compare Quantities

Objectives

- Use an inequality to represent a relationship between quantities.

Students will use a greater-than or less-than symbol to write a number sentence that compares quantities in a practical situation.

View or print the Compare Quantities activity page. Students should copy the problems from the Activity Book into their Math Notebook as necessary and solve them there.

1. Discuss the Worked Examples with students. Tell students that there are two expressions in this situation.

2. Have students identify the two different expressions. Remind students that an expression can be a number, such as 8.

3. Ask students what math operation shows 4 racks with 3 pretzels on each rack. Guide students to see that equal groups, with the same number in each group, indicate multiplication.

4. Have students compare the two expressions. Guide students to think of 4×3 as 12. Tell students that thinking of each expression as a number makes it easier to compare.

5. Remind students that the comparison symbol points to the lesser quantity and opens to the greater quantity. Tell students that because 12 is greater than 8, 4×3 is greater than 8.

6. Guide students to complete each section of Problems 1 and 2.

7. Have students write a number sentence for each situation in Problems 3–8. Remind them that the expressions should match the situations and the symbols should compare the quantities.

Tips

Have students use different-colored highlighters to identify each part of the situation.

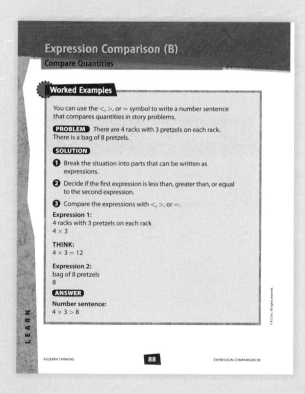

Expression Comparison (B)
Compare Quantities

Worked Examples

You can use the $<$, $>$, or $=$ symbol to write a number sentence that compares quantities in story problems.

PROBLEM There are 4 racks with 3 pretzels on each rack. There is a bag of 8 pretzels.

SOLUTION

❶ Break the situation into parts that can be written as expressions.

❷ Decide if the first expression is less than, greater than, or equal to the second expression.

❸ Compare the expressions with $<$, $>$, or $=$.

Expression 1:
4 racks with 3 pretzels on each rack
4×3

THINK:
$4 \times 3 = 12$

Expression 2:
bag of 8 pretzels
8

ANSWER

Number sentence:
$4 \times 3 > 8$

ALGEBRA THINKING   88   EXPRESSION COMPARISON (B)

Write an expression to match the situation. Then, write a number sentence to compare the numbers that are in the expression.

1. Mr. Weaver has 25 peanuts and gives the same number of peanuts to each of his 5 children. Mrs. Mead has 4 peanuts.

Expression 1:
25 peanuts to each of 5 children
$25 \square 5 \div$
Think:
$25 \square 5 = 5 \div$

Expression 2:
? peanuts **4 peanuts**
? **4**
Number sentence:
? **$25 \div 5 > 4$**

2. Lola has 10 rings. Kari has 2 rings on each of 5 fingers.

Expression 1:
? rings **10**

Expression 2:   **5**
2 ? rings on each of ? fingers
Think:
? **$2 \times 5 = 10$**
Number sentence:
? **$10 = 2 \times 5$**

Write a number sentence to compare the numbers that are in the situation.

3. There are 45 children in the red line and 23 in the blue line for the roller coaster. There are 62 children in line for the fun house. **$45 + 23 > 62$**

4. There are 72 prizes at the duck booth, and 49 prizes are given away. There are 56 prizes at the bottle booth. **$72 - 49 < 56$**

5. There are 3 riders on the swings. On the cars there are 30 riders separated equally into 5 groups. **$3 < 30 \div 5$**

6. Each of 5 children tosses 3 rings. Mike tosses 8 rings. **$5 \times 3 > 8$**

7. There are 22 candy apples, and 18 are eaten. Seven children buy drinks. **$22 - 18 < 7$**

8. Naomi plays games for 45 minutes. Allie plays skee ball for 10 minutes and ring toss for 20 minutes. **$45 > 10 + 20$**

ALGEBRA THINKING   89   EXPRESSION COMPARISON (B)

TRY IT Write Expressions

- Use an inequality to represent a relationship between quantities.

Students will practice writing expressions and number sentences to describe quantities in a given situation. View or print the Write Expressions activity page and read the directions with students.

Students should copy the problems from the Activity Book into their Math Notebook as necessary and solve them there.

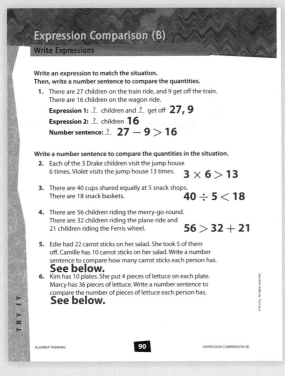

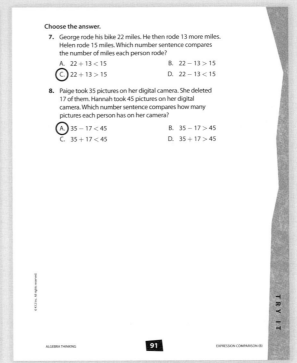

Additional Answers

5. **Example:** $22 - 5 > 10$; Other correct answers are acceptable.

6. **Example:** $10 \times 4 > 36$; Other correct answers are acceptable.

CHECKPOINT

- Use an inequality to represent a relationship between quantities.

Students will complete an online Checkpoint. If necessary, read the directions, problems, and answer choices to students and help them with keyboard or mouse operations.

Missing Symbols

▶ Lesson Objectives

Select the appropriate symbol to show an operation or a relationship that makes a number sentence true.

▶ Prerequisite Skills

- Write and solve addition or subtraction number sentences to represent problem-solving situations with sums and minuends up through 1,000.
- Use an equation to represent a relationship between quantities.
- Use an Inequality to represent a relationship between quantities.

Materials to Gather

SUPPLIED

Make It True activity page

blocks – E (3 yellow)

ALSO NEEDED

clear tape

marker

▶ Content Background

An expression is a combination of numbers and symbols that represents a given value. For example, $2 + 3$ and $4 - 3 + ?$ are expressions. Also, a number alone, such as 5, is an expression. An expression does not include relational symbols, such as $=$, $<$, and $>$, in the way number sentences do.

Operation symbols ($+$, $-$, $\times$, $\div$) and relation symbols ($<$, $>$, $=$) make number sentences true. Operation symbols show an action to be performed with numbers, while relation symbols show the relationship between numbers and quantities. When working with students, avoid the term *relation symbols*. Instead, use the term *comparison symbols* or *symbols that compare expressions* to show whether two expressions are equal or one is greater than or less than the other. It is important that students focus on the meaning of operation symbols and relation or comparison symbols to be sure that number sentences show true relationships between quantities.

▶ Advance Preparation

Place a piece of clear tape on 3 yellow E blocks. Write a comparison symbol ($<$, $>$, $=$) on each.

GET READY Number Sentences

Students will review the meaning and use of operation symbols $(+, -, \times, \div)$ and comparison symbols $(<, >, =)$. The operation symbols tell students which operation to do. The comparison symbols compare the expressions to indicate whether they are equal or whether one is greater than or less than another. Students will also review how to represent a story problem with a number sentence, and they will solve a story problem.

Objectives

- Write and solve addition or subtraction number sentences to represent problem-solving situations with sums and minuends up through 1,000.
- Use an equation to represent a relationship between quantities.
- Use an inequality to represent a relationship between quantities.

LEARN Missing Operation Symbols

Students will use their knowledge of operation symbols $(+, -, \times, \div)$ to determine which operation symbol can be used to make a number sentence true. Remind students that when they see an expression on one side of a number sentence, they should find its value. For example, if they see the number sentence $5 + 5 = 2 \stackrel{?}{=} 8$, they should first find the value of $5 + 5$. Then they should figure out the correct operation symbol for the other side of the number sentence. In this example, they should be able to fill in the correct operation symbol to show that $5 + 5 = 2 + 8$.

Objectives

- Select the appropriate symbol to show an operation or a relationship that makes a number sentence true.

LEARN Find the Symbol

Students will put the correct comparison symbol in number sentences to make the number sentences true.

  Gather the labeled blocks. During the activity, students should write the number sentences in their Math Notebook.

Objectives

- Select the appropriate symbol to show an operation or a relationship that makes a number sentence true.

Tips

Ask students to write their own true number sentences by using at least one operation symbol and one comparison symbol.

1. Show students the comparison symbols $(<, >, =)$ on the yellow blocks. Explain that comparison symbols tell whether an expression is less than, greater than, or equal to another expression.

2. Write $10 + 10 \stackrel{?}{=} 20$ large enough so that students can place a labeled block on the number sentence for the answer.

3. Have students look at both sides and decide whether they are equal or not.

   Ask: What is the value of $10 + 10$? Is it the same as 20? If not, is it greater than 20 or less than 20?

   Say: Place the correct symbol between the $10 + 10$ and the 20.
   Correct symbol: $=$

4. Repeat with the following number sentences:
   - $10 - 10 \stackrel{?}{=} 20$ Correct symbol: $<$
   - $10 \times 10 \stackrel{?}{=} 20$ Correct symbol: $>$

   Review the greater-than and less-than symbols. Demonstrate that each symbol opens toward the greater number and points at the lesser number. Ask students to think of ways to remember this fact.

5. Explain that sometimes the comparison symbol is on the left in the number sentence. Write these problems. Have students fill in the correct comparison symbol to make the number sentence true.

- 30 $\underline{\ ?\ }$ 20 + 20   Correct symbol: $<$
- 30 $\underline{\ ?\ }$ 30 − 0   Correct symbol: $=$
- 30 $\underline{\ ?\ }$ 25 − 25   Correct symbol: $>$
- 30 $\underline{\ ?\ }$ 25 + 3   Correct symbol: $>$

6. Challenge students to place the correct comparison symbol into number sentences with two operation symbols, such as the following:

- 5 + 4 $\underline{\ ?\ }$ 10 − 2   Correct answer: $>$
- 8 − 3 $\underline{\ ?\ }$ 4 + 1   Correct answer: $=$

TRY IT   Make It True

OFFLINE **10**min

Objectives

Students will decide which operation or comparison symbol is needed to make a true number sentence. View or print the Make It True activity page and read the directions with students.

Students should copy the problems from the Activity Book into their Math Notebook as necessary and solve them there.

- Select the appropriate symbol to show an operation or a relationship that makes a number sentence true.

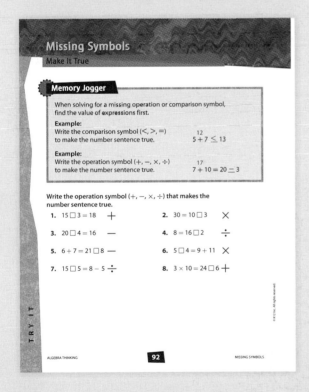

Missing Symbols

Make It True

Memory Jogger

When solving for a missing operation or comparison symbol, find the value of expressions first.

Example:
Write the comparison symbol ($<$, $>$, $=$) to make the number sentence true.

$5 + 7 \overset{12}{\leq} 13$

Example:
Write the operation symbol ($+$, $−$, $\times$, $\div$) to make the number sentence true.

$7 + 10 = 20 \overset{17}{-} 3$

Write the operation symbol ($+$, $−$, $\times$, $\div$) that makes the number sentence true.

1. $15 \ \square \ 3 = 18$ $+$
2. $30 = 10 \ \square \ 3$ $\times$
3. $20 \ \square \ 4 = 16$ $-$
4. $8 = 16 \ \square \ 2$ $\div$
5. $6 + 7 = 21 \ \square \ 8$ $-$
6. $5 \ \square \ 4 = 9 + 11$ $\times$
7. $15 \ \square \ 5 = 8 - 5$ $\div$
8. $3 \times 10 = 24 \ \square \ 6$ $+$

TRY IT

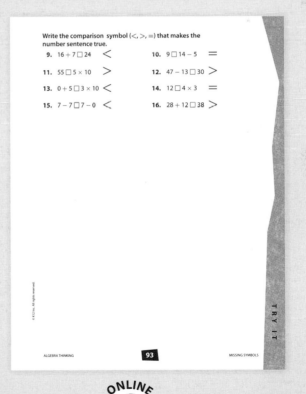

Write the comparison symbol ($<$, $>$, $=$) that makes the number sentence true.

9. $16 + 7 \ \square \ 24$ $<$
10. $9 \ \square \ 14 - 5$ $=$
11. $55 \ \square \ 5 \times 10$ $>$
12. $47 - 13 \ \square \ 30$ $>$
13. $0 + 5 \ \square \ 3 \times 10$ $<$
14. $12 \ \square \ 4 \times 3$ $=$
15. $7 - 7 \ \square \ 7 - 0$ $<$
16. $28 + 12 \ \square \ 38$ $>$

TRY IT

ONLINE **10**min

CHECKPOINT

Objectives

Students will complete an online Checkpoint. If necessary, read the directions, problems, and answer choices to students and help them with keyboard or mouse operations.

- Select the appropriate symbol to show an operation or a relationship that makes a number sentence true.

Missing Values (A)

Lesson Overview

GET READY Choose the Sentence	10 minutes	**ONLINE**
LEARN Choose the Symbol	15 minutes	**ONLINE**
LEARN True Statements	25 minutes	**OFFLINE**
TRY IT What's Missing?	10 minutes	**OFFLINE**

▶ Lesson Objectives

- Use an equation to represent a relationship between quantities.
- Use an inequality to represent a relationship between quantities.
- Determine a missing number in an equation or inequality.

▶ Prerequisite Skills

Write and solve addition or subtraction number sentences to represent problem-solving situations with sums and minuends up through 1,000.

▶ Content Background

Students will use their understanding of operation symbols ($+$, $-$, $\times$, $\div$), relation symbols ($<$, $>$, $=$), and inverse operations to find a missing value that will make a number sentence true. Students will see problems such as the following:

- $30 = 25 + \square$
- $10 + 20 = 3 \times \square$
- $17 > 9 + \square$

Students will learn that number sentences with an equals symbol and one missing value, such as the first two examples, have only one correct answer. They will learn that a number sentence with a greater-than or less-than symbol (an inequality), such as the last example, can be true with a range of different values in the blank space. As students complete these types of problems, they will become more fluent with expressions, number sentences, and the type of thinking that will be useful for algebra in the future.

▶ Advance Preparation

Label a set of small sticky notes with numbers 0 through 9. They should be small enough that students can stick them on the page.

Materials to Gather

SUPPLIED

True Statements activity page

What's Missing? activity page

ALSO NEEDED

sticky notes, small – labeled 0–9

GET READY Choose the Sentence

ONLINE 10min

Students will review the use of number sentences to represent a relationship between quantities. First they will decide which number sentence can be used to solve a story problem. Then they will decide which number sentence compares two expressions. Finally, students will solve a story problem.

LEARN Choose the Symbol

ONLINE 15min

Students will identify the two expressions that make up a number sentence. Remind students that expressions have numbers and operation symbols, while number sentences are made up of expressions with a comparison symbol between them, showing whether the expressions are equal or one expression is greater than or less than the other. After identifying the expressions in a number sentence, students will decide which comparison symbol will make the number sentence true.

> **Tips**
>
> Mention that when reading the greater-than and less-than symbols, students can read the symbols left to right. If the left side is the greater opening ($>$), students read "greater than." If the left side is the smaller point ($<$), students read "less than."

LEARN True Statements

OFFLINE 25min

Students will create expressions to make number sentences true. Then they will use a set of numbered sticky notes to fill in missing values and make true number sentences. Finally, they will write missing values in number sentences.

View or print the True Statements activity page. Students should copy the problems from the Activity Book into their Math Notebook as necessary and solve them there. Set aside the sticky notes until later in the activity.

1. Discuss the Worked Examples with students.
2. Have students look at Problem 1. Ask them to identify the expression on the left side of the equals symbol and to simplify the expression by finding its value. $5 + 7$; 12
3. Point to the right side of the number sentence. Ask students what two numbers added together have the same value as $5 + 7$, or 12. Encourage students to name numbers other than 5 and 7 that have a sum of 12, such as $6 + 6$ or $8 + 4$.
4. Explain that the numbers 8 and 4 make the number sentence true because the quantity on each side of the equals symbol is the same. Tell students that the numbers 9 and 4 would make the number sentence false because the value of 9 and 4 is 13, not 12.

> **Tips**
>
> You may wish to have students place a clear plastic sheet over the activity page and use an erasable marker for exercises that don't require the sticky notes. If you have numbered counters or tiles, you can use them instead of sticky notes.

5. Have students complete Problems 2–6. They should find the value of the given expression and then identify numbers that have a sum or difference of the same value. Check students' work.

6. Have students look at Problems 7 and 8. Point out that these problems use the less-than and greater-than symbols rather than the equals symbol. Explain that the best strategy is to solve them as though there is an equals symbol and then adjust the numbers so that one expression is greater than or less than the other. In Problem 7, have students simplify the expression on the right first to find that its value is 4 (because $8 - 4 = 4$). Explain that they need to create an expression with a difference less than 4. Any expression with a value less than 4 will work. Use the same strategy to solve Problem 8.

7. Display the sticky notes numbered 0–9. Tell students they will use the sticky notes to complete Problems 9–15. Explain that they have 10 notes and there are 10 empty boxes. Emphasize that each note will be used only once to complete the problems. Students should place the notes in the boxes on the activity page to make each number sentence true.

8. Guide students to complete the problems with only one box first and then use the remaining notes to complete the problems with two boxes. Note that some problems would normally have more than one possible answer; however, because each note can be used only one time, there is only one correct way to place the 10 notes so that each number sentence is true.

9. As students complete the problems, ask questions such as the following, using their answers from the activity page:
   • What number subtracted from 5 equals 4? 1
   • What two numbers added together equal 5? 2, 3
   • What number added to 4 equals 4? 0

10. Direct students' attention to Problems 16–21. Tell students they will use the sticky notes again to make these number sentences true. Ask students what differences they see in Problems 16–21. Explain that generally with less-than and greater-than symbols, there is more than one possible answer. Remind students that since each note can be used only once, there is only one correct way to place the 10 notes so every number sentence is true. Be sure students complete the problems in order so possible solutions are narrowed down with each subsequent problem.

11. As students complete the problems, ask questions such as the following, using their answers from the activity page:
   • What numbers added together have a value less than 2? 0, 1
   • What numbers added together have a value less than 6? 2, 3
   • What number added to 6 has a sum less than 11? 4

12. Have students set aside the sticky notes and look at Problems 22–27. Explain that some of these missing numbers are greater than 9 and some have more than one possible solution. Ask questions such as the following:
   • What number added to 9 equals 17? 8
   • What number added to 9 is greater than 17? any number greater than 8
   • What number is greater than the sum of 8 and 9? any number greater than 17

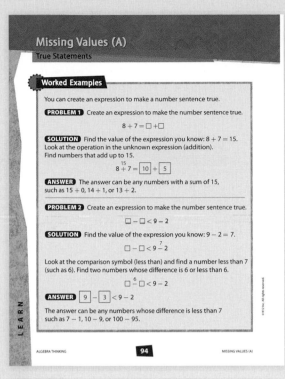

Missing Values (A)
True Statements

Worked Examples

You can create an expression to make a number sentence true.

PROBLEM 1 Create an expression to make the number sentence true.

$$8 + 7 = \square + \square$$

SOLUTION Find the value of the expression you know: $8 + 7 = 15$.
Look at the operation in the unknown expression (addition).
Find numbers that add up to 15.

$$\overset{15}{8 + 7} = \boxed{10} + \boxed{5}$$

ANSWER The answer can be any numbers with a sum of 15, such as $15 + 0$, $14 + 1$, or $13 + 2$.

PROBLEM 2 Create an expression to make the number sentence true.

$$\square - \square < 9 - 2$$

SOLUTION Find the value of the expression you know: $9 - 2 = 7$.

$$\square - \square < \overset{7}{9 - 2}$$

Look at the comparison symbol (less than) and find a number less than 7 (such as 6). Find two numbers whose difference is 6 or less than 6.

$$\overset{6}{\square - \square} < 9 - 2$$

ANSWER $\boxed{9} - \boxed{3} < 9 - 2$

The answer can be any numbers whose difference is less than 7 such as $7 - 1$, $10 - 9$, or $100 - 95$.

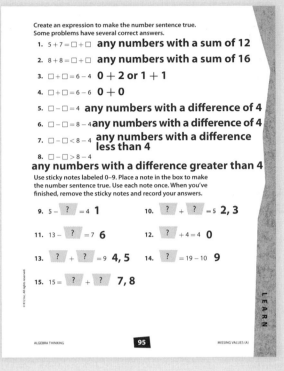

Create an expression to make the number sentence true.
Some problems have several correct answers.

1. $5 + 7 = \square + \square$ **any numbers with a sum of 12**

2. $8 + 8 = \square + \square$ **any numbers with a sum of 16**

3. $\square + \square = 6 - 4$ **0 + 2 or 1 + 1**

4. $\square + \square = 6 - 6$ **0 + 0**

5. $\square - \square = 4$ **any numbers with a difference of 4**

6. $\square - \square = 8 - 4$ **any numbers with a difference of 4**

7. $\square - \square < 8 - 4$ **any numbers with a difference less than 4**

8. $\square - \square > 8 - 4$ **any numbers with a difference greater than 4**

Use sticky notes labeled 0–9. Place a note in the box to make the number sentence true. Use each note once. When you've finished, remove the sticky notes and record your answers.

9. $5 - \boxed{?} = 4$ **1**   10. $\boxed{?} + \boxed{?} = 5$ **2, 3**

11. $13 - \boxed{?} = 7$ **6**   12. $\boxed{?} + 4 = 4$ **0**

13. $\boxed{?} + \boxed{?} = 9$ **4, 5**   14. $\boxed{?} = 19 - 10$ **9**

15. $15 = \boxed{?} + \boxed{?}$ **7, 8**

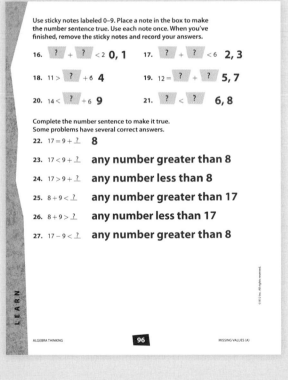

Use sticky notes labeled 0–9. Place a note in the box to make the number sentence true. Use each note once. When you've finished, remove the sticky notes and record your answers.

16. $\boxed{?} + \boxed{?} < 2$ **0, 1**   17. $\boxed{?} + \boxed{?} < 6$ **2, 3**

18. $11 > \boxed{?} + 6$ **4**   19. $12 = \boxed{?} + \boxed{?}$ **5, 7**

20. $14 < \boxed{?} + 6$ **9**   21. $\boxed{?} < \boxed{?}$ **6, 8**

Complete the number sentence to make it true.
Some problems have several correct answers.

22. $17 = 9 + \underline{?}$ **8**

23. $17 < 9 + \underline{?}$ **any number greater than 8**

24. $17 > 9 + \underline{?}$ **any number less than 8**

25. $8 + 9 < \underline{?}$ **any number greater than 17**

26. $8 + 9 > \underline{?}$ **any number less than 17**

27. $17 - 9 < \underline{?}$ **any number greater than 8**

TRY IT What's Missing?

Objectives

- Determine a missing number in an equation or an inequality.

Students will practice writing a missing number to make a number sentence true. View or print the What's Missing? activity page and read the directions with students.

Students should copy the problems from the Activity Book into their Math Notebook as necessary and solve them there.

Tips

Remind students that some exercises have more than one correct answer.

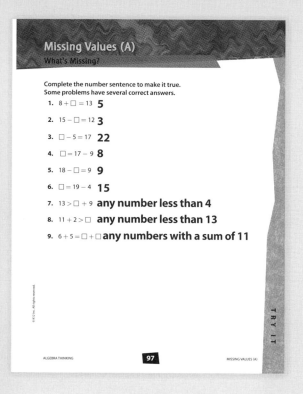

Missing Values (A)
What's Missing?

Complete the number sentence to make it true.
Some problems have several correct answers.

1. $8 + \square = 13$ **5**

2. $15 - \square = 12$ **3**

3. $\square - 5 = 17$ **22**

4. $\square = 17 - 9$ **8**

5. $18 - \square = 9$ **9**

6. $\square = 19 - 4$ **15**

7. $13 > \square + 9$ **any number less than 4**

8. $11 + 2 > \square$ **any number less than 13**

9. $6 + 5 = \square + \square$ **any numbers with a sum of 11**

ALGEBRA THINKING   97   MISSING VALUES (A)

TRY IT

Missing Values (B)

Lesson Overview

LEARN Use Inverse Relationships	15 minutes	**ONLINE**
LEARN Multiplication and Division	20 minutes	**OFFLINE**
LEARN Use Letters for Missing Values	15 minutes	**OFFLINE**
TRY IT Missing Values in Number Sentences	10 minutes	**OFFLINE**

▶ Lesson Objectives

Determine a missing number in an equation or an inequality.

▶ Prerequisite Skills

- Write and solve addition or subtraction number sentences to represent problem-solving situations with sums and minuends up through 1,000.
- Use an equation to represent a relationship between quantities.
- Use an inequality to represent a relationship between quantities.

▶ Content Background

Students will continue to use their understanding of operation symbols $(+, -, \times, \div)$, relation symbols $(<, >, =)$, and inverse operations to find a missing value that will make a number sentence true. Students will see problems such as the following:

- $30 = 25 + \square$
- $10 + 20 = 3 \times \square$
- $17 > 9 + \square$

Students will learn that number sentences with an equals symbol and one missing value, such as the first two examples, have only one correct answer. They will learn that a number sentence with a greater-than or less-than symbol (an inequality), such as the last example, can be true with a range of different values in the blank space. As students complete these types of problems, they will become more fluent with expressions, number sentences, and the type of thinking that will be more useful for algebra in the future.

▶ Advance Preparation

Print the Centimeter Grid Paper. Cut two rectangles 3 rows by 5 columns from the paper. Keep the unused paper for use in the activity.

Materials to Gather

SUPPLIED

Multiplication and Division activity page

Using Letters for Missing Values activity page

Missing Values in Number Sentences activity page

blocks – B (15 of any color)

Centimeter Grid Paper (printout)

ALSO NEEDED

scissors, adult

LEARN Use Inverse Relationships

Students will use part-part-total charts and the inverse relationship of addition and subtraction to help them find missing numbers in number sentences. Provide paper and pencil for student calculations.

Objectives

- Determine a missing number in an equation or an inequality.

LEARN Multiplication and Division

Students will use arrays and the inverse relationship of multiplication and division to help them find missing numbers in number sentences. Remind students that an array is an arrangement of objects in rows and columns. Also remind them that rows are horizontal—they go across from left to right—and columns are vertical, or up-and-down.

Gather the blocks, scissors, and rectangles you prepared from the Centimeter Grid Paper printout. Set the rectangles aside until later in the activity. View or print the Multiplication and Division activity page. Students should copy the problems from the Activity Book into their Math Notebook as necessary and solve them there.

1. Tell students that expressions can include any operation. They have already worked with addition and subtraction expressions; now they will work with multiplication and division expressions.

2. Discuss the Worked Examples with students. Go over the multiplication problems. Explain that multiplication involves equal groups and that an array is one way to arrange objects so that each row shows an equal group.

3. Have students look at Problem 1 on the activity page. Ask students to use their B blocks to show 3 groups of 5 circles as illustrated on the activity page. Tell students that when there are 3 groups of 5, they say "3 times 5" and write 3×5. Point to 3×5 on the activity page.

4. Tell students that they can use what they know about multiplication to solve number sentences. Work through each number sentence in Problem 1, relating back to the array as necessary. Then ask students how each expression is alike. The value of each expression is 15.

5. Guide students through the number sentences in Problem 2. Have students see how each previous number sentence helps them complete the next number sentence. Have them compare the values of each expression and see that again, they all have a value of 15. Have students note the different ways 15 is shown.

6. Have students complete the number sentences in Problems 3 and 4. As students complete the number sentences in each problem, have them identify the value of each expression. The value of each expression in Problem 3 is 40 and the value of each expression in Problem 4 is 16

7. Point out the grid in Problem 5. Remind students that they have seen multiplication as combining equal groups, such as 3 groups of 5 equals 15. Display one of the prepared rectangle grids to show 3 rows of 5 as on the activity page.

Objectives

- Determine a missing number in an equation or an inequality.

Tips

Allow students to use B blocks or grid paper to make arrays or grids.

8. Explain that the grid can also show that 5 groups of 3 equals 15. Turn the rectangle so that it shows 5 rows of 3.

9. Explain that division is the opposite of multiplication. It undoes multiplication; it is the inverse operation of multiplication. Tell students that division is separating a total amount into equal groups. Write 15 divided by 3 equals 5. Show students one of the rectangles you prepared. Cut the rows of the rectangle into 3 separate strips of 5 squares to show division. Point out that the total, 15, is separated into 3 equal groups and there are 5 squares in each group.

10. Display the other prepared rectangle grid. Explain that the grid can also show 15 divided by 5 equals 3. Cut the rows of this rectangle into 5 separate strips of 3 squares. Point out that the total, 15, is separated into 5 equal groups and there are 3 squares in each group. Use the cut-up rectangles as a guide to help students complete the number sentences in Problem 5.

11. Point to Problem 6, and have students complete the first sentence below the grid. Emphasize that when students need to solve a division problem, they can think of the related multiplication problem. Point to $20 \div 5 = \square$. Guide students to think: How many groups of 5 make 20? 4 groups of 5 equals 20, or $4 \times 5 = 20$, and therefore $20 \div 5 = 4$

12. Guide students to complete the other number sentences in Problem 6, using the grid and the related multiplication facts. Look back at the Worked Examples. Direct students' attention to the division problems and see if they can explain how the grid in Worked Examples Problem 2 can help solve the division number sentences.

13. Have students complete the remaining problems. Guide them to find the value of the complete expression to determine the value of the missing number. Remind them to use multiplication to find the missing number in the division expressions.

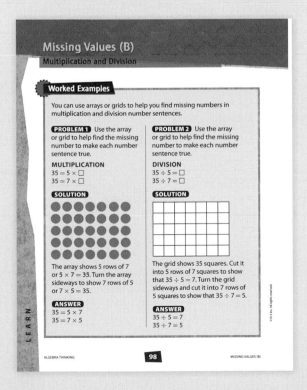

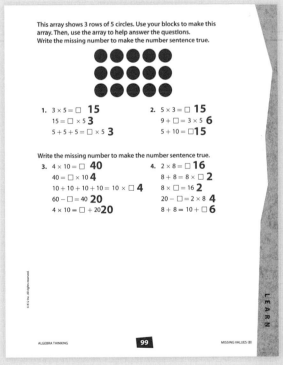

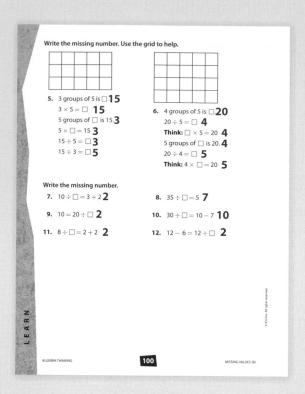

Write the missing number. Use the grid to help.

5. 3 groups of 5 is ☐ **15**
3 × 5 = ☐ **15**
5 groups of ☐ is 15. **3**
5 × ☐ = 15 **3**
15 ÷ 5 = ☐ **3**
15 ÷ 3 = ☐ **5**

6. 4 groups of 5 is ☐ **20**
20 ÷ 5 = ☐ **4**
Think: ☐ × 5 = 20 **4**
5 groups of ☐ is 20. **4**
20 ÷ 4 = ☐ **5**
Think: 4 × ☐ = 20 **5**

Write the missing number.

7. 10 ÷ ☐ = 3 + 2 **2**

8. 35 ÷ ☐ = 5 **7**

9. 10 = 20 ÷ ☐ **2**

10. 30 ÷ ☐ = 10 − 7 **10**

11. 8 ÷ ☐ = 2 + 2 **2**

12. 12 − 6 = 12 ÷ ☐ **2**

ONLINE

LEARN Use Letters for Missing Values

15 min

Objectives

- Determine a missing number in an equation or an inequality.

Students will complete addition and subtraction equations to show what is happening in a story problem using letters to show missing values.

View or print the Use Letters for Missing Values activity page. Students should copy the problems from the Activity Book into their math notebook as necessary and solve them there.

1. Read the Worked Examples Problem 1 with students. Review with students that they are completing a subtraction equation in which the difference is represented by the letter y. Explain that any letter could be used to show the missing value. Encourage students to simplify the equation by solving for y. **72**

2. Read the Worked Examples Problem 2 with students. Point out that in this example they are completing an addition equation in which one of the addends is represented by the letter b. Encourage students to simplify the equation by solving for b using inverse operations. $175 - 50 = 125$; $125 + 50 = 175$

3. Have students complete Problems 1–4 on their own. Point out that they are completing each of the problems using the information in the story problem. To extend the activity, have students find the value of the missing value.

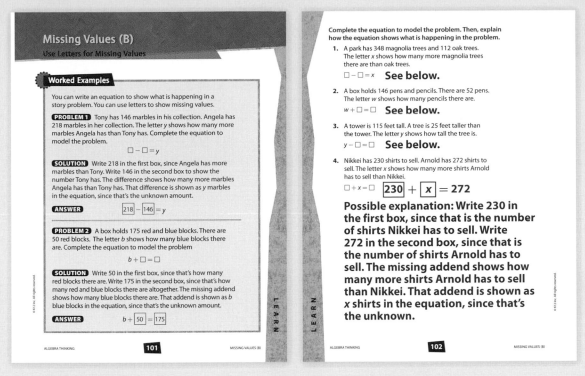

Missing Values (B)
Use Letters for Missing Values

Worked Examples

You can write an equation to show what is happening in a story problem. You can use letters to show missing values.

PROBLEM 1 Tony has 146 marbles in his collection. Angela has 218 marbles in her collection. The letter y shows how many more marbles Angela has than Tony has. Complete the equation to model the problem.

$$\square - \square = y$$

SOLUTION Write 218 in the first box, since Angela has more marbles than Tony. Write 146 in the second box to show the number Tony has. The difference shows how many more marbles Angela has than Tony has. That difference is shown as y marbles in the equation, since that's the unknown amount.

ANSWER $\boxed{218} - \boxed{146} = y$

PROBLEM 2 A box holds 175 red and blue blocks. There are 50 red blocks. The letter b shows how many blue blocks there are. Complete the equation to model the problem

$$b + \square = \square$$

SOLUTION Write 50 in the first box, since that's how many red blocks there are. Write 175 in the second box, since that's how many red and blue blocks there are altogether. The missing addend shows how many blue blocks there are. That addend is shown as b blue blocks in the equation, since that's the unknown amount.

ANSWER $b + \boxed{50} = \boxed{175}$

Complete the equation to model the problem. Then, explain how the equation shows what is happening in the problem.

1. A park has 348 magnolia trees and 112 oak trees. The letter x shows how many more magnolia trees there are than oak trees.

   $\square - \square = x$　**See below.**

2. A box holds 146 pens and pencils. There are 52 pens. The letter w shows how many pencils there are.

   $w + \square = \square$　**See below.**

3. A tower is 115 feet tall. A tree is 25 feet taller than the tower. The letter y shows how tall the tree is.

   $y - \square = \square$　**See below.**

4. Nikkei has 230 shirts to sell. Arnold has 272 shirts to sell. The letter x shows how many more shirts Arnold has to sell than Nikkei.

   $\square + x = \square$　$\boxed{230} + \boxed{x} = 272$

   Possible explanation: Write 230 in the first box, since that is the number of shirts Nikkei has to sell. Write 272 in the second box, since that is the number of shirts Arnold has to sell. The missing addend shows how many more shirts Arnold has to sell than Nikkei. That addend is shown as x shirts in the equation, since that's the unknown.

Additonal Answers

1. $348 - 112 = x$; **Possible explanation:** Write 348 in the first box, since there are more magnolia trees than oak trees. Write 112 in the second box to show the number of oak trees. The difference shows how many more magnolia trees there are than oak trees. That difference is shown as x magnolia trees in the equation, since that's the unknown.

2. $w + 52 = 146$; **Possible explanation:** Write 52 in the first box, since that is the number of pens. Write 146 in the second box, since that is the number of pens and pencils altogether. The missing addend shows how many pencils there are. That addend is shown as w pencils in the equation, since that's the unknown.

3. $y - 115 = 25$; **Possible explanation:** Write 115 in the first box, since that is how tall the tower is. Write 25 in the second box to show how much taller the tree is than the tower. The height of the tree is shown as y in the equation, since that's the unknown.

TRY IT Missing Values in Number Sentences

Objectives

- Determine a missing number in an equation or an inequality.

Students will practice using everything they know about operations and expressions to determine the missing value in a number sentence. In problems such as $? \times 3 = 10 - 4$, remind students to find the value of the expression, $10 - 4$, first. When students cannot do a problem in their head, they should be encouraged to use everything they know about the operations. They may make a part-part-total chart for addition and subtraction, make arrays or use a grid for multiplication or division, and use inverse relationships (or opposite operations) to help solve problems with any of the four operations.

View or print the Missing Values in Number Sentences activity page and read the directions with students. They should copy the problems from the Activity Book into their Math Notebook as necessary and solve them there.

Tips

Remind students that addition and subtraction are inverse, or opposite, operations, as are multiplication and division. They can use inverse operations to find missing values in expressions.

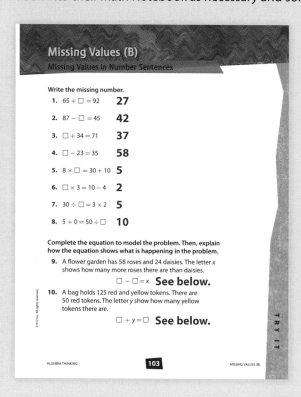

Missing Values (B)
Missing Values in Number Sentences

Write the missing number.

1. $65 + \square = 92$ **27**
2. $87 - \square = 45$ **42**
3. $\square + 34 = 71$ **37**
4. $\square - 23 = 35$ **58**
5. $8 \times \square = 30 + 10$ **5**
6. $\square \times 3 = 10 - 4$ **2**
7. $30 \div \square = 3 \times 2$ **5**
8. $5 + 0 = 50 \div \square$ **10**

Complete the equation to model the problem. Then, explain how the equation shows what is happening in the problem.

9. A flower garden has 58 roses and 24 daisies. The letter x shows how many more roses there are than daisies.

$\square - \square = x$ **See below.**

10. A bag holds 125 red and yellow tokens. There are 50 red tokens. The letter y show how many yellow tokens there are.

$\square + y = \square$ **See below.**

ALGEBRA THINKING   103   MISSING VALUES (B)

Additonal Answers

9. $58 - 24 = x$; **Possible explanation:** Write 58 in the first box, since there are more roses than daisies. Write 24 in the second box to show the number of daisies. The difference shows how many more roses there are than daisies. That difference is shown as x daisies in the equation, since that's the unknown.

10. $50 + y = 125$; **Possible explanation:** Write 50 in the first box, since that is the number of red tokens. Write 125 in the second box, since that is the number of red and yellow tokens in all. The missing addend shows how many yellow tokens there are. That addend is shown as y yellow tokens in the equation, since that's the unknown.

Missing Values (C)

▶ Lesson Objectives

Determine a missing number in an equation or an inequality.

▶ Prerequisite Skills

- Write and solve addition or subtraction number sentences to represent problem-solving situations with sums and minuends up through 1,000.
- Use an equation to represent a relationship between quantities.
- Use an inequality to represent a relationship between quantities.

▶ Content Background

Students will continue to use their understanding of operation symbols $(+, -, \times, \div)$, relation symbols $(<, >, =)$, and inverse operations to find a missing value that will make a number sentence true. Students will see problems such as the following:

- $30 = 25 + \square$
- $10 + 20 = 3 \times \square$
- $17 > 9 + \square$

Students will learn that number sentences with an equals symbol and one missing value, such as the first two examples, have only one correct answer. They will learn that a number sentence with a greater-than or less-than symbol (an inequality), such as the last example, can be true with a range of different values in the blank space. As students complete these types of problems, they will become more fluent with expressions, number sentences, and the type of thinking that will be more useful for algebra in the future.

When students are asked to simplify, they are being asked to find a value that is equal to another value but more simple to understand. For example, to simplify 2×5, they would write 10.

Materials to Gather

SUPPLIED
Compare to Find Missing Values activity page
Simplify and Solve activity page

LEARN Add or Subtract and Compare

Students will decide which of three answer choices makes a number sentence true. In some of the problems, they will simplify by adding or subtracting to find the value of an expression. Then they will compare the expressions on each side of the comparison symbol. Guide students to see that it is easiest to find the answer that makes the expressions equal and then decide how to make one expression greater than or less than the other. Provide paper and pencil for students calculations.

Objectives

- Determine a missing number in an equation or an inequality.

LEARN Compare to Find Missing Values

Students will determine the missing number in number sentences in which they have to compare the two sides of the number sentence.

View or print the Compare to Find Missing Values activity page. Students should copy the problems from the Activity Book into their Math Notebook as necessary and solve them there.

1. Tell students that they will learn how to find a missing number in a number sentence when they have to compare the two sides of the number sentence.

2. Have students read aloud the number sentence in the Worked Examples: $2 \times 5 < 5 + ?$

   Ask: What is the expression on the left? 2×5

   Ask: What is the expression on the right? $5 + ?$

   Ask: What comparison symbol separates the two expressions? $<$; less-than symbol

3. Have students read the first two lines of the solution.

   Ask: What is the small, raised 10? It is the value of 5×2.

   Ask: Which expression is the unknown expression, or the one that you don't know the value of? $5 + ?$; the expression on the right

4. Have students read the rest of the solution.

   Ask: Why does the 6 make this number sentence true? The 6 added to the 5 equals 11. We already simplified 2×5 to get 10. The number sentence now says 10 is less than 11, which is true.

5. Have students read the answer.

   Ask: Why can the answer be any number that is greater than 6? As long as 10 is less than the value of the expression on the right side, the number sentence is correct. When number sentences have a less-than or a greater-than symbol, there can be more than one correct answer.

6. Guide students through each problem, helping them simplify expressions. They should write answers for the Think statements when provided. Encourage students to find the number that would make the expressions equal, and then decide if the missing number should be greater or less.

Objectives

- Determine a missing number in an equation or an inequality.

Tips

Have students place a clear plastic sheet over the activity page and use a dry-erase marker to write the missing numbers.

Remind students that some exercises have more than one correct answer.

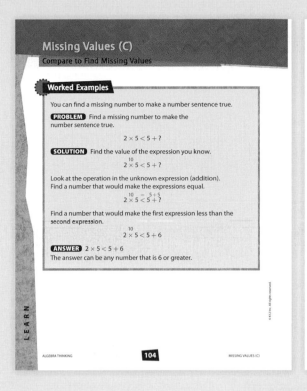

Missing Values (C)
Compare to Find Missing Values

Worked Examples

You can find a missing number to make a number sentence true.

PROBLEM Find a missing number to make the number sentence true.

$$2 \times 5 < 5 + ?$$

SOLUTION Find the value of the expression you know.

$$\overset{10}{2 \times 5} < 5 + ?$$

Look at the operation in the unknown expression (addition). Find a number that would make the expressions equal.

$$\overset{10}{2 \times 5} = \overset{5+5}{5 + ?}$$

Find a number that would make the first expression less than the second expression.

$$\overset{10}{2 \times 5} < 5 + 6$$

ANSWER $2 \times 5 < 5 + 6$
The answer can be any number that is 6 or greater.

ALGEBRA THINKING   **104**   MISSING VALUES (C)

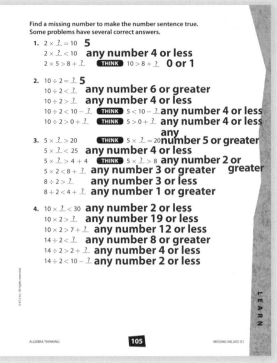

Find a missing number to make the number sentence true.
Some problems have several correct answers.

1. $2 \times ? = 10$ **5**
   $2 \times ? < 10$ **any number 4 or less**
   $2 \times 5 > 8 + ?$ **THINK** $10 > 8 + ?$ **0 or 1**

2. $10 \div 2 = ?$ **5**
   $10 \div 2 < ?$ **any number 6 or greater**
   $10 \div 2 > ?$ **any number 4 or less**
   $10 \div 2 < 10 - ?$ **THINK** $5 < 10 - ?$ **any number 4 or less**
   $10 \div 2 > 0 + ?$ **THINK** $5 > 0 + ?$ **any number 4 or less**

3. $5 \times ? > 20$ **THINK** $5 \times ? = 20$ **any number 5 or greater**
   $5 \times ? < 25$ **any number 4 or less**
   $5 \times ? > 4 + 4$ **THINK** $5 \times ? > 8$ **any number 2 or greater**
   $5 \times 2 < 8 + ?$ **any number 3 or greater**
   $8 \div 2 > ?$ **any number 3 or less**
   $8 \div 2 < 4 + ?$ **any number 1 or greater**

4. $10 \times ? < 30$ **any number 2 or less**
   $10 \times 2 > ?$ **any number 19 or less**
   $10 \times 2 > 7 + ?$ **any number 12 or less**
   $14 \div 2 < ?$ **any number 8 or greater**
   $14 \div 2 > 2 + ?$ **any number 4 or less**
   $14 \div 2 < 10 - ?$ **any number 2 or less**

ALGEBRA THINKING   **105**   MISSING VALUES (C)

OFFLINE

15 min

TRY IT Simplify and Solve

Objectives

- Determine a missing number in an equation or an inequality.

Students will practice finding missing values in number sentences. When number sentences with missing values have a greater-than or less-than symbol, there can be more than one correct answer. Remind students that they have to find only one number that makes the number sentence true. View or print the Simplify and Solve activity page and read the directions with students.

Students should copy the problems from the Activity Book into their Math Notebook as necessary and solve them there.

Tips   Remind students to look for the number that makes the expressions equal and then find a number that makes the unknown expression either greater or less, whichever is correct for solving the problem.

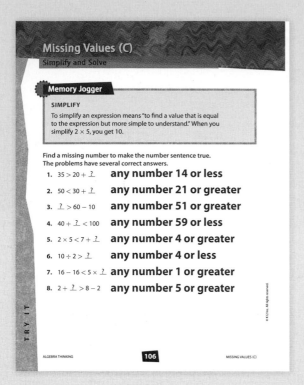

Missing Values (C)
Simplify and Solve

Memory Jogger

SIMPLIFY

To simplify an expression means "to find a value that is equal to the expression but more simple to understand." When you simplify 2 × 5, you get 10.

Find a missing number to make the number sentence true.
The problems have several correct answers.

1. 35 > 20 + ?   **any number 14 or less**
2. 50 < 30 + ?   **any number 21 or greater**
3. ? > 60 − 10   **any number 51 or greater**
4. 40 + ? < 100   **any number 59 or less**
5. 2 × 5 < 7 + ?   **any number 4 or greater**
6. 10 ÷ 2 > ?   **any number 4 or less**
7. 16 − 16 < 5 × ?   **any number 1 or greater**
8. 2 + ? > 8 − 2   **any number 5 or greater**

TRY IT

CHECKPOINT

ONLINE 10 min

Students will complete an online Checkpoint. If necessary, read the directions, problems, and answer choices to students and help them with keyboard or mouse operations.

Objectives

- Determine a missing number in an equation or an inequality.

Number Patterns

Lesson Overview

GET READY What's the Pattern?	5 minutes	**OFFLINE**
LEARN What Comes Next?	10 minutes	**OFFLINE**
LEARN Find the Rule	10 minutes	**OFFLINE**
LEARN Look for Multiplication Patterns	10 minutes	**OFFLINE**
TRY IT Describe and Extend	15 minutes	**OFFLINE**
CHECKPOINT	10 minutes	**ONLINE**

▶ ## Lesson Objectives

- Extend a linear pattern, such as stating what number comes next in a series.
- Recognize and describe a linear pattern, such as counting by 5s or multiplying 5 times a number to reach 100, by its rule.
- Identify patterns in addition or multiplication facts.

▶ ## Prerequisite Skills

- Describe linear patterns, such as 3, 6, 9, using wheels on 1 tricycle, 2 tricycles, 3 tricycles as an example.
- Determine a next term and extend a linear pattern, such as 3, 6, 9, … as the wheels on 1 tricycle, 2 tricycles, 3 tricycles, and extending it to 12 wheels on 4 tricycles as an example.

Materials to Gather

SUPPLIED

Find the Rule activity page

Look for Multiplication Patterns activity page

Describe and Extend activity page

▶ ## Content Background

Students will describe and extend linear patterns.

A linear pattern is a number pattern in which each successive number increases or decreases by the same value. A rule describes a linear pattern. You can use a rule to extend a pattern. For example, if the rule is "add 5," the numbers increase by 5. To find the next number, add 5 to the last number shown.

- **Linear pattern:** 5, 10, 15, 20
- **Rule:** add 5
- **Next number:** 25 (20 + 5)

Skip counting creates a linear pattern. For example, skip counting by 2s creates the linear pattern 2, 4, 6, 8, …. The rule for this pattern is "add 2."

Students will look for odd and even patterns in products when multiplying two odd factors, two even factors, and one odd and one even factor. For example, when multiplying two odd factors, the product is always an odd number: $3 \times 5 = 15$. When multiplying two even factors, the product is always an even number: $4 \times 6 = 24$. When multiplying odd and even factors, the product is always even: $3 \times 6 = 18$.

OFFLINE
5 min

Objectives

Students will identify a pattern and find the next number in a sequence. They will see an example of how patterns can represent things in everyday situations. Have students record patterns and rules in their Math Notebook.

1. Tell students you are going to look at number patterns. Start counting by 2s, saying 2, 4, 6, and ask student to continue the pattern until 20. 8, 10, 12, 14, 16, 18, 20

2. **Ask:** Can you say a rule that tells how to get the next number in the pattern? The rule is "add 2."

3. Count by 2s, saying 74, 76, 78. Have students continue the pattern for a few more numbers. Ask for the rule for getting the next number. 80, 82, 84; The rule is "add 2."

4. Count by 2s, saying 83, 85, 87. Have students continue the pattern and say the rule. 89, 91, 93; The rule is "add 2."

   Say: Patterns describe things that we see every day. Note that one hand has 5 fingers (write 5), two hands have 10 fingers (write 10), and so on.

   Have students write 5, 10, _?_, _?_, _?_ in their Math Notebook. Have students continue the pattern and say the rule. Notice that each time we add a hand we add 5 more fingers. The rule is "add 5."

5. Have students write answers for the following questions:

   Ask: Here's a pattern that can show the number of wheels on tricycles. If I have zero tricycles, how many wheels do I have? I have zero wheels. Students write 0.

   Ask: If I have one tricycle, how many wheels do I have? Students write 3.

   Ask: If I have one more tricycle, how many wheels do I have? Students write 6.

   Have students continue the pattern and say the rule. 9, 12, 15; The rule is "add 3."

Objectives

- Describe linear patterns, such as 3, 6, 9, using wheels on 1 tricycle, 2 tricycles, 3 tricycles as an example.

- Determine a next term and extend a linear pattern, such as 3, 6, 9, … as the wheels on 1 tricycle, 2 tricycles, 3 tricycles, and extending it to 12 wheels on 4 tricycles as an example.

OFFLINE
10 min

LEARN What Comes Next?

Students will fill in missing numbers in patterns and state the rule for the pattern. They will then use what they know about patterns to fill in missing numbers in charts. Emphasize that charts can be used to organize information.

1. Explain to students that they can use rules to find the next number in many patterns. Write the following pattern, showing the missing numbers as blanks. Have students write the missing numbers and say the rule. If students have difficulty, have them look at the 39 and see how much is added to get to 43.

   - 31, _?_, 39, 43, _?_, 51. **Rule:** plus 4; **Answer:** 31, 35, 39, 43, 47, 51

2. Write these patterns and have students fill in the missing numbers and say the rule. If students have difficulty, remind them that rules can involve subtraction as well as addition.

   - 100, 90, _?_, _?_, 60, _?_ **Rule:** subtract 10; **Answer:** 100, 90, 80, 70, 60, 50

   - _?_, 94, 90, _?_, 82, _?_, _?_ **Rule:** subtract 4; **Answer:** 98, 94, 90, 86, 82, 78, 74

Objectives

- Extend a linear pattern, such as stating what number comes next in a series.

3. For further practice, give students a starting number and a rule and have them create number patterns. For example, give the starting number 30 and the rule "subtract 5." Students should write the number pattern 30, 25, 20, 15, 10, 5, 0. Vary the starting number and the rule. Challenge students with a rule that combines two operations such as "add 10, subtract 3." A number pattern with that type of rule might look like this: 0, 7, 14, 21, 28, ….

4. Explain to students that patterns can be helpful in counting things in everyday situations. Have students make the following charts and use what they know about patterns to fill in the missing numbers:

Ticket Prices	
Number of tickets	Price
1	$5
2	$10
3	$15
4	$20
5	$25
6	$30
7	$35
8	$40
9	$45

Seats	
Number of rows	Seats in each row
1	14
2	28
3	42
4	56
5	70

5. Ask students what rule they used to fill out the Ticket Prices chart. Some students will say they added 5 to the previous amount. Some students may notice that you can multiply the number of tickets in the left column by 5 to get the amount in the right column. Explain to students that there's an advantage to using the number in the left column to get the number in the right right. If they want to know how much 100 tickets would cost, they would simply multiply by 5 rather than adding 5 to the previous amount 100 times.

LEARN Find the Rule

Students will describe and extend number patterns. View or print the Find the Rule activity page and read the directions with students. They should copy the problems from the Activity Book into their Math Notebook as necessary and solve them there.

1. Discuss the Worked Examples with students. Ask them to read the first sentence and the problem.

    Ask: What is the pattern? 4, 8, 12, 16

    Ask: Why did Sarah see that pattern when she counted the legs of horses? Horses have 4 legs.

2. Have students read the solution and the answer.

    Ask: Why is "add 4" the answer? Each number is 4 more than the number just before it in the pattern.

3. Have students complete Problems 1–4.

4. Read the information in the Problem 5 chart. Have students copy the chart into their Math Notebook. Have them describe the pattern in their own words.
    1 nest, 2 eggs; 2 nests, 4 eggs; 3 nests, 6 eggs …

    Ask: What is the rule? double the number of nests, or multiply the number of nests by 2

    Say: That rule will help us know how many eggs would be in any number of nests without having to count eggs. Write the rule under the chart. multiply by 2

    Ask: How many eggs would there be in 20 nests? 40 eggs

5. Go through a similar explanation for Problem 6.

6. Have students solve Problem 7. They may draw a chart to help them.

Objectives

- Recognize and describe a linear pattern, such as counting by 5s or multiplying 5 times a number to reach 100, by its rule.

Tips

If you have a plastic sheet cover, you may want to place it over the activity page. Students can then use a dry-erase marker to write the rule for each chart.

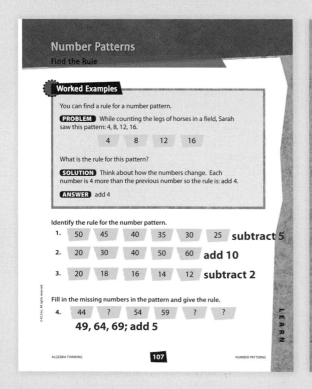

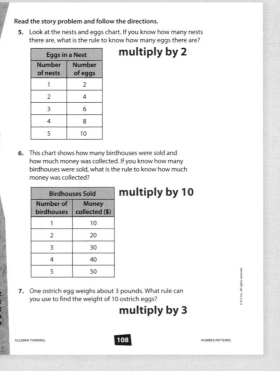

LEARN Look for Multiplication Patterns

Objectives

- Identify patterns in addition or multiplication facts.

Students will explore the pattern of odd and even numbers in products when two factors are both odd or both even or one factor is odd and the other one is even.

View or print the Look for Multiplication Patterns activity page. Students should copy the problems from the Activity Book into their Math Notebook as necessary and solve them there.

1. Read the Worked Examples with students. Review with students how to use the multiplication table. Point out that the factors are in the shaded squares along one side and along the bottom of the table. The product can be found where the row and column of the two chosen factors intersect. Have students practice using the multiplication table several times before working through the Worked Examples.

2. Have students complete Problems 1–4 on their own. When they finish, ask them these questions:

   - What pattern do you see in the product when you multiply two odd numbers? The product is odd.

   - What pattern do you see in the product when you multiply an even number and an odd number? The product is even.

3. Point out to students that they have learned three multiplication patterns. Suggest they copy the following rules in their Math Notebook for later reference:

$$\text{even} \times \text{even} = \text{even}$$

$$\text{odd} \times \text{odd} = \text{odd}$$

$$\text{even} \times \text{odd} = \text{even}$$

Number Patterns
Look for Multiplication Patterns

Worked Examples

10	0	10	20	30	40	50	60	70	80	90	100
9	0	9	18	27	36	45	54	63	72	81	90
8	0	8	16	24	32	40	48	56	64	72	80
7	0	7	14	21	28	35	42	49	56	63	70
6	0	6	12	18	24	30	36	42	48	54	60
5	0	5	10	15	20	25	30	35	40	45	50
4	0	4	8	12	16	20	24	28	32	36	40
3	0	3	6	9	12	15	18	21	24	27	30
2	0	2	4	6	8	10	12	14	16	18	20
1	0	1	2	3	4	5	6	7	8	9	10
0	0	0	0	0	0	0	0	0	0	0	0
	0	1	2	3	4	5	6	7	8	9	10

PROBLEM Choose 2 even factors and multiply them. Do you get an even number or an odd number?

Is the product of 2 even numbers even or odd? Use the multiplication table to help you answer this question.

SOLUTION

❶ Pick 2 and 6. When you multiply these numbers you get 12, which is an even number. Try 4 and 8. The product is 32, which is even. Try 10 and 6. The product is 60, which is even.

❷ Look at the multiplication table. Every time you multiply 2 even numbers, you get another even number.

ALGEBRA THINKING   109   NUMBER PATTERNS

Use the multiplication table to answer. Choose 2 odd factors and multiply them.

1. Do you get an even number or an odd number?
odd
2. Is the product of 2 odd numbers even or odd? Use more pairs of numbers from the multiplication table to help you answer this question.
odd

Use the multiplication table to answer. Choose an even factor and an odd factor, and then multiply them.

3. Do you get an even number or an odd number?
even
4. What kind of number do you get when you multiply an even number and an odd number? Use more pairs of factors from the multiplication table to help you answer this question.
even

ALGEBRA THINKING   110   NUMBER PATTERNS

TRY IT Describe and Extend

Students will practice extending patterns. View or print the Describe and Extend activity page and read the directions with students.

Students should copy the problems from the Activity Book into their Math Notebook as necessary and solve them there.

- Extend a linear pattern, such as stating what number comes next in a series.
- Recognize and describe a linear pattern, such as counting by 5s or multiplying 5 times a number to reach 100, by its rule.
- Identify patterns in addition or multiplication facts.

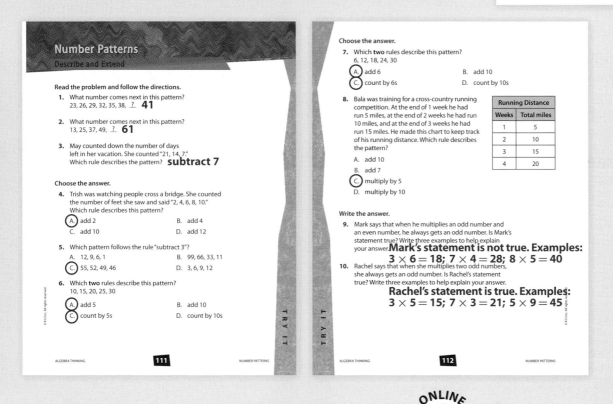

Number Patterns
Describe and Extend

Read the problem and follow the directions.

1. What number comes next in this pattern?
   23, 26, 29, 32, 35, 38, ? **41**

2. What number comes next in this pattern?
   13, 25, 37, 49, ? **61**

3. May counted down the number of days left in her vacation. She counted "21, 14, 7." Which rule describes the pattern? **subtract 7**

Choose the answer.

4. Trish was watching people cross a bridge. She counted the number of feet she saw and said "2, 4, 6, 8, 10." Which rule describes this pattern?
   (A.) add 2   B. add 4
   C. add 10   D. add 12

5. Which pattern follows the rule "subtract 3"?
   A. 12, 9, 6, 1   B. 99, 66, 33, 11
   (C.) 55, 52, 49, 46   D. 3, 6, 9, 12

6. Which **two** rules describe this pattern?
   10, 15, 20, 25, 30
   (A.) add 5   B. add 10
   (C.) count by 5s D. count by 10s

Choose the answer.

7. Which **two** rules describe this pattern?
   6, 12, 18, 24, 30
   (A.) add 6   B. add 10
   (C.) count by 6s D. count by 10s

8. Bala was training for a cross-country running competition. At the end of 1 week he had run 5 miles, at the end of 2 weeks he had run 10 miles, and at the end of 3 weeks he had run 15 miles. He made this chart to keep track of his running distance. Which rule describes the pattern?
   A. add 10
   B. add 7
   (C.) multiply by 5
   D. multiply by 10

Running Distance	
Weeks	Total miles
1	5
2	10
3	15
4	20

Write the answer.

9. Mark says that when he multiplies an odd number and an even number, he always gets an odd number. Is Mark's statement true? Write three examples to help explain your answer. **Mark's statement is not true. Examples: $3 \times 6 = 18$; $7 \times 4 = 28$; $8 \times 5 = 40$**

10. Rachel says that when she multiplies two odd numbers, she always gets an odd number. Is Rachel's statement true? Write three examples to help explain your answer. **Rachel's statement is true. Examples: $3 \times 5 = 15$; $7 \times 3 = 21$; $5 \times 9 = 45$**

ALGEBRA THINKING   111   NUMBER PATTERNS

ALGEBRA THINKING   112   NUMBER PATTERNS

CHECKPOINT

Students will complete an online Checkpoint. If necessary, read the directions, problems, and answer choices to students and help them with keyboard or mouse operations.

- Extend a linear pattern, such as stating what number comes next in a series.
- Recognize and describe a linear pattern, such as counting by 5s or multiplying 5 times a number to reach 100, by its rule.
- Identify patterns in addition or multiplication facts.

Story Problems and Patterns (A)

Lesson Overview

GET READY Number Patterns	10 minutes	**ONLINE**
LEARN Find the Pattern	15 minutes	**ONLINE**
LEARN Story Problems	15 minutes	**OFFLINE**
LEARN Look for Addition Patterns	10 minutes	**OFFLINE**
TRY IT Tables and Patterns	10 minutes	**OFFLINE**

▶ Lesson Objectives

- Solve a simple story problem that involves a function.
- Identify patterns in addition or multiplication facts.
- Identify odd and even numbers and describe their characteristics.

▶ Prerequisite Skills

- Solve problems involving simple number patterns.
- Extend a linear pattern, such as stating what number comes next in a series.
- Recognize and describe a linear pattern, such as counting by 5s or multiplying 5 times a number to reach 100, by its rule.

▶ Content Background

Students will use linear pattern rules to solve simple story problems.

A linear pattern is a number pattern in which each successive number increases or decreases by the same value. A rule describes a linear pattern.

Skip counting creates a linear pattern. For example, skip counting by 2s creates the linear pattern 2, 4, 6, 8, …. The rule for this pattern is "add 2."

▶ Advance Preparation

Print two copies of the Input-Output Tables.

Materials to Gather

SUPPLIED

Story Problems activity page

Look for Addition Patterns activity page

Tables and Patterns activity page

Input-Output Tables (printout)

GET READY Number Patterns

ONLINE 10min

Students will review different rules for creating and continuing numerical patterns. They will then use patterns to solve everyday problems.

Objectives

- Solve problems involving simple number patterns.
- Extend a linear pattern, such as stating what number comes next in a series.
- Recognize and describe a linear pattern, such as counting by 5s or multiplying 5 times a number to reach 100, by its rule.

LEARN Find the Pattern

Students will solve simple story problems that involve patterns. They will use a function machine. In this machine, a number goes in and is changed using a rule such as "add 5" or "multiply by 2." Then the machine sends the changed number out. Students can keep track of the numbers that go in and come out using a T chart, also called an input-output table. The input-output table has two columns: input and output. Students will use the patterns they see in the table to figure out the rule that is changing the numbers.

Objectives

• Solve a simple story problem that involves a function.

Tips

If students have difficulty with patterns, use input numbers that are sequential so students can see the pattern.

LEARN Story Problems

Students will fill in missing numbers for a given rule in an input-output table. They will also solve simple story problems by using an input-output table. They will identify and extend a pattern to solve the problems. Model for students how to organize the information from a story problem into an input-output table.

Gather the Input-Output Tables printout. Set the printout aside until later in the activity. View or print the Story Problems activity page. Students should copy the problems from the Activity Book into their Math Notebook as necessary and solve them there.

Objectives

• Solve a simple story problem that involves a function.

Tips

Provide counting objects or paper and pencil for students to complete calculations.

1. Explain to students that certain types of story problems work just like a function machine, in which a number goes in and the machine adds to it, multiplies it, or does other operations on it, and another number comes out. For these problems, it's helpful to use an input-output table.

2. Have students look at the Worked Examples. The table shows the number of crayons needed for different numbers of students. Since 1 student needs 5 crayons, they could imagine that 1 goes in and 5 comes out of a function machine. They see that 2 students need 10 crayons, so 2 goes into the machine and 10 comes out. Since 3 students need 15 crayons, they can say that if 3 goes into the machine, 15 comes out.

   Ask: Can you find the rule that says what the machine does to the number that goes in so that it becomes the number that comes out? The rule is "multiply by 5."

   Using this rule, students can figure out how many crayons they'll need for 10 students or 100 students without building the whole chart.

3. Emphasize that students can build the chart one step at a time by adding 5 crayons for each new student, or they can look at the chart and multiply the number of students by 5 to find out how many crayons are needed for any number of students.

4. Have students complete Problems 1–4 on their own. Give students the Input-Output Tables printout. They can use the printout to create the input-output table to solve Problem 4.

Number of students	Number of crayons
1	5
2	10
3	15
4	**20**
5	**25**
10	**50**
100	**500**

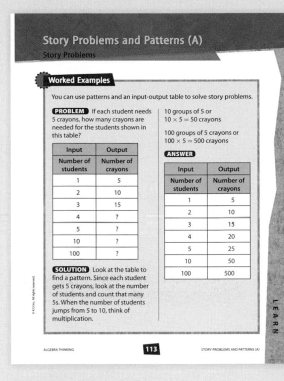

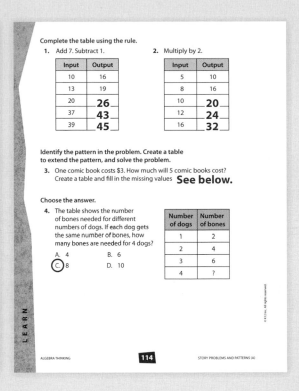

Additional Answers

3. $15

Number of comic books	Total price
1	$3
2	$6
3	$9
4	$12
5	$15

LEARN Look for Addition Patterns

OFFLINE **10** min

Objectives

- Identify odd and even numbers and describe their characteristics.

Students will explore the pattern of odd and even numbers in sums when two addends are both odd, both even, one odd and one even.

View or print the Look for Addition Patterns activity page. Students should copy the problems from the Activity Book into their Math Notebook as necessary and solve them there.

1. Read the Worked Examples problem with students. If necessary, review with students how to use the addition table. Point out that the addends are in the shaded squares along one side and bottom of the table. The sum can be found where the row and column of the two chosen addends intersect. Have students practice using the addition table several times before working through the Worked Examples problem.

2. Have students complete Problems 1–4 on their own. When they finish, ask students what pattern they see in the sum when they add two odd numbers. The sum is even. Ask them what pattern they see in the sum when they add an even number and an odd number. The sum is odd.

3. Point out to students that they have used an addition table to learn three addition patterns. Suggest they copy the following rules in their Math Notebook for later reference:

$$\text{even} + \text{even} = \text{even}$$

$$\text{odd} + \text{odd} = \text{even}$$

$$\text{even} + \text{odd} = \text{odd}$$

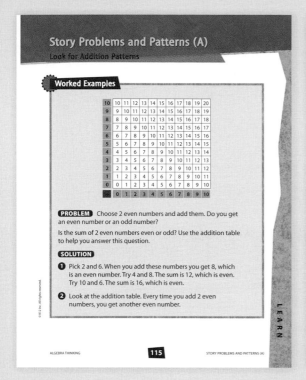

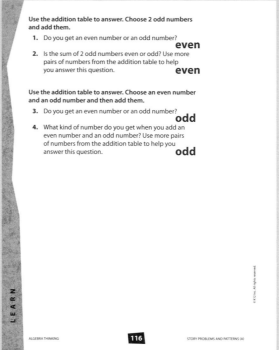

TRY IT Tables and Patterns

OFFLINE 10 min

Objectives

Students will practice solving story problems by identifying and extending patterns using an input-output table. Gather the Input-Output Tables printout. View or print the Tables and Patterns activity page and read the directions with students.

Students should copy the problems from the Activity Book into their Math Notebook as necessary and solve them there.

- Solve a simple story problem that involves a function.
- Identify patterns in addition or multiplication facts.

Tips   Have students create their tables on the Input-Output Tables printout. Also, have counting objects or paper and pencil available for students to complete their calculations.

Story Problems and Patterns (A)
Tables and Patterns

Read the problem and solve.

1. Complete the input-output table by using the rule "add 5, subtract 2."

Input	Output
32	35
34	37
36	**39**
38	**41**
40	**43**

2. Complete the input-output table by using the rule "subtract 5, add 3."

Input	Output
5	3
10	8
15	**13**
20	**18**
25	**23**

3. LaBella is making a sign showing the cost to ski at Big Ski Hill. She wants to charge $12 per hour.

Big Ski Hill Prices	
Hours	Total cost
1	$12
2	$24
3	**$36**
4	**$48**

4. Frank is making a sign for his ice rink showing the cost to skate. He wants to charge $8 an hour.

Ice-Skating Prices	
Hours	Total cost
1	$8
2	$16
3	**$24**
4	**$32**

T R Y   I T

Identify the pattern. Create a table to extend the pattern and solve.

5. It takes Anne 10 minutes to walk once around her block. She knows it will take 20 minutes to walk around the block 2 times and 30 minutes to walk around the block 3 times. How many minutes will it take Anne to walk around the block 5 times?   **See below.**

Write the answer.

6. Scott says that when he adds an odd number and an even number, he always gets an odd number. Is Scott correct? Write three examples to help explain your answer.
   See below.

7. Nichi says that when she adds two odd numbers, she always gets an odd number. Is Nichi correct? Write three examples to help explain your answer.
   See below.

8. Carmen says that when she adds two even numbers, she always gets an even number. Is Carmen correct? Write three examples to help explain your answer.
   See below.

T R Y   I T

Additional Answers

5. 50

Block	Minutes
1	10
2	20
3	30
4	40
5	50

6. Scott is correct. **Examples:** $3 + 6 = 9$; $8 + 7 = 15$; $5 + 8 = 13$

7. Nichi is not correct. **Examples:** $3 + 5 = 8$; $7 + 3 = 10$; $5 + 9 = 14$

8. Carmen is correct. **Examples:** $6 + 2 = 8$; $6 + 8 = 14$; $8 + 4 = 12$

Story Problems and Patterns (B)

Lesson Overview

GET READY Boat Games	5 minutes	**ONLINE**
LEARN Beach Math	15 minutes	**OFFLINE**
LEARN Look for Multiplication Patterns	15 minutes	**OFFLINE**
TRY IT Make a Chart	15 minutes	**OFFLINE**
CHECKPOINT	10 minutes	**ONLINE**

▶ Lesson Objectives

- Solve a simple story problem that involves a function.
- Identify patterns in addition or multiplication facts.

▶ Prerequisite Skills

- Solve problems involving simple number patterns.
- Extend a linear pattern, such as stating what number comes next in a series.
- Recognize and describe a linear pattern, such as counting by 5s or multiplying 5 times a number to reach 100, by its rule.

▶ Content Background

Students will continue to use linear pattern rules to solve simple story problems.
  A linear pattern is a number pattern in which each successive number increases or decreases by the same value. A rule describes a linear pattern.
  Skip counting creates a linear pattern. For example, skip counting by 2s creates the linear pattern 2, 4, 6, 8, …. The rule for this pattern is "add 2."

▶ Advance Preparation

Print the Input-Output Tables.

Materials to Gather

SUPPLIED

Beach Math activity page
Look for Multiplication Patterns activity page
Make a Chart activity page
Input-Output Tables (printout)

ONLINE
5 min

GET READY Boat Games

Students will review extending number patterns by counting on or repeatedly adding or subtracting a number. They will enter the number that will fill in the blank in the pattern. Students may repeat the game to try to improve their score.

Objectives

- Solve problems involving simple number patterns.
- Extend a linear pattern, such as stating what number comes next in a series.
- Recognize and describe a linear pattern, such as counting by 5s or multiplying 5 times a number to reach 100, by its rule.

LEARN Beach Math

Students will use patterns counting on by a number, repeatedly adding a number, or multiplying by a number to solve problems. Gather the Input-Output Tables printout. View or print the Beach Math activity page. Students should copy the problems from the Activity Book into their Math Notebook as necessary and solve them there.

1. Discuss the Worked Examples with students. Explain to students that 1 skateboard has 4 wheels.

2. Explain that to find the number of wheels on 2 skateboards, students can add 4 plus 4 to get 8.

3. Work together to go over the table. Show students that one way to create the table is by repeatedly adding 4 to find how many wheels are needed for 10 skateboards.

4. Ask students if they can identify another pattern in the number of wheels. Students may notice that the number of wheels increases by 4 each time and therefore they can also count by 4s to extend the pattern and find the answer. Point out that the number of skateboards times 4 equals the number of wheels.

5. Have students complete Problems 1–6 on their own. Ask them to describe the patterns they see in the input-output tables. Encourage them to describe the patterns in terms of counting by a number, repeatedly adding a number, or multiplying the input by a number.

6. Give students the Input-Output Tables printout. Students can use the printout to create the input-output tables to solve the rest of the story problems on the activity page.

Objectives

- Solve a simple story problem that involves a function.

Tips

Be sure students understand how to create and label the input-output tables on the Input-Output Tables printout.

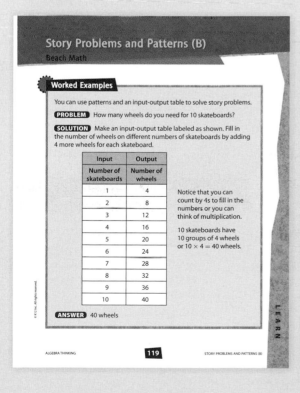

Story Problems and Patterns (B)
Beach Math

Worked Examples

You can use patterns and an input-output table to solve story problems.

PROBLEM How many wheels do you need for 10 skateboards?

SOLUTION Make an input-output table labeled as shown. Fill in the number of wheels on different numbers of skateboards by adding 4 more wheels for each skateboard.

Input	Output
Number of skateboards	Number of wheels
1	4
2	8
3	12
4	16
5	20
6	24
7	28
8	32
9	36
10	40

Notice that you can count by 4s to fill in the numbers or you can think of multiplication.

10 skateboards have 10 groups of 4 wheels or 10 × 4 = 40 wheels.

ANSWER 40 wheels

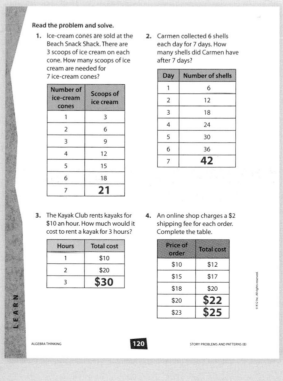

Read the problem and solve.

1. Ice-cream cones are sold at the Beach Snack Shack. There are 3 scoops of ice cream on each cone. How many scoops of ice cream are needed for 7 ice-cream cones?

Number of ice-cream cones	Scoops of ice cream
1	3
2	6
3	9
4	12
5	15
6	18
7	**21**

2. Carmen collected 6 shells each day for 7 days. How many shells did Carmen have after 7 days?

Day	Number of shells
1	6
2	12
3	18
4	24
5	30
6	36
7	**42**

3. The Kayak Club rents kayaks for $10 an hour. How much would it cost to rent a kayak for 3 hours?

Hours	Total cost
1	$10
2	$20
3	**$30**

4. An online shop charges a $2 shipping fee for each order. Complete the table.

Price of order	Total cost
$10	$12
$15	$17
$18	$20
$20	**$22**
$23	**$25**

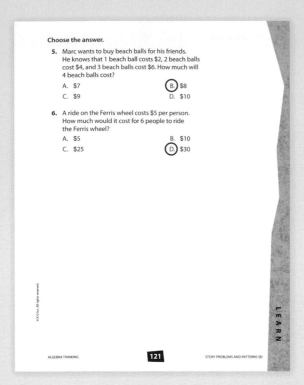

Choose the answer.

5. Marc wants to buy beach balls for his friends. He knows that 1 beach ball costs $2, 2 beach balls cost $4, and 3 beach balls cost $6. How much will 4 beach balls cost?

A. $7

B. $8

C. $9

D. $10

6. A ride on the Ferris wheel costs $5 per person. How much would it cost for 6 people to ride the Ferris wheel?

A. $5

B. $10

C. $25

D. $30

LEARN Look for Multiplication Patterns

OFFLINE 15 min

Objectives

- Identify patterns in addition or multiplication facts.

Students will explore number patterns using a multiplication table. They will describe the pattern they see when 2, 3, 4, or 5 are multiplied by any number.

View or print the Look for Multiplication Patterns activity page. Students should copy the problems from the Activity Book into their math notebook as necessary and solve them there.

1. Read the Worked Examples problem with students. Review with students how to use the multiplication table. Point out that the factors are in the shaded squares along one side and bottom of the table. The product can be found where the row and column of the two chosen factors intersect. Have students practice using the multiplication table several times before working through the Worked Examples problem.

2. Have students complete Problems 1–9 on their own. When they finish, ask students these questions:

   - What pattern do you see in the product when you multiply by 2?
     The product is even. (Students may also say that the product always ends in 0, 2, 4, 6, or 8.)

   - What pattern do you see in the product when you multiply by 5?
     The product is odd. (Students may also say that the product always ends in 0 or 5.)

   - What pattern do you see in the product when you multiply by 4?
     The product is even.

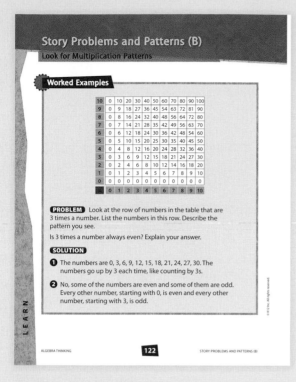

Worked Examples (page 122)

Story Problems and Patterns (B)
Look for Multiplication Patterns

10	0	10	20	30	40	50	60	70	80	90	100
9	0	9	18	27	36	45	54	63	72	81	90
8	0	8	16	24	32	40	48	56	64	72	80
7	0	7	14	21	28	35	42	49	56	63	70
6	0	6	12	18	24	30	36	42	48	54	60
5	0	5	10	15	20	25	30	35	40	45	50
4	0	4	8	12	16	20	24	28	32	36	40
3	0	3	6	9	12	15	18	21	24	27	30
2	0	2	4	6	8	10	12	14	16	18	20
1	0	1	2	3	4	5	6	7	8	9	10
0	0	0	0	0	0	0	0	0	0	0	0
	0	1	2	3	4	5	6	7	8	9	10

PROBLEM Look at the row of numbers in the table that are 3 times a number. List the numbers in this row. Describe the pattern you see.

Is 3 times a number always even? Explain your answer.

SOLUTION

❶ The numbers are 0, 3, 6, 9, 12, 15, 18, 21, 24, 27, 30. The numbers go up by 3 each time, like counting by 3s.

❷ No, some of the numbers are even and some of them are odd. Every other number, starting with 0, is even and every other number, starting with 3, is odd.

ALGEBRA THINKING   **122**   STORY PROBLEMS AND PATTERNS (B)

(page 123)

Use the multiplication table to answer. Look at the row of numbers in the table that are 2 times a number.

1. List the numbers in this row. Describe the pattern you see.
   See below.
2. Is 2 times a number even or odd? Explain your answer.
   See below.
3. Show that 2 times a number can always be written as the sum of 2 equal numbers. Give two examples.
   See below.

Use the multiplication table to answer. Look at the numbers in the table that are 5 times a number.

4. List the numbers in this row. Describe the pattern you see.
   See below.
5. Is 5 times a number always odd? Explain your answer.
   See below.

Use the multiplication table to answer. Look at the row of numbers in the table that are 4 times a number.

6. List the numbers in this row. Describe the pattern you see.
   See below.
7. Is 4 times a number even or odd? Explain your answer.
   See below.
8. Show that 4 times a number can always be written as the sum of 2 equal numbers. Give two examples.
   See below.
9. Why do you think that 4 times a number or 2 times a number can always be written as the sum of 2 equal numbers?

   Possible answer: Because 4 and 2 are even numbers. When one of two factors is even, the product is always even.

ALGEBRA THINKING   **123**   STORY PROBLEMS AND PATTERNS (B)

Additional Answers

1. 0, 2, 4, 6, 8, 10, 12, 14, 16, 18, 20; The pattern is "add 2."
2. even; **Possible explanation:** Every number, starting with 0, is even.
3. **Possible examples:** $2 \times 4 = 8$; $4 + 4 = 8$; $2 \times 7 = 14$; $7 + 7 = 14$
4. 0, 5, 10, 15, 20, 25, 30, 35, 40, 45, 50; The pattern is "add 5."
5. No, some numbers are even and some of them are odd. Every other number, starting with 0, is even and every other number, starting with 5, is odd.
6. 0, 4, 8, 12, 16, 20, 24, 28, 32, 36, 40; The pattern is "add 4."
7. even; **Possible explanation:** Every number, starting with 0, is even.
8. **Possible examples:** $4 \times 3 = 12$, $6 + 6 = 12$; $4 \times 6 = 24$, $12 + 12 = 24$

TRY IT   Make a Chart

OFFLINE 15 min

Students will solve story problems by completing input-output tables. View or print the Make a Chart activity page. Gather the Input-Output Tables printout Students can use the printout to create the tables to solve each story problem.

Tips   Be sure students understand how to set up and label the columns in the input-output tables.

Objectives

- Solve a simple story problem that involves a function.

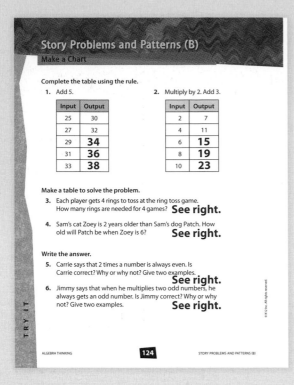

Story Problems and Patterns (B)
Make a Chart

Complete the table using the rule.

1. Add 5.

Input	Output
25	30
27	32
29	**34**
31	**36**
33	**38**

2. Multiply by 2. Add 3.

Input	Output
2	7
4	11
6	**15**
8	**19**
10	**23**

Make a table to solve the problem.

3. Each player gets 4 rings to toss at the ring toss game. How many rings are needed for 4 games? **See right.**

4. Sam's cat Zoey is 2 years older than Sam's dog Patch. How old will Patch be when Zoey is 6? **See right.**

Write the answer.

5. Carrie says that 2 times a number is always even. Is Carrie correct? Why or why not? Give two examples. **See right.**

6. Jimmy says that when he multiplies two odd numbers, he always gets an odd number. Is Jimmy correct? Why or why not? Give two examples. **See right.**

TRY IT

ALGEBRA THINKING   **124**   STORY PROBLEMS AND PATTERNS (B)

Additional Answers

3. 16 rings

Games	Number of rings
1	4
2	8
3	12
4	16

4. 4 years old

Zoey's age	Patch's age
2	0
3	1
4	2
5	3
6	4

5. Carrie is correct. The number 2 is an even number. When one of two factors is even, the product is even. **Possible examples:** $2 \times 6 = 12$; $2 \times 9 = 18$

6. Jimmy is correct. When two odd numbers are multiplied, the product is always odd. **Possible examples:** $3 \times 5 = 15$; $7 \times 9 = 63$.

ONLINE
10 min

CHECKPOINT

Objectives

Students will complete an online Checkpoint. If necessary, read the directions, problems, and answer choices to students and help them with keyboard or mouse operations.

- Solve a simple story problem that involves a function.

Core Focus
Use Letters for Unknown Values

Lesson Overview

GET READY Choose the Number Sentence	15 minutes	ONLINE
LEARN Letters for Unknown Values	20 minutes	ONLINE
TRY IT Solve Problems with Unknown Values	15 minutes	OFFLINE
CHECKPOINT	10 minutes	ONLINE

▶ Lesson Objectives

- Determine a missing number in an equation or an inequality.
- Use a variable to represent an unknown number in an equation.

▶ Prerequisite Skills

- Write and solve addition or subtraction number sentences to represent problem-solving situations with sums and minuends up through 1,000.
- Use an equation to represent a relationship between quantities.
- Use an inequality to represent a relationship between quantities.

▶ Content Background

Students will use their understanding of operation symbols ($+, -, \times, \div$), and inverse operations to find an unknown value that will make a number sentence true. Unknown values will be represented with letters rather than the customary question mark or box. Students will see and work with problems such as the following:

$$40 = x + 25$$
$$32 + 46 = y$$
$$w - 13 = 72$$

Students will learn that number sentences with an equals symbol and one unknown value, such as the examples above, have only one correct answer. As students complete these types of problems, they will become more fluent with expressions, number sentences, and the type of thinking that will be useful for algebra in the future.

When students are asked to simplify, they are being ask to find a value that is equal to another value but simpler to understand. For example, to simplify $24 + 12 = y$, they would write $36 = y$ or $y = 36$.

▶ Common Errors and Misconceptions

- Students might have a difficult time understanding that a letter can represent different values or that different letters can represent the same value. They commonly interpret a letter as representing a specific number. For example, students might think that $7w + 22 = 78$ and $7x + 22 = 78$ have different answers because they don't understand that w and x represent the same number.
- Students might not understand the use of letters for unknown values partly because there are limited examples in elementary grades. Students

see equations such as $53 = 5$ tens $+ \square$ ones in which the unknown has a specific value. They also see boxes and letters that represent a specific unknown, such as $7 + \square = 10$ or $7 + x = 10$. Students rarely see cases in which letters represent general unknown values or patterns.

- Students might not understand that letters in algebraic expressions and equations represent different values.

- Students might see equations such as $5 + a = 12$ as merely abstract symbols with little or no connection to everyday situations.

GET READY Choose the Number Sentence

ONLINE 15min

Students will review the use of number sentences to represent a relationship between quantities. First they will decide which number sentence can be used to solve a story problem. Then they will decide which number sentence compares two expressions. Finally students will determine which operations to use to solve several story problems.

Objectives

- Write and solve addition or subtraction number sentences to represent problem-solving situations with sums and minuends up through 1,000.
- Use an equation to represent a relationship between quantities.
- Use an inequality to represent a relationship between quantities

LEARN Letters for Unknown Values

ONLINE 20min

Students will learn how to solve real-world story problems involving number sentences with a single unknown value represented by a letter. The letters represent different unknown values, such as an addend, a minuend, a sum, or a difference. After reviewing how to solve for an unknown value, students will then select an equation that can be used to represent a given situation and determine the unknown value in the equation.

Objectives

- Determine a missing number in an equation or an inequality.

TRY IT Solve Problems with Unknown Values

OFFLINE 15min

Students will solve story problems with unknown values by modeling and solving equations that use a letter to represent the unknown value. Students will also explain how the equation shows what is happening in the problem and then simplify and solve the equation.

View or print the Solve Problems with Unknown Values activity page and read the directions with students.

Students should copy the problems from the Activity Book into their Math Notebook as necessary and solve them there.

Objectives

- Determine a missing number in an equation or an inequality.
- Use a variable to represent an unknown number in an equation.

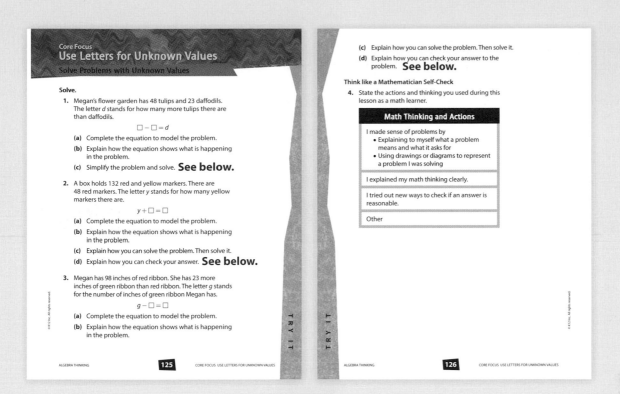

Answers

1. (a) $48 - 23 = d$

(b) The number 48 goes in the first box since there are more tulips than daffodils. The number 23 goes in the second box to show the number of daffodils. The difference shows how many more tulips there are. That difference is shown as d in the equation since that is the unknown value.

(c) $48 - 23 = 25; d = 25$; There are 25 more tulips than daffodils.

2. (a) $y + 48 = 132$

(b) The number 48 goes in the first box since that is the number of red markers. The number 132 goes in the second box since that is the total number of red and yellow markers. The missing addend y stands for how many yellow markers there are.

(c) I can use inverse operations to solve the problem: $132 - 48 = 84$; $y = 84$; There are 84 yellow markers.

(d) I can check the problem by putting the value for y in the equation. If the equation is true, my answer is correct. $84 + 48 = 132$; My answer is correct.

3. (a) $g - 23 = 98$ or $g - 98 = 23$

(b) Sample explanation: The number 23 goes in the first box since that is how much longer the green ribbon is. The number 98 goes in the second box since that is how long the red ribbon is. The missing value g stands for how long the green ribbon is.

(c) I can use inverse operations to solve the problem: $23 + 98 = 121$; $g = 121$; The green ribbon is 121 inches long.

(d) I can check the problem by putting the value for g in the equation. If the equation is true, my answer is correct. $121 - 23 = 98$; My answer is correct.

Objectives

Students will complete an online Checkpoint. If necessary, read the directions, problems, and answer choices to students and help them with keyboard or mouse operations.

- Determine a missing number in an equation or an inequality.
- Use a variable to represent an unknown number in an equation.

Unit Review

Lesson Overview

UNIT REVIEW Look Back	10 minutes	ONLINE
UNIT REVIEW Checkpoint Practice	50 minutes	ONLINE
⤷ UNIT REVIEW Prepare for the Checkpoint		

▶ Lesson Objectives

- Use a mathematical expression to represent a relationship between quantities.
- Use an equation to represent a relationship between quantities.
- Use an inequality to represent a relationship between quantities.
- Select the appropriate symbol to show an operation or a relationship that makes a number sentence true.
- Determine a missing number in an equation or an inequality.
- Extend a linear pattern, such as stating what number comes next in a series.
- Recognize and describe a linear pattern, such as counting by 5s or multiplying 5 times a number to reach 100, by its rule.
- Identify patterns in addition or multiplication facts.
- Solve a simple story problem that involves a function.
- Identify odd and even numbers and describe their characteristics.
- Use a variable to represent an unknown number in an equation.

Materials to Gather

There are no materials to gather for this lesson.

▶ Advance Preparation

In this lesson, students will have an opportunity to review previous activities in the Algebra Thinking unit. Look at the suggested activities in Unit Review: Prepare for the Checkpoint online and gather any needed materials.

UNIT REVIEW Look Back ONLINE 10min

Objectives

- Review unit objectives.

Students will review key concepts from the unit to prepare for the Unit Checkpoint.

UNIT REVIEW Checkpoint Practice ONLINE 50min

Objectives

- Review unit objectives.

Students will complete an online Checkpoint Practice to prepare for the Unit Checkpoint. If necessary, read the directions, problems, and answer choices to students. Have students answer the problems on their own. Carefully review the answers with students.

⤷ UNIT REVIEW Prepare for the Checkpoint

What you do next depends on how students performed in the previous activity, Unit Review: Checkpoint Practice. If students had difficulty with any of the problems, complete the appropriate review activity listed in the table online.

Unit Checkpoint

UNIT CHECKPOINT Online   60 minutes   **ONLINE**

▶ Unit Objectives

This lesson assesses the following objectives:

- Use a mathematical expression to represent a relationship between quantities.
- Use an equation to represent a relationship between quantities.
- Use an inequality to represent a relationship between quantities.
- Select the appropriate symbol to show an operation or a relationship that makes a number sentence true.
- Determine a missing number in an equation or an inequality.
- Extend a linear pattern, such as stating what number comes next in a series.
- Recognize and describe a linear pattern, such as counting by 5s or multiplying 5 times a number to reach 100, by its rule.
- Identify patterns in addition or multiplication facts.
- Solve a simple story problem that involves a function.
- Identify odd and even numbers and describe their characteristics.
- Use a variable to represent an unknown number in an equation.

Materials to Gather

There are no materials to gather for this lesson.

ONLINE
60min

UNIT CHECKPOINT Online

Objectives

- Assess unit objectives.

Students will complete the Unit Checkpoint online. If necessary, read the directions, problems, and answer choices to students and help them with keyboard or mouse operations.

Extended Problems: Reasoning

USE WHAT YOU KNOW Offline | 60 minutes | **OFFLINE**

▶ Lesson Objectives

This lesson assesses the following objectives:

- Use a mathematical expression to represent a relationship between quantities.

- Use an equation to represent a relationship between quantities.

- Determine a missing number in an equation or an inequality.

- Extend a linear pattern, such as stating what number comes next in a series.

- Recognize and describe a linear pattern, such as counting by 5s or multiplying 5 times a number to reach 100, by its rule.

- Solve a simple story problem that involves a function.

- Assess the reasonableness of answers using mental computation and estimation strategies, including rounding.

- Solve multistep word problems using whole numbers.

- Analyze complex problems using mathematical knowledge and skills.

Materials to Gather

SUPPLIED

Extended Problems: Reasoning (printout)

Extended Problems: Reasoning Answer Key (printout)

USE WHAT YOU KNOW Offline

60min

The Extended Problems: Reasoning and its answer key are located online in the Resources section for this unit in the Online Book Menu of *Math+ Purple Lesson Guide*. Give students the Extended Problems: Reasoning. Read the directions, problems, and answer choices to students, if necessary.

You will grade this assignment.

- Students should complete the assignment on their own.

- Students should submit the completed assignment to you.

Objectives

- Analyze complex problems using mathematical knowledge and skills.

Geometry

- Identify right angles in geometric figures or everyday objects.
- Identify the measure of an angle in a geometric figure or an everyday object as greater than or less than a right angle.
- Identify, describe, and classify a polygon according to the number of its sides.
- Identify attributes of isosceles, equilateral, and right triangles.
- Identify attributes of parallelograms, rectangles, and squares.
- Know how to define and sketch different quadrilaterals.
- Define and identify attributes of different quadrilaterals.

▶ Big Ideas

- Geometric figures can be described and classified by the shapes of their faces and by how many faces, sides, edges, or vertices they have.
- Shapes can be constructed from other shapes.

▶ Unit Introduction

In this unit, students will learn about both two-dimensional and three-dimensional geometric figures. They will learn to see those figures in the world and will learn how to describe with mathematical language the many attributes of the figures. They will learn that square corners are right angles, and they'll recognize when an angle is greater than, less than, or equal to a right angle.

Students will use their shape blocks and an online geoboard to learn to describe and classify polygons according to the number of sides. They will identify attributes of triangles and will learn to recognize isosceles, equilateral, and right triangles. They'll also identify attributes of parallelograms, rectangles, and squares. Finally they will look at three-dimensional solid figures, including spheres, cones, cylinders, rectangular solids, and triangular and rectangular pyramids. Students will learn to identify the solids and describe them by the number and shape of their faces and the number of vertices. They will also see how three-dimensional figures can be put together to make other figures.

▶ Keywords

angle	face	rectangle
angle measure	intersecting lines	rectangular prism
attributes	isosceles triangle	rectangular pyramid
base of a figure	line	right angle
cone	parallel	rotate
cube	parallel lines	scalene triangle
cylinder	parallelogram	side of a polygon
degree	plane figure	solid figure
edge	polygon	sphere
equilateral	prism	square
equilateral triangle	quadrilateral	triangular prism
	ray	triangular pyramid
		vertex (plural: vertices)

Right Angles and Other Angles

▶ Lesson Objectives

- Identify right angles in geometric figures or everyday objects.
- Identify the measure of an angle in a geometric figure or an everyday object as greater than or less than a right angle.

▶ Prerequisite Skills

Classify plane figures according to similarities and differences, such as triangle, square, rectangle, circle, oval.

▶ Content Background

Students will learn to identify right angles in geometric figures and everyday objects. They will also learn to identify angles by comparing them to the measures of a right angle and deciding if they are greater than, less than, or equal to a right angle.

Avoid using the words *bigger* and *smaller* with students. Do not use phrases like *the angle is bigger/smaller* or *the opening is bigger/smaller*. Those terms and phrases lead students to incorrectly assume that an angle with longer sides has a greater measure.

In geometry, students use the terms *lines*, *rays*, and *angles*.

line   ray   angle

An angle is made of two rays that share an endpoint, called a *vertex*.

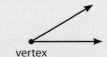

vertex

The rays of the angle are called the *sides* of the angle. When the sides of an angle form a square corner, the angle is called a *right angle* and can be marked with a square corner marker. An angle that is less than a right angle is called an *acute angle*. An angle that is greater than a right angle is called an *obtuse angle*.

Materials to Gather

SUPPLIED

blocks – A, B, C, D, E, F, G, H, I, J, K, L, M, N (3 of each)

ALSO NEEDED

index card

household objects – pipe cleaner, 2 drinking straws

household objects – twist tie (optional)

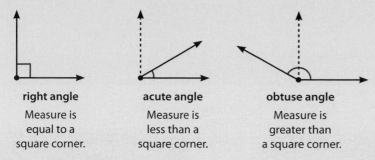

right angle
Measure is
equal to a
square corner.

acute angle
Measure is
less than a
square corner.

obtuse angle
Measure is
greater than
a square corner.

Angles are measured by how much of a rotation has been made between the sides. The rotation is measured in degrees, and a right angle (an angle with a square corner) is 90°.

▶ Common Errors and Misconceptions

- Students might not recognize angles as important parts of figures.
- Students might focus on the length of the line segments that form an angle's sides, the tilt of the top line segment, the area enclosed by the sides, or the proximity of the two sides rather than look at the actual size of the angle. For example, students might indicate that in the two triangles shown here, angle *A* is smaller than angle *X*.

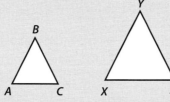

▶ Advance Preparation

Gather a pipe cleaner and 2 drinking straws.

GET READY Name That Shape

OFFLINE
5min

Students will review the names of shapes and their attributes. Gather the blocks.

1. Lay out the blocks in random order.
2. Have students sort the blocks by shape.
3. As students pick up each block, ask them to explain how they know that the block has that particular shape. Encourage them to use math vocabulary. Explanations may include the following:

   - A circle is round (A, B blocks).
   - A triangle has 3 sides (F, H, J, K blocks).
   - A rectangle has 4 sides and square corners (C, D, E, G blocks).
   - A square has 4 equal sides and square corners (E, G blocks).
   - A trapezoid has 4 sides. Two of the sides are parallel (M blocks). (Students might describe *parallel* without using the exact term. They will learn it in future lessons.)

Objectives

- Classify plane figures according to similarities and differences, such as triangle, square, rectangle, circle, oval.

Tips

Remind students that this activity is a review. If they do not remember the names or attributes of the shapes, reinforce vocabulary along with the shapes' sides and angles.

- A rhombus has 4 equal sides (L, G blocks).

- A hexagon has 6 sides (N block).

- A parallelogram has 4 sides. Both pairs of opposite sides are parallel (L, I blocks). (Students may or may not recognize this shape. The shape will be covered in future lessons.)

LEARN Recognize Right Angles

OFFLINE 15 min

Students will learn the definition of an angle. They will identify a right angle in everyday objects and geometric figures. They will recognize angles that are less than a right angle and greater than a right angle.

Gather the blocks, index card, pipe cleaner, and drinking straws.

1. Define an angle as a corner where two lines meet. Tell students that they will learn about angles and that angles are all around them.

2. Have students hold their index finger and thumb straight up in the air, and then move their thumb away from their index finger gradually. Explain that students are making angles with greater and greater measures.

3. Take one of the blocks, choose a vertex, and have students trace that angle with their finger. Students should use their finger to move out from the vertex along one side of the block, then go back to that vertex and trace along the other side. Point out that students are tracing an angle on the block. Repeat the process on paper. Trace a block and have students trace an angle by choosing a vertex and tracing along the two sides that extend from that vertex.

4. Model more examples of angles on the blocks by pointing out where 2 sides meet to form an angle. Allow time for students to identify other angles on the blocks. Point out that the circle has no angles.

5. Show students a square and ask what kind of shape could fit in its corners. squares

   Tell students that the angles on the square are called *right angles*. Explain that a right angle is an angle that forms when two lines meet to form a square corner.

6. Ask students to find another shape with right angles and to point out two sides that make a right angle. Students should choose a different rectangular piece or one of the right triangles and point to 2 sides that meet to form a right angle or square.

7. Give students an index card and ask if it has right angles. Yes

   Draw two lines on the card, very close to the edge, with arrows. Put a square corner marker in the corner to show a right angle. Write "right angle" near the corner of the card. Tell students that all the corners of the card are right angles and that sometimes people use the square corner marker to show that there is a right angle.

right angle

Objectives

- Identify right angles in geometric figures or everyday objects.

- Identify the measure of an angle in a geometric figure or an everyday object as greater than or less than a right angle.

Tips

If you wish, substitute a twist tie for the pipe cleaner in this activity.

8. **Say:** We can use the index card to check whether an angle is a right angle.

   Hold the card up to the corner of a rectangular block. Point out how the corners match, which shows the right angle in the rectangle. Have students match the card to something in the room that has a right angle such as a book, a cabinet door, or the corner of a rectangular or square table.

9. Give students 1 minute to go around the room and point out as many right angles as possible. Students should use the index card to help them recognize objects with right angles. Explain that the lengths of the sides of an object do not matter. Any object that has a square corner has a right angle. A big poster on a wall has a right angle, and a small index card has a right angle.

10. Show students an analog clock or watch. Discuss two times when a clock shows a right angle, 3:00 and 9:00.

11. Have students use a pipe cleaner to make a right angle. Have them check that their right-angle pipe cleaner is a right angle by wrapping it around the corner of a table or laying one side on the top of a table and having the other side go down over the edge of the table. They can also check their angle using the index card.

12. Have students open and close the angle to show angles greater than a right angle and less than a right angle. Have them put straws on the end of the bent pipe cleaner to show that the lengths of the sides of the angle don't affect the measure of the angle.

LEARN Greater Than, Less Than a Right Angle   **10**min ONLINE

Students will learn that an angle is made up of two rays that share a vertex. They will identify angles as right angles, as angles that are greater than right angles, and as angles that are less than right angles.

Objectives

- Identify right angles in geometric figures or everyday objects.
- Identify the measure of an angle in a geometric figure or an everyday object as greater than or less than a right angle.

LEARN Geoboard Fun   **15**min ONLINE

Students will use the Geoboard Learning Tool to create shapes that have right angles, angles greater than 90°, and angles less than 90°.

Objectives

- Identify right angles in geometric figures or everyday objects.
- Identify the measure of an angle in a geometric figure or an everyday object as greater than or less than a right angle.

DIRECTIONS FOR USING THE GEOBOARD LEARNING TOOL

1. Click Lesson Mode. If necessary, click Menu and Help to review the instructions for the learning tool.

2. To make the angles, have students use two rubber bands. Have them make a 90° angle, or right angle, by following these steps:
   - Drag a rubber band and make a vertical segment of any length.
   - Drag another rubber band and make a horizontal segment that connects to an end of the first rubber band to make a right angle.

3. Have students make the following angles:
   - an angle that measures less than 90°
   - an angle that measures greater than 90°

4. Have students make shapes that have different types of angles. To make the shapes, they will use one rubber band. Have them make these shapes:

- a 4-sided shape that has 4 right angles
- a 5-sided shape that has 2 right angles (If students have difficulty, they can make a 4-sided shape and stretch 1 side. Refer to the illustration for an example.)
- a triangle with 1 right angle and 2 angles less than 90°

Students' angles and shapes should be similar to the following:

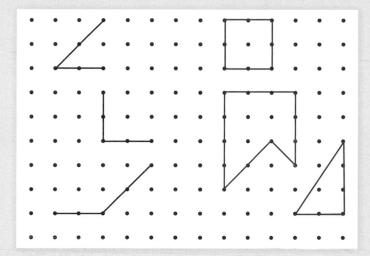

TRY IT Right Angles

ONLINE 10 min

Students will complete an online Try It. If necessary, read the directions, problems, and answer choices to students and help them with keyboard or mouse operations.

Objectives

- Identify right angles in geometric figures or everyday objects.
- Identify the measure of an angle in a geometric figure or an everyday object as greater than or less than a right angle.

CHECKPOINT

ONLINE 5 min

Students will complete an online Checkpoint. If necessary, read the directions, problems, and answer choices to students and help them with keyboard or mouse operations.

Objectives

- Identify right angles in geometric figures or everyday objects.
- Identify the measure of an angle in a geometric figure or an everyday object as greater than or less than a right angle.

Identify and Classify Polygons

Lesson Overview

GET READY Play a Shape Game	5 minutes	**OFFLINE**
LEARN Toothpick Polygons	20 minutes	**OFFLINE**
LEARN Create and Identify Polygons	15 minutes	**ONLINE**
TRY IT Name Polygons	10 minutes	**OFFLINE**
CHECKPOINT	10 minutes	**ONLINE**

▶ Lesson Objectives

Identify, describe, and classify a polygon according to the number of its sides.

▶ Prerequisite Skills

- Identify and describe plane figures according to the number of sides and vertices, such as triangle, square, rectangle, circle, oval.
- Classify plane figures according to similarities and differences, such as triangle, square, rectangle, circle, oval.

▶ Content Background

In this lesson, students will learn to identify, describe, and classify common geometric shapes according to the number of straight sides. They will learn the names for common polygons up through 10 sides.

Students are familiar with a variety of shapes. They will learn that all straight-sided, closed figures are called polygons and that *polygon* means "many-sided figure." A polygon is classified by its number of sides. Students know that all 3-sided figures are triangles. They may also know that 4-sided figures have different names, such as quadrilateral, parallelogram, square, rhombus, rectangle, and trapezoid. Students will learn that the term *quadrilateral* is used to describe all 4-sided figures. They will learn the names for other common polygons, such as the 5-sided pentagon, the 6-sided hexagon, and other polygons up through 10 sides.

When students use the online Geoboard Learning Tool, they will see the words *convex* and *concave*. At this level, it's sufficient to just mention to students that a concave figure "caves in," whereas a convex figure does not.

A figure that lies on a flat surface, or in two dimensions, is called a *plane figure*. Plane figures include those with straight sides (polygons) as well as those with curved sides, such as circles. It's important to use the term *plane figure* with students, but they are not required to use the term.

▶ Common Errors and Misconceptions

- Students might misinterpret which characteristics define a shape. For example, they may see a triangle that has three equal sides and think that all triangles must have three equal sides. Actually, any shape with only 3 sides is a triangle.

Materials to Gather

SUPPLIED

blocks – A, B, C, D, E, F, G, H, I, J, K, L, M, N (1 of each)

Name Polygons activity page

Dot Paper (printout)

ALSO NEEDED

household objects – 60 toothpicks

index cards – 9

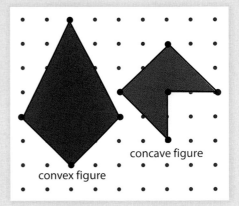

concave figure

convex figure

- Students might not recognize that a shape might be positioned different ways. For example, students might not recognize that the second shape shown here is a square.
- Students might inappropriately use *converse reasoning* when classifying shapes. For example, they might say, "All squares have 4 sides. This shape has 4 sides, so it must be a square."

▶ Advance Preparation

Print the Dot Paper.
  Gather 60 toothpicks.

▶ Safety

Supervise students as they work with toothpicks, paper clips, and other pointy items.

GET READY Play a Shape Game

OFFLINE 5min

Students will play the game Guess My Shape to identify, describe, and classify plane figures according to the number of sides and vertices.
  Gather the blocks.

1. Hide a block in your hand.

   Say: I'm hiding a block. You can ask Yes and No questions about its attributes to guess which block it is. You can ask about the shape's sides and vertices and the types of angles, but you may not ask about its color. And you can ask if it's a certain shape only once, when you're certain what shape it is.

2. Guide students to ask questions such as the following:
   - Does it have exactly 3 sides?
   - Does it have a square corner?
   - Does it have a right angle?
   - Does it have a vertex?
   - Does it have a curved side?
   - Are all sides equal?
   - Is it big?
   - Does it have more than 3 sides?

3. Have students ask questions until they know which block you are hiding. They should state the shape of the block. Uncover the block to show whether they gave the correct answer.

4. Repeat Steps 1–3 two or three times as time allows. Trade roles so students choose the block and you ask the questions.

Objectives

- Identify and describe plane figures according to the number of sides and vertices, such as triangle, square, rectangle, circle, oval.
- Classify plane figures according to similarities and differences, such as triangle, square, rectangle, circle, oval.

Tips

Explain to students that a shape with more than 3 sides, such as a square, has 3 sides, but not exactly 3 sides. Guide students to ask about attributes that narrow the possibilities.

LEARN Toothpick Polygons

OFFLINE 20min

Students will use toothpicks to construct polygons with 3 through 10 sides. They will create shape flash cards.
  Gather the toothpicks, blocks, and index cards.

Objectives

- Identify, describe, and classify a polygon according to the number of its sides.

1. Tell students that they have seen many shapes and will now learn more about how to describe them. Ask students to use three toothpicks to make a closed shape. Explain that a closed shape is like a fence with no openings.

   Ask: What shape did you make? triangle

   Ask students to identify each side of the triangle. Have them feel a side with their finger and realize that when they reach a corner, or vertex, it's the beginning of a new side. Ask students to point out a vertex where 2 sides meet.

2. Break some toothpicks and make two more triangles of different shapes. Show one with a right angle. Show the triangles in different orientations so that they're turned in different ways.

   Ask: How do you know that all of these shapes are triangles? They all have 3 sides.

   Tell students that any closed figure with exactly 3 sides is called a triangle. Point out that *tri–* means "three" and that a triangle has 3 angles. Ask students what other words they can think of that start with *tri–*. Examples: tricycle, tripod, triplets

3. Have students write "triangle" on one side of an index card. Then on the other side of the card, have them draw a small picture of a triangle with a 3 inside it. Place the card above the toothpick triangles. Leave the triangles in place.

4. Give students four toothpicks and have them make a 4-sided closed figure.

   Ask: What shape did you make? square or rhombus

   Remind students that a rhombus has 4 equal sides but it doesn't have to have right angles like a square.

5. Break some toothpicks and have students use different-sized pieces to make two more 4-sided figures.

   Tell students that there is a special word to describe all 4-sided figures that are closed and have no lines that cross. That word is *quadrilateral*. *Quad–* means four and *–lateral* means "side"; *quadrilateral* means "four sided." Ask students what other words they can think of that start with *quad–*. Example: quadruplets

6. Have students write "quadrilateral" on one side of an index card. Then on the other side of the card, have them draw a small picture of a quadrilateral with a 4 inside it. Place the card above the toothpick quadrilaterals.

   Say: A quadrilateral is any closed figure that has 4 sides that don't cross over each other. So squares, rhombuses, trapezoids, rectangles, and all other 4-sided figures are quadrilaterals.

7. Draw the figure shown that is closed and has no lines that cross. Explain to students that quadrilaterals can also have sides that "cave in." As long as a closed figure has 4 straight sides and the lines don't cross each other, it's a quadrilateral.

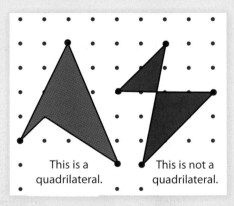

This is a quadrilateral.   This is not a quadrilateral.

8. Have students continue to create toothpick figures, learn the correct names, and make shape flash cards for the following figures:

   - pentagon – 5-sided closed figure
   - hexagon – 6-sided closed figure
   - septagon – 7-sided closed figure (*heptagon* is another name for a 7-sided closed figure.)
   - octagon – 8-sided closed figure
   - nonagon – 9-sided closed figure
   - decagon – 10-sided closed figure

9. Tell students that there is one word to describe all closed figures with straight sides. That word is *polygon*. Have students say "polygon." Explain that *polygon* means "many sided." Have students write the word "polygon" on an index card and place it above all the toothpick figures.

   Ask: Which of the figures you made or drew are polygons? all of them

   Explain that polygons are made of straight lines that don't cross and that connect to make a closed figure.

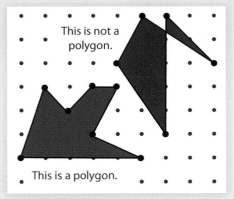

This is not a polygon.

This is a polygon.

10. Have students look at the blocks. Ask the following questions. Allow students to look at their index cards for help.
    - Which blocks are polygons? all except the circles
    - Which are triangles? F, H, J, K
    - Which are quadrilaterals? C, D, E, G, I, L, M
    - What other type of polygon do we have among the blocks? hexagon: N block

11. Encourage students to practice memorizing the names of polygons by using their shape flash cards.

ONLINE
15min

LEARN Create and Identify Polygons

Students will use the Geoboard Learning Tool to create and name polygons. Remind students that a polygon is a closed figure with straight sides that don't cross each other. Remind them that they have learned the names of many types of polygons.

DIRECTIONS FOR USING THE GEOBOARD LEARNING TOOL

1. Click Lesson Mode. If necessary, click Menu and Help to review the instructions for the learning tool.

2. Have students make a shape, such as a triangle, on the Geoboard.

3. Have students click Show Info to see the name of the shape. Point out the word *concave* or *convex* next to the shape's name. Tell students that a shape is concave if it "caves in" or has an inward dent. Otherwise, it is convex. (Students at this level are not expected to remember those names.)

4. Have students make the following polygons on one screen:
   - triangle: green
   - pentagon: orange
   - septagon: yellow
   - nonagon: blue
   - quadrilateral: blue
   - hexagon: red
   - octagon: purple
   - decagon: green

   Here are sample polygons:

triangle   quadrilateral   pentagon   hexagon   septagon   octagon   nonagon   decagon

   Students can decide how they want each figure to look as long as it has the correct number of sides and is a polygon. The color names are a key for you to use in identifying the sample polygons in the illustration. Students can use any color for any polygon. Remember that their polygons can look different from these polygons.

Objectives

- Identify, describe, and classify a polygon according to the number of its sides.

Tips

Allow students to use Dot Paper printouts to create their own polygon designs offline.

TRY IT Name Polygons

Objectives

Students will practice identifying, describing, and classifying a polygon according to the number of sides it has. Gather the Dot Paper. View or print the Name Polygons activity page and read the directions with students.

Students should copy the problems from the Activity Book into their Math Notebook as necessary and solve them there.

- Identify, describe, and classify a polygon according to the number of its sides.

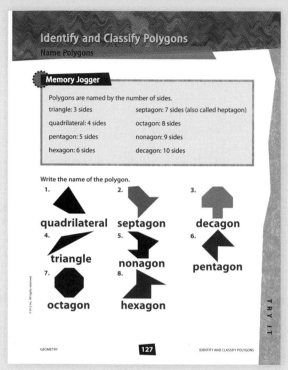

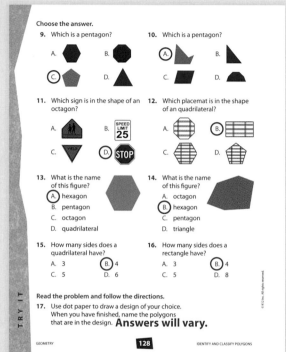

CHECKPOINT

Objectives

Students will complete an online Checkpoint. If necessary, read the directions, problems, and answer choices to students and help them with keyboard or mouse operations.

- Identify, describe, and classify a polygon according to the number of its sides.

Triangles

▶ Lesson Objectives

Identify attributes of isosceles, equilateral, and right triangles.

▶ Prerequisite Skills

Identify and describe plane figures according to the number of sides and vertices, such as triangle, square, rectangle, circle, oval.

▶ Content Background

Students will learn to identify different types of triangles.
Isosceles triangles have at least 2 equal sides.

isosceles triangle

Equilateral triangles have 3 equal sides.

equilateral triangle

An equilateral triangle is a special type of isosceles triangle, but students should name a triangle as equilateral if all 3 sides are the same length.
Right triangles have a right angle.

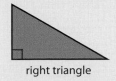

right triangle

Materials to Gather

SUPPLIED

blocks – A, B, C, D, E, F, G, H, I, J, K, L, M, N (1 of each)

Dot Paper (printout)

Isometric Dot Paper (printout)

ALSO NEEDED

index cards – 6

scissors, pointed-end safety

household objects – 6 toothpicks

Students will use two types of dot paper—regular dot paper and isometric dot paper—to draw polygons. On isometric dot paper, the dots are in a triangular pattern where each dot is 1 unit from the dots that surround it. An equilateral triangle with a side unit of 1 is the smallest triangle that can be shown on isometric dot paper. This paper is designed so that it's easy to draw equilateral triangles and parallelograms that have equal side lengths but are not squares (nonsquare rhombuses).

On regular dot paper that uses a square grid pattern, a square is the smallest polygon that has side lengths of 1 unit. Notice that the distance between diagonal points on the regular dot paper is greater than 1 unit, which makes it difficult to draw an equilateral triangle on this paper.

The Geoboard Learning Tool has options to use these different types of grids.

square grid

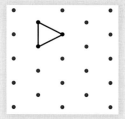
isometric grid

▶ Common Errors and Misconceptions

Students might misinterpret which characteristics define a shape. For example, they may see a triangle that has three equal sides and think that all triangles must have 3 equal sides. Actually, any shape with only 3 sides is a triangle.

▶ Advance Preparation

Print the Dot Paper and Isometric Dot Paper.
Gather 6 toothpicks.

▶ Safety

Supervise students as they work with toothpicks, paper clips, and other pointy items.

Make sure students handle the scissors carefully and be sure to store them in a safe place.

GET READY Shape Comparison

OFFLINE
5min

Objectives

Students will sort shapes into groups of triangles and quadrilaterals and will describe the differences among the shapes in each group.
Gather the blocks.

- Identify and describe plane figures according to the number of sides and vertices, such as triangle, square, rectangle, circle, oval.

1. Lay out the blocks in random order.

2. **Ask:** What is a 3-sided figure called? triangle

3. Have students make a pile of all the triangles and describe the differences between them. They may notice that some are big, some are small, some have right angles, some have sides that are the same length, and some

4. **Ask:** What is a 4-sided figure called? quadrilateral

5. Have students make a pile of all the quadrilaterals and describe the differences between them. They may notice that some are squares, some are rectangles, some are rhombuses, some are parallelograms, some have sides that are all the same length, and some have opposite sides that are the same length.

6. Explain to students that they might know more words to describe quadrilaterals and that in this lesson, they will learn more ways to describe the different types of triangles.

LEARN Attributes of Three Triangles

OFFLINE **25**min

Students will learn to identify right, isosceles, and equilateral triangles and describe their attributes.

Gather the blocks, index cards, toothpicks, and scissors, and the two types of dot paper.

RIGHT TRIANGLES

1. **Say:** You know about different types of triangles. Now let's learn new ways to describe and group them.

   Have students cut a diagonal from the bottom edge to the side edge of an index card as shown.

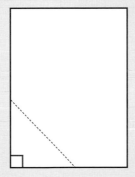

   Ask students to explain what they notice about the angles in the triangle. Guide students to see that one of the angles is a right angle. Have students draw a square corner marker on the triangle to show the right angle.

2. Have students identify the blocks that are right triangles. F, H, J

   Tell students that these triangles are called right triangles because they have a right angle in them. Have students write "right triangle" on one side of an index card. On the other side, have them draw a picture of a right triangle with a square corner marker to signify the right angle.

3. Emphasize that the lengths of the sides of a right angle do not affect the angle. Therefore, a triangle of any size that has a right angle is a right triangle. Have students match up the right angles on the F, H, and J blocks to model that any size triangle that has a right angle is a right triangle.

   As time permits, have students draw right triangles on the Dot Paper (square grid).

ISOSCELES TRIANGLES

4. Give students a new index card. Have them fold the card in half and cut a diagonal line from the bottom right to the left side as shown.

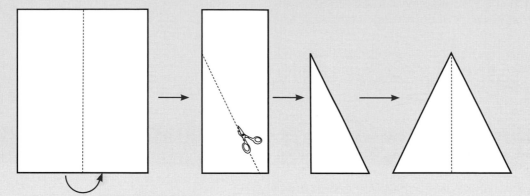

Ask students to explain what they notice about the sides of the triangle. Guide them to see that 2 of the sides are the same length. Turn the triangle so that it has a different orientation. Some students have difficulty seeing that 2 sides of a triangle are the same length if the triangle is turned at an odd angle.

5. Have students identify the triangle blocks that have 2 sides the same length. F, H, J, K

Students can check to see that the sides of one triangle are equal by comparing them to the same side of another triangle. Tell them that triangles that have 2 equal-length sides are called isosceles triangles. Have them write "isosceles triangle" on one side of an index card. On the other side, have students draw a picture of an isosceles triangle.

As time permits, have students draw isosceles triangles on the Dot Paper (square grid or isometic grid).

6. **Ask:** What are the names of the two special triangles? What makes them special? A right triangle has a right angle, and an isosceles triangle has at least 2 equal sides.

7. Have students identify the blocks that are both right triangles and isosceles triangles. F, H, J

EQUILATERAL TRIANGLES

8. Tell students there is one more special triangle. Explain that this triangle has 3 sides that have equal lengths. Give students three toothpicks. Have them create a triangle with the toothpicks.

Ask students to explain what they notice about the sides of the triangle. Guide them to see that the 3 sides of the triangle have the same length. Have them look at the triangle from different orientations. Some students have difficulty seeing that a triangle is equilateral if the triangle is at an odd angle.

9. Have students identify the triangle block that has 3 equal sides. K

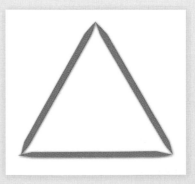

Tell students this triangle is called an equilateral triangle because it has 3 equal-length sides. Have them write "equilateral triangle" on one side of an index card. On the other side, have students draw a picture of an equilateral triangle.

As time permits, have students draw equilateral triangles on Isometric Dot Paper. As a challenge, have them draw an equilateral triangle on Dot Paper (square grid).

10. Present the following questions to students and allow them to share their answers:

- Are all equilateral triangles isosceles triangles? Guide students to see that since isosceles triangles have at least 2 equal sides and equilateral triangles have 3 equal sides, all equilateral triangles are isosceles triangles.

- Can an equilateral triangle be a right triangle? Use toothpicks to show students that this is not possible. A right angle made with two toothpicks cannot be closed to make a triangle with a third toothpick because the third toothpick is too short.

11. Review that the term *equilateral* means "equal-sided." Tell students that just as there are equilateral triangles, there are also equilateral polygons. Any polygon with all equal sides is called an equilateral polygon. Examples are the square and hexagon blocks.

12. Summarize and review right, isosceles, and equilateral triangles and their attributes.

LEARN Three Types of Triangles

ONLINE 10 min

Objectives

- Identify attributes of isosceles, equilateral, and right triangles.

Students will identify right, isosceles, and equilateral triangles using marks such as a square corner marker to signify a right angle in a right triangle, or tick marks to signify the equal sides of an isosceles or equilateral triangle. Help students recognize that the triangles can be turned so that equal sides or right angles are not as easy to see.

Tips

If students have difficulty recognizing isosceles triangles or right triangles when they are turned in an odd way, take the blocks and turn them in an odd way and have students practice picking out which are right triangles, isosceles triangles, and equilateral triangles.

isosceles triangle

equilateral triangle

right triangle

TRY IT Triangle Practice

ONLINE 10 min

Objectives

- Identify attributes of isosceles, equilateral, and right triangles.

Students will complete an online Try It. If necessary, read the directions, problems, and answer choices to students and help them with keyboard or mouse operations.

CHECKPOINT

ONLINE 10 min

Objectives

- Identify attributes of isosceles, equilateral, and right triangles.

Students will complete an online Checkpoint. If necessary, read the directions, problems, and answer choices to students and help them with keyboard or mouse operations.

Parallelograms

Lesson Overview

GET READY Shape Design		5 minutes	**ONLINE**
LEARN What Is a Parallelogram?		20 minutes	**OFFLINE**
LEARN Side Lengths of Parallelograms		15 minutes	**ONLINE**
TRY IT Parallelogram Practice		10 minutes	**OFFLINE**
CHECKPOINT		10 minutes	**ONLINE**

▶ Lesson Objectives

Identify attributes of parallelograms, rectangles, and squares.

▶ Prerequisite Skills

Identify and describe plane figures according to the number of sides and vertices, such as triangle, square, rectangle, circle, oval.

▶ Content Background

Students will learn how to identify parallelograms. They will recognize that rectangles are special parallelograms and squares are special rectangles.

Polygons are classified by the number of sides they have. Quadrilaterals are polygons with 4 sides. Among quadrilaterals are parallelograms. Parallelograms have parallel opposite sides that are equal in length. Identify a parallelogram by looking at the sides and the angles. Rectangles, rhombuses, and squares are special types of parallelograms. The illustration shows the relationship between the sides and angles in different types of parallelograms. Notice the tick marks. Sides with one tick mark have the same length and those with two tick marks have the same length. The square in the corner indicates a right angle.

A square is not only a square but also a rectangle, a rhombus, and a parallelogram. A rectangle is always a parallelogram, but it is only a square when its sides are equal. A rhombus is always a parallelogram, but it is only a square when its angles are right angles.

▶ Common Errors and Misconceptions

- Students might misinterpret which characteristics define a shape. For example, they may see a triangle that has 3 equal sides and think that all triangles must have 3 equal sides. Actually, any shape with only 3 sides is a triangle.

Materials to Gather

SUPPLIED

blocks – A, B, C, D, E, F, G, H, I, J, K, L, M, N (2 of each)

Dot Paper (printout)

Parallelogram Practice activity page

ALSO NEEDED

index cards – 4

paper, printer – 1 sheet

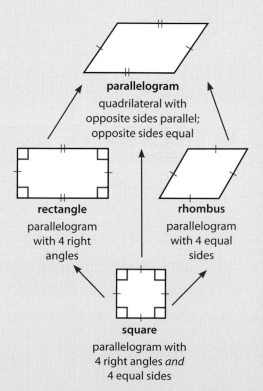

parallelogram
quadrilateral with opposite sides parallel; opposite sides equal

rectangle
parallelogram with 4 right angles

rhombus
parallelogram with 4 equal sides

square
parallelogram with 4 right angles *and* 4 equal sides

- Students might not recognize that a shape might be positioned different ways. For example, students might not recognize that the second shape is a square.

- Students might inappropriately use *converse reasoning* when classifying shapes. For example, they might say, "All squares have 4 sides. This shape has 4 sides, so it must be a square."

▶ Advance Preparation

Print two copies of the Dot Paper.
Draw a parallelogram on one copy of the Dot Paper.

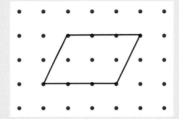

GET READY Shape Design

ONLINE
5min

Students will use polygons to make a design on the online Geoboard. Have students look at both the isometric grid and the regular grid before starting their design.

Students can use their ideas from this activity to create further designs on the Dot Paper and Isometric Dot Paper.

DIRECTIONS FOR USING THE GEOBOARD LEARNING TOOL

1. Click Lesson Mode. If necessary, click Menu and Help to review the instructions for the learning tool.

2. Have students make a complex figure on the Geoboard. Encourage students to use as many of the following shapes as possible to create their design: square, rectangle, rhombus, triangle, pentagon, hexagon, septagon, octagon, nonagon, decagon, and right triangle. Students may use either the isometric grid or the regular grid.

3. Have students identify and describe the figures in their design by name and attributes.

Objectives

- Identify and describe plane figures according to the number of sides and vertices, such as triangle, square, rectangle, circle, oval.

Tips

Sit with students during the activity. Ask them to explain how they know the name of each figure in their design.

Students will learn the attributes of parallelograms. They will identify and sort special types of parallelograms (rhombuses, rectangles, and squares).

Gather the parallelogram you have drawn on the Dot Paper, printer paper, blocks, and index cards.

1. Remind students that polygons are closed figures with straight sides and no lines crossing. Tell them that in this lesson, they're going to look more closely at 4-sided polygons. Explain that 4-sided polygons are called *quadrilaterals*.

2. Introduce the term *parallel lines*. Give examples of parallel lines such as the lines on binder paper or the rails on a train track. Have the students draw parallel lines on the dot paper. Then have them describe parallel lines in their own words and tell where they see them in the world. Guide students to understand that parallel lines never cross and provide additional examples: top and bottom of windows, doors, and some furniture; the tracks of skiers and the tracks of a car after it goes through a puddle; and the 10-yard lines of a football field. Conclude by telling students that anywhere there are rectangles, there are parallel lines.

3. Have students draw a rectangle and a square on separate index cards. Remind them that these are both quadrilaterals. Have them note that opposite sides have the same length and are parallel.

4. Show students the parallelogram on the Dot Paper. Have them tell the number of sides in the shape. 4

   Ask: Are any of the lines parallel? Yes, the opposite sides

   Ask: Are any of the sides the same length? Yes, opposite sides

   Explain that the shape is a parallelogram.

   Say: A parallelogram is a special quadrilateral. Its opposite sides are parallel and equal in length.

   Have students write "parallelogram" on one side of an index card and draw a picture of a parallelogram on the other side.

   Ask: Is a rectangle a parallelogram? Yes

   Ask: Are all parallelograms rectangles? No, some parallelograms look like they are slanting to the side and don't have right angles like a rectangle.

5. Show students the trapezoid block (M block) without naming it. Ask if it is a parallelogram and have students explain why or why not. Students should notice that the trapezoid has only one set of parallel sides. To be a parallelogram, the other two sides would also need to be parallel.

6. Have students sort the parallelogram-shaped blocks. Display a rhombus (L block). Ask students to describe the shape according to number of sides, lengths of sides, and parallel lines. 4 sides, all sides equal in length, opposite sides parallel

   Explain that this shape is a rhombus.

   Say: A rhombus is a quadrilateral with 4 equal sides.

   Have students write "rhombus" on one side of an index card and draw a picture of a rhombus on the other side.

7. Ask the following questions and have students explain their answers:
   - Is a rhombus a parallelogram? Yes, opposite sides are parallel.
   - Are all parallelograms rhombuses? No, only those with all sides the same length.
   - Can a rhombus be a rectangle? Yes, if all angles are right angles.
   - Can a rhombus be a square? Yes, if all angles are right angles.
   - Are all rhombuses squares? No, some rhombuses do not have right angles.

8. Ask the following questions and have students explain their answers:
   - Is a square a parallelogram? Yes, it has opposite sides that are parallel and of equal length.
   - Is a square a rectangle? Yes, it has 4 right angles.
   - Is a square a rhombus? Yes, it has 4 equal-length sides.

   Remind students that a shape with sides of equal length is equilateral, and that squares and rhombuses are equilateral polygons.

9. Have students find as many different-shaped rectangles as they can among the blocks and put them near the rectangle card. If necessary, remind students that squares are rectangles. C, D, E, G

   Leave the rectangles in place and have students find different-shaped rhombuses and put them near the rhombus card. E, G, L

   Ask students if there are any blocks that are both rectangles and rhombuses. squares (E and G blocks)

10. Turn a blank sheet of printer paper horizontally. Draw the diagram shown. Use the diagram to organize the blocks. Point to the appropriate section of the diagram to emphasize each step of the directions.
    Say: Put rectangles in the left oval labeled "rectangles" and rhombuses in the right oval labeled "rhombuses." If there are shapes that are both rectangles and rhombuses, put them in the center where the two ovals overlap.

11. Have students sort the blocks into the diagram. Have them describe which type of blocks go into the overlapping section. the blocks that are squares, because they are rectangles and rhombuses

    Tell students that this type of diagram is called a *Venn diagram* and it is sometimes used to sort objects.

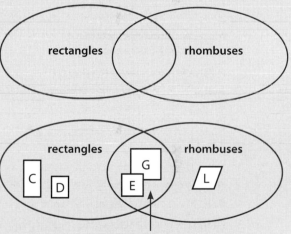

objects that are rectangles and rhombuses

ONLINE

15min

LEARN Side Lengths of Parallelograms

Objectives

- Identify attributes of parallelograms, rectangles, and squares.

Students will practice making lines parallel. They will then review the attributes of parallelograms and the special parallelograms, including the following:

- rectangles: parallelograms with all right angles
- squares: parallelograms with all right angles *and* all sides equal

TRY IT Parallelogram Practice

Students will practice identifying attributes of parallelograms, rectangles, and squares. Gather the Dot Paper. View or print the Parallelogram Practice activity page and read the directions with students.

Students should copy the problems from the Activity Book into their Math Notebook as necessary and solve them there.

Tips   Allow students to draw on the Dot Paper, use the blocks, or refer to the diagrams from the Side Lengths of Parallelograms online activity to answer the questions.

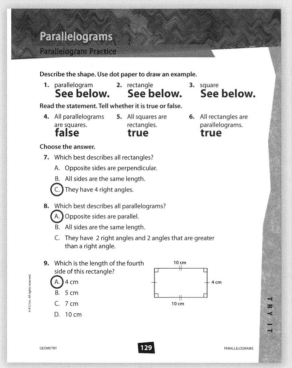

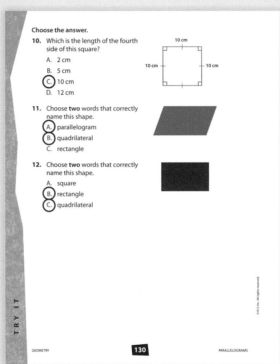

Additional Answers

1. a 4-sided polygon with opposite sides parallel
   Sample drawing:

2. a 4-sided polygon with opposite sides the same length and parallel and 4 right angles
   Sample drawing:

3. a 4-sided polygon with opposite sides parallel, all sides the same length, and 4 right angles
   Sample drawing:

CHECKPOINT

Students will complete an online Checkpoint. If necessary, read the directions, problems, and answer choices to students and help them with keyboard or mouse operations.

Core Focus
Quadrilaterals

▶ Lesson Objectives

- Know how to define and sketch different quadrilaterals.
- Define and identify attributes of different quadrilaterals.

▶ Prerequisite Skills

Identify, describe, and classify a polygon according to the number of its sides.

▶ Content Background

Students will learn how to define and classify different quadrilaterals.

A plane figure is a figure that lies on a flat or two-dimensional surface. A polygon is a closed plane figure with straight sides that do not cross each other. A quadrilateral is a 4-sided polygon. Many quadrilaterals have special names based on characteristics, such as the lengths or their sides, their angle measurements, and whether opposite sides are parallel. A drawing of a plane geometric figure often shows tick marks on the sides of the figure. Identical tick marks show sides that are equal in length. If 2 or more sides have the same number of tick marks, those sides are equal in length. A small square in a corner shows that the angle is a right angle.

Here is a list of common quadrilaterals and their definitions.

- parallelogram – quadrilateral with opposite sides parallel and also equal in length
- rectangle – quadrilateral with 4 right angles and opposite sides parallel and also equal in length
- rhombus – quadrilateral with opposite sides parallel and all 4 sides equal in length
- square – quadrilateral with 4 right angles, opposite sides parallel, and all 4 sides equal in length
- trapezoid – quadrilateral with only 1 pair of opposite sides parallel

If a 4-sided polygon does not fit into a specific category, it is simply called a *quadrilateral*. At this level, it is sufficient for students to identify quadrilaterals according to the definitions above, but this lesson will also show that some quadrilaterals fall into overlapping categories.

The following relationships exist among quadrilaterals:

- A square is also a special type of rectangle, a special type of rhombus, and a special type of parallelogram.
- A rectangle is also a special type of parallelogram.
- A rhombus is also a special type of parallelogram.

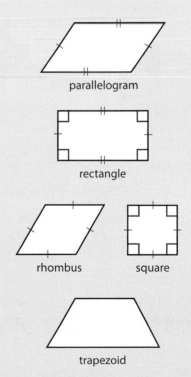

parallelogram

rectangle

rhombus   square

trapezoid

GET READY Polygons

Objectives

- Identify, describe, and classify a polygon according to the number of its sides.

Students will use the Geoboard Learning Tool to create and name polygons. Remind students that a polygon is a closed figure with straight sides that don't cross each other. Remind them that they have learned the names of many types of polygons.

DIRECTIONS FOR USING THE GEOBOARD LEARNING TOOL

1. Click Lesson Mode. If necessary, click Menu and Help to review instructions for the learning tool

2. Have students make a shape, such as a triangle, on the Geoboard.

3. Have students click Show Info to see the name of the shape. Point out the word *concave* or *convex* next the shape's name. Tell students that a shape is concave if it "caves in" or has an inward dent. Otherwise, it is convex. (Students at this level are not expected to remember those names.)

4. Have students make the following polygons on one screen:

- triangle: green
- quadrilateral: blue
- pentagon: orange
- hexagon: red
- septagon: yellow
- octagon: purple
- nonagon: blue
- decagon: green

   Students can decide how they want each figure to look as long as it has the correct number of sides and is a polygon. The color names are a key for you to use in identifying the sample polygons in the illustration. Students can use any color for any polygon. Remember that their polygons can look different from these polygons, as long as they have the correct number of sides.

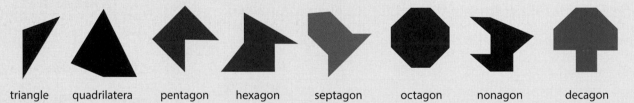

| triangle | quadrilatera | pentagon | hexagon | septagon | octagon | nonagon | decagon |

LEARN Classifying Quadrilaterals

Objectives

- Know how to define and sketch different quadrilaterals.
- Define and identify attributes of different quadrilaterals.

Students will learn the definitions of different quadrilaterals. They will recognize quadrilaterals in the environment and then play a Hidden Pictures game in which they uncover a hidden picture by using clues to identify different kinds of quadrilaterals.

TRY IT Attributes of Quadrilaterals

Objectives

Students will identify, compare, and describe quadrilaterals. View or print the Attributes of Quadrilaterals activity page and read the directions with students.

Students should copy the problems from the Activity Book into their Math Notebook as necessary and solve them there.

- Know how to define and sketch different quadrilaterals.
- Define and identify attributes of different quadrilaterals.

Core Focus
Quadrilaterals
Attributes of Quadrilaterals

Solve.

1. Daily drew these two quadrilaterals.

   A   B

   (a) What is the name of each quadrilateral?
   (b) How are the two quadrilaterals alike?
   (c) How are the two quadrilaterals different?
   See below.

2. Sonia drew these two quadrilaterals.

   A   B

   (a) What is the name of each quadrilateral?
   (b) How are the two quadrilaterals alike?
   (c) How are the two quadrilaterals different?
   See below.

3. Stan drew this quadrilateral. He said it was a square. Is Stan correct? Explain.
   See below.

GEOMETRY   131   CORE FOCUS QUADRILATERALS

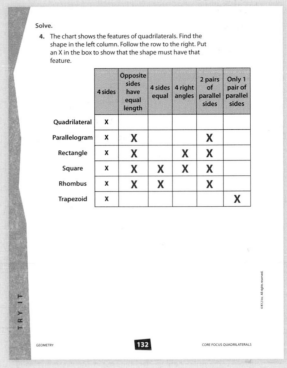

Solve.

4. The chart shows the features of quadrilaterals. Find the shape in the left column. Follow the row to the right. Put an X in the box to show that the shape must have that feature.

	4 sides	Opposite sides have equal length	4 sides equal	4 right angles	2 pairs of parallel sides	Only 1 pair of parallel sides
Quadrilateral	X					
Parallelogram	X	X			X	
Rectangle	X	X		X	X	
Square	X	X	X	X	X	
Rhombus	X	X	X		X	
Trapezoid	X					X

GEOMETRY   132   CORE FOCUS QUADRILATERALS

Think like a Mathematician Self-Check

5. State the actions and thinking you used during this lesson as a math learner.

Math Thinking and Actions
I made sense of problems by • Explaining to myself what a problem means and what it asks for • Using drawings or diagrams to represent a problem I was solving
I explained my math thinking clearly.
I tried out new ways to check if an answer is reasonable.
Other

GEOMETRY   133   CORE FOCUS QUADRILATERALS

Additional Answers

1. **(a)** Quadrilateral A is a rectangle and Quadrilateral B is a trapezoid.

   (b) They each have 4 sides and 4 angles.

   (c) The rectangle has 4 right angles with opposite sides equal in length and parallel. The trapezoid has 2 angles that are less than a right angle, 2 angles that are greater than a right angle, and one pair of parallel sides that are not equal in length.

2. **(a)** Quadrilateral A is a square and Quadrilateral B is a parallelogram.

   (b) Both are parallelograms. They each have 4 sides, 4 angles, and opposite sides equal in length and parallel.

   (c) The square has 4 right angles and the parallelogram has 2 angles greater than a right angle and 2 angles less than a right angle. The square has all 4 sides the same length, and the parallelogram does not.

3. Stan is not correct. Possible explanation: Stan drew a rhombus. A rhombus does not have any right angles. A square has 4 right angles.

ONLINE
10min

Objectives

- Know how to define and sketch different quadrilaterals.
- Define and identify attributes of different quadrilaterals.

Students will complete an online Checkpoint. If necessary, read the directions, problems, and answer choices to students and help them with keyboard or mouse operations.

Unit Review

Lesson Overview

UNIT REVIEW Look Back	10 minutes	**ONLINE**
UNIT REVIEW Checkpoint Practice	50 minutes	**ONLINE**
⏩ **UNIT REVIEW** Prepare for the Checkpoint		

▶ Unit Objectives

This lesson reviews the following objectives:

- Identify right angles in geometric figures or everyday objects.
- Identify the measure of an angle in a geometric figure or an everyday object as greater than or less than a right angle.
- Identify, describe, and classify a polygon according to the number of its sides.
- Identify attributes of isosceles, equilateral, and right triangles.
- Identify attributes of parallelograms, rectangles, and squares.
- Know how to define and sketch different quadrilaterals.
- Define and identify attributes of different quadrilaterals.

Materials to Gather

There are no materials to gather for this lesson.

▶ Advance Preparation

In this lesson, students will have an opportunity to review previous activities in the Geometry unit. Look at the suggested activities in Unit Review: Prepare for the Checkpoint online and gather any needed materials.

UNIT REVIEW Look Back

ONLINE **10**min

Objectives

- Review unit objectives.

Students will review key concepts from the unit to prepare for the Unit Checkpoint.

UNIT REVIEW Checkpoint Practice

ONLINE **50**min

Objectives

- Review unit objectives.

Students will complete an online Checkpoint Practice to prepare for the Unit Checkpoint. If necessary, read the directions, problems, and answer choices to students. Have students answer the problems on their own. Review any missed problems with students.

⏩ UNIT REVIEW Prepare for the Checkpoint

What you do next depends on how students performed in the previous activity, Unit Review: Checkpoint Practice. If students had difficulty with any of the problems, complete the appropriate review activity listed in the table online.

Unit Checkpoint

UNIT CHECKPOINT Online   60 minutes   **ONLINE**

▶ Unit Objectives

This lesson assesses the following objectives:

- Identify right angles in geometric figures or everyday objects.
- Identify the measure of an angle in a geometric figure or an everyday object as greater than or less than a right angle.
- Identify, describe, and classify a polygon according to the number of its sides.
- Identify attributes of isosceles, equilateral, and right triangles.
- Identify attributes of parallelograms, rectangles, and squares.
- Know how to define and sketch different quadrilaterals.
- Define and identify attributes of different quadrilaterals.

Materials to Gather

There are no materials to gather for this lesson.

UNIT CHECKPOINT Online   ONLINE **60**min

Students will complete the Unit Checkpoint online. If necessary, read the directions, problems, and answer choices to students and help them with keyboard or mouse operations.

Objectives

- Assess unit objectives.

Extended Problems: Reasoning

Lesson Overview

USE WHAT YOU KNOW Offline	60 minutes	**OFFLINE**

▶ Lesson Objectives

This lesson assesses the following objectives:

- Identify right angles in geometric figures or everyday objects.
- Identify, describe, and classify a polygon according to the number of its sides.
- Know how to define and sketch different quadrilaterals.
- Identify attributes of isosceles, equilateral, and right triangles.
- Identify attributes of parallelograms, rectangles, and squares.
- Draw quadrilaterals that are not rhombuses, rectangles, or squares.
- Identity and name shapes that share specific attributes.
- Analyze complex problems using mathematical knowledge and skills.

Materials to Gather

SUPPLIED

Extended Problems: Reasoning (printout)

Extended Problems: Reasoning Answer Key (printout)

USE WHAT YOU KNOW Offline
OFFLINE
60min

The Extended Problems: Reasoning and its answer key are located online in the Resources section for this unit in the Online Book Menu of *Math+ Purple Lesson Guide*. Give students the Extended Problems: Reasoning. Read the directions, problems, and answer choices to students, if necessary.

You will grade this assignment.

- Students should complete the assignment on their own.
- Students should submit the completed assignment to you.

Objectives

- Analyze complex problems using mathematical knowledge and skills.

Semester Review

Lesson Overview

SEMESTER REVIEW Look Back	20 minutes	**ONLINE**
SEMESTER REVIEW Checkpoint Practice	40 minutes	**ONLINE**
➔ **SEMESTER REVIEW** Prepare for the Checkpoint		

▶ Semester Objectives

- Compare whole numbers through 1,000.
- Order three or more whole numbers through 1,000.
- Round whole numbers through 1,000 to the nearest ten.
- Round whole numbers through 1,000 to the nearest hundred.
- Find the sum or difference of two whole numbers with sums and minuends up through 1,000.
- Identify odd and even numbers and describe their characteristics.
- Recognize and solve a story problem in which two quantities are compared by the use of addition or subtraction.
- Recognize and solve a story problem in which one quantity must be change to equal another quantity.
- Use an equation to represent a relationship between quantities.
- Use an inequality to represent a relationship between quantities.
- Select the appropriate symbol to show an operation or a relationship that makes a number sentence true.
- Determine a missing number in an equation or an inequality.
- Extend a linear pattern, such as stating what number comes next in a series.
- Solve a simple story problem that involves a function.
- Use an area model to explain multiplication.
- Explain and apply the commutative property of multiplication.
- Demonstrate automatic recall of multiplication facts.
- Explain and apply the associative property of multiplication.
- Solve a multiplication problem involving a multidigit factor and a one-digit factor.
- Use multiplication to solve a story problem that involves equal groups.
- Use multiplication to solve a story problem that involves equal measures.
- Use objects or sketches to solve a division problem.
- Demonstrate understanding that division by zero is undefined.
- Recognize the meaning of the three symbols for division.
- Demonstrate an understanding of the inverse relationship between multiplication and division.
- Use the inverse relationship of multiplication and division to compute and check results.
- Use division to solve a story problem that involves equal groups.
- Use division to solve a story problem that involves equal measures.

- Identify right angles in geometric figures or everyday objects.
- Identify, describe, and classify a polygon according to the number of its sides.
- Identify attributes of isosceles, equilateral, and right triangles.
- Identify attributes of parallelograms, rectangles, and squares.
- Know how to define and sketch different quadrilaterals.

▶ Advance Preparation

In this lesson, students will have an opportunity to review previous activities from the semester. Look at the suggested activities in Semester Review: Prepare for the Checkpoint online and be prepared to gather any needed materials.

SEMESTER REVIEW Look Back

ONLINE 20min

Objectives

- Review semester objectives.

As students prepare to complete the semester, they should refresh their knowledge of the math they have learned thus far. You may notice that some of the objectives in the Semester Review are not necessarily included in the Semester Checkpoint. Some of these concepts are particularly important to review in order to be successful with the upcoming topics students will encounter, and others contribute to a greater understanding of the concepts that are being assessed. Therefore, a complete review of the objectives in this lesson is recommended.

To review, first students will practice multiplication and division facts using the Fast Facts Learning Tool. Then they will play a Super Genius game, which includes problems that span the topics covered this semester. If students answer a problem incorrectly, the correct answer will display. Be sure to help students understand why the answer is correct before they move on to the next problem. If they miss several problems, have students play the game again. When students finish playing the Super Genius game, they are given the opportunity to review polygons using the Geoboard Learning Tool.

SEMESTER REVIEW Checkpoint Practice

ONLINE 40min

Objectives

- Review semester objectives.

Students will complete an online Checkpoint Practice to prepare for the Semester Checkpoint. If necessary, read the directions, problems, and answer choices to students. Have students answer the problems on their own. Review any missed problems with students.

▶ SEMESTER REVIEW Prepare for the Checkpoint

What you do next depends on how students performed in the previous activity, Semester Review: Checkpoint Practice. If students had difficulty with any of the problems, complete the appropriate review activity listed in the Unit Review tables online.

Because there are many concepts to review, consider using the Your Choice day to continue preparing for the Semester Checkpoint.

Semester Checkpoint 1

SEMESTER CHECKPOINT Online 　　　　　　　　　　　　　　　　　60 minutes ｜ **ONLINE**

▶ Semester Objectives

- Identify the place value for each digit in whole numbers through 1,000.
- Order three or more whole numbers through 1,000.
- Round whole numbers through 1,000 to the nearest ten.
- Round whole numbers through 1,000 to the nearest hundred.
- Find the sum or difference of two whole numbers with sums and minuends up through 1,000.
- Identify odd and even numbers and describe their characteristics.
- Recognize and solve a story problem in which two quantities are compared by the use of addition or subtraction.
- Recognize and solve a story problem in which one quantity must be changed to equal another quantity.
- Use an equation to represent a relationship between quantities.
- Use an inequality to represent a relationship between quantities.
- Select the appropriate symbol to show an operation or a relationship that makes a number sentence true.
- Determine a missing number in an equation or an inequality.
- Extend a linear pattern, such as stating what number comes next in a series.
- Solve a simple story problem that involves a function.
- Use an area model to explain multiplication.
- Explain and apply the commutative property of multiplication.
- Demonstrate automatic recall of multiplication facts.
- Explain and apply the associative property of multiplication.
- Solve a multiplication problem involving a multidigit factor and a one-digit factor.
- Use multiplication to solve a story problem that involves equal groups.
- Use multiplication to solve a story problem that involves equal measures.
- Use objects or sketches to solve a division problem.
- Demonstrate understanding that division by zero is undefined.
- Recognize the meaning of the three symbols for division.
- Demonstrate an understanding of the inverse relationship between multiplication and division.
- Use the inverse relationship of multiplication and division to compute and check results.
- Use division to solve a story problem that involves equal groups.
- Use division to solve a story problem that involves equal measures.
- Identify right angles in geometric figures or everyday objects.
- Identify, describe, and classify a polygon according to the number of its sides.

Materials to Gather

There are no materials to gather for this lesson.

- Identify attributes of isosceles, equilateral, and right triangles.
- Identify attributes of parallelograms, rectangles, and squares.
- Know how to define and sketch different quadrilaterals.

SEMESTER CHECKPOINT Online

ONLINE 60min

Students will complete this part of Semester Checkpoint online. If necessary, read the directions, problems, and answer choices to students and help them with keyboard or mouse operations.

Objectives

- Assess semester objectives.

Semester Checkpoint 2

SEMESTER CHECKPOINT Offline | 60 minutes | **OFFLINE**

▶ Semester Objectives

- Round whole numbers through 1,000 to the nearest hundred.
- Find the sum or difference of two whole numbers with sums and minuends up through 1,000.
- Recognize and solve a story problem in which two quantities are compared by the use of addition or subtraction.
- Use an equation to represent a relationship between quantities.
- Select the appropriate symbol to show an operation or a relationship that makes a number sentence true.
- Determine a missing number in an equation or an inequality.
- Use an area model to explain multiplication.
- Demonstrate automatic recall of multiplication facts.
- Use multiplication to solve a story problem that involves equal groups.
- Use objects or sketches to solve a division problem.
- Demonstrate an understanding of the inverse relationship between multiplication and division.
- Use the inverse relationship of multiplication and division to compute and check results.
- Use division to solve a story problem that involves equal groups.
- Identify, describe, and classify a polygon according to the number of its sides.
- Identify attributes of parallelograms, rectangles, and squares.
- Know how to define and sketch different quadrilaterals.

Materials to Gather

Semester Checkpoint 2 (printout)
Semester Checkpoint 2 Answer Key (printout)

SEMESTER CHECKPOINT Offline

OFFLINE
60min

Objectives

- Assess semester objectives.

This part of the Semester Checkpoint and its answer key are located in the Resources section for this unit in the Online Book Menu of *Math+ Purple Lesson Guide*. Give students the Semester Checkpoint 2. Have students complete the Semester Checkpoint 2 on their own. Use the answer key to score the Semester Checkpoint 2, and then enter the results online.

Whole Numbers and Multiple Operations

▶ Unit Objectives

- Use the order of operations to evaluate an expression.
- Solve a story problem involving two or more operations.
- Represent a story problem with an equation.
- Determine whether addition, subtraction, multiplication, or division is the appropriate operation to use to solve a story problem and solve the problem.

▶ Big Ideas

- The use of letters, numbers, and mathematical symbols makes possible the translation of complex situations or long word statements into concise mathematical sentences or expressions.
- The order of operations dictates the order in which operations are to be performed. The order of operations ensures that any numerical expression has exactly one correct value.

▶ Unit Introduction

Students have skills with addition, subtraction, multiplication, and division. They have solved many story problems involving each of these operations. They will now see a wide range of story problems and determine which operation is needed to solve the problem. Students will also begin to work with problems that include more than one operation, such as $2 + 10 \times 3 = ?$ A problem like that would have two possible answers if no agreement existed on which operation should be done first. For that agreement, there are the rules in mathematics called the *order of operations*. In this unit, students will use the proper order of operations to find the value of expressions with more than one operation. They will then solve story problems involving more than one operation.

▶ Keywords

associative property
commutative property
expression
order of operations

Use the Order of Operations

GET READY Use Properties to Add or Multiply	10 minutes	**OFFLINE**
LEARN Follow the Order of Operations	15 minutes	**OFFLINE**
LEARN Find the Value of Expressions	10 minutes	**ONLINE**
TRY IT Practice Finding the Value	15 minutes	**OFFLINE**
CHECKPOINT	10 minutes	**ONLINE**

▶ Lesson Objectives

Use the order of operations to evaluate an expression.

Materials to Gather

SUPPLIED

Practice Finding the Value activity page

▶ Prerequisite Skills

Use the commutative and associative properties to simplify expressions.

▶ Content Background

Students will learn about the order of operations and apply the rules to find the value of expressions that involve more than one operation.

The *order of operations* is the set of rules used to evaluate math expressions or solve number sentences. An *expression* is a set of numbers and operations; for example, $3 + 5 \times 4 - 7$. When an expression is written with an equals symbol and a place for the solution, as in $3 + 5 \times 4 - 7 = ?$, use the terms *number sentence* or *equation*. The international mathematics community developed the order of operations to use when a problem has more than one operation.

When doing division problems, avoid using the phrase *goes into*. For example, in the problem $5\overline{)40}$, avoid saying "5 goes into 40." While students may be splitting 40 "into" 5 groups, it makes no sense to say that "5 *goes into* 40." They should consistently relate what they are doing to division. The phrase *goes into* becomes a rote phrase that has no meaning for students. Students should say "40 divided by 5" or "5 divides 40." Learning the words that will help with understanding the math will benefit students as they progress to higher mathematics.

RULES FOR THE ORDER OF OPERATIONS WITH NO PARENTHESES

Multiply or divide from left to right in the order that the $\times$ or $\div$ symbols appear. Then add or subtract from left to right in the order that the $+$ or $-$ symbols appear.

The rules for the order of operations prevent confusion when performing computations with more than one operation. Without the rules, students would get different answers depending on which operations they completed first. For example, using the order of operations for $7 + 2 \times 3 = ?$ gives the correct answer 13. The rules say to multiply and divide first so $7 + 2 \times 3$ becomes $7 + 6$. However, when the order of operations is not followed, students are likely to start at the left and say $7 + 2 = 9$ and 9×3 is 27. Order of operations enables everyone in the world to agree that the answer is 13, not 27.

Students will not use parentheses in this lesson. The goal is for them to learn and understand the rules when there are no parentheses. However, at a later time, students will learn that by inserting parentheses in a computation problem, they can change or clarify the order in which operations are performed.

GET READY Use Properties to Add or Multiply

OFFLINE
10 min

Objectives

- Use the commutative and associative properties to simplify expressions.

Students will review the commutative and associative properties of addition and multiplication and apply these properties to simplify expressions.

1. Review the commutative and associative properties of addition through an example.
   - **Say:** The commutative property of addition states that changing the order of the numbers in an addition problem does not change the answer.
   - **Say:** The associative property of addition states that grouping the numbers in an addition problem in different ways does not change the answer.
   - Have students write the expression $40 + 34 + 10$ in their Math Notebook. Remind them that this is an expression because it has numbers and operation symbols. (If it had an equals symbol, it would be a number sentence or equation rather than just an expression.)
   - Ask students how they could change the order of the numbers to make the problem easier to add. You could change the order of 34 and 10 so the expression is $40 + 10 + 34$.
   - Remind students that when they change the order of numbers in an addition problem, they are using the commutative property.
   - **Ask:** Which two numbers would you add first? $40 + 10$
   - Remind students that when they group numbers in an addition problem to make it easier to add, they are using the associative property of addition.

$$40 + 10 + 34$$
$$\vee$$
$$50 + 34 = 84$$

2. Review the commutative and associative properties of multiplication through an example.
   - **Say:** The commutative property of multiplication states that changing the order of the factors does not change the product.
   - **Say:** The associative property of multiplication states that grouping factors in different ways does not change the product.
   - Have students write the expression $5 \times 7 \times 2$ in their Math Notebook.
   - Have students change the order to make the numbers easier to multiply. They may change the order of the 7 and 2, or they may change the order of the 5 and 7. Remind them that changing the order is an example of the commutative property of multiplication.
   - Have students group 5×2 and multiply those first to get 10. Note that the 5×2 might be on the left or right depending on how students changed the order. They should then multiply by 7 to get 70. Tell students they have just used the associative property of multiplication.

two ways to multiply $5 \times 7 \times 2$

$5 \times 2 \times 7$	$7 \times 5 \times 2$
$\vee$	$\vee$
$10 \times 7 = 70$	$7 \times 10 = 70$

3. Have students use the commutative and associative properties of addition and multiplication to find the value of each expression.

   - $61 + 15 + 9$ $61 + 9 + 15 = 85$
   - $7 + 56 + 13$ $7 + 13 + 56 = 76$
   - $4 \times 9 \times 5$ $4 \times 5 \times 9 = 180$
   - $5 \times 9 \times 2$ $5 \times 2 \times 9 = 90$

LEARN Follow the Order of Operations

OFFLINE
15 min

Students will learn the order of operations and find the value of expressions that have more than one operation.

1. Explain to students that they know the four basic operations (addition, subtraction, multiplication, and division) and that they will use these operations throughout their life to solve problems.

2. Tell students that most problems they have seen so far involved only one operation, but now they will solve problems with more than one operation.

   Say: To find the value of an expression with more than one operation, you need rules to tell you how to find the value correctly.

3. Write the expression $7 + 2 \times 3$. Ask students to find the value of the expression. Most students will calculate from left to right and get the value of 27. Others might multiply first and then add to get the value of 13. Ask students to share their answers and explain how they found the value.

4. Tell students that problems like this one might seem to have two reasonable answers. However, there is only one correct answer. Explain that there are rules so everyone knows what the one correct answer is.

   Say: These rules are called the order of operations. They tell you what order to calculate in so that everyone around the world finds the same value.

5. Go back to the original problem and explain that the value is 13.

6. Present the order of operations to students.

   - Multiply or divide from left to right in the order that the $\times$ or $\div$ symbols appear.
   - Then add or subtract from left to right in the order that the $+$ or $-$ symbols appear.

7. Have students write the rules in their Math Notebook.

8. Ask students to look back at the expression $7 + 2 \times 3$ and explain how using the order of operations results in the correct answer, 13. First you multiply 2×3 and get a product of 6. Then you add $7 + 6$ and get a sum of 13.

9. Write the expression $20 - 5 \times 2$. Ask students to use the order of operations rules to find the correct answer. 10

   If students don't get 10 for the answer, show how the correct answer is found by multiplying first and then subtracting: $5 \times 2 = 10$ and $20 - 10 = 10$.

10. Write the expression $60 - 10 \div 2 \times 3$. Have students record each step as they find the value.

Ask: Will you multiply or divide first? How do you know? divide; The rules say to multiply or divide from left to right in the order the symbols appear, and in this problem division appears first.

Ask: What is 10 divided by 2? 5

Say: Now multiply 5 times 3 and then subtract.

Ask: What is the value of the expression? $60 - 15 = 45$

11. Have students practice using the order of operations to find the value of the following expressions:

- $72 \div 8 - 5 \quad 9 - 5 = 4$
- $9 + 6 \div 3 \quad 9 + 2 = 11$
- $8 + 6 \times 5 - 3 \quad 8 + 30 - 3 = 35$
- $20 + 12 \div 4 - 2 \times 5 \quad 20 + 3 - 10 = 13$

ONLINE

LEARN Find the Value of Expressions

Objectives

- Use the order of operations to evaluate an expression.

Students will use the order of operations to find the value of expressions. Remind students that when doing problems with multiple operations, they should

- Multiply or divide from left to right in the order the $\times$ or $\div$ symbols appear.
- Then add or subtract from left to right in the order the $+$ or $-$ symbols appear.

Tips Have students say each step in finding the value of each expression.

OFFLINE

TRY IT Practice Finding the Value

Objectives

- Use the order of operations to evaluate an expression.

Students will practice using the order of operations to find the value of expressions. View or print the Practice Finding the Value activity page and read the directions with students.

Students should copy the problems from the Activity Book into their Math Notebook as necessary and solve them there.

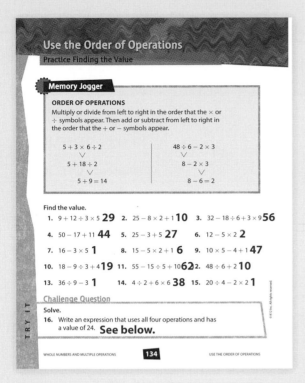

Additional Answers

16. Answers will vary. The expression should include all four operations (addition, subtraction, multiplication, and division) and have a value of 24.

   Sample answer: $3 \times 4 + 12 \div 2 + 8 - 2$; Students may also come up with clever answers that use ones or zeros such as $24 \div 24 \times 1 - 1 + 24$ or $1 \div 1 \times 0 - 0 + 24$.

CHECKPOINT

ONLINE 10 min

Students will complete an online Checkpoint. If necessary, read the directions, questions, and answer choices to students and help them with keyboard or mouse operations.

Objectives

- Use the order of operations to evaluate an expression.

Choose the Correct Operation (A)

Lesson Overview

GET READY Create Silly Story Problems	5 minutes	**OFFLINE**
LEARN Add or Subtract to Solve	10 minutes	**OFFLINE**
LEARN Multiply or Divide to Solve	10 minutes	**OFFLINE**
LEARN Operations and Unknown Values	10 minutes	**OFFLINE**
LEARN Identify the Operation and Solve	15 minutes	**ONLINE**
TRY IT Choose the Operation and Solve	10 minutes	**ONLINE**

▶ Lesson Objectives

Determine whether addition, subtraction, multiplication, or division is the appropriate operation to use to solve a story problem and solve the problem.

▶ Prerequisite Skills

- Write and solve addition or subtraction number sentences to represent problem-solving situations with sums and minuends up through 1,000.
- Create a story problem that can be represented by a multiplication number sentence.
- Create a story problem that can be represented by a division number sentence.

▶ Content Background

Students will learn to identify which operation—addition, subtraction, multiplication, or division—is appropriate to use to solve a story problem. Then they will solve the problem. They should be able to explain why they know a given operation is the correct one. When students do addition problems, they are combining amounts; for subtraction they are finding the difference between two numbers; with multiplication they are finding the total when there are several equal amounts; and with division they have a total amount that is being divided into equal groups.

Problem solving is a part of daily life. To become good problem solvers, students need to recognize when a new problem is similar to a problem they have already solved. Instead of treating every problem they encounter as new, students can build on their previous experiences with problems and develop strategies to solve similar problems. Knowing they have successfully completed similar problems will help students become confident problem solvers.

Students have solved a variety of problems using the four basic operations: addition, subtraction, multiplication, and division. When they see a new problem, they need to first decide which operation should be used to solve it. Then they can write a number sentence to solve the problem.

Materials to Gather

SUPPLIED

Add or Subtract to Solve activity page

Multiply or Divide to Solve activity page

Operations and Unknown Values activity page

▶ Common Errors and Misconceptions

- Students might have difficulty solving nonstandard problems, problems requiring multiple steps, or problems with extra information. Avoid introducing students to techniques that work for one-step problems but do not work for multistep problems, such as associating key words with particular operations.

- Students might quickly read through a problem and immediately begin to compute with the numbers, often choosing the wrong operation because they did not take time to read through and understand the context of the problem. Students need to learn to use "slow-down" mechanisms that can help them concentrate on thoroughly understanding a problem before they solve it.

GET READY Create Silly Story Problems

OFFLINE
5min

Students will create humorous multiplication and division story problems. They will not solve the problems, but they will explain how they know which operation to use to solve them.

There are no materials to gather for this activity.

1. **Say:** You know how to solve many kinds of story problems and you have written your own story problems. You are going to make up silly story problems and tell which operation, multiplication or division, to use to solve the problems.

2. Discuss with students how multiplication and division story problems are different. Multiplication problems often describe combining equal groups to find a total while division problems separate a total into equal groups.

3. Write the numbers 3, 5, 30, and 50. Explain to students that they will use these numbers to make up a story problem that can be solved using multiplication, and then make up a problem that can be solved using division.

4. Tell students that their problems should be about banana slugs, elves, or another subject they find interesting or humorous. Share the following examples with students:

   - Three elves each invited 30 banana slugs for lunch. How many banana slugs came to lunch in all?

   - Fifty banana slugs are seated evenly at 5 tables. How many banana slugs are seated at each table?

5. Explain to students that they do not need to solve their story problem or write a number sentence. Have them simply say their story problem and explain how they know which operation to use to solve it.

6. If time permits, have students make up an addition or a subtraction problem.

Objectives

- Write and solve addition or subtraction number sentences to represent problem-solving situations with sums and minuends up through 1,000.

- Create a story problem that can be represented by a multiplication number sentence.

- Create a story problem that can be represented by a division number sentence.

Tips

If you wish, change the numbers and use this type of activity during car rides or around the dinner table.

LEARN Add or Subtract to Solve

Objectives

- Determine whether addition, subtraction, multiplication, or division is the appropriate operation to use to solve a story problem and solve the problem.

Students will identify the correct operation and number sentence that can be used to solve an addition or subtraction story problem. They will write the number sentence and solve the problem. View or print the Add or Subtract to Solve activity page and read the directions with students.

Students should copy the problems from the Activity Book into their Math Notebook as necessary and solve them there.

1. To start, ask students how they know whether to add or subtract when they do story problems. **Example:** You add when you combine groups and subtract when you take some away or want to find out how much more one group has than the other.

2. Read each of the following situations to students. Ask them whether they would add or subtract to solve the problem. Have them explain how they know which operation to use. Have students focus on the operation for these four problems rather than solving them.

   - Kelly kayaked 14 miles. Brian kayaked 11 miles. How many more miles did Kelly kayak than Brian? Subtract to find the difference.

   - There are 453 campers are eating in the dining hall and 278 campers are eating hamburgers. The rest are eating hot dogs. How many campers are eating hot dogs? Subtract the number of people eating hamburgers from the total to find out how many people are eating hot dogs.

   - There are 143 campers who want to kayak in the lake. Everyone who kayaks needs a paddle. There are 121 paddles. How many more paddles are needed so that everyone can kayak? Subtract to find out how many more paddles are needed.

   - Kelly has 21 pieces of ribbon. She gives 14 pieces away. How many pieces does Kelly have left? Subtract the number given away from the total number of pieces (separation from a group).

3. Read the Worked Example on the activity page with students. Have them answer the questions in the Solution.

   - What are you asked to find in the story problem? the number of adults who visited the park Thursday

   - Would a picture or model help you understand the problem? **Example:** Yes, you could draw a long bar to show the total. Underneath, you could draw shorter bars to show the number of children and the number of adults, which you don't know yet.

984 people	
237 children	? adults

   - Which operation will you use? subtraction

   - How do you know that you should use that operation? because you have to find the difference between the number of adults and the number of children

   - What number sentence will you use to solve the story problem? $984 - 237 = ?$

4. Have students read Problem 1. Guide students to answer each question from the Worked Example as it relates to Problem 1.

- What are you asked to find in the story problem? the number of people at the park after it started raining
- Would a picture or model help you understand the problem? Answers may vary.
- Which operation will you use? subtraction
- How do you know that you should use that operation? **Example:** In the problem, you take some away from a group; you know you have to subtract to find the remaining amount.
- What number sentence will you use to solve the story problem? $756 - 284 = ?$

5. Have students write the number sentence and subtract to answer the question.

6. Have students solve Problems 2–5 on their own. They should identify the operation, the number sentence, and the solution for each problem in their Math Notebook.

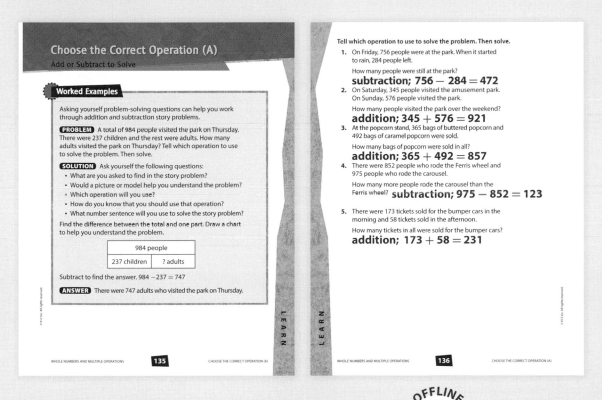

Choose the Correct Operation (A)
Add or Subtract to Solve

Worked Examples

Asking yourself problem-solving questions can help you work through addition and subtraction story problems.

PROBLEM A total of 984 people visited the park on Thursday. There were 237 children and the rest were adults. How many adults visited the park on Thursday? Tell which operation to use to solve the problem. Then solve.

SOLUTION Ask yourself the following questions:
- What are you asked to find in the story problem?
- Would a picture or model help you understand the problem?
- Which operation will you use?
- How do you know that you should use that operation?
- What number sentence will you use to solve the story problem?

Find the difference between the total and one part. Draw a chart to help you understand the problem.

984 people	
237 children	? adults

Subtract to find the answer. $984 - 237 = 747$

ANSWER There were 747 adults who visited the park on Thursday.

Tell which operation to use to solve the problem. Then solve.

1. On Friday, 756 people were at the park. When it started to rain, 284 people left.
   How many people were still at the park?
   subtraction; $756 - 284 = 472$
2. On Saturday, 345 people visited the amusement park. On Sunday, 576 people visited the park.
   How many people visited the park over the weekend?
   addition; $345 + 576 = 921$
3. At the popcorn stand, 365 bags of buttered popcorn and 492 bags of caramel popcorn were sold.
   How many bags of popcorn were sold in all?
   addition; $365 + 492 = 857$
4. There were 852 people who rode the Ferris wheel and 975 people who rode the carousel.
   How many more people rode the carousel than the Ferris wheel? **subtraction; $975 - 852 = 123$**
5. There were 173 tickets sold for the bumper cars in the morning and 58 tickets sold in the afternoon.
   How many tickets in all were sold for the bumper cars?
   addition; $173 + 58 = 231$

WHOLE NUMBERS AND MULTIPLE OPERATIONS   135   CHOOSE THE CORRECT OPERATION (A)

WHOLE NUMBERS AND MULTIPLE OPERATIONS   136   CHOOSE THE CORRECT OPERATION (A)

LEARN Multiply or Divide to Solve

OFFLINE
10 min

Objectives

Students will identify the correct operation and number sentence to use to solve a multiplication or division story problem. They will write the number sentence and solve the problem.

1. Ask students to share an example of a story problem that is solved using multiplication. **Example:** I had 3 fish tanks. Each tank had 9 fish in it. I bought a bigger tank so that I could put all the fish together. How many fish are in the bigger tank?

- Determine whether addition, subtraction, multiplication, or division is the appropriate operation to use to solve a story problem and solve the problem.

2. Share the following division situations with students. Ask students to explain why they can use division to solve each problem. (Students do not have to solve the problem or to identify which problems involve separating and which involve sharing.) Answers should include that division involves separating objects into equal groups or sharing a group equally.

   - Kelly is packing lunches. She has 32 carrot sticks. She puts 4 carrot sticks in each lunch. How many lunches does Kelly pack?

   - Kelly and Brian share 24 baseball cards equally. How many cards does each person get?

   - Brian buys 18 granola bars to take to play practice. Each person eats 2 granola bars until all the granola bars are eaten. How many people eat granola bars?

3. View or print the Multiply or Divide to Solve activity page. Read the Worked Example with students. Have them answer the questions in the Solution.

   - What are you asked to find in the story problem? the total number of squares in the quilt

   - Would a picture or model help you understand the problem? **Example:** Yes, you could make a sketch of 9 rows with 12 squares in each row.

   - Which operation will you use? multiplication

   - How do you know that you should use that operation? because there are 9 equal groups of 12

   - What number sentence will you use to solve the story problem? $9 \times 12 = ?$

4. Have students read Problem 1. Guide students to answer each question from the Worked Example as it relates to Problem 1.

   - What are you asked to find in the story problem? how many days it will take to sell all the paintbrushes

   - Would a picture or model help you understand the problem? **Example:** No, you don't need a picture or model; you can just use the numbers.

   - Which operation will you use? division

   - How do you know that you should use that operation? **Example:** You know the total number of objects and the number in each group; you know that you can use division to find the total number of equal groups.

   - What number sentence will you use to solve the story problem? $54 \div 6 = ?$

5. Have students write the number sentence and divide to answer the question.

6. Have students solve Problems 2–5 on their own. They should identify the operation, the number sentence, and the solution in their Math Notebook.

7. Have students look at Problems 2 and 4 for similarities in the language. Guide them to see that both problems ask them to find a total or to combine parts.

8. Then have students look at Problems 1, 3, and 5 for similarities. Guide them to see that all three problems involve dividing a whole into equal parts or equally sharing a total.

9. Point out that both multiplication and division problems use some of the same words, such as *each*. Tell students that looking for specific words will not indicate which operation to use. Explain that identifying the overall meaning of the story problem will indicate which operation to use.

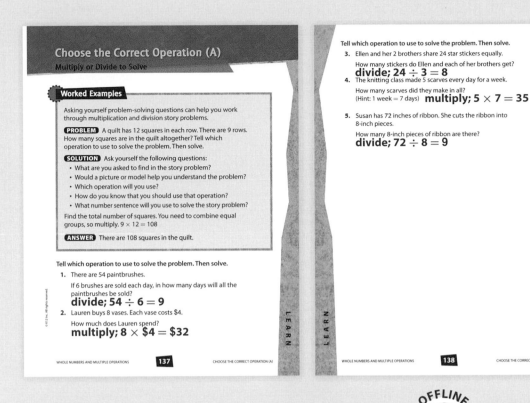

Choose the Correct Operation (A)
Multiply or Divide to Solve

Worked Examples

Asking yourself problem-solving questions can help you work through multiplication and division story problems.

PROBLEM A quilt has 12 squares in each row. There are 9 rows. How many squares are in the quilt altogether? Tell which operation to use to solve the problem. Then solve.

SOLUTION Ask yourself the following questions:
• What are you asked to find in the story problem?
• Would a picture or model help you understand the problem?
• Which operation will you use?
• How do you know that you should use that operation?
• What number sentence will you use to solve the story problem?

Find the total number of squares. You need to combine equal groups, so multiply. $9 \times 12 = 108$

ANSWER There are 108 squares in the quilt.

Tell which operation to use to solve the problem. Then solve.

1. There are 54 paintbrushes.

   If 6 brushes are sold each day, in how many days will all the paintbrushes be sold?
   divide; $54 \div 6 = 9$

2. Lauren buys 8 vases. Each vase costs $4.

   How much does Lauren spend?
   multiply; $8 \times \$4 = \$32$

WHOLE NUMBERS AND MULTIPLE OPERATIONS   **137**   CHOOSE THE CORRECT OPERATION (A)

Tell which operation to use to solve the problem. Then solve.

3. Ellen and her 2 brothers share 24 star stickers equally.

   How many stickers do Ellen and each of her brothers get?
   divide; $24 \div 3 = 8$

4. The knitting class made 5 scarves every day for a week.

   How many scarves did they make in all?
   (Hint: 1 week = 7 days) **multiply; $5 \times 7 = 35$**

5. Susan has 72 inches of ribbon. She cuts the ribbon into 8-inch pieces.

   How many 8-inch pieces of ribbon are there?
   divide; $72 \div 8 = 9$

WHOLE NUMBERS AND MULTIPLE OPERATIONS   **138**   CHOOSE THE CORRECT OPERATION (A)

LEARN Operations and Unknown Values

OFFLINE **10** min

Objectives

• Determine whether addition, subtraction, multiplication, or division is the appropriate operation to use to solve a story problem and solve the problem.

Students will learn to choose the correct operation so that an equation with an unknown value models a problem.

View or print the Operations and Unknown Values activity page and read the directions with students. They should copy the problems into their Math Notebook as necessary and solve them there.

1. Read Problem 1 in the Worked Examples with students. Talk with students about addition and subtraction, and determine which of these operations they should choose so that the equation models the problem. If students are having difficulty, talk about everyday examples where addition and subtraction would be used.

   • addition: You have two amounts that you want to put together.

   • subtraction: You have an amount and you want to take some away, or you want to compare your amount with another one.

2. Have students complete Problems 1–3, referring to Problem 1 in the Worked Examples as necessary. For each problem, have students explain why they chose the operation they did. Guide them in verbalizing the meaning of the operation, as shown in Step 1.

3. Read Problem 2 in the Worked Examples with students. Talk with students about multiplication and division, and determine which of these operations they should choose so that the equation models the problem. If students are having difficulty, talk about everyday examples where multiplication and division would be used.

   • multiplication: You have a certain number of groups of objects that all have the amount in them, or you know how many rows and columns you have in an array.

- division: You want to share a certain amount equally or find out how many equal groups you can create with a certain amount.

4. Have students complete Problems 4–6, referring to Problem 2 in the Worked Examples as necessary. For each problem, have students explain why they chose the operation they did. Guide them in verbalizing the meaning of the operation, as shown in Step 3.

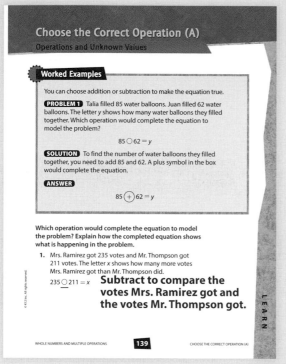

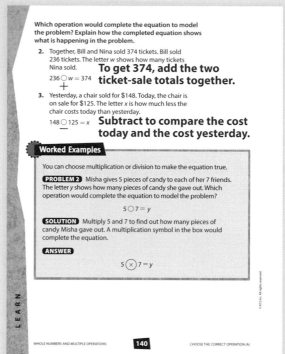

Additional Answers

4. $40 \div 8 = x$

   Forty apples are shared equally with 8 people. Divide 40 by 8 to find how many apples each person gets.

5. $5 \times w = 15$

   To get 15, multiply 5 by how many pictures he painted each day. If students point out that the painter might have painted a different number of pictures each day but still painted 15 in 5 days, tell them that this problem is just showing how many pictures he would have painted each day if he had painted at a steady pace.

LEARN Identify the Operation and Solve

ONLINE
15 min

Objectives

- Determine whether addition, subtraction, multiplication, or division is the appropriate operation to use to solve a story problem and solve the problem.

Students will decide which operation—addition, subtraction, multiplication, or division—is appropriate to use to solve a story problem. Then they will create the equation to solve the story problem and solve.

You should sit with students as they complete this activity. Ask the following questions as students work to solve each story problem:

- What are you asked to find in the story problem?
- Would a picture or model help you understand the problem?
- Which operation will you use?
- How do you know that you should use that operation?
- What number sentence will you use to solve the story problem?

TRY IT Choose the Operation and Solve

ONLINE
10 min

Objectives

- Determine whether addition, subtraction, multiplication, or division is the appropriate operation to use to solve a story problem and solve the problem.

Students will complete an online Try It. If necessary, read the directions, problems, and answer choices to students and help them with keyboard or mouse operations.

Choose the Correct Operation (B)

Lesson Overview

LEARN Explain Thinking About Solutions	15 minutes	**OFFLINE**
LEARN Solve Circus Story Problems	10 minutes	**OFFLINE**
LEARN Understanding Operations	15 minutes	**OFFLINE**
TRY IT Choose the Operation at Camp	10 minutes	**OFFLINE**
CHECKPOINT	10 minutes	**ONLINE**

▶ Lesson Objectives

Determine whether addition, subtraction, multiplication, or division is the appropriate operation to use to solve a story problem and solve the problem.

▶ Prerequisite Skills

- Write and solve addition or subtraction number sentences to represent problem-solving situations with sums and minuends up through 1,000.
- Create a story problem that can be represented by a multiplication number sentence.
- Create a story problem that can be represented by a division number sentence.

▶ Content Background

Students will continue to learn to identify which operation—addition, subtraction, multiplication, or division—is appropriate to use to solve a story problem and then solve the problem. They should be able to explain why they know a given operation is the correct one. When students do addition problems, they are combining amounts; for subtraction they are finding the difference between two numbers; with multiplication they are finding the total when there are several equal amounts; and with division, they have a total amount that is being divided into equal groups.

Problem solving is a part of daily life. To become good problem solvers, students need to recognize when a new problem is similar to a problem they have already solved. Instead of treating every problem they encounter as new, students can build on their previous experiences with problems and develop strategies to solve similar problems. Knowing they have successfully completed similar problems will help students become confident problem solvers.

Students have solved a variety of problems using the four basic operations: addition, subtraction, multiplication, and division. When they see a new problem, they need to first decide which operation should be used to solve it. Then they can write a number sentence to solve the problem.

Materials to Gather

SUPPLIED

Explain Thinking About Solutions activity page

Solve Circus Story Problems activity page

Understanding Operations activity page

Choose the Operation at Camp activity page

ALSO NEEDED

index card (optional)

▶ Common Errors and Misconceptions

- Students might have difficulty solving nonstandard problems, problems requiring multiple steps, or problems with extra information. Avoid introducing students to techniques that work for one-step problems but do not work for multistep problems, such as associating key words with particular operations.

- Students might quickly read through a problem and immediately begin to compute with the numbers, often choosing the wrong operation because they did not take time to read through and understand the context of the problem. Students need to learn to use "slow-down" mechanisms that can help them concentrate on thoroughly understanding a problem before they solve it.

LEARN Explain Thinking About Solutions

OFFLINE **15**min

Students will explain their thinking to solve a story problem. They will solve the problem and label the answer.

1. View or print the Explain Thinking About Solutions activity page. Read the Worked Example with students.

2. Discuss the problem-solving questions students should ask themselves as they work to solve story problems.

   - What are you asked to find in the story problem?
   - Would a picture or model help you understand the problem?
   - Which operation will you use?
   - How do you know that you should use that operation?
   - What number sentence will you use to solve the story problem?

   Point out to students how the solution to the Worked Example addresses all the problem-solving questions. Also point out that the question asked for a cost and thus the answer had to be a dollar amount. Tell students that a number alone wouldn't have been enough to answer the question. A statement that includes a label is needed to explain and give meaning to the number.

3. Read Problem 1 with students. Ask students the problem-solving questions listed in Step 2, and have them answer. Make sure they understand how to find the information in the story problem to answer each question. Have them write and solve the number sentence in their Math Notebook.

4. Read Problem 2 with students. Have students tell you the problem-solving questions they would ask and answer. Then have them write and solve the number sentence in their Math Notebook.

5. Repeat Step 4 for Problem 3.

Objectives

- Determine whether addition, subtraction, multiplication, or division is the appropriate operation to use to solve a story problem and solve the problem.

Tips

Write the questions from Step 2 on an index card for students to use as a reference when solving story problems.

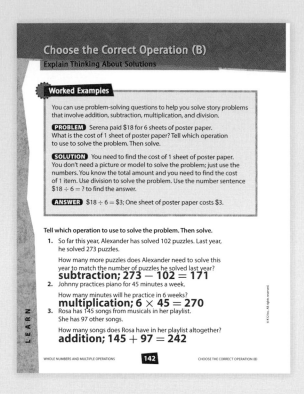

LEARN Solve Circus Story Problems

OFFLINE
10min

Objectives

Students will identify the correct operation and number sentence to solve a story problem. They will write the number sentence and label the answer.

- Determine whether addition, subtraction, multiplication, or division is the appropriate operation to use to solve a story problem and solve the problem.

1. To begin, review with students the problem-solving questions they can use to solve story problems:
   - What are you asked to find in the story problem?
   - Would a picture or model help you understand the problem?
   - Which operation will you use?
   - How do you know that you should use that operation?
   - What number sentence will you use to solve the story problem?

2. View or print the Solve Circus Story Problems activity page. Read the Worked Example with students.

   Say: The solution to this problem shows how the problem-solving questions were used. One of those questions is "Which operation will you use?" When you have a story problem, how do you decide which operation to use?
   Example: You read the problem; think about what the question is asking; and decide whether to add, subtract, multiply, or divide.

   Tell students that these steps will help them solve any story problem.

3. Work with students to solve Problems 1–4. Encourage them to think about how to solve each problem by asking and answering the problem-solving questions. If they are having trouble deciding which operation to use, they should read the problem; think about what question is being asked; draw a picture if necessary; and decide whether they will add, subtract, multiply or divide to answer the question.

4. Have students review their solutions and check that the answer to Problem 3 has a label.

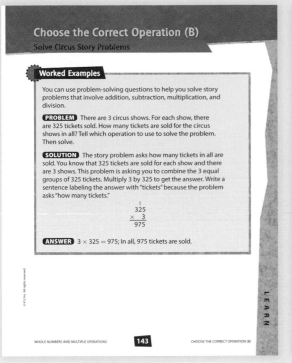

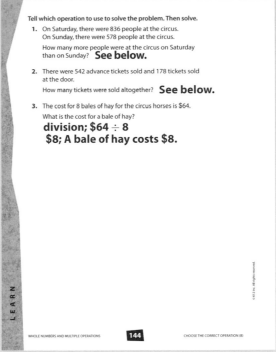

Choose the Correct Operation (B)

Solve Circus Story Problems

Worked Examples

You can use problem-solving questions to help you solve story problems that involve addition, subtraction, multiplication, and division.

PROBLEM There are 3 circus shows. For each show, there are 325 tickets sold. How many tickets are sold for the circus shows in all? Tell which operation to use to solve the problem. Then solve.

SOLUTION The story problem asks how many tickets in all are sold. You know that 325 tickets are sold for each show and there are 3 shows. This problem is asking you to combine the 3 equal groups of 325 tickets. Multiply 3 by 325 to get the answer. Write a sentence labeling the answer with "tickets" because the problem asks "how many tickets."

$$\begin{array}{r} \scriptstyle 1 \\ 325 \\ \times \quad 3 \\ \hline 975 \end{array}$$

ANSWER $3 \times 325 = 975$; In all, 975 tickets are sold.

LEARN

LEARN

Tell which operation to use to solve the problem. Then solve.

1. On Saturday, there were 836 people at the circus. On Sunday, there were 578 people at the circus.
   How many more people were at the circus on Saturday than on Sunday? **See below.**
2. There were 542 advance tickets sold and 178 tickets sold at the door.
   How many tickets were sold altogether? **See below.**
3. The cost for 8 bales of hay for the circus horses is $64.
   What is the cost for a bale of hay?
   division; $64 ÷ 8
   $8; A bale of hay costs $8.

Additional Answers

1. subtraction; $836 - 578 = 258$; There were 258 more people at the circus on Saturday.
2. addition; $542 + 178 = 720$; In all, 720 tickets were sold.

LEARN Understanding Operations

OFFLINE 15 min

Objectives

- Determine whether addition, subtraction, multiplication, or division is the appropriate operation to use to solve a story problem and solve the problem.

Students will learn to choose the correct operation so that an equation models a problem.

View or print the Understanding Operations activity page and read the directions with students. They should copy the problems into their Math Notebook as necessary and solve them there.

1. Read the Worked Example with students. Talk with students about the four operations and determine which of these operations they should choose so that the equation models the problem. If students are struggling, discuss simple everyday examples that involve each of the four operations.
   - addition: You have two amounts that you want to put together.
   - subtraction: You have an amount and you want to take some away, or you want to compare your amount with another one.
   - multiplication: You have a certain number of groups of objects that all have the amount in them, or you know how many rows and columns you have in an array.
   - division: You want to share a certain amount equally or find out how many equal groups you can create with a certain amount.
2. Alternately, have students choose any operation and see why that operation does or does not work in the equation.

3. Have students complete Problems 1–4, referring to the Worked Example as necessary. For each problem, have students explain why they chose the operation they did. Guide them in verbalizing the meaning of the operation, as shown in Step 1.

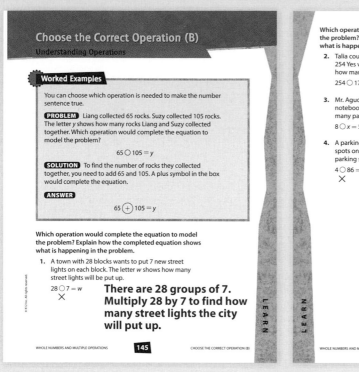

Additional Answers

2. $254 \ominus 176 = y$

There were 254 Yes votes and 176 No votes. Subtract to compare the Yes votes and the No votes.

3. $8 \otimes x = 56$

There are an unknown number of packages, with 8 notebooks in each package to make a total of 56 notebooks. Find what number multiplied by 8 equals 56 to find how many packages Mr. Aguda needs to buy.

TRY IT Choose the Operation at Camp

OFFLINE

10 min

Students will practice determining whether to add, subtract, multiply, or divide to solve a story problem and then solve the problem. View or print the Choose the Operation at Camp activity page and read the directions with students.

Students should copy the problems from the Activity Book into their Math Notebook as necessary and solve them there.

Objectives

- Determine whether addition, subtraction, multiplication, or division is the appropriate operation to use to solve a story problem and solve the problem.

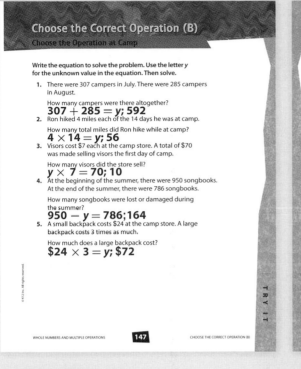

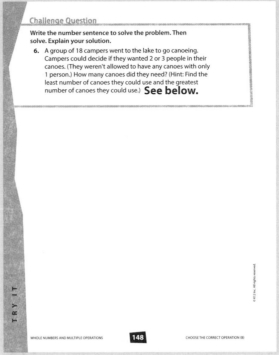

Additional Answers

6. They would need at least 6 canoes and at most 9 canoes.

Explanation: $18 \div 3 = 6$

If they put 3 people in each canoe, they would need 6 canoes.

Explanation: $18 \div 2 = 9$

If they put 2 people in each canoe, they would need 9 canoes.

ONLINE
10 min

CHECKPOINT

Objectives

Students will complete an online Checkpoint. If necessary, read the directions, problems, and answer choices to students and help them with keyboard or mouse operations.

- Determine whether addition, subtraction, multiplication, or division is the appropriate operation to use to solve a story problem and solve the problem.

Use More Than One Operation (A)

▶ **Lesson Objectives**

Solve a story problem involving two or more operations.

▶ **Prerequisite Skills**

Determine whether addition, subtraction, multiplication, or division is the appropriate operation to use to solve a story problem and solve the problem.

▶ **Content Background**

Students will learn to solve a problem with multiple steps and involving more than one operation.

Problem solving is a part of daily life. To become good problem solvers, students need to recognize when a new problem is similar to a problem they have already solved. Instead of treating every problem they encounter as new, students can build on their previous experiences with problems and develop strategies to solve similar problems. Knowing they have successfully completed similar problems will help students become confident problem solvers.

Students have solved a wide variety of story problems using the four basic operations: addition, subtraction, multiplication, and division. They will now use their problem-solving skills to solve problems that involve more than one operation.

▶ **Common Errors and Misconceptions**

- Students might have difficulty solving nonstandard problems, problems requiring multiple steps, or problems with extra information. Avoid introducing students to techniques that work for one-step problems but do not work for multistep problems, such as associating key words with particular operations.

- Students might quickly read through a problem and immediately begin to compute with the numbers, often choosing the wrong operation because they did not take time to read through and understand the context of the problem. Students need to learn to use "slow-down" mechanisms that can help them concentrate on thoroughly understanding a problem before they solve it.

Materials to Gather

SUPPLIED

Problems with More Than One Step activity page

GET READY Choose the Operation

Students will choose the correct operation to solve a story problem and then solve it.

Objectives

- Determine whether addition, subtraction, multiplication, or division is the appropriate operation to use to solve a story problem and solve the problem.

OFFLINE
20min

LEARN Problems with More Than One Step

Objectives

Students will solve story problems using two or more operations.

- Solve a story problem involving two or more operations.

1. View or print the Problems with More Than One Step activity page. Read the Worked Example with students. Have them answer the problem-solving questions aloud. Make sure they understand how the answer was reached before continuing.

2. Read Problem 1 with students. Ask them to explain their thinking about how they would solve the problem. Encourage them to share the problem-solving questions and answers they use to work through solving the problem.

3. Have students solve Problem 1. Emphasize the importance of including a label in the answer. Remind students that labels explain and give meaning to the answers.

4. Have students solve Problems 2–4 on their own. Students should record their answers in their Math Notebook.

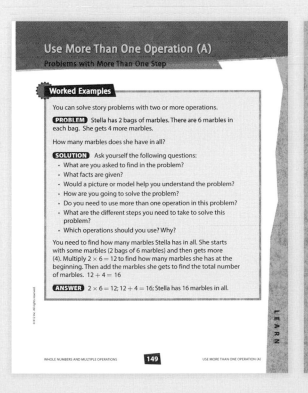

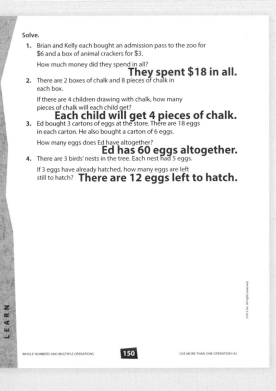

LEARN Problem Solving at the Carousel

ONLINE 20min

Objectives

- Solve a story problem involving two or more operations.

Students will use information in a chart to practice solving story problems that involve more than one step and more than one operation. They should do the calculations in their Math Notebook and enter the answers online.

Tips   Encourage students to use the problem-solving questions to help them solve the story problems.

TRY IT Problems with Two or More Operations

ONLINE 15min

Objectives

- Solve a story problem involving two or more operations.

Students will complete an online Try It. If necessary, read the directions, problems, and answer choices to students and help them with keyboard or mouse operations.

Use More Than One Operation (B)

GET READY Solve Problems at the Circus	5 minutes	**ONLINE**
LEARN Problem-Solving Questions	20 minutes	**OFFLINE**
TRY IT More Than One Operation	25 minutes	**OFFLINE**
CHECKPOINT	10 minutes	**ONLINE**

▶ Lesson Objectives

Solve a story problem involving two or more operations.

▶ Prerequisite Skills

Determine whether addition, subtraction, multiplication, or division is the appropriate operation to use to solve a story problem and solve the problem.

▶ Content Background

Students will continue to learn to solve a problem with multiple steps and involving more than one operation.

Problem solving is a part of daily life. To become good problem solvers, students need to recognize when a new problem is similar to a problem they have already solved. Instead of treating every problem they encounter as new, students can build on their previous experiences with problems and develop strategies to solve similar problems. Knowing they have successfully completed similar problems will help students become confident problem solvers.

Students have solved a wide variety of story problems using the four basic operations: addition, subtraction, multiplication, and division. They will now use their problem-solving skills to solve problems that involve more than one operation.

▶ Common Errors and Misconceptions

- Students might have difficulty solving nonstandard problems, problems requiring multiple steps, or problems with extra information. Avoid introducing students to techniques that work for one-step problems but do not work for multistep problems, such as associating key words with particular operations.

- Students might quickly read through a problem and immediately begin to compute with the numbers, often choosing the wrong operation because they did not take time to read through and understand the context of the problem. Students need to learn to use "slow-down" mechanisms that can help them concentrate on thoroughly understanding a problem before they solve it.

Materials to Gather

SUPPLIED

Problem-Solving Questions activity page

More Than One Operation activity page

GET READY Solve Problems at the Circus

Objectives

- Determine whether addition, subtraction, multiplication, or division is the appropriate operation to use to solve a story problem and solve the problem.

Students will complete an online activity to practice choosing the correct operation to solve a story problem. Then students will solve story problems.

LEARN Problem-Solving Questions

Objectives

- Solve a story problem involving two or more operations.

Students will use problem-solving questions to help them solve story problems involving two or more operations.

1. Review with students the problem-solving questions they can use to solve story problems:
   - What are you asked to find in the problem?
   - What facts are given?
   - Would a picture or model help you solve the problem?
   - How are you going to solve this problem?
   - Do you need to use more than one operation for this problem?
   - What are the different steps you need to take to solve this problem?
   - Which operations should you use? Why?

2. View or print the Problem-Solving Questions activity page. Read the Worked Example with students. Point out that some of the problem-solving questions are answered in the solution. Make sure students understand how the answer was reached before continuing with the story problems. They should copy the problems from the Activity Book into their Math Notebook as necessary and solve them there.

3. Read Problem 1 with students. Ask students to explain their thinking about how they would solve the problem. Encourage them to share the problem-solving questions and answers they use to work through solving the problem.

4. Have students solve Problem 1. Emphasize the importance of including a label in the answer. Remind students that labels explain and give meaning to the answers.

5. Have students solve Problems 2 and 3 on their own. They should record their answers in their Math Notebook.

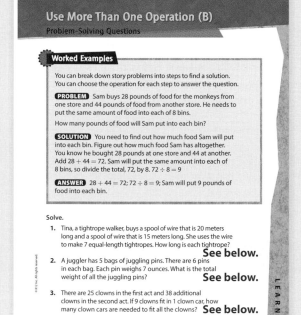

Additional Answers

1. Each tightrope is 5 meters long.
2. The pins weigh 210 ounces altogether.
3. The clowns need 7 clown cars.

TRY IT More Than One Operation

Objectives

- Solve a story problem involving two or more operations.

Students will practice solving story problems with more than one operation. View or print the More Than One Operation activity page and read the directions with students.

Students should copy the problems from the Activity Book into their Math Notebook as necessary and solve them there.

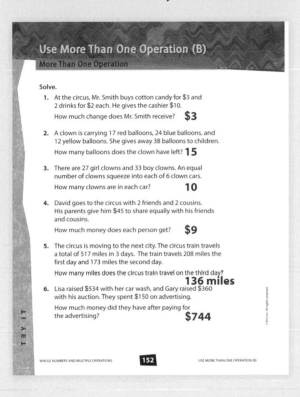

Use More Than One Operation (B)

More Than One Operation

Solve.

1. At the circus, Mr. Smith buys cotton candy for $3 and 2 drinks for $2 each. He gives the cashier $10.

   How much change does Mr. Smith receive? **$3**

2. A clown is carrying 17 red balloons, 24 blue balloons, and 12 yellow balloons. She gives away 38 balloons to children.

   How many balloons does the clown have left? **15**

3. There are 27 girl clowns and 33 boy clowns. An equal number of clowns squeeze into each of 6 clown cars.

   How many clowns are in each car? **10**

4. David goes to the circus with 2 friends and 2 cousins. His parents give him $45 to share equally with his friends and cousins.

   How much money does each person get? **$9**

5. The circus is moving to the next city. The circus train travels a total of 517 miles in 3 days. The train travels 208 miles the first day and 173 miles the second day.

   How many miles does the circus train travel on the third day?
   136 miles

6. Lisa raised $534 with her car wash, and Gary raised $360 with his auction. They spent $150 on advertising.

   How much money did they have after paying for the advertising? **$744**

WHOLE NUMBERS AND MULTIPLE OPERATIONS **152** USE MORE THAN ONE OPERATION (B)

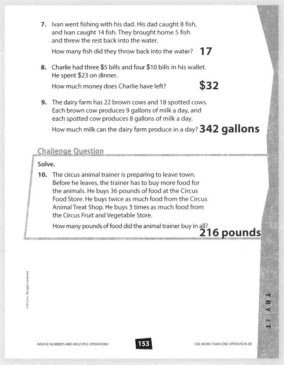

7. Ivan went fishing with his dad. His dad caught 8 fish, and Ivan caught 14 fish. They brought home 5 fish and threw the rest back into the water.

   How many fish did they throw back into the water? **17**

8. Charlie had three $5 bills and four $10 bills in his wallet. He spent $23 on dinner.

   How much money does Charlie have left? **$32**

9. The dairy farm has 22 brown cows and 18 spotted cows. Each brown cow produces 9 gallons of milk a day, and each spotted cow produces 8 gallons of milk a day.

   How much milk can the dairy farm produce in a day? **342 gallons**

Challenge Question

Solve.

10. The circus animal trainer is preparing to leave town. Before he leaves, the trainer has to buy more food for the animals. He buys 36 pounds of food at the Circus Food Store. He buys twice as much food from the Circus Animal Treat Shop. He buys 3 times as much food from the Circus Fruit and Vegetable Store.

    How many pounds of food did the animal trainer buy in all?
    216 pounds

WHOLE NUMBERS AND MULTIPLE OPERATIONS **153** USE MORE THAN ONE OPERATION (B)

CHECKPOINT

Objectives

- Solve a story problem involving two or more operations.

Students will complete an online Checkpoint. If necessary, read the directions, problems, and answer choices to students and help them with keyboard or mouse operations.

Core Focus
Identify More Than One Operation

Lesson Overview

GET READY Select the Correct Operation	5 minutes	**ONLINE**
LEARN Farmer's Market Math	15 minutes	**ONLINE**
LEARN Use the Order of Operations	15 minutes	**OFFLINE**
TRY IT Multiple Operations	15 minutes	**OFFLINE**
CHECKPOINT	10 minutes	**ONLINE**

▶ ## Lesson Objectives

- Use the order of operations to evaluate an expression.
- Solve a story problem involving two or more operations.
- Represent a story problem with an equation.

▶ ## Prerequisite Skills

Determine whether addition, subtraction, multiplication, or division is the appropriate operation to use to solve a story problem and solve the problem.

▶ ## Content Background

Students will review how to use multiple steps to solve a problem that involves more than one operation.

Problem solving is a part of daily life. To become good problem solvers, students need to recognize when a new problem is similar to a problem they have already solved. Instead of treating every problem they encounter as new, students can build on their previous experiences with problems and develop strategies to solve similar problems. Knowing they have successfully completed similar problems will help students become confident problem solvers.

Students have solved a wide variety of story problems using the four basic operations: addition, subtraction, multiplication, and division. They will now use their problem-solving skills to solve problems that involve more than one operation.

▶ ## Common Errors and Misconceptions

- Students might have difficulty solving nonstandard problems, problems requiring multiple steps, or problems with extra information. Avoid introducing students to techniques that work for one-step problems but do not work for multistep problems, such as associating key words with particular operations.
- Students might quickly read through a problem and immediately begin to compute with the numbers, often choosing the wrong operation because they did not take time to read through and understand the context of the problem. Students need to learn to use "slow-down" mechanisms that can help them concentrate on thoroughly understanding a problem before they solve it.

Materials to Gather

SUPPLIED

Use the Order of Operations activity page

Multiple Operations activity page

GET READY Select the Correct Operation

ONLINE **5**min

Objectives

Students will choose the correct operation to solve a story problem and then will solve it.

- Determine whether addition, subtraction, multiplication, or division is the appropriate operation to use to solve a story problem and solve a problem.

LEARN Farmer's Market Math

ONLINE **15**min

Objectives

Students will use a step-by-step chart to help them solve story problems that involve more than one step and more than one operation. They will follow a problem-solving strategy to help them identify what they are asked to find, what facts are given in the problem, what steps they need to take, and what operations they need to use to solve the problem.

- Solve a story problem involving two or more operations.

LEARN Use the Order of Operations

OFFLINE **15**min

Objectives

Students will learn how to interpret multistep story problems as expressions and equations which they solve using the order of operations. View or print the Use the Order of Operations activity page.

1. Review the Worked Example with students. Remind them that they should follow the order of operations as they solve an equation or evaluate an expression. They should

   - Multiply or divide from left to right in the order the $\times$ or $\div$ symbols appear.

   - Then add or subtract from left to right in the order the $+$ or $-$ symbols appear.

2. Have students complete Problems 1–3 on their own. Students should copy the problems from the Activity Book into their math Notebook as necessary and solve them there.

- Use the order of operations to evaluate an expression.
- Solve a story problem involving two or more operations.
- Represent a story problem with an equation.

| **Tips** | Encourage students to use the problem-solving questions to help them solve the story problems. |

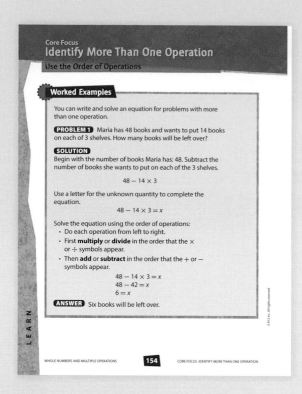

Identify More Than One Operation
Use the Order of Operations

Worked Examples

You can write and solve an equation for problems with more than one operation.

PROBLEM 1 Maria has 48 books and wants to put 14 books on each of 3 shelves. How many books will be left over?

SOLUTION
Begin with the number of books Maria has: 48. Subtract the number of books she wants to put on each of the 3 shelves.

$$48 - 14 \times 3$$

Use a letter for the unknown quantity to complete the equation.

$$48 - 14 \times 3 = x$$

Solve the equation using the order of operations:
- Do each operation from left to right.
- First **multiply** or **divide** in the order that the $\times$ or $\div$ symbols appear.
- Then **add** or **subtract** in the order that the $+$ or $-$ symbols appear.

$$48 - 14 \times 3 = x$$
$$48 - 42 = x$$
$$6 = x$$

ANSWER Six books will be left over.

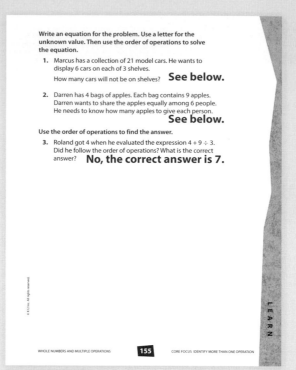

Write an equation for the problem. Use a letter for the unknown value. Then use the order of operations to solve the equation.

1. Marcus has a collection of 21 model cars. He wants to display 6 cars on each of 3 shelves.
   How many cars will not be on shelves?   **See below.**

2. Darren has 4 bags of apples. Each bag contains 9 apples. Darren wants to share the apples equally among 6 people. He needs to know how many apples to give each person.
   See below.

Use the order of operations to find the answer.

3. Roland got 4 when he evaluated the expression $4 + 9 \div 3$. Did he follow the order of operations? What is the correct answer?   **No, the correct answer is 7.**

Additional Answers

1. $21 - 6 \times 3 = x$; $21 - 18 = x$; $3 = x$; Three cars will not be on shelves.

2. $4 \times 9 \div 6 = x$; $36 \div 6 = x$; $6 = x$; Darren will give each person 6 apples.

TRY IT Multiple Operations

OFFLINE
15 min

Students will practice determining which operations to use to solve a problem and then solving problems that require more than one step. View or print the Multiple Operations activity page. Students should copy the problems into their Math Notebook and solve them there.

Objectives

- Use the order of operations to evaluate an expression.
- Solve a story problem involving two or more operations.

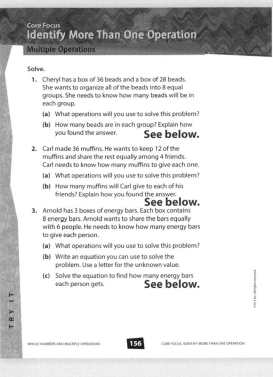

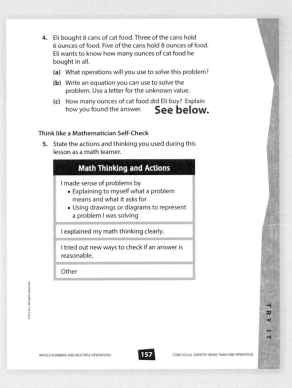

Answers

1. **(a)** I will add and then I will divide.

   (b) 8 beads; **Possible explanation:** First I added the number of beads in each box to find the total number of beads: $36 + 28 = 64$. Then I divided the total number of beads by 8, which is the number of groups: $64 \div 8 = 8$.

2. **(a)** I will subtract and then I will divide.

   (b) 6 muffins; **Possible explanation:** First, I subtracted the number of muffins Carl wants to keep from the number of muffins he made: $36 - 12 = 24$. Then, I divided the difference by 4, the number of friends Carl wants to give the remaining muffins to: $24 \div 4 = 6$.

3. **(a)** I will multiply and then I will divide.

   (b) Possible equation: $3 \times 8 \div 6 = x$.

   (c) Each person gets 4 energy bars: $3 \times 8 \div 6 = 4$.

4. **(a)** I will multiply twice and then I will add.

   (b) Possible equation: $3 \times 6 + 5 \times 8 = x$.

   (c) 58 ounces; **Possible explanation:** First, I multiplied 3 of the cans by 6: $3 \times 6 = 18$. Then, I multiplied 5 of the cans by 8: $5 \times 8 = 40$. Then, I added the two products to find the total number of ounces: $18 + 40 = 58$.

ONLINE

10 min

CHECKPOINT

Students will complete an online Checkpoint. If necessary, read the directions, problems, and answer choices to students and help them with keyboard or mouse operations.

Objectives

- Solve a story problem involving two or more operations.
- Represent a story problem with an equation.

Unit Review

Lesson Overview

UNIT REVIEW Look Back	10 minutes	**ONLINE**
UNIT REVIEW Checkpoint Practice	50 minutes	**ONLINE**
⤐ **UNIT REVIEW** Prepare for the Checkpoint		

▶ Unit Objectives

- Use the order of operations to evaluate an expression.
- Determine whether addition, subtraction, multiplication, or division is the appropriate operation to use to solve a story problem and solve the problem.
- Solve a story problem involving two or more operations.
- Represent a story problem with an equation.

▶ Advance Preparation

In this lesson, students will have an opportunity to review previous activities in the Whole Numbers and Multiple Operations unit. Look at the suggested activities in Unit Review: Prepare for the Checkpoint online and gather any needed materials.

Materials to Gather

There are no materials to gather for this lesson.

UNIT REVIEW Look Back ONLINE **10**min

Students will review key concepts from the unit to prepare for the Unit Checkpoint.

Objectives

- Review unit objectives.

UNIT REVIEW Checkpoint Practice ONLINE **50**min

Students will complete an online Checkpoint Practice to prepare for the Unit Checkpoint. If necessary, read the directions, problems, and answer choices to students. Have students answer the problems on their own. Review any missed problems with students.

Objectives

- Review unit objectives.

⤐ **UNIT REVIEW** Prepare for the Checkpoint

What you do next depends on how students performed in the previous activity, Unit Review: Checkpoint Practice. If students had difficulty with any of the problems, complete the appropriate review activity listed in the table online.

Unit Checkpoint

UNIT CHECKPOINT Online | 60 minutes | **ONLINE**

▶ Unit Objectives

- Use the order of operations to evaluate an expression.
- Determine whether addition, subtraction, multiplication, or division is the appropriate operation to use to solve a story problem and solve the problem.
- Solve a story problem involving two or more operations.
- Represent a story problem with an equation.

Materials to Gather

There are no materials to gather for this lesson.

ONLINE
60min

UNIT CHECKPOINT Online

Objectives

- Assess unit objectives.

Students will complete the Unit Checkpoint online. If necessary, read the directions, problems, and answer choices to students and help them with keyboard or mouse operations.

Extended Problems: Reasoning

GRADED ASSIGNMENT   60 minutes   **OFFLINE**

▶ Lesson Objectives

- Use the order of operations to evaluate an expression.
- Determine whether addition, subtraction, multiplication, or division is the appropriate operation to use to solve a story problem and solve the problem.
- Solve a story problem involving two or more operations.
- Analyze complex problems using mathematical knowledge and skills.

Materials to Gather

SUPPLIED

Extended Problems: Reasoning (printout)

GRADED ASSIGNMENT

Objectives

Open the Extended Problems: Reasoning. Read the directions, problems, and answer choices to students, if necessary.
   You will grade this assignment.

- Students should complete the assignment on their own.
- Students should submit the completed assignment to you.
- Enter the results online.

- Analyze complex problems using mathematical knowledge and skills.

Fractions and Probability

- Explain that a fraction can be used to represent the relationship of a part to a whole and a rational number on the number line.
- Write the fraction represented by a drawing that shows parts of a whole or a rational number on the number line.
- Use a sketch to represent a fraction.
- Recognize and determine equivalent fractions.
- Explain why two given fractions are equivalent.
- Compare and order unit fractions, such as $\frac{1}{4}$, and fractions with like denominators, such as $\frac{2}{6}$ and $\frac{4}{6}$, by using objects or sketches.
- Compare and order fractions with like numerators by using objects or sketches.
- Recognize that the comparison of two fractions is only valid if the wholes are identical.

- Identify whether specific events are certain, likely, unlikely, or impossible.
- Identify and systematically record the possible outcomes for a simple event.
- Summarize and display the results of a probability experiment in a clear and organized way.
- Draw a scaled picture graph or bar graph to represent a data set with several categories.
- Solve one- and two-step "how many more" and "how many fewer" problems using information presented in scaled picture graphs or bar graphs.
- Use the results of a probability experiment to predict future events.
- Explain why $a = \frac{a}{1}$.
- Explain why $\frac{a}{a} = 1$.
- Demonstrate how fractions and whole numbers can be plotted on a number line.

■ Big Ideas

- Fractions represent the ratio of a part to a whole, including a part of a set to the whole set.
- A rational number (a fraction) is any number that can be written as a ratio of one integer to another integer.

■ Unit Opener

In this unit, students will explore fractions, decimals, and early probability concepts. They will explain that fractions can be seen as part of a whole, such as when they have half a cookie; or as a rational number on the number line. Students will recognize that the number above the fraction bar is the numerator and the number below the fraction bar is the denominator. They will recognize that as the denominator gets greater, the fractional pieces become smaller, and they will recognize that a fraction such as $\frac{1}{5}$ is less than $\frac{1}{4}$. Students will learn the relationship between fractions and decimals and explain that a fraction and a decimal can represent the same quantity. They will look at simple notions of probability, identifying whether specific events are certain, likely, unlikely, or impossible. They will identify and record possible outcomes for a simple event. They will learn about tally charts, line plots, and bar graphs, and they will use the results of a probability experiment to predict future events.

■ Keywords

decimal	fractions with like denominators	mixed number
denominator		numerator
equivalent fractions	fractions with unlike denominators	outcomes
fraction		predict an outcome
fraction bar	improper fraction	probability

Represent and Name Fractions (A)

Lesson Overview

GET READY Fraction Meanings and Names	10 minutes	**ONLINE**
LEARN Fractions of Areas	15 minutes	**OFFLINE**
LEARN Name and Show Parts of a Whole	20 minutes	**ONLINE**
TRY IT Name Fractions	15 minutes	**OFFLINE**

▶ ## Lesson Objectives

- Explain that a fraction can be used to represent the relationship of a part to a whole and a rational number on the number line.
- Write the fraction represented by a drawing that shows parts of a whole or a rational number on the number line.
- Use a sketch to represent a fraction.

▶ ## Prerequisite Skills

- Demonstrate that a fraction can represent the relationship of equal parts to a whole.
- Write the fraction represented by a drawing that shows parts of a whole.

▶ ## Content Background

Students will learn that a fraction can represent the relationship of a part to a whole. They will draw a sketch to show a fraction and write the fraction represented by a drawing. Avoid using the term *rational numbers* with students.

Fractions are numbers that can represent whole numbers and parts of a whole. Fractions can be shown as parts of a whole, parts of a set, or as a location on a number line.

Although a fraction can represent many different relationships, a fraction as part of a whole is most familiar. A set of 3 slices of 8 equal-sized slices in a whole pizza is a part-of-a-whole comparison written as $\frac{3}{8}$. If there is a combination of 1 whole pizza and 3 equal-sized slices of another 8-slice pizza of the same size, the part-of-a-whole comparison is $1\frac{3}{8}$. Remember that when discussing fractions as a part of a whole, all the parts must be the same size and shape, and all the wholes must also be the same size and shape.

Numbers that have a whole and a fraction are called mixed numbers. The mixed number $1\frac{3}{8}$ can also be written as an improper fraction. Since 1 whole is $\frac{8}{8}$, $1\frac{3}{8}$ would be $\frac{8}{8}$ plus $\frac{3}{8}$, or $\frac{11}{8}$. When the numerator is greater than the denominator, the fraction is called an improper fraction.

$$\frac{3}{4} \qquad\qquad 1\frac{3}{4} \qquad\qquad \frac{7}{4}$$

fraction mixed number improper fraction

Materials to Gather

SUPPLIED

Fractions of Areas activity page

Name Fractions activity page

Although students will most often see fractions written with a horizontal fraction bar in math, such as $\frac{2}{3}$ or $5\frac{5}{6}$, they will occasionally see a diagonal fraction bar, such as 2/3 or 5 5/6. Students will very likely see the diagonal fraction bar in everyday experiences, but be sure they understand that using the horizontal fraction bar in their work makes problems involving fractions easier to interpret and solve.

▶ Common Errors and Misconceptions

- Students might view the numerator and denominator of a fraction as separate, isolated numbers that can be operated on independently. This may lead to students "memorizing" rather than understanding fraction algorithms and then using them incorrectly.

- Students might not understand the difference between fractions and whole numbers. Fractions are parts of whole numbers. Examples of fractions include $\frac{4}{5}$, $\frac{7}{100}$, and $2\frac{1}{2}$. Examples of whole numbers include 4, 6, and 10. Whole numbers may be written as fractions but always with a denominator of 1, such as $\frac{4}{1}$, $\frac{6}{1}$, or $\frac{10}{1}$.

- Students might think that a fraction compares one part to another part rather than recognizing that a fraction compares one part to the whole.

GET READY Fraction Meanings and Names

ONLINE
10 min

Students will review the meaning of fractions. They also will name fractions as equal parts of a whole.

Objectives

- Demonstrate that a fraction can represent the relationship of equal parts to a whole.

- Write the fraction represented by a drawing that shows parts of a whole.

LEARN Fractions of Areas

OFFLINE
15 min

Students will use fractions to express what part of the area of a shape is shaded. View or print the Fractions of Areas activity page and read the directions with students. They should copy the problems into their Math Notebook as necessary and solve them there.

1. Remind students that the area of a figure is simply the amount of space inside the figure.

2. Read the Worked Example with students. Show students that the area, or space inside the large rectangle, is divided into 4 equal sections. Discuss how fractions can name parts of wholes, so the part of the area of the rectangle that is shaded is one-fourth of the entire area.

3. Have students complete Problems 1–7, referring to the Worked Example as necessary. Emphasize that the particular fraction is that part of the entire area of the shape. If students have difficulty, you can have them write how many parts are shaded and how many parts there are in all. Then they can write the fraction from those two numbers.

Objectives

- Explain that a fraction can be used to represent the relationship of a part to a whole and a rational number on a number line.

- Write the fraction represented by a drawing that shows parts of a whole or a rational number on a number line.

4. When students finish, review Problem 7. Guide them to recognize that even though the equal parts in the different squares are different shapes, they each represent the same area because the squares are the same shape and size. Point out that $\frac{1}{4}$ of a figure can have different shapes.

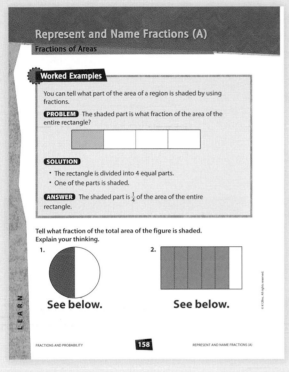

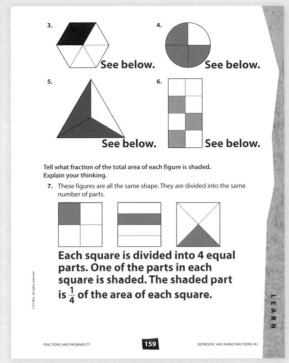

Additional Answers

1. The circle is divided into 2 equal parts. One of the parts is shaded. The shaded part is $\frac{1}{2}$ of the area of the entire circle.

2. The rectangle is divided into 6 equal parts. Five of the parts are shaded. The shaded part is $\frac{5}{6}$ of the area of the entire rectangle.

3. The hexagon is divided into 6 equal parts. Two of the parts are shaded. The shaded part is $\frac{2}{6}$ of the area of the entire rectangle.

4. The circle is divided into 4 equal parts. Three of the parts are shaded. The shaded part is $\frac{3}{4}$ of the area of the entire circle.

5. The triangle is divided into 3 equal parts. Two of the parts are shaded. The shaded part is $\frac{2}{3}$ of the area of the entire triangle.

6. The rectangle is divided into 8 equal parts. Three of the parts are shaded. The shaded part is $\frac{3}{8}$ of the area of the entire rectangle.

LEARN Name and Show Parts of a Whole

Students will identify the fraction that names the shaded part of a whole. They will recognize that the whole must have equal-sized parts. They will also see that the numerator shows the number of parts shaded and the denominator shows the number of parts in a whole. Student will learn that a number greater than 1 can be a mixed number, or it can be written as an improper fraction. For example, $1\frac{2}{3}$ can also be written as $\frac{5}{3}$.

Tips

Have students count the number of parts in each shape. Write that number as the denominator (the number below the fraction bar) before focusing on the number of shaded parts.

Objectives

- Explain that a fraction can be used to represent the relationship of a part to a whole and a rational number on a number line.

- Write the fraction represented by a drawing that shows parts of a whole or a rational number on the number line.

- Use a sketch to represent a fraction.

TRY IT Name Fractions

Students will practice representing and naming fractions. View or print the Name Fractions activity page in their Activity Book and read the directions with students.

Students should copy the problems from the Activity Book into their Math Notebook as necessary and solve them there.

Objectives

- Explain that a fraction can be used to represent the relationship of a part to a whole and a rational number on the number line.

- Write the fraction represented by a drawing that shows parts of a whole or a rational number on the number line.

- Use a sketch to represent a fraction.

Choose the answer.

7. Jeff said that this model shows $2\frac{3}{8}$ shaded. Eliza said that this model shows $\frac{19}{8}$ shaded. Who is correct?

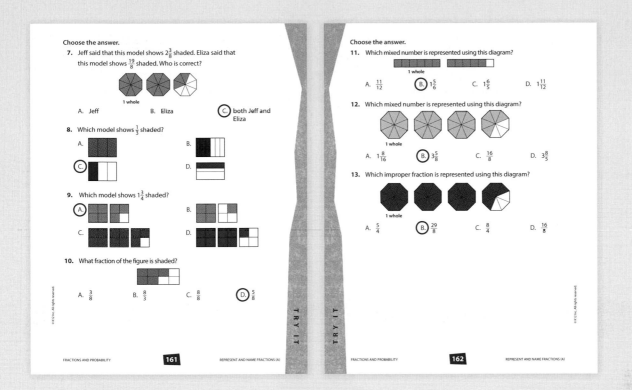

1 whole

   A. Jeff   B. Eliza   (C.) both Jeff and Eliza

8. Which model shows $\frac{1}{3}$ shaded?

   A.   B.

   (C.)   D.

9. Which model shows $1\frac{3}{4}$ shaded?

   (A.)   B.

   C.   D.

10. What fraction of the figure is shaded?

   A. $\frac{3}{8}$ B. $\frac{8}{3}$ C. $\frac{8}{8}$ (D.) $\frac{5}{8}$

T R Y   I T

Choose the answer.

11. Which mixed number is represented using this diagram?

1 whole

   A. $\frac{11}{12}$ (B.) $1\frac{5}{6}$ C. $1\frac{6}{5}$ D. $1\frac{11}{12}$

12. Which mixed number is represented using this diagram?

1 whole

   A. $1\frac{8}{16}$ (B.) $3\frac{5}{8}$ C. $\frac{16}{8}$ D. $3\frac{8}{5}$

13. Which improper fraction is represented using this diagram?

1 whole

   A. $\frac{5}{4}$ (B.) $\frac{29}{8}$ C. $\frac{8}{4}$ D. $\frac{16}{8}$

T R Y   I T

Represent and Name Fractions (B)

Lesson Overview

GET READY Write Fractions	10 minutes	**ONLINE**
LEARN Fractions on a Number Line	25 minutes	**OFFLINE**
TRY IT Represent Fractions	15 minutes	**OFFLINE**
CHECKPOINT	10 minutes	**ONLINE**

▶ Lesson Objectives

- Explain that a fraction can be used to represent the relationship of a part to a whole and a rational number on the number line.
- Write the fraction represented by a drawing that shows parts of a whole or a rational number on the number line.
- Use a sketch to represent a fraction.

▶ Prerequisite Skills

- Demonstrate how fractions and whole numbers can be plotted on a number line.
- Write the fraction represented by a drawing that shows parts of a whole or a rational number on the number line.

▶ Content Background

Students will continue to learn that a fraction can represent the relationship of a part to a whole and a rational number on the number line. They will draw a sketch to show a fraction and write the fraction represented by a drawing. Avoid using the term *rational numbers* with students.

Fractions are numbers that can represent whole numbers and parts of a whole. Fractions can be shown as parts of a whole or as a location on a number line.

Although a fraction can represent many different relationships, a fraction as part of a whole is most familiar. A set of 3 slices of 8 equal-sized slices in a whole pizza is a part-of-a-whole comparison written as $\frac{3}{8}$. If there is a combination of 1 whole pizza and 3 equal-sized slices of another 8-slice pizza of the same size, the part-of-a-whole comparison is $1\frac{3}{8}$. Remember that when discussing fractions as a part of a whole, all the parts must be the same size and shape, and all the wholes must also be the same size and shape.

Materials to Gather

SUPPLIED

number lines from Number Line Creator Tool

Represent Fractions activity page

Numbers that have a whole and a fraction are called mixed numbers. The mixed number $1\frac{3}{8}$ can also be written as an improper fraction. Since 1 whole is $\frac{8}{8}$, $1\frac{3}{8}$ would be $\frac{8}{8}$ plus $\frac{3}{8}$, or $\frac{11}{8}$. When the numerator is greater than the denominator, the fraction is called an improper fraction.

$$\frac{3}{4}$$

fraction

$$1\frac{3}{4}$$

mixed number

$$\frac{7}{4}$$

improper fraction

Fractions are a part of the larger set of rational numbers. Every rational number has a specific location along the number line. For example, $\frac{3}{4}$ is located at the point exactly $\frac{3}{4}$ of the distance from 0 to 1 on the number line, and $5\frac{3}{8}$ is located at the point exactly $\frac{3}{8}$ of the distance from 5 to 6.

Although students will most often see fractions written with a horizontal fraction bar in math, such as $\frac{2}{3}$ or $5\frac{5}{6}$, they will occasionally see a diagonal fraction bar, such as 2/3 or 5 5/6. Students will very likely see the diagonal fraction bar in everyday experiences, but be sure they understand that using the horizontal fraction bar in their work makes problems involving fractions easier to interpret and solve.

▶ Common Errors and Misconceptions

- Students might view the numerator and denominator of a fraction as separate, isolated numbers that can be operated on independently. This may lead to students "memorizing" rather than understanding fraction algorithms, and then using them incorrectly.

- Students might not understand the difference between fractions and whole numbers. Fractions are parts of whole numbers. Examples of fractions include $\frac{4}{6}$, $\frac{7}{8}$, and $2\frac{1}{2}$. Examples of whole numbers include 4, 6, and 10. Whole numbers may be written as fractions, but always with a denominator of 1, such as $\frac{4}{1}$, $\frac{6}{1}$, or $\frac{10}{1}$.

- Students might have difficulty understanding how different models represent fractions because they often see fractions represented as parts of circles—for example, pie and pizza illustrations. They might not recognize, for example, that the following models also represent the fraction $\frac{3}{8}$.

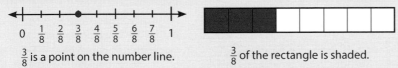

$\frac{3}{8}$ is a point on the number line. $\frac{3}{8}$ of the rectangle is shaded.

- Students might think that a fraction always represents the size of a part of a whole or a location on the number line, and so might not understand that a fraction can also represent a relationship, such as a quotient or a ratio of one quantity to another.

- Students might think that a fraction compares one part to another part rather than recognizing that a fraction compares one part to the whole.

▶ Advance Preparation

Use the Number Line Creator Tool to make six number lines, three to a page. Print the number lines.

DIRECTIONS FOR USING THE NUMBER LINE CREATOR TOOL

To create number lines for thirds:

1. Set Range:	2. Select Options:	3. Print Number Line:
• Start Number Line at: 0 • End Number Line at: 4	• Tick Marks: ones, thirds • Labels: ones • Label Format: fractions	• Page Orientation: landscape • Number Lines per Sheet: 3

To create number lines for fourths:

1. Set Range:	2. Select Options:	3. Print Number Line:
• Start Number Line at: 0 • End Number Line at: 4	• Tick Marks: ones, fourths • Labels: ones • Label Format: fractions	• Page Orientation: landscape • Number Lines per Sheet: 3

GET READY Write Fractions

ONLINE 10 min

Students will review number lines and fractions on the number line. Remind them that a fraction is a special kind of number used to show amounts less than 1. On the number line a fraction, such as $\frac{3}{4}$, can be seen as marking a point three-fourths of the distance from 0 to 1.

Objectives

- Demonstrate how fractions and whole numbers can be plotted on a number line.
- Write the fraction represented by a drawing that show parts of a whole or a rational number on the number line.

LEARN Fractions on a Number Line

OFFLINE 25 min

Students will label fractions, improper fractions, and mixed numbers on a number line. Gather the printed number lines from the Number Line Creator Tool.

1. Tell students that fractions can be shown on a number line. Give them the sheet of number lines that have the tick marks for thirds. Remind students that they have seen whole numbers on a number line.

2. Have students imagine that the tick marks show the hops that a miniature frog would have to take to get to 1.

   Ask: How many hops would it take to get to 1? 3

   Ask: How much of the distance would the frog go with each hop? $\frac{1}{3}$

   Ask: How far would the frog go in 3 hops? $\frac{3}{3}$ or 1

Objectives

- Explain that a fraction can be used to represent the relationship of a part to a whole and a rational number on the number line.
- Write the fraction represented by a drawing that shows parts of a whole or a rational number on the number line.
- Use a sketch to represent a fraction.

3. Guide students to find and label the fractions on the number line. $\frac{1}{3}, \frac{2}{3}, \frac{3}{3}, \frac{4}{3}$, and so on

Then have students count aloud, saying both the fraction and whole number. $\frac{1}{3}, \frac{2}{3}, \frac{3}{3}$ equals 1; $\frac{4}{3}, \frac{5}{3}, \frac{6}{3}$ equals 2; and so on

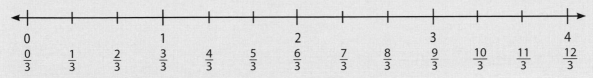

4. Tell students that a number line can be divided into different numbers of equal sections to show different fractions.

   Say: If there were four sections between each whole number, the number line would be divided into fourths and each tick mark would show $\frac{1}{4}$.

5. Give students the sheet of number lines that have the tick marks for fourths. Have students look at one of these lines and explain why it shows fourths even though there are only three tick marks between each whole number. It shows fourths because there are four sections. The tick marks are $\frac{1}{4}, \frac{2}{4}$, and $\frac{3}{4}$ and the fourth tick mark is $\frac{4}{4}$ or 1.

6. Guide students to find and label the fractions on the number line and say each one. $\frac{1}{4}, \frac{2}{4}, \frac{3}{4}, \frac{4}{4}$ equals 1; $\frac{5}{4}, \frac{6}{4}, \frac{7}{4}, \frac{8}{4}$ equals 2; and so on

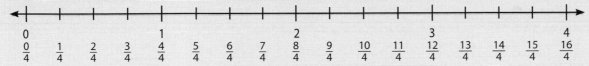

7. Refer to the number line that the students marked in thirds. Guide students to write the mixed numbers for the improper fractions on a new number line marked in thirds. Have students count aloud by thirds again from 0 to 4, using mixed numbers. $\frac{1}{3}, \frac{2}{3}, \frac{3}{3}$ equals 1; $1\frac{1}{3}, 1\frac{2}{3}, 1\frac{3}{3}$ equals 2; $2\frac{1}{3}, 2\frac{2}{3}, 2\frac{3}{3}$ equals 3; and so on

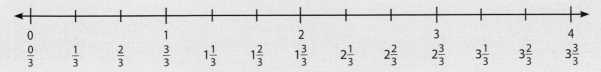

8. After students are comfortable counting, ask them to locate the following fractions on the number line: $\frac{2}{3}, 1\frac{1}{3}$, and $2\frac{2}{3}$.

9. Have students go back to the number line they labeled in fourths. Have them label a new fourths number line with mixed numbers. $\frac{1}{4}, \frac{2}{4}, \frac{3}{4}, \frac{4}{4}$ equals 1; $1\frac{1}{4}, 1\frac{2}{4}, 1\frac{3}{4}, 1\frac{4}{4}$ equals 2; $2\frac{1}{4}, 2\frac{2}{4}, 2\frac{3}{4}, 2\frac{4}{4}$ equals 3; and so on

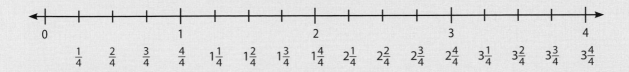

10. As time permits, say various fractions, mixed numbers, and improper fractions and have students find them on the number lines. For mixed numbers, have students say the fraction as an improper fraction.

   Remind students that they have now seen fractions as part of a whole and as a number on the number line.

| Tips | Have students look at the two number lines they marked in thirds and remind them that while improper fractions and mixed numbers look very different, numbers such as $\frac{4}{3}$ and $1\frac{1}{3}$ stand for exactly the same amount, just as $\frac{3}{3}$ and 1 stand for the same amount. |

TRY IT Represent Fractions

OFFLINE 15 min

Objectives

Students will practice sketching the same fraction in two ways—as part of a whole and as a number on a number line. They will practice identifying fractions sketched in multiple ways. View or print the Represent Fractions activity page and read the directions with students.

   Students should copy the problems from the Activity Book into their Math Notebook as necessary and solve them there.

- Explain that a fraction can be used to represent the relationship of a part to a whole and a rational number on the number line.

- Write the fraction represented by a drawing that shows parts of a whole or a rational number on the number line.

- Use a sketch to represent a fraction.

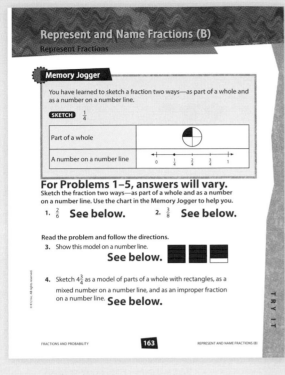

Represent and Name Fractions (B)
Represent Fractions

Memory Jogger

You have learned to sketch a fraction two ways—as part of a whole and as a number on a number line.

SKETCH $\frac{1}{4}$

Part of a whole	
A number on a number line	

For Problems 1–5, answers will vary.

Sketch the fraction two ways—as part of a whole and as a number on a number line. Use the chart in the Memory Jogger to help you.

1. $\frac{2}{6}$ **See below.**   2. $\frac{3}{8}$ **See below.**

Read the problem and follow the directions.

3. Show this model on a number line.   **See below.**

4. Sketch $4\frac{3}{4}$ as a model of parts of a whole with rectangles, as a mixed number on a number line, and as an improper fraction on a number line. **See below.**

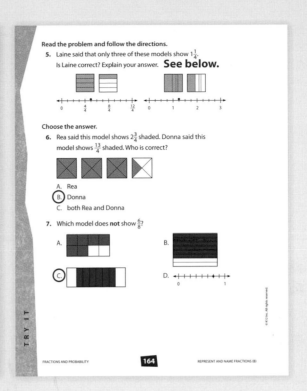

Read the problem and follow the directions.

5. Laine said that only three of these models show $1\frac{1}{4}$. Is Laine correct? Explain your answer. **See below.**

Choose the answer.

6. Rea said this model shows $2\frac{3}{4}$ shaded. Donna said this model shows $\frac{13}{4}$ shaded. Who is correct?

A. Rea
B. Donna
C. both Rea and Donna

7. Which model does **not** show $\frac{6}{8}$?

A.
B.
C.
D.

Additional Answers

1.

2.
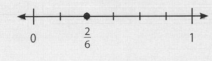

3.

4.
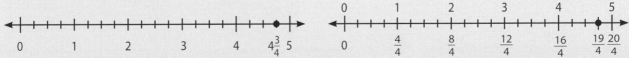

5. Yes. **Sample explanation:** The first model shows $1\frac{1}{4}$ shaded blue. The second model doesn't show $1\frac{1}{4}$ because all of the sections are not the same size and same shape. The first number line shows a dot at $\frac{5}{4}$, which is the same as $1\frac{1}{4}$. The second number line shows a dot at $1\frac{1}{4}$.

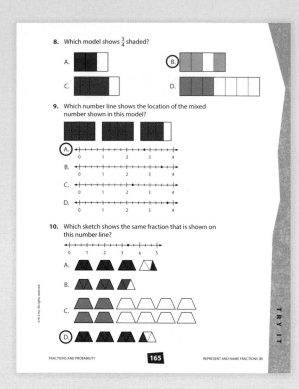

8. Which model shows $\frac{3}{4}$ shaded?

A.

B.

C.

D.

9. Which number line shows the location of the mixed number shown in this model?

A.
0 1 2 3 4

B.
0 1 2 3 4

C.
0 1 2 3 4

D.
0 1 2 3 4

10. Which sketch shows the same fraction that is shown on this number line?

0 1 2 3 4 5

A.

B.

C.

D.

T R Y   I T

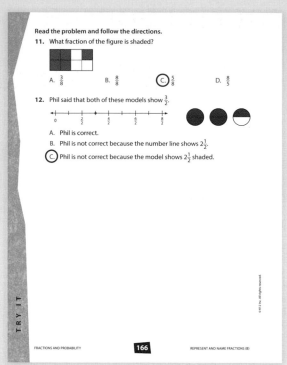

T R Y   I T

Read the problem and follow the directions.

11. What fraction of the figure is shaded?

A. $\frac{3}{8}$ B. $\frac{8}{8}$ C. $\frac{5}{8}$ D. $\frac{8}{5}$

12. Phil said that both of these models show $\frac{3}{2}$.

0   $\frac{2}{2}$ $\frac{4}{2}$ $\frac{5}{2}$ $\frac{6}{2}$

A. Phil is correct.

B. Phil is not correct because the number line shows $2\frac{1}{2}$.

C. Phil is not correct because the model shows $2\frac{1}{2}$ shaded.

ONLINE
10min

CHECKPOINT

Objectives

Students will complete an online Checkpoint. If necessary, read the directions, problems, and answer choices to students and help them with keyboard or mouse operations.

- Explain that a fraction can be used to represent the relationship of a part to a whole and a rational number on the number line.

- Write the fraction represented by a drawing that shows parts of a whole or a rational number on the number line.

- Use a sketch to represent a fraction.

Equivalent Fractions

Lesson Overview

GET READY Fractions Two Ways	5 minutes	ONLINE
LEARN Model Equivalent Fractions	10 minutes	ONLINE
LEARN Fraction Equivalents	10 minutes	ONLINE
LEARN Fractions and Fraction Strips	10 minutes	ONLINE
TRY IT Explain Equivalent Fractions	15 minutes	OFFLINE
CHECKPOINT	10 minutes	ONLINE

▶ Lesson Objectives

- Recognize and determine equivalent fractions.
- Explain why two given fractions are equivalent.

Materials to Gather

SUPPLIED

Explain Equivalent Fractions activity page

▶ Prerequisite Skills

- Explain that a fraction can be used to represent the relationship of a part to a whole and a rational number on the number line.
- Write the fraction represented by a drawing that shows parts of a whole or a rational number on a number line.
- Use a sketch to represent a fraction.

▶ Content Background

Students may already have a basic understanding of the different interpretations of fractions as part of a whole and a location on a number line. In this lesson, students will learn about equivalent fractions and explain why two fractions are equivalent.

Fractions are equivalent when they represent the same value. For example, $\frac{1}{2} = \frac{2}{4} = \frac{3}{6}$. Equivalent fractions can be shown as equal parts of a whole and as locations on a number line that are the same distance from 0.

▶ Common Errors and Misconceptions

- Students might not understand the difference between fractions and whole numbers. Fractions are parts of whole numbers. Examples of fractions include $\frac{4}{6}$, $\frac{7}{8}$, and $2\frac{1}{2}$. Examples of whole numbers include 4, 6, and 10. Whole numbers may be written as fractions but always with a denominator of 1, such as $\frac{4}{1}$, $\frac{6}{1}$, or $\frac{8}{1}$.
- Students might have difficulty understanding how different models represent fractions because they often see fractions represented as parts of circles, such as pie and pizza illustrations. They might recognize, for example, that area models and number lines can also represent fractions.

- Students might think that a fraction compares one part to another part, rather than recognizing that a fraction compares one part or several parts to the whole.

- Students might have difficulty understanding that numbers can look different, but still represent the same amount. For example, students might find it difficult to understand that though the numbers $\frac{1}{2}$, $\frac{2}{4}$, and $\frac{3}{6}$ look different, they are all equivalent, or represent the same part of a whole or location on the number line.

GET READY   Fractions Two Ways

 ONLINE 5 min

Students will focus on the meaning of a fraction's numerator and denominator as they use area models and number lines to represent the same fractions.

Objectives

- Explain that a fraction can be used to represent the relationship of a part to a whole and a rational number on the number line.

- Write the fraction represented by a drawing that shows parts of a whole or a rational number on a number line.

- Use a sketch to represent a fraction.

LEARN Model Equivalent Fractions

 ONLINE 10 min

Students will compare models of equivalent fractions to see that equivalent fractions are fractions with the same value. They will see how equivalent fractions can be modeled with shapes and number lines

Objectives

- Recognize and determine equivalent fractions.

LEARN Fraction Equivalents

 ONLINE 10 min

Students will use number lines to find equivalent fractions.

Objectives

- Recognize and determine equivalent fractions.

- Explain why two given fractions are equivalent.

LEARN Fractions and Fraction Strips

ONLINE 10 min

Students will use the Fraction Strips Learning Tool to learn how they can use fraction strips to represent equivalent fractions

Objectives

- Recognize and determine equivalent fractions.

- Explain why two given fractions are equivalent.

DIRECTIONS FOR USING THE FRACTION STRIPS LEARNING TOOL

1. Read the instructions and click Start.

2. Click the equivalent chart reference icon in the lower left of the screen to show students the various combinations of fractions that are equivalent to a whole, or 1.

3. **Say:** The top fraction strip represents a whole, or 1. Look at the fraction strips below 1.

   Ask: How many one-eighths $\left(\frac{1}{8}\right)$ are equal to 1 whole? 8 one-eighths

   Ask: How many one-thirds $\left(\frac{1}{3}\right)$ are equal to 1 whole? 3 one-thirds

4. **Say:** Since $\frac{3}{3}$ and $\frac{8}{8}$ both equal 1 whole, we know that $\frac{8}{8}$ and $\frac{3}{3}$ are equivalent fractions. They have the same value. Now we are going to drag the fraction strips to find other fractions that are equivalent.

   Click the X in the upper right of the chart to close it.

5. Tell students that they will use the fractions strips to show how many one-eighths $\left(\frac{1}{8}\right)$ are equivalent to three-fourths $\left(\frac{3}{4}\right)$. Have students drag three $\frac{1}{4}$ strips from the top bar to the left section of the screen and place them side by side. Have students name the fraction modeled.

6. Have students begin dragging $\frac{1}{8}$ strips from the top bar to line up directly under the three $\frac{1}{4}$ strips. Direct them to drag $\frac{1}{8}$ strips until they fill the space under the three $\frac{3}{4}$ strips. Then have the students count the number of $\frac{1}{8}$ strips that is equivalent to three $\frac{1}{4}$ strips and name the fraction modeled 6; $\frac{6}{8}$ Tell students that $\frac{6}{8}$ is equivalent to $\frac{3}{4}$.

7. Repeat Steps 5 and 6 with the following combinations of fractions:
   - Show two $\frac{1}{3}$ strips, and have students find the equivalent number of $\frac{1}{6}$ strips. Have students name both fractions and state the equivalency. $\frac{2}{3} = \frac{4}{6}$
   - Show two $\frac{1}{4}$ strips and have students find the equivalent number of $\frac{1}{8}$ strips. Have students name both fractions and state the equivalency. $\frac{2}{4} = \frac{4}{8}$

8. Have students create different sets of equivalent fractions that are less than or equal to 1 by using the fraction strips.

OFFLINE

| TRY IT Explain Equivalent Fractions | **15** min | Objectives |

Students will practice identifying and explaining why two fractions are equivalent. View or print the Explain Equivalent Fractions activity page and read the directions with students.

Students should copy the problems from the Activity Book into their math Notebook as necessary and solve them there.

- Recognize and determine equivalent fractions.
- Explain why two given fractions are equivalent.

Answers

1. The equal-sized squares show that you shade the same amount if you shade $\frac{3}{4}$ of the rectangle or $\frac{6}{8}$ of the rectangle, so $\frac{3}{4}$ and $\frac{6}{8}$ are equivalent fractions.

2. The equal-sized squares show that you shade the same amount if you shade $\frac{1}{2}$ of the square or $\frac{4}{8}$ of the square, so $\frac{1}{2}$ and $\frac{4}{8}$ are equivalent fractions.

3. Yes, $\frac{2}{6}$ and $\frac{1}{3}$ are equivalent. **Sample explanation:** If a rectangle is divided into 6 equal-sized sections and you shade 2 of them, you will have shaded the same part of the rectangle as if you had divided the rectangle into 3 equal-sized sections and shaded 1 of them.

4. Yes, $\frac{2}{8}$ and $\frac{1}{4}$ are equivalent. **Sample explanation:** If a rectangle is divided into 8 equal-sized sections and you shade 2 of them, you will have shaded the same part of the rectangle as if you had divided it into 4 equal-sized sections and shaded 1 of them.

5. Yes, $\frac{2}{4}$ is equivalent to $\frac{4}{8}$. **Sample explanation:** Show the fractions on number lines. The fractions are on the same place on the number line.

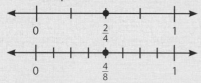

6. Yes, $\frac{2}{4}$ is equivalent to $\frac{1}{2}$. **Sample explanation:** Show the fractions on number lines. The fractions are on the same place on the number line.

7. No, $\frac{5}{6}$ is not equivalent to $\frac{2}{3}$. **Sample explanation:** Show the fractions on number lines. The fractions are not on the same place on the number line.

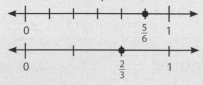

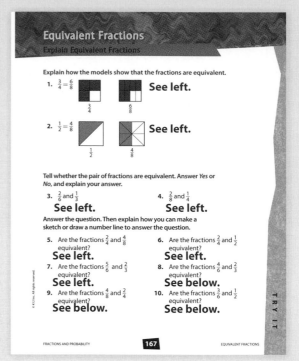

Equivalent Fractions
Explain Equivalent Fractions

Explain how the models show that the fractions are equivalent.

1. $\frac{3}{4} = \frac{6}{8}$ **See left.**

   $\frac{3}{4}$ $\frac{6}{8}$

2. $\frac{1}{2} = \frac{4}{8}$ **See left.**

   $\frac{1}{2}$ $\frac{4}{8}$

Tell whether the pair of fractions are equivalent. Answer *Yes* or *No*, and explain your answer.

3. $\frac{2}{6}$ and $\frac{1}{3}$ 4. $\frac{2}{8}$ and $\frac{1}{4}$
   See left.   **See left.**

Answer the question. Then explain how you can make a sketch or draw a number line to answer the question.

5. Are the fractions $\frac{2}{4}$ and $\frac{4}{8}$ equivalent?   6. Are the fractions $\frac{2}{4}$ and $\frac{1}{2}$ equivalent?
   See left.   **See left.**

7. Are the fractions $\frac{5}{6}$ and $\frac{2}{3}$ equivalent?   8. Are the fractions $\frac{4}{6}$ and $\frac{2}{3}$ equivalent?
   See left.   **See below.**

9. Are the fractions $\frac{4}{8}$ and $\frac{2}{4}$ equivalent?   10. Are the fractions $\frac{3}{6}$ and $\frac{1}{2}$ equivalent?
   See below.   **See below.**

FRACTIONS AND PROBABILITY   **167**   EQUIVALENT FRACTIONS

TRY IT

8. Yes, $\frac{4}{6}$ is equivalent to $\frac{2}{3}$. **Sample explanation:** Sketch equal-sized rectangles and shade $\frac{4}{6}$ and $\frac{2}{3}$. The same amount is shaded on each rectangle.

9. Yes, $\frac{4}{8}$ is equivalent to $\frac{2}{4}$. **Sample explanation:** Show the fractions on number lines. The fractions are on the same place on the number line.

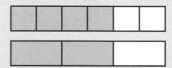

10. Yes, $\frac{3}{6}$ is equivalent $\frac{1}{2}$. **Sample explanation:** Show the fractions on number lines. The fractions are on the same place on the number line.

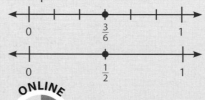

ONLINE

10 min

CHECKPOINT

Objectives

Students will complete an online Checkpoint. If necessary, read the directions, problems, and answer choices to students and help them with keyboard or mouse operations.

- Recognize and determine equivalent fractions.

Compare and Order Fractions (A)

Lesson Overview

GET READY Identify and Order Fractions	10 minutes	**ONLINE**
LEARN Compare Fractions on a Number Line	20 minutes	**ONLINE**
LEARN Fractions and Fraction Strips	20 minutes	**ONLINE**
TRY IT Compare Fractions	10 minutes	**OFFLINE**

▶ Lesson Objectives

Compare and order unit fractions, such as $\frac{1}{4}$, and fractions with like denominators, such as $\frac{2}{6}$ and $\frac{4}{6}$, by using objects or sketches.

▶ Prerequisite Skills

Use concrete objects or given drawings to compare unit fractions.

▶ Content Background

Students will learn to identify and compare fractions with like and unlike denominators using $<$, $>$, and $=$.

   Students will use the comparison symbols of $<$, $>$, and $=$ to compare fractions. The denominator, or the number below the fraction bar, of a fraction tells how many equal pieces the whole has been divided into. It is important for students to understand that as the denominator increases, the size of each piece decreases.

$\frac{1}{2}$

$\frac{1}{4}$

$\frac{1}{6}$

$\frac{1}{8}$

▶ Common Errors and Misconceptions

- Students might view the numerator and denominator of a fraction as separate, isolated numbers that can be operated on independently. This may lead to students "memorizing" rather than understanding fraction algorithms, and then using them incorrectly.

- Students might not understand the difference between fractions and whole numbers. Fractions are parts of whole numbers. Examples of fractions include $\frac{4}{6}$, $\frac{7}{8}$, and $2\frac{1}{2}$. Examples of whole numbers include 4, 6, and 10. Whole numbers may be written as fractions, but always with a denominator of 1, such as $\frac{4}{1}$, $\frac{6}{1}$, or $\frac{10}{1}$.

Materials to Gather

SUPPLIED

Compare Fractions activity page

- Students might have difficulty understanding how different models represent fractions because they often see fractions represented as parts of circles—for example, pie and pizza illustrations. They might not recognize, for example, that the following models all represent the fraction $\frac{3}{8}$.

$\frac{3}{8}$ is a point on the number line. $\frac{3}{8}$ of the rectangle is shaded.

- Students might think that a fraction always represents the size of a part of a whole or a location on the number line, and so might not understand that a fraction can also represent a relationship, such as a quotient or a ratio of one quantity to another.

- Students might think that a fraction compares one part to another part rather than recognizing that a fraction compares one part to the whole.

GET READY Identify and Order Fractions

ONLINE 10 min

Students will compare and order unit fractions. Unit fractions have 1 in the numerator. Students will see that with unit fractions, the greater the denominator, the less value the fraction has. Help them recognize that the denominator, below the fraction bar, tells how many parts are in a whole and the numerator, above the fraction bar, tells how many parts are shaded.

Objectives

- Use concrete objects or given drawings to compare unit fractions.

LEARN Compare Fractions on a Number Line

ONLINE 20 min

Students will use the Different Ways to Show Fractions Learning Tool to see that unit fractions (fractions that have 1 in the numerator), such as $\frac{1}{2}, \frac{1}{3}, \frac{1}{4}$, can be compared by looking at the denominator. The greater the denominator, the less value the unit fraction has. Students will also see that when two fractions have the same denominator, such as $\frac{3}{8}$ and $\frac{5}{8}$, the fraction with the greater numerator has the greater value. The fraction $\frac{5}{8}$ is greater than $\frac{3}{8}$ because $\frac{5}{8}$ has more eighths.

Objectives

- Compare and order unit fractions, such as $\frac{1}{4}$, and fractions with like denominators, such as $\frac{2}{6}$ and $\frac{4}{6}$, by using objects or sketches.

DIRECTIONS FOR USING THE DIFFERENT WAYS TO SHOW FRACTIONS LEARNING TOOL

1. Click Parts of a Whole.
2. Click Show Number Line.
3. Have students click the square to show one whole.

   Say: Fractions can be shown as part of a whole or as a number on the number line.

4. Have students click the + symbol in the lower right of the screen a few times and watch the number line.

   Ask: What happens to the number line as you click the + symbol? It gets divided into more and more sections that are smaller.

   Ask: What happens to the denominator as you click the + symbol? It increases with each click.

   Ask: What happens to the square? It gets more parts.

5. Have students watch the number line as they click the + symbol until the denominator is 8.

   Say: What happens to the sections on the number line as the denominator increases? The sections get smaller.

6. Have students do the following:

   - Click the − symbol in the lower right until the denominator is back to 1. See that the sections of the number line get bigger.
   - Click the square to show 1. See how the number line shows 1.
   - Click the + symbol to show halves. Click $\frac{1}{2}$ of the square. Notice how the number line shows $\frac{1}{2}$.

   Ask: Is $\frac{1}{2}$ greater than or less than 1 whole? less

7. Click the + symbol to show thirds and then click one section of the square to show $\frac{1}{3}$.

   Ask: Is $\frac{1}{3}$ greater than or less than $\frac{1}{2}$? less

8. Repeat Step 7 to show the unit fractions $\frac{1}{4}$, $\frac{1}{5}$, $\frac{1}{6}$, ... to $\frac{1}{8}$. Each time, ask students whether the current fraction is greater than or less than the previous fraction. It will always be less than the previous fraction, which they will be able to see as they watch the number line.

   Remind students that when the denominator is greater, the parts are smaller. So if they compare fractions that have a 1 in the numerator, they can always say that the fraction with the greatest denominator will have the least value.

9. Look at $\frac{1}{8}$ on the number line. Have students click two more sections of the square to show $\frac{3}{8}$ and notice that $\frac{3}{8}$ is to the right of $\frac{1}{8}$ on the number line.

   Ask: Which is greater: $\frac{3}{8}$ or $\frac{1}{8}$? $\frac{3}{8}$

10. Have students click two more parts to show $\frac{5}{8}$.

    Ask: Which is greater: $\frac{3}{8}$ or $\frac{5}{8}$? $\frac{5}{8}$

    Ask: Without making the fraction, answer this question: Which would be greater, $\frac{3}{8}$ or $\frac{6}{8}$, and how do you know? The answer is $\frac{6}{8}$, because it has more eighths, and because it's to the right on the number line.

    Say: When two fractions have the same denominator, the fraction with the greater numerator has the greater value.

LEARN Fractions and Fraction Strips

ONLINE
20 min

Students will use the Fraction Strips Learning Tool to compare unit fractions and fractions with the same denominator. After they use the learning tool, they will put fractions in order from least to greatest and from greatest to least.

DIRECTIONS FOR USING THE FRACTION STRIPS LEARNING TOOL

1. Read the instructions, and click Start.

2. Click the equivalent chart reference icon in the lower-left corner of the screen to show students the many combinations of fractions that are equivalent to a whole, or 1.

Objectives

- Compare and order unit fractions, such as $\frac{1}{4}$, and fractions with like denominators, such as $\frac{2}{6}$ and $\frac{4}{6}$, by using objects or sketches.

3. **Say:** The top fraction strip represents a whole, or 1. Look at the fraction strips below 1.

   Ask: How many one-thirds $\left(\frac{1}{3}\right)$ are equal to 1 whole? 3 one-thirds

   Ask: How many one-eighths $\left(\frac{1}{8}\right)$ are equal to 1 whole? 8 one-eighths

4. **Say:** Since $\frac{3}{3}$ and $\frac{8}{8}$ both equal 1 whole, we know that $\frac{8}{8}$ and $\frac{3}{3}$ are equal to each other. They have the same value.

   Click the X in the upper-right corner of the chart to close it.

5. Tell students that they will use the fraction strips to compare fractions. Have students drag a 1-whole strip from the top bar to the top of the screen's left section.

6. Next have students drag a $\frac{1}{2}$ strip under the 1 whole.

   Ask: Which fraction is greater? 1 whole

7. Repeat Step 6 with fraction strips for $\frac{1}{3}, \frac{1}{4}, \frac{1}{6}$, and $\frac{1}{8}$. Have students line up the strips from greatest to least, one under the other. Have them state each comparison. Example: $\frac{1}{6}$ is less than $\frac{1}{4}$ $\left(\text{or } \frac{1}{4} \text{ is greater than } \frac{1}{6}\right)$.

   Remind students that the greater the denominator, the smaller each part of the whole is.

8. Have students use the middle section to compare $\frac{5}{8}$ and $\frac{3}{8}$. Have them drag five $\frac{1}{8}$ strips, and underneath those strips, drag three $\frac{1}{8}$ strips.

   Ask: How do $\frac{5}{8}$ and $\frac{3}{8}$ compare with each other? $\frac{5}{8}$ is greater than $\frac{3}{8}$ $\left(\text{or } \frac{3}{8} \text{ is less than } \frac{5}{8}\right)$.

9. Do a few more. Have students compare $\frac{1}{4}$ and $\frac{3}{4}$; have them compare $\frac{2}{6}$ and $\frac{4}{6}$.

   Say: When you compare two fractions with the same denominator, the number in the numerator determines which fraction is greater.

TRY IT Compare Fractions

OFFLINE
10 min

Objectives

Students will practice identifying and comparing fractions as part of a whole and as a location on a number line. They will use $<$, $>$, or $=$ to compare fractions. View or print the Compare Fractions activity page and read the directions with students.

Students should copy the problems from the Activity Book into their Math Notebook as necessary and solve them there.

- Compare and order unit fractions, such as $\frac{1}{4}$, and fractions with like denominators, such as $\frac{2}{6}$ and $\frac{4}{6}$, by using objects or sketches.

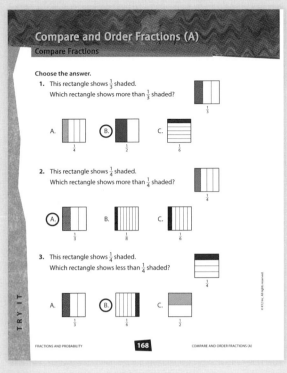

Compare and Order Fractions (A)
Compare Fractions

Choose the answer.

1. This rectangle shows $\frac{1}{3}$ shaded.
Which rectangle shows more than $\frac{1}{3}$ shaded?

A. $\frac{1}{4}$ (B.) $\frac{1}{2}$ C. $\frac{1}{6}$

2. This rectangle shows $\frac{1}{4}$ shaded.
Which rectangle shows more than $\frac{1}{4}$ shaded?

(A.) $\frac{1}{3}$ B. $\frac{1}{8}$ C. $\frac{1}{6}$

3. This rectangle shows $\frac{1}{4}$ shaded.
Which rectangle shows less than $\frac{1}{4}$ shaded?

A. $\frac{1}{3}$ (B.) $\frac{1}{6}$ C. $\frac{1}{2}$

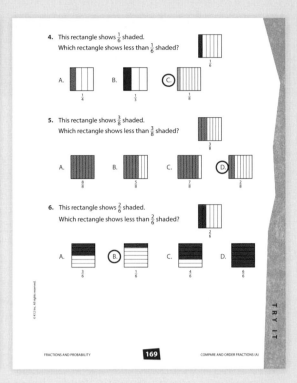

4. This rectangle shows $\frac{1}{6}$ shaded.
Which rectangle shows less than $\frac{1}{6}$ shaded?

A. $\frac{1}{4}$ B. $\frac{1}{3}$ (C.) $\frac{1}{8}$

5. This rectangle shows $\frac{3}{8}$ shaded.
Which rectangle shows less than $\frac{3}{8}$ shaded?

A. $\frac{8}{8}$ B. $\frac{5}{8}$ C. $\frac{7}{8}$ (D.) $\frac{2}{8}$

6. This rectangle shows $\frac{2}{6}$ shaded.
Which rectangle shows less than $\frac{2}{6}$ shaded?

A. $\frac{3}{6}$ (B.) $\frac{1}{6}$ C. $\frac{4}{6}$ D. $\frac{6}{6}$

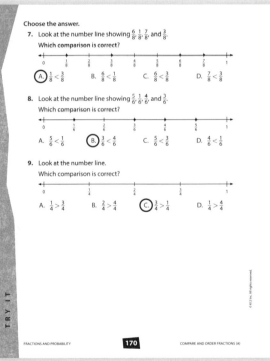

Choose the answer.

7. Look at the number line showing $\frac{6}{8}, \frac{1}{8}, \frac{7}{8},$ and $\frac{3}{8}$.
Which comparison is correct?

(A.) $\frac{1}{8} < \frac{3}{8}$ B. $\frac{6}{8} < \frac{1}{8}$ C. $\frac{6}{8} < \frac{3}{8}$ D. $\frac{7}{8} < \frac{3}{8}$

8. Look at the number line showing $\frac{5}{6}, \frac{1}{6}, \frac{4}{6},$ and $\frac{3}{6}$.
Which comparison is correct?

A. $\frac{5}{6} < \frac{1}{6}$ (B.) $\frac{3}{6} < \frac{4}{6}$ C. $\frac{5}{6} < \frac{3}{6}$ D. $\frac{4}{6} < \frac{1}{6}$

9. Look at the number line.
Which comparison is correct?

A. $\frac{1}{4} > \frac{3}{4}$ B. $\frac{2}{4} > \frac{4}{4}$ (C.) $\frac{3}{4} > \frac{1}{4}$ D. $\frac{1}{4} > \frac{4}{4}$

Compare and Order Fractions (B)

Lesson Overview

LEARN Compare with Fraction Strips	15 minutes	OFFLINE
LEARN Use Number Lines to Compare Fractions	20 minutes	OFFLINE
TRY IT Compare and Order with Models	15 minutes	OFFLINE
CHECKPOINT	10 minutes	ONLINE

▶ ## Lesson Objectives

Compare and order unit fractions, such as $\frac{1}{4}$, and fractions with like denominators, such as $\frac{2}{6}$ and $\frac{4}{6}$, by using objects or sketches.

▶ ## Prerequisite Skills

Use concrete objects or given drawings to compare unit fractions.

▶ ## Content Background

Students will continue to learn to identify and compare fractions with like and unlike denominators using $<$, $>$, or $=$.

Students will use the comparison symbols of $<$, $>$, or $=$ to compare fractions. The denominator, or the number below the fraction bar, of a fraction tells how many equal pieces the whole has been divided into. It is important for students to understand that as the denominator increases, the size of each piece decreases.

$\frac{1}{2}$

$\frac{1}{4}$

$\frac{1}{6}$

$\frac{1}{8}$

Materials to Gather

SUPPLIED

Fraction Strips (printout)

Whole to Twelfths Number Lines (printout)

Use Number Lines to Compare Fractions activity page

Compare and Order with Models activity page

ALSO NEEDED

straightedge

▶ ## Common Errors and Misconceptions

- Students might view the numerator and denominator of a fraction as separate, isolated numbers that can be operated on independently. This may lead to students "memorizing" rather than understanding fraction algorithms, and then using them incorrectly.

- Students might not understand the difference between fractions and whole numbers. Fractions are parts of whole numbers. Examples of fractions include $\frac{4}{6}$, $\frac{7}{8}$, and $2\frac{1}{2}$. Examples of whole numbers include 4, 6, and 10. Whole numbers may be written as fractions, but always with a denominator of 1, such as $\frac{4}{1}$, $\frac{6}{1}$, or $\frac{10}{1}$.

- Students might have difficulty understanding how different models represent fractions because they often see fractions represented as parts of circles—for example, pie and pizza illustrations. They might not recognize, for example, that the following models all represent the fraction $\frac{3}{8}$.

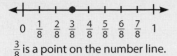

$\frac{3}{8}$ is a point on the number line.

$\frac{3}{8}$ of the rectangle is shaded.

- Students might think that a fraction always represents the size of a part of a whole, number of items in a set, or a location on the number line, and so might not understand that a fraction can also represent a relationship, such as a quotient or a ratio of one quantity to another.

- Students might think that a fraction compares one part to another part rather than recognizing that a fraction compares one part to the whole.

▶ Advance Preparation

Print the Fraction Strips and the Whole to Twelfths Number Lines.

LEARN Compare with Fraction Strips

OFFLINE
15 min

Objectives

- Compare and order unit fractions, such as $\frac{1}{4}$, and fractions with like denominators, such as $\frac{2}{6}$ and $\frac{4}{6}$, by using objects or sketches.

Students will use fraction strips to compare and order fractions using $<$, $>$, or $=$. They will also use fraction strips to order fractions from least to greatest and from greatest to least.

Gather the Fraction Strips printout.

1. Introduce the fraction strips to students. Explain that the first row shows one whole and each row after that shows fractions of a whole. Mention that the fraction strips do not include elevenths.

2. Have students look at the second row. Tell them that this row shows $\frac{1}{2}$ two times. Ask them how many halves it takes to make a whole. 2

   Have students look at the third row. Tell them that this row shows $\frac{1}{3}$ three times. Ask them how many thirds it takes to make a whole. 3

3. Repeat Step 2 for each remaining row on the printout. Make sure students understand that if a row shows fourths, there are 4 parts that make a whole and if a row shows twelfths, there are 12 parts that make a whole. Emphasize that as the denominator increases, the fraction sections get smaller.

4. Explain how to use fraction strips to compare fractions, as follows:

   - Have students look at the fraction strips and identify the $\frac{1}{3}$ strip and the $\frac{1}{4}$ strip. Then ask which is greater, $\frac{1}{3}$ or $\frac{1}{4}$. $\frac{1}{3}$

   - Emphasize that if a whole is divided into 3 equal parts, the parts are bigger than if a whole is divided into 4 equal parts.

   - Have students find a fraction that is less than $\frac{1}{4}$. Students should identify any fraction below $\frac{1}{4}$ $\left(\frac{1}{5}, \frac{1}{6}, \frac{1}{7}, \frac{1}{8}, \frac{1}{9}, \frac{1}{10}, \text{ or } \frac{1}{12}\right)$ as less than $\frac{1}{4}$. Explain that these fraction pieces are all smaller than $\frac{1}{4}$.

   - Explain that you can go straight up or down on the fraction strips to find fractions that are equal to one another.

Say: Look at $\frac{1}{2}$. The fraction $\frac{1}{2}$ is equal to $\frac{2}{4}$. Find other fractions equal to $\frac{1}{2}$. $\frac{3}{6}, \frac{4}{8}, \frac{5}{10}$, and $\frac{6}{12}$

5. Ask students to use the fraction strips to compare these fractions:

- $\frac{1}{8} \; \underline{\;?\;} \; \frac{1}{4} \quad <$
- $\frac{1}{2} \; \underline{\;?\;} \; \frac{1}{8} \quad >$
- $\frac{1}{4} \; \underline{\;?\;} \; \frac{1}{3} \quad <$
- $\frac{1}{6} \; \underline{\;?\;} \; \frac{1}{8} \quad >$
- $\frac{1}{6} \; \underline{\;?\;} \; \frac{1}{4} \quad <$
- $\frac{1}{3} \; \underline{\;?\;} \; \frac{1}{2} \quad <$

6. Have students use the fraction strips to order the following fractions:

- $\frac{1}{4}, \frac{1}{2}, \frac{1}{3}$ least to greatest $\quad \frac{1}{4}, \frac{1}{3}, \frac{1}{2}$
- $\frac{1}{6}, \frac{1}{8}, \frac{1}{4}$ greatest to least $\quad \frac{1}{4}, \frac{1}{6}, \frac{1}{8}$

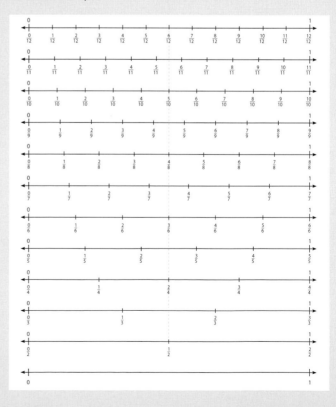

LEARN Use Number Lines to Compare Fractions 20 min

OFFLINE

Students will use number lines to compare fractions.

View or print the Use Number Lines to Compare Fractions activity page. Gather the Whole to Twelfths Number Lines printout and the straightedge (index card or ruler).

1. Introduce the stacked number lines to students. Explain that the stacked number lines are similar to fraction strips. The difference is that here the fractions are just points on a number line, not part of a whole strip.

   Say: All the points shown here exist on every number line. However, if they all appeared on the same line, they'd be too close together to see clearly. The stacked number lines are a way to see the points separately.

2. Point out that each number line goes from 0 to 1 and that along the right side are all the fractions that equal 1 whole. Emphasize that the fractions equal to 1 whole are all equal, or equivalent, fractions. Have students point to 1 whole on the bottom strip. Then have them move their finger up to $\frac{1}{2}, \frac{1}{3}, \frac{1}{4}$, continuing up to $\frac{1}{12}$. Students will see that these unit fractions decrease in value as the denominator increases.

3. Tell students that the stacked number line is another way to compare fractions to identify greater, lesser, or equal fractions. Show students how to use a straightedge to see fractions that have the same value. Line up a straightedge with the line showing fractions that equal $\frac{1}{2}$. By lining up the straightedge with a given fraction, students can tell which fractions are greater than, less than, or equal to the given fraction.

Objectives

- Compare and order unit fractions, such as $\frac{1}{4}$, and fractions with like denominators, such as $\frac{2}{6}$ and $\frac{4}{6}$, by using objects or sketches.

4. Read the first Worked Example with students. Then have students complete Problems 1–8, referring to the Worked Example as needed. Students may use the Whole to Twelfths Number Lines printout.

5. Read the second Worked Example with students. Then have students complete Problems 9–14, referring to the Worked Example as needed. Students may use the Whole to Twelfths Number Lines printout.

6. Have students complete Problems 15–19. Have them explain how they solved the problems.

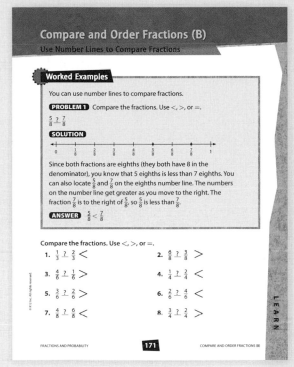

Compare and Order Fractions (B)
Use Number Lines to Compare Fractions

Worked Examples

You can use number lines to compare fractions.

PROBLEM 1 Compare the fractions. Use $<$, $>$, or $=$.

$\frac{5}{8} \ ? \ \frac{7}{8}$

SOLUTION

Since both fractions are eighths (they both have 8 in the denominator), you know that 5 eighths is less than 7 eighths. You can also locate $\frac{5}{8}$ and $\frac{7}{8}$ on the eighths number line. The numbers on the number line get greater as you move to the right. The fraction $\frac{7}{8}$ is to the right of $\frac{5}{8}$, so $\frac{5}{8}$ is less than $\frac{7}{8}$.

ANSWER $\frac{5}{8} < \frac{7}{8}$

Compare the fractions. Use $<$, $>$, or $=$.

1. $\frac{1}{3} \ ? \ \frac{2}{3}$ $<$
2. $\frac{6}{8} \ ? \ \frac{3}{8}$ $>$
3. $\frac{4}{6} \ ? \ \frac{1}{6}$ $>$
4. $\frac{1}{4} \ ? \ \frac{2}{4}$ $<$
5. $\frac{3}{6} \ ? \ \frac{2}{6}$ $>$
6. $\frac{2}{6} \ ? \ \frac{4}{6}$ $<$
7. $\frac{4}{8} \ ? \ \frac{6}{8}$ $<$
8. $\frac{3}{4} \ ? \ \frac{2}{4}$ $>$

FRACTIONS AND PROBABILITY **171** COMPARE AND ORDER FRACTIONS (B)

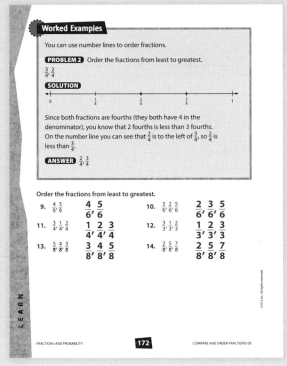

Worked Examples

You can use number lines to order fractions.

PROBLEM 2 Order the fractions from least to greatest.

$\frac{3}{4}, \frac{2}{4}$

SOLUTION

Since both fractions are fourths (they both have 4 in the denominator), you know that 2 fourths is less than 3 fourths. On the number line you can see that $\frac{2}{4}$ is to the left of $\frac{3}{4}$, so $\frac{2}{4}$ is less than $\frac{3}{4}$.

ANSWER $\frac{2}{4}, \frac{3}{4}$

Order the fractions from least to greatest.

9. $\frac{4}{6}, \frac{5}{6}$ $\quad \frac{4}{6}, \frac{5}{6}$
10. $\frac{3}{6}, \frac{2}{6}, \frac{5}{6}$ $\quad \frac{2}{6}, \frac{3}{6}, \frac{5}{6}$
11. $\frac{3}{4}, \frac{1}{4}, \frac{2}{4}$ $\quad \frac{1}{4}, \frac{2}{4}, \frac{3}{4}$
12. $\frac{3}{3}, \frac{1}{3}, \frac{2}{3}$ $\quad \frac{1}{3}, \frac{2}{3}, \frac{3}{3}$
13. $\frac{5}{8}, \frac{4}{8}, \frac{3}{8}$ $\quad \frac{3}{8}, \frac{4}{8}, \frac{5}{8}$
14. $\frac{2}{8}, \frac{5}{8}, \frac{7}{8}$ $\quad \frac{2}{8}, \frac{5}{8}, \frac{7}{8}$

FRACTIONS AND PROBABILITY **172** COMPARE AND ORDER FRACTIONS (B)

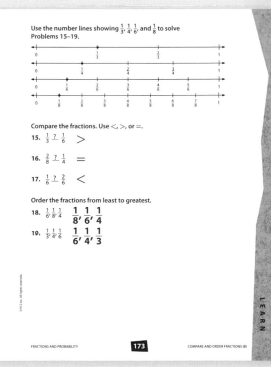

Use the number lines showing $\frac{1}{3}, \frac{1}{4}, \frac{1}{6},$ and $\frac{1}{8}$ to solve Problems 15–19.

Compare the fractions. Use $<$, $>$, or $=$.

15. $\frac{1}{3} \ ? \ \frac{1}{6}$ $>$

16. $\frac{2}{8} \ ? \ \frac{1}{4}$ $=$

17. $\frac{1}{6} \ ? \ \frac{2}{6}$ $<$

Order the fractions from least to greatest.

18. $\frac{1}{6}, \frac{1}{8}, \frac{1}{4}$ $\quad \frac{1}{8}, \frac{1}{6}, \frac{1}{4}$

19. $\frac{1}{3}, \frac{1}{4}, \frac{1}{6}$ $\quad \frac{1}{6}, \frac{1}{4}, \frac{1}{3}$

FRACTIONS AND PROBABILITY **173** COMPARE AND ORDER FRACTIONS (B)

TRY IT Compare and Order with Models

Objectives

Students will practice comparing and ordering fractions with like and unlike denominators. They will use stacked number lines and illustrations to make the comparisons. View or print the Compare and Order with Models activity page in their Activity Book and read the directions with students.

Students should copy the problems from the Activity Book into their Math Notebook as necessary and solve them there.

- Compare and order unit fractions, such as $\frac{1}{4}$, and fractions with like denominators, such as $\frac{2}{6}$ and $\frac{4}{6}$, by using objects or sketches.

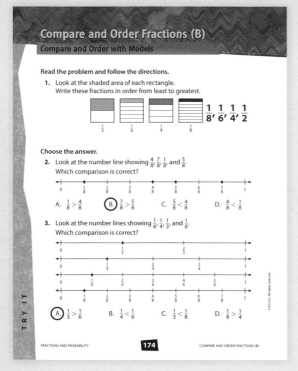

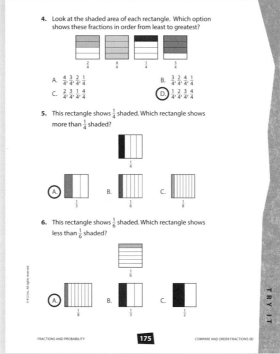

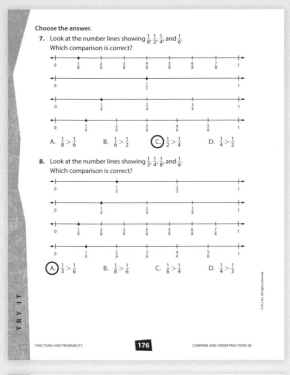

Choose the answer.

7. Look at the number lines showing $\frac{1}{8}, \frac{1}{2}, \frac{1}{4},$ and $\frac{1}{6}$. Which comparison is correct?

A. $\frac{1}{8} > \frac{1}{6}$ B. $\frac{1}{6} > \frac{1}{2}$ C. (circled) $\frac{1}{2} > \frac{1}{4}$ D. $\frac{1}{4} > \frac{1}{2}$

8. Look at the number lines showing $\frac{1}{3}, \frac{1}{4}, \frac{1}{8},$ and $\frac{1}{6}$. Which comparison is correct?

A. (circled) $\frac{1}{3} > \frac{1}{6}$ B. $\frac{1}{8} > \frac{1}{6}$ C. $\frac{1}{6} > \frac{1}{4}$ D. $\frac{1}{4} > \frac{1}{3}$

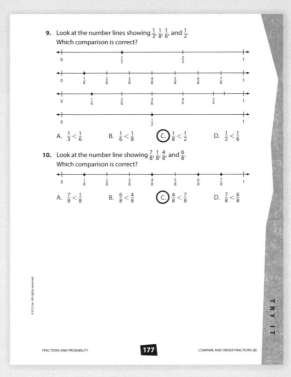

9. Look at the number lines showing $\frac{1}{3}, \frac{1}{8}, \frac{1}{6},$ and $\frac{1}{2}$. Which comparison is correct?

A. $\frac{1}{3} < \frac{1}{6}$ B. $\frac{1}{6} < \frac{1}{8}$ C. (circled) $\frac{1}{8} < \frac{1}{2}$ D. $\frac{1}{2} < \frac{1}{6}$

10. Look at the number line showing $\frac{7}{8}, \frac{1}{8}, \frac{4}{8},$ and $\frac{6}{8}$. Which comparison is correct?

A. $\frac{7}{8} < \frac{1}{8}$ B. $\frac{6}{8} < \frac{4}{8}$ C. (circled) $\frac{4}{8} < \frac{7}{8}$ D. $\frac{7}{8} < \frac{6}{8}$

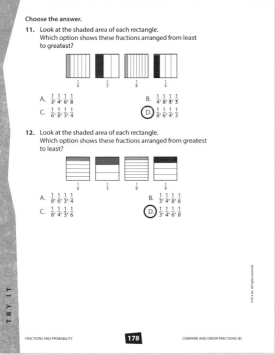

Choose the answer.

11. Look at the shaded area of each rectangle. Which option shows these fractions arranged from least to greatest?

$\frac{1}{6}$ $\frac{1}{3}$ $\frac{1}{8}$ $\frac{1}{4}$

A. $\frac{1}{3}, \frac{1}{4}, \frac{1}{6}, \frac{1}{8}$ B. $\frac{1}{4}, \frac{1}{6}, \frac{1}{8}, \frac{1}{3}$

C. $\frac{1}{6}, \frac{1}{8}, \frac{1}{3}, \frac{1}{4}$ D. (circled) $\frac{1}{8}, \frac{1}{6}, \frac{1}{4}, \frac{1}{3}$

12. Look at the shaded area of each rectangle. Which option shows these fractions arranged from greatest to least?

$\frac{1}{6}$ $\frac{1}{3}$ $\frac{1}{8}$ $\frac{1}{4}$

A. $\frac{1}{8}, \frac{1}{6}, \frac{1}{3}, \frac{1}{4}$ B. $\frac{1}{3}, \frac{1}{4}, \frac{1}{8}, \frac{1}{6}$

C. $\frac{1}{8}, \frac{1}{4}, \frac{1}{3}, \frac{1}{6}$ D. (circled) $\frac{1}{3}, \frac{1}{4}, \frac{1}{6}, \frac{1}{8}$

CHECKPOINT

ONLINE 10 min

Students will complete an online Checkpoint. If necessary, read the directions, problems, and answer choices to students and help them with keyboard or mouse operations.

Objectives

- Compare and order unit fractions, such as $\frac{1}{4}$, and fractions with like denominators, such as $\frac{2}{6}$ and $\frac{4}{6}$, by using objects or sketches.

COMPARE AND ORDER FRACTIONS (B) **335**

Compare and Prove

Lesson Overview

GET READY Equivalent Fractions of Shapes	5 minutes	**ONLINE**
LEARN Compare Distances on Number Lines	15 minutes	**ONLINE**
LEARN Compare and Explain	15 minutes	**OFFLINE**
TRY IT Explain Comparing and Ordering	15 minutes	**OFFLINE**
CHECKPOINT	10 minutes	**ONLINE**

▶ ## Lesson Objectives

- Compare and order unit fractions, such as $\frac{1}{4}$, and fractions with like denominators, such as $\frac{2}{6}$ and $\frac{4}{6}$, by using objects or sketches.
- Compare and order fractions with like numerators by using objects or sketches.
- Recognize that the comparison of two fractions is only valid if the wholes are identical.

▶ ## Prerequisite Skills

Identify a few simple equivalent fractions, such as $\frac{1}{2} = \frac{2}{4}$.

▶ ## Content Background

Students will learn how to identify and compare fractions with like numerators and different denominators using number lines, area models, and reasoning. Students will also learn that the comparison of two fractions is only valid if the wholes are identical.

Students will use the comparison symbols of $<$, $>$, and $=$ to compare fractions. The denominator, or the number below the fraction bar, of a fraction tells how many equal pieces the whole has been divided into. It is important for students to understand that as the denominator increases, the size of each piece decreases.

$\frac{1}{2}$

$\frac{1}{4}$

$\frac{1}{6}$

$\frac{1}{8}$

▶ ## Common Errors and Misconceptions

- Students might view the numerator and denominator of a fraction as separate, isolated numbers that can be operated on independently. This may lead to students "memorizing" rather than understanding fraction algorithms and then using them incorrectly.

Materials to Gather

SUPPLIED

Fraction Strips (printout)

Whole to Twelfths Number Lines (printout)

Compare and Explain activity page

Explain Comparing and Ordering activity page

- Students might not understand the difference between fractions and whole numbers. Fractions are parts of whole numbers. Examples of fractions include $\frac{4}{6}$, $\frac{7}{8}$, and $2\frac{1}{2}$. Examples of whole numbers include 4, 6, and 8. Whole numbers may be written as fractions but always with a denominator of 1, such as $\frac{4}{1}$, $\frac{6}{1}$, or $\frac{8}{1}$.

- Students may have difficulty understanding how different models represent fractions because they often see fractions represented as parts of circles—for example, pie and pizza illustrations. They might not recognize, for example, that fractions can be represented on number lines and with area models.

- Students might think that a fraction compares one part to another part rather than recognizing that a fraction compares one part to the whole.

▶ Advance Preparation

Print the Fraction Strips and the Whole to Twelfths Number Lines.

ONLINE 5 min

GET READY Equivalent Fractions of Shapes

Students will review that equivalent fractions are fractions with the same value. They will see how equivalent fractions can be modeled with shapes.

Objectives

- Identify a few simple equivalent fractions, such as $\frac{1}{2} = \frac{2}{4}$.

ONLINE 15 min

LEARN Compare Distances on Number Lines

Students will compare fractions with different numerators and like denominators and fractions with like numerators and different denominators by comparing distances on number lines.

Objectives

- Compare and order unit fractions, such as $\frac{1}{4}$, and fractions with like denominators, such as $\frac{2}{6}$ and $\frac{4}{6}$, by using objects or sketches.
- Compare and order fractions with like numerators by using objects or sketches.

OFFLINE 15 min

LEARN Compare and Explain

Students will use reasoning to explain why comparisons of fractions are only valid when the wholes are identical.

View or print the Compare and Explain activity page and read the directions with students. They should copy the problems into their Math Notebook as necessary and solve them there.

Objectives

- Recognize that the comparison of two fractions is only valid if the wholes are identical.

1. Remind students that the area of a figure is simply the amount of space inside the figure.

2. Read the first Worked Example with students. Point out that the two wholes, the two pizzas, are exactly the same size, but they are divided differently. Mario's pizza is divided into sixths and Dan's pizza is divided into eighths. Remind students that a sixth is larger than an eighth. If necessary, draw an area model to illustrate. Then guide students to conclude that two-sixths will be larger than two-eighths.

3. Read and review the second Worked Example with students. Point out that this time the two wholes are different sizes. To compare fractions, the wholes have to be the same size, so you cannot use the fractions to compare the pieces of pizza in this case.

4. Have students complete Problems 1 and 2, referring to the Worked Examples as necessary. Students should draw sketches of the situations if necessary. Emphasize that two fractions can only be compared if the whole is the same size and shape.

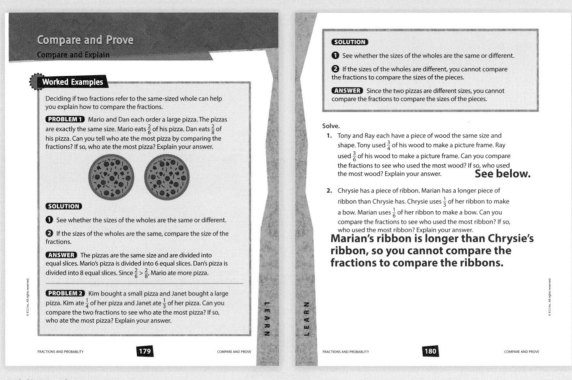

Additional Answer

1. The pieces of wood are the same shape and size, so I can compare the size of the fractions. Since fourths are larger than sixths, $\frac{3}{4} > \frac{3}{6}$. Tony used more wood than Ray did.

TRY IT Explain Comparing and Ordering

OFFLINE 15 min

Students will practice identifying and comparing fractions as part of a whole and as locations on number lines. They will also use reasoning to explain the comparisons they make. Gather the Fraction Strips and Whole to Twelfths Number Lines printouts. View or print the Explain Comparing and Ordering activity and read the directions with students. They should refer to the Fraction Strips and Whole to Twelfths Number Lines printouts for support as they compare the fractions. Remind students that they can only compare different fractions if they refer to the same whole.

Students should copy the problems from the Activity Book into their Math Notebook as necessary and solve them there.

Objectives

- Compare and order unit fractions, such as $\frac{1}{4}$, and fractions with like denominators, such as $\frac{2}{6}$ and $\frac{4}{6}$, by using objects or sketches.
- Compare and order fractions with like numerators by using objects or sketches.
- Recognize that the comparison of two fractions is only valid if the wholes are identical.

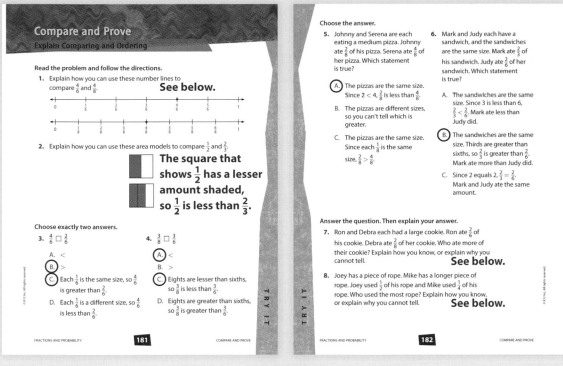

Additional Answers

1. The distance from zero to $\frac{4}{6}$ is greater than the distance from zero to $\frac{4}{8}$, so $\frac{4}{6}$ is greater than $\frac{4}{8}$.

7. Ron ate more of his cookie. **Sample explanation:** The cookies are the same size. Sixths are greater than eighths, so $\frac{2}{6} > \frac{2}{8}$.

8. **Sample answer:** Since the ropes are not the same length, you cannot compare the fractions to compare the ropes.

CHECKPONT

ONLINE
10 min

Objectives

Students will complete an online Checkpoint. If necessary, read the directions, problems, and answer choices to students and help them with keyboard or mouse operations.

- Compare and order unit fractions, such as $\frac{1}{4}$, and fractions with like denominators, such as $\frac{2}{6}$ and $\frac{4}{6}$, by using objects or sketches.
- Compare and order fractions with like numerators by using objects or sketches.
- Recognize that the comparison of two fractions is only valid if the wholes are identical.

Probability

Lesson Overview

LEARN Certain, Likely, Unlikely, Impossible	20 minutes	**ONLINE**
LEARN Outcomes	15 minutes	**ONLINE**
TRY IT What Is the Probability?	15 minutes	**ONLINE**
CHECKPOINT	10 minutes	**ONLINE**

▶ Lesson Objectives

Identify whether specific events are certain, likely, unlikely, or impossible.

▶ Content Background

In this lesson, students will learn to describe the likelihood of an event occurring as certain, likely, unlikely, or impossible. This lesson is an introductory lesson on probability.

For students to understand the concepts that form the foundation of mathematical probability, they must first learn about the likelihood of something happening or not happening. By using the image of a number line between and including 0 and 1, students will begin to visually position given events between 0 (impossible) and 1 (certain), as shown in the illustration.

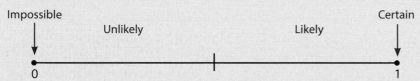

Students will not do formal probability at this level but will learn to identify potential outcomes and consider whether they are certain, likely, unlikely, or impossible. When they determine actual probability values, they will discover that probabilities that are not impossible or certain are expressed as fractions between 0 and 1, sometimes also expressed as decimals and percents.

The probability of an event occurring is not the same as the odds that an event will occur. The terms *probability* and *odds* should not be used interchangeably. If the probability of an event is $\frac{3}{5}$, the odds are 3 to 2.

Materials to Gather

There are no materials to gather for this lesson.

LEARN Certain, Likely, Unlikely, Impossible

ONLINE 20min

Students will learn about probability and consider whether the likelihood of an event occurring is certain, likely, unlikely, or impossible. They will also learn to identify equally likely outcomes, such as flipping heads or tails with a coin.

Objectives

- Identify whether specific events are certain, likely, unlikely, or impossible.

LEARN Outcomes

ONLINE 15min

Objectives

Students will describe the probability of an event occurring as certain, likely, unlikely, or impossible.

- Identify whether specific events are certain, likely, unlikely, or impossible.

TRY IT What Is the Probability?

ONLINE 15min

Objectives

Students will complete an online Try It. If necessary, read the directions, problems, and answer choices to students and help them with keyboard or mouse operations.

- Identify whether specific events are certain, likely, unlikely, or impossible.

CHECKPOINT

ONLINE 10min

Objectives

Students will complete an online Checkpoint. If necessary, read the directions, problems, and answer choices to students and help them with keyboard or mouse operations.

- Identify whether specific events are certain, likely, unlikely, or impossible.

Identify, Record, and Display Outcomes

▶ Lesson Objectives

- Identify and systematically record the possible outcomes for a simple event.
- Summarize and display the results of a probability experiment in a clear and organized way.

▶ Prerequisite Skills

- Systematically record numerical data.
- Identify whether specific events are certain, likely, unlikely, or impossible.
- Represent the same data set with more than one representation, such as a tally, picture graph, or bar graph.

▶ Content Background

Students will learn to record data from probability experiments as tally marks in tally charts and then represent that information in line plots and bar graphs.

It is important for students to understand the possible outcomes in a situation and represent these outcomes as data in a clear and organized way. They will learn to use tally marks, tally charts, line plots, and bar graphs as tools for collecting, recording, and displaying data.

Materials to Gather

SUPPLIED

blocks – E (4 yellow, 3 blue)

Data Display (printout)

Find the Outcome activity page

ALSO NEEDED

household objects – paper bag, coin

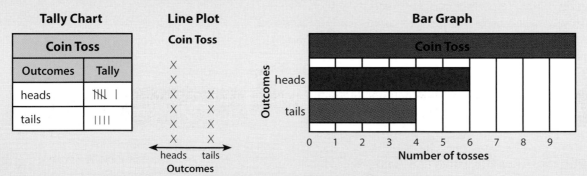

When analyzing probability problems, students should be able to list the possible outcomes of each event. Diagrams and tables are effective ways to organize possible outcomes. Students should also be able to state whether the probability of each event is likely, unlikely, impossible, or certain.

▶ Advance Preparation

Print the Data Display.

Gather a paper bag for Learn: Data Display and a coin for Try It: Find the Outcome.

GET READY Compare Data

ONLINE 5min

Students will see data in a picture graph and will identify the tally chart and bar graph that show the same data. Point out that the charts show the same data different ways. In the picture graph, students count the symbols to see how many people prefer a certain type of fruit. In the tally chart, they count the tally marks. In the bar graph, they look at the numbers to the left of the bars.

Objectives

- Systematically record numerical data.
- Identify whether specific events are certain, likely, unlikely, or impossible.
- Represent the same data set with more than one representation, such as a tally, picture graph, or bar graph.

LEARN Chart the Outcomes

ONLINE 15min

Students will learn to identify possible outcomes for tossing a coin, rolling a number cube, and spinning a spinner. They will also identify outcomes that are not possible for spinning a spinner or rolling a number cube. They'll see that it's impossible to land on a color that isn't on the spinner or to land on a number that isn't on the cube. Toward the end of the activity, students will use an online spinner do a probability experiment. They will see how the data from the experiment are displayed in a tally chart and bar graph.

Objectives

- Identify and systematically record the possible outcomes for a simple event.
- Summarize and display the results of a probability experiment in a clear and organized way.

DIRECTIONS FOR USING THE TALLY CHARTS AND BAR GRAPHS LEARNING TOOL

1. Click Begin.
2. Have students spin the spinner until one outcome has 10 tally marks.
3. Explain to students that it's important to collect, record, and organize the data from probability experiments in a way that can be easily understood by others.

LEARN Data Display

OFFLINE 20min

Students will gather data and complete a tally chart, a line plot, and a vertical bar graph (a graph with bars that are vertical rather than horizontal).

Gather the E blocks, paper bag, and Data Display printout.

1. Give students the Data Display printout. Tell them that in this activity, they'll carry out an experiment and record the results in the tally chart, line plot, and bar graph on the printout.
2. Have students place the yellow and blue squares in the paper bag.

Objectives

- Identify and systematically record the possible outcomes for a simple event.
- Summarize and display the results of a probability experiment in a clear and organized way.

3. Ask students to identify the possible outcomes when picking 1 square out of the bag. Student should explain that picking a yellow square or a blue square are the possible outcomes.

Tell students that since there are 4 yellow squares out of 7 squares total, the chance of picking a yellow square is 4 out of 7. Relate this to fractions by saying that the chance of picking a yellow square is $\frac{4}{7}$.

4. Have students draw 1 square out of the bag. Have them record the result in the tally chart in the printout. Students should then place the square back in the bag and draw again. They should repeat this step until they have made a total of 10 draws.

5. Have students use the data in the tally chart to complete the line plot.

6. Have students use the data in the tally chart to complete the bar graph. The graph will have vertical bars showing how many yellow squares and blue squares were drawn.

7. **Say:** The the line plot and the bar graph show the same data. However, you must count the Xs to determine values on the line plot and use the scale to determine the value of each bar on the bar graph.

TRY IT Find the Outcome

Students will practice identifying the outcomes and the data of different probability experiments, such as tossing a coin, spinning a spinner, and rolling a number cube. Gather the coin. View or print the Find the Outcome activity page and read the directions with students.

Students should copy the problems from the Activity Book into their Math Notebook as necessary and solve them there.

Objectives

- Identify and systematically record the possible outcomes for a simple event.

- Summarize and display the results of a probability experiment in a clear and organized way.

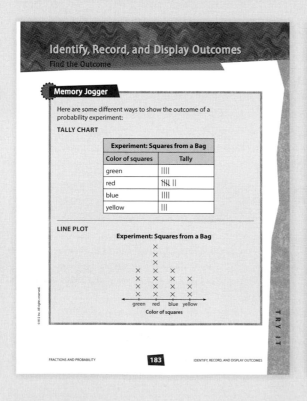

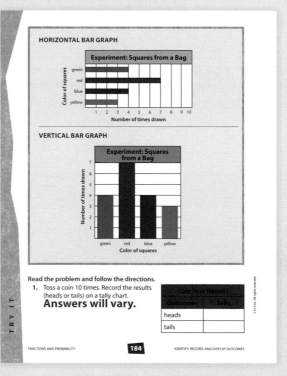

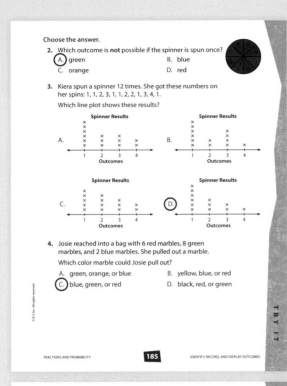

Choose the answer.

2. Which outcome is **not** possible if the spinner is spun once?
   (A.) green
   B. blue
   C. orange
   D. red

3. Kiera spun a spinner 12 times. She got these numbers on her spins: 1, 1, 2, 3, 1, 1, 2, 2, 1, 3, 4, 1.

   Which line plot shows these results?

A. Spinner Results

B. Spinner Results

C. Spinner Results

(D.) Spinner Results

4. Josie reached into a bag with 6 red marbles, 8 green marbles, and 2 blue marbles. She pulled out a marble.

   Which color marble could Josie pull out?

   A. green, orange, or blue
   B. yellow, blue, or red
   (C.) blue, green, or red
   D. black, red, or green

T R Y   I T

---

5. Niki spun a spinner 20 times and recorded the results on this tally chart.

   Which bar graph correctly shows these results?

Spinner Results	
Color	Tally
yellow	ⅢⅢ ⅢⅠ
orange	ⅢⅢ ⅡⅠ
green	ⅢⅠ

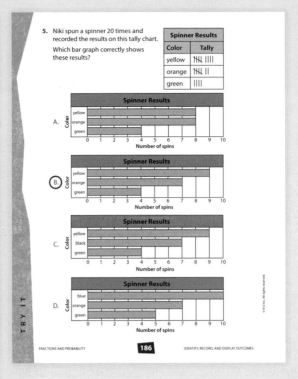

A. Spinner Results

(B.) Spinner Results

C. Spinner Results

D. Spinner Results

T R Y   I T

---

6. Which outcome is **not** possible if one ball is taken out of this jar?
   A. purple ball
   (B.) green ball
   C. brown ball
   D. white ball

7. Geoff rolled a number cube 15 times. He rolled these numbers: 3, 6, 4, 2, 3, 1, 5, 6, 6, 4, 2, 5, 3, 2, 4. Which tally chart shows these results?

(A.)
Number Cube Results	
Number	Tally
1	Ⅰ
2	ⅢⅠ
3	ⅢⅠ
4	ⅢⅠ
5	Ⅱ
6	ⅢⅠ

B.
Number Cube Results	
Number	Tally
1	Ⅰ
2	Ⅱ
3	ⅢⅠ
4	ⅢⅠ
5	ⅢⅠ
6	ⅢⅠ

C.
Number Cube Results	
Number	Tally
1	ⅢⅠ
2	ⅢⅠ
3	ⅢⅠ
4	ⅢⅠ
5	Ⅱ
6	ⅢⅠ

D.
Number Cube Results	
Number	Tally
1	Ⅰ
2	Ⅰ
3	ⅢⅠ
4	Ⅱ
5	Ⅱ
6	ⅢⅠ

T R Y   I T

ONLINE
10min

CHECKPOINT

Students will complete an online Checkpoint. If necessary, read the directions, problems, and answer choices to students and help them with keyboard or mouse operations.

Objectives

- Identify and systematically record the possible outcomes for a simple event.
- Summarize and display the results of a probability experiment in a clear and organized way.

Scaled Graphs (A)

Lesson Overview

GET READY Match Data Displays	5 minutes	**ONLINE**
LEARN Create Scaled Picture Graphs	20 minutes	**OFFLINE**
LEARN Interpret Scaled Picture Graphs	10 minutes	**ONLINE**

▶ Lesson Objectives
- Draw a scaled picture graph to represent a data set with several categories.
- Solve one- and two-step "how many more" and "how many fewer" problems using information presented in scaled picture graphs.

▶ Prerequisite Skills
Represent the same data set with more than one representation, such as a tally, picture graph, or bar graph.

▶ Content Background
Students will build on their previous knowledge of picture graphs to create and interpret scaled picture graphs with several categories. A scaled picture graph is one in which each symbol represents more than one object.

▶ Advance Preparation
Print three copies of the Scaled Picture Graph.

Materials to Gather

SUPPLIED
Scaled Picture Graph (printout)
Create Scaled Picture Graphs activity page

GET READY Match Data Displays

ONLINE
5min

Students will review representations such as bar graphs, tally charts, and picture graphs that show the same data set. As students progress through the activity, have them ask themselves questions such as the following:
- What are the categories?
- Which chart or graph shows the same numbers for each category as the chart or graph in the question?

Objectives
- Represent the same data set with more than one representation, such as a tally, picture graph, or bar graph.

LEARN Create Scaled Picture Graphs

OFFLINE
20min

Objectives

- Draw a scaled picture graph to represent a data set with several categories.

Students will build on their previous knowledge of picture graphs to create scaled picture graphs with several categories.

Gather the Scaled Picture Graph printouts and view or print the Create Scaled Picture Graphs activity page.

1. Read the Worked Example with students.

   Ask: What is the problem asking us to do? Complete the picture graph by drawing circles for the balloons.

   Ask: What is the key used for? The key says that every circle we draw is equal to 2 balloons.

   Ask: How many circles should we draw for the red balloons? There are 14 red balloons. Since $14 = 2 + 2 + 2 + 2 + 2 + 2 + 2$, we draw 7 circles.

   Ask: How many circles should we draw for the blue balloons? There are 8 red balloons. Since $8 = 2 + 2 + 2 + 2$, we draw 4 circles.

2. Have students complete Problems 1–3, referring to the Worked Example as needed. They should create their picture graphs using the Scaled Picture Graphs printouts. Be sure that students include a title, appropriate labels, and a key for each of their graphs.

Scaled Graphs (A)

Create Scaled Picture Graphs

Worked Examples

Picture graphs can be created using a scale, such as each symbol equals 2 balloons.

PROBLEM There are 14 red balloons and 8 blue balloons. Complete the picture graph by drawing circles to represent the correct number of balloons.

Number of Balloons	
red balloons	?
blue balloons	?
Key: Each symbol = 2 balloons.	

SOLUTION Each circle equals 2 balloons.

For the 14 red balloons, draw 7 circles, because $2 + 2 + 2 + 2 + 2 + 2 + 2 = 14$.

For the 8 blue balloons, draw 4 circles, because $2 + 2 + 2 + 2 = 8$.

ANSWER

Number of Balloons	
red balloons	○○○○○○○
blue balloons	○○○○
Key: Each symbol = 2 balloons.	

Complete the picture graph.

1. Beth is selling 20 green shirts, 15 blue shirts, and 30 white shirts. Use squares as symbols to represent shirts.

Number of Shirts	
green shirts	■ ■ ■ ■
blue shirts	■ ■ ■
white shirts	■ ■ ■ ■ ■ ■
Key: Each symbol = 5 shirts.	

2. Ms. Leung asked Arno, Lilly, Pat, and Sven how many pages they read. Arno read 8 pages, Lilly read 20 pages, Pat read 12 pages, and Sven read 16 pages. Use happy faces as symbols to represent pages read.

Number of Pages Read	
Arno	☺ ☺
Lilly	☺ ☺ ☺ ☺ ☺
Pat	☺ ☺ ☺
Sven	☺ ☺ ☺ ☺
Key: Each symbol = 4 pages.	

FRACTIONS AND PROBABILITY   188   SCALED GRAPHS (A)

FRACTIONS AND PROBABILITY   189   SCALED GRAPHS (A)

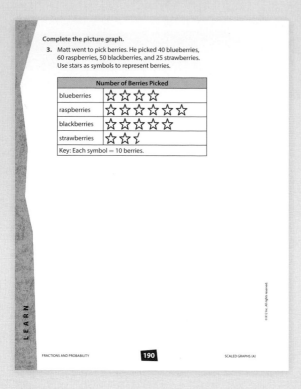

Complete the picture graph.

3. Matt went to pick berries. He picked 40 blueberries, 60 raspberries, 50 blackberries, and 25 strawberries. Use stars as symbols to represent berries.

Number of Berries Picked	
blueberries	☆ ☆ ☆ ☆
raspberries	☆ ☆ ☆ ☆ ☆ ☆
blackberries	☆ ☆ ☆ ☆ ☆
strawberries	☆ ☆ ⯪
Key: Each symbol = 10 berries.	

LEARN

LEARN Interpret Scaled Picture Graphs

ONLINE
10min

Objectives

Students will interpret and answer questions about picture graphs online.

- Solve one- and two-step "how many more" and "how many fewer" problems using information presented in scaled picture graphs.

Scaled Graphs (B)

Lesson Overview

GET READY Bar Graph Questions	10 minutes	**ONLINE**
LEARN Create Scaled Bar Graphs	20 minutes	**OFFLINE**
LEARN Interpret Scaled Bar Graphs	20 minutes	**OFFLINE**

▶ Lesson Objectives

- Draw a scaled bar graph to represent a data set with several categories.
- Solve one- and two-step "how many more" and "how many fewer" problems using information presented in scaled bar graphs.

▶ Prerequisite Skills

Ask and answer simple questions related to data representations.

▶ Content Background

Students will build on their previous knowledge of bar graphs to create and interpret scaled bar graphs with several categories. A scaled bar graph is one in which a scale greater than one unit for each line is used along the vertical axis.

▶ Advance Preparation

Print two copies of the Scaled Bar Graph.

Materials to Gather

SUPPLIED

Scaled Bar Graph (printout)

Create Scaled Bar Graphs activity page

Interpret Scaled Bar Graphs activity page

GET READY Bar Graph Questions

ONLINE 10 min

Students will answer questions about data in vertical and horizontal bar graphs. They will also create and answer their own questions about the data. Encourage students to ask a variety of questions; for example, have them ask one that asks about the quantities, one that asks about the most or the fewest, and one that compares two quantities.

Objectives

- Ask and answer simple questions related to data representations.

LEARN Create Scaled Bar Graphs

OFFLINE 20 min

Students will build on their previous knowledge of bar graphs to create scaled bar graphs with several categories.

Gather the Scaled Bar Graph printouts and view or print the Create Scaled Bar Graphs activity page.

1. Read the Worked Example with students.

    Ask: What is the problem asking us to do? Create a bar graph for the number of bicycles that were sold on each day.

    Ask: What does each horizontal line of the graph represent? The numbers go by 10s and there is a line between each number. Each line is 5 bicycles.

Objectives

- Draw a scaled bar graph to represent a data set with several categories.

Ask: How many lines up should each bar go? For Thursday, the bar should go up to 10, which is the second line. For Friday, the bar should go up to 25, which is the fifth line. For Saturday, the line should go up to 30, which is the sixth line. For Sunday, the bar should go up to 5, which is the first line.

2. Have students complete Problems 1 and 2, referring to the Worked Example as needed. They should create the bar graphs using the Scaled Bar Graphs printouts. Be sure that students include a title and appropriate labels for each of their graphs.

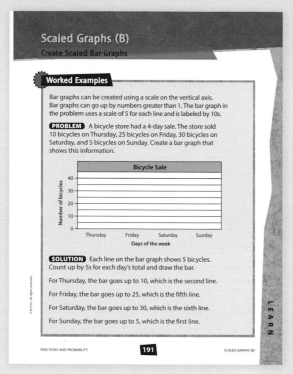

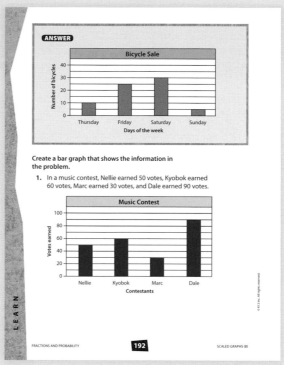

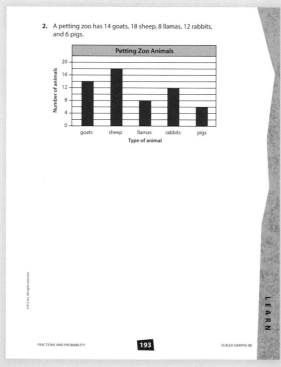

LEARN Interpret Scaled Bar Graphs

Students will build on their previous knowledge of bar graphs to interpret scaled bar graphs with several categories.

View or print the Interpret Scaled Bar Graphs activity page.

- Solve one- and two-step "how many more" and "how many fewer" problems using information presented in scaled bar graphs.

1. Read the Worked Example with students.

Ask: What is the problem asking us to do? Look at the bar graph and use it to answer the questions.

Ask: How much does each line represent? The numbers go up by 4s. There are lines halfway between, so each line represents 2 snacks.

Ask: How can you find out how many more apples than doughnuts were sold? First, look at the bar graph to find how many apples were sold and how many doughnuts were sold. Then, subtract to find the difference.

Ask: How can you find out how much Anthony made on the sale of cupcakes and apples? Find out how many cupcakes he sold and multiply by 2, or double that number, to find the amount he made. Then add that amount to the amount he made selling apples at $1 each.

2. Have students complete Problems 1 and 2, referring to the Worked Example as needed. Students should copy the problems into their Math Notebook as necessary and solve them there.

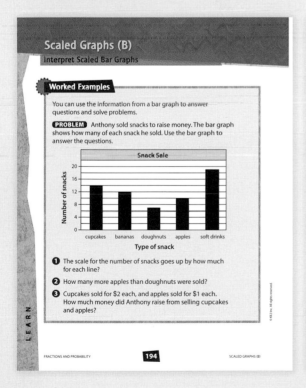

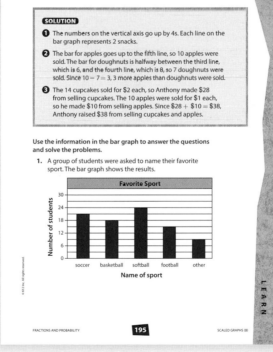

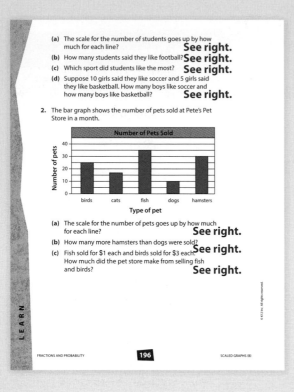

(a) The scale for the number of students goes up by how much for each line? **See right.**

(b) How many students said they like football? **See right.**

(c) Which sport did students like the most? **See right.**

(d) Suppose 10 girls said they like soccer and 5 girls said they like basketball. How many boys like soccer and how many boys like basketball? **See right.**

2. The bar graph shows the number of pets sold at Pete's Pet Store in a month.

Number of Pets Sold

(a) The scale for the number of pets goes up by how much for each line? **See right.**

(b) How many more hamsters than dogs were sold? **See right.**

(c) Fish sold for $1 each and birds sold for $3 each. How much did the pet store make from selling fish and birds? **See right.**

Answers

1. **(a)** The numbers on the vertical axis go up by 6. Each line represents 3 students.

    (b) Fifteen students like football.

    (c) Softball is the favorite sport.

    (d) The total for soccer is 21, and $21 - 10 = 11$. Eleven boys like soccer. The total for basketball is 18, and $18 - 5 = 13$. Thirteen boys like basketball.

2. **(a)** The numbers on the vertical axis go up by 10. Each line represents 5 pets.

    (b) Thirty hamsters were sold. Ten dogs were sold. $30 - 10 = 20$; Twenty more hamsters than dogs were sold.

    (c) The 35 fish sold for $1 each, or $35, and the 25 birds were sold for $3 each, or $75. $35 + $75 = $110; The store made $110 from selling fish and birds.

Use Data to Make Predictions

Lesson Overview

GET READY Compare Tally Charts and Bar Graphs	5 minutes	**ONLINE**
LEARN Squares from a Bag	20 minutes	**OFFLINE**
LEARN What Will Happen Next?	10 minutes	**OFFLINE**
TRY IT Make a Prediction	15 minutes	**OFFLINE**
CHECKPOINT	10 minutes	**ONLINE**

▶ Lesson Objectives

Use the results of a probability experiment to predict future events.

▶ Prerequisite Skills

Summarize and display the results of a probability experiment in a clear and organized way.

▶ Content Background

Students will learn to use the results of a probability experiment to predict future events. For example, they can look at the results of drawing a colored square from a bag to predict the chance of certain colored squares being pulled from the bag in the future.

Although students will not do formal probability at this level, it is important that they understand that the likelihood of something happening or not happening can be described as impossible, unlikely, likely, or certain. When they determine actual probability values, they will discover that probabilities that are not impossible or certain are expressed as fractions between 0 and 1, sometimes as decimals and as percents.

The probability of an event occurring is not the same as the odds that an event will occur. The terms *probability* and *odds* should not be used interchangeably. If the probability of an event is $\frac{3}{5}$, the odds are 3 to 2.

In this lesson, students will record the results of probability experiments in tally charts, line plots, and bar graphs. Avoid using the term *bar chart* with students. The term *bar graph* is the correct term.

▶ Advance Preparation

Place the 10 blue and 2 red squares in a paper bag. Do not let students see how many of each color are in the bag.

Materials to Gather

SUPPLIED
blocks – E (10 blue, 2 red)
What Will Happen Next? activity page
Make a Prediction activity page

ALSO NEEDED
household objects – paper bag

Draw two copies of this chart in students' Math Notebook:

Experiment: Squares from a Bag	
Color of squares	Tally

GET READY Compare Tally Charts and Bar Graphs

Students will look at data in a tally chart and choose the bar graph that displays the tally chart data correctly.

Objectives

- Summarize and display the results of a probability experiment in a clear and organized way.

LEARN Squares from a Bag

Students will do a probability experiment by selecting colored squares out of a bag. They will use the results to predict what would happen if they continued the experiment.

Gather the prepared bag of squares. Students will write tally marks on the chart you drew in their Math Notebook.

Objectives

- Use the results of a probability experiment to predict future events.

1. Discuss how past experiences are often used to predict future events. For example, if a family lives in a place where summer days are usually hot, they can be pretty sure it will not snow in the summer. If a girl wants to run into a friend at the park, she might go at the most popular times. She wouldn't expect to run into her friend if she went to the park at 6:00 in the morning. It's possible, but not likely.

2. **Say:** A dog had several litters of puppies in the past. There were three or four puppies in each litter. How many puppies would you expect the dog to have in the next litter? three or four puppies

   Ask students to explain how they made this prediction. Students might say that they know that each of the previous litters had three or four puppies and they used what they know about the past to predict what might happen in the future.

3. Show students the bag.

   Say: There are at least two colors of squares in this bag. Let's do an experiment where you draw squares from the bag 20 times and record the outcomes. Then you'll use that information to predict what will happen if you repeat the experiment. After that, you'll repeat the experiment and compare those results to your prediction.

4. Have students draw a square from the bag, record the color, and place a tally mark on the tally chart. Have them return the square to the bag. Have them repeat this 19 times for a total of 20 tally marks.

5. At the end of the experiment, ask students to discuss and explain the results. They may find that they drew a blue square more often than a red one.

6. Have students predict the results if they drew squares from the bag 20 more times. Most likely, students will predict that they would continue to draw a greater number of blue squares.

7. Repeat the experiment. Have students choose a square from the bag 20 times and record the outcomes in the second tally chart. At the end of the experiment, have students review the data and explain if their prediction was correct.

8. Show students the squares from the bag. Ask them to compare the number of blue squares and the number of red squares. Talk about how the number of blue and red squares affected the results of the experiment. Also, discuss how the information that there are 15 blue squares and 2 red squares helps confirm their predictions.

LEARN What Will Happen Next?

10 min OFFLINE

Objectives

- Use the results of a probability experiment to predict future events.

Students will use results from probability experiments, displayed in tally charts, line plots, and bar graphs, to make predictions about future events. View or print the What Will Happen Next? activity page and read the directions with students. Students should copy the problems from the Activity Book into their Math Notebook as necessary and solve them there.

1. Read the Worked Example with students. Have them look at the spinner. Point out that the section labeled yo-yos takes up half the space on the spinner; it's much larger than the other three sections. Have students summarize the problem in their own words.

2. Guide students through Problems 1–3. For each problem, discuss the results of the experiment. Have students use the results shown in the charts and graphs to make predictions about future events. Use the following questions to guide students:

   - Which outcome occurred the most?

   - Which outcome occurred the least?

   - If this experiment were repeated, which outcome would be most likely and least likely to occur?

Worked Examples

You can use data to make predictions for future events.

PROBLEM At a carnival, a giant wheel is spun to see which prize you win. The bar graph shows the prizes given out each day for 4 days. Use the data to predict which prize will be given out the most times on the fifth day.

SOLUTION Far more yo-yos were given out than any other prize. And the yo-yo section of the spinner is much larger than any other section. So yo-yos will probably be given out the most times on the fifth day.

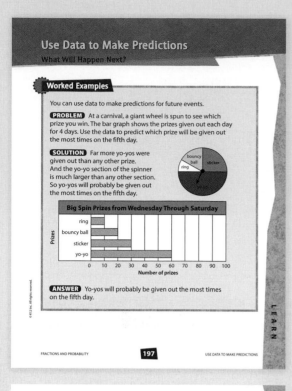

ANSWER Yo-yos will probably be given out the most times on the fifth day.

Use the data to predict future events.

1. Eddie tosses a number cube with the numbers 1, 2, and 3 on it. The line plot shows the results of his tosses. If he tosses the cube 30 more times, predict which number is likely to show the most times. **3**

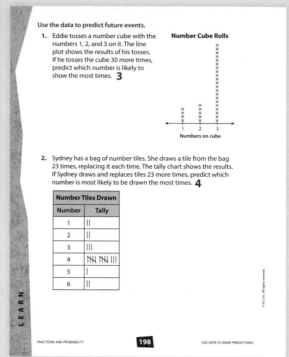

2. Sydney has a bag of number tiles. She draws a tile from the bag 23 times, replacing it each time. The tally chart shows the results. If Sydney draws and replaces tiles 23 more times, predict which number is most likely to be drawn the most times. **4**

Number Tiles Drawn	
Number	Tally
1	II
2	II
3	III
4	ꟷꟷꟷ ꟷꟷꟷ III
5	I
6	II

---

3. Brady spins the spinner 36 times. He records the outcomes in the line plot. Predict the color that would most likely be spun the most if Brady spins the spinner 36 more times.

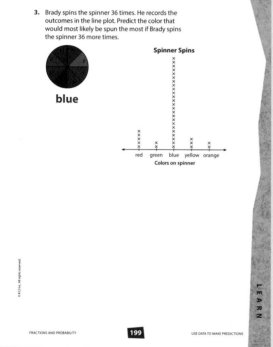

blue

TRY IT Make a Prediction

Students will practice using data from probability experiments to predict what is most likely or least likely to happen in future events. View or print the Make a Prediction activity page and read the directions with students.

Students should copy the problems from the Activity Book into their Math Notebook as necessary and solve them there.

- Use the results of a probability experiment to predict future events.

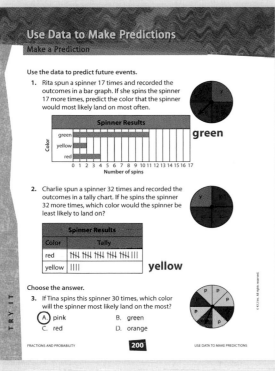

Use Data to Make Predictions
Make a Prediction

Use the data to predict future events.

1. Rita spun a spinner 17 times and recorded the outcomes in a bar graph. If she spins the spinner 17 more times, predict the color that the spinner would most likely land on most often.

Spinner Results

green

2. Charlie spun a spinner 32 times and recorded the outcomes in a tally chart. If he spins the spinner 32 more times, which color would the spinner be least likely to land on?

Spinner Results	
Color	Tally
red	卌 卌 卌 卌 卌 卌 III
yellow	IIII

yellow

Choose the answer.

3. If Tina spins this spinner 30 times, which color will the spinner most likely land on the most?
   A. pink   B. green
   C. red   D. orange

FRACTIONS AND PROBABILITY   **200**   USE DATA TO MAKE PREDICTIONS

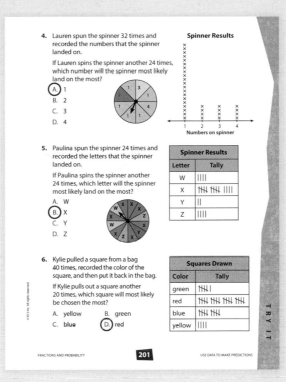

4. Lauren spun the spinner 32 times and recorded the numbers that the spinner landed on.
   If Lauren spins the spinner another 24 times, which number will the spinner most likely land on the most?
   A. 1
   B. 2
   C. 3
   D. 4

Spinner Results

5. Paulina spun the spinner 24 times and recorded the letters that the spinner landed on.
   If Paulina spins the spinner another 24 times, which letter will the spinner most likely land on the most?
   A. W
   B. X
   C. Y
   D. Z

Spinner Results	
Letter	Tally
W	IIII
X	卌 卌 IIII
Y	II
Z	IIII

6. Kylie pulled a square from a bag 40 times, recorded the color of the square, and then put it back in the bag.
   If Kylie pulls out a square another 20 times, which square will most likely be chosen the most?
   A. yellow   B. green
   C. blue   D. red

Squares Drawn	
Color	Tally
green	卌 I
red	卌 卌 卌 卌
blue	卌 卌
yellow	IIII

FRACTIONS AND PROBABILITY   **201**   USE DATA TO MAKE PREDICTIONS

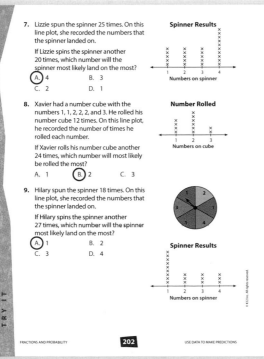

7. Lizzie spun the spinner 25 times. On this line plot, she recorded the numbers that the spinner landed on.
   If Lizzie spins the spinner another 20 times, which number will the spinner most likely land on the most?
   A. 4   B. 3
   C. 2   D. 1

Spinner Results

8. Xavier had a number cube with the numbers 1, 1, 2, 2, 2, and 3. He rolled his number cube 12 times. On this line plot, he recorded the number of times he rolled each number.
   If Xavier rolls his number cube another 24 times, which number will most likely be rolled the most?
   A. 1   B. 2   C. 3

Number Rolled

9. Hilary spun the spinner 18 times. On this line plot, she recorded the numbers that the spinner landed on.
   If Hilary spins the spinner another 27 times, which number will the spinner most likely land on the most?
   A. 1   B. 2
   C. 3   D. 4

Spinner Results

FRACTIONS AND PROBABILITY   **202**   USE DATA TO MAKE PREDICTIONS

ONLINE
10min

Students will complete an online Checkpoint. If necessary, read the directions, problems, and answer choices to students and help them with keyboard or mouse operations.

- Use the results of a probability experiment to predict future events.

Core Focus
More About Fractions

Lesson Overview

GET READY Frog-Hopping Fractions	5 minutes	**ONLINE**
LEARN Whole Numbers as Fractions	10 minutes	**OFFLINE**
LEARN Fractions Equal to One	10 minutes	**OFFLINE**
LEARN Mixed Numbers	15 minutes	**ONLINE**
TRY IT Fractions and Mixed Numbers	10 minutes	**OFFLINE**
CHECKPOINT	10 minutes	**ONLINE**

▶ Lesson Objectives

- Explain why $a = \frac{a}{1}$.
- Explain why $\frac{a}{a} = 1$.
- Demonstrate how fractions and whole numbers can be plotted on a number line.

Materials to Gather

SUPPLIED

Centimeter Grid Paper (printout)

Whole Numbers as Fractions
  activity page

Fraction and Mixed Numbers
  activity page

▶ Prerequisite Skills

Explain why two given fractions are equivalent.

▶ Content Background

Students will learn to represent a fraction as a part of a whole and explain why a whole, or 1, can be expressed as a fraction with a numerator and denominator that are equal positive integers, such as $\frac{4}{4}$, $\frac{6}{6}$, or $\frac{8}{8}$. Students will also learn that any whole number can be written as a fraction with a denominator of 1 by graphing the numbers on the number line.

Students will review the fact that a mixed number is a number with a whole-number part and a fractional part. The numbers $1\frac{2}{3}$, $5\frac{2}{6}$, or $3\frac{5}{8}$ are all mixed numbers. Students will learn how to locate mixed numbers on the number line.

▶ Advance Preparation

Print the Centimeter Grid Paper. On the grid paper, sketch five rectangles. Draw vertical lines to divide four of the rectangles into equal sections as follows: one rectangle with 2 equal sections, one rectangle with 4 equal sections, one rectangle with 6 equal sections, and one rectangle with 8 equal sections. Do not divide the fifth rectangle.

GET READY Frog-Hopping Fractions

ONLINE 5 min

Objectives

- Explain why two given fractions are equivalent.

Students will practice naming fractions on a number line. They will see that equivalent fractions represent the same location on a number line.

LEARN Whole Numbers as Fractions

OFFLINE 10 min

Objectives

- Explain why $a = \frac{a}{1}$.

Students will use a number line diagram to explain why any whole number can be written as a fraction with a denominator of 1; for example $3 = \frac{3}{1}, 15 = \frac{15}{1}$.

View or print the Whole Numbers as Fractions activity page and read the directions with students.

Students should copy the problems from the Activity Book into their Math Notebook as necessary and solve them there.

1. Read and review the Worked Example with students. Remind students that the whole numbers are 0 and the counting numbers: 1, 2, 3, 4, 5, and so on.

2. Direct students to the top number line. Have them count the number of whole units along the number line diagram. 4

   Point out that each segment is 1 whole because it is not divided into smaller parts such as halves, thirds, or fourths.

3. Discuss with students how the number line represents 4 wholes, so each number along the number line can be written as a fraction with a denominator of 1.

   Ask: What does the denominator represent? how many equal parts the whole is divided into What does the numerator represent? the number of equal parts

4. Have students identify each whole number on the number line as a fraction: $\frac{1}{1}, \frac{2}{1}, \frac{3}{1}, \frac{4}{1}$.

5. Show students the rectangle model. Point out that the shapes are all wholes—they are not divided into parts—so the denominator is 1. There are 4 wholes, so the numerator is 4.

6. Have students complete Problems 1 and 2, referring to the Worked Example as necessary. Emphasize that any whole number can be written as a fraction with a denominator of 1.

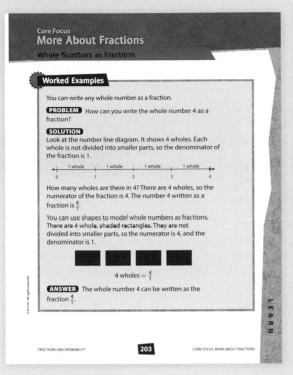

Additional Answers

1. (a)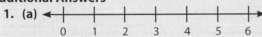

   (b) **Possible answer:** I can write each whole number as a fraction with a denominator of 1. $\frac{1}{1}, \frac{2}{1}, \frac{3}{1}, \frac{4}{1}, \frac{5}{1}, \frac{6}{1}$

OFFLINE

10 min

LEARN Fractions Equal to One

Objectives

- Explain why $\frac{a}{a} = 1$.

Gather the rectangles you sketched on the Centimeter Grid Paper.

1. Have students refer to the rectangle that you drew that shows fourths. Have them shade in one part of the rectangle and tell you what fraction the rectangle represents. $\frac{1}{4}$ Then have them shade the rest of the sections, one by one, and tell you what fraction each model represents. $\frac{2}{4}, \frac{3}{4}, \frac{4}{4}$

2. Explain to students that when all 4 of the sections are shaded, the whole figure is shaded, so $\frac{4}{4} = 1$.

3. Repeat Steps 1 and 2 for the rectangles that show halves and sixths. Point out that $\frac{2}{2} = 1$ and $\frac{6}{6} = 1$.

4. Help students understand that whenever the numerator of a fraction (the parts shaded) equals the denominator of the fraction (the total number of parts), the fraction equals 1.

5. Have students shade the other rectangle to show 1 and write the corresponding fraction. $\frac{8}{8}$

6. Have students draw another shape that shows 1, such as a rectangle divided into thirds with all thirds shaded. Have them tell you what fraction the model represents. $\frac{3}{3}$

7. Have student sketch a number line to show fourths. Have them label the fourths from 0 to 1. Pont out that $\frac{4}{4}$ is located at the same point on the number line as 1, so the number line also shows that $\frac{4}{4} = 1$.

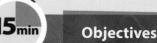
ONLINE
15min

LEARN Mixed Numbers

Objectives

Students will learn to locate mixed numbers on a number line. They will learn to first find the whole-number part of the mixed number. Then they will count on by the fractional part to locate the mixed number on the number line.

- Demonstrate how fractions and mixed numbers can be plotted on a number line.

OFFLINE
10min

TRY IT Fractions and Mixed Numbers

Objectives

Students will practice identifying and locating mixed numbers on the number line. They will demonstrate an understanding that whenever the numerator of a fraction equals the denominator of the fraction, the fraction equals 1. They will also demonstrate an understanding that whole numbers can be written as fractions with 1 as the denominator. View or print the Fractions and Mixed Numbers activity page and read the directions with students.

Students should copy the problems from the Activity Book into their Math Notebook as necessary and solve them there.

- Explain why $\frac{a}{a} = 1$.
- Explain why $a = \frac{a}{1}$.
- Demonstrate how fractions and mixed numbers can be plotted on a number line.

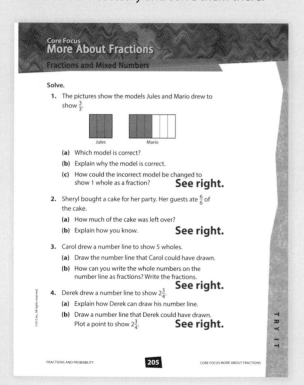

Answers

1. (a) The model Jules drew is correct.

    (b) Possible explanation: The fraction $\frac{3}{3}$ is the same as 1 whole. The model is divided into 3 equal parts and all 3 of the parts are shaded, so the whole model is shaded.

    (c) If Mario shaded all of his model, it would show $\frac{6}{6} = 1$ whole.

2. (a) None of the cake was leftover.

    (b) Possible explanation: The fraction $\frac{6}{6}$ is the same as 1 whole. Since $\frac{6}{6}$ of the cake was eaten, all of the cake was eaten and none was leftover.

3. (a)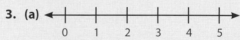

    (b) Posible answer: I can write each whole number as a fraction with a denominator of 1. $\frac{1}{1}, \frac{2}{1}, \frac{3}{1}, \frac{4}{1}, \frac{5}{1}$

4. (a) Possible explanation: Derek can draw a number line that shows 0 to 3 divided into fourths.

    (b) Check students' number lines. The number lines should show 0 to 3 divided into fourths with a point at the $2\frac{3}{4}$ tick mark.

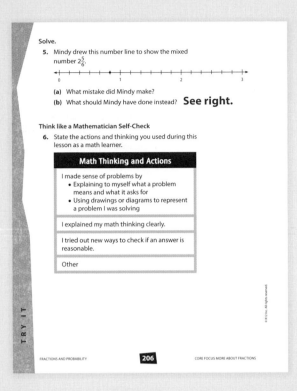

Answers

5. (a) Possible answer: Mindy did not count the whole-number part of the mixed number.

(b) Mindy should have counted $\frac{5}{6}$ from 2 to find where to draw the point for $2\frac{5}{6}$.

ONLINE

10 min

CHECKPOINT

Students will complete an online Checkpoint. If necessary, read the directions, problems, and answer choices to students and help them with keyboard or mouse operations.

Objectives

- Explain why $\frac{a}{a} = 1$.
- Explain why $a = \frac{a}{1}$.
- Demonstrate how fractions and mixed numbers can be plotted on a number line.

Unit Review

Lesson Overview		
UNIT REVIEW Look Back	10 minutes	**ONLINE**
UNIT REVIEW Checkpoint Practice	50 minutes	**ONLINE**
⤵ **UNIT REVIEW** Prepare for the Checkpoint		

▶ Unit Objectives

- Explain that a fraction can be used to represent the relationship of a part to a whole and a rational number on the number line.
- Write the fraction represented by a drawing that shows parts of a whole or a rational number on the number line.
- Use a sketch to represent a fraction.
- Recognize and determine equivalent fractions.
- Explain why two given fractions are equivalent.
- Compare and order unit fractions, such as $\frac{1}{4}$, and fractions with like denominators, such as $\frac{2}{6}$ and $\frac{4}{6}$, by using objects or sketches.
- Compare and order fractions with like numerators by using objects or sketches.
- Recognize that the comparison of two fractions is only valid if the wholes are identical.
- Identify whether specific events are certain, likely, unlikely, or impossible.
- Identify and systematically record the possible outcomes for a simple event.
- Summarize and display the results of a probability experiment in a clear and organized way.
- Draw a scaled picture graph or bar graph to represent a data set with several categories.
- Solve one- and two-step "how many more" and "how many fewer" problems using information presented in scaled picture graphs or bar graphs.
- Use the results of a probability experiment to predict future events.
- Explain why $a = \frac{a}{1}$.
- Explain why $\frac{a}{a} = 1$.
- Demonstrate how fractions and whole numbers can be plotted on a number line.

Materials to Gather

There are no materials to gather for this lesson.

▶ Advance Preparation

In this lesson, students will have an opportunity to review previous activities in the Fractions and Probability unit. Look at the suggested activities in Unit Review: Prepare for the Checkpoint online and gather any needed materials.

ONLINE
10min

Objectives

- Review unit objectives.

Students will review key concepts from the unit to prepare for the Unit Checkpoint.

ONLINE
50min

Objectives

- Review unit objectives.

Students will complete an online Checkpoint Practice to prepare for the Unit Checkpoint. If necessary, read the directions, problems, and answer choices to students. Have students answer the problems on their own. Review any missed problems with students.

➔ UNIT REVIEW Prepare for the Checkpoint

What you do next depends on how students performed in the previous activity, Unit Review: Checkpoint Practice. If students had difficulty with any of the problems, complete the appropriate review activity listed in the table online.

Unit Checkpoint

▶ Unit Objectives

- Explain that a fraction can be used to represent the relationship of a part to a whole and a rational number on the number line.
- Write the fraction represented by a drawing that shows parts of a whole or a rational number on the number line.
- Use a sketch to represent a fraction.
- Recognize and determine equivalent fractions.
- Explain why two given fractions are equivalent.
- Compare and order unit fractions, such as $\frac{1}{4}$, and fractions with like denominators, such as $\frac{2}{6}$ and $\frac{4}{6}$, by using objects or sketches.
- Compare and order fractions with like numerators by using objects or sketches.
- Recognize that the comparison of two fractions is only valid if the wholes are identical.
- Identify whether specific events are certain, likely, unlikely, or impossible.
- Identify and systematically record the possible outcomes for a simple event.
- Summarize and display the results of a probability experiment in a clear and organized way.
- Draw a scaled picture graph or bar graph to represent a data set with several categories.
- Solve one- and two-step "how many more" and "how many fewer" problems using information presented in scaled picture graphs or bar graphs.
- Use the results of a probability experiment to predict future events.
- Explain why $a = \frac{a}{1}$.
- Explain why $\frac{a}{a} = 1$.
- Demonstrate how fractions and whole numbers can be plotted on a number line.

Materials to Gather

There are no materials to gather for this lesson.

UNIT CHECKPOINT Online

ONLINE 60min

Students will complete the Unit Checkpoint online. If necessary, read the directions, problems, and answer choices to students and help them with keyboard or mouse operations.

Objectives

- Assess unit objectives.

Extended Problems: Real-World Application

USE WHAT YOU KNOW Offline | 60 minutes | **OFFLINE**

▶ Lesson Objectives

- Explain that a fraction can be used to represent the relationship of a part to a whole and a rational number on the number line.
- Write the fraction represented by a drawing that shows parts of a whole or a rational number on the number line.
- Use a sketch to represent a fraction.
- Recognize and determine equivalent fractions.
- Solve one- and two-step "how many more" and "how many fewer" problems using information presented in scaled bar graphs.
- Recognize and describe a linear pattern, such as counting by 5s or multiplying 5 times a number to reach 100, by its rule.
- Extend a linear pattern, such as stating what number comes next in a series.
- Identify, describe, and classify a polygon according to the number of its sides.
- Partition shapes into parts with equal areas. Express the area of each part as a unit fraction of the whole.
- Solve two-step word problems, limited to whole numbers.
- Apply mathematical knowledge and skills to evaluate and analyze real-world situations.

Materials to Gather

SUPPLIED

Extended Problems: Real-World Application (printout)

USE WHAT YOU KNOW Offline

OFFLINE 60min

Open the Extended Problems: Real-World Application. Read the directions, problems, and answer choices to students, if necessary.
The teacher will grade this assignment.

- Students should save the graded assignment to their computer. In the filename, they should replace "studentname" with their last name followed by their first initial.
- Students should complete the assignment on their own.
- Students should submit the completed assignment according to the teacher's instructions.

Objectives

- Apply mathematical knowledge and skills to evaluate and analyze real-world situations.

Measurement:
Length and Time

▶ Unit Objectives

- Identify the appropriate tools for measuring the length of an object.
- Identify the appropriate metric or English units for measuring the length of an object.
- Estimate and measure the length of an object to the nearest centimeter.
- Estimate the length of an object to the nearest $\frac{1}{2}$ inch and measure the length to the nearest $\frac{1}{4}$ inch.
- Interpret and display data on a line plot.
- Collect measurement data and display the data in a line plot.
- Tell time to the nearest minute.
- Determine elapsed time to the nearest minute.
- Solve word problems involving addition and subtraction of time intervals in minutes.
- Represent problems involving time intervals in minutes on a number-line diagram.

▶ Big Ideas

Measurement is the process of repeatedly using a unit over a quantity to determine how much you have.

▶ Unit Introduction

In this unit, students will explore measurement of length and time. They will start by identifying tools for measuring the length of an object. They will use metric units to estimate measurements and precisely measure to the nearest centimeter. They will use English units to estimate measurements to the nearest half inch and precisely measure to the nearest quarter inch. Students will learn to tell time to the nearest minute and find elapsed time between a starting time and an ending time.

▶ Keywords

centimeter (cm)
elapsed time
English system of
    measurement
foot (ft)
inch (in.)

kilometer (km)
measurement
meter (m)
metric system of
    measurement

mile (mi)
standard unit
yard (yd)

Tools and Units for Measuring Length

Lesson Overview

GET READY Measure Height in Feet and Inches	5 minutes	**OFFLINE**
LEARN Different Measurement Tools	5 minutes	**OFFLINE**
LEARN English and Metric Units of Length	15 minutes	**OFFLINE**
LEARN Appropriate Tools and Units	15 minutes	**ONLINE**
TRY IT Choose the Tool and Unit	10 minutes	**ONLINE**
CHECKPOINT	10 minutes	**ONLINE**

► Lesson Objectives

- Identify the appropriate tools for measuring the length of an object.
- Identify the appropriate metric or English units for measuring the length of an object.

► Prerequisite Skills

Measure the length of objects by repeating a standard unit.

► Content Background

Students will learn to identify tools for measuring the length of objects. They will learn the appropriate unit of measure in the metric system of measurement (centimeters, meters, and kilometers) and the English system of measurement (inches, feet, yards, and miles).

Students experience measurement every day. Their clothing and shoes are a particular size. They travel distances by foot, by car, by bus, or on their bicycles. They carry things that are heavy. They tell time and identify what day it is. They know if the weather is hot or cold. All of these experiences require some knowledge of measurement.

In this lesson, the term *length* is used interchangeably to mean length, width, height, or depth. Note that when measurements are abbreviated (cm, m, km, in., ft, yd, and mi), only the abbreviation for *inch* has a period. The period is added to avoid confusion with the word *in*.

Materials to Gather

SUPPLIED

There are no supplied materials to gather for this lesson.

ALSO NEEDED

ruler, dual-scale

tape, masking

▶ Common Errors and Misconceptions

Students often have difficulty giving the correct measure of an object when the object is not aligned with the 0-end of a ruler. For example, they might think that this pencil is 4 inches long because the right end of the pencil aligns with the 4-inch mark. The pencil is actually only 3 inches long because the left end of the pencil aligns with the 1-inch mark.

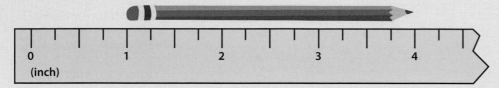

GET READY Measure Height in Feet and Inches OFFLINE 5min

Objectives

Students will use a ruler to measure their height in feet and inches. Gather the ruler and tape.

1. Show students a 12-inch ruler and point to the inch marks on the ruler.

   Ask: What is the name of each unit on this ruler? inch

2. Point out that the ruler is 12 inches long, and the length of the entire ruler is 1 foot.

3. Have students stand with their back against a wall. Place the ruler flat on the top of their head. One end of the ruler should be touching the wall. Place a small piece of masking tape on the wall so that the top edge of the tape is just under the ruler.

4. Guide students to use the ruler to measure their height in feet and inches. Students should place the 0-end of the ruler on the floor and work their way up the wall by repeatedly using the foot unit. Show students how to use a finger to mark the ending point of the first foot. Then have them slide the ruler so the 0-end aligns with their finger as they measure the next foot.

5. Record the number of whole feet. Explain how to add the extra inches that don't make up a whole foot. Help students find their height to the nearest half inch. If students are unfamiliar with reading the half-inch marks on a ruler, explain that a ruler is like a number line; the halfway mark between each inch marks the half-inch point. Have them record their height in feet and inches.

6. Have students record their height in feet and inches in the front of their Math Notebook. Encourage them to use abbreviations, such as 3 ft 10 in. Point out the period in the abbreviation for inches. Add a note that at the end of the year, students can measure their height again and compare the measurements.

* Measure the length of objects by repeating a standard unit.

Tips

If students have difficulty marking the end of each foot with a finger, use masking tape to mark each foot.

LEARN Different Measurement Tools

Objectives

- Identify the appropriate tools for measuring the length of an object.

Students will identify different kinds of measurement tools, such as a clock for measuring time and a thermometer for measuring temperature. They will also locate measuring tools in their environment.

There are no materials to gather for this activity.

1. Tell students that they use measurement all the time. Explain that they make informal measurements when they make statements like these:

   - That's a long way to walk.
   - That's so small (or large).
   - That's really heavy.
   - It's very hot (or cold) outside.
   - It's too early.

2. Discuss with students what they are measuring in each of the statements in Step 1. Explain that they are indicating a way to measure distance, size, weight, temperature, and time.

3. Explain that measuring tools are needed to make accurate measurements. Ask students what tool they use for measuring each of the following:

   - time clock or watch
   - an object's weight scale
   - how hot it is outside thermometer
   - a person's height or the length of a board ruler, tape measure, yardstick, or meterstick
   - how far away something is map or odometer in a car

   Students may be familiar with a car odometer, but they probably don't know what it's called. You may wish to show students a picture of an odometer.

4. Explain to students that they need the correct tool to measure accurately.

   Say: You cannot measure temperature with a clock or the distance to New York with a thermometer.

5. Have students look around their environment and locate as many measuring tools as they can find. For example, help them locate clocks, measuring cups and spoons, rulers, tape measures, thermometers, and scales.

Tips

Allow students to look at books, magazines, or the Internet for examples of measuring tools.

Car odometers measure miles.

LEARN English and Metric Units of Length

Objectives

- Identify the appropriate tools for measuring the length of an object.
- Identify the appropriate metric or English units for measuring the length of an object.

Students will learn about the English and metric units for measuring length, including the inch, foot, yard, mile, centimeter, meter, and kilometer.

Gather the ruler.

1. Discuss with students that if they need to find the length of an object, they must use a measurement tool. Explain that the terms *length* and *width* are used interchangeably at times. For instance, if you have a long table, you might measure the length, but when you want to see if it will fit in a certain place, you might ask "How wide is it?" and refer to the same measure.

   Have students look at some common objects nearby and identify the length and width to see that in some instances, they have to decide which is which.

2. **Say:** It's important to know the unit you will use to measure the length of an object. Look at the ruler. Notice that one side of the ruler is divided into inches and the other side is divided into centimeters.

3. Explain that the units of length or distance in the English system of measurement are inches, feet, yards, and miles. Have students identify inches on the ruler. Explain that miles measure long distances.

4. Explain that some of the units of length or distance in the metric system of measurement are centimeters, meters, and kilometers. Have students identify centimeters on the ruler. Explain that kilometers measure long distances.

5. Tell students that they have to use a unit, such as an inch or a centimeter, to measure the length of an object.

6. Point to the side of the ruler labeled in inches.

   Ask: What units are on this side of the ruler? inches

7. Guide students to see that the ruler is 12 inches long, which is the same as 1 foot. Have students find one object in the room that is about 1 inch in length and one object that is about 1 foot in length or height.

8. Explain that there is another unit of length in the English system of measurement called a *yard*. If there is a measuring tape or yardstick available, show students 1 yard. Otherwise, measure 3 feet along a table edge, or other piece of furniture, to give students a sense of 1 yard.

9. Explain that, for many people, a yard is about the distance from their nose to the tip of their fingers when they are facing forward with an arm outstretched to the side. Demonstrate this distance for students.

10. Point to the metric side of the ruler labeled in centimeters.

    Ask: What units are on this side of the ruler? centimeters

11. Explain that centimeters are units of the metric system used to measure shorter lengths. Tell students that 100 centimeters equals 1 meter. Explain that 1 meter is about 3 inches longer than 1 yard, so meters and yards are used to measure the same types of objects. Have students find one object in the room that is about 1 centimeter in length and one object that is about 1 meter in length or height.

12. Tell students that the metric system also has a unit called a *decimeter*. A decimeter is the length of 10 centimeters. It is the unit between a centimeter and a meter. Explain that decimeters are not used as frequently as the English system's foot. Instead in the metric system, lengths are usually measured in centimeters or meters.

13. **Say:** We could use *yards* or *meters* to describe the distance we travel in a car or on a train or airplane. But we'd need so many yards or meters that the number would be huge. Instead, we use greater units of measure to describe longer distances. In the English system, we use miles. In the metric system, we use kilometers.

    Go over some familiar distances with students. Discuss about how far it is to the library or to a relative's home, or to other places students commonly visit.

LEARN Appropriate Tools and Units

ONLINE 15min

Students will identify the most appropriate tool and unit of measure for measuring the length of different types of objects, such as the length of a straw or the width of a room.

Objectives

- Identify the appropriate tools for measuring the length of an object.
- Identify the appropriate metric or English units for measuring the length of an object.

TRY IT Choose the Tool and Unit

ONLINE 10min

Students will complete an online Try It. If necessary, read the directions, problems, and answer choices to students and help them with keyboard or mouse operations.

Objectives

- Identify the appropriate tools for measuring the length of an object.
- Identify the appropriate metric or English units for measuring the length of an object.

CHECKPOINT

ONLINE 10min

Students will complete an online Checkpoint. If necessary, read the directions, problems, and answer choices to students and help them with keyboard or mouse operations.

Objectives

- Identify the appropriate tools for measuring the length of an object.
- Identify the appropriate metric or English units for measuring the length of an object.

Estimate and Measure Centimeters

Lesson Overview

GET READY Hand Measurements	10 minutes	OFFLINE
LEARN Round to the Nearest Centimeter	15 minutes	OFFLINE
LEARN Estimate and Measure	15 minutes	OFFLINE
TRY IT Centimeter Measures	10 minutes	OFFLINE
CHECKPOINT	10 minutes	ONLINE

▶ Lesson Objectives

Estimate and measure the length of an object to the nearest centimeter.

▶ Prerequisite Skills

- Identify centimeters on a ruler and measure the length of an object to the nearest centimeter.
- Estimate the length of an object to the nearest inch or centimeter.

▶ Content Background

Students will learn to estimate and measure in centimeters.

Avoid using the words *round up* or *round down* with students. Use *round to the nearest centimeter* instead.

Estimating and measuring objects is an important skill. When judging whether an object will fit in a given space, students estimate the length, width, and height of the object. Then they compare the estimates to the given space to determine if the object will fit. Students often use familiar benchmark measurements when estimating and measuring. They may know that a large paper clip is about 1 centimeter wide, a dime is about 2 centimeters across, and a child's finger is about 1 centimeter wide. Benchmark measurements help students judge the measure of other objects.

Note that when measurements are abbreviated (cm, m, km, in., ft, yd, and mi), only the abbreviation for *inch* has a period. The period is added to avoid confusion with the word *in*.

▶ Common Errors and Misconceptions

Students often have difficulty giving the correct measure of an object when the object is not aligned with the 0-end of a ruler. For example, they might think that this pencil is 4 inches long because the right end of the pencil aligns with the 4-inch mark. The pencil is actually only 3 inches long because the left end of the pencil aligns with the 1-inch mark.

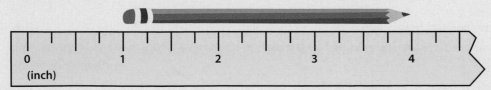

Materials to Gather

SUPPLIED

Centimeter Ruler (printout)

Round to the Nearest Centimeter activity page

Centimeter Measures activity page

ALSO NEEDED

scissors, adult

ruler, dual-scale

index card

household objects – various lengths (3 objects less than 15 cm, 3 objects between 20 and 30 cm, and 2 objects greater than 30 cm)

▶ Advance Preparation

For the Learn: Round to the Nearest Centimeter activity, print the Centimeter Ruler and cut it out. The printed ruler has decimals and fractions, which students will need for the activity.

For the Learn: Estimate and Measure activity, gather three objects that are less than 15 centimeters long, three objects that are between 20 and 30 centimeters long, and two objects that are greater than 30 centimeters long.

GET READY Hand Measurements

OFFLINE 10 min ▶

Objectives

- Identify centimeters on a ruler and measure the length of an object to the nearest centimeter.
- Estimate the length of an object to the nearest inch or centimeter.

Students will measure their hand span in centimeters. They will use this measurement as a benchmark to estimate the length, width, or height of objects. Students will compare the estimate to the actual measurement in centimeters. Gather the index card and ruler.

1. **Say:** When you need to measure an object, you won't always have a measurement tool handy. But if you know the measure of a part of your body, you can use it as a measurement tool.

2. Explain that students will measure their hand span in centimeters and use this measurement to estimate the length, width, and height of objects.

3. Give students the ruler. Have them point to the side of the ruler marked in centimeters (cm). Mention that the abbreviation for *centimeter* and *centimeters* is *cm*. Students may see the abbreviation on rulers and other everyday objects.

4. Have students spread their fingers as wide as they can and place them on the ruler so that their thumb is on the 0-mark. Help students determine their hand span to the nearest centimeter.

5. Have students record the measure of their hand span on the index card.

hand span: 14 cm

6. Find an object that is approximately 1 to 3 hand spans long (or wide or high). Have students use their hand span to estimate the length, width, or height of the object.

7. Help students use their hand span to measure the object. Have them place their left hand span on the object to start measuring and then put their right hand span next to it, making sure the hands do not overlap. If the object is more than 2 hand spans long, have students use the first hand to cross over and continue measuring where the second hand span ended. If a student's hand span is 14 cm and the object measured is about 2 hand spans long, add 14 cm plus 14 cm to get an estimate of 28 cm. Most objects won't be an exact number of hand spans. Students will have to estimate how many centimeters the partial hand span is.

8. Have students use the ruler to measure the length of the object in centimeters. Then have them compare their estimate with the actual length.

LEARN Round to the Nearest Centimeter

Students will measure line segments and round the measurements to the nearest centimeter. Mention to students that in most instances when they use measuring devices, they measure things exactly. In this activity, they are making "rough" measurements, so they are rounding to the nearest centimeter. After students finish the activity page, have them measure actual objects to the nearest centimeter.

Gather the cut-out centimeter ruler. View or print the Round to the Nearest Centimeter activity page and read the directions with students.

Students should copy the problems from the Activity Book into their Math Notebook as necessary and solve them there.

1. Tell students they will be measuring lines to the nearest centimeter. Have them find the edge of the centimeter ruler and point to the centimeter marks on the ruler.

2. Explain that lengths of objects are not usually an exact number of centimeters. When a measurement falls between two centimeters, the measurement rounds to the nearest centimeter. If the measurement falls before the halfway mark, it is rounded to the lesser centimeter. If the measurement falls on or after the halfway mark, it is rounded to the greater centimeter.

3. Have students look at the centimeter and half-centimeter markings on the ruler. Emphasize that the marks on a centimeter ruler are just like those on a number line.

4. Explain how $\frac{1}{2}$ on a number line is the same as $\frac{1}{2}$ centimeter on a centimeter ruler.

    Have students find the $\frac{1}{2}$ cm mark. Guide students to find the $1\frac{1}{2}$ cm, $2\frac{1}{2}$ cm, $3\frac{1}{2}$ cm, and so on, marks on the ruler.

5. Have students look at the Worked Example on the activity page. Be sure they understand how to measure the length of a line. Students should align the beginning of the line with the 0-mark of the ruler. Then they should identify the mark on the ruler where the line ends. Review the rules for rounding the length to the nearest centimeter.

6. Have students measure the length of the line in Problem 1. Ask them whether the line ends before the halfway mark or after it. Students should explain that the line ends after the halfway mark so the length, to the nearest centimeter, is 1 cm.

7. Have students complete Problems 2–7. Guide them in measuring each line segment and rounding the measurement to the nearest centimeter.

8. Discuss with students that because the line segment in Problem 3 measures exactly halfway between 4 and 5 centimeters, the length is rounded to the greater centimeter, or 5 cm. Make sure students apply the same rule to Problems 6 and 7.

9. As time allows, have students measure the length of objects of their choice to the nearest centimeter.

Objectives

- Estimate and measure the length of an object to the nearest centimeter.

Tips

Remind students to align the beginning of each line with the 0-mark on the ruler.

Note that many printers scale documents to fit to a printable area by default. Be sure to turn off page scaling so that documents print at 100% of their intended size.

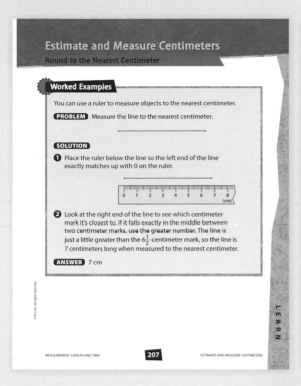

Estimate and Measure Centimeters
Round to the Nearest Centimeter

Worked Examples

You can use a ruler to measure objects to the nearest centimeter.

PROBLEM Measure the line to the nearest centimeter.

SOLUTION

❶ Place the ruler below the line so the left end of the line exactly matches up with 0 on the ruler.

❷ Look at the right end of the line to see which centimeter mark it's closest to. If it falls exactly in the middle between two centimeter marks, use the greater number. The line is just a little greater than the $6\frac{1}{2}$-centimeter mark, so the line is 7 centimeters long when measured to the nearest centimeter.

ANSWER 7 cm

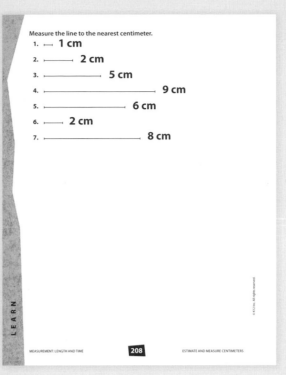

Measure the line to the nearest centimeter.

1. ⊢— 1 cm
2. ⊢——— 2 cm
3. ⊢————— 5 cm
4. ⊢————————— 9 cm
5. ⊢——————— 6 cm
6. ⊢— 2 cm
7. ⊢————————— 8 cm

LEARN Estimate and Measure

OFFLINE 15 min

Students will measure everyday objects in centimeters and use these measurements to estimate the measurements of other objects.

Gather the ruler, the index card with the student's hand-span measurement (from the Get Ready activity), and the household objects to measure.

1. Tell students that they will estimate and measure the length of objects to the nearest centimeter. Have students identify the centimeter side of the ruler.

2. Ask students to identify an object that measures about 1 centimeter long. They may suggest a ones cube. Explain that they should think of 1 centimeter as the length of a ones cube, or whatever object they identified, when estimating length.

3. Remind students that when they measure objects, they must match up the beginning of the object with the 0-mark on the ruler. This mark is not on the edge of most rulers, so students must adjust the ruler and the object to align at 0.

4. Show students one of the objects that measures less than 15 centimeters. Tell them which dimension of the object they will measure in centimeters. For example, students might measure the height of a cup.

5. Have students measure the object in centimeters. Remind them that if the length does not measure exactly to a centimeter line, they must round it to the nearest centimeter. If the measurement falls before the halfway mark, they should round to the lesser centimeter. If the measurement falls on or after the halfway mark, they should round to the greater centimeter.

Objectives

- Estimate and measure the length of an object to the nearest centimeter.

Tips

Review how to round a measurement to the nearest centimeter.

6. Have students write the name of the object and its measurement to the nearest centimeter in their Math Notebook. Students may abbreviate *centimeters* as *cm*. Tell them that they now have a known measure and they can use this measure to estimate the length of other objects.

7. Show students the next object that measures less than 15 centimeters. Tell them which dimension of the object they will measure. Have students use a known measure to estimate the measurement of the object. For example, they may know that the height of the cup is 13 cm or the width of a dime is about 2 cm. Students should compare the known measure with the new object to make an estimate.

8. Have students measure the object and record the measurement. Have them compare their estimate with the actual measurement.

9. Repeat Steps 7 and 8 with the third object that's less than 15 centimeters in length.

10. Present the smallest object that has a measure of 20 to 30 centimeters. Have students estimate its length, keeping in mind known measurements. Then have them measure the object with the ruler and compare their estimate with the actual measurement.

11. Have students estimate and measure the remaining items that are 20 to 30 centimeters long. Encourage them to compare and describe their estimates with the actual measurements.

12. Have students look at the index card and note the width of their hand span. Then have them use their hand span to estimate the measure of the two objects that are greater than 30 cm. After estimating, have them measure the objects with the ruler.

TRY IT Centimeter Measures

OFFLINE

10 min

Objectives

- Estimate and measure the length of an object to the nearest centimeter.

Students will practice estimating and measuring items in centimeters. Remind them that when they measure an object to the nearest centimeter, if the measure is exactly to the half-centimeter mark or past that mark, they should round to the greater centimeter. View or print the Centimeter Measures activity page and read the directions with students.

Students should copy the problems from the Activity Book into their Math Notebook as necessary and solve them there.

Point out to students that sometimes an object is held up to a ruler but isn't aligned with the 0 on the ruler as Problem 2 illustrates. Discuss ways to find the lengths of such objects. Students can count forward from the beginning of the object, or subtract the amount to the left of the object from the length.

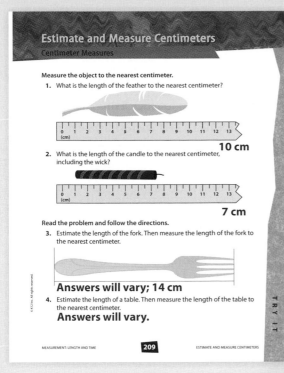

Estimate and Measure Centimeters
Centimeter Measures

Measure the object to the nearest centimeter.

1. What is the length of the feather to the nearest centimeter?

10 cm

2. What is the length of the candle to the nearest centimeter, including the wick?

7 cm

Read the problem and follow the directions.

3. Estimate the length of the fork. Then measure the length of the fork to the nearest centimeter.

Answers will vary; 14 cm

4. Estimate the length of a table. Then measure the length of the table to the nearest centimeter.
Answers will vary.

T R Y   I T

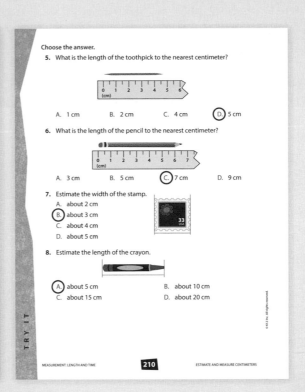

Choose the answer.

5. What is the length of the toothpick to the nearest centimeter?

A. 1 cm B. 2 cm C. 4 cm D. 5 cm

6. What is the length of the pencil to the nearest centimeter?

A. 3 cm B. 5 cm C. 7 cm D. 9 cm

7. Estimate the width of the stamp.
A. about 2 cm
B. about 3 cm
C. about 4 cm
D. about 5 cm

8. Estimate the length of the crayon.

A. about 5 cm B. about 10 cm
C. about 15 cm D. about 20 cm

T R Y   I T

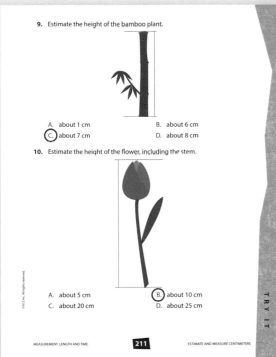

9. Estimate the height of the bamboo plant.

A. about 1 cm B. about 6 cm
C. about 7 cm D. about 8 cm

10. Estimate the height of the flower, including the stem.

A. about 5 cm B. about 10 cm
C. about 20 cm D. about 25 cm

T R Y   I T

ONLINE
10min

CHECKPOINT

Students will complete an online Checkpoint. If necessary, read the directions, problems, and answer choices to students and help them with keyboard or mouse operations.

Objectives

- Estimate and measure the length of an object to the nearest centimeter.

Estimate and Measure Inches (A)

Lesson Overview

GET READY Measure in Inches	10 minutes	OFFLINE
LEARN Measure to the Nearest Quarter Inch	20 minutes	OFFLINE
LEARN Measure Everyday Objects	20 minutes	OFFLINE
TRY IT Find the Nearest Quarter Inch	10 minutes	OFFLINE

▶ Lesson Objectives

Estimate the length of an object to the nearest $\frac{1}{2}$ inch and measure the length to the nearest $\frac{1}{4}$ inch.

▶ Prerequisite Skills

- Identify inches on a ruler and measure the length of an object to the nearest inch.
- Estimate the length of an object to the nearest inch or centimeter.

▶ Content Background

Students will learn to estimate and measure in inches. They will estimate to the nearest half inch and measure to the nearest quarter inch.

Estimating and measuring objects is an important skill. When judging whether an object will fit in a given space, students estimate the length, width, and height of the object. Then they compare the estimates to the given space to determine if the object will fit. Students often use familiar benchmark measurements when estimating and measuring. For instance, they may be familiar with $8\frac{1}{2} \times 11$ inch notebook paper. Students may use this information to estimate the length of an object or judge whether it will fit in a given space.

Note that when measurements are abbreviated (cm, m, km, in., ft, yd, and mi), only the abbreviation for *inch* has a period. The period is added to avoid confusion with the word *in*.

▶ Common Errors and Misconceptions

Students often have difficulty giving the correct measure of an object when the object is not aligned with the 0-end of a ruler. For example, they might think that this pencil is 4 inches long because the right end of the pencil aligns with the 4-inch mark. The pencil is actually only 3 inches long because the left end of the pencil aligns with the 1-inch mark.

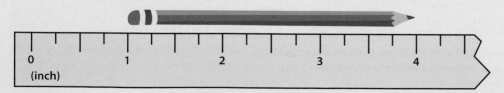

Materials to Gather

SUPPLIED

Measure to the Nearest Quarter Inch activity page

Find the Nearest Quarter Inch activity page

ALSO NEEDED

ruler, dual-scale

index card – 3 by 5 inches (2)

tape, masking

▶ Advance Preparation

Put a piece of masking tape across the length of a ruler in a way that doesn't cover up the inch markings or numbers. Write small labels on the tape to illustrate what the ruler marks mean. Write $\frac{1}{4}$, $\frac{1}{2}$, $\frac{3}{4}$, $1\frac{1}{2}$, and $2\frac{1}{2}$ in the correct places on the ruler. If students have difficulties as you measure during the activity, write more fractions on the tape.

GET READY Measure in Inches

OFFLINE 10 min

Students will measure the length of an index card to the nearest inch and use that measurement to estimate the length of other objects.
   Gather the ruler and index card.

1. Give students the ruler. Have them point to the side of the ruler marked in inches (in.). Tell them that the abbreviation for *inch* and *inches* is *in.* with a period after it. They may see the abbreviation on rulers and other everyday objects.

2. Give students the index card. Explain that they are to measure the length of the index card to the nearest inch. Remind them that the length is the longer side. Students should determine that the length is 5 inches.

3. Have students gather objects that they think have a measure of about 5 inches. Encourage them to use the index card as a known measure of 5 inches.

4. Explain that students should use the index card to estimate the length, width, or height of the objects. Then have them use the ruler to find the actual length, width, or height. Have them compare their estimates with the actual measurements.

Objectives

- Identify inches on a ruler and measure the length of an object to the nearest inch.
- Estimate the length of an object to the nearest inch or centimeter.

LEARN Measure to the Nearest Quarter Inch

OFFLINE 20 min

Students will learn how to measure objects to the nearest quarter inch. Gather the ruler marked with fractions. View or print the Measure to the Nearest Quarter Inch activity page and read the directions with students.
   Students should copy the problems from the Activity Book into their Math Notebook as necessary and solve them there.

1. Ask students what they know about quarters. They may relate quarters to the fraction $\frac{1}{4}$, the coin, or a whole divided into four equal parts. Emphasize that when a whole is divided into quarters, there are four equal parts. Also emphasize that the word *whole* means a unit of measure such as 1 inch. Say that a quarter of an inch is $\frac{1}{4}$ of the way to 1 inch. Tell students they will learn to measure length to the nearest quarter inch.

2. Tell students that the ruler is like a number line that shows halves, fourths, eighths, and even sixteenths. Have students count the small lines between two numbers to see that there are 16 tiny lines that make up a whole. The distance between each small line is one-sixteenth of an inch. Note that students will not need to use one-sixteenths.

Objectives

- Estimate the length of an object to the nearest $\frac{1}{2}$ inch and measure the length to the nearest $\frac{1}{4}$ inch.

Tips

Remind students to align the beginning of each line with the 0-mark on the ruler.

3. Ask students to point out the half-inch markings on the ruler. Explain that the half-inch marks divide each inch into two equal parts. Point out the quarter-inch marks. Explain that the quarter-inch marks, $\frac{1}{4}$, $\frac{2}{4}$, $\frac{3}{4}$, and $\frac{4}{4}$, divide each inch into four equal parts. Emphasize that $\frac{2}{4}$ is equal to $\frac{1}{2}$. Point out the eighth-inch marks and explain that these markings divide each inch into eight equal parts.

4. Tell students that they will measure line segments to the nearest $\frac{1}{4}$ inch.

   Ask: How many $\frac{1}{4}$ inches are in one inch? 4

   Explain that sometimes a line may measure to the $1\frac{2}{4}$ mark on the ruler. Remind students that $1\frac{2}{4}$ inches is the same as $1\frac{1}{2}$ inches, so that particular measure to the nearest quarter inch is $1\frac{1}{2}$ inches. Also, a line might measure $1\frac{4}{4}$ inches, which is the same as 2 inches. Be sure students understand that when measuring to the nearest quarter inch, the answer may not always be given in quarter inches. Sometimes it will be given in halves or wholes.

5. Review how to measure the length of a line. Students should align the beginning of the line with the 0-mark on the ruler. Then they should identify the nearest quarter-inch mark on the ruler where the line ends to determine the length to the nearest quarter inch. Remind students that if a line measures exactly halfway between two quarter-inch marks, they use the greater measure.

6. Direct students' attention to the Worked Example. Read the example with them. Then have them complete Problems 1–6. Guide them in measuring each line segment to the nearest quarter inch.

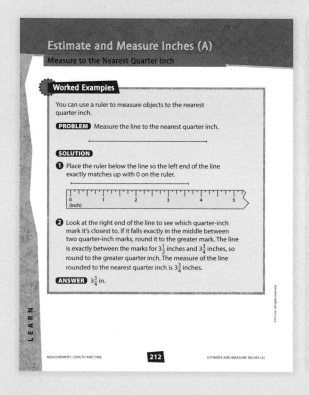

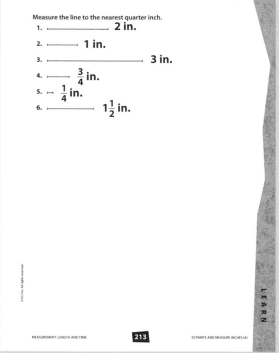

LEARN Measure Everyday Objects

Students will use a known measurement to estimate the measure of other objects. Students will measure the objects to the nearest quarter inch.
 Gather the ruler and index card.

1. Review what it means to measure to the nearest quarter inch. Remind students that 4 quarter inches equal 1 whole inch. Also remind them that measurements such as $2\frac{1}{2}$ inches and 3 inches can represent lengths to the nearest quarter inch.

2. Tell students that they will determine known measurements and use them to estimate the length of objects. Then they will measure the objects to the nearest quarter inch and compare their estimates to the actual measurements.

3. Have students find and measure a part of their hand that is about 1 inch and record it on the index card. For example, they may identify the length of part of their thumb, the width of two fingers, or the distance from the tip of the finger to the knuckle.

4. Have students also measure their hand span by spreading their fingers as wide as they can and placing them on the ruler so their thumb is on the 0-mark. Help students determine their hand span and record it on the index card.

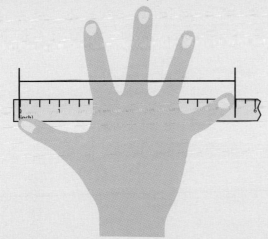

5. Ask students to look at the two measures and try to memorize them. The goal is for students to use a known measure to estimate the length of other objects.

6. Choose an object in the room for students to measure. Have them estimate the measure of its length, width, or height. Remind students to use one of the known measures—the part of the hand they measured or their hand span—to make the estimate.

7. Give students the ruler and have them measure the object to the nearest quarter inch. Check to make sure students measured to the nearest quarter inch correctly.

8. Have students compare their estimate with the actual measure. If students made estimates that are close to the actual measure, have them find a longer object to estimate and measure. If students did not estimate well, have them find another object about the same size to estimate and measure.

9. Have students continue to practice estimating and measuring objects. Make sure they measure different-sized objects and different dimensions (length, width, and height).

TRY IT Find the Nearest Quarter Inch

Objectives

Students will practice estimating and measuring to the nearest quarter inch. View or print the Find the Nearest Quarter Inch activity page and read the directions with students.

Students should copy the problems from the Activity Book into their Math Notebook as necessary and solve them there.

Remind students that sometimes an object is held up to a ruler but isn't aligned with the 0-mark on the ruler as Problems 4 and 11 illustrate. Remind students that they can count forward from the beginning of the object, or subtract the amount to the left of the object from the length.

- Estimate the length of an object to the nearest $\frac{1}{2}$ inch and measure the length to the nearest $\frac{1}{4}$ inch.

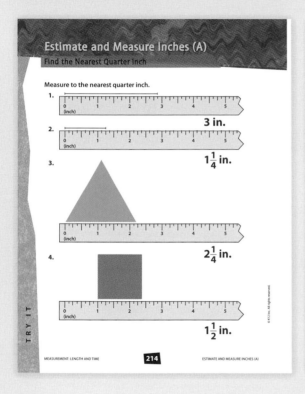

Estimate and Measure Inches (A)

Find the Nearest Quarter Inch

Measure to the nearest quarter inch.

1.

3 in.

2.

$1\frac{1}{4}$ **in.**

3.

$2\frac{1}{4}$ **in.**

4.

$1\frac{1}{2}$ **in.**

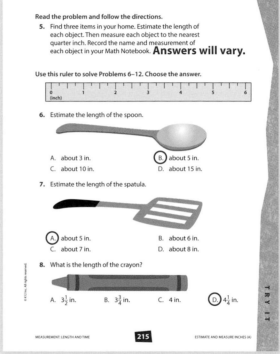

Read the problem and follow the directions.

5. Find three items in your home. Estimate the length of each object. Then measure each object to the nearest quarter inch. Record the name and measurement of each object in your Math Notebook. **Answers will vary.**

Use this ruler to solve Problems 6–12. Choose the answer.

6. Estimate the length of the spoon.

   A. about 3 in.   **B.** about 5 in.
   C. about 10 in.   D. about 15 in.

7. Estimate the length of the spatula.

   A. about 5 in.   B. about 6 in.
   C. about 7 in.   D. about 8 in.

8. What is the length of the crayon?

   A. $3\frac{1}{2}$ in.   B. $3\frac{3}{4}$ in.   C. 4 in.   **D.** $4\frac{1}{4}$ in.

TRY IT

Use this ruler to solve Problems 6–12. Choose the answer.

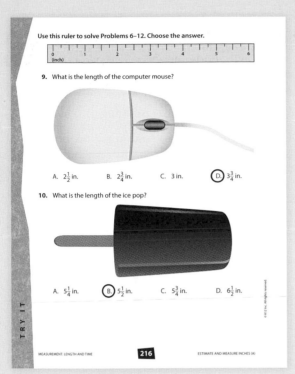

9. What is the length of the computer mouse?

A. $2\frac{1}{2}$ in.   B. $2\frac{3}{4}$ in.   C. 3 in.   (D.) $3\frac{3}{4}$ in.

10. What is the length of the ice pop?

A. $5\frac{1}{4}$ in.   (B.) $5\frac{1}{2}$ in.   C. $5\frac{3}{4}$ in.   D. $6\frac{1}{2}$ in.

Use this ruler to solve Problems 6–12. Choose the answer.

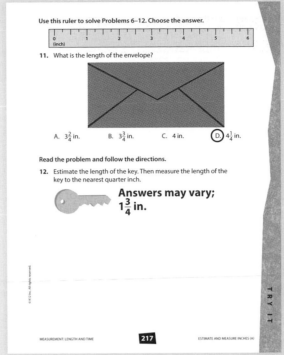

11. What is the length of the envelope?

A. $3\frac{2}{4}$ in.   B. $3\frac{3}{4}$ in.   C. 4 in.   (D.) $4\frac{1}{4}$ in.

Read the problem and follow the directions.

12. Estimate the length of the key. Then measure the length of the key to the nearest quarter inch.

Answers may vary;
$1\frac{3}{4}$ in.

Estimate and Measure Inches (B)

Lesson Overview

GET READY Draw and Measure Lines	5 minutes	OFFLINE
LEARN Use Hand Spans to Estimate Measures	15 minutes	OFFLINE
LEARN Estimate-and-Measure Game	15 minutes	OFFLINE
TRY IT Measure to a Quarter Inch	15 minutes	OFFLINE
CHECKPOINT	10 minutes	ONLINE

▶ **Lesson Objectives**

Estimate the length of an object to the nearest $\frac{1}{2}$ inch and measure the length to the nearest $\frac{1}{4}$ inch.

▶ **Prerequisite Skills**

- Identify inches on a ruler and measure the length of an object to the nearest inch.
- Estimate the length of an object to the nearest inch or centimeter.

▶ **Content Background**

Students will continue to learn to estimate and measure in inches. They will estimate to the nearest half inch and measure to the nearest quarter inch.

Estimating and measuring objects is an important skill. When judging whether an object will fit in a given space, students estimate the length, width, and height of the object. Then they compare the estimates to the given space to determine if the object will fit. Students often use familiar benchmark measurements when estimating and measuring. For instance, they may be familiar with $8\frac{1}{2} \times 11$ inch notebook paper. Students may use this information to estimate the length of an object or judge whether it will fill a given space.

Note that when measurements are abbreviated (cm, m, km, in., ft, yd, and mi), only the abbreviation for *inch* has a period. The period is added to avoid confusion with the word *in*.

▶ **Common Errors and Misconceptions**

Students often have difficulty giving the correct measure of an object when the object is not aligned with the 0-end of a ruler. For example, they might think that this pencil is 4 inches long because the right end of the pencil aligns with the 4-inch mark. The pencil is actually only 3 inches long because the left end of the pencil aligns with the 1-inch mark.

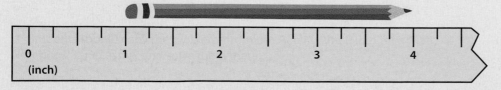

Materials to Gather

SUPPLIED
Measure to a Quarter Inch activity page

ALSO NEEDED
index cards – 20
ruler, dual-scale

▶ Advance Preparation

On index cards, write the names of readily available objects and a measurable characteristic of each object, such as a pencil's length, a drinking-glass's height, a chair's width, a table's length, a marker's width, and a pair of scissors' widest opening. Students will use the index cards to play a game in which they will estimate the length of objects and then measure the objects.

GET READY Draw and Measure Lines

OFFLINE 5 min

Students will practice drawing lines of a given length without a measuring tool. They will then measure the lines to check for accuracy.

Gather the ruler.

1. Ask students to draw a line 2 inches long without using a measuring tool.

2. Give students a ruler and have them measure the line. Have students compare the length of their line to the 2-inch mark on the ruler.

3. Repeat Steps 1 and 2 with a 3-inch line.

4. Challenge students to draw longer lines and line lengths ending in half inches as they become more comfortable with the process. Ask them to draw lines that are $2\frac{1}{2}$ and $3\frac{1}{2}$ inches long.

Objectives

- Identify inches on a ruler and measure the length of an object to the nearest inch.

- Estimate the length of an object to the nearest inch or centimeter.

Tips

Remind students to align the beginning of each line with the 0-mark on the ruler.

LEARN Use Hand Spans to Estimate Measures

OFFLINE 15 min

Students will measure parts of their hand and use those known measurements to estimate the length of other objects.

Gather the ruler.

1. Have students extend their four fingers (index finger through pinky finger) straight out, with all fingers touching. Have them measure the width of these four fingers by holding a ruler with the other hand. Students should measure the width to the nearest half inch.

Objectives

- Estimate the length of an object to the nearest $\frac{1}{2}$ inch and measure the length to the nearest $\frac{1}{4}$ inch.

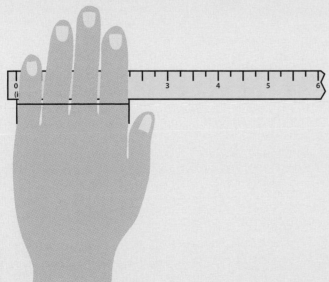

2. Have students record the width of their four fingers and any lesser widths they may find helpful. If students don't already have the other two found measures, their hand span and a 1-inch length such as the width of two fingers, have them record those measurements.

3. Have students gather several objects from their surroundings. Ask them to choose part of an object to measure. Explain that they will use the measurement tools on their hands to estimate the length, width, or height of the object. For example, if students want to find the width of a picture frame, they will estimate by using their hand span. If a hand span is 5 inches and the frame is a little more than 2 hand spans, students may estimate the width to be 11 inches.

4. After students estimate the length, width, or height of the object, have them use a ruler to find the actual measurement to the nearest quarter inch. Students should compare their estimate with the actual measurement.

5. Have students continue practicing estimating and measuring. When they are comfortable with their estimates to the nearest inch, have them estimate measures to the nearest half inch and quarter inch.

OFFLINE 15 min

LEARN Estimate-and-Measure Game

Play a game with students to practice estimating and measuring various objects. Students will earn points based on how close their estimate is to the actual measure of the object.

Gather the ruler and labeled index cards.

1. Place the index cards face down in a pile. The first player takes the top card, identifies the object, and estimates the given measurement. If the card says "a pencil's length," students choose whatever pencil they wish. If it says "chair's width," they choose any chair to measure. Remind players to use a known measure (such as a hand span) to estimate. Then the player uses a ruler to find the actual measure of the object. Players get a point for every inch of the actual measure, and they subtract 2 points for each inch that their estimate was off. For instance, if students estimated an object was 2 feet or 24 inches long, and its actual length was 21 inches long, they would be 3 inches off from the actual measure, so they get 21 points minus $2 \times 3 = 6$. So their score would be $21 - 6 = 15$.

Place the card on the bottom of the pile when the turn is over.

2. Have the next player take the top card from the pile, identify the object, estimate the measurement, find the actual measurement, and calculate the score.

3. Continue playing. The player with the highest score when all the cards have been used is the winner. To continue playing, reuse the cards with the rule that players pick different objects from ones they picked in the previous game.

Objectives

- Estimate the length of an object to the nearest $\frac{1}{2}$ inch and measure the length to the nearest $\frac{1}{4}$ inch.

Tips

Write the points on an index card for each player. Have students help refine the scoring system. They can add bonus points for estimating very close to the actual measurement, or for estimating objects that are greater than 3 hand spans, or for meeting other challenges that come up during the game.

TRY IT Measure to a Quarter Inch

Objectives

Students will practice estimating to the nearest half inch and measuring to the nearest quarter inch. Remind students to adjust their measure if an object is not matched up with the 0-mark on the ruler. Gather the ruler. View or print the Measure to a Quarter Inch activity page and read the directions with students.

Students should copy the problems from the Activity Book into their Math Notebook as necessary and solve them there.

- Estimate the length of an object to the nearest $\frac{1}{2}$ inch and measure the length to the nearest $\frac{1}{4}$ inch.

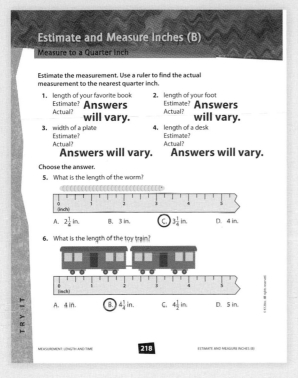

Estimate and Measure Inches (B)
Measure to a Quarter Inch

Estimate the measurement. Use a ruler to find the actual measurement to the nearest quarter inch.

1. length of your favorite book
   Estimate? **Answers**
   Actual? **will vary.**

2. length of your foot
   Estimate? **Answers**
   Actual? **will vary.**

3. width of a plate
   Estimate?
   Actual?
   Answers will vary.

4. length of a desk
   Estimate?
   Actual?
   Answers will vary.

Choose the answer.

5. What is the length of the worm?

   A. $2\frac{1}{4}$ in.　　B. 3 in.　　**C.** $3\frac{1}{4}$ in.　　D. 4 in.

6. What is the length of the toy train?

   A. 4 in.　　**B.** $4\frac{1}{4}$ in.　　C. $4\frac{1}{2}$ in.　　D. 5 in.

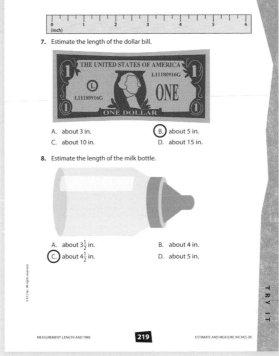

7. Estimate the length of the dollar bill.

   A. about 3 in.　　**B.** about 5 in.
   C. about 10 in.　　D. about 15 in.

8. Estimate the length of the milk bottle.

   A. about $3\frac{1}{2}$ in.　　B. about 4 in.
   C. about $4\frac{1}{2}$ in.　　D. about 5 in.

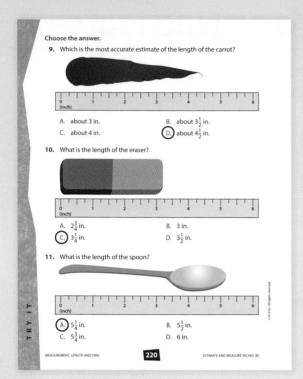

Choose the answer.

9. Which is the most accurate estimate of the length of the carrot?

A. about 3 in. B. about $3\frac{1}{2}$ in.
C. about 4 in. D. about $4\frac{1}{2}$ in.

10. What is the length of the eraser?

A. $2\frac{3}{4}$ in. B. 3 in.
C. $3\frac{1}{4}$ in. D. $3\frac{1}{2}$ in.

11. What is the length of the spoon?

A. $5\frac{1}{4}$ in. B. $5\frac{1}{2}$ in.
C. $5\frac{3}{4}$ in. D. 6 in.

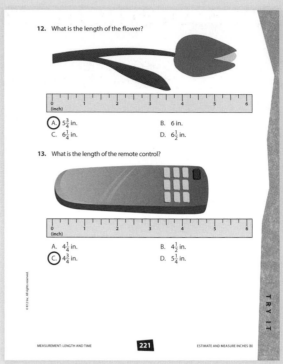

12. What is the length of the flower?

A. $5\frac{3}{4}$ in. B. 6 in.
C. $6\frac{1}{4}$ in. D. $6\frac{1}{2}$ in.

13. What is the length of the remote control?

A. $4\frac{1}{4}$ in. B. $4\frac{1}{2}$ in.
C. $4\frac{3}{4}$ in. D. $5\frac{1}{4}$ in.

14. What is the length of the caterpillar?

A. 2 in. B. $2\frac{1}{4}$ in.
C. $2\frac{1}{2}$ in. D. $2\frac{3}{4}$ in.

15. What is the height of the doll?

A. $5\frac{1}{4}$ in. B. $5\frac{1}{2}$ in.
C. $5\frac{3}{4}$ in. D. $6\frac{3}{4}$ in.

CHECKPOINT

ONLINE 10 min

Students will complete an online Checkpoint. If necessary, read the directions, problems, and answer choices to students and help them with keyboard or mouse operations.

Objectives

- Estimate the length of an object to the nearest $\frac{1}{2}$ inch and measure the length to the nearest $\frac{1}{4}$ inch.

Display Measurement Data in Line Plots

Lesson Overview

LEARN Create Line Plots	20 minutes	**OFFLINE**
LEARN Show Measurements on Line Plots	20 minutes	**OFFLINE**

▶ **Lesson Objectives**
- Interpret and display data on a line plot.
- Collect measurement data and display the data in a line plot.

▶ **Content Background**

Students will build on their previous knowledge of measuring objects and creating line plots.

▶ **Advance Preparation**

Print two copies of the Blank Number Lines.

Materials to Gather

SUPPLIED

Create Line Plots activity page

Show Measurements on Line Plots activity page

Blank Number Lines (printout)

ALSO NEEDED

ruler, dual-scale

LEARN Create Line Plots

OFFLINE 20 min

Students will use given data sets to create and interpret line plots.
    View or print the Create Line Plots activity page. Gather the Blank Number Lines.

1. Read the directions and Problem 1 with students.

    Ask: What is the problem asking us to do? Make a line plot for the data set and then tell what number appears most often.

    Say: First find the least and greatest numbers in the data set. Then use those numbers, and the numbers in between, to label a number line for your line plot.

    Ask: What are the least and greatest numbers in this data set? 2 and 7

    Say: Now let's look at each number in the data set. Every time we see a number, we put an X above the number line over that number. We need to be sure to keep the Xs the same size so that they are lined up with each other both up and down and side to side.

    Show students how to place the Xs for the first 5 numbers in the data set and have them complete the line plot for the remaining 6 numbers.

    Ask: What is the number that appears the most in the data set? The plot shows that 5 has the most Xs in the data set. So 5 is the number that appears most often.

2. Have students complete Problems 2–4. Students should use the Blank Number Lines to create the line plots.

Objectives
- Interpret and display data on a line plot.

Tips

When making a line plot, have students cross out the numbers in the data set when they put them on the line plot. Crossing out helps keep track of the numbers they have already used.

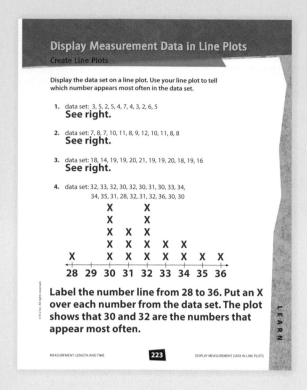

Display Measurement Data in Line Plots
Create Line Plots

Display the data set on a line plot. Use your line plot to tell which number appears most often in the data set.

1. data set: 3, 5, 2, 5, 4, 7, 4, 3, 2, 6, 5
   See right.

2. data set: 7, 8, 7, 10, 11, 8, 9, 12, 10, 11, 8, 8
   See right.

3. data set: 18, 14, 19, 19, 20, 21, 19, 19, 20, 18, 19, 16
   See right.

4. data set: 32, 33, 32, 30, 32, 30, 31, 30, 33, 34,
   34, 35, 31, 28, 32, 31, 32, 36, 30, 30

```
        X       X
        X       X
        X   X   X
        X   X   X   X   X
    X   X   X   X   X   X   X
   28  29  30  31  32  33  34  35  36
```

Label the number line from 28 to 36. Put an X over each number from the data set. The plot shows that 30 and 32 are the numbers that appear most often.

MEASUREMENT: LENGTH AND TIME   **223**   DISPLAY MEASUREMENT DATA IN LINE PLOTS

L E A R N

Additional Answers

1.
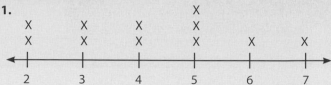

Label the number line from 2 to 7. Put an X over each number from the data set. The plot shows that 5 is the number that appears most often.

2.
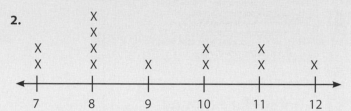

Label the number line from 7 to 12. Put an X over each number from the data set. The plot shows that 8 is the number that appears most often.

3.
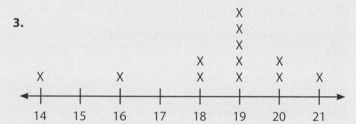

Label the number line from 14 to 21. Put an X over each number from the data set. The plot shows that 19 is the number that appears most often.

OFFLINE

20min

LEARN Show Measurements on Line Plots

Objectives

- Collect measurement data and display the data in a line plot.

Students will build on their previous knowledge of measuring objects and creating line plots.

View or print the Show Measurements on Line Plots activity page. Gather the ruler and the Blank Number Lines.

1. Read the Worked Example with students.

   Ask: What is the problem asking us to do? Use a ruler to measure each pencil to the nearest quarter inch. Then create a line plot that shows those measurements.

   Ask: Why is it easier to write the measurements in order? Writing the measurements in order makes plotting easier.

   Ask: How can you create the line plot and be sure you've plotted all your measurements? I plot an X on the line plot over the measurement. I cross out the measurement from the list so that I don't lose track of what I plotted.

2. Have students complete Problems 1 and 2, referring to the Worked Example as needed. Students should use the Blank Decimal Number Lines to create the line plots.

Tips

Have students cross out the measurements they've recorded as they plot them.

LEARN Time to the Nearest Minute

Students will use the Clock Learning Tool to tell time to the nearest minute. They will say the time two different ways.

DIRECTIONS FOR USING THE CLOCK LEARNING TOOL

1. Click Begin and choose the following:
   - Click the clock display button.
   - Uncheck the digital clock box.

2. Drag the minute hand to set the clock to 12:05.

3. Point to the light-blue 5 on the outer ring of the clock. Explain that the light-blue numbers on the outer ring of the clock tell how many minutes after the hour it is. Point out that those numbers are like skip counting by 5s.

4. Have students click the speaker button and listen as the time is read.

5. To show students how 12:05 is written and how it would display on a digital clock, choose the following:
   - Click the clock display button.
   - Check the digital clock box.

   Say: Another way to say this time is 5 minutes after 12.

6. Repeat Steps 2–5 for the following times, allowing students to move the minute hand. Point out the corresponding light blue numbers for each time.
   - 1:25 one twenty-five; 25 minutes after 1
   - 2:40 two forty; 40 minutes after 2
   - 3:55 three fifty-five; 55 minutes after 3

7. Set the clock to exactly 4:00.

8. Have students drag the minute hand very slowly around the clock. Have them look at the time on the digital clock as the minute hand moves. Emphasize that each tick mark on the clock represents one minute. Point out that the time on the digital clock advances by 1-minute intervals as they drag the minute hand around the clock. Continue until students get to 4:59 and then finally move to 5:00.

9. Have students click the + button under the minutes on the digital clock. They will find that the minutes display does not necessarily increase by one with every click. Have students verify for themselves that the display on the digital clock matches the time shown on the analog clock.

10. Change the settings again to the following:
    - Click the clock display button.
    - Uncheck the digital clock box.

11. Move the minute hand to the following times. Have students read the time two different ways.
    - 4:37 four thirty-seven; 37 minutes after 4
    - 11:52 eleven fifty-two; 52 minutes after 11
    - 8:49 eight forty-nine; 49 minutes after 8
    - 5:13 five thirteen; 13 minutes after 5

Tips

Throughout the day, have students look at an analog clock, with hour and minute hands, and state the time.

LEARN Read the Time More Than One Way

Students will use the Clock Learning Tool to learn how to read the time as both the number of minutes after an hour and the number of minutes before the next hour. For example, they'll learn that 2:40 is both 40 minutes after 2 and 20 minutes before 3. They will show times on an analog clock.

- Tell time to the nearest minute.

Tips

If students have difficulty setting the hands for a particular time, have them use the the digital clock to practice setting times and checking them.

DIRECTIONS FOR USING THE CLOCK LEARNING TOOL

1. Click Begin and choose the following:
    - Click the clock display button.
    - Uncheck the digital clock box.

2. Drag the minute hand around the clock to show 5:45.

    Say: The time shown is 5:45 or 45 minutes after 5. There is another way to say this time. Since the time will be 6:00 in 15 minutes, you can say this time as 15 minutes before 6 or 15 minutes till 6. You can also say this as quarter till 6.

3. Point to the light-blue numbers around the outer edge of the clock. Explain that when the minute hand is on one of these multiples of 5, students should skip count by 5s to the next hour to see how many minutes there are until that hour.

4. Drag the minute hand back to show 5:40. Have students count the number of minutes before 6.

    Ask: Now that you know how many minutes there are before 6, how do you read this time? 20 minutes before 6; 20 minutes till 6; 40 minutes after 5

5. Drag the minute hand around the clock to show 7:51.

    Say: The time shown is 7:51 or 51 minutes after 7. There is another way to say this time. Since the time will be 8:00 in 9 minutes, you can say this time as 9 minutes before 8 or 9 minutes till 8. You can see that there are 4 minutes until the next 5, which is 7:55, and then 5 more minutes, so altogether there are 9 minutes until 8.

6. Drag the minute hand around the clock to show 10:38.

    Ask: What time is shown? 10:38, or 38 minutes after 10

    Say: There is another way to say this time.

    Ask students how they could figure out how many minutes it is before 11. Students could figure it out in any of the following ways.

    - Start at 38 and count 2 minutes to 40; skip count by 5s, stepping from number to number on the clock (5, 10, 15, 20); then add the 2 minutes to get 22 minutes till 11.

    - Start at 11 o'clock and skip count by 5s going backward on the clock from number to number—5, 10, 15, 20—then 21, 22 to get to 10:38.

    - Count up by 10s from 38 to 60 without using the clock (starting at 38, 48, then 58, and 2 more is 60) to get 22 minutes till 11.

    - Simply subtract 38 minutes from 60 minutes. Since 60 − 38 = 22, the time is 22 minutes before 11, or 22 minutes till 11.

7. Repeat Step 6 with the following times. Allow students to choose the strategy that works best for them to determine the answer.

    - 12:35 35 minutes after 12; 25 minutes before 1; 25 minutes till 1
    - 2:49 49 minutes after 2; 11 minutes before 3; 11 minutes till 3

8. Have students drag the minute hand around the clock to show the times in each of the following situations. Then have them press the speaker button to see if they're correct.

   • Serena leaves for swim practice at 4:30 p.m.
   • Alexander arrived at the party at 3:05 p.m.
   • The sun rose this morning at 7:43 a.m.
   • The tide of the ocean is at its lowest today at 9:58 p.m.

9. Have students move the clock hands to show each of the following times. Check their work. The speaker button will give the time in only one way. For instance, it will say, "The time is 7:35." Check that students are comfortable also giving the time as 35 minutes after 7 and 25 minutes before 8.

   • Rosa left for play rehearsal at 14 minutes after 7. 7:14
   • Johnny left for the park at 10 minutes before 2. 1:50
   • Ron's baseball game ended at 12 minutes till 6. 5:48
   • The moonrise tonight is at 26 minutes after 9. 9:26

TRY IT Show and Tell Time

OFFLINE
15 min

Objectives

Students will practice telling time to the minute. View or print the Show and Tell Time activity page and read the directions with students.

   Students should copy the problems from the Activity Book into their Math Notebook as necessary and solve them there.

• Tell time to the nearest minute.

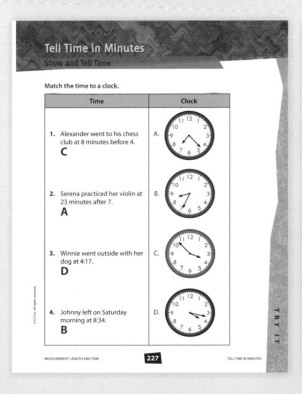

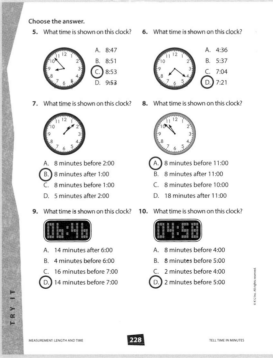

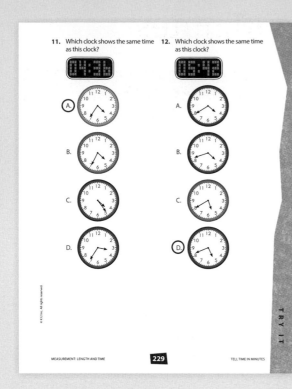

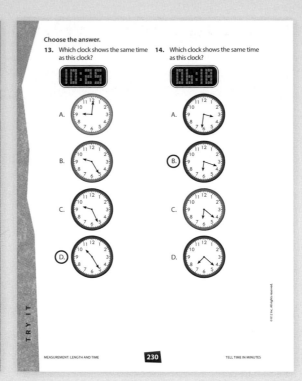

CHECKPOINT

ONLINE 10min

Students will complete an online Checkpoint. If necessary, read the directions, problems, and answer choices to students and help them with keyboard or mouse operations.

Objectives

- Tell time to the nearest minute.

Determine Elapsed Time in Minutes

Lesson Overview

GET READY Passing Time	5 minutes	**ONLINE**
LEARN Time Spent	20 minutes	**ONLINE**
LEARN Across A.M. and P.M.	20 minutes	**ONLINE**
TRY IT How Much Time?	15 minutes	**OFFLINE**

▶ Lesson Objectives

Determine elapsed time to the nearest minute.

▶ Prerequisite Skills

Determine elapsed time in hours, such as 11:00 a.m. to 4:00 p.m.

Materials to Gather

SUPPLIED
Time Spent (printout)
Across A.M. and P.M. (printout)
How Much Time? activity page

▶ Content Background

Students will learn to determine elapsed time. Elapsed time is the amount of time that passes between a starting and ending time. Students will also learn to find the end time of an activity given the start time and the elapsed time.

Elapsed time can include elapsed hours, elapsed days, elapsed months, or other time periods. Students need to understand that when counting to determine elapsed time, such as hours, they count beginning with the hour after the starting time. For example, if students are counting how many hours there are between 2:00 p.m. to 7:00 p.m., they begin counting at 3:00—that is, 3:00, 4:00, 5:00, 6:00, 7:00—to find that there are 5 hours between 2:00 p.m. and 7:00 p.m. Students should use this counting principle in any type of counting-on situation, either from a number or from another starting point such as time.

▶ Advance Preparation

Print the Time Spent printout and the Across A.M. and P.M. printout.

GET READY Passing Time

ONLINE
5min

Students will determine elapsed time in hours. Explain to students that elapsed time is the time that passes between a starting time and an ending time.

Objectives

- Determine elapsed time in hours, such as 11:00 a.m. to 4:00 p.m.

Tips	Have students find 3 more than 5 by counting on: 6, 7, 8. Apply this counting-on strategy to find 3 hours after 5:00 by counting on hours: 6:00, 7:00, 8:00.

LEARN Time Spent

Students will use the Clock Learning Tool to learn how to find elapsed times and ending times in story problems. Elapsed time is the amount of time that passes between two times. The story problems in this activity use times that don't cross 12:00 noon or 12:00 midnight, so answers will not include a.m. and p.m.

Gather the Time Spent printout.

DIRECTIONS FOR USING THE CLOCK LEARNING TOOL

1. Click Begin.

2. Explain that elapsed time is the amount of time that passes between a start time and an end time. Tell students that when they know the time an activity starts and the time it ends, they can find the elapsed time.

   Say: Moving the minute hand 1 full circle equals 1 hour. When you figure elapsed time, start by moving the minute hand around the clock 1 full circle for each hour that has passed. Then move the minute hand the number of minutes.

3. Give students the printout and have them read Problem 1.

   • Have students drag the minute hand around the analog clock until the time is 3:10, the starting time in Problem 1.

   • Tell students that they will need to drag the minute hand to 4:55, the ending time, and count forward while doing so.

   • Have them move the minute hand 1 full rotation and count aloud "1 hour." They should make a note on the printout that they have counted 1 hour.

   • For counting 55 minutes, have them first move the minute hand 30 minutes from 4:10 to 4:40. Then have them move the hand and count by 5-minute intervals, starting with 30, until they reach 4:55. They will say, "30, 35, 40, 45" as they reach 4:55 on the clock. Have them make a note on the printout that they counted 45 minutes. They have written 1 hour and 45 minutes as the elapsed time.

   Ask: How long did the movie last? 1 hour and 45 minutes

4. Have students read Problem 2 on the printout and move the clock hands to 9:40.

   • Ask students to move the minute hand and count the number of minutes until 10 o'clock and then count another 12 minutes. Have them make a note of 20 minutes plus 12 minutes on the printout.

   • Explain that they moved the hand to 10 o'clock as a way to help them count the minutes easily. When they counted 20 minutes to reach 10 o'clock and then added 12 minutes, it was easier than counting minute-by-minute.

   Ask: How many minutes were the muffins in the oven? 32 minutes

5. Explain that students can count forward first by hours and then by minutes to get to the target time, or they can use the method of counting minutes forward to the next whole hour and then count on by hours. Either way, remind them to record the hours and minutes as they count forward.

6. Have students read Problems 3 and 4. Help them count as they move the minute hand. Help them keep track of the hours and minutes and record their answers on the printout.

   Ask: In Problem 3, how long was Kelly at the zoo? 4 hours and 25 minutes

   Ask: In Problem 4, how long was the plane in the air? 6 hours and 32 minutes

7. Have students read Problem 5. Explain that they can identify the end time when the problem gives them the start time and the elapsed time.

   - Have students set the clock to 2:10.

   - Have them move the minute hand forward 2 hours and 7 minutes. Help them count as they move the hand around the clock.

   Ask: What time did the movie end? 4:17

8. Have students complete Problems 6–8 on the printout. Help them as necessary with counting the hours and minutes as they move the minute hand of the learning tool.

   Ask: In Problem 6, what time did Mr. Walters return home? 9:53

   Ask: In Problem 7, what time did Lee's karate class end? 5:10

   Ask: In Problem 8, what time did Becky finish her art project? 9:05

LEARN Across A.M. and P.M.

ONLINE
20min

Objectives

- Determine elapsed time to the nearest minute.

Students will learn how to find the elapsed time in story problems that give a start and end time for events that cross over 12:00 noon or 12:00 midnight. They will also learn how to find the end time of events when the elapsed time crosses over 12:00 noon or 12:00 midnight.

Gather the Across A.M. and P.M. printout.

DIRECTIONS FOR USING THE CLOCK LEARNING TOOL

1. Click Begin.

2. Remind students that elapsed time is the amount of time that passes between a start time and an end time. Tell students that they will learn about elapsed time that crosses from a.m. to p.m. and from p.m. to a.m.

3. Give students the printout and have them read Problem 1.

   - Have students drag the minute hand around the analog clock until the time is 10:30 a.m., the starting time in Problem 1.

   - Tell students that, to find out how long Jake spends at the museum, they will need to drag the minute hand to 1:43 p.m., the ending time, and count forward while doing so.

   - Have them move the minute hand 3 full rotations and count aloud "1 hour, 2 hours, 3 hours." They should make a note on the printout that they have counted 3 hours.

   - As they drag the minute hand past 12 o'clock, have them observe that a.m. changes to p.m., the word *noon* appears, and the sun pops up.

   - Tell students that now they have to count from 1:30 p.m. to 1:43 p.m. to complete the elapsed time. Have them move the minute hand 10 minutes and then 3 minutes.

   - **Say:** 1:30 to 1:40 is 10 minutes, and 1:40 to 1:43 is 3 minutes, for 13 minutes.

- Have students make a note on the printout that they counted 13 minutes. They should see that their notes show 3 hours and 13 minutes.

   Ask: How long did Jake spend at the museum? 3 hours and 13 minutes

4. Have students read Problem 2 on the printout and drag the minute hand to set the time to 11:50 a.m.

   - Ask students to first drag the minute hand and count the number of minutes until noon, which is 10 minutes. They should make a note of 10 minutes on their printout.

   - Then they should drag the minute hand and count another 1 hour and 27 minutes to get to 1:27 p.m. and make a note of that time span. Then they should add 1 hour and 27 minutes to 10 minutes for a total of 1 hour and 37 minutes.

   - Explain that they can use that method of counting time before 12 o'clock and then after 12 o'clock and then adding the two times together.

5. Repeat Steps 3 and 4 to guide students to complete Problems 3 and 4 on the printout. As students move the clock hands in Problem 4, have them note that when the clock shows 12 midnight, the word *midnight* appears and the moon appears.

   Ask: How much time did Tyler spend at the zoo? 3 hours and 52 minutes

   Ask: How much time did Eddie sleep? 9 hours and 31 minutes

6. Tell students they will now find the end time of events that cross from a.m. to p.m. and from p.m. to a.m. They will be given the start time and elapsed time.

7. Have students read Problem 5 and drag the minute hand to set the clock to 11:30 a.m.

   - Have students start by moving the minute hand 7 full rotations, counting aloud by hours as they go. The clock will show 6:30 p.m.

   - Have students move the minute hand 20 minutes past 6:30 p.m.

   Ask: What time does the clock show and what is the answer to Problem 5? 6:50 p.m.

8. Have students read Problems 6–8 and guide them to find the end times by using the learning tool.

   Ask: What time did Mrs. Kish finish painting the dining room? 2:43 p.m.

   Ask: What time does Tonya's dance class end? 12:20 p.m.

   Ask: What time did Monica wake up? 7:22 a.m.

Tips Allow students to try finding elapsed time across 12:00 noon and 12:00 midnight by visualizing the clock hands moving forward. Begin by giving them some short elapsed-time problems.

TRY IT How Much Time?

Students will practice determining elapsed time to the nearest minute. They also will practice finding the end time when they are given the start time and elapsed time. View or print the How Much Time? activity page and read the directions with students.

• Determine elapsed time to the nearest minute.

Students should copy the problems from the Activity Book into their Math Notebook as necessary and solve them there.

Tips   Have students show the start time on a clock drawing. Then have them count forward on the model to determine the elapsed time.

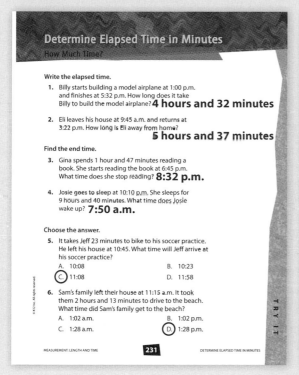

Determine Elapsed Time in Minutes
How Much Time?

Write the elapsed time.

1. Billy starts building a model airplane at 1:00 p.m. and finishes at 5:32 p.m. How long does it take Billy to build the model airplane? **4 hours and 32 minutes**

2. Eli leaves his house at 9:45 a.m. and returns at 3:22 p.m. How long is Eli away from home?
   5 hours and 37 minutes

Find the end time.

3. Gina spends 1 hour and 47 minutes reading a book. She starts reading the book at 6:45 p.m. What time does she stop reading? **8:32 p.m.**

4. Josie goes to sleep at 10:10 p.m. She sleeps for 9 hours and 40 minutes. What time does Josie wake up? **7:50 a.m.**

Choose the answer.

5. It takes Jeff 23 minutes to bike to his soccer practice. He left his house at 10:45. What time will Jeff arrive at his soccer practice?
   A. 10:08   B. 10:23
   (C) 11:08   D. 11:58

6. Sam's family left their house at 11:15 a.m. It took them 2 hours and 13 minutes to drive to the beach. What time did Sam's family get to the beach?
   A. 1:02 a.m.   B. 1:02 p.m.
   C. 1:28 a.m.   (D) 1:28 p.m.

MEASUREMENT: LENGTH AND TIME   **231**   DETERMINE ELAPSED TIME IN MINUTES

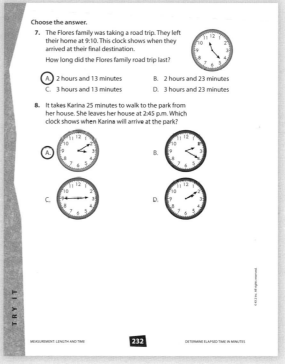

Choose the answer.

7. The Flores family was taking a road trip. They left their home at 9:10. This clock shows when they arrived at their final destination.

   How long did the Flores family road trip last?

   (A) 2 hours and 13 minutes   B. 2 hours and 23 minutes
   C. 3 hours and 13 minutes   D. 3 hours and 23 minutes

8. It takes Karina 25 minutes to walk to the park from her house. She leaves her house at 2:45 p.m. Which clock shows when Karina will arrive at the park?

   (A)   B.

   C.   D.

MEASUREMENT: LENGTH AND TIME   **232**   DETERMINE ELAPSED TIME IN MINUTES

Measure and Display Time Intervals

Lesson Overview

LEARN Problem Solving with Time Intervals   20 minutes   **OFFLINE**

▶ Lesson Objectives

- Solve word problems involving addition and subtraction of time intervals in minutes.
- Represent problems involving time intervals in minutes on a number-line diagram.

▶ Content Background

Students will build on their previous knowledge of number-line addition and subtraction to solve problems involving the addition and subtraction of time intervals.

LEARN Problem Solving with Time Intervals   OFFLINE 20min

Students will build on their previous knowledge of number-line addition and subtraction to solve problems involving the addition and subtraction of time intervals.

View or print the Problem Solving with Time Intervals activity page.

1. Read the Worked Example with students.

   Ask: What is the problem asking us to do? Use the number line to find what time Priscilla finished playing.

   Ask: How many minutes are between the marks on the number line? 5

   Ask: How can you use the number line to find the answer? First, start at 3:15. Move 2 marks for the 10 minutes of bicycle riding time, then 3 more marks for the 15 minutes of time spent playing catch. The answer is where I end up on the number line.

   Ask: What is the solution? Priscilla finished playing at 3:40 p.m.

2. Have students complete Problems 1–5, referring to the Worked Example as needed. Students should copy the problems into their Math Notebook as necessary and solve them there.

Objectives

- Solve word problems involving addition and subtraction of time intervals in minutes.
- Represent problems involving time intervals in minutes on a number-line diagram.

Tips

Be sure students pay close attention when moving from morning times (a.m.) to afternoon times (p.m.).

Also, when students subtract time intervals, emphasize that they should begin at the ending time and work backward through the time intervals, moving left on the number line.

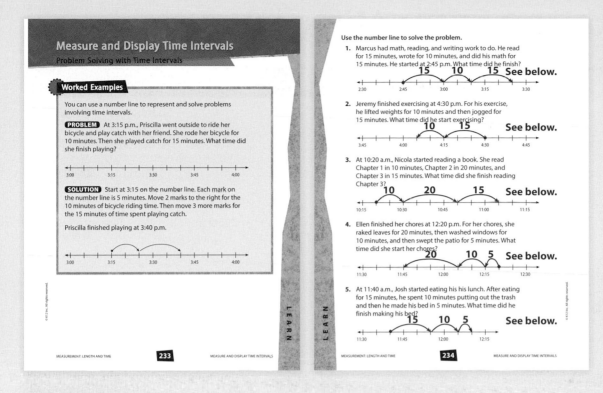

Measure and Display Time Intervals
Problem Solving with Time Intervals

Worked Examples

You can use a number line to represent and solve problems involving time intervals.

PROBLEM At 3:15 p.m., Priscilla went outside to ride her bicycle and play catch with her friend. She rode her bicycle for 10 minutes. Then she played catch for 15 minutes. What time did she finish playing?

SOLUTION Start at 3:15 on the number line. Each mark on the number line is 5 minutes. Move 2 marks to the right for the 10 minutes of bicycle riding time. Then move 3 more marks for the 15 minutes of time spent playing catch.

Priscilla finished playing at 3:40 p.m.

Use the number line to solve the problem.

1. Marcus had math, reading, and writing work to do. He read for 15 minutes, wrote for 10 minutes, and did his math for 15 minutes. He started at 2:45 p.m. What time did he finish? **See below.**

2. Jeremy finished exercising at 4:30 p.m. For his exercise, he lifted weights for 10 minutes and then jogged for 15 minutes. What time did he start exercising? **See below.**

3. At 10:20 a.m., Nicola started reading a book. She read Chapter 1 in 10 minutes, Chapter 2 in 20 minutes, and Chapter 3 in 15 minutes. What time did she finish reading Chapter 3? **See below.**

4. Ellen finished her chores at 12:20 p.m. For her chores, she raked leaves for 20 minutes, then washed windows for 10 minutes, and then swept the patio for 5 minutes. What time did she start her chores? **See below.**

5. At 11:40 a.m., Josh started eating his his lunch. After eating for 15 minutes, he spent 10 minutes putting out the trash and then he made his bed in 5 minutes. What time did he finish making his bed? **See below.**

MEASUREMENT: LENGTH AND TIME **233** MEASURE AND DISPLAY TIME INTERVALS

MEASUREMENT: LENGTH AND TIME **234** MEASURE AND DISPLAY TIME INTERVALS

Additional Answers

1. Start at 2:45 on the number line. Marcus finished at 3:25 p.m.

2. Start at 4:30 on the number line and work backward. Jeremy started at 4:05 p.m.

3. Start at 10:20 on the number line. Nicola finished reading Chapter 3 at 11:05 a.m.

4. Start at 12:20 on the number line and work backward. Ellen started at 11:45 a.m.

5. Start at 11:40 on the number line. Josh finished making his bed at 12:10 p.m.

Core Focus
Elapsed Time to the Minute

▶ Lesson Objectives

- Determine elapsed time to the nearest minute.
- Solve word problems involving addition and subtraction of time intervals in minutes.

▶ Prerequisite Skills.

Tell time to the nearest minute.

▶ Content Background

Students will review how to determine elapsed time and will practice determining how to find elapsed time to the nearest minute. Elapsed time is the amount of time that passes between a starting and an ending time. Students will learn to find the ending time of an activity given the starting time and the elapsed time. They will also learn to count back from an ending time to determine a starting time.

   Elapsed time can include elapsed hours, elapsed days, elapsed months, or other time periods. Students need to understand that when counting to determine elapsed time, such as hours, they start counting with the hour after the starting time. For example, if students are counting how many hours there are between 2:00 p.m. to 7:00 p.m., they begin counting at 3:00 p.m—that is, 3:00, 4:00, 5:00, 6:00, 7:00—to find that there are 5 hours between 2:00 p.m. and 7:00 p.m.

Materials to Gather

SUPPLIED

Elapsed Time activity page

Find Elapsed Time activity page

ONLINE

10min

GET READY Time to the Nearest Minute

Objectives

- Tell time to the nearest minute

Students will use the Clock Learning Tool to review telling time to the nearest minute.

DIRECTIONS FOR USING THE CLOCK LEARNING TOOL

1. Click Begin and choose the following:
   - Click the clock display button.
   - Uncheck the digital clock box.

2. Drag the minute hand to set the clock to 1:15. Ask students what time the clock says.

3. Remind students that the light-blue numbers on the outer ring of the clock tell how many minutes after the hour it is, and that these numbers are skip-counted by 5s.

4. Move the minute hand to the following times and have students tell you each time.
   - 4:28
   - 10:56
   - 9:12
   - 2:01

5. Tell students the following times and have them set the clock by moving the minute hand.
   - 3:13
   - 1:34
   - 5:49
   - 11:59

LEARN Elapsed Time on the Clock

ONLINE **10**min

Objectives

- Determine elapsed time to the nearest minute.

Students will determine elapsed time in hours and minutes using clock models. Remind students that elapsed time is the amount of time between a starting time and an ending time.

Tips | Have students use counting on as a strategy. For example, to find 2 hours and 3 minutes after 4:05, count on by 2 hours and then by 3 minutes: 5:05, 6:05; 6:06, 6:07, 6:08.

LEARN Elapsed Time

OFFLINE **15**min

Objectives

- Solve word problems involving addition and subtraction of time intervals in minutes.

Students will use their knowledge of elapsed time to solve problems. They will determine the amount of elapsed time from a starting time and an ending time. They will determine an ending time given the starting time and elapsed time.

  View or print the Elapsed Time activity page and read the directions with students.

1. Read the first Worked Example with students.

   Ask: What are you asked to find? what time the soccer team finishes doing drills.

   Ask: How can you find how much time the team spent running and doing drills? Add the two times together.

   Tell students they can use a clock model or a number line to find what time it is after 52 minutes.

   Say: You can count on by 10 minutes. Start at 10:35. 10:45 is 10 minutes. 10:55 is 20 minutes. 11:05 is 30 minutes. 11:15 is 40 minutes. 11:25 is 50 minutes. 11:27 is 52 minutes.

2. Read and review the second Worked Example with students.

Ask: What are you asked to find? what time Don arrived at the mall.

Ask: What information can you use to find the solution? I can use the amount of time Don spent at the shoe store and eating lunch, and the time that Don left the mall.

Ask: How can you use the starting time and elapsed time to find the solution? I can add 34 minutes and 28 minutes to find that Don was there for 62 minutes altogether. Then I can find what time it was 62 minutes before 12:30.

Say: You can count backward from 12:30. 62 minutes is 1 hour and two minutes. One hour before 12:30 p.m. is 11:30 a.m. Two minutes before 11:30 is 11:28 a.m.

Ask: What is the solution? Don arrived at the mall at 11:28 a.m.

3. Have students complete Problems 1 and 2, referring to the Worked Examples as needed. Students should copy the problems into their Math Notebook as necessary and solve them there.

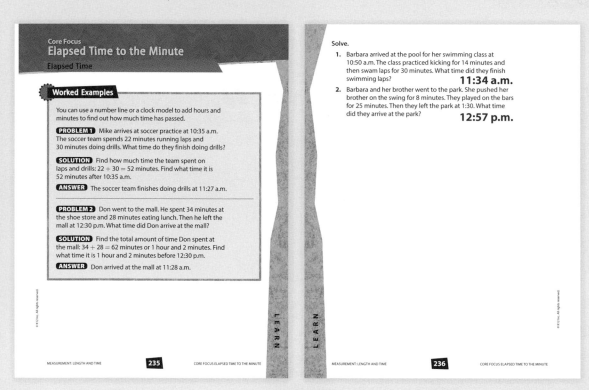

Core Focus
Elapsed Time to the Minute
Elapsed Time

Worked Examples

You can use a number line or a clock model to add hours and minutes to find out how much time has passed.

PROBLEM 1 Mike arrives at soccer practice at 10:35 a.m. The soccer team spends 22 minutes running laps and 30 minutes doing drills. What time do they finish doing drills?

SOLUTION Find how much time the team spent on laps and drills: 22 + 30 = 52 minutes. Find what time it is 52 minutes after 10:35 a.m.

ANSWER The soccer team finishes doing drills at 11:27 a.m.

PROBLEM 2 Don went to the mall. He spent 34 minutes at the shoe store and 28 minutes eating lunch. Then he left the mall at 12:30 p.m. What time did Don arrive at the mall?

SOLUTION Find the total amount of time Don spent at the mall: 34 + 28 = 62 minutes or 1 hour and 2 minutes. Find what time it is 1 hour and 2 minutes before 12:30 p.m.

ANSWER Don arrived at the mall at 11:28 a.m.

Solve.

1. Barbara arrived at the pool for her swimming class at 10:50 a.m. The class practiced kicking for 14 minutes and then swam laps for 30 minutes. What time did they finish swimming laps?   **11:34 a.m.**

2. Barbara and her brother went to the park. She pushed her brother on the swing for 8 minutes. They played on the bars for 25 minutes. Then they left the park at 1:30. What time did they arrive at the park?   **12:57 p.m.**

TRY IT Find Elapsed Time

Objectives

- Determine elapsed time to the nearest minute.
- Solve word problems involving addition and subtraction of time intervals in minutes.

Students will practice determining elapsed time to the nearest minute. They will also practice finding the ending time when they are given the starting time and elapsed time.

View or print the Find Elapsed Time activity page and read the directions with students. They should copy the problems from the Activity Book into their Math Notebook as necessary and solve them there.

Tips   Have students show the starting time on a clock drawing. Then have them count forward on the model to determine the elapsed time.

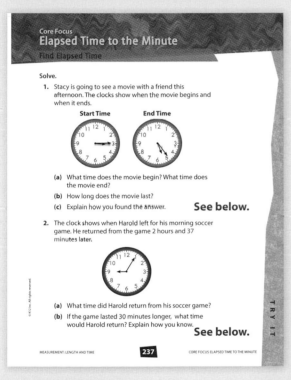

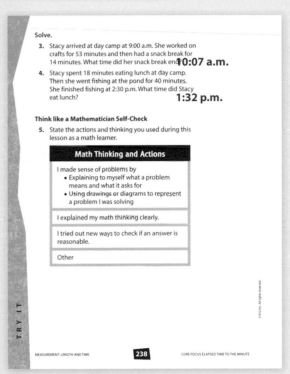

Additional Answers

1. **(a)** The movie begins at 3:15 p.m. and ends at 5:24 p.m.

   (b) The movie lasts 2 hours and 9 minutes.

   (c) Possible explanation: I counted 2 hours from 3:15 to 5:15. Then I counted 9 minutes from 5:15 to 5:24.

2. **(a)** Harold returned at 11:42 a.m.

   (b) 12:12 p.m. **Possible explanation:** I counted on 30 minutes from 11:42.

CHECKPOINT

Objectives

- Determine elapsed time to the nearest minute.
- Solve word problems involving addition and subtraction of time intervals in minutes.

Students will complete an online Checkpoint. If necessary, read the directions, problems, and answer choices to students and help them with keyboard or mouse operations.

Unit Review

Lesson Overview

UNIT REVIEW Look Back	10 minutes	**ONLINE**
UNIT REVIEW Checkpoint Practice	50 minutes	**ONLINE**
⏩ **UNIT REVIEW** Prepare for the Checkpoint		

▶ Unit Objectives

- Identify the appropriate tools for measuring the length of an object.
- Identify the appropriate metric or English units for measuring the length of an object.
- Estimate and measure the length of an object to the nearest centimeter.
- Estimate the length of an object to the nearest $\frac{1}{2}$ inch and measure the length to the nearest $\frac{1}{4}$ inch.
- Interpret and display data on a line plot.
- Collect measurement data and display the data in a line plot.
- Tell time to the nearest minute.
- Determine elapsed time to the nearest minute.
- Solve word problems involving addition and subtraction of time intervals in minutes.
- Represent problems involving time intervals in minutes on a number line.

▶ Advance Preparation

In this lesson, students will have an opportunity to review previous activities in the Measurement: Length and Time unit. Look at the suggested activities in Unit Review: Prepare for the Checkpoint online and gather any needed materials.

Materials to Gather

There are no materials to gather for this lesson.

ONLINE **10min**

UNIT REVIEW Look Back

Students will review key concepts from the unit to prepare for the Unit Checkpoint.

Objectives

- Review unit objectives.

ONLINE **50min**

UNIT REVIEW Checkpoint Practice

Students will complete an online Checkpoint Practice to prepare for the Unit Checkpoint. If necessary, read the directions, problems, and answer choices to students. Have students answer the problems on their own. Carefully review the answers with students.

Objectives

- Review unit objectives.

⏩ UNIT REVIEW Prepare for the Checkpoint

What you do next depends on how students performed in the previous activity, Unit Review: Checkpoint Practice. If students had difficulty with any of the problems, complete the appropriate review activity listed in the table online.

Unit Checkpoint

UNIT CHECKPOINT Online	60 minutes	**ONLINE**

▶ Unit Objectives

- Identify the appropriate tools for measuring the length of an object.
- Identify the appropriate metric or English units for measuring the length of an object.
- Estimate and measure the length of an object to the nearest centimeter.
- Estimate the length of an object to the nearest $\frac{1}{2}$ inch and measure the length to the nearest $\frac{1}{4}$ inch.
- Interpret and display data on a line plot.
- Collect measurement data and display the data in a line plot.
- Tell time to the nearest minute.
- Determine elapsed time to the nearest minute.
- Solve word problems involving addition and subtraction of time intervals in minutes.
- Represent problems involving time intervals in minutes on a number line.

Materials to Gather

There are no materials to gather for this lesson.

ONLINE
60min

UNIT CHECKPOINT Online

Students will complete the Unit Checkpoint online. If necessary, read the directions, problems, and answer choices to students and help them with keyboard or mouse operations.

Objectives

- Assess unit objectives.

Extended Problems: Reasoning

GRADED ASSIGNMENT   60 minutes   **OFFLINE**

▶ Lesson Objectives

- Identify the appropriate metric or English units for measuring the length of an object.
- Estimate the length of an object to the nearest $\frac{1}{2}$ inch and measure the length to the nearest $\frac{1}{4}$ inch.
- Determine elapsed time to the nearest minute.
- Collect measurement data and display the data in a line plot.
- Solve word problems involving addition and subtraction of time intervals in minutes.
- Compare fractions by reasoning about their size.
- Analyze complex problems using mathematical knowledge and skills.

Materials to Gather

SUPPLIED

Extended Problems: Reasoning (printout)

GRADED ASSIGNMENT   **60** min   **Objectives**

Open the Extended Problems: Reasoning. Read the directions, problems, and answer choices to students, if necessary.

You will grade this assignment.

- Analyze complex problems using mathematical knowledge and skills.

- Students should complete the assignment on their own.
- Students should submit the completed assignment to you.
- Enter the results online.

Measurement: Capacity and Weight

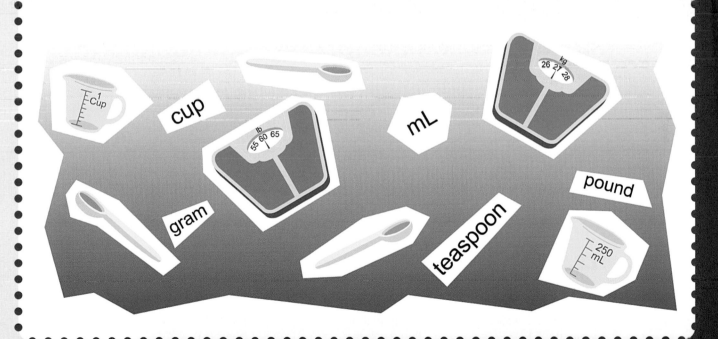

▶ Unit Objectives

- Identify the appropriate tools for measuring liquid volume.
- Identify the appropriate metric and English units for measuring liquid volume.
- Estimate and measure liquid volume to the nearest liter.
- Estimate and measure liquid volume to the nearest cup.
- Identify the appropriate tools for measuring the weight or mass of an object.
- Identify the appropriate metric and English units for measuring the weight or mass of an object.
- Estimate and measure the mass of an object to the nearest gram.
- Estimate and measure the weight of an object to the nearest ounce.
- Write a simple unit conversion, such as inches to feet, as an expression or an equation.
- Use a simple unit conversion, such as centimeters to meters, to solve a problem.
- Solve a unit-conversion story problem by using multiplication or division.
- Solve one-step word problems involving volume.
- Solve one-step word problems involving mass.

▶ Big Ideas

Measurement is the process of repeatedly using a unit over a quantity to determine how much you have.

▶ Unit Introduction

In this unit, students will extend their understanding of measurement of weight, mass, and liquid volume. They will identify appropriate metric and English measurement tools and will become familiar with the units in each measurement system. Students will estimate liquid measures to the nearest liter and cup, and they will estimate weight to the nearest ounce and mass to the nearest gram. They will use their understanding of measurement units to write simple unit conversions such as inches to feet, or centimeters to meters. Finally they will use unit conversions to solve story problems.

▶ Keywords

capacity	gallon (gal)	ounce (oz)
cup (c)	gram (g)	pint (pt)
equivalent measures	kilogram (kg)	pound (lb)
estimate (n.)	liquid volume	quart (qt)
estimate (v.)	liter (L)	teaspoon (t)
expression	mass	tablespoon (T)
fluid ounce (fl oz)	milliliter (mL)	weight

Capacity

Lesson Overview

GET READY Chart Liquid Measures	5 minutes	OFFLINE
LEARN Tools and English Units	15 minutes	OFFLINE
LEARN Tools and Metric Units	20 minutes	OFFLINE
TRY IT Tools and Units to Measure Capacity	10 minutes	OFFLINE
CHECKPOINT	10 minutes	ONLINE

▶ ## Lesson Objectives

- Identify the appropriate tools for measuring liquid volume.
- Identify the appropriate metric and English units for measuring liquid volume.

▶ ## Prerequisite Skills

Measure and compare capacities by using a standard unit (for example, use a measuring cup to measure contents of a water bottle).

▶ ## Content Background

Students will learn which tools and units are used to measure liquid volume, or capacity. They will learn about both metric and English units.

Students will have experiences throughout their lives measuring or judging amounts of liquid volume or capacity. Such experiences might include measuring in cooking, making lemonade, drinking an adequate amount of water in a day, equally sharing a bottle of water with a friend, and deciding how much juice to buy for a large group. As adults, they might mix paints, make homemade cleaning solutions with vinegar and baking soda, and possibly mix chemicals.

Throughout this lesson, the term *capacity* will be used interchangeably with *liquid volume*. Students will use both the metric and English systems of measuring liquids. Within the metric system, students will work with milliliters (mL) and liters (L) as the units of measure. Within the English system (also known as the customary system), they will work with teaspoons (t), tablespoons (T), fluid ounces (fl oz), cups (c), pints (pt), quarts (qt), and gallons (gal) as the units of measure. Students will use a variety of measuring spoons, cups, and marked containers in their work.

▶ ## Advance Preparation

For the Get Ready: Chart Liquid Measures activity, have commercial containers or packaging for liquids available from the pantry, refrigerator, or recycling bin. Bottles, cans, and jars should indicate liquid measures, including milliliters (mL), liters (L), fluid ounces (fl oz), cups (c), pints (pt), quarts (qt), and gallons (gal).

Materials to Gather

SUPPLIED

base-10 ones cube

base-10 thousands cube

Tools and Units to Measure Capacity activity page

ALSO NEEDED

household objects – labeled commercial containers for various liquids, tablespoon, teaspoon, 1-cup liquid measuring cup, 250-milliliter liquid measuring cup

containers, transparent beverage – pint, quart, gallon, half-liter, 1 liter, 2 liter

water

index cards – 13

marker, permanent

tape, masking

For the Learn: Tools and English Units activity, copy this chart in the Math Notebook:

_____ teaspoons = 1 tablespoon
_____ tablespoons = 1 cup
_____ cups = 1 pint
_____ pints = 1 quart
_____ quarts = 1 gallon

For the Learn: Tools and English Units activity, label seven index cards with the following: **English measures**, **teaspoon**, **tablespoon**, **cup**, **pint**, **quart**, and **gallon**. Mix them up in a pile. Gather a liquid measuring cup and beverage containers in three different sizes (pint, quart, and gallon). Use the measuring cup to pour exactly 2 cups of water into the pint container. (Use a funnel if needed.) Mark the level of the liquid on the container with a permanent marker or the bottom edge of a piece of masking tape. Pour exactly 2 pints (4 cups) of water into the quart container and mark the level of the liquid on the container. Pour exactly 4 quarts into the gallon container and mark the level of the liquid on the container. Empty all containers.

For the Learn: Tools and Metric Units activity, label six index cards with the following: **metric measures**, **1 mL**, **250 mL**, **half-liter**, **1 liter**, and **2 liter**. Mix them up in a pile. Gather a liquid measuring cup marked in milliliters up to 250 mL and beverage containers in three different sizes (half-liter, 1 liter, and 2 liter). Pour exactly 500 mL into the half-liter container. Mark the level of the liquid on the container with a permanent marker or the bottom edge of a piece of masking tape. Pour exactly 1,000 mL into the 1-liter container and mark the level of the liquid on the container. Pour exactly 2,000 mL into the 2-liter container and mark the level of the liquid on the container. Empty all containers.

OFFLINE

GET READY Chart Liquid Measures

5 min

Objectives

Students will find labels on cans, jars, and bottles that contain liquids to see how the contents are measured. They will make a chart of their findings.

Gather the labeled commercial containers for liquids.

1. Have students make a three-column chart in their Math Notebook. The columns should be labeled **Type of liquid**, **English measure**, and **Metric measure**.

2. Have students examine the commercial containers to see how the contents are measured.

3. Direct students to list their findings on the chart, recording both the English and metric measures.

4. Mention to students that liquids are often labeled on containers in fluid ounces, but cooking requires measuring in cups. Tell them that 1 cup is 8 fluid ounces. Have students notice the abbreviations on the containers. They will learn more about the abbreviations in later lessons.

5. Summarize the activity by discussing the various English and metric units for measuring liquid volume.

- Measure and compare capacities by using a standard unit (for example, use a measuring cup to measure contents of a water bottle).

Type of liquid	English measure	Metric measure
can of soup: serving size	$\frac{1}{2}$ cup	120 mL
vanilla	1 fl oz	29 mL
milk	1 gal	3.78 L

LEARN Tools and English Units

Students will explore tools and English units for measuring liquid volume.
Gather the index cards labeled with English units; teaspoon, tablespoon, and 1-cup liquid measuring cup; pint, quart, and gallon containers. Arrange the measuring tools in order—teaspoon, tablespoon, cup, pint, quart, and gallon. Have students turn to the prepared chart in their Math Notebook.

1. Tell students they will be working with tools and measuring units in the English system. Explain that they will be filling a tool with water and pouring the water into the next measuring tool until that tool is filled.

2. Have students fill the first tool—the teaspoon—with water and pour the water into the tablespoon. Guide students to continue filling the teaspoon with water and pouring it into the tablespoon until the tablespoon is filled. Students should count as they work.

3. Have students record the number of teaspoons in the chart in their notebook.

4. As students work, have them explain their actions. For example, "I am using a measuring spoon that measures in teaspoons to fill this tablespoon."

5. Have students take the water-filled tablespoon and pour the water into the next measuring tool—the 1-cup liquid measuring cup. Students should then continue filling the tablespoon with water and pouring the water into the cup until the cup is filled.

6. Have students record the number of tablespoons in a cup and explain their actions. For example, "I am now using a measuring spoon that measures in tablespoons to fill this cup."

7. Continue with the next container, repeating Steps 2–4 until students have filled the last measuring tool—the gallon container. (Students may want to use a funnel.)

8. Once the gallon container is full, place the **English measures** card on the table. Have students line up the measuring tools in order from least to greatest capacity. Have students name each tool and the unit it measures. For the pint, quart, and gallon containers, the name of the tool can be "container", or whatever the container actually is, such as a juice bottle.

9. Have students put the index card for each measuring unit next to the appropriate container.

Objectives

- Identify the appropriate tools for measuring liquid volume.
- Identify the appropriate metric and English units for measuring liquid volume.

Tips

Have students work on a surface near a sink or provide them with a large container filled with water.

$\underline{\quad 3 \quad}$ teaspoons = 1 tablespoon
$\underline{\quad 16 \quad}$ tablespoons = 1 cup
$\underline{\quad 2 \quad}$ cups = 1 pint
$\underline{\quad 2 \quad}$ pints = 1 quart
$\underline{\quad 4 \quad}$ quarts = 1 gallon

LEARN Tools and Metric Units

Students will explore tools and metric units for measuring liquid volume.
Gather the base-10 cubes; index cards labeled with metric units; 250-milliliter liquid measuring cup; and half-pint, 1-liter, and 2-liter containers. Arrange the measuring tools in order—250-milliliter liquid measuring cup, half-liter container, 1-liter container, and 2-liter container.

1. Display the base-10 ones cube.

   Say: If the ones cube were hollow, it would hold exactly 1 mL of liquid. So a milliliter is not very much liquid.

2. Display the base-10 thousands cube.

   Ask: How many ones cubes are in this thousands cube? 1,000

Objectives

- Identify the appropriate tools for measuring liquid volume.
- Identify the appropriate metric and English units for measuring liquid volume.

3. Explain that if the thousands cube were hollow, it would hold 1,000 milliliters, which is the same as a liter.

4. Tell students that they will be working with tools and measuring units in the metric system. Explain that they will be filling a tool with water and pouring the water into the next measuring tool until that tool is filled.

5. In the Math Notebook, write the following for students to complete as they fill the containers:

___ mL = 1 half-liter

___ mL = 1 liter

___ mL = 2 liters

6. Have students fill the first tool—the 250-milliliter measuring cup—with water and pour the water into the half-liter container. Guide students to continue filling the cup with water and pouring it into the container until the water level reaches the mark. They should count as they work. (Students may want to use a funnel.)

7. Have students explain their actions. For example, "I am using a measuring cup that measures 250 milliliters to fill this half-liter container."

8. Guide students to calculate the number of milliliters in the half-liter container. 500 mL

   Have students record their findings for each container in their notebook. Explain that mL is the abbreviation for milliliter.

9. Have students use the half-liter container to fill the next container—the 1-liter container.

10. Have students explain their actions and determine the number of milliliters needed to fill the 1-liter container. 1,000 mL

11. Have students compare the 1-liter capacity to the base-10 thousands cube. Remind them that if the thousands cube could be filled with water, it would hold 1,000 mL, which is the same as 1 liter.

12. Have students continue the process using the 1-liter container to fill the 2-liter container. Have students explain their actions and complete the chart indicating the number of milliliters equal to 2 liters. 2,000 mL

13. Once the 2-liter container is full, place the **metric measures** card on the table. Have students line up the measuring tools (including the base-10 ones cube and thousands cube) in order from least capacity to greatest. Have students name each tool and the unit it measures. The thousands cube and liter container should be together, since they have the same capacity. For the half-liter, 1-liter, and 2-liter containers, the name of the tool can be "container" or whatever the container actually is, such as a water bottle.

14. Have students put the index card for each measuring unit next to the appropriate container.

_500_ mL = 1 half-liter
_1,000_ mL = 1 liter
_2,000_ mL = 2 liters

OFFLINE

10 min

TRY IT Tools and Units to Measure Capacity

Students will practice identifying the appropriate tool or unit for measuring liquid volume. View or print the Tools and Units to Measure Capacity activity page and read the directions with students.

Students should copy the problems from the Activity Book into their Math Notebook as necessary and solve them there.

Capacity
Tools and Units to Measure Capacity

Circle the tools or units that match the description.

1. Tools that measure capacity, or liquid volume:

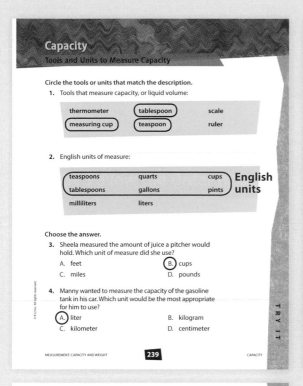

thermometer   (tablespoon)   scale
(measuring cup)   (teaspoon)   ruler

2. English units of measure:

(teaspoons)   (quarts)   (cups)   **English units**
(tablespoons)   (gallons)   (pints)
milliliters   liters

Choose the answer.

3. Sheela measured the amount of juice a pitcher would hold. Which unit of measure did she use?
- A. feet
- (B.) cups
- C. miles
- D. pounds

4. Manny wanted to measure the capacity of the gasoline tank in his car. Which unit would be the most appropriate for him to use?
- (A.) liter
- B. kilogram
- C. kilometer
- D. centimeter

TRY IT

Choose the answer.

5. Lena washed a load of clothes. How much water did the washing machine likely hold when it was full?
- A. 30 fluid ounces
- B. 30 cups
- C. 30 pints
- (D.) 30 gallons

6. How much liquid is the spoon most likely to hold?
- A. 15 liters
- B. 15 meters
- C. 15 centimeters
- (D.) 15 milliliters

7. The capacity of which container is most likely measured in gallons?

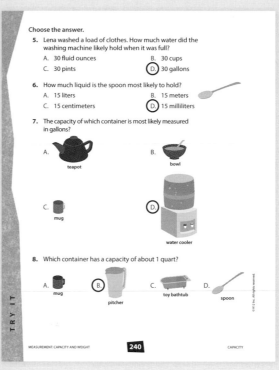

A. teapot   B. bowl   C. mug   (D.) water cooler

8. Which container has a capacity of about 1 quart?

A. mug   (B.) pitcher   C. toy bathtub   D. spoon

TRY IT

---

9. Marilyn's plant needs 8 fluid ounces of water twice a week. Which is the **best** tool to use to measure the amount of water the plant needs for 1 week?
- A. ruler
- B. balance
- C. thermometer
- (D.) measuring cup

10. Clarissa is baking a cake. She needs to measure some milk for the batter. Which measurement tool should Clarissa use?

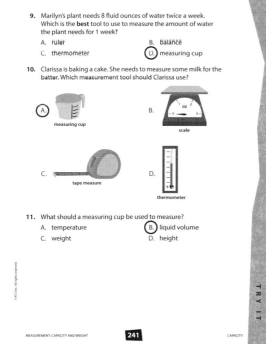

(A.) measuring cup   B. scale   C. tape measure   D. thermometer

11. What should a measuring cup be used to measure?
- A. temperature
- (B.) liquid volume
- C. weight
- D. height

TRY IT

ONLINE 10 min

CHECKPOINT

Students will complete an online Checkpoint. If necessary, read the directions, problems, and answer choices to students and help them with keyboard or mouse operations.

Objectives

- Identify the appropriate tools for measuring liquid volume.
- Identify the appropriate metric and English units for measuring liquid volume.

Measure to the Nearest Liter

GET READY Milliliters and Liters	5 minutes	**ONLINE**
LEARN Estimate and Measure in Liters	30 minutes	**OFFLINE**
TRY IT Identify Volume	15 minutes	**OFFLINE**
CHECKPOINT	10 minutes	**ONLINE**

▶ **Lesson Objectives**

Estimate and measure liquid volume to the nearest liter.

▶ **Prerequisite Skills**

Identify the appropriate metric and English units for measuring liquid volume.

▶ **Content Background**

Students will learn to estimate the capacity of various containers in liters. Students will then use a liter container to find the actual capacity of each container.

While many quantities need to be measured precisely, some can simply be estimated. Estimation is important for students, since it focuses them on which unit is being used in the measurement and helps them develop a greater feel for the size of that unit. Most students view estimating as a fun guessing game. They will learn that the more they estimate and check their estimates, the better they will become in estimating measures. Measuring precisely is a key skill as well; not doing so can lead to undesirable results, such as a fallen cake, a salty stew, or a watery milk shake.

When finding actual measures, students need to take special care in both using and reading the measuring instrument accurately. They should understand that all measures that the average person makes are only close approximations, both because of the lack of precision of the tools used in daily life and because of human error.

Students will have experiences throughout their lives measuring or judging amounts of liquid volume, or capacity. Such experiences might include measuring in cooking, making lemonade, drinking an adequate amount of water in a day, equally sharing a bottle of water with a friend, and deciding how much juice to buy for a large group. As adults, they might mix paints, make homemade cleaning solutions with vinegar and baking soda, and possibly mix chemicals.

▶ **Common Errors and Misconceptions**

Students might have difficulty knowing how to read the numbers on a measurement scale. They may count the number of tick marks starting with 0 (on a ruler, or scale on the side of a volume measure, for example) rather than the units between the marks. Students may treat the 1 tick mark as the starting point instead of the 0 or place the edge of an object at the 1-inch tick mark rather than the 0 tick mark. Students might have the same problems when reading a volume measure (on a measuring jug, for example).

Materials to Gather

SUPPLIED

Identify Volume activity page

ALSO NEEDED

household objects – various containers that hold more than 1 liter, 250-milliliter liquid measuring cup

container, transparent beverage – 1 liter

water

index cards – 4

markers, permanent – 2 colors

tape, masking

▶ Advance Preparation

On two index cards, write the following in one color: **milliliter** and **liter**. On two index cards, write the following abbreviations in another color: **mL** and **L**. On the back of all four cards, write **Metric Capacity Units**.

Gather containers such as pitchers, buckets and plastic trash containers of varying sizes, and other containers that can hold water.

GET READY Milliliters and Liters

Students will be shown an object that holds liquid and will identify whether the liquid volume would be measured in milliliters or liters. Explain to students that when they measure an amount of liquid, they are measuring liquid volume. When they find how much liquid a container holds, they measure the liquid capacity of the container. They should say, "The volume of liquid is 1 liter" or "The capacity of the container is 1 liter."

Have students write the words *volume* and *capacity* in their Math Notebook.

Objectives

• Identify the appropriate metric and English units for measuring liquid volume.

LEARN Estimate and Measure in Liters

Students will estimate the capacity of containers in liters. They will then use a 1-liter container to find the actual measurement of each container.

Gather the labeled index cards, markers, measuring cup, tape, and containers.

1. Lay out the index cards with the **Metric Capacity Units** side showing.

2. Turn over the card that says **milliliter** first, followed by the card that says liter. Put these cards side by side. Turn over the cards with the abbreviations and give them to students. Have students place each abbreviation card under the word they think the abbreviation matches. They should learn how to say and recognize each word and how to recognize and write each abbreviation.

3. Have students fill the measuring cup 4 times. Have them pour the water (a total of 1,000 mL) into a 1-liter container, such as a large water or soda bottle. Have them mark the level of the liquid on the container with a permanent marker or with the bottom edge of a piece of masking tape. Tell students their bottle now holds 1 liter. Explain that they'll be using this bottle to measure the number of liters other containers can hold.

4. Tell students they will be estimating how many liters will fill a variety of containers before actually measuring to see how close their estimates were. Let them know that the more they practice estimating, the easier it will be.

5. Have students make a three-column chart in their Math Notebook. The columns should be labeled **Container**, **My estimate**, and **Actual liters**.

Objectives

• Estimate and measure liquid volume to the nearest liter.

Tips

Have students work on a surface near a sink or provide them with a large container filled with water.

When students are filling the 1-liter container, make sure that the liquid is level with the line they drew or masking tape they placed.

6. Have students move from one container to the next (in any order), first recording on the chart the type of container and then making an estimate of how many liters it will hold. When measuring the capacity of cooking pots or bowls, students should pick a height near the top of the pot or bowl, mark that spot with tape, and then estimate how many liters it would take to fill it to that level. Since people usually don't fill pots to the brim when cooking, students don't need to measure to the brim. They should measure to the nearest liter.

7. Have students fill their bottle to the liter mark, and then pour the water into one of the containers. (Students may want to use the funnel.) They should count the liters as they fill the container with their liter bottle. Ask students to come up with a good way to keep track of the number of liters (such as tally marks or laying down an index card or tile for each liter they pour). They should record the actual measurement on their chart to the nearest liter. Have them repeat this process until they've measured the capacity of all the containers.

8. Have students estimate and then measure the capacity of the kitchen sink or another nearby sink. Use a drain plug and then fill the sink 1 liter at a time to find the actual measure. This activity will provide a valuable reference point for students as they estimate larger capacities. A typical kitchen sink holds about 20 liters of water.

9. Have students review their estimates and measurements to see how close they were.

10. Tell students that the measures most people make are only very close approximations because of the lack of precision of the tools used in daily life and because of human error.

TRY IT Identify Volume

OFFLINE
15 min

Objectives

- Estimate and measure liquid volume to the nearest liter.

Students will practice estimating and identifying the liquid volume of various objects. View or print the Identify Volume activity page and read the directions with students. Remind them that they can think about the capacity of items they know to estimate the capacity of other items. Some measurements that may be helpful include a kitchen sink, which typically holds about 20 liters, and a bathtub, which typically holds about 160 liters.

Students should copy the problems from the Activity Book into their Math Notebook as necessary and solve them there.

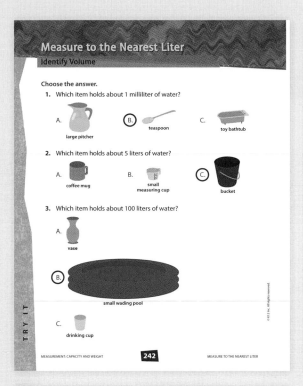

Measure to the Nearest Liter
Identify Volume

Choose the answer.

1. Which item holds about 1 milliliter of water?

   A. large pitcher   (B.) teaspoon   C. toy bathtub

2. Which item holds about 5 liters of water?

   A. coffee mug   B. small measuring cup   (C.) bucket

3. Which item holds about 100 liters of water?

   A. vase

   (B.) small wading pool

   C. drinking cup

MEASUREMENT: CAPACITY AND WEIGHT   **242**   MEASURE TO THE NEAREST LITER

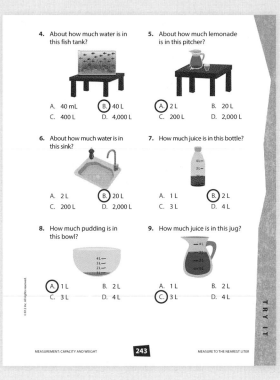

4. About how much water is in this fish tank?

   A. 40 mL   (B.) 40 L
   C. 400 L   D. 4,000 L

5. About how much lemonade is in this pitcher?

   (A.) 2 L   B. 20 L
   C. 200 L   D. 2,000 L

6. About how much water is in this sink?

   A. 2 L   (B.) 20 L
   C. 200 L   D. 2,000 L

7. How much juice is in this bottle?

   A. 1 L   (B.) 2 L
   C. 3 L   D. 4 L

8. How much pudding is in this bowl?

   (A.) 1 L   B. 2 L
   C. 3 L   D. 4 L

9. How much juice is in this jug?

   A. 1 L   B. 2 L
   (C.) 3 L   D. 4 L

MEASUREMENT: CAPACITY AND WEIGHT   **243**   MEASURE TO THE NEAREST LITER

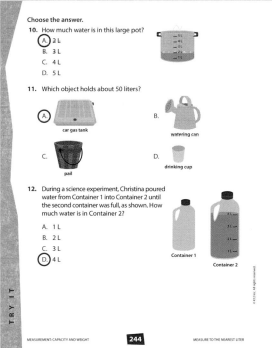

Choose the answer.

10. How much water is in this large pot?

    (A.) 2 L
    B. 3 L
    C. 4 L
    D. 5 L

11. Which object holds about 50 liters?

    (A.) car gas tank   B. watering can

    C. pail   D. drinking cup

12. During a science experiment, Christina poured water from Container 1 into Container 2 until the second container was full, as shown. How much water is in Container 2?

    A. 1 L
    B. 2 L
    C. 3 L
    (D.) 4 L

    Container 1   Container 2

MEASUREMENT: CAPACITY AND WEIGHT   **244**   MEASURE TO THE NEAREST LITER

CHECKPOINT

ONLINE 10 min

Students will complete an online Checkpoint. If necessary, read the directions, problems, and answer choices to students and help them with keyboard or mouse operations.

Objectives

- Estimate and measure liquid volume to the nearest liter.

English Units of Capacity

GET READY Identify English Capacity Units	5 minutes	ONLINE
LEARN Abbreviation Match	5 minutes	ONLINE
LEARN Estimate and Measure Capacity	25 minutes	OFFLINE
TRY IT Estimate Capacity in English Units	15 minutes	OFFLINE
CHECKPOINT	10 minutes	ONLINE

▶ Lesson Objectives

Estimate and measure liquid volume to the nearest cup.

▶ Prerequisite Skills

Identify the appropriate metric and English units for measuring liquid volume.

▶ Content Background

Students will learn to estimate and measure capacity in English units. They will fill various containers with cups of water and explore equivalent measurements of a pint, a quart, and a gallon.

While many quantities need to be measured precisely, some can simply be estimated. Estimation is important for students, since it focuses them on which unit is being used in the measurement and helps them develop a greater feel for the size of a unit. Most students view estimating as a fun guessing game. They will learn that the more they estimate and check their estimates, the better they will become at estimating measures. Measuring precisely is also a key skill, since not doing so can lead to undesirable results, such as a fallen cake, a salty stew, or a watery milkshake.

When finding actual measures, students need to take special care in both using and reading the measuring instrument accurately. They should understand that all measures that the average person makes are only close approximations because of the lack of precision of the tools used in daily life and because of human error.

Students will have experiences throughout their lives measuring or judging amounts of liquid volume, or capacity. Such experiences might include measuring in cooking, making lemonade, drinking an adequate amount of water in a day, equally sharing a bottle of water with a friend, and deciding how much juice to buy for a large group. As adults, they might mix paints, make homemade cleaning solutions with vinegar and baking soda, and possibly mix chemicals.

▶ Advance Preparation

Gather the containers. Suggestions include pitchers, buckets and plastic trash containers of varying sizes, and other containers that can hold water.

Materials to Gather

SUPPLIED

Estimate Capacity in English Units activity page

ALSO NEEDED

household objects – 8-ounce liquid measuring cup

transparent beverage containers – pint, quart, gallon

various containers that hold more than 1 cup

water

GET READY Identify English Capacity Units

ONLINE 5min

Objectives

- Identify the appropriate metric and English units for measuring liquid volume.

Students will identify English units of measure for capacity. Remind them that the capacity of a container is the amount it holds, and that when they're measuring the amount of liquid in a container, they're measuring the liquid volume. Seven units of capacity are used in this activity: teaspoon, tablespoon, fluid ounce, cup, pint, quart, and gallon. If students mix up the terms *ounce* and *fluid ounce*, remind them that ounces are used when measuring weight and fluid ounces are used to measure an amount or volume of liquid.

LEARN Abbreviation Match

ONLINE 5min

Objectives

- Estimate and measure liquid volume to the nearest cup.

Students will practice reading English units of capacity. Then they will match abbreviations to English capacity units. Encourage students to remember the abbreviations. Remind them that there are no periods in these abbreviations.

Students will see the following English units to measure capacity, along with their abbreviations:

- teaspoon (t)
- tablespoon (T)
- fluid ounce (fl oz)
- cup (c)
- pint (pt)
- quart (qt)
- gallon (gal)

LEARN Estimate and Measure Capacity

OFFLINE 25min

Objectives

- Estimate and measure liquid volume to the nearest cup.

Students will estimate and measure the capacity of various containers in English units.
Gather the measuring cup; pint, quart, and gallon containers; and other containers of various sizes.

1. Show students how to fill the measuring cup to the 1-cup mark.
2. Explain to students that 1 cup is also 8 fluid ounces. Remind them that when measuring for cooking, people often measure in cups, but that food packaging often lists the liquid volume in fluid ounces. Students should be familiar with both units of measure.
3. Tell students that they'll estimate how many cups will fill different containers, and then they'll measure to see how many cups each container holds.

   Say: The more you practice estimating and measuring, the easier it will be.

4. Have students make a three-column chart in their Math Notebook. The columns should be labeled **Container**, **My estimate**, and **Actual cups**.
5. Have students choose one of the smaller containers. Guide them to write a name for the container or draw a picture of it in the first column.

   Ask: How many cups do you think will fill this container?

6. Have students record their estimate in the second column.

Tips

Have students work near a sink, in a bathtub, or outdoors to control any spills. Allow them to use a funnel for the smaller containers, if you wish.

7. Have students measure how many cups the container actually holds by pouring 1 cup of water at a time into the container. (Students may want to use the funnel.) Check that they are filling the measuring cup to the 1-cup mark each time. Help them keep track of the number of cups by using tally marks or counters. Guide students to record the closest cup measure.

8. Have students compare the actual capacity to their estimate.

9. Have students repeat Steps 5–7 with each of the other containers. They may know from past experience how many cups a pint, quart, and gallon hold. When they work with each container, encourage them to remember those equivalencies.

10. Have students estimate and then measure the capacity of the kitchen sink or another nearby sink. Use a drain plug and then fill the sink 1 gallon at a time to find the actual measure. This action will provide a valuable reference point for students as they estimate larger capacities. A typical kitchen sink holds about 5 to 6 gallons of water.

11. Summarize by telling students that the measures most people make are only close approximations both because of the lack of precision of the tools used in daily life and because of human error.

OFFLINE

TRY IT Estimate Capacity in English Units   15 min

Objectives

Students will practice estimating capacity in English units. View or print the Estimate Capacity in English Units activity page and read the directions with students. Remind them that they can think about the capacity of items they know to estimate the capacity of other items. Some measurements that may be helpful include a kitchen sink, which is typically holds about 5 to 6 gallons, and a bathtub, which typically holds about 40 gallons.

Students should copy the problems from the Activity Book into their Math Notebook as necessary and solve them there.

- Estimate and measure liquid volume to the nearest cup.

Tips

Provide cup and gallon containers for reference, if you wish.

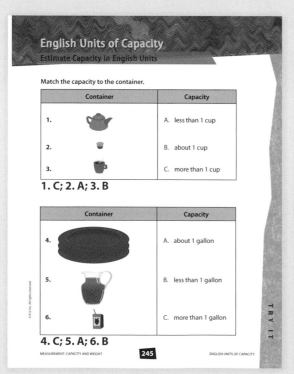

English Units of Capacity
Estimate Capacity in English Units

Match the capacity to the container.

Container	Capacity
1.	A. less than 1 cup
2.	B. about 1 cup
3.	C. more than 1 cup

1. C; 2. A; 3. B

Container	Capacity
4.	A. about 1 gallon
5.	B. less than 1 gallon
6.	C. more than 1 gallon

4. C; 5. A; 6. B

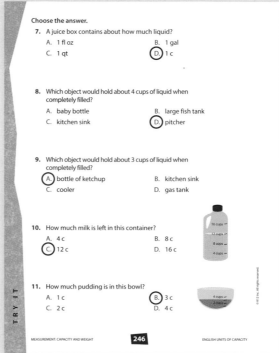

Choose the answer.

7. A juice box contains about how much liquid?
    A. 1 fl oz   B. 1 gal
    C. 1 qt   D. 1 c

8. Which object would hold about 4 cups of liquid when completely filled?
    A. baby bottle   B. large fish tank
    C. kitchen sink   D. pitcher

9. Which object would hold about 3 cups of liquid when completely filled?
    A. bottle of ketchup   B. kitchen sink
    C. cooler   D. gas tank

10. How much milk is left in this container?
    A. 4 c   B. 8 c
    C. 12 c   D. 16 c

11. How much pudding is in this bowl?
    A. 1 c   B. 3 c
    C. 2 c   D. 4 c

T R Y I T

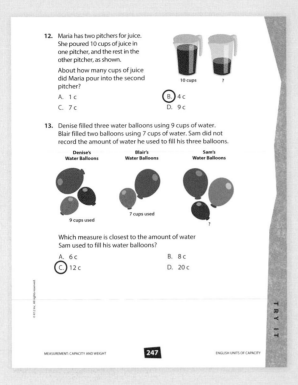

12. Maria has two pitchers for juice. She poured 10 cups of juice in one pitcher, and the rest in the other pitcher, as shown.

About how many cups of juice did Maria pour into the second pitcher?

10 cups   ?

A. 1 c

B. 4 c

C. 7 c

D. 9 c

13. Denise filled three water balloons using 9 cups of water. Blair filled two balloons using 7 cups of water. Sam did not record the amount of water he used to fill his three balloons.

Denise's Water Balloons   Blair's Water Balloons   Sam's Water Balloons

9 cups used   7 cups used   ?

Which measure is closest to the amount of water Sam used to fill his water balloons?

A. 6 c

B. 8 c

C. 12 c

D. 20 c

TRY IT

MEASUREMENT: CAPACITY AND WEIGHT   **247**   ENGLISH UNITS OF CAPACITY

ONLINE

10min

CHECKPOINT

Students will complete an online Checkpoint. If necessary, read the directions, problems, and answer choices to students and help them with keyboard or mouse operations.

Objectives

- Estimate and measure liquid volume to the nearest cup.

Measure in English and Metric Units

Lesson Overview

GET READY Heavier and Lighter	10 minutes	OFFLINE
LEARN Units to Measure Weight and Mass	20 minutes	OFFLINE
LEARN Tools to Measure Weight and Mass	10 minutes	ONLINE
TRY IT Measure Weight and Mass	10 minutes	ONLINE
CHECKPOINT	10 minutes	ONLINE

▶ Lesson Objectives

- Identify the appropriate tools for measuring the weight or mass of an object.
- Identify the appropriate metric and English units for measuring the weight or mass of an object.

▶ Prerequisite Skills

- Compare objects by weight (heavier and lighter).
- Use a nonstandard unit to describe the weight of an object and compare the weights of two or more objects (for example, the pencil is as heavy as 12 paper clips, and the marker is as heavy as 19 paper clips).

▶ Content Background

Students will learn the units to measure weight and mass in the English and metric systems. They will gain an understanding of ounces and pounds, and of grams and kilograms. They will also learn the different tools that can be used to measure weight and mass.

MEASUREMENT OF WEIGHT

Students will have experiences throughout their lives measuring or judging how much objects weigh. Some examples might include weighing themselves or a pet, measuring in cooking, and knowing how long to bake something if directions are given by weight. As adults, they might need to weigh items to be mailed for proper postage, decide how much produce to buy when priced by the pound, estimate how much potato salad to buy when serving a meal to a large group of people, and weigh luggage before flying.

Students will use both the metric and English systems of measuring weight. Within the metric system, they will work with grams (g) and kilograms (kg) as the units of measure. Within the English system (also known as the customary system), they will work with ounces (oz) and pounds (lb) as the units of measure. They will see a variety of types of scales used to weigh objects.

THE DIFFERENCES BETWEEN WEIGHT AND MASS

Weight is the measurement of the pull of gravity on an object, while *mass* is a measurement of the amount of matter something contains. The mass of an object doesn't change when an object's location changes. Weight, on the other hand, does change with location. For example, a baseball on the earth has one

Materials to Gather

SUPPLIED

base-10 ones cubes – 28

ALSO NEEDED

household objects – 2 objects that are about the same size but are different weights, 10 nickels, 9 quarters, 1 $1 bill, 1 banana, 1 orange, 4 sticks of butter (1 lb), 1 can of soup, 1 paper clip, 3 plastic bags (small, clear, resealable)

mass. On the moon, it has the same mass. On the earth, it has one weight; on the moon, it weighs less.

The difference between weight and mass will be introduced later in students' math education. For now, be sure students are aware that the units to measure weight include pounds and ounces and the units to measure mass include grams and kilograms.

▶ Advance Preparation

Gather the various household objects. Place the base-10 ones cubes in a plastic bag, the quarters in a second plastic bag, and the nickels in a third plastic bag.

GET READY Heavier and Lighter

OFFLINE 10 min

Students will explore weight by comparing two objects they hold in their hands. Gather the two objects that are similar in size but different in weight.

Show students the two objects. Ask them which one they think is heavier. Then have them hold the two objects, one in each hand. Have them compare the weights, saying which object is heavier and which is lighter.

Turn the activity into a game in which you look at nearby objects, pick up two objects at a time, and have students guess which one will feel heavier. Then give students the objects so they can judge the weights. Trade places with students, having them pick objects. Then make them guess and compare the objects. Look for objects in every room, such as a knickknack, shoe, couch pillow, bowl, small cooking pot, crayon, and fork. Try to select pairs of objects close in weight but different enough so that anyone holding the objects can tell which one is heavier.

Objectives

- Compare objects by weight (heavier and lighter).
- Use a nonstandard unit to describe the weight of an object and compare the weights of two or more objects (for example, the pencil is as heavy as 12 paper clips, and the marker is as heavy as 19 paper clips).

LEARN Units to Measure Weight and Mass

OFFLINE 20 min

Students will learn the metric and English units used to measure mass and weight. They will also be introduced to the weights of common objects in ounces and pounds, and the mass of objects in grams and kilograms, giving them a general frame of reference for those units of measure. Gather the various household objects.

Explain to students that there are two systems of measurement—the metric system and the English system (sometimes called the customary system). There are different units in each system. Tell students they will explore two units of weight in the English system, the ounce and the pound.

ENGLISH UNITS

1. Show students the bag of base-10 ones cubes. Explain that all these cubes together weigh about 1 ounce.

2. Remove 5 quarters from the bag and give them to students. Explain to students that the 5 quarters also weigh about 1 ounce. Students may compare the ones cubes and the quarters to see that they have about the same weight.

Objectives

- Identify the appropriate tools for measuring the weight or mass of an object.
- Identify the appropriate metric and English units for measuring the weight or mass of an object.

Tips

Make a two-column chart. Label the columns **English units** and **Metric units**. Write "ounce" and "pound" under the **English units** head. Write "gram" and "kilogram" under the **metric units** head.

3. Explain to students that it is helpful to use various objects in their environment as found measures, or known amounts, when weighing other objects. Now that they know what an ounce feels like, they can look for other objects that can be weighed in ounces. Have students identify one more object that weighs about 1 ounce.

4. Have students work with the following objects to identify found measures. They should have the 5 quarters handy.

   • Give students a stick of butter to hold. Ask them if they think the stick of butter weighs more or less than 1 ounce. more

     Tell students that the stick of butter (if packaged 4 to a pound) weighs 4 ounces.

   • Give students an average-sized orange and ask them to compare its weight to the quarters and the butter. The orange weighs more than the quarters and the butter. Tell students that the orange weighs about 12 ounces.

   • Give students a can of soup and explain that it weighs more than the other objects they've worked with. Tell them that the can weighs about 13 ounces. Explain that 16 ounces equals 1 pound and that the can of soup is close to 1 pound.

5. Show students 1 pound of butter. Tell them it weighs 16 ounces, or 1 pound. Allow them to hold the butter and compare its weight to the lighter objects (orange, can of soup).

6. Allow students to identify a variety of objects in their environment that weigh about 1 pound.

METRIC UNITS

7. Tell students that now they will explore two units in the metric system, the gram and the kilogram. Explain that in the metric system, when measuring in grams and kilograms, they say they're measuring the mass of an object.

8. Give students a single base-10 ones cube, a small paper clip, and a $1 bill. Tell them that the mass of each object is about 1 gram. Allow them to pick up each object and compare the masses. Students should notice that the masses are similar. Have them identify other objects that have a mass of about 1 gram.

9. Have students work with the following objects to identify found measures:

   • Give students a nickel. Tell them that the mass of a nickel is about 5 grams. Discuss with students that the mass of 1 nickel is the same as the mass of 5 base-10 ones cubes or 5 small paper clips.

   • Give students the bag of 9 quarters. Explain that the mass of these quarters is about 50 grams. For comparison, tell them that this is 10 times more than the mass of 1 nickel. Students would need 10 nickels to equal 50 grams.

   • Give students a banana. Explain that the mass of a banana is about 170 grams.

   • Give students the can of soup. Discuss that in the metric system, the mass of the can is about 350 grams.

10. Tell students that 1,000 grams equals 1 kilogram. Ask them to find objects labeled in grams that add up to 1,000 grams. Place these objects together to help students understand the measure of 1 kilogram.

11. Ask students to identify other objects in their environment that have a mass of about 1 kilogram.

LEARN Tools to Measure Weight and Mass

Students will learn about various tools to measure weight and mass. They will see a variety of scales and balances, and they'll learn which units correspond to the different tools.

After students have studied the scales, take them to the local grocery or hardware store. Allow them to identify the different scales used in the stores. Have them find the weight or mass of fruits and vegetables at the grocery store and compare the weight of different-sized boxes of nails at the hardware store. Some hardware stores sell nails by the pound and have a scale that students can see. Have students note whether the scales give the weight or mass in English or metric units or both.

- Identify the appropriate tools for measuring the weight or mass of an object.
- Identify the appropriate metric and English units for measuring the weight or mass of an object.

TRY IT Measure Weight and Mass

Students will complete an online Try It. If necessary, read the directions, problems, and answer choices to students and help them with keyboard or mouse operations.

- Identify the appropriate tools for measuring the weight or mass of an object.
- Identify the appropriate metric and English units for measuring the weight or mass of an object.

CHECKPOINT

Students will complete an online Checkpoint. If necessary, read the directions, problems, and answer choices to students and help them with keyboard or mouse operations.

- Identify the appropriate tools for measuring the weight or mass of an object.
- Identify the appropriate metric and English units for measuring the weight or mass of an object.

Measure in Grams

▶ Lesson Objectives

Estimate and measure the mass of an object to the nearest gram.

▶ Prerequisite Skills

Identify the appropriate metric and English units for measuring the mass or weight of an object.

▶ Content Background

Students will learn to measure and estimate the mass of an object to the nearest gram. In this lesson, they will use the metric system of measuring mass. Within the metric system, they will work with grams (g) and kilograms (kg) as the units of measure.

Students will have experiences throughout their lives measuring or judging how much objects weigh. Some examples include weighing themselves or a pet, measuring in cooking, and knowing how long to bake something by its weight. As adults, they might need to weigh items to be mailed for proper postage, decide how much produce to buy when priced by the pound, estimate how much potato salad to buy when serving a meal to a large group of people, and weigh luggage before flying.

Weight is the measurement of the pull of gravity on an object and *mass* is a measurement of the amount of matter something contains. The mass of an object doesn't change when an object's location changes. Weight, on the other hand, does change with location. For example, a baseball on the earth has one mass. On the moon, it has the same mass. On the earth, it has one weight; on the moon, it weighs less.

The difference between weight and mass will be introduced later in students' math education. For now, be sure students are aware that the units to measure weight include pounds and ounces, while the units to measure mass include grams and kilograms.

Materials to Gather

SUPPLIED

base-10 ones cubes – 50

Metric Units of Mass activity page

ALSO NEEDED

balance supplies – 2 paper clips, 2 rubber bands, pointed-end safety scissors, 3 wooden skewers or other thin sticks about 9 inches long, masking tape, dental floss or sturdy lightweight string, 2 small identical containers (transparent or translucent, such as clear plastic cups), 2 medium identical containers (such as disposable plastic containers for leftovers)

household objects – 5 nickels, 9 quarters, 1 $1 bill, 4 sticks of butter (1 lb), 1 can of soup (350 g), 1 cup of yogurt, deck of cards, cell phone, roll of coins

index cards – 10 (4 labeled)

markers, permanent – 2 colors

While many quantities need to be measured precisely, some can simply be estimated. Estimation is important for students, since it focuses them on which unit is being used in the measurement and helps them develop a greater feel for the size of that unit. Most students view estimating as a fun guessing game. They will learn that the more they estimate and check their estimates, the better they will become at estimating measures. Measuring precisely is also a key skill; not doing so can lead to undesirable results, such as a fallen cake, a salty stew, or a watery milkshake.

When finding actual measures, students need to take special care in both using and reading the measuring instrument accurately.

▶ Advance Preparation

For the Learn: Gram and Kilogram activity, on two index cards, write the following in one color: **gram** and **kilogram**. On two index cards, write the following abbreviations in another color: **g** and **kg**. On the back of all four cards, write **Metric Units of Mass**.

For the Learn: Use a Balance activity and the Learn: Compare Masses activity, make a hanging balance. Test the balance to make sure it works.

PREPARE THE CUPS

An asterisk * marks steps that students might help with.

*1. Place a thick rubber band around the rim of each of 2 identical, lightweight, transparent or translucent cups.

*2. Cut 2 equal lengths of string about 18 inches long.

*3. For each cup, tie each end of a string to the rubber band, with the ends of the string on opposite sides of the cup rim.

*4. Attach a paper clip to the middle of each string as a loop from which the cup will hang.

PREPARE THE BALANCE BEAM

5. Gather 3 wooden chopsticks, bamboo skewers, or other thin sticks. If the sticks have pointed ends, remove the sharp points.

6. Make grooves on the sticks where strings will be secured. Mark the center of the sticks, and make a groove with the blade of a pair of scissors. Measure one-half inch from each end of the sticks, and make a groove in each place.

7. Cut a string about 12 inches long. Tie a loop at one end. Tie the other end to the middle of the sticks at the groove. The groove should be deep enough to hold the string in place, but you may use tape to secure the string if necessary.

8. Hang both cups by their paper clips over the grooves at each end of the beam. You may tape the paper clips to the beam.

HANG AND TEST

9. Hang the balance so the cups are just a few inches above a flat surface. The balance is sensitive. Only a few grams difference in the cups can tip it and tangle the strings. A surface below the balance helps prevent that problem.

You may hang the balance from a ruler on a table with heavy objects on one end of the ruler. The other end of the ruler would stick out from the edge of the table. A chair under the balance can provide a flat surface so that the balance won't tilt too much when objects are placed in the cups.

10. If the balance beam (the sticks) is horizontal, then the cups are balanced. If the balance beam isn't horizontal, check that the paper clips and center string haven't moved. If they are in place, then add some tape to the bottom of the lighter cup until the stick is horizontal.

11. Put a base-10 ones cube (a centimeter cube) in each cup and look at the balance beam to make sure it's balanced. Adjust as necessary.

12. Decide where you will hang the balance when you do the lesson: a table, chair, open cupboard doorknob above a counter, or even a low tree branch with a chair or table under it. If no surface underneath is available, be sure a helper holds the cups while you place objects in them.

▶ Safety

Make sure students handle the scissors carefully and be sure to store them in a safe place.

Handle the materials carefully when constructing the balance and be sure to store them in a safe place.

GET READY Find the Weight or Mass

ONLINE 5min

Students will identify the most appropriate weight for a given object or group of objects. The activity reinforces students' grasp of various units of measure.

Objectives

- Identify the appropriate metric and English units for measuring the mass or weight of an object.

LEARN Gram and Kilogram

OFFLINE 5min

Students will learn the abbreviations for the metric units of mass—gram and kilogram. Gather the labeled index cards, one base-10 ones cube, and $1 bill.

1. Tell students that they will measure the mass of objects using metric units.

2. Tell students that they will focus on two metric units for mass—grams and kilograms. Explain that a gram is a small unit of measure. A $1 bill and a base-10 ones cube each have a mass of about 1 gram. Let students hold a base-10 ones cube and a $1 bill so that they get a sense of what 1 gram feels like. Also explain that a kilogram is 1,000 grams. Tell students that 1,000 ones cubes, 1,000 $1 bills, and 9 sticks of butter each have a mass of about 1 kilogram.

3. Lay out the index cards with the **Metric Units of Mass** side showing. Turn them over. Put the spelled-out units next to each other and give students the abbreviation cards. Have students place each abbreviation card under the word they think the abbreviation matches.

4. Discuss the words and abbreviations. By the end of the activity, students should be able to say and recognize all the words and abbreviations.

5. Have students choose a card. If the card shows an abbreviation, have them say the unit it represents. If the card shows a word, have them write the abbreviation.

Objectives

- Estimate and measure the mass of an object to the nearest gram.

Tips

Have students locate the weight or mass on labels of packaged food in their kitchen. Have them note that the labels show both metric and English units.

LEARN Use a Balance

Objectives

- Estimate and measure the mass of an object to the nearest gram.

Students will measure the mass of objects to the nearest gram.
Gather the hanging balance, base-10 cubes, blank index cards, nickels, quarters, $1 bill, and other small objects to measure.

1. Set up the hanging balance. Explain to students that they will be using a homemade balance, and explain how it works.

2. Set out the objects to measure and an index card for each.

3. Explain that the base-10 ones cube has a mass of about 1 gram and that students can use ones cubes to compare masses.

4. Have students place a ones cube in each cup to test the balance. Then have them balance a ones cube with a $1 bill.

5. Have students find the mass of a nickel in grams by adding ones cubes to the opposite cup until the balance is even. Count the ones cubes to determine the mass in grams. close to 5 g

   Ask: if a nickel is 5 grams, does that mean a penny is 1 gram? No. You can't mix up units of measure for mass and money.

6. Ask students to pick an object and use the ones cubes to find its mass. They may also use nickels as 5-gram weights to counterbalance their objects. Have them write the object's name on the card and put the mass in grams in the upper right corner using the abbreviation *g* for grams. Repeat with one other object.

7. Have students look over all the objects and try to arrange them in order from the one they think has the least mass to the one with the greatest. Have them include objects they've already compared.

8. As students guess and measure the mass of each object, have them write its name in the center of the card and the mass in the upper right corner.

9. As students get more information about the mass of different objects, encourage them to rearrange the objects they ordered from least to greatest.

10. As students get comfortable, have them estimate the mass of an object before they compare it and put their guess in the lower left corner of the card.

11. If students don't have enough cubes as counterweights, encourage them to use heavier objects whose mass they know. For instance, they can use 9 quarters to represent 50 grams.

12. When students have found the mass of all the objects, have them pick five of the most memorable objects to record in their Math Notebook. Have them record each object's name, the estimate, and the actual mass.

Objectives

- Estimate and measure the mass of an object to the nearest gram.

Students will use a balance to measure the mass of heavier objects to the nearest gram and explore objects that have a mass of about a kilogram.

Gather the hanging balance and larger containers; base-10 cubes; blank index cards; nickels; quarters; butter; and other objects to measure, such as a cup of yogurt, can of soup, deck of cards, cell phone, and roll of coins.

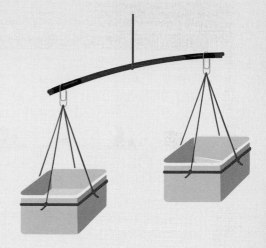

1. Show students the hanging balance. Review how to use it. Explain that the thin balance beam is perfect for measuring items in grams but is too thin to compare full kilograms. Remind students that 1 kilogram is the same as 1,000 grams. Tell students that they can compare 500-gram masses with the balance if they use bigger containers. Have students replace the small containers with larger containers by carefully removing the rubber bands and placing them around larger containers. Check that the balance is level. If necessary, add extra strings to keep the container from tipping when objects are placed in it.

2. Set out the various larger household objects and an index card for each item. Explain that a stick of butter has a mass of about 113 grams, 4 sticks of butter have a mass of about 450 grams, and 9 quarters plus 4 sticks of butter have a mass of about 500 grams. Tell students that they can use these known masses and the base-10 ones cubes to compare masses and find the mass of a larger object in grams.

3. Have students place a can of soup in one container of the balance and sticks of butter and ones cubes in the opposite container until the balance is level.

   Ask: How many sticks of butter and ones cubes are in the container that is opposite the container holding the can of soup? about 3 sticks of butter and 10 ones cubes

   Ask: So what is the mass of a can of soup in grams? close to 350 g

4. Ask students to pick an object and use the sticks of butter, can of soup, quarters, or base-10 ones cubes to estimate its mass to the nearest gram. They may also use nickels as 5-gram weights to counterbalance the objects. Have students write the object's name on an index card and put the mass in grams in the upper right corner using the abbreviation *g* for grams.

5. Repeat Step 4 for another object.

6. Have students explore what 1 kilogram feels like by combining objects to find a total mass of around 1,000 grams. An example might include a can of soup, cup of yogurt, and 4 sticks of butter.

7. Have students look for objects that have the mass labeled, such as a bag of nuts, candle, or jar of baby food. Challenge them to find items of different masses and use the balance to compare the masses of known and unknown objects. Have them write sentences describing the masses by using the words *more* and *less* and then estimate each mass. A cell phone has less mass than a stick of butter. The estimated mass of the cell phone is about 90 grams.

   As students gain more experience in estimating and measuring masses, they will refine their intuitive sense of relative masses of objects.

TRY IT Metric Units of Mass

- Estimate and measure the mass of an object to the nearest gram.

Students will practice judging the mass of objects in grams. View or print the Metric Units of Mass activity page and read the directions with students.

Students should copy the problems from the Activity Book into their Math Notebook as necessary and solve them there.

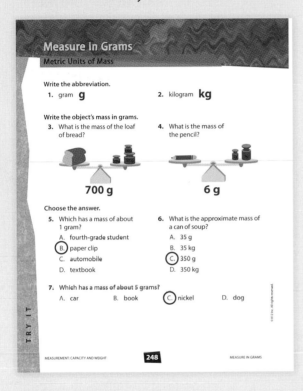

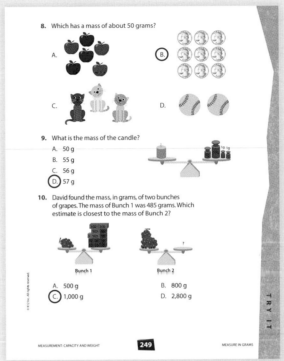

CHECKPOINT

- Estimate and measure the mass of an object to the nearest gram.

Students will complete an online Checkpoint. If necessary, read the directions, problems, and answer choices to students and help them with keyboard or mouse operations.

Measure Weight in Ounces and Pounds

Lesson Overview

GET READY Match Scales to Objects	5 minutes	**ONLINE**
LEARN Identify Ounces and Pounds	5 minutes	**ONLINE**
LEARN Compare Weights with a Balance	25 minutes	**OFFLINE**
TRY IT Estimate and Measure Weight	15 minutes	**OFFLINE**
CHECKPOINT	10 minutes	**ONLINE**

▶ Lesson Objectives

Estimate and measure the weight of an object to the nearest ounce.

▶ Prerequisite Skills

Identify the appropriate tools for measuring the weight or mass of an object.

▶ Content Background

Students will learn to estimate and measure the weight or mass of objects to the nearest ounce. They will also explore measuring objects in pounds.

ESTIMATION AND PRECISE MEASUREMENT

While many quantities need to be measured precisely, some can simply be estimated. Estimation is important for students, since it focuses them on which unit is being used in the measurement and helps them develop a greater feel for the size of that unit. Most students view estimating as a fun guessing game. They will learn that the more they estimate and check their estimates, the better they will become at estimating measures. Measuring precisely is also a key skill, since not doing so can lead to undesirable results, such as a fallen cake, a salty stew, or a watery milkshake.

When finding actual measures, students need to take special care in both using and reading the measuring instrument accurately. They should understand that all measures that the average person makes are only close approximations, both because of the lack of precision of the tools used in daily life and because of human error.

THE DIFFERENCES BETWEEN WEIGHT AND MASS

Weight is the measurement of the pull of gravity on an object, while *mass* is a measurement of the amount of matter something contains. The mass of an object doesn't change when an object's location changes. Weight, on the other hand, does change with location. For example, a baseball on the earth has one mass. On the moon, it has the same mass. On the earth, it has one weight; on the moon, it weighs less.

The difference between weight and mass will be introduced later in students' math education. For now, be sure students are aware that the units to measure weight include pounds and ounces, while the units to measure mass include grams and kilograms.

Materials to Gather

SUPPLIED

base-10 ones cubes – 28

Estimate and Measure Weight activity page

ALSO NEEDED

hanging balance from Measure in Grams lesson

balance supplies –2 rubber bands (large, thick), pointed-end safety scissors, 3 wooden skewer or other thin sticks about 9 inches long, masking tape, dental floss or sturdy lightweight string, 2 medium identical containers (such as disposable plastic containers for leftovers)

household objects – 10 quarters, 4 small objects that weight about 1 ounce (such as small nail clippers, large binder clip, glue stick, and small nail clippers), 4–6 objects that weigh about 1 pound (such as keys, marbles, canned goods, and boxed foods), plastic bag (small, clear, resealable)

index cards – 6

▶ Advance Preparation

For the Learn: Compare Weights with a Balance activity, gather various household objects and the hanging balance from the Measure in Grams lesson. If you do not have the hanging balance, refer to the Measure in Grams lesson in the Lesson Guide for instructions on how to create it. Modify the hanging balance.

1. Tape three wooden skewers or other thin sticks together to make a heavier balance beam. (If the sticks have pointed ends, remove the sharp points.) Replace the single-stick beam with this one.

2. If the containers are not large enough to hold a pound of butter or a few pieces of fruit, replace them with larger ones. To do so, remove the rubber bands from previous containers and carefully place them around the upper lip of the larger containers. It's helpful if the containers have a lip so that the rubber bands don't pull off with heavier weights.

The new version should look similar to the illustration. Be sure each paper clip sits in a groove that is either cut in the sticks (with scissors) or made by wrapping tape around the stick on either side of the paper clip.

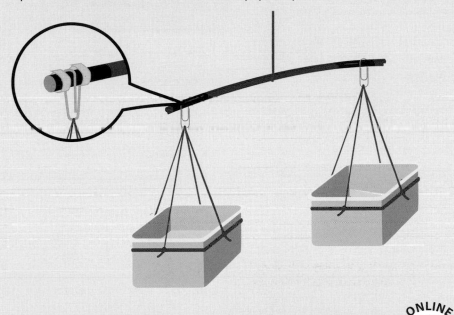

GET READY Match Scales to Objects

Students will match each object with the correct type of scale used to measure the weight or mass of the object. When students complete the matching, they will learn about a type of large scale.

Objectives

- Identify the appropriate tools for measuring the weight or mass of an object.

LEARN Identify Ounces and Pounds

Students will learn that ounces and pounds are two English units for measuring weight. They will see common items that weigh 1 ounce and that weigh 1 pound. They will learn why pound is abbreviated as lb and why ounce is abbreviated as oz. They also will match each abbreviation to the correct word.

LEARN Compare Weights with a Balance

Students will compare the weights of different objects to known weights. They will record the weight of each object in ounces or pounds.

Gather the hanging balance, quarters, base-10 ones cubes, index cards, sticks of butter, and household objects.

1. Set up the hanging balance from a table, chair, plant hook, open cupboard door, coat rack, or any place it can hang freely. Try to hang the balance no more than a few inches above a flat surface. That way, when it's unbalanced, the heavier container will touch the surface rather than tilt the beam too far and cause the strings to tangle. Explain to students how the balance works.

2. Set out the household objects and an index card for each object.

3. Explain that 5 quarters or 28 base-10 ones cubes weigh about 1 ounce and that the quarters (or ones cubes) can be used to compare weights of different objects.

4. Have students place 5 quarters in each container to test the balance. Explain that when the balance beam is horizontal, the balance is level. If it isn't level, check that the paper clips holding the containers are in the correct position and that the string holding the balance beam is still in the groove. If it still doesn't balance, add tape to the bottom of the lighter container until it is balanced. This small adjustment should not greatly affect the performance of the balance. Then have students test the balance again with 5 quarters in one container and 28 ones cubes in the other.

5. Tell students to remove the quarters and ones cubes from the containers.

    •   Explain that a stick of butter weighs 4 ounces. Have them label an index card stick of butter and write 4 oz in the upper right corner.

    •   Have students place 5 quarters in one container and a stick of butter in the other. Then have them place small objects in the container with the quarters until the two sides balance.

    •   Have students remove the small objects from the container and place them in a plastic bag labeled 3 oz.

    Students now have the following weights:

    •   1 oz: 5 quarters or 28 ones cubes

    •   2 oz: 10 quarters

    •   3 oz: bag of small objects

    •   4 oz: stick of butter

Objectives

•   Estimate and measure the weight of an object to the nearest ounce.

Objectives

•   Estimate and measure the weight of an object to the nearest ounce.

Tips

Put 28 base-10 ones cubes in a lightweight sandwich bag to make a 1-ounce weight.

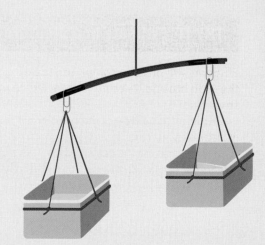

6. Ask students to pick an object from those gathered and use their homemade weights to find its weight. They may also use multiple sticks of butter to counterbalance their object. (Each stick is a 4-ounce weight.) Have students write the object name on an index card and record the weight in ounces in the upper right corner, using the abbreviation *oz* for *ounces*. Repeat this step with one other object.

7. Tell students to look over all the objects gathered and try to arrange them by weight from the least to the greatest. Have students include the objects they already weighed in the lineup.

8. Have students check the order of their objects by weighing the objects one at a time.

    •   Have them create index cards for each object that doesn't have one yet. Have them write the name of the object in the center of the card.

    •   Before they weigh each object, have them estimate the weight in ounces and write their guess in the lower left corner of the corresponding card.

    •   After they weigh each object, have them write the actual weight in ounces in the upper right corner of its card.

    •   As students get more information about the weight of different objects, encourage them to rearrange the objects in their least-to-greatest line. If they are trying to find the weight of something heavy, encourage them to use heavier objects for which they know the weight. For instance, they can use a banana (about 6 ounces), can of soup (about 13 ounces), or other homemade weights.

9. Have students feel the weight of 4 sticks of butter. Explain that this is what 1 pound feels like. Have students put the pound of butter in one container. Have them choose other items that they think might weigh about a pound, such as a number of potatoes, pieces of fruit, vegetables, or other objects. Have them balance the objects with the pound of butter to find out whether the objects weigh more or less than a pound.

10. When students have a good sense of a pound and have weighed all the objects from Step 8, have them choose five of the most memorable objects to record in their Math Notebook. Have them write down each object's name, the estimate, and the actual weight.

TRY IT Estimate and Measure Weight

OFFLINE
15 min

Objectives

•   Estimate and measure the weight of an object to the nearest ounce.

Students will practice comparing the weights of objects in ounces. View or print the Estimate and Measure Weight activity page and read the directions with students.

Students should copy the problems from the Activity Book into their Math Notebook as necessary and solve them there. In Problems 2–4, help students read the marks on the scale shown in the problem. Explain to students that by looking at the labeled marks on a scale, they can determine the value of the unlabeled marks.

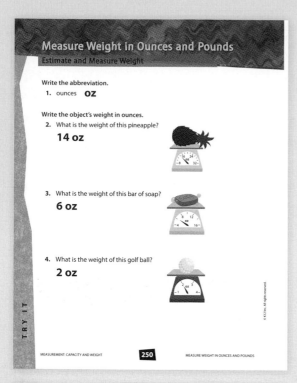

Measure Weight in Ounces and Pounds
Estimate and Measure Weight

Write the abbreviation.

1. ounces **OZ**

Write the object's weight in ounces.

2. What is the weight of this pineapple?
   14 oz

3. What is the weight of this bar of soap?
   6 oz

4. What is the weight of this golf ball?
   2 oz

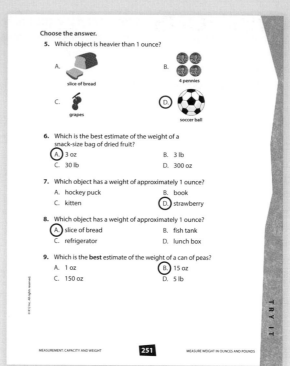

Choose the answer.

5. Which object is heavier than 1 ounce?
   A. slice of bread
   B. 4 pennies
   C. grapes
   D. (soccer ball)

6. Which is the best estimate of the weight of a snack-size bag of dried fruit?
   A. 3 oz
   B. 3 lb
   C. 30 lb
   D. 300 oz

7. Which object has a weight of approximately 1 ounce?
   A. hockey puck
   B. book
   C. kitten
   D. strawberry

8. Which object has a weight of approximately 1 ounce?
   A. slice of bread
   B. fish tank
   C. refrigerator
   D. lunch box

9. Which is the **best** estimate of the weight of a can of peas?
   A. 1 oz
   B. 15 oz
   C. 150 oz
   D. 5 lb

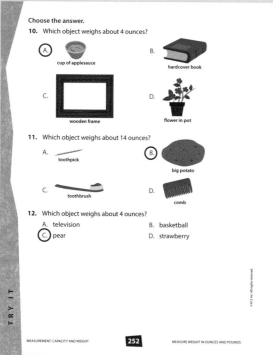

Choose the answer.

10. Which object weighs about 4 ounces?
    A. cup of applesauce
    B. hardcover book
    C. wooden frame
    D. flower in pot

11. Which object weighs about 14 ounces?
    A. toothpick
    B. big potato
    C. toothbrush
    D. comb

12. Which object weighs about 4 ounces?
    A. television
    B. basketball
    C. pear
    D. strawberry

CHECKPOINT

ONLINE 10 min

Students will complete an online Checkpoint. If necessary, read the directions, problems, and answer choices to students and help them with keyboard or mouse operations.

Objectives

- Estimate and measure the weight of an object to the nearest ounce.

Unit Conversions

Lesson Overview		
GET READY Time Relationships	5 minutes	**ONLINE**
LEARN Measurement Match	15 minutes	**ONLINE**
LEARN Convert Units of Measure	25 minutes	**OFFLINE**
TRY IT Write the Conversion	10 minutes	**OFFLINE**
CHECKPOINT	5 minutes	**ONLINE**

▶ Lesson Objectives

Write a simple unit conversion, such as inches to feet, as an expression or an equation.

▶ Prerequisite Skills

- Identify relationships between units of time, such as minutes in an hour, days in a month, weeks in a year.
- Use a mathematical expression to represent a relationship between quantities.

▶ Content Background

In this lesson, students will learn how to convert one measurement unit to another. They will write expressions to represent conversions. For example, since there are 12 inches in a foot, the number of inches in 5 feet is represented by the expression 5×12.

Expressions can be numbers only, or symbols and numbers together, that represent a value. Expressions do not include $<$, $>$, and $=$ symbols. Number sentences, on the other hand, compare quantities using $<$, $>$, and $=$ symbols. When a number sentence has an equals symbol, it can be called an equation. An equation shows that two values are equal. Since equations are one kind of number sentence, continue to use the term *number sentence* with students rather than *equation*.

Students will use number sentences to represent unit conversions (for example, 12 inches = 1 foot). They will also work on memorizing common unit conversions. In everyday life, students will have many opportunities to convert one measurement unit to another. They may need to convert inches to feet for one purpose, or feet to inches for another. They also may need to convert grams to kilograms, cups to ounces, quarters to dollars, minutes to hours, or even dozens to individual items. To be smart consumers, students will benefit from memorizing many of the common conversions they see in this lesson.

Materials to Gather

SUPPLIED

Measurement Conversion Chart (printout)

Convert Units of Measure activity page

Write the Conversion activity page

▶ Common Errors and Misconceptions

Students might incorrectly reason that when a greater number of units is given, they need to divide to convert the units, and when a lesser number of units is given, they need to multiply. Students also might think they need to divide if the given number of units is a multiple of the conversion unit. For example, in the problem 144 feet = ? inches, students might automatically divide 144 by 12 because 144 is a multiple of 12, rather than realize that they are converting a larger unit to a smaller unit, so they have to multiply.

▶ Advance Preparation

Print the Measurement Conversion Chart.

GET READY Time Relationships

ONLINE 5 min

Students will answer questions about units of time. They'll also write number sentences to show the relationship between units. Learning to write these relationships as number sentences is the first step in being able to convert one unit to another.

Objectives

- Identify relationships between units of time, such as minutes in an hour, days in a month, weeks in a year.
- Use a mathematical expression to represent a relationship between quantities.

LEARN Measurement Match

ONLINE 15 min

Students will learn about unit conversions. They'll also practice matching smaller and larger units of measure.
  Gather the Measurement Conversion Chart.

1. Have students look over the measurement conversions on the chart. Ask them to point out any conversions that are familiar. Discuss any conversions that are new to students or that they do not understand.

2. Have students go through the online screens that show unit conversions. Encourage them to find each one on the Measurement Conversion Chart. Then have them match the smaller units to the larger ones as directed.

Objectives

- Write a simple unit conversion, such as inches to feet, as an expression or an equation.

LEARN Convert Units of Measure

OFFLINE 25 min

Students will write unit conversions as expressions and number sentences. Gather the Measurement Conversion Chart. View or print the Convert Units of Measure activity page and read the directions with students.
  Students should copy the problems from the Activity Book into their Math Notebook as necessary and solve them there.

1. Review the Measurement Conversion Chart with students. Explain that people use these unit conversions to change, or convert, measurements from one unit to another. For instance, have students find the conversion 12 inches = 1 foot. Explain that they can find the number of inches in 2 feet

---

by using the expression 2 × 12. Remind students that expressions represent quantities. Expressions can have numbers and symbols, but they do not include the comparison symbols <, >, or =.

Say: When you solve the conversion, write a number sentence to show equal values. The number sentence 2 × 12 = 24 is used to show that 2 feet = 24 inches.

Remind students that number sentences do include the comparison symbols <, >, or =.

Say: Notice that when you changed from a larger unit (feet) to a smaller unit (inches), you multiplied. If the problem was to find how many feet are in 24 inches, you would be changing 24 inches (smaller units) into feet (larger units) and you would divide.

2. Read the first Worked Example with students. Have them explain in their own words why they need to multiply, not divide, to solve this problem. **Sample explanation:** I'm changing feet to inches. Since there are 12 inches in each foot, I will multiply by 5 to find how many inches are in 5 feet. When I'm changing larger units to smaller units, I need to multiply.

3. Repeat Step 2 for the second Worked Example. Note that this example requires changing smaller units to larger units; therefore, students will divide.

4. Guide students through Problem 1. Prompt them with questions such as the following:

   - What are the two measures in the problem? ounces and pounds
   - What do you need to find to solve the problem? how many ounces are in 7 pounds
   - What conversion number sentence compares the two measures? 16 ounces = 1 pound
   - Are you changing larger units to smaller units, or smaller units to larger ones? larger units to smaller ones
   - Will you multiply or divide? multiply
   - What expression will you write to convert the units? 7 × 16
   - What number sentence could you write to convert the units? 7 × 16 = 112

5. Have students complete Problems 2–5. Encourage them to refer to the Worked Examples for the steps to follow. Students may use abbreviations when writing their conversion number sentences.

Tips

Show items to help students visualize the conversions, such as a 1-foot ruler marked in inches, a carton of 1 dozen eggs, and a measuring cup marked in fluid ounces.

Worked Examples

You can write an expression and a number sentence to convert one unit of measure to another.

PROBLEM 1 Write and solve a number sentence to show how many inches there are in 5 feet.

SOLUTION

❶ Look for the two measures in the problem.
The measures are inches and feet.

❷ Identify what you need to find to solve the problem.
You need to find the number of inches in 5 feet.

❸ Write the conversion number sentence that compares the two measures. The number sentence 12 inches = 1 foot compares the measures.

❹ Identify which unit of measure you have. Is it the larger unit or the smaller unit? You have 5 feet and you want to know how many inches that is. You're changing from larger units (feet) to smaller units (inches).

❺ Decide whether you will multiply or divide. Multiply if you're changing larger units to smaller units. You will have more of the smaller units. Multiply the number of units you're converting (5) by the number of smaller units (12) in the conversion number sentence.

Multiply. You have 5 feet, and you know there are 12 inches in each foot. So multiply 5 × 12 to find the total number of inches.

❻ Write the number sentence.
Number sentence: 5 × 12 = ?

ANSWER 5 × 12 = 60
There are 60 inches in 5 feet.

PROBLEM 2 Write and solve a number sentence to show how many yards equal 12 feet.

SOLUTION

❶ Look for the two measures in the problem.
The measures are feet and yards.

❷ Identify what you need to find to solve the problem.
You need to find the number of yards in 12 feet.

❸ Write the conversion number sentence that compares the two measures. The number sentence 3 feet = 1 yard compares the measures.

❹ Identify which unit of measure you have. Is it the larger unit or the smaller unit? You have 12 feet, and you want to know how many yards that is. You're changing from smaller units (feet) to larger units (yards).

❺ Decide if you will multiply or divide. Divide if you're changing smaller units to larger units. You will have fewer of the larger units. Divide the number of units you're converting (12) by the number of smaller units (3) in the conversion number sentence.

Divide. You have 12 feet, and you know that 3 feet equal 1 yard. So divide 12 ÷ 3 to find the number of yards.

❻ Write the number sentence.
Number sentence: 12 ÷ 3 = ?

ANSWER 12 ÷ 3 = 4
So 4 yards equal 12 feet.

Write the expression.

1. How many ounces are in 7 pounds?
(16 ounces = 1 pound) **7 × 16**

2. How many items are in 3 dozen?
(12 items = 1 dozen) **3 × 12**

Write and solve the number sentence.

3. How many quarts are in 16 pints?
(2 pints = 1 quart)   **16 ÷ 2 = ?**
                      16 ÷ 2 = 8
4. How many minutes are in 5 hours?
(60 minutes = 1 hour) **5 × 60 = ?**
                       5 × 60 = 300
5. How many dollars are equal to 24 quarters?
(4 quarters = 1 dollar) **24 ÷ 4 = ?**
                         24 ÷ 4 = 6

TRY IT Write the Conversion

OFFLINE 10 min

Students will practice writing simple unit conversions as an expression or a number sentence. View or print the Write the Conversion activity page and read the directions with students.

Students should copy the problems from the Activity Book into their Math Notebook as necessary.

Objectives

- Write a simple unit conversion, such as inches to feet, as an expression or an equation.

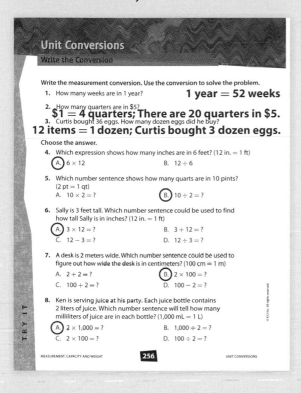

Unit Conversions
Write the Conversion

Write the measurement conversion. Use the conversion to solve the problem.

1. How many weeks are in 1 year? **1 year = 52 weeks**

2. How many quarters are in $5?
$1 = 4 quarters; There are 20 quarters in $5.

3. Curtis bought 36 eggs. How many dozen eggs did he buy?
12 items = 1 dozen; Curtis bought 3 dozen eggs.

Choose the answer.

4. Which expression shows how many inches are in 6 feet? (12 in. = 1 ft)
   A. 6 × 12   B. 12 ÷ 6

5. Which number sentence shows how many quarts are in 10 pints? (2 pt = 1 qt)
   A. 10 × 2 = ?   B. 10 ÷ 2 = ?

6. Sally is 3 feet tall. Which number sentence could be used to find how tall Sally is in inches? (12 in. = 1 ft)
   A. 3 × 12 = ?   B. 3 + 12 = ?
   C. 12 − 3 = ?   D. 12 ÷ 3 = ?

7. A desk is 2 meters wide. Which number sentence could be used to figure out how wide the desk is in centimeters? (100 cm = 1 m)
   A. 2 + 2 = ?   B. 2 × 100 = ?
   C. 100 ÷ 2 = ?   D. 100 − 2 = ?

8. Ken is serving juice at his party. Each juice bottle contains 2 liters of juice. Which number sentence will tell how many milliliters of juice are in each bottle? (1,000 mL = 1 L)
   A. 2 × 1,000 = ?   B. 1,000 ÷ 2 = ?
   C. 2 × 100 = ?   D. 100 ÷ 2 = ?

MEASUREMENT: CAPACITY AND WEIGHT   **256**   UNIT CONVERSIONS

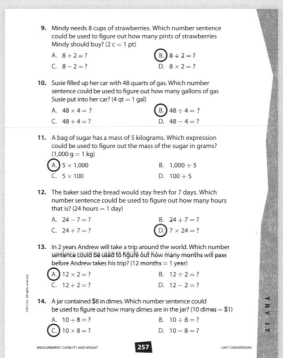

9. Mindy needs 8 cups of strawberries. Which number sentence could be used to figure out how many pints of strawberries Mindy should buy? (2 c = 1 pt)
   A. 8 + 2 = ?   B. 8 ÷ 2 = ?
   C. 8 − 2 = ?   D. 8 × 2 = ?

10. Susie filled up her car with 48 quarts of gas. Which number sentence could be used to figure out how many gallons of gas Susie put into her car? (4 qt = 1 gal)
    A. 48 × 4 = ?   B. 48 ÷ 4 = ?
    C. 48 + 4 = ?   D. 48 − 4 = ?

11. A bag of sugar has a mass of 5 kilograms. Which expression could be used to figure out the mass of the sugar in grams? (1,000 g = 1 kg)
    A. 5 × 1,000   B. 1,000 ÷ 5
    C. 5 × 100   D. 100 ÷ 5

12. The baker said the bread would stay fresh for 7 days. Which number sentence could be used to figure out how many hours that is? (24 hours = 1 day)
    A. 24 − 7 = ?   B. 24 ÷ 7 = ?
    C. 24 + 7 = ?   D. 7 × 24 = ?

13. In 2 years Andrew will take a trip around the world. Which number sentence could be used to figure out how many months will pass before Andrew takes his trip? (12 months = 1 year)
    A. 12 × 2 = ?   B. 12 ÷ 2 = ?
    C. 12 + 2 = ?   D. 12 − 2 = ?

14. A jar contained $8 in dimes. Which number sentence could be used to figure out how many dimes are in the jar? (10 dimes = $1)
    A. 10 + 8 = ?   B. 10 ÷ 8 = ?
    C. 10 × 8 = ?   D. 10 − 8 = ?

MEASUREMENT: CAPACITY AND WEIGHT   **257**   UNIT CONVERSIONS

CHECKPOINT

ONLINE 5 min

Students will complete an online Checkpoint. If necessary, read the directions, problems, and answer choices to students and help them with keyboard or mouse operations.

Objectives

- Write a simple unit conversion, such as inches to feet, as an expression or an equation.

Measurement Conversions (A)

GET READY Conversion Match-Up	10 minutes	**ONLINE**
LEARN Multiply or Divide to Convert	15 minutes	**ONLINE**
LEARN Conversion Stories	20 minutes	**OFFLINE**
TRY IT Convert and Solve	15 minutes	**OFFLINE**

▶ Lesson Objectives

- Use a simple unit conversion, such as centimeters to meters, to solve a problem.
- Solve a unit-conversion story problem by using multiplication or division.

▶ Prerequisite Skills

Write a simple unit conversion, such as inches to feet, as an expression or an equation.

▶ Content Background

In this lesson, students will learn to use a simple unit conversion, such as centimeters to meters, to solve a problem. They will also learn to use multiplication or division to solve unit-conversion story problems.

   Knowing when to multiply or divide is a key skill students need when converting measurements. They will continue to practice and memorize measurement conversions. They will apply these skills and use multiplication and division to solve story problems involving measurement conversions. Students may need to convert inches to feet, grams to kilograms, cups to ounces, quarters to dollars, minutes to hours, or dozens to individual items. They will learn tips to determine whether to multiply or divide to solve the measurement conversion problems.

▶ Common Errors and Misconceptions

Students might incorrectly reason that when a greater number of units is given, they need to divide to convert the units, and when a lesser number of units is given, they need to multiply. Students also might think they need to divide if the given number of units is a multiple of the conversion unit. For example, in the problem 144 feet = ? inches, students might automatically divide 144 by 12 because 144 is a multiple of 12, rather than realize that they are converting a larger unit to a smaller unit, so they have to multiply.

▶ Advance Preparation

Print the Measurement Conversion Chart.

Materials to Gather

SUPPLIED

Measurement Conversion Chart (printout)

Conversion Stories activity page

Convert and Solve activity page

GET READY Conversion Match-Up

ONLINE 10 min

Students will practice matching up the parts of conversion sentences.
    Gather the Measurement Conversion Chart. Review the conversions with students before doing the online activity.

Objectives

- Write a simple unit conversion, such as inches to feet, as an expression or an equation.

LEARN Multiply or Divide to Convert

ONLINE 15 min

Students will identify whether they need to multiply or divide to convert units. Remind students that when changing from a larger unit such as feet to a smaller unit such as inches, they can think: 1 foot = 12 inches, so 2 feet would be 2×12 inches. They will soon become accustomed to the idea that when converting from larger units to smaller units, they multiply. And they will know that when going from larger units to smaller units, they divide.
    Gather the Measurement Conversion Chart. Allow students to refer to the chart as needed while they complete the online activity.

Objectives

- Use a simple unit conversion, such as centimeters to meters, to solve a problem.
- Solve a unit-conversion story problem by using multiplication or division.

LEARN Conversion Stories

OFFLINE 20 min

Students will use multiplication or division to solve unit-conversion story problems. Encourage them to use any strategy they are comfortable with to solve problems. For example, at times using repeated subtraction to solve division problems will be easier for students. Their understanding will increase as they apply their own techniques. Gather the Measurement Conversion Chart. View or print the Conversion Stories activity page and read the directions with students.
    Students should copy the problems from the Activity Book into their Math Notebook as necessary and solve them there.

Objectives

- Use a simple unit conversion, such as centimeters to meters, to solve a problem.
- Solve a unit-conversion story problem by using multiplication or division.

1. Review with students what a number sentence is and how number sentences are used in measurement conversions.

    Say: A number sentence compares quantities using $<$, $>$, or $=$. When you say 12 inches = 1 foot, you are using a number sentence to show two equal values. To convert 2 feet into inches, you would write the number sentence $2 \times 12 = ?$ and then find the answer.

2. Read the first Worked Example with students. Have them find the conversion 60 seconds = 1 minute on the Measurement Conversion Chart.

3. Have students explain in their own words why they need to multiply, not divide, to solve this problem. **Sample explanation:** Since there are 60 seconds in 1 minute, there would be 2×60 seconds in 2 minutes. When I'm changing larger units to smaller units, I need to multiply.

4. Read the second Worked Example with students. Point out that this story problem is a 2-step problem. First subtract to find the number of quarters remaining. Then divide the remaining quarters by 4 to convert them to dollars.

5. Have students explain in their own words why they need to divide, not multiply, to solve this problem. **Sample explanation:** I'm changing quarters to dollars. Dollars are the larger units. When I'm changing smaller units to larger units, I need to divide.

6. Guide students through Problem 1. Prompt them with questions such as:

   - What are the two measures in the problem? feet and yards

   - What do you need to find to solve the problem? how many yards of ribbon Rosa has

   - What conversion number sentence compares the two measures? 3 feet = 1 yard

   - Are you changing larger units to smaller units, or smaller units to larger ones? smaller units to larger ones

   - Will you multiply or divide? divide

   - What number sentence will you write to convert the units? $12 \div 3 = 4$

7. Have students complete Problems 2–4. Encourage them to refer to the Worked Examples for the steps to follow. Students should use the Measurement Conversion Chart to find the conversions they need. Encourage them to use abbreviations for units of measure whenever possible. (Note: Problems 3 and 4 are 2-step story problems. If needed, help students identify the steps and the operations to complete them.)

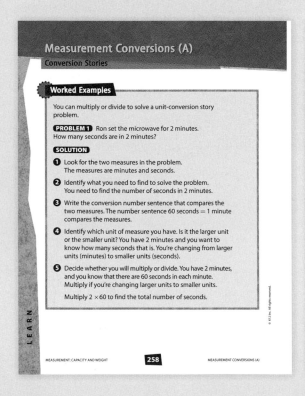

Measurement Conversions (A)
Conversion Stories

Worked Examples

You can multiply or divide to solve a unit-conversion story problem.

PROBLEM 1 Ron set the microwave for 2 minutes. How many seconds are in 2 minutes?

SOLUTION

❶ Look for the two measures in the problem. The measures are minutes and seconds.

❷ Identify what you need to find to solve the problem. You need to find the number of seconds in 2 minutes.

❸ Write the conversion number sentence that compares the two measures. The number sentence 60 seconds = 1 minute compares the measures.

❹ Identify which unit of measure you have. Is it the larger unit or the smaller unit? You have 2 minutes and you want to know how many seconds that is. You're changing from larger units (minutes) to smaller units (seconds).

❺ Decide whether you will multiply or divide. You have 2 minutes, and you know that there are 60 seconds in each minute. Multiply if you're changing larger units to smaller units.

Multiply 2×60 to find the total number of seconds.

MEASUREMENT: CAPACITY AND WEIGHT   **258**   MEASUREMENT CONVERSIONS (A)

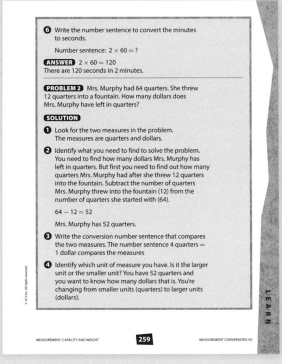

❻ Write the number sentence to convert the minutes to seconds.

Number sentence: $2 \times 60 = ?$

ANSWER $2 \times 60 = 120$
There are 120 seconds in 2 minutes.

PROBLEM 2 Mrs. Murphy had 64 quarters. She threw 12 quarters into a fountain. How many dollars does Mrs. Murphy have left in quarters?

SOLUTION

❶ Look for the two measures in the problem. The measures are quarters and dollars.

❷ Identify what you need to find to solve the problem. You need to find how many dollars Mrs. Murphy has left in quarters. But first you need to find out how many quarters Mrs. Murphy had after she threw 12 quarters into the fountain. Subtract the number of quarters Mrs. Murphy threw into the fountain (12) from the number of quarters she started with (64).

$64 - 12 = 52$

Mrs. Murphy has 52 quarters.

❸ Write the conversion number sentence that compares the two measures. The number sentence 4 quarters = 1 dollar compares the measures

❹ Identify which unit of measure you have. Is it the larger unit or the smaller unit? You have 52 quarters and you want to know how many dollars that is. You're changing from smaller units (quarters) to larger units (dollars).

MEASUREMENT: CAPACITY AND WEIGHT   **259**   MEASUREMENT CONVERSIONS (A)

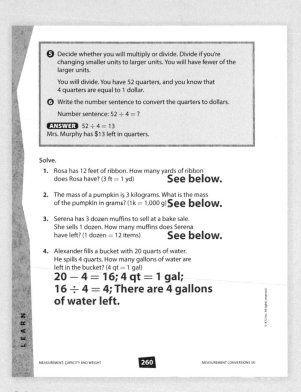

Additional Answers

1. 3 ft = 1 yd; 12 ÷ 3 = 4; Rosa has 4 yards of ribbon.

2. 1,000 g = 1 kg; 3 × 1,000 = 3,000; The mass is 3,000 grams.

3. 3 − 1 = 2; 12 items = 1 dozen; 2 × 12 = 24; Serena has 24 muffins.

TRY IT Convert and Solve

OFFLINE
15 min

Students will practice using multiplication and division to solve unit-conversion problems. Have students turn to the Convert and Solve activity page in their Activity Book and read the directions with them.

Students should copy the problems from the Activity Book into their Math Notebook as necessary and solve them there.

Tips — Encourage students to use repeated addition if they are having difficulty multiplying and to use repeated subtraction if they are having difficulty dividing.

Objectives

- Use a simple unit conversion, such as centimeters to meters, to solve a problem.
- Solve a unit-conversion story problem by using multiplication or division.

Convert and Solve

Solve.

1. Since 10 dimes equal 1 dollar, how many dimes equal 6 dollars?

   $6 \times 10 = 60;$ **So 60 dimes equal 6 dollars.**

2. There are 2 pints in 1 quart. How many quarts equal 14 pints?

   $14 \div 2 = 7$ **quarts; So 7 quarts equal 14 pints.**

3. Cole's cat Bix is 3 years old. He wants to figure out Bix's age in months. There are 12 months in a year. How many months are in 3 years?

   3×12 (or $12 + 12 + 12$) $= 36;$ **There are 36 months in 3 years.**

4. Katrina has 4 liters of juice to serve at her party. Her mom brings home another liter of juice. How many milliliters of juice does Katrina have altogether? (1,000 mL = 1 L)

   $4 + 1 = 5;$ $5 \times 1,000 = 5,000;$ **Katrina has 5,000 milliliters.**

5. Jackson has 6 meters of rope. He uses 1 meter of rope as a lasso. How many centimeters of rope does he have left? (1 m = 100 cm)

   $6 - 1 = 5;$ $5 \times 100 = 500;$ **Jackson has 500 centimeters of rope left.**

6. Beth bought 3 dozen eggs. How many eggs did she buy? (12 items = 1 dozen)

   $3 \times 12 = 36;$ **Beth bought 36 eggs.**

7. Tiffany biked 2 kilometers. How many meters did she bike? (1,000 m = 1 km)

   $2 \times 1,000 = 2,000;$ **Tiffany biked 2,000 meters.**

8. Four hours is equivalent to how many minutes? (60 minutes = 1 hour)

   $4 \times 60 = 240;$ **So 4 hours is equivalent to 240 minutes.**

9. How many gallons are in 24 quarts? (4 quarts = 1 gallon)

   $24 \div 4 = 6;$ **There are 6 gallons in 24 quarts.**

Choose the answer.

10. How many quarters are equal to 4 dollars? (4 quarters = 1 dollar)

    A. 1   B. 4

    C. 16   D. 20

11. Jan is riding her bike 9 kilometers to her grandmother's house. She has biked 2 kilometers already. How many more meters does Jan have to bike? (1,000 m = 1 km)

    A. 70 m   B. 700 m

    C. 7,000 m   D. 70,000 m

12. Jorge found two jars filled with pennies. One jar held $2 and the other jar held $3. How many pennies did Jorge find? (100 pennies = $1)

    A. 5   B. 20

    C. 500   D. 1,000

13. Della has 3 pounds of apples for a fruit salad. Each apple weighs about 6 ounces. Della knows there are 16 ounces in a pound. How many apples does Della have for the fruit salad?

    A. 2   **B.** 8

    C. 24   D. 48

Measurement Conversions (B)

GET READY Match Measurements	5 minutes	ONLINE
LEARN Conversion Story Problems	10 minutes	ONLINE
LEARN Solve and Convert Answers	20 minutes	OFFLINE
TRY IT Measurement Problems	15 minutes	OFFLINE
CHECKPOINT	10 minutes	ONLINE

▶ Lesson Objectives

- Use a simple unit conversion, such as centimeters to meters, to solve a problem.
- Solve a unit-conversion story problem by using multiplication or division.

▶ Prerequisite Skills

Write a simple unit conversion, such as inches to feet, as an expression or an equation.

▶ Content Background

Students will continue to use a simple unit conversion, such as centimeters to meters, to solve a problem. They will also use multiplication or division to solve unit-conversion story problems.

Knowing when to multiply or divide is a key skill students need when converting measurements. They will continue to practice and memorize measurement conversions. They will apply these skills and use multiplication and division to solve story problems involving measurement conversions. They may need to convert inches to feet, grams to kilograms, cups to ounces, quarters to dollars, minutes to hours, or dozens to individual items. They will learn tips to determine whether to multiply or divide to solve the measurement-conversion problems.

▶ Common Errors and Misconceptions

Students might incorrectly reason that when a greater number of units is given, they need to divide to convert the units, and when a lesser number of units is given, they need to multiply. Students also might think they need to divide if the given number of units is a multiple of the conversion unit. For example, in the problem 144 feet = ? inches, students might automatically divide 144 by 12 because 144 is a multiple of 12, rather than realize that they are converting a larger unit to a smaller unit, so they have to multiply.

▶ Advance Preparation

Print the Measurement Conversion Chart.

Materials to Gather

SUPPLIED

Measurement Conversion Chart (printout)

Solve and Convert Answers activity page

Measurement Problems activity page

GET READY Match Measurements

ONLINE
5min

Students will match measurements that show equal amounts, such as 12 inches and 1 foot. Gather the Measurement Conversion Chart. Students may use the chart during this activity. However, the goal is to help students begin to memorize the equivalencies.

Objectives

- Write a simple unit conversion, such as inches to feet, as an expression or an equation.

Tips

Have students repeat this activity several times to help them memorize equivalent measures.

LEARN Conversion Story Problems

ONLINE
10min

Students will identify the correct number sentence to solve a measurement-conversion story problem.

  Gather the Measurement Conversion Chart. Students may refer to the chart as needed.

Objectives

- Use a simple unit conversion, such as centimeters to meters, to solve a problem.
- Solve a unit-conversion story problem by using multiplication or division.

LEARN Solve and Convert Answers

OFFLINE
20min

Students will solve measurement story problems and then use multiplication or division to convert the units in the solution. Gather the Measurement Conversion Chart. View or print the Solve and Convert Answers activity page and read the directions with students.

  Students should copy the problems from the Activity Book into their Math Notebook as necessary and solve them there.

1. Read the first Worked Example with students.
2. **Ask:** What number sentence shows how many muffins Mrs. Ford baked altogether? $24 + 12 = 36$
3. Go through each step of the Worked Example, helping students identify the measures, decide whether to multiply or divide, and write the number sentence that will solve the problem.
4. Read the second Worked Example with students. Point out that this story problem is a 2-step problem. Help students understand that since they're changing the larger unit of time (hours) to a smaller unit of time (minutes), they will multiply.
5. Use the Worked Examples to help students complete Problems 1–4. Students may use the Measurement Conversion Chart as needed. Encourage them to use abbreviations for units of measure whenever possible. (Note: These problems are 2-step story problems. If needed, help students identify the steps and the operations to complete them.)

Objectives

- Use a simple unit conversion, such as centimeters to meters, to solve a problem.
- Solve a unit-conversion story problem by using multiplication or division.

Tips

Encourage students to become familiar with all the units on the Measurement Conversion Chart.

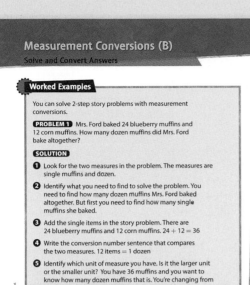

Measurement Conversions (B)
Solve and Convert Answers

Worked Examples

You can solve 2-step story problems with measurement conversions.

PROBLEM 1 Mrs. Ford baked 24 blueberry muffins and 12 corn muffins. How many dozen muffins did Mrs. Ford bake altogether?

SOLUTION

❶ Look for the two measures in the problem. The measures are single muffins and dozen.

❷ Identify what you need to find to solve the problem. You need to find how many dozen muffins Mrs. Ford baked altogether. But first you need to find how many single muffins she baked.

❸ Add the single items in the story problem. There are 24 blueberry muffins and 12 corn muffins. 24 + 12 = 36

❹ Write the conversion number sentence that compares the two measures. 12 items = 1 dozen

❺ Identify which unit of measure you have. Is it the larger unit or the smaller unit? You have 36 muffins and you want to know how many dozen muffins that is. You're changing from smaller units (single muffins) to larger units (dozens).

❻ Decide whether you will multiply or divide. You have 36 muffins, and you know that there are 12 muffins in a dozen. Divide 36 ÷ 12 to find the total number of muffins.

❼ Write the number sentence to convert the single muffins to dozens. 36 ÷ 12 = ?

ANSWER 36 ÷ 12 = 3; Mrs. Ford baked 3 dozen muffins.

PROBLEM 2 The trip to Florida takes 22 hours. Ali's family has traveled for 19 hours so far. How many more minutes do they still have to travel?

SOLUTION

❶ Look for the two measures in the problem. The measures are hours and minutes.

❷ Identify what you need to find to solve the problem. You need to find how many more minutes Ali's family has to travel. But first you need to find out how many hours they have to travel.

❸ Subtract the number of hours Ali's family has traveled (19) from the total hours the trip takes (22). 22 − 19 = 3

❹ Write the conversion number sentence that compares the two measures in this problem. 1 hour = 60 minutes

❺ Identify which unit of measure you have. Is it the larger unit or the smaller unit? You have 3 hours and you want to know how many minutes that is. You're changing from larger units (hours) to smaller units (minutes).

❻ Decide whether you will multiply or divide. You have 3 hours and you know there are 60 minutes in each hour, so multiply 3 × 60 to find the number of minutes in 3 hours.

❼ Write the number sentence to convert 3 hours to minutes. 3 × 60 = ?

ANSWER 3 × 60 = 180; Ali's family still has to travel 180 minutes.

Solve.

1. Sharon collected 46 nickels. Mark collected 34 nickels. How many dollars did they collect altogether? (20 nickels = $1) **See below.**

2. The water container holds 5 liters. The soccer team drank 3 liters. How many milliliters of water are left? (1 L = 1,000 mL) **See below.**

3. Theo mixes 6 pints of fruit juice and 3 pints of soda water to make one batch of punch. How many cups are in one batch of punch? (1 pt = 2 c) **See below.**

4. The distance between the start and finish of the turtle race is 400 centimeters. Winnie's turtle has crawled 200 centimeters so far. How many more meters does Winnie's turtle need to crawl to reach the finish line? (100 cm = 1 m)

 400 − 200 = 200; 100 cm = 1 m; 200 ÷ 100 = 2; Winnie's turtle needs to crawl 2 more meters.

Additional Answers

1. 46 + 34 = 80; 20 nickels = $1; 80 ÷ 20 = 4; They collected $4.

2. 5 − 3 = 2; 1 L = 1,000 mL; 2 × 1,000 = 2,000; There are 2,000 milliliters of water left.

3. 6 + 3 = 9; 1 pt = 2 c; 9 × 2 = 18; There are 18 cups in one batch of punch.

TRY IT Measurement Problems

Objectives

- Use a simple unit conversion, such as centimeters to meters, to solve a problem.

- Solve a unit-conversion story problem by using multiplication or division.

Students will practice using multiplication and division to solve unit-conversion story problems. View or print the Measurement Problems activity page and read the directions with students.

Students should copy the problems from the Activity Book into their Math Notebook as necessary and solve them there. Have students use whatever strategies they are most comfortable with to figure out the conversions. For example in Problem 1, when finding out how many days are in 72 hours, some students will find it easier to subtract 24 hours repeatedly to get the solution. Using these strategies assures that students understand what they're doing rather than following a rote method.

Measurement Conversions (B)
Measurement Problems

Write the number sentence.

1. There are 24 hours in 1 day. The baby is 72 hours old.
   How many days old is the baby? **72 ÷ 24 = ?**

2. There are 16 ounces in 1 pound. The baby weighs 8 pounds.
   How many ounces does the baby weigh?
   8 × 16 = ?

Solve.

3. There are 4 quarters in $1. Jimmy wants to spend $5 at the arcade. How many quarters should he bring?
   5 × 4 = 20; He should bring 20 quarters.

4. There are 3 feet in 1 yard. Mr. Porter has 30 feet of fencing. He uses 21 feet to make a chicken pen. How many yards of fencing does Mr. Porter have left?
   30 − 21 = 9; 9 ÷ 3 = 3; He has 3 yards left.

5. How many quarters are the same as $6?
   (4 quarters = $1) **6 × 4 = 24;**
   So $6 is the same as 24 quarters.

6. Adrienne bought 6 quarts of milk. How many pints of milk did Adrienne buy? (2 pt = 1 qt)
   6 × 2 = 12; She bought 12 pints.

Choose the answer.

7. The recipe calls for 16 fluid ounces of buttermilk and 8 fluid ounces of regular milk. How many cups of milk are needed?
   (8 fl oz = 1 c)
   (A.) 3 c   B. 24 c   C. 64 c   D. 192 c

T R Y I T

---

8. Marcus is taking two books back to the library. Each book has a mass of 2 kilograms. What is the total mass of the books, in grams?
   (1,000 g = 1 kg)
   A. 200 g   B. 400 g   C. 1,000 g   **(D)** 4,000 g

9. Dave is planning to run 3 kilometers and then walk 4 kilometers. How many meters is Dave planning to cover?
   (1,000 m = 1 km)
   A. 100 m   B. 700 m   C. 1,000 m   **(D)** 7,000 m

10. Theresa bought 4 dozen brown eggs and 1 dozen white eggs. What is the total number of eggs that Theresa bought?
    (12 items = 1 dozen)
    A. 48   **(B.)** 60   C. 72   D. 120

T R Y I T

CHECKPOINT

Objectives

- Solve a unit-conversion story problem by using multiplication or division.

- Use a simple unit conversion, such as centimeters to meters, to solve a problem.

Students will complete an online Checkpoint. If necessary, read the directions, problems, and answer choices to students and help them with keyboard or mouse operations.

Tips Suggest that students record the different units and the basic conversion in each problem before they solve the problem.

---

458 **MEASUREMENT: CAPACITY AND WEIGHT**

Core Focus
Problems Using Volume and Mass

▶ Lesson Objectives

- Solve one-step word problems involving volume.
- Solve one-step word problems involving mass.

▶ Prerequisite Skills.

- Identify the appropriate metric and English units for measuring liquid volume.
- Identify the appropriate metric and English units for measuring the mass or weight of an object.

▶ Content Background

Students will use their knowledge of metric liquid volume and mass to solve simple 1-step story problems.

Throughout their lives, students will have experiences in which they will measure or judge amounts of liquid volume, or capacity. These experiences might include measuring liquid used in cooking, making lemonade, drinking an adequate daily amount of water, equally sharing a bottle of water with a friend, and deciding how much juice to buy for a large group. When they become adults, students might mix paints, make a homemade cleaning solution with vinegar and baking soda, and possibly mix chemicals.

Students will also have experiences throughout their lives in which they will measure or judge the mass or weight of objects. Some examples include weighing themselves or a pet, measuring the mass of ingredients used in cooking, and figuring out how long to bake something according to its weight. When students become adults, they might need to weigh items to be mailed to determine the proper postage, decide how much produce to buy when it is priced by the gram or kilogram, estimate how much potato salad to buy when serving a meal to a large group of people, and weigh luggage before flying.

Weight is the measure of the pull of gravity on an object, and mass is a measurement of the amount of matter something contains. The *mass* of an object doesn't change when an object's location changes. Weight, on the other hand, does change with location. For example, a baseball on the earth has a certain mass and on the moon, it has the same mass. On the earth, the basketball has one weight; on the moon, it weighs less.

Materials to Gather

SUPPLIED

Volume Story Problems activity page

Mass Story Problems activity page

Volume and Mass Story Problems activity page

The difference between weight and mass will be introduced later in students' math education. For now, make sure students are aware that units used to measure weight include pounds and ounces and units used to measure mass include grams and kilograms.

GET READY Units of Volume and Mass

ONLINE
5min

Objectives

- Identify the appropriate metric and English units for measuring liquid volume.
- Identify the appropriate metric and English units for measuring the mass or weight of an object.

Students will be shown an object that holds liquid and will identify whether the liquid volume would be measured in milliliters or liters. Review with students that when they measure an amount of liquid, they are measuring liquid volume. When they figure out how much liquid a container holds, they measure the liquid capacity of the container. They should say, "The volume of liquid is 1 liter," or "The capacity of the container is 1 liter."

Students will also identify the most appropriate metric unit of mass of a given object. Both parts of the activity reinforce students' grasp of various units of metric measure.

LEARN Volume Story Problems

OFFLINE
15min

Objectives

- Solve one-step word problems involving volume.

Students will solve simple one-step story problems that involve operations with the metric units of volume, liters and milliliters. View or print the Volume Story Problems activity page and read the directions with students.

Students should copy the problems from the Activity Book into their Math Notebook as necessary and solve them there

1. Read the first Worked Example with students.

   Ask: What are you asked to find in this problem? how many liters of fruit punch Maria will need in all

   Ask: What information are you given? the amount of fruit punch for each table and the number of tables

   Ask: How many groups are there? 6 groups, or tables

   Ask: How many items are there for each group? 3 liters for each group or table

2. Have students explain in their own words why they need to multiply to solve the problem. **Sample explanation:** Since there are 3 items or liters for each table and there are 6 tables, I need to multiply to find the total number of liters.

   Ask: What number sentence can you write to solve the problem? $6 \times 3 = 18$

3. Read the second Worked Example with students.

   Ask: What are you asked to find in this problem? how much water is in each bottle.

   Ask: What information are you given? The amount of water there is and the number of bottles it will be poured into.

   Ask: How many groups are there? 8 groups or water bottles What number sentence can you write to solve the problem? $24 \div 8 = 3$

4. Have students complete Problems 1–4. Encourage them to refer to the Worked Examples to remember the steps they should follow.

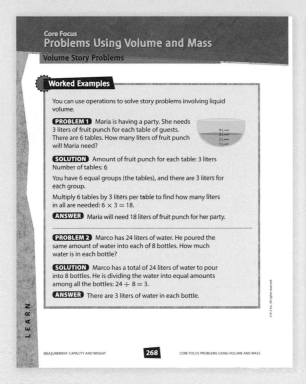

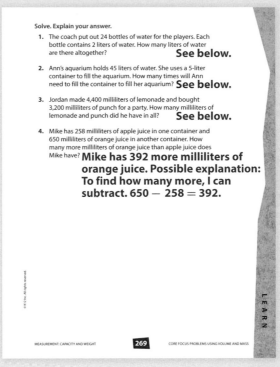

Additional Answers

1. There are 48 liters of water. **Possible explanation:** Since there are 24 bottles and each bottle contains 2 liters, I can multiply 24 times 2 to find the answer.

2. 9 times; **Possible explanation:** Since the container that Ann is using holds 5 liters, I can divide 45 by 5 to find how many times Ann will need to fill the 5-liter container.

3. He had 7,600 milliliters altogether. **Possible explanation:** 4,400 milliliters of lemonade + 3,200 milliliters of punch = 7,600 milliliters in all.

LEARN Mass Story Problems

OFFLINE **15 min**

Objectives

- Solve one-step word problems involving mass.

Students will solve simple 1-step story problems that involve operations with the metric units of mass, kilograms and grams. View or print the Mass Story Problems activity page and read the directions with students.

Students should copy the problems from the Activity Book into their Math Notebook as necessary and solve them there

1. Read the first Worked Example with students.

   Ask: What are you asked to find in this problem? the total mass of all the bricks

   Ask: What information are you given? the number of bricks and the mass of each brick

   Ask: What is the mass of each brick? 3 kilograms

   Ask: How many bricks are there in all? 25

2. Have students explain in their own words why they need to multiply to solve the problem. **Sample explanation:** Since each brick has a mass of 3 kilograms and there are 25 bricks in all, I need to multiply to find the total mass of all the bricks.

Ask: What number sentence can you write to solve the problem? $25 \times 3 = 75$

3. Read the second Worked Example with students. Have students complete Problems 1–4. Encourage them to refer to the Worked Examples to remember the steps they should follow.

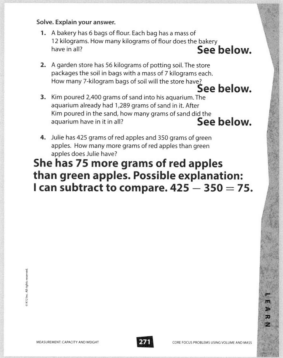

Additional Answers

1. The bakery has 72 kilograms of flour in all. **Possible explanation:** Since there are 6 bags and each bag contains 12 kilograms, I can multiply 6 times 12 to find the answer.

3. The aquarium had 3,689 grams of sand in all. **Possible explanation:** Since there were 1,289 grams of sand in the aquarium already and Kim added 2,400 grams, I can add the two amounts to find the total.

2. 8 bags; **Possible explanation:** Since each bag contains 7 kilograms, I can divide 56 by 7 to find how many bags of soil the store will have.

TRY IT Volume and Mass Story Problems

Students will practice solving simple 1-step problems involving metric units of volume and mass. View or print the Volume and Mass Story Problems activity page. Students should copy the problems into their Math Notebook and solve them there.

Objectives
- Solve one-step word problems involving mass.
- Solve one-step word problems involving volume.

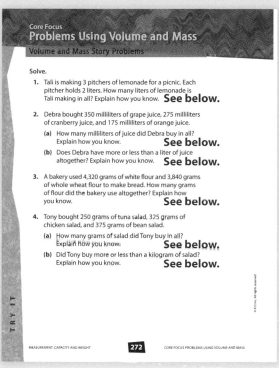

Core Focus
Problems Using Volume and Mass
Volume and Mass Story Problems

Solve.

1. Tali is making 3 pitchers of lemonade for a picnic. Each pitcher holds 2 liters. How many liters of lemonade is Tali making in all? Explain how you know. **See below.**

2. Debra bought 350 milliliters of grape juice, 275 milliliters of cranberry juice, and 175 milliliters of orange juice.

   (a) How many milliliters of juice did Debra buy in all? Explain how you know. **See below.**

   (b) Does Debra have more or less than a liter of juice altogether? Explain how you know. **See below.**

3. A bakery used 4,320 grams of white flour and 3,840 grams of whole wheat flour to make bread. How many grams of flour did the bakery use altogether? Explain how you know. **See below.**

4. Tony bought 250 grams of tuna salad, 325 grams of chicken salad, and 375 grams of bean salad.

   (a) How many grams of salad did Tony buy in all? Explain how you know. **See below.**

   (b) Did Tony buy more or less than a kilogram of salad? Explain how you know. **See below.**

MEASUREMENT: CAPACITY AND WEIGHT **272** CORE FOCUS PROBLEMS USING VOLUME AND MASS

Think like a Mathematician Self-Check

5. State the actions and thinking you used during this lesson as a math learner.

Math Thinking and Actions
I made sense of problems by • Explaining to myself what a problem means and what it asks for • Using drawings or diagrams to represent a problem I was solving
I explained my math thinking clearly.
I tried out new ways to check if an answer is reasonable.
Other

MEASUREMENT: CAPACITY AND WEIGHT **273** CORE FOCUS PROBLEMS USING VOLUME AND MASS

Answers

1. 6 liters; **Possible explanation:** Each pitcher hold 2 liters and there are 3 pitchers, so I multiply 2 times 3 to find the answer.

3. The bakery used 8,160 grams of flour. **Possible explanation:** I added the mass of the white flour and the mass of the whole wheat flour to find the total mass of the flour.

2. (a) Debra bought 800 milliliters of juice. **Possible explanation:** I can add to find the total amount: $350 + 275 + 175 = 800$.

   (b) Debra has less than a liter of juice. **Possible explanation:** There are 1,000 milliliters in 1 liter. Debra has 800 milliliters of juice. $800 < 1,000$.

4. (a) 950 grams; **Possible explanation:** I added the mass of each type of salad Tony bought to find the total number of grams: $250 + 325 + 375 = 950$ grams.

   (b) Tony bought less than a kilogram of salad. **Possible explanation:** There are 1,000 grams in a kilogram. Tony bought 950 grams of salad. $950 < 1,000$.

CHECKPOINT

Students will complete an online Checkpoint. If necessary, read the directions, problems, and answer choices to students and help them with keyboard or mouse operations.

Objectives
- Solve one-step word problems involving mass.
- Solve one-step word problems involving volume.

Unit Review

UNIT REVIEW Look Back	10 minutes	**ONLINE**
UNIT REVIEW Checkpoint Practice	50 minutes	**ONLINE**
⏩ **UNIT REVIEW** Prepare for the Checkpoint		

▶ Unit Objectives

- Identify the appropriate tools for measuring liquid volume.
- Identify the appropriate metric and English units for measuring liquid volume.
- Estimate and measure liquid volume to the nearest liter.
- Estimate and measure liquid volume to the nearest cup.
- Identify the appropriate tools for measuring the weight or mass of an object.
- Identify the appropriate metric and English units for measuring the weight or mass of an object.
- Estimate and measure the mass of an object to the nearest gram.
- Estimate and measure the weight of an object to the nearest ounce.
- Write a simple unit conversion, such as inches to feet, as an expression or an equation.
- Use a simple unit conversion, such as centimeters to meters, to solve a problem.
- Solve a unit-conversion story problem by using multiplication or division.
- Solve one-step word problems involving volume.
- Solve one-step word problems involving mass.

Materials to Gather

There are no materials to gather for this lesson.

▶ Advance Preparation

In this lesson, students will have an opportunity to review previous activities in the Measurement: Capacity and Weight unit. Look at the suggested activities in Unit Review: Prepare for the Checkpoint online and gather any needed materials.

ONLINE
10 min

UNIT REVIEW Look Back

Students will review key concepts from the unit to prepare for the Unit Checkpoint.

Objectives

- Review unit objectives.

ONLINE

50min

Objectives

- Review unit objectives.

Students will complete an online Checkpoint Practice to prepare for the Unit Checkpoint. If necessary, read the directions, problems, and answer choices to students. Have students answer the problems on their own. Review any missed problems with students.

➔ UNIT REVIEW Prepare for the Checkpoint

What you do next depends on how students performed in the previous activity, Unit Review: Checkpoint Practice. If students had difficulty with any of the problems, complete the appropriate review activity listed in the table online.

Unit Checkpoint

UNIT CHECKPOINT Online	60 minutes	**ONLINE**

▶ Unit Objectives

- Identify the appropriate tools for measuring liquid volume.
- Identify the appropriate metric and English units for measuring liquid volume.
- Estimate and measure liquid volume to the nearest liter.
- Estimate and measure liquid volume to the nearest cup.
- Identify the appropriate tools for measuring the weight or mass of an object.
- Identify the appropriate metric and English units for measuring the weight or mass of an object.
- Estimate and measure the mass of an object to the nearest gram.
- Estimate and measure the weight of an object to the nearest ounce.
- Write a simple unit conversion, such as inches to feet, as an expression or an equation.
- Use a simple unit conversion, such as centimeters to meters, to solve a problem.
- Solve a unit-conversion story problem by using multiplication or division.
- Solve one-step word problems involving volume.
- Solve one-step word problems involving mass.

Materials to Gather

There are no materials to gather for this lesson.

UNIT CHECKPOINT Online ONLINE **60**min

Objectives

- Assess unit objectives.

Students will complete the Unit Checkpoint online. If necessary, read the directions, problems, and answer choices to students and help them with keyboard or mouse operations.

Extended Problems: Real-World Application

GRADED ASSIGNMENT   60 minutes **OFFLINE**

▶ Lesson Objectives

- Identify the appropriate metric and English units for measuring liquid volume.
- Identify the appropriate metric and English units for measuring the weight or mass of an object.
- Measure and estimate masses of objects using standard units of grams (g) or kilograms (kg).
- Solve one-step word problems involving mass.
- Solve one-step word problems involving volume.
- Draw a scaled bar graph to represent a data set with several categories.
- Solve simple comparison problems using information from a bar graph.
- Solve word problems involving measurements and arrays using multiplication or division within 100.
- Apply mathematical knowledge and skills to evaluate and analyze real-world situations.

Materials to Gather

SUPPLIED

Extended Problems: Real-World Application (printout)

GRADED ASSIGNMENT

OFFLINE
60min

Objectives

Open the Extended Problems: Real-World Application. Read the directions, problems, and answer choices to students, if necessary.
   You will grade this assignment.

- Students should complete the assignment on their own.
- Students should submit the completed assignment to you.
- Enter the results online.

- Apply mathematical knowledge and skills to evaluate and analyze real-world situations.

Mathematical Reasoning

▶ Unit Objectives

- Analyze a story problem by identifying the question, recognizing relevant information, and developing a solution strategy.

- Demonstrate when and how to break a multistep story problem into simpler steps.

- Apply strategies and results from a simpler story problem to either a more complex problem or to a similar problem.

- Explain mathematical reasoning in a story problem by using words, numbers, symbols, charts, graphs, tables, diagrams, or models.

- Determine the answer to a story problem to a specific degree of accuracy, such as hundreds or tens.

- Explain the advantages of exact answers and approximate answers to story problems.

- Check the accuracy of a calculation in a story problem.

▶ Big Ideas

- The use of letters, numbers, and mathematical symbols makes possible the translation of complex situations or long word statements into concise mathematical sentences or expressions.

- Estimation is a useful tool in problem solving.

▶ Unit Introduction

In this unit, students will develop strategies to solve story problems by identifying the question they must answer; determining when and how to break a multistep problem into simpler parts; and using words, numbers, graphs, tables, and models to explain their problem-solving reasoning about problem situations. They will learn the importance of estimating to verify the reasonableness of answers. They will find that some story problems require an exact answer while others may need only an approximate solution. As students learn to analyze problems, they will use a variety of strategies to solve story problems, explain the advantage of using a particular strategy for a given problem, compute answers to a given degree of accuracy, check the accuracy of their answer, and be able to explain their reasoning by following a 4-step problem-solving plan: (1) understand the problem; (2) devise a plan; (3) carry out the plan; and (4) look back.

▶ Keywords

approximate (v.)	expression	reasoning
degree of accuracy	reasonableness	strategy
estimate (n.)		

Analyze Story Problems (A)

Lesson Overview

GET READY The Yo-Yo Train	5 minutes	**ONLINE**
LEARN Identify Needed Facts	15 minutes	**ONLINE**
LEARN Necessary Information	15 minutes	**ONLINE**
LEARN Sort Problem Facts	10 minutes	**ONLINE**
TRY IT Needed and Unneeded Facts	15 minutes	**ONLINE**

▶ Lesson Objectives

Analyze a story problem by identifying the question, recognizing relevant information, and developing a solution strategy.

▶ Prerequisite Skills

Determine whether addition, subtraction, multiplication, or division is the appropriate operation to use to solve a story problem and solve the problem.

▶ Content Background

Students will learn to identify the question in a story problem. They will also learn to identify the information they need and the information they don't need to solve a story problem.

Solving a story problem is a strategic process; it is often not a straightforward one. The following 4-step problem-solving method was developed by George Pólya, and it is an effective way to solve a variety of story problems: (1) understand the problem; (2) devise a plan; (3) carry out the plan; and (4) look back.

If students have difficulty with the first step of this process—understand the problem—it will interfere with their ability to solve the problem. The secret to success is in students' ability to carefully read the problem, reword the problem, analyze the question, and find relationships among the given pieces of information. Once students complete these steps, they can recognize relevant and irrelevant information and gain the confidence to proceed to the second step—devise a plan. They devise their plan by deciding on an effective strategy for solving the problem.

In this lesson, students will focus on the first step of Pólya's problem-solving plan. They will focus on identifying the question and the relevant and irrelevant information. Students should realize that there is often more than one way to solve a problem and more than one strategy they can use. By using many different strategies, they learn to be flexible in their problem solving and learn that some strategies are more efficient than others.

GET READY The Yo-Yo Train

ONLINE
5min

Objectives

- Determine whether addition, subtraction, multiplication, or division is the appropriate operation to use to solve a story problem and solve the problem.

Students will solve a multistep story problem about a yo-yo train. The problem involves adding and subtracting distances.

1. Read the online problem with students. Discuss strategies to solve the problem.
2. Guide students to solve the problem and explain their steps. They might mentally add and subtract, add and subtract on paper, or sketch a number line to help them keep track of the forward and backward distances.

   Ask: What information in the problem is not needed? the statement that the train stopped for 30 minutes
3. Have students enter their answer and check it.

LEARN Identify Needed Facts

ONLINE
15min

Objectives

- Analyze a story problem by identifying the question, recognizing relevant information, and developing a solution strategy.

Students will identify the question in a given story problem, the facts they need to solve the problem, and the facts they do not need. Explain to students that when they are figuring out problems in everyday life, they can follow these same steps. They should consider all the information, then decide what information they need and what they do not need to solve the problem.

LEARN Necessary Information

ONLINE
15min

Objectives

- Analyze a story problem by identifying the question, recognizing relevant information, and developing a solution strategy.

Students will identify the necessary and unnecessary information in a story problem. They will also identify additional information needed to solve a problem. The focus is on understanding the problem and deciding what information they need. Have students ask themselves, "Do I understand all the words in the problem?"

Discuss the meaning of any unknown words in the story problem. As students do the activity, ask them the following questions:

- What is the question I have to answer?
- What information in the problem is needed to answer the question?
- What information in the problem is not needed?

Explain that information that is needed is the necessary information. The information that is not needed is the unnecessary information. In some cases there may also be missing information. Students should get into the habit of asking themselves what (if any) information is not given in the problem, but is needed to answer the question. Explain to students that when they are figuring out problems in everyday life, they can follow these same steps. They should consider all the information, then decide what information they need and what they do not need to solve the problem.

LEARN Sort Problem Facts

Students will identify which given facts are needed and which are not needed to solve different story problem questions.

Objectives

- Analyze a story problem by identifying the question, recognizing relevant information, and developing a solution strategy.

TRY IT Needed and Unneeded Facts

ONLINE 15min

Students will complete an online Try It. If necessary, read the directions, problems, and answer choices to students and help them with keyboard or mouse operations.

Objectives

- Analyze a story problem by identifying the question, recognizing relevant information, and developing a solution strategy.

Analyze Story Problems (B)

Lesson Overview

LEARN Problem-Solving Plan	15 minutes	**ONLINE**
LEARN Plan a Solution Strategy	30 minutes	**OFFLINE**
TRY IT Understand and Plan	15 minutes	**OFFLINE**

▶ Lesson Objectives

Analyze a story problem by identifying the question, recognizing relevant information, and developing a solution strategy.

▶ Prerequisite Skills

Determine whether addition, subtraction, multiplication, or division is the appropriate operation to use to solve a story problem and solve the problem.

▶ Content Background

Solving a story problem is a strategic process; it is often not a straightforward one. The following 4-step problem-solving method was developed by George Pólya, and it is an effective way to solve a variety of story problems: (1) understand the problem; (2) devise a plan; (3) carry out the plan; and (4) look back.

   If students have difficulty with the first step of this process—understand the problem—it will interfere with their ability to solve the problem. The secret to success is in students' ability to carefully read the problem, reword the problem, analyze the question, and find relationships among the given pieces of information. Once students complete these steps, they can recognize relevant and irrelevant information and gain the confidence to proceed to the second step—devise a plan. They devise their plan by deciding on an effective strategy for solving the problem.

   Students should realize that there is often more than one way to solve a problem and more than one strategy they can use. By using many different strategies, they learn to be flexible in their problem solving and learn that some strategies are more efficient than others.

▶ Advance Preparation

Print the Problem-Solving Plan.

Materials to Gather

SUPPLIED

Problem-Solving Plan (printout)

Plan a Solution Strategy activity page

Understand and Plan activity page

ONLINE

15 min

LEARN Problem-Solving Plan

Students will become familiar with Pólya's 4-step problem-solving plan, review the steps to understanding the problem, and learn about devising a plan. Devising a plan involves picking a strategy that makes the problem easier to solve.

Objectives

- Analyze a story problem by identifying the question, recognizing relevant information, and developing a solution strategy.

LEARN Plan a Solution Strategy

Objectives

- Analyze a story problem by identifying the question, recognizing relevant information, and developing a solution strategy.

Students will read a story problem and identify the question, the facts they need, and the facts they do not need. They'll develop a plan to solve it. Students will not be expected to solve the problem yet; instead, they will focus on the first two steps of the problem-solving plan. Gather the Problem-Solving Plan. View or print the Plan a Solution Strategy activity page and read the directions with students.

Students should copy the problems from the Activity Book to their Math Notebook as necessary and solve them there.

1. Give students the Problem-Solving Plan. Tell them that in this activity, they'll be focusing on the first two steps of the plan.

2. Read the story problem in the Worked Example with students.

   Say: The first step in solving the problem is to understand it. Read the problem again and look for any words you do not understand.

   Explain that the word *block* has several meanings. Make sure students know that the block in this problem is a city block from one corner to the next. Also make sure they know what it means to say that Joanna rode "3 times as many blocks."

3. Read the solution and answer with students. Make sure they understand why they don't need to know how far Joanna lives from her friend to solve this story problem.

4. Point out that this particular problem contains several smaller problems. (First students need to find how far Joanna rode the second day. Then students need to find out how far she rode in all.) Explain that many problems are made up of several smaller problems. Remind students that they have done multistep problems of this type in the past. Tell them that now they're learning to analyze multistep problems so they'll have more strategies to use in the future.

5. Have students look at the first step on the Problem-Solving Plan. Point out that they've completed this step for the problem in the Worked Example. Tell them that now they can devise a plan to solve the problem, which is the second step of the Problem-Solving Plan.

6. Tell students that making a table can be a good way to organize information. Mention that there are different ways to show information in a table, and that any way that organizes the information clearly is okay. Point out that the Worked Example shows two different ways to organize the information.

   Say: Another person might not use a table. That person might go straight to a number sentence and write $14 + 3 \times 14 = ?$ In this case, without a table to separate the parts of the problem, the person would need to use the rules for the order of operations. He or she would do the multiplication first and then do the addition.

7. Have students look at the second step on the Problem-Solving Plan. Point out the two strategies you've just discussed (make a table, chart, or graph; and translate into a number sentence).

8. Have students read Problem 1 and complete the table. Guide them to complete the problem.

9. Have students read Problem 2 and complete the table. Have them complete the problem. Students may refer to the Problem-Solving Plan for ideas on strategies they can use. If they cannot choose a strategy, suggest they use the "draw a picture or diagram" strategy and the "translate into a number sentence" strategy. Students do not need to solve the problems.

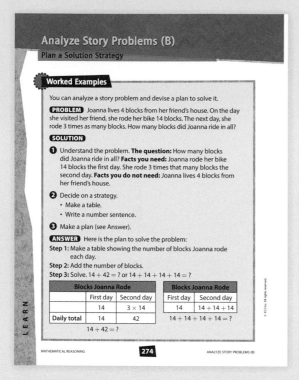

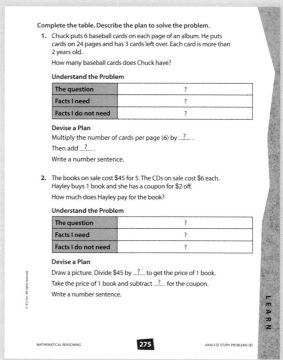

Additional Answers

1. **Question:** How many baseball cards does Chuck have?

    Facts I need: the number of cards on each page (6)

    the number of pages (24)

    the number of cards left over (3)

    Facts I do not need: The cards are 2 years old.

    Sample plan: Multiply the number of cards per page (6) by the number of pages (24). Then add the leftover cards (3). Write a number sentence.

2. **Question:** How much does Hayley pay for the book?

    Facts I need: Books on sale cost $45 for 5.

    Hayley buys 1 book.

    She has a coupon for $2 off.

    Facts I do not need: CDs on sale cost $6 each.

    Sample plan: Draw a picture. Divide $45 by 5 to get the price of 1 book. Take the price of 1 book and subtract $2 for the coupon. Write a number sentence.

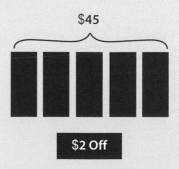

TRY IT Understand and Plan

Objectives

Students will practice devising a plan for solving a problem by deciding which strategy makes it easier to solve. View or print the Understand and Plan activity page and read the directions with students.

Students should copy the problems from the Activity Book into their Math Notebook as necessary and solve them there.

- Analyze a story problem by identifying the question, recognizing relevant information, and developing a solution strategy.

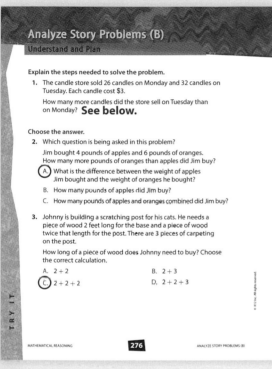

Analyze Story Problems (B)
Understand and Plan

Explain the steps needed to solve the problem.

1. The candle store sold 26 candles on Monday and 32 candles on Tuesday. Each candle cost $3.

   How many more candles did the store sell on Tuesday than on Monday? **See below.**

Choose the answer.

2. Which question is being asked in this problem?

   Jim bought 4 pounds of apples and 6 pounds of oranges. How many more pounds of oranges than apples did Jim buy?

   A. What is the difference between the weight of apples Jim bought and the weight of oranges he bought?

   B. How many pounds of apples did Jim buy?

   C. How many pounds of apples and oranges combined did Jim buy?

3. Johnny is building a scratching post for his cats. He needs a piece of wood 2 feet long for the base and a piece of wood twice that length for the post. There are 3 pieces of carpeting on the post.

   How long of a piece of wood does Johnny need to buy? Choose the correct calculation.

   A. $2 + 2$ B. $2 + 3$

   C. $2 + 2 + 2$ D. $2 + 3 + 3$

4. Which information is necessary to solve this problem?

   There were 58 blackbirds and 6 sparrows sitting in a tree. At 12:30 p.m., 26 more blackbirds landed on the tree, and 12 blackbirds flew away.

   How many blackbirds were left on the tree?

   A. 58 blackbirds, 26 blackbirds, 12 blackbirds

   B. 58 blackbirds, 26 blackbirds, 6 sparrows, 12 blackbirds

   C. 58 blackbirds, 12:30 p.m., 12 blackbirds

5. Which option shows steps that could be used to solve this problem?

   Joanne drove 126 miles the first day. She drove twice as far the second day.

   How far did Joanne drive in 2 days?

   A. Add 126 and 126 and then multiply by 2.

   B. Add 126 and 126 and then divide by 2.

   C. Multiply 126 by 2 and then add 126.

6. Which **two** options show steps that could be used to solve this problem?

   Olivia has two soup mixes in her cupboard. One mix makes 18 ounces of soup and one mix makes 24 ounces of soup. Each bowl holds 6 ounces of soup.

   How many bowls of soup can Olivia make?

   A. **Step 1:** Divide 18 by 6.
      Step 2: Divide 24 by 6.
      Step 3: Add the two quotients.

   B. **Step 1:** Add 18 and 24.
      Step 2: Divide the sum by 6.

   C. **Step 1:** Divide 18 by 6.
      Step 2: Divide 24 by 6.
      Step 3: Subtract the two quotients.

Choose the answer.

7. Which **two** options show steps that could be used to solve this problem?

   Tickets to a concert cost $25 for adults and $13 for children.

   How much would tickets cost for 3 adults and 3 children?

   A. **Step 1:** Subtract $13 from $25.
      Step 2: Multiply the answer by 3.

   B. **Step 1:** Multiply $25 by 3.
      Step 2: Multiply $13 by 3.
      Step 3: Add the two products.

   C. **Step 1:** Add $25 and $13.
      Step 2: Multiply the answer by 3.

Additional Answer

1. **Example:** Subtract the number of candles sold on Monday from the number of candles sold on Tuesday.

Analyze Story Problems (C)

▶ Lesson Objectives

Analyze a story problem by identifying the question, recognizing relevant information, and developing a solution strategy.

▶ Prerequisite Skills

Determine whether addition, subtraction, multiplication, or division is the appropriate operation to use to solve a story problem and solve the problem.

▶ Content Background

Students will use the first 2 steps of the 4-step problem-solving plan to analyze story problems and create solution strategies. They will learn to identify the question in a story problem. They'll also learn to identify the information they need and the information they do not need to solve the problem.

Solving a story problem is a strategic process; it is often not a straightforward one. The following 4-step problem-solving method was developed by George Pólya, and it is an effective way to solve a variety of story problems: (1) understand the problem; (2) devise a plan; (3) carry out the plan; and (4) look back.

If students have difficulty with the first step of this process—understand the problem—it can interfere with their ability to solve the problem. The secret to success is in students' ability to carefully read the problem, reword the problem, analyze the question, and find relationships among the given pieces of information. Once students complete these steps, they can recognize relevant and irrelevant information and gain the confidence to proceed to the second step—devise a plan. They devise their plan by deciding on an effective strategy for solving the problem.

In this lesson, students will continue to focus on the first step of Pólya's problem-solving plan. They will focus on identifying the question and the relevant and irrelevant information. Students should realize that there is often more than one way to solve a problem and more than one strategy they can use. By using many different strategies, they learn to be flexible in their problem solving and learn that some strategies are more efficient than others.

Materials to Gather

SUPPLIED

Problem-Solving Plan (printout)

Amusement Park Fun activity page

What Are the Steps? activity page

▶ Advance Preparation

Print the Problem-Solving Plan. Save it for use throughout the lesson.
For the Learn: Bakery Stories activity, write the following two problems:

- **Problem 1:** The baker used 25 cups of white flour, 2 cups of whole wheat flour, and 7 cups of sugar each day. How much flour did the baker use in 5 days?

- **Problem 2:** The baker sold 50 boxes of cookies and 20 pies on Saturday. She sold 30 boxes of cookies on Sunday. If the baker sold each box of cookies for $8, how much money did she earn selling cookies on Saturday and Sunday?

GET READY Wildlife Count

OFFLINE **5**min

Objectives

- Determine whether addition, subtraction, multiplication, or division is the appropriate operation to use to solve a story problem and solve the problem.

Students will use what they know about the problem-solving plan to solve a unique story problem that requires common knowledge about animals to get all the needed information.
Gather the Problem-Solving Plan.

1. Give students the Problem-Solving Plan. Review the first two steps of the plan with them.

2. Present the following problem to students:
   - The wildlife count showed that there were 90 deer, 60 birds, and 20 snakes. How many feet were there?

3. Have students follow the Problem-Solving Plan to explain what they understand about the problem, which information they need, and which information they do not need. Students should also recognize that they need to know that deer have 4 feet, birds have 2 feet, and snakes have no feet. needed: the number of deer and the number of birds; not needed: the number of snakes

4. Have students share their their plan to solve the problem and the order in which they would complete the steps. Answers may include multiplying 4 times 90, multiplying 2 times 60, and adding the two products.
   $90 \times 4 = 360$
   $60 \times 2 = 120$
   $360 + 120 = 480$
   There are 480 feet in the wildlife count.

LEARN Bakery Stories

OFFLINE **15**min

Objectives

- Analyze a story problem by identifying the question, recognizing relevant information, and developing a solution strategy.

Students will explain the first two steps for solving a multistep story problem.
Gather the Problem-Solving Plan and the two problems you wrote.

1. Have students read the first story problem. Refer to the Problem-Solving Plan and have students ask themselves the questions listed in the first step.

2. Have students ask themselves the following questions to check their understanding of the problem:

   • What question do I need to answer? How much flour did the baker use in 5 days?

   • What facts do I need? The baker used 25 cups of white flour and 2 cups of whole wheat flour each day.

   • What facts do I not need? The baker used 7 cups of sugar each day.

3. Tell students that once they understand the problem, they need to devise a plan to solve it. Refer to the second step of the Problem-Solving Plan. Have students ask themselves the following questions:

   • What are some strategies I've used before that might be good for this problem?

   • Is this a multistep problem?

   • Is there a picture or diagram I could draw?

   • Can I model the problem with objects?

   • What steps will I use to solve the problem?

4. Have students explain the strategies they will use and the steps to solving the problem.

5. Point out that some students might solve the problem by multiplying 5 × 25, multiplying 5 × 2, and then adding the products.

   Point out that other students might solve the problem by adding 25 + 2 and then multiplying 5 × 27.

   Ask students which way is easier for them and have them explain why, which will give insights into how they problem solve.

6. Have students read the second story problem and ask themselves the questions listed in the first step of the Problem-Solving Plan.

7. Have students ask themselves the following questions to check their understanding of the problem:

   • What question do I need to answer? How much money did the baker earn selling cookies on Saturday and Sunday?

   • What facts do I need? The baker sold 50 boxes of cookies on Saturday. She sold 30 boxes of cookies on Sunday. The baker sold each box of cookies for $8.

   • What facts do I not need? She sold 20 pies on Saturday.

8. Remind students that once they understand the problem, they need to devise a plan to solve it. Refer to the second step of the Problem-Solving Plan. Have students ask themselves the the questions in Step 3 above.

9. Have students explain the strategies they will use and the steps to solving the problem.

10. Point out that some students might solve the problem by multiplying $8 × 50, multiplying $8 × 30, and then adding the products. Explain that others might add all the cookies together, 50 + 30, and then multiply, $8 × 80. Discuss with students which method they think is easier.

LEARN Amusement Park Fun

Students will analyze a story problem and devise a plan to solve it. Gather the Problem-Solving Plan. View or print the Amusement Park Fun activity page and read the directions with students.

Students should copy the problems from the Activity Book into their Math Notebook as necessary and solve them there.

1. Read the Worked Example with students. Point out that the solution shows two different strategies that can be used to answer the question. Tell students that they may use any strategy that helps them solve a problem.

2. Read Problem 1 with students. Refer to the Problem-Solving Plan and have students ask themselves the questions listed in the first step.

3. Have students complete the chart to check their understanding of the question and separate the facts into those needed and those not needed.

4. Guide students to devise a plan to solve the problem. Refer to the second step in the Problem-Solving Plan. Have students ask themselves the following questions:

   - What are some strategies I've used before that might be good for this problem?
   - Is this a multistep problem?
   - Is there a picture or diagram I could draw?
   - Can I model the problem with objects?
   - What steps will I use to solve the problem?

5. Have students record their plan to solve the problem.

6. Repeat Steps 1–5 above for Problems 2–5.

Objectives

- Analyze a story problem by identifying the question, recognizing relevant information, and developing a solution strategy.

Tips

Encourage students to use a variety of strategies to solve the problems.

Analyze Story Problems (C)
Amusement Park Fun

Worked Examples

You can analyze a story problem and devise a plan to solve it.

PROBLEM Describe the plan to solve the problem.
- The day camp counselors are taking 42 children and 8 adults to an amusement park. They have 5 buses and 3 vans. If they take only the buses and put same number of people on each bus, how many people will ride on each bus?

SOLUTION 1

❶ Understand the problem.
You need to make a plan to solve the problem.
The question: How many people will ride on each bus?
Facts you need: There are 42 children and 8 adults going to the amusement park. They will ride in 5 buses. The same number of people will ride on each bus. **Facts you do not need:** They have 3 vans.

❷ Decide on a strategy.
- Use logical reasoning to make a list of steps.
- Translate into a number sentence.

❸ Make the plan (see Answer).

ANSWER Here is the plan to solve the problem:
Step 1: Add 42 + 8 to find how many people will ride on buses.
   $42 + 8 = 50$
Step 2: Divide the total by 5 to find out how many will be on each bus.
Step 3: Solve. $50 ÷ 5 = ?$

MATHEMATICAL REASONING   279   ANALYZE STORY PROBLEMS (C)

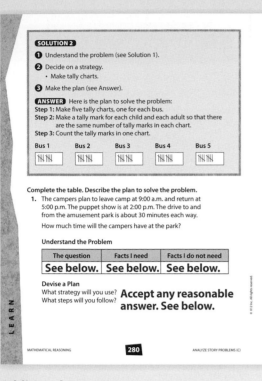

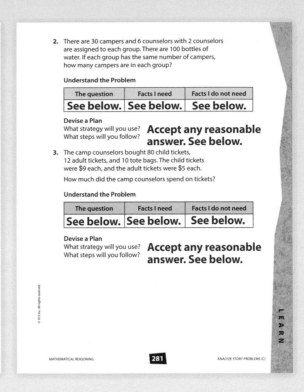

Additional Answers

1.

The question	Facts I need	Facts I do not need
How much time will the campers have at the park?	The campers plan to leave camp at 9:00 a.m. and return at 5:00 p.m. The drive to and from the amusement park is about 30 minutes each way.	The puppet show is at 2:00 p.m.

Example:

Step 1: Find how many hours there are between 9:00 a.m. and 5:00 p.m.

Step 2: Subtract 30 minutes twice to take away the time spent driving.

2.

The question	Facts I need	Facts I do not need
How many campers are in each group?	There are 30 campers and 6 counselors, with 2 counselors assigned to each group.	There are 100 bottles of water.

Example:

Step 1: Divide 6 by 2 to find how many groups.

Step 2: Divide 30 by the quotient to find how many campers are in each group.

3.

The question	Facts I need	Facts I do not need
How much did the camp counselors spend on tickets?	The camp counselors bought 80 child tickets and 12 adult tickets. The child tickets were $9 each, and the adult tickets were $5 each.	They bought 10 tote bags.

Example:

Step 1: Multiply $9 × 80 to get the cost of the child tickets.

Step 2: Multiply $5 × 12 to find the cost of the adult tickets.

Step 3: Add the products.

4.

The question	Facts I need	Facts I do not need
How much did each patch cost?	Counselor Tim spent $20 on 4 patches.	Counselor Tim spent $6 on snacks.

Example: Divide $20 by 4 to find how much each patch costs.

5.

The question	Facts I need	Facts I do not need
How many miles did the bus drivers drive on the way home?	The bus drivers drove 20 miles to the amusement park. They drove an additional 2 miles when they had to take a detour on the way home.	They parked for 6 hours.

Example: Add 20 + 2 to find the total number of miles driven on the way home.

OFFLINE
10min

TRY IT What Are the Steps?

Objectives

Students will practice analyzing a story problem and making a plan to solve the problem. View or print the What Are the Steps? activity page and read the directions with students.

Students should copy the problems from the Activity Book into their Math Notebook as necessary and solve them there.

- Analyze a story problem by identifying the question, recognizing relevant information, and developing a solution strategy.

Tips   Allow students to refer to the Problem-Solving Plan if needed.

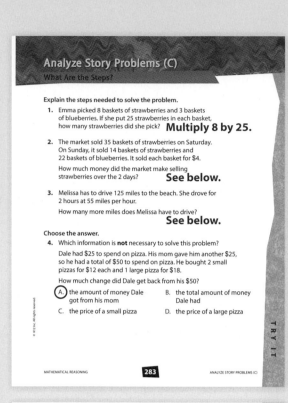

Analyze Story Problems (C)
What Are the Steps?

Explain the steps needed to solve the problem.

1. Emma picked 8 baskets of strawberries and 3 baskets of blueberries. If she put 25 strawberries in each basket, how many strawberries did she pick? **Multiply 8 by 25.**

2. The market sold 35 baskets of strawberries on Saturday. On Sunday, it sold 14 baskets of strawberries and 22 baskets of blueberries. It sold each basket for $4.

    How much money did the market make selling strawberries over the 2 days?   **See below.**

3. Melissa has to drive 125 miles to the beach. She drove for 2 hours at 55 miles per hour.

    How many more miles does Melissa have to drive?   **See below.**

Choose the answer.

4. Which information is **not** necessary to solve this problem?

    Dale had $25 to spend on pizza. His mom gave him another $25, so he had a total of $50 to spend on pizza. He bought 2 small pizzas for $12 each and 1 large pizza for $18.

    How much change did Dale get back from his $50?

    (A.) the amount of money Dale got from his mom
    B. the total amount of money Dale had
    C. the price of a small pizza
    D. the price of a large pizza

TRY IT

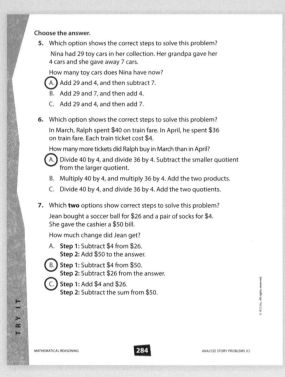

Choose the answer.

5. Which option shows the correct steps to solve this problem?

    Nina had 29 toy cars in her collection. Her grandpa gave her 4 cars and she gave away 7 cars.

    How many toy cars does Nina have now?

    (A.) Add 29 and 4, and then subtract 7.
    B. Add 29 and 7, and then add 4.
    C. Add 29 and 4, and then add 7.

6. Which option shows the correct steps to solve this problem?

    In March, Ralph spent $40 on train fare. In April, he spent $36 on train fare. Each train ticket cost $4.

    How many more tickets did Ralph buy in March than in April?

    (A.) Divide 40 by 4, and divide 36 by 4. Subtract the smaller quotient from the larger quotient.
    B. Multiply 40 by 4, and multiply 36 by 4. Add the two products.
    C. Divide 40 by 4, and divide 36 by 4. Add the two quotients.

7. Which **two** options show correct steps to solve this problem?

    Jean bought a soccer ball for $26 and a pair of socks for $4. She gave the cashier a $50 bill.

    How much change did Jean get?

    A. **Step 1:** Subtract $4 from $26.
       Step 2: Add $50 to the answer.
    (B.) **Step 1:** Subtract $4 from $50.
       Step 2: Subtract $26 from the answer.
    (C.) **Step 1:** Add $4 and $26.
       Step 2: Subtract the sum from $50.

TRY IT

8. Which **two** options show correct steps to solve this problem?

    There were 2 times as many red lights as white lights on a strand of lights. There were 10 white lights on each strand.

    How many red lights were on 4 strands of lights?

    (A.) **Step 1:** Multiply 10 by 2.
       Step 2: Multiply the answer by 4.
    B. **Step 1:** Add 10 and 4.
       Step 2: Multiply the answer by 2.
    (C.) **Step 1:** Multiply 10 by 4.
       Step 2: Multiply the answer by 2.

TRY IT

Additional Answers

2. **Step 1:** Add the 35 + 14 (number of baskets of strawberries).
   Step 2: Multiply the sum by $4.
   Or
   Step 1: Multiply 35 × $4.
   Step 2: Multiply 14 × $4.
   Step 3: Add the products.

3. **Example:** Multiply the number of hours by the number of miles driven per hour (2 × 55). Subtract this number from 125 to figure out how many more miles Melissa has to drive.

CHECKPOINT

ONLINE
10min

Objectives

Students will complete an online Checkpoint. If necessary, read the directions, problems, and answer choices to students and help them with keyboard or mouse operations.

- Analyze a story problem by identifying the question, recognizing relevant information, and developing a solution strategy.

Understand Multistep Problems

Lesson Overview

GET READY Choose the Operation	5 minutes	ONLINE
LEARN Organize Information in a Problem	10 minutes	ONLINE
LEARN Make a Plan	20 minutes	OFFLINE
TRY IT Stepping Through Multistep Problems	15 minutes	OFFLINE
CHECKPOINT	10 minutes	ONLINE

▶ **Lesson Objectives**

Demonstrate when and how to break a multistep story problem into simpler steps.

▶ **Prerequisite Skills**

Determine whether addition, subtraction, multiplication, or division is the appropriate operation to use to solve a story problem and solve the problem.

▶ **Content Background**

In this lesson, students will learn to solve multistep problems by making a plan and breaking the problem into simpler steps.

Solving a story problem is a strategic process; it is often not a straightforward one. The following 4-step problem-solving method was developed by George Pólya, and it is an effective way to solve a variety of story problems: (1) understand the problem; (2) devise a plan; (3) carry out the plan; and (4) look back.

Although students use many problem-solving strategies—including invented strategies of their own—one strategy they can use when solving a multistep problem is to break the problem into simpler parts. Solving smaller problems can help students feel more confident when solving more complex problems. In this lesson, students will focus on when and how to break apart a story problem into simpler parts.

▶ **Advance Preparation**

Print the Problem-Solving Plan.

Materials to Gather

SUPPLIED
Problem-Solving Plan (printout)
Make a Plan activity page
Stepping Through Multistep Problems activity page

GET READY Choose the Operation

ONLINE
5min

Students will read a story problem and decide whether addition, subtraction, multiplication, or division should be used to solve the problem.

Objectives

• Determine whether addition, subtraction, multiplication, or division is the appropriate operation to use to solve a story problem and solve the problem.

LEARN Organize Information in a Problem

Students will use a problem-solving plan to solve a multistep problem. They will break the multistep problem into simpler problems. The strategy they will use will be to make a table to organize the information. The table will help students do each part of the problem.

- Demonstrate when and how to break a multistep story problem into simpler steps.

LEARN Make a Plan

Students will learn to break multistep problems into simpler problems. For this activity, they should focus on the steps to solve the problems. They do not need to get final answers but should record the steps they would use to get an answer. Gather the Problem-Solving Plan. View or print the Make a Plan activity page and read the directions with students.

Students should copy the problems from the Activity Book into their Math Notebook as necessary and solve them there.

- Demonstrate when and how to break a multistep story problem into simpler steps.

Tips

Note that students should be expected only to make a plan. They do not need to solve the problem.

1. Give students the Problem-Solving Plan. Review the first two steps of the plan with students.

2. Tell students that when devising a plan to solve the problem, they should ask themselves questions like these:
   - Is this a multistep problem?
   - What are some strategies I've used before that might be good for this problem?
   - Is there a picture or diagram I could draw?
   - Can I model the problem with objects?
   - What steps will I use to solve the problem?

3. Read the Worked Example with students. Point out that this problem is a multistep problem. Remind students that they should break multistep problems into simpler parts to solve them.

   Ask: Suppose Jaime's mother had only a $20 bill and she asked for change. What new step would be needed to find out how much change she received? I would need to subtract the total cost of food from $20.

4. Have students read Problem 1. Have them go through the problem and explain the steps to solve the problem. Students should recognize that they must first find how far the family bicycled and then add the distance the family traveled by train.

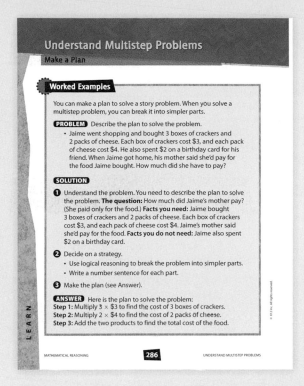

Understand Multistep Problems
Make a Plan

Worked Examples

You can make a plan to solve a story problem. When you solve a multistep problem, you can break it into simpler parts.

PROBLEM Describe the plan to solve the problem.

- Jaime went shopping and bought 3 boxes of crackers and 2 packs of cheese. Each box of crackers cost $3, and each pack of cheese cost $4. He also spent $2 on a birthday card for his friend. When Jaime got home, his mother said she'd pay for the food Jaime bought. How much did she have to pay?

SOLUTION

❶ Understand the problem. You need to describe the plan to solve the problem. **The question:** How much did Jaime's mother pay? (She paid only for the food.) **Facts you need:** Jaime bought 3 boxes of crackers and 2 packs of cheese. Each box of crackers cost $3, and each pack of cheese cost $4. Jaime's mother said she'd pay for the food. **Facts you do not need:** Jaime also spent $2 on a birthday card.

❷ Decide on a strategy.
- Use logical reasoning to break the problem into simpler parts.
- Write a number sentence for each part.

❸ Make the plan (see Answer).

ANSWER Here is the plan to solve the problem:
Step 1: Multiply 3 × $3 to find the cost of 3 boxes of crackers.
Step 2: Multiply 2 × $4 to find the cost of 2 packs of cheese.
Step 3: Add the two products to find the total cost of the food.

Describe the plan to solve the problem.

1. The Stewart family bicycled 46 miles each day for 5 days. Then they took a wilderness train 525 miles, arriving in Oz at 7:30 p.m.

How far did the Stewart family travel?

Step 1: Multiply 5 times 46 miles.
Step 2: Add 525 to the product.

TRY IT Stepping Through Multistep Problems

OFFLINE 15 min

Objectives

Students will practice identifying the steps needed to solve a multistep problem. View or print the Stepping Through Multistep Problems activity page and read the directions with students.

Students should copy the problems from the Activity Book into their Math Notebook as necessary and solve them there.

- Demonstrate when and how to break a multistep story problem into simpler steps.

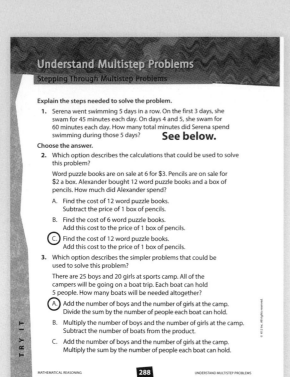

Understand Multistep Problems
Stepping Through Multistep Problems

Explain the steps needed to solve the problem.

1. Serena went swimming 5 days in a row. On the first 3 days, she swam for 45 minutes each day. On days 4 and 5, she swam for 60 minutes each day. How many total minutes did Serena spend swimming during those 5 days? **See below.**

Choose the answer.

2. Which option describes the calculations that could be used to solve this problem?

   Word puzzle books are on sale at 6 for $3. Pencils are on sale for $2 a box. Alexander bought 12 word puzzle books and a box of pencils. How much did Alexander spend?

   A. Find the cost of 12 word puzzle books. Subtract the price of 1 box of pencils.

   B. Find the cost of 6 word puzzle books. Add this cost to the price of 1 box of pencils.

   C. Find the cost of 12 word puzzle books. Add this cost to the price of 1 box of pencils. ⃝

3. Which option describes the simpler problems that could be used to solve this problem?

   There are 25 boys and 20 girls at sports camp. All of the campers will be going on a boat trip. Each boat can hold 5 people. How many boats will be needed altogether?

   A. Add the number of boys and the number of girls at the camp. Divide the sum by the number of people each boat can hold. ⃝

   B. Multiply the number of boys and the number of girls at the camp. Subtract the number of boats from the product.

   C. Add the number of boys and the number of girls at the camp. Multiply the sum by the number of people each boat can hold.

4. Which option describes the calculations that could be used to solve this problem?

   The Hudson family drove 96 miles each day for 3 days. They then flew 652 miles. How far did the Hudson family travel?

   A. Divide 96 by 3. Then add 652.

   B. Multiply 96 by 3. Then add 652. ⃝

   C. Multiply 96 by 3. Then subtract that product from 652.

5. Which option describes the calculations that could be used to solve this problem?

   Janine rode 34 miles on her bike the first day of her trip. On the second day, she rode twice as far. How far did Janine ride in 2 days?

   A. Add 34 and 2. Then add 2 to the sum.

   B. Multiply 34 by 2. Then add 34. ⃝

   C. Divide 34 by 2. Then add 2.

6. Which option describes the calculations that could be used to solve this problem?

   Noah earned $32 one week and $40 the following week. He makes $8 an hour. How many hours did Noah work in 2 weeks?

   A. Divide $32 by $8. Then add $40.

   B. Divide $32 by 8. Divide $40 by 8. Multiply the two quotients.

   C. Divide $32 by 8. Divide $40 by 8. Add the two quotients. ⃝

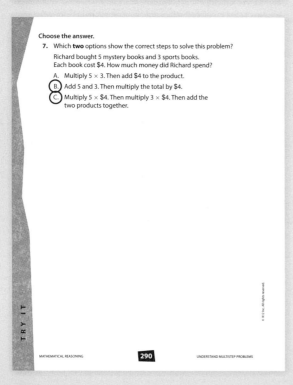

Choose the answer.

7. Which **two** options show the correct steps to solve this problem?

   Richard bought 5 mystery books and 3 sports books. Each book cost $4. How much money did Richard spend?

   A. Multiply 5 × 3. Then add $4 to the product.

   B. Add 5 and 3. Then multiply the total by $4. ⃝

   C. Multiply 5 × $4. Then multiply 3 × $4. Then add the two products together. ⃝

Additional Answer

1. **Possible explanation:** Multiply 3 × 45. Multiply 2 × 60. Add the products.

CHECKPOINT

ONLINE

10min

Objectives

Students will complete an online Checkpoint. If necessary, read the directions, problems, and answer choices to students and help them with keyboard or mouse operations.

• Demonstrate when and how to break a multistep story problem into simpler steps.

Strategies to Solve Complex Problems

Lesson Overview

GET READY Break Down Complex Problems	5 minutes	**ONLINE**
LEARN Problem-Solving Strategies	15 minutes	**OFFLINE**
LEARN Learn More Strategies	15 minutes	**OFFLINE**
TRY IT Strategy Practice	15 minutes	**OFFLINE**
CHECKPOINT	10 minutes	**ONLINE**

▶ Lesson Objectives

Apply strategies and results from a simpler story problem to either a more complex problem or to a similar problem.

▶ Prerequisite Skills

- Demonstrate an understanding of connections between similar addition or subtraction computation problems, involving sums and minuends up through 1,000.
- Analyze a story problem by identifying the question, recognizing relevant information, and developing a solution strategy.
- Demonstrate when and how to break a multistep story problem into simpler steps.

▶ Content Background

Students will learn to apply strategies or results from a simpler problem to a more complex problem.

Effective problem solvers use certain strategies over and over to solve different problems. For students to do this, they need to recognize similarities between problems. One problem-solving strategy they can employ is to use a simpler problem to solve a more complex problem. When using this strategy, students begin to see that instead of treating each problem as a new experience, they can apply successful strategies used in solving simple problems to solve more complex problems. More complex problems can include problems with greater numbers, problems with fractions and decimals, and multistep problems.

The following 4-step problem-solving plan was developed by George Pólya, and it is an effective way to solve a variety of story problems: (1) understand the problem; (2) devise a plan; (3) carry out the plan; and (4) look back. As students work on simple and complex problems, they should follow this plan. It is in the "devise a plan" step that students will decide if they can use a simpler problem to solve a more complex one.

▶ Advance Preparation

Print the Problem-Solving Plan. Save it for use throughout the lesson.

Materials to Gather

SUPPLIED

blocks – K (10 green)

Problem-Solving Plan (printout)

Problem-Solving Strategies activity page

Learn More Strategies activity page

Strategy Practice activity page

GET READY Break Down Complex Problems

ONLINE
5min

Objectives

Students will read questions related to a story problem and decide if they would need to break the problem down into simpler steps to solve it.

- Demonstrate an understanding of connections between similar addition or subtraction computation problems, involving sums and minuends up through 1,000.

- Analyze a story problem by identifying the question, recognizing relevant information, and developing a solution strategy.

- Demonstrate when and how to break a multistep story problem into simpler steps.

LEARN Problem-Solving Strategies

Objectives

- Apply strategies and results from a simpler story problem to either a more complex problem or to a similar problem.

Students will use the draw-a-sketch strategy and the guess-and-test strategy to understand and solve problems. They will will use charts and tables to organize the information. Gather the Problem-Solving Plan. View or print the Problem-Solving Strategies activity page and read the directions with students.

   Students should copy the problems from the Activity Book into their Math Notebook as necessary and solve them there.

1. Tell students that they will use the draw-a-sketch strategy and the guess-and-test strategy to understand and solve story problems.

2. Review the Problem-Solving Plan with students. Emphasize the second step, "devise a plan," and draw students' attention to the list of possible problem-solving strategies.

3. Read the first Worked Example with students. Go over each part of the Problem-Solving Plan as you go through the problem. When students are ready to calculate 8×14, ask them to make an estimate. They can think of it as 8×15 and calculate 8×10 plus 8×5 and add $80 + 40 = 120$ to get an estimate. Be sure students understand and can verify the answer.

4. Have students look at Problem 1. Discuss how this problem is similar to the Worked Example. Ask students how many beads are in each pattern. 4 red, 5 clear, and 4 black for a total of 13 beads in each pattern

   Ask: How many clear beads are in each pattern? 5

   Ask: How many copies of the pattern will it take to use 15 clear beads? 3

   Ask: How many beads will be in 1 necklace? $3 \times 13 = 39$ beads in 1 necklace

   Ask: How can you find out how many beads are in 4 necklaces? multiply 4×39

   Ask: How could you estimate your answer? multiply 4×40 to get an estimate of 160

5. Read the second Worked Example with students. This problem employs the guess-and-test strategy, using a table to keep track of the guesses. Discuss the benefits of using the table to organize the information generated with the guess-and-test strategy.

6. Have students do Problem 2, following the steps in the second Worked Example. In this problem the numbers are greater, so students may start with guesses that are multiples of 10. They may guess 10 for the number of tulips, and find that it's too low. They may jump to 20 and find that it's too high. A guess of 15 will work.

Have students do the "look back" step to make sure they answered the question asked in the problem and did their calculations correctly.

Remind students that they are getting experience with a wide range of strategies that will help them be better problem solvers.

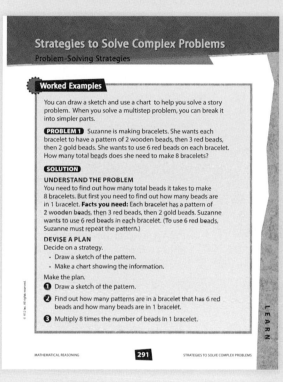

Strategies to Solve Complex Problems
Problem-Solving Strategies

Worked Examples

You can draw a sketch and use a chart to help you solve a story problem. When you solve a multistep problem, you can break it into simpler parts.

PROBLEM 1 Suzanne is making bracelets. She wants each bracelet to have a pattern of 2 wooden beads, then 3 red beads, then 2 gold beads. She wants to use 6 red beads on each bracelet. How many total beads does she need to make 8 bracelets?

SOLUTION

UNDERSTAND THE PROBLEM
You need to find out how many total beads it takes to make 8 bracelets. But first you need to find out how many beads are in 1 bracelet. **Facts you need:** Each bracelet has a pattern of 2 wooden beads, then 3 red beads, then 2 gold beads. Suzanne wants to use 6 red beads in each bracelet. (To use 6 red beads, Suzanne must repeat the pattern.)

DEVISE A PLAN
Decide on a strategy.
· Draw a sketch of the pattern.
· Make a chart showing the information.

Make the plan.
❶ Draw a sketch of the pattern.

❷ Find out how many patterns are in a bracelet that has 6 red beads and how many beads are in 1 bracelet.

❸ Multiply 8 times the number of beads in 1 bracelet.

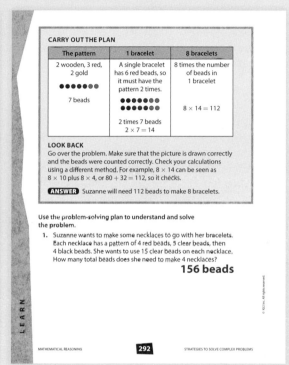

CARRY OUT THE PLAN

The pattern	1 bracelet	8 bracelets
2 wooden, 3 red, 2 gold ●●●●●●● 7 beads	A single bracelet has 6 red beads, so it must have the pattern 2 times. ●●●●●●● ●●●●●●● 2 times 7 beads $2 \times 7 = 14$	8 times the number of beads in 1 bracelet $8 \times 14 = 112$

LOOK BACK
Go over the problem. Make sure that the picture is drawn correctly and the beads were counted correctly. Check your calculations using a different method. For example, 8×14 can be seen as 8×10 plus 8×4, or $80 + 32 = 112$, so it checks.

ANSWER Suzanne will need 112 beads to make 8 bracelets.

Use the problem-solving plan to understand and solve the problem.

1. Suzanne wants to make some necklaces to go with her bracelets. Each necklace has a pattern of 4 red beads, 5 clear beads, then 4 black beads. She wants to use 15 clear beads on each necklace. How many total beads does she need to make 4 necklaces?

156 beads

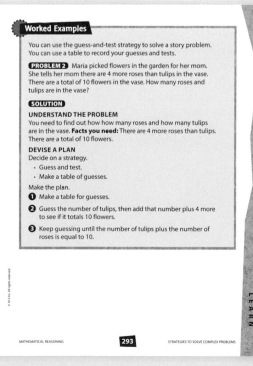

Worked Examples

You can use the guess-and-test strategy to solve a story problem. You can use a table to record your guesses and tests.

PROBLEM 2 Maria picked flowers in the garden for her mom. She tells her mom there are 4 more roses than tulips in the vase. There are a total of 10 flowers in the vase. How many roses and tulips are in the vase?

SOLUTION

UNDERSTAND THE PROBLEM
You need to find out how how many roses and how many tulips are in the vase. **Facts you need:** There are 4 more roses than tulips. There are a total of 10 flowers.

DEVISE A PLAN
Decide on a strategy.
· Guess and test.
· Make a table of guesses.

Make the plan.
❶ Make a table for guesses.

❷ Guess the number of tulips, then add that number plus 4 more to see if it totals 10 flowers.

❸ Keep guessing until the number of tulips plus the number of roses is equal to 10.

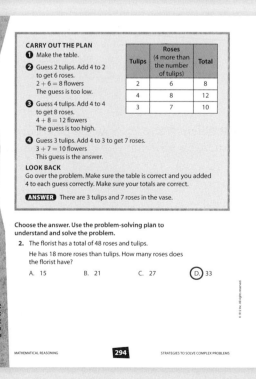

CARRY OUT THE PLAN
❶ Make the table.

❷ Guess 2 tulips. Add 4 to 2 to get 6 roses.
$2 + 6 = 8$ flowers
The guess is too low.

❸ Guess 4 tulips. Add 4 to 4 to get 8 roses.
$4 + 8 = 12$ flowers
The guess is too high.

❹ Guess 3 tulips. Add 4 to 3 to get 7 roses.
$3 + 7 = 10$ flowers
This guess is the answer.

Tulips	Roses (4 more than the number of tulips)	Total
2	6	8
4	8	12
3	7	10

LOOK BACK
Go over the problem. Make sure the table is correct and you added 4 to each guess correctly. Make sure your totals are correct.

ANSWER There are 3 tulips and 7 roses in the vase.

Choose the answer. Use the problem-solving plan to understand and solve the problem.

2. The florist has a total of 48 roses and tulips.
He has 18 more roses than tulips. How many roses does the florist have?

A. 15　　　　B. 21　　　　C. 27　　　　(D.) 33

LEARN Learn More Strategies

Objectives

- Apply strategies and results from a simpler story problem to either a more complex problem or to a similar problem.

Students will use tables and models to understand and solve story problems. They will use the results from a simpler problem-solving activity to solve a more complex problem. Gather the K blocks and the Problem-Solving Plan. View or print the Learn More Strategies activity page and read the directions with students.

Students should copy the problems from the Activity Book into their Math Notebook as necessary and solve them there.

1. Read the first Worked Example with students. Use the Problem-Solving Plan to guide students through the problem. Emphasize the benefit of using a table to organize the information in the problem. Discuss how students can use the answer from the first part of the problem to answer the second question.

2. Have students complete Problem 1 on their own.

3. Read the second Worked Example with students. Explain that the problem in this Worked Example is a complex problem, but if it is broken down into smaller, simpler problems, it becomes easier to solve.

4. Have students solve Problem 2 on their own.

5. Discuss with students that these were difficult problems but that by making a plan and using several strategies, the problems were much easier to solve.

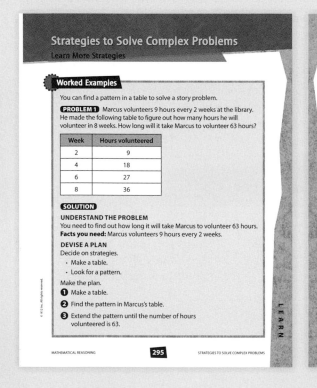

Strategies to Solve Complex Problems
Learn More Strategies

Worked Examples

You can find a pattern in a table to solve a story problem.

PROBLEM 1 Marcus volunteers 9 hours every 2 weeks at the library. He made the following table to figure out how many hours he will volunteer in 8 weeks. How long will it take Marcus to volunteer 63 hours?

Week	Hours volunteered
2	9
4	18
6	27
8	36

SOLUTION

UNDERSTAND THE PROBLEM
You need to find out how long it will take Marcus to volunteer 63 hours.
Facts you need: Marcus volunteers 9 hours every 2 weeks.

DEVISE A PLAN
Decide on strategies.
- Make a table.
- Look for a pattern.

Make the plan.
1. Make a table.
2. Find the pattern in Marcus's table.
3. Extend the pattern until the number of hours volunteered is 63.

MATHEMATICAL REASONING **295** STRATEGIES TO SOLVE COMPLEX PROBLEMS

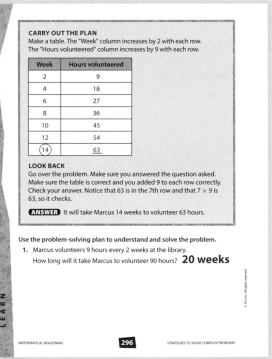

CARRY OUT THE PLAN
Make a table. The "Week" column increases by 2 with each row. The "Hours volunteered" column increases by 9 with each row.

Week	Hours volunteered
2	9
4	18
6	27
8	36
10	45
12	54
(14)	63

LOOK BACK
Go over the problem. Make sure you answered the question asked. Make sure the table is correct and you added 9 to each row correctly. Check your answer. Notice that 63 is in the 7th row and that 7×9 is 63, so it checks.

ANSWER It will take Marcus 14 weeks to volunteer 63 hours.

Use the problem-solving plan to understand and solve the problem.
1. Marcus volunteers 9 hours every 2 weeks at the library.
   How long will it take Marcus to volunteer 90 hours? **20 weeks**

MATHEMATICAL REASONING **296** STRATEGIES TO SOLVE COMPLEX PROBLEMS

Worked Examples

You can solve some story problems by solving simpler problems using a table. You can look for a pattern in that table and then use the pattern to solve the more complex problem.

PROBLEM 2 What is the distance around 50 triangular animal pens when they are set next to each other as shown? Each side = 1 unit, and all sides are the same length.

SOLUTION

UNDERSTAND THE PROBLEM
You need to find the distance around 50 triangular animal pens.
Facts you need: There are 50 triangular animal pens arranged as shown. Each side is 1 unit.

DEVISE A PLAN
Decide on strategies.
- Make a table.
- Use a model or drawing.
- Solve easier problems.
- Look for a pattern.

Make the plan.
❶ Make a table showing number of triangles and the distance around.
❷ Use a model or drawing and count to find the distance around 1 pen, then 2 pens, then 3 pens, and so on. Record the distances in the table.
❸ Find a pattern.
❹ Extend the pattern to find out what the distance around 50 triangular pens would be.

CARRY OUT THE PLAN
❶ Make the table.

Triangles	Distance around (units)
1	
2	
3	

❷ Model the problem and enter the information in the table.

Triangles	Distance around (units)
1	3
2	4
3	5
4	6
5	7
6	8
7	9

❸ Find the pattern. The pattern seems to be that the distance around is 2 more than the number of triangles.

❹ Extend the pattern. If the distance around is 2 more than the number of triangles, then for 10 triangles the distance around should be 12. Test to see if this is true.

Triangles	Distance around (units)
10	12

The pattern works.
For 50 triangles, the distance around would be 50 + 2 = 52.

Triangles	Distance around (units)
50	52

LOOK BACK
Go over the problem. Make sure you answered the question asked. Make sure the table is correct. Look for another way to explain it. Notice that with 10 triangles, there are 5 sides that make the distance along the top of the figure and 5 that make the distance along the bottom. So there are 5 + 5 sides on the top and bottom and 2 end sides that make the total distance of 12 units around the animal pens. If there were 50 triangles, there would be 25 + 25 sides on the top and bottom and 2 end sides, for a total of 52 units around the pens.

ANSWER The distance around 50 animal pens, arranged as shown, is 52 units.

Use the problem-solving plan to understand and solve the problem.

2. What is the distance around 100 triangular animal pens when they are set next to each other as shown? Each side = 1 unit, and all sides are the same length.

102 units

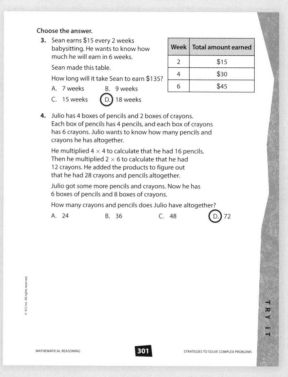

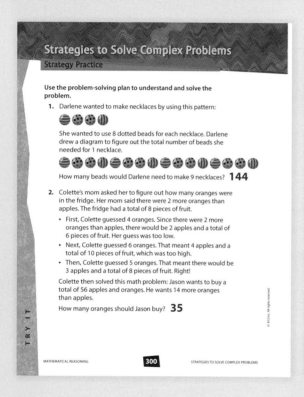

TRY IT Strategy Practice

Students will practice using a variety of strategies to solve complex story problems. Gather the Problem-Solving Plan. View or print the Strategy Practice activity page and read the directions with students.

Students should copy the problems from the Activity Book into their Math Notebook as necessary and solve them there.

- Apply strategies and results from a simpler story problem to either a more complex problem or to a similar problem.

Tips Allow students to refer to the Problem-Solving Plan if needed.

CHECKPOINT

Students will complete an online Checkpoint. If necessary, read the directions, problems, and answer choices to students and help them with keyboard or mouse operations.

- Apply strategies and results from a simpler story problem to either a more complex problem or to a similar problem.

Story Problem Reasoning (A)

Lesson Overview

LEARN Three Strategies	20 minutes	ONLINE
LEARN Work Backward	20 minutes	ONLINE
TRY IT Story Problem Practice	20 minutes	OFFLINE

▶ Lesson Objectives

Explain mathematical reasoning in a story problem by using words, numbers, symbols, charts, graphs, tables, diagrams, or models.

▶ Prerequisite Skills

- Justify the procedures selected for addition or subtraction problem-solving situations with sums or minuends up through 1,000.

- Apply strategies and results from a simpler story problem to either a more complex problem or to a similar problem.

▶ Content Background

Students will use different representations to solve story problems and explain their reasoning. They might use diagrams, drawings, or number lines as they work backward or guess and test.

Having students solve a variety of story problems will help them gain confidence so they can solve problems efficiently using a variety of representations. The different representations include, but are not limited to, words, numbers, symbols, charts, graphs, tables, diagrams, and models. One of the most important skills students need to learn is how to explain and justify which strategies are most efficient for them and why. Math helps students learn how to verbalize and write their reasons for making the choices they have made. A strategy that is efficient for one student may not be efficient for another. Encourage students to invent mathematically valid strategies that work best for them in solving new problems.

The following 4-step problem-solving plan was developed by George Pólya, and it is an effective way to solve a variety of story problems: (1) understand the problem; (2) devise a plan; (3) carry out the plan; and (4) look back. The goal of this lesson is to help students become flexible in their thinking, increase their ability to choose a strategy, organize the information in a problem, make a plan, carry out the plan, and look back and be confident in their answer. The only way to know if students have achieved this goal is if they become expert explainers. Effective problem solvers are able to explain what they do during each step.

▶ Advance Preparation

Print the Problem-Solving Plan. Save it for use throughout the lesson.

Materials to Gather

SUPPLIED

Problem-Solving Plan (printout)

Story Problem Practice activity page

LEARN Three Strategies

Objectives

- Explain mathematical reasoning in a story problem by using words, numbers, symbols, charts, graphs, tables, diagrams, or models.

Students will see that there is often more than one way to solve a story problem, using different strategies. The focus of the activity is more on how students explain their strategies than on the final answer itself.

When students are asked to choose a strategy and work the problem using that strategy, have them write the solution in their Math Notebook. Then have them explain their work to you in terms of the problem-solving plan before moving on. Gather the Problem-Solving Plan.

LEARN Work Backward

Objectives

- Explain mathematical reasoning in a story problem by using words, numbers, symbols, charts, graphs, tables, diagrams, or models.

Students will work with problems that are most easily solved by working backward. They'll see that using a diagram often helps with this type of problem, as well.

Again, students' explanations are the focus of this activity, even more so than the final answer to the problems. Gather the Problem-Solving Plan. Have students explain the working of the problems to you in terms of this plan.

TRY IT Story Problem Practice

Objectives

- Explain mathematical reasoning in a story problem by using words, numbers, symbols, charts, graphs, tables, diagrams, or models.

Students will practice using different representations to explain their solutions to story problems. Remind them that they may use tables, drawings, time lines, and any other representations that help them solve the problems. View or print the Story Problem Practice activity page and read the directions with students.

Students should copy the problems from the Activity Book into their Math Notebook as necessary and solve them there.

Tips Allow students to use the Problem-Solving Plan to guide them in solving the story problems.

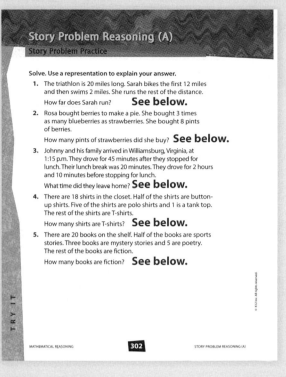

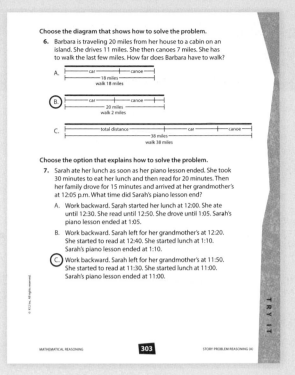

Additional Answers

1. 6 miles; Accept any reasonable answer that shows students explaining their solution.

2. 2 pints; Accept any reasonable answer that shows students explaining their solution.

3. 10:00 a.m.; Accept any reasonable answer that shows students explaining their solution.

4. 3; Accept any reasonable answer that shows students explaining their solution.

5. 2; Accept any reasonable answer that shows students explaining their solution.

Story Problem Reasoning (B)

Lesson Overview

GET READY 100 Rhombuses	5 minutes	ONLINE
LEARN Numbers and Tables	20 minutes	OFFLINE
TRY IT Justify Solutions	25 minutes	OFFLINE
CHECKPOINT	10 minutes	ONLINE

▶ Lesson Objectives

Explain mathematical reasoning in a story problem by using words, numbers, symbols, charts, graphs, tables, diagrams, or models.

▶ Prerequisite Skills

Apply strategies and results from a simpler story problem to either a more complex problem or to a similar problem.

▶ Content Background

Students will continue to use different representations to solve story problems and explain their reasoning. Specifically they will use tables and the work backward strategy.

Having students solve a variety of story problems will help them gain confidence so that they can solve problems efficiently using a variety of representations. The different representations include, but are not limited to, words, numbers, symbols, charts, graphs, tables, and diagrams or models. One of the most important skills for students to learn is how to explain and justify which strategies are most efficient for them and why. Math helps students learn how to verbalize and write their reasons for making the choices they have made. A strategy that is efficient for one student may not be efficient for another. Encourage students to invent mathematically valid strategies that work best for them in solving new problems.

The following 4-step problem-solving plan was developed by George Pólya, and it is an effective way to solve a variety of story problems: (1) understand the problem; (2) devise a plan; (3) carry out the plan; and (4) look back. The goal of this lesson is to help students become flexible in their thinking, increase their ability to choose a strategy, organize the information in a problem, make a plan, carry out the plan, and look back and be confident in their answer. The only way to know if students have achieved this goal is if they become expert explainers. Effective problem solvers are able to explain what they do during each step.

Materials to Gather

SUPPLIED

blocks – L (optional)
base-10 blocks (optional)
Problem-Solving Plan (printout)
Justify Solutions activity page

Advance Preparation

Print the Problem-Solving Plan. Save it for use throughout this lesson.

For the Learn: Numbers and Tables activity, copy the following two problems into the students' Math Notebook, one problem per page:

Problem 1: Ron said, "I am thinking of a secret number. Add 7 to this number. Multiply the sum by 6. The answer is 54." What is Ron's secret number?

Problem 2: Serena's swim team hires 3 coaches for every 22 swimmers. This season, the team hired 12 coaches. How many swimmers are on the team?

GET READY   100 Rhombuses

ONLINE 5 min

In this activity, students will use the pattern in a simpler problem to solve a more difficult problem. The problem involves using small rhombus shapes to make a big rhombus shape. Remind students that a rhombus is a 4-sided shape whose sides are equal in length.

Objectives

- Apply strategies and results from a simpler story problem to either a more complex problem or to a similar problem.

Tips   If students have difficulty understanding the problem, have them model the pictures with rhombuses (L blocks).

LEARN   Numbers and Tables

OFFLINE 20 min

Students will use a table and the work backward strategy to solve story problems and explain their solutions.

Gather the Problem-Solving Plan. Have students turn to the two problems you copied in their Math Notebook.

Objectives

- Explain mathematical reasoning in a story problem by using words, numbers, symbols, charts, graphs, tables, diagrams, or models.

PROBLEM 1

1. Tell students they will continue to solve problems using the Problem-Solving Plan. Have students read the first problem that you wrote in their Math Notebook:
   - Ron said, "I am thinking of a secret number. Add 7 to this number. Multiply the sum by 6. The answer is 54." What is Ron's secret number?

   Work through the following steps together, and refer to the Problem-Solving Plan to make sure students understand the problem.

2. Have students ask themselves the following questions as they work through the first two steps of the plan:
   - What operations can I use to solve the problem?
   - How did I solve problems like this in the past?

3. If students are having difficulty, mention that since they know the final number in the problem, the work backward strategy would be one good choice.

Tips

Allow students to use counters or base-10 blocks to help them calculate the numbers in the table.

Explain that students can start with the fact that 6 times the secret number plus 7 is 54. They don't know what the secret number plus 7 is, but they do know that when they multiply the sum by 6, they get 54. Start on the right side of the page under the problem in the Math Notebook and write the following number sentence. Be sure that the box is large enough to write a solution in it. Ask students if they can figure out what number goes in the box. They need to find what number times 6 equals 54.

$$\boxed{\text{secret number}} \times 6 = 54$$

Using the inverse of multiplication, students can solve $54 \div 6$ to find that the number in the box would be 9. Have students write 9 in the box.

4. If students can complete the problem at this point, have them share and carry out their plan. Encourage students to explain which steps they are following and which math skills they are using.

   If students are still having difficulty, explain that Ron's secret number plus 7 is 9. Under the completed number sentence, write this number sentence:

$$\boxed{\boxed{\text{secret number}} + 7} = 9, \text{so} \, \underline{} + 7 = 9$$

   Now students only have to figure out what number plus 7 equals 9.

   This time, using the inverse of addition, students can solve $9 - 7 = ?$ to get 2 as Ron's secret number.

   Work with students until they get an answer. If their answer isn't correct, don't mention it; let them go through the steps to discover what is wrong.

5. Have students look at their answer and ask themselves the following questions:

   • Did I answer the question?

   • Does my answer make sense when I reread the problem?

   • If I start with my answer, add 7, and then multiply by 6, do I get 54?

PROBLEM 2

6. Have students read the second problem you wrote in their Math Notebook:

   • Serena's swim team hires 3 coaches for every 22 swimmers. This season, the team hired 12 coaches. How many swimmers are on the team?

   Ask students to explain the problem in their own words and explain a strategy for solving it. Have them describe the steps of their plan before solving it.

7. If students have difficulty, mention that when they're given one amount, such as 3 coaches for every 22 players, a table can be a useful strategy. Show students how to make a table like the one here.

Coaches				
Swimmers				

8. Discuss the quantities given in the problem, and show students how to use those quantities to complete the table.

   Say: You know that for every 3 coaches, there are 22 swimmers.

9. Write the numbers 3 and 22 in the second column. Then guide students through completing the table with the following questions:

Coaches	3			
Swimmers	22			

   - If there are 3 more coaches, how many how many coaches will there be? 6
   - If there are 6 coaches, how many swimmers will there be? 44
   - If there is another set of coaches, how many coaches will there be? 9
   - If there are 9 coaches, how many swimmers will there be? 66
   - If there is another set of coaches, how many coaches will there be? 12
   - How many swimmers will there be for 12 coaches? 88

Coaches	3	6	9	12
Swimmers	22	44	66	88

10. Have students look at the answer and compare it to the question in the problem to see if it makes sense.

> **Tips**
> If students suggest simply multiplying 4 by 22 to get the answer, have them fully explain why that would work. Then have them look at the table as an alternate strategy.

TRY IT Justify Solutions

OFFLINE
25min

Students will practice using different representations to explain their solutions to story problems. View or print the Justify Solutions activity page and read the directions with students.

Students should copy the problems from the Activity Book into their Math Notebook as necessary and solve them there.

> **Tips**
> Allow students to use the Problem-Solving Plan to guide them in solving the story problems.

Objectives

- Explain mathematical reasoning in a story problem by using words, numbers, symbols, charts, graphs, tables, diagrams, or models.

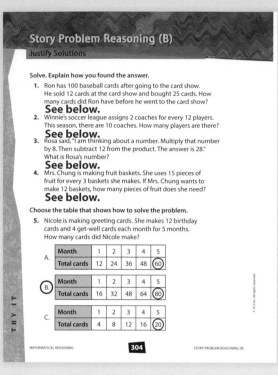

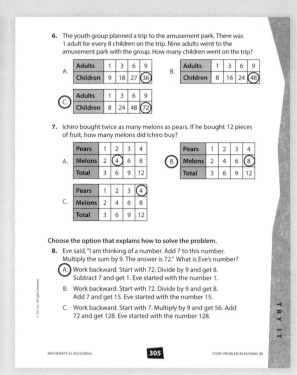

Additional Answers

1. 87; Accept any reasonable explanation. Students may use the work backward strategy and explain that before Ron bought the 25 cards, he had 100 − 25, or 75, cards. And before he sold the 12 cards, he had 75 + 12, or 87, cards.

2. 60; Accept any reasonable explanation. Students may explain that they used a table like the following:

Coaches	2	4	6	8	10
Players	12	24	36	48	60

3. 5; Accept any reasonable explanation. Students may explain that they used the work backward strategy and opposite operations to find that 28 + 12 = 40; 40 ÷ 8 = 5.

4. 60; Accept any reasonable explanation. Students may explain that they used a table like the following:

Baskets	3	6	9	12
Fruit pieces	15	30	45	60

ONLINE
10min

CHECKPOINT

Students will complete an online Checkpoint. If necessary, read the directions, questions, and answer choices to students and help them with keyboard or mouse operations.

Objectives

- Explain mathematical reasoning in a story problem by using words, numbers, symbols, charts, graphs, tables, diagrams, or models.

Exact and Approximate Solutions

Lesson Overview

GET READY Estimate Solutions	5 minutes	**ONLINE**
LEARN Exact or Approximate	15 minutes	**ONLINE**
LEARN Rounded Answers	15 minutes	**OFFLINE**
TRY IT Accurate Solutions	15 minutes	**OFFLINE**
CHECKPOINT	10 minutes	**ONLINE**

▶ Lesson Objectives

- Determine the answer to a story problem to a specific degree of accuracy, such as hundreds or tens.
- Explain the advantages of exact answers and approximate answers to story problems.

▶ Prerequisite Skills

- Round whole numbers through 1,000 to the nearest ten.
- Round whole numbers through 1,000 to the nearest hundred.
- Use estimation to predict a solution to a story problem and to determine whether calculations are reasonable.
- Explain mathematical reasoning in a story problem by using words, numbers, symbols, charts, graphs, tables, diagrams, or models.

Materials to Gather

SUPPLIED
Rounded Answers activity page
Accurate Solutions activity page

▶ Content Background

Students will learn to determine an answer in a problem situation to a specific degree of accuracy, and they will explain the advantages of an exact answer in some situations and an approximate answer in other situations.

Finding an answer to a specific degree of accuracy is not the same as estimating. When estimating, students round the numbers in a problem to make the problem easier to solve. When finding an answer to a specific degree of accuracy, they round only the answer to make it easier to remember or to work with.

An estimate, or an approximate calculation, is sufficient and appropriate in many situations. Students should understand that in math problems *an estimate* is a mathematical term that means "about how many" and that different everyday situations require different degrees of accuracy. Yet, in some situations, estimation is inappropriate. For example, a pharmacist should not estimate when filling a prescription. Students will learn to base their choice of an appropriate estimation strategy on the context of each story problem.

The following 4-step problem-solving method was developed by George Pólya, and it is an effective way to solve a variety of story problems: (1) understand the problem; (2) devise a plan; (3) carry out the plan; and (4) look back.

GET READY Estimate Solutions

Students will estimate the solution to a story problem and will find out if their estimate was reasonable or unreasonable.

Tips   Allow students to use a number line to help with estimates.

Objectives

- Round whole numbers through 1,000 to the nearest ten.
- Round whole numbers through 1,000 to the nearest hundred.
- Use estimation to predict a solution to a story problem and to determine whether calculations are reasonable.
- Explain mathematical reasoning in a story problem by using words, numbers, symbols, charts, graphs, tables, diagrams, or models.

LEARN Exact or Approximate

Students will decide if a situation gives an exact amount or an approximate amount. Also, they will round whole numbers to the nearest ten or hundred. Discuss with students the idea that in some situations they need to know an exact amount, such as how much flour to put in a cake, or what time the train leaves. At other times an approximate amount is fine, such as when they want to know about how much something costs, or around what time someone will be home.

Objectives

- Determine the answer to a story problem to a specific degree of accuracy, such as hundreds or tens.
- Explain the advantages of exact answers and approximate answers to story problems.

LEARN Rounded Answers

Students will learn to round an answer in a story-problem situation. They'll also learn to explain the advantages of an exact answer in some situations and an approximate answer in other situations. View or print the Rounded Answers activity page and read the directions with students.

Students should copy the problems from the Activity Book into their Math Notebook as necessary and solve them there.

Objectives

- Determine the answer to a story problem to a specific degree of accuracy, such as hundreds or tens.
- Explain the advantages of exact answers and approximate answers to story problems.

1. Explain to students when they would use an exact answer in some situations and an estimate in others.

   Say: One way to estimate the answer to a story problem is to round the numbers before calculating, which makes the calculation easier. At other times you may want to calculate an exact answer but then round it to a friendly number that's easier to remember. Sometimes a problem only asks for an answer to a certain degree of accuracy, such as to the nearest ten or hundred.

2. Review the Worked Example with students.

3. Have students read Problem 1. Guide students to solve the problem and find an exact answer. Then tell students that they should round the answer to the nearest hundred.

   Ask: The exact answer is 796. How do you know which hundred to round to? I look at the digit in the tens place and see that it is a 9, so I know the nearest hundred is 800 rather than 700.

4. Have students solve Problem 2 on their own. Offer guidance as needed.

   Say: Sometimes there are advantages to having an exact answer, and sometimes it's more convenient to round the number to a specific degree of accuracy.

5. Have students read Problem 3. Explain that they do not need to calculate or round answers for this problem. Discuss with students that an estimate, or approximate answer, is appropriate when deciding if there is enough money, but an exact amount is needed when paying a bill.

6. Discuss Problems 4 and 5 with students. Have students answer the problems on their own.

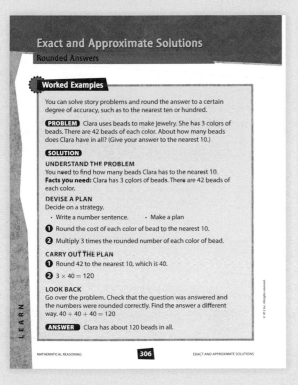

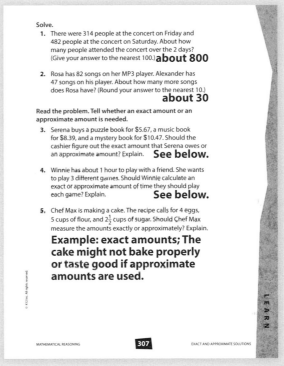

Additional Answers

3. **Example:** exact amount; Serena doesn't want to overpay and the store doesn't want Serena to underpay.

4. **Example:** approximate amount; Winnie can use an approximate amount of time because an exact amount of time is not necessary.

TRY IT Accurate Solutions

Objectives

Students will practice determining an answer to a specific degree of accuracy and explaining the advantages of exact and approximate answers. View or print the Accurate Solutions activity page and read the directions students.

Students should copy the problems from the Activity Book into their Math Notebook as necessary and solve them there.

- Determine the answer to a story problem to a specific degree of accuracy, such as hundreds or tens.
- Explain the advantages of exact answers and approximate answers to story problems.

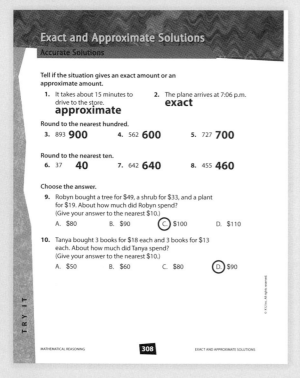

Exact and Approximate Solutions
Accurate Solutions

Tell if the situation gives an exact amount or an approximate amount.

1. It takes about 15 minutes to drive to the store.
approximate

2. The plane arrives at 7:06 p.m.
exact

Round to the nearest hundred.

3. 893 **900**   4. 562 **600**   5. 727 **700**

Round to the nearest ten.

6. 37 **40**   7. 642 **640**   8. 455 **460**

Choose the answer.

9. Robyn bought a tree for $49, a shrub for $33, and a plant for $19. About how much did Robyn spend?
(Give your answer to the nearest $10.)
A. $80   B. $90   (C.) $100   D. $110

10. Tanya bought 3 books for $18 each and 3 books for $13 each. About how much did Tanya spend?
(Give your answer to the nearest $10.)
A. $50   B. $60   C. $80   (D.) $90

11. The computer factory made 936 computer chips one week. Of these, 293 were faulty and had to be thrown away. About how many computer chips were left?
(Give your answer to the nearest 100 chips.)
A. 500   (B.) 600   C. 700   D. 800

12. A flower shop has 132 red roses and 259 yellow roses. About how many red and yellow roses does the shop have?
(Give your answer to the nearest 10.)
A. 350   B. 380   (C.) 390   D. 400

CHECKPOINT

Objectives

Students will complete an online Checkpoint. If necessary, read the directions, problems, and answer choices to students and help them with keyboard or mouse operations.

- Determine the answer to a story problme to a specific degree of accuracy, such as hundreds or tens.
- Explain the advantages of exact answers and approximate answers to story problems.

Core Focus
Solve and Check for Accuracy

Lesson Overview

GET READY Check Calculations	5 minutes	OFFLINE
LEARN Check Answers	15 minutes	ONLINE
LEARN Solve and Check	20 minutes	OFFLINE
TRY IT Look Back and Check	10 minutes	OFFLINE
CHECKPOINT	10 minutes	ONLINE

▶ ## Lesson Objectives

- Check the accuracy of a calculation in a story problem.
- Explain mathematical reasoning in a story problem by using words, numbers, symbols, charts, graphs, tables, diagrams, or models.

▶ ## Prerequisite Skills

Check the accuracy of calculations from the context of addition or subtraction problem-solving situations with sums and minuends up through 1,000 with regrouping.

▶ ## Content Background

In this lesson, students will check answers to story problems and analyze the calculations for accuracy. This lesson focuses on the "look back" step of the 4-step problem-solving plan.

The following 4-step problem-solving plan was developed by George Pólya, and it is an effective way to solve a variety of story problems: (1) understand the problem; (2) devise a plan; (3) carry out the plan; and (4) look back. As students solve story problems using the problem-solving plan, an important aspect of the "look back" step is checking the accuracy of the work.

Students know that the opposite of addition is subtraction and the opposite of multiplication is division. The term used to describe these opposite pairs of operations is *inverse operations*. Students can check their calculations using inverse operations. For example, when they see $300 + 400 = 700$, they can subtract $700 - 400 = 300$ to check that the answer is correct. When they see $900 - 600 = 300$, they can check the calculation by adding $300 + 600 = 900$. The same principle applies with multiplication and division. If $10 \times 3 = 30$, then $30 \div 3 = 10$; and if $42 \div 6 = 7$, then $7 \times 6 = 42$. Students can use this and other invented strategies to check that their calculations are accurate.

▶ ## Advance Preparation

Print the Problem-Solving Plan. Save it for use throughout the lesson.

For the Get Ready: Check Calculations activity, write the following two story problems on index cards, one per card:

- **Problem 1:** Ron solved this problem: The auditorium can seat 452 people. There are 370 people sitting in the auditorium. How many seats are empty? Ron's answer: 182 seats

Materials to Gather

SUPPLIED
Problem-Solving Plan (printout)
Solve and Check activity page
Look Back and Check activity page

ALSO NEEDED
index cards – 2

- **Problem 2:** Winnie solved this problem: Tonya and her friends collected 356 cans to take to the recycling center. Mike and his friends collected 372 cans. How many cans did they collect altogether? Winnie's answer: 728 cans

GET READY Check Calculations

ONLINE 5min

Students will use inverse operations to check the answers to story problems. Gather the index cards on which you have written the story problems.

1. Have students read the first story problem and Ron's answer.

2. Have students write the subtraction problem vertically with Ron's answer shown. Have students check the answer by using the inverse operation, addition.

   Ask: What numbers will you add together to check Ron's answer? 370 and 182

   Have students write the addition problem vertically and find the sum.

3. Guide students to see that the sum does not match the total number of seats in the auditorium; therefore, Ron made an error in his calculation. Ask students to explain what Ron did wrong and give the correct answer. When he subtracted, he regrouped but forgot to cross out the 4 in the hundreds place; correct answer: 82 seats.

4. Have students read the second story problem and Winnie's answer.

5. Have students write down the addition problem vertically with Winnie's answer shown. Tell students to use an inverse operation to check Winnie's answer.

   Ask: Which inverse operation will you use to check the answer? subtraction

6. Have students write the subtraction problem vertically and find the difference.

   Ask: Is Winnie's answer correct? How do you know? Yes, the difference matches the other addend.

Objectives

- Check the accuracy of calculations from the context of addition or subtraction problem-solving situations with sums and minuends up through 1,000 with regrouping.

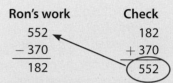

Ron's work	Check
552	182
− 370	+ 370
182	552

Ron is incorrect.

The correct solution is:

452	82
− 370	+ 370
82	452

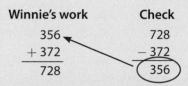

Winnie's work	Check
356	728
+ 372	− 372
728	356

LEARN Check Answers

ONLINE 15min

Student will use the 4-step problem-solving plan to solve story problems and focus on explaining the solution by using words, numbers, pictures, charts, or equations. The main goal is to have students identify a strategy for checking their answers to determine if they are reasonable and/or accurate.

Objectives

- Check the accuracy of a calculation in a story problem.

- Explain mathematical reasoning in a story problem by using words, numbers, symbols, charts, graphs, tables, diagrams, or models.

LEARN Solve and Check

Objectives

- Check the accuracy of a calculation in a story problem.

Students will solve problems using the 4-step problem-solving plan with a focus on the "look back" step. They will estimate answers, do calculations, and check accuracy to verify their answers. Gather the Problem-Solving Plan. View or print the Solve and Check activity page and read the directions with students.

Students should copy the problems from the Activity Book into their Math Notebook as necessary and solve them there.

1. Have students look at the Problem-Solving Plan. Review the steps of the plan. Tell students that in this lesson they will focus on the "look back" step of the plan. Discuss how students will check their answer using estimation and inverse operations.

2. Have students read the Worked Example. Guide them through each step of the plan to solve the problem. Ask these questions as students work through each step:

   Understand the problem.

   - Do you understand the problem?
   - What are you asked to find?
   - Can you sketch or model the problem?
   - What information do you have? What do you need? What do you not need?

   Devise a plan.

   - What strategy can you use?
   - How many steps do you need?
   - Which operations do you need?

   Carry out the plan.

   - How can you show your work?

3. Point to the "look back" step. Have students work backward to be sure that their answer makes sense.

   Ask: What inverse operation do you use to check division? multiplication

   Ask: What inverse operation do you use to check subtraction? addition

4. Have students use inverse operations to check the calculations. Explain that the calculation is correct if the final answer matches the original amount of 34 books. Ask students these final questions to complete the example problem and check understanding:

   - Did you answer exactly what the question asked?
   - How do you decide if the answer makes sense?
   - How did you use inverse operations to check the calculation?
   - Have you forgotten anything?

5. Have students read Problem 1 and use the Problem-Solving Plan as they work through the problem. Have them concentrate on the "look back" step when they verify their answers. Use the questions in Steps 2 and 4 to guide students through the plan. Encourage students to use both estimation and inverse operations to check their work.

6. Repeat Step 5 for Problem 2.

7. Have students read Problems 3–6 on the activity page. Explain that they need to check the work for each problem and explain whether it is correct or incorrect. Students may estimate, use inverse operations, or invent a method to check the calculations. Emphasize that students need to be able to explain how they checked the answers and determine the error if there is one.

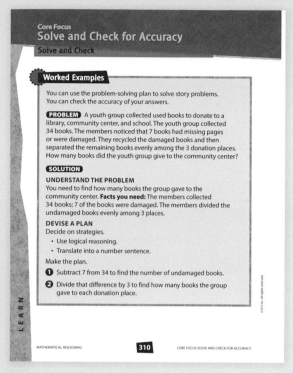

Core Focus
Solve and Check for Accuracy
Solve and Check

Worked Examples

You can use the problem-solving plan to solve story problems. You can check the accuracy of your answers.

PROBLEM A youth group collected used books to donate to a library, community center, and school. The youth group collected 34 books. The members noticed that 7 books had missing pages or were damaged. They recycled the damaged books and then separated the remaining books evenly among the 3 donation places. How many books did the youth group give to the community center?

SOLUTION

UNDERSTAND THE PROBLEM
You need to find how many books the group gave to the community center. **Facts you need:** The members collected 34 books; 7 of the books were damaged. The members divided the undamaged books evenly among 3 places.

DEVISE A PLAN
Decide on strategies.
• Use logical reasoning.
• Translate into a number sentence.

Make the plan.
❶ Subtract 7 from 34 to find the number of undamaged books.
❷ Divide that difference by 3 to find how many books the group gave to each donation place.

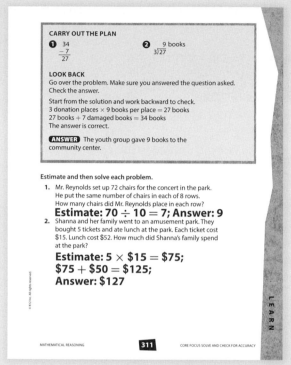

CARRY OUT THE PLAN
❶ 34
   −7
   —
   27

❷ 9 books
   3)27

LOOK BACK
Go over the problem. Make sure you answered the question asked. Check the answer.

Start from the solution and work backward to check.
3 donation places × 9 books per place = 27 books
27 books + 7 damaged books = 34 books
The answer is correct.

ANSWER The youth group gave 9 books to the community center.

Estimate and then solve each problem.
1. Mr. Reynolds set up 72 chairs for the concert in the park. He put the same number of chairs in each of 8 rows. How many chairs did Mr. Reynolds place in each row?
Estimate: 70 ÷ 10 = 7; Answer: 9
2. Shanna and her family went to an amusement park. They bought 5 tickets and ate lunch at the park. Each ticket cost $15. Lunch cost $52. How much did Shanna's family spend at the park?

Estimate: 5 × $15 = $75;
$75 + $50 = $125;
Answer: $127

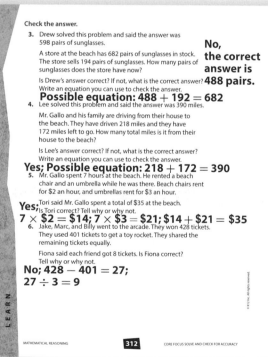

Check the answer.
3. Drew solved this problem and said the answer was 598 pairs of sunglasses.

A store at the beach has 682 pairs of sunglasses in stock. The store sells 194 pairs of sunglasses. How many pairs of sunglasses does the store have now?

Is Drew's answer correct? If not, what is the correct answer? Write an equation you can use to check the answer.
No, the correct answer is 488 pairs.
Possible equation: 488 + 192 = 682

4. Lee solved this problem and said the answer was 390 miles.

Mr. Gallo and his family are driving from their house to the beach. They have driven 218 miles and they have 172 miles left to go. How many total miles is it from their house to the beach?

Is Lee's answer correct? If not, what is the correct answer? Write an equation you can use to check the answer.
Yes; Possible equation: 218 + 172 = 390

5. Mr. Gallo spent 7 hours at the beach. He rented a beach chair and an umbrella while he was there. Beach chairs rent for $2 an hour, and umbrellas rent for $3 an hour.

Tori said Mr. Gallo spent a total of $35 at the beach. Is Tori correct? Tell why or why not.
Yes; 7 × $2 = $14; 7 × $3 = $21; $14 + $21 = $35

6. Jake, Marc, and Billy went to the arcade. They won 428 tickets. They used 401 tickets to get a toy rocket. They shared the remaining tickets equally.

Fiona said each friend got 8 tickets. Is Fiona correct? Tell why or why not.
No; 428 − 401 = 27;
27 ÷ 3 = 9

TRY IT Look Back and Check

OFFLINE 10 min

Students will practice checking the solution to story problems. View or print the Look Back and Check activity page and read the directions with students.

Students should copy the problems from the Activity Book into their Math Notebook as necessary and solve them there.

Objectives

- Check the accuracy of a calculation in a story problem.

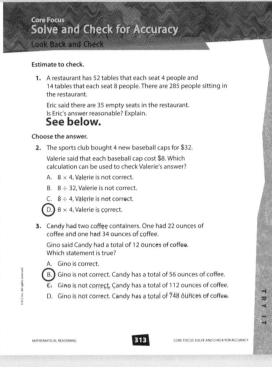

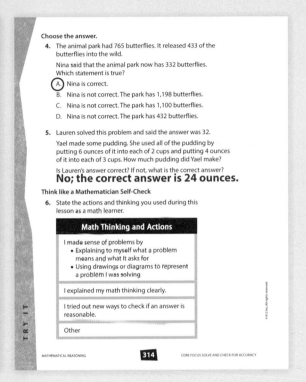

Additional Answer

1. Erics's answer is reasonable.
   Estimate: $50 \times 4 = 200$
   $15 \times 8 = 120$
   $200 + 120 = 320$ seats
   320 seats $- 290$ people $= 30$ empty seats

CHECKPOINT

ONLINE 10 min

Students will complete an online Checkpoint. If necessary, read the directions, problems, and answer choices to students and help them with keyboard or mouse operations.

Objectives

- Check the accuracy of a calculation in a story problem.

Unit Review

▶ Unit Objectives

- Analyze a story problem by identifying the question, recognizing relevant information, and developing a solution strategy.

- Demonstrate when and how to break a multistep story problem into simpler steps.

- Apply strategies and results from a simpler story problem to either a more complex problem or to a similar problem.

- Explain mathematical reasoning in a story problem by using words, numbers, symbols, charts, graphs, tables, diagrams, or models.

- Determine the answer to a story problem to a specific degree of accuracy, such as hundreds or tens.

- Explain the advantages of exact answers and approximate answers to story problems.

- Check the accuracy of a calculation in a story problem.

Materials to Gather

There are no materials to gather for this lesson.

▶ Advance Preparation

In this lesson, students will have an opportunity to review previous activities in the Mathematical Reasoning unit. Look at the suggested activities in Unit Review: Prepare for the Checkpoint online and gather any needed materials.

UNIT REVIEW Look Back

ONLINE **10**min

Objectives

- Review unit objectives.

Students will review key concepts from the unit to prepare for the Unit Checkpoint.

UNIT REVIEW Checkpoint Practice

ONLINE **50**min

Objectives

- Review unit objectives.

Students will complete an online Checkpoint Practice to prepare for the Unit Checkpoint. If necessary, read the directions, problems, and answer choices to students. Have students answer the problems on their own. Review any missed problems with students.

⇥ UNIT REVIEW Prepare for the Checkpoint

What you do next depends on how students performed in the previous activity, Unit Review: Checkpoint Practice. If students had difficulty with any of the problems, complete the appropriate review activity listed in the table online.

Unit Checkpoint

| **UNIT CHECKPOINT** Online | 60 minutes | **ONLINE** |

▶ Unit Objectives

- Analyze a story problem by identifying the question, recognizing relevant information, and developing a solution strategy.
- Demonstrate when and how to break a multistep story problem into simpler steps.
- Apply strategies and results from a simpler story problem to either a more complex problem or to a similar problem.
- Explain mathematical reasoning in a story problem by using words, numbers, symbols, charts, graphs, tables, diagrams, or models.
- Determine the answer to a story problem to a specific degree of accuracy, such as hundreds or tens.
- Explain the advantages of exact answers and approximate answers to story problems.
- Check the accuracy of a calculation in a story problem.

Materials to Gather

There are no materials to gather for this lesson.

UNIT CHECKPOINT Online

Students will complete the Unit Checkpoint online. If necessary, read the directions, problems, and answer choices to students and help them with keyboard or mouse operations.

Objectives

- Assess unit objectives.

Extended Problems: Reasoning

Lesson Overview

GRADED ASSIGNMENT ⋮ 60 minutes ⋮ **OFFLINE**

▶ Lesson Objectives

- Analyze a story problem by identifying the question, recognizing relevant information, and developing a solution strategy.
- Demonstrate when and how to break a multistep story problem into simpler steps.
- Apply strategies and results from a simpler story problem to either a more complex problem or to a similar problem.
- Explain mathematical reasoning in a story problem by using words, numbers, symbols, charts, graphs, tables, diagrams, or models.
- Express the solution to a story problem clearly and logically with appropriate mathematical notation, terms, and accurate language.
- Check the accuracy of a calculation in a story problem.
- Make, check, and verify predictions about the quantity, size, and shape of objects and groups of objects.
- Solve addition word problems within 100 involving lengths that are given in the same units.
- Solve two-step word problems, limited to whole numbers.
- Analyze complex problems using mathematical knowledge and skills.

Materials to Gather

SUPPLIED

Extended Problems: Reasoning
  (printout)

GRADED ASSIGNMENT

OFFLINE
60min

Open the Extended Problems: Reasoning. Read the directions, problems, and answer choices to students, if necessary.
  You will grade this assignment.

- Students should complete the assignment on their own.
- Students should submit the completed assignment to you.
- Enter the results online.

Objectives

- Analyze complex problems using mathematical knowledge and skills.

Perimeter and Area

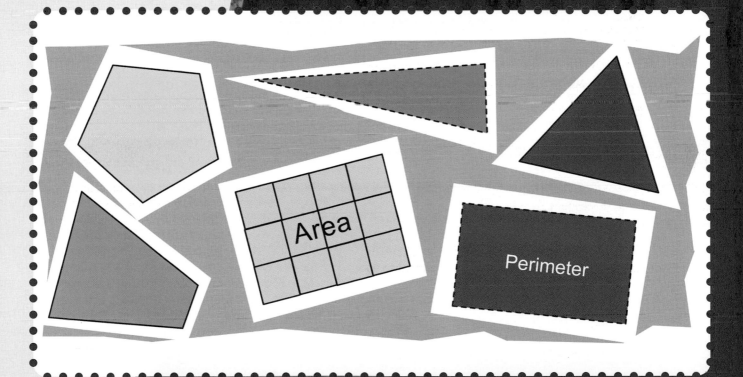

▶ Unit Objectives

- Determine the perimeter of a polygon with whole-number side lengths.
- Given the whole-number perimeter of a polygon, students will find the whole-number length of an unknown side.
- Given the perimeter of an everyday object in a story problem, find the whole-number length of an unknown side.
- Decompose composite figures formed by rectangles into non-overlapping rectangles to determine the area of the original figure using the additive property of area.

- Use multiplication or division to solve a story problem involving rectangular area.
- Define and demonstrate understanding of the area of any plane figure.
- Demonstrate understanding that rectangles that have the same area can have different perimeters.
- Demonstrate understanding that rectangles that have the same perimeter can have different areas.

▶ Big Ideas

- Geometric figures can be described and classified by the shapes of their faces and by how many faces, sides, edges, or vertices they have.
- Every geometric figure has several useful aspects that can be measured, calculated, or approximated. Area is a measure of how much material is needed to cover a plane figure.

▶ Unit Introduction

In this unit, students will learn about perimeter and area. They will learn that *perimeter* is the measure of the distance around an object, and that perimeter is measured in centimeters, inches, or other units of length. They will find the perimeter of polygons with whole-number side lengths. Students will then learn that *area* is the measure of the space inside two-dimensional figures, and that area is measured in square units. They will use multiplication or division to solve story problems involving rectangular area. Students will not use formulas to find perimeter or area, but will focus on developing an understanding and use that understanding to find these measures by their own methods.

▶ Keywords

area
grid

line segment
perimeter

side
square unit

Find the Perimeter of Objects

Lesson Overview

GET READY Draw and Name Polygons	10 minutes	OFFLINE
LEARN Identify Perimeter	10 minutes	OFFLINE
LEARN Measure Perimeter	20 minutes	OFFLINE
TRY IT Perimeter of Polygons	10 minutes	OFFLINE
CHECKPOINT	10 minutes	ONLINE

▶ ## Lesson Objectives

Determine the perimeter of a polygon with whole-number side lengths.

▶ ## Prerequisite Skills

Identify, describe, and classify a polygon according to the number of its sides.

▶ ## Content Background

Students will learn that the distance around an object or a shape is called the *perimeter*. They'll learn that perimeter is measured in centimeters, inches, or other units of length.

The side lengths of a shape must be known if the perimeter is to be determined. Often the side lengths of the shape can be found by using the properties of the shape. For example, rectangles have opposite sides that are equal, so the perimeter can be found when only one length and one width are known. Students can apply their knowledge of properties of shapes to find the perimeter of more complex figures. They will not use a particular rule or formula to find perimeter. Instead, they will use their understanding of perimeter to determine that they can find the distance around an object by adding the side lengths of a given shape.

▶ ## Advance Preparation

Print the Centimeter Grid Paper and several copies of the Isometric Dot Paper.

For the Learn: Measure Perimeter activity, students will need shapes that have been drawn on the dot paper. They may use the shapes from the Get Ready, or you may draw the following shapes in advance:

Materials to Gather

SUPPLIED

blocks – K, L, M, N (3 of each); E (8)
Isometric Dot Paper (printout)
Centimeter Grid Paper (printout)
Measure Perimeter activity page
Perimeter of Polygons activity page

ALSO NEEDED

ruler, dual-scale
household objects – string (4 ft)
index card
pipe cleaner or long twist tie
crayons or markers, coloring – 2
scissors, adult

triangle quadrilateral pentagon hexagon septagon octagon nonagon decagon

Objectives

- Identify, describe, and classify a polygon according to the number of its sides.

Students will draw polygons and name figures with 3 to 10 sides.

Gather the Isometric Dot Paper.

Have students use the dot paper to draw and label the polygons shown. Encourage them to draw shapes in such a way that they always draw a line through one of the nearest dots as shown, which will make it easy to reuse the shapes in the Learn: Measure Perimeter activity.

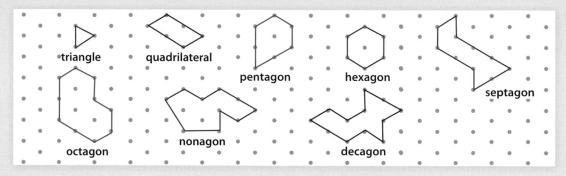

Polygons with lines like those shown in red cannot be reused. However, if students want to draw these sorts of lines, they can draw new shapes in the perimeter activity.

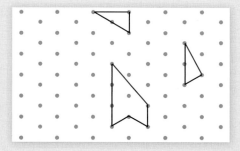

Objectives

- Determine the perimeter of a polygon with whole-number side lengths.

Students will learn about perimeter by measuring around the outside of a shape or an object.

Gather the blocks, ruler, string, index card, markers or crayons, scissors, and pipe cleaner or twist tie.

1. Tell students that in everyday life, there are times when they'll need to know the distance around a shape or an object. For example, they might need to know the distance that joggers run around a track, the length of a fence around a garden, or how long the wood is around the sides of a sandbox. The distance around a shape or an object is called the *perimeter*.

2. Write the word *perimeter* on an index card and draw arrows around the edge as shown.

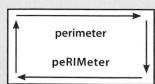

3. Have students trace around the edge of the card with their finger to show the perimeter. Tell students that they can remember it because the word *rim* is part of the word *perimeter*. Students can think of perimeter as the distance around the rim of an object.

4. Have students run their finger around the perimeter of a table. Have them point out the perimeter of the room they're in.

5. Explain to students that perimeter is a measurement of the distance around a shape or an object. Tell them that perimeter can be measured in inches, feet, yards, and even miles.

6. Give students a K block (small green triangle). Have them use a ruler to measure one side in inches. Bend a pipe cleaner or twist tie tightly around the perimeter of the triangle. Cut it at the end of the third side. Straighten it out and measure it (3 inches). Have students trace the K block, write **1 inch** next to each side, and write **perimeter = 3 inches** under the picture.

1 inch

perimeter = 3 inches

7. Pick up the other blocks.

   Ask: If the length of one side of the green triangle is 1 inch, how long is the length of one side of each of the other blocks in this group?

   Students should determine that all block pieces have 1-inch side lengths, except for one side of the trapezoid. They can find the perimeter of each block by counting the side lengths in inches. Have them find the length of the longest side of the trapezoid by using the edge of one of the other pieces. Have them trace each shape, label the lengths of the sides, and write **perimeter = ? inches** below the shape. (In place of the question mark, students should write the measurement.)

8. Have students estimate and then determine the perimeter of the L block (blue rhombus), the N block (yellow hexagon), and the M block (red trapezoid). Have them record the perimeter under each of their tracings.
   L block: 4 inches, N block: 6 inches, M block: 5 inches

9. Have students put together two green triangles to form a rhombus. Explain that when two triangles are put together, one side of each is now on the inside, so the outside edges form a rhombus. The new rhombus has the same perimeter as the rhombus block.

10. Show students that the perimeter of a group of blocks can vary, depending on how the blocks are arranged. First have students use four E blocks (squares) to make a 2 by 2 square, and have them find the perimeter. 8 inches

    Then give them four more squares and ask them to make a shape with a different perimeter.

    Ask: Why do the two arrangements of four squares have different perimeters? When more sides are on the inside of the design, there are fewer sides around the outside, so the perimeter is less.

perimeter = 8 inches   perimeter = 10 inches

11. Have students use any 10 blocks to create a design. Have them estimate the perimeter of the design and then find the exact perimeter. Emphasize that since perimeter is a distance, it needs to be measured with a unit of measure. Have them write the perimeter of their design. Then have them use the same 10 blocks to create a new design with a different perimeter. Have students estimate the perimeter and then find the exact perimeter.

12. Have students look again at the index card. Have them hold up the string and show how much of it they think would equal the perimeter of the card. Have students mark the distance on the string and estimate the length to that mark in inches. Then have them use the string to go around the perimeter of the card. Mark the actual perimeter on the string in a different color. (Note that measuring with string is always an approximation because string stretches and measuring with it is often not exact.) Have students use what they know about the index card to calculate the exact perimeter. Example for a 3×5 card: $3 + 5 + 3 + 5 = 16$ inches

Have students compare their estimate to the exact length.

LEARN Measure Perimeter

OFFLINE 20 min

Students will measure the perimeter of different shapes. Gather the Centimeter Grid Paper and the shapes drawn on dot paper. View or print the Measure Perimeter activity page and read the directions with students.

Students should copy the problems from the Activity Book into their Math Notebook as necessary and solve them there.

1. Show students the Centimeter Grid Paper. Explain that each square on the paper is 1 centimeter on each side. Tell students that they can draw shapes on the grid paper and know the exact perimeter as long as they stay on the lines. Point out that a diagonal line drawn between corners of any square would not be 1 centimeter. Have students draw three different rectangles on the centimeter grid paper and determine the perimeter of each. Be sure students do not use diagonal lines to make the rectangles.

2. Have students describe how they found the perimeter of each rectangle. Encourage them to share any shortcuts they may have discovered for finding the perimeter.

3. Have students draw a rectangle that is 15 centimeters long and 3 centimeters wide. Ask them how they would find the perimeter of this rectangle. Students should understand that they do not have to count each side length because they know that opposite sides of rectangles are equal. Therefore, they can think $15 + 15 + 3 + 3$.

4. Have students make several interesting geometric shapes on the grid paper. Make sure each shape has only square corners. Have students find the perimeter of each shape.

Objectives

- Determine the perimeter of a polygon with whole-number side lengths.

Tips

Remind students not to draw diagonal lines on the Centimeter Grid Paper. The length of a diagonal line is greater than 1 unit.

5. Have students look at the prepared shapes on the dot paper. Have them hold the paper horizontally. Tell them that the dots are spaced in such a way that some are closer together than others. Point to a diagonal or vertical row of dots. Tell students that the distance between two adjacent dots in any of these rows is 1 unit. Next point to a horizontal row of dots. Tell students that these dots are more than 1 unit apart.

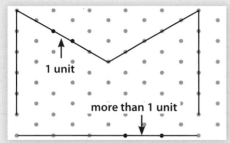

6. Have students find the perimeter of any shapes on the dot paper with sides that only pass through dots that are 1 unit apart. Explain that if a shape has lines connecting dots that are farther apart than 1 unit, they can't be sure of the perimeter. (In this illustration, the perimeter of the shapes with red lines is unknown.) Have students write the measurement below each shape as $P = ?$ (In place of the question mark, students should write the measurement.) Tell students that the abbreviation for *perimeter* is an uppercase P.

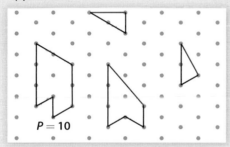

7. Focus students' attention on the Measure Perimeter activity page. Go over the Worked Example. Make sure students understand both ways of finding the perimeter. They can add all the sides, or if there are several sides that are equal length, they can multiply to find the total for those sides.

8. Have students look at Problems 1–4. Guide them through each problem. Encourage them to explain what they know about each shape before they find the perimeter. For example, when students are finding the perimeter of the square, remind them that a square has 4 equal sides, so if they know the length of one side, they know the length of the other 3 sides. When finding the perimeter of a rectangle, remind students that opposite sides are equal. Tell them that the tick marks (short lines) on the sides of the triangle in Problem 3 and the pentagon in Problem 4 show that those sides have equal lengths.

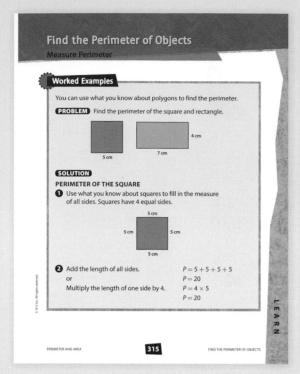

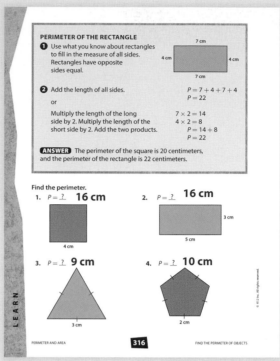

TRY IT Perimeter of Polygons

OFFLINE 10 min

Students will practice finding the perimeter of different shapes and objects. View or print the Perimeter of Polygons activity page and read the directions with students.

Students should copy the problems from the Activity Book into their Math Notebook as necessary and solve them there.

Remind students that perimeter is the distance around the outside of a shape or object. Also point out that tick marks on the sides of a shape indicate that those sides are the same length. In Problem 9, help students see that they can determine the lengths of the unmarked sides by looking at the lengths on the sides opposite them.

Objectives

- Determine the perimeter of a polygon with whole-number side lengths.

Tips

If students have difficulty with Problems 4 and 9, have them draw the figures on grid paper.

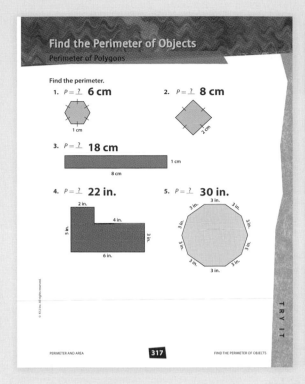

Find the perimeter.

1. $P = ?$ **6 cm**

1 cm

2. $P = ?$ **8 cm**

2 cm

3. $P = ?$ **18 cm**

8 cm

1 cm

4. $P = ?$ **22 in.**

2 in.
4 in.
5 in.
3 in.
6 in.

5. $P = ?$ **30 in.**

3 in. 3 in. 3 in. 3 in. 3 in. 3 in. 3 in. 3 in. 3 in. 3 in.

TRY IT

PERIMETER AND AREA — **317** — FIND THE PERIMETER OF OBJECTS

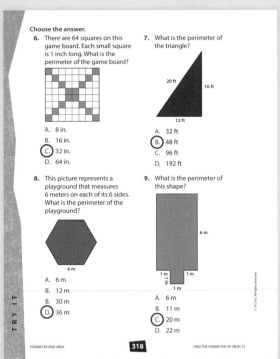

Choose the answer.

6. There are 64 squares on this game board. Each small square is 1 inch long. What is the perimeter of the game board?

A. 8 in.
B. 16 in.
C. 32 in.
D. 64 in.

7. What is the perimeter of the triangle?

20 ft
16 ft
12 ft

A. 32 ft
B. 48 ft
C. 96 ft
D. 192 ft

8. This picture represents a playground that measures 6 meters on each of its 6 sides. What is the perimeter of the playground?

6 m

A. 6 m
B. 12 m
B. 30 m
D. 36 m

9. What is the perimeter of this shape?

6 m
1 m 1 m 1 m
1 m

A. 6 m
B. 11 m
C. 20 m
D. 22 m

TRY IT

PERIMETER AND AREA — **318** — FIND THE PERIMETER OF OBJECTS

ONLINE
10 min

CHECKPOINT

Students will complete an online Checkpoint. If necessary, read the directions, problems, and answer choices to students and help them with keyboard or mouse operations.

Objectives

- Determine the perimeter of a polygon with whole-number side lengths.

Find the Missing Side Length

LEARN Find the Missing Length   20 minutes   **OFFLINE**

▶ Lesson Objectives

Given the whole-number perimeter of a polygon, students will find the whole-number length of an unknown side.

▶ Content Background

Students will find the missing side length of a polygon for two different cases. They will find the missing side length when they are given the perimeter and the lengths of the other sides. Next students will find the side lengths of a regular polygon (all equal sides) when the perimeter is known.

Materials to Gather

SUPPLIED

Find the Missing Length activity page

LEARN Find the Missing Length

OFFLINE
20min

Objectives

- Given the whole-number perimeter of a polygon, students will find the whole-number length of an unknown side.

View or print the Find the Missing Length activity page.

1. Read Problem 1 in the Worked Examples with students.

   Ask: What is the problem asking you to do? Find the missing side length.

   Ask: What information are you given? I am given the perimeter, which is 27 inches. I am also given the lengths of all but 1 side.

   Ask: How can you use the information to find the answer? Add up all of the side lengths that are shown on the polygon. Then subtract that sum from the perimeter.

   Ask: What is the answer? The missing side length is 3 inches.

2. Read Problem 2 in the Worked Examples with students.

   Ask: What is the problem asking you to do? Find the lengths of each side.

   Ask: What information are you given? I know the perimeter, which is 27 centimeters. Also, all the side lengths are equal in an equilateral triangle.

   Ask: How can you use the information to find the answer? Since all side lengths are equal, I can divide 27 by 3 to get the length of each side.

   Ask: What is the answer? The length of each side is 9 centimeters.

3. Have students complete Problems 1–4, referring to the Worked Examples as needed. Students should copy the problems into their Math Notebook as necessary and solve them there.

Find the Missing Side Length
Find the Missing Length

Worked Examples

You can find the missing side length of a polygon if you know the perimeter and the lengths of the other sides.

PROBLEM 1 The perimeter of the polygon is 27 inches. What is the missing side length?

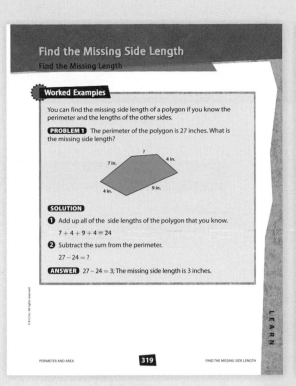

SOLUTION

❶ Add up all of the side lengths of the polygon that you know.

$7 + 4 + 9 + 4 = 24$

❷ Subtract the sum from the perimeter.

$27 - 24 = ?$

ANSWER $27 - 24 = 3$; The missing side length is 3 inches.

L E A R N

You can find the length of a side of a regular polygon when you know the perimeter.

PROBLEM 2 The perimeter of the equilateral triangle is 27 centimeters. What is the length of each side?

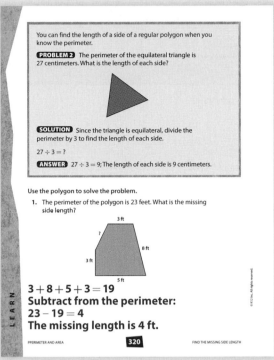

SOLUTION Since the triangle is equilateral, divide the perimeter by 3 to find the length of each side.

$27 \div 3 = ?$

ANSWER $27 \div 3 = 9$; The length of each side is 9 centimeters.

Use the polygon to solve the problem.

1. The perimeter of the polygon is 23 feet. What is the missing side length?

3 ft

?

8 ft

3 ft

5 ft

$3 + 8 + 5 + 3 = 19$
Subtract from the perimeter:
$23 - 19 = 4$
The missing length is 4 ft.

L E A R N

---

2. The perimeter of the pentagon is 35 inches. All sides are the same length. What is the length of each side?

7 in.

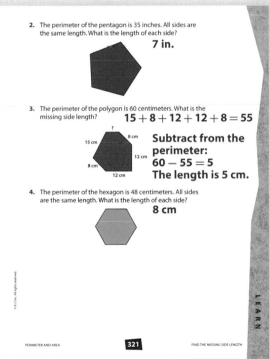

3. The perimeter of the polygon is 60 centimeters. What is the missing side length?

$15 + 8 + 12 + 12 + 8 = 55$

?

8 cm

15 cm

12 cm

8 cm

12 cm

Subtract from the perimeter:
$60 - 55 = 5$
The length is 5 cm.

4. The perimeter of the hexagon is 48 centimeters. All sides are the same length. What is the length of each side?

8 cm

L E A R N

Find Unknown Lengths of Real Objects

LEARN Find Everyday Side Lengths | 20 minutes | **OFFLINE**

▶ Lesson Objectives

Given the perimeter of an everyday object in a story problem, find the whole-number length of an unknown side.

▶ Content Background

Students will learn how to find missing side lengths of everyday objects, when given the perimeter.

Materials to Gather

SUPPLIED

Find Everyday Side Lengths
   activity page

LEARN Find Everyday Side Lengths

OFFLINE
20min

View or print the Find Everyday Side Lengths activity page.

1. Read the Worked Example with students.

   Ask: What is the problem asking you to do? Find the missing side length of the corkboard.

   Ask: What information is given in the problem? The perimeter is 10 feet, and the length of the top side is 3 feet.

   Ask: What sides of the corkboard have the same length? The top and bottom sides have the same length of 3 feet. The left and right sides also have the same length because the corkboard is a rectangle.

   Ask: How can you use the perimeter to find the answer? Subtract the top and bottom side lengths from the perimeter. Then divide the result by 2 to find the missing side length.

   Ask: What is the answer to the problem? The missing side length is 2 feet.

2. Have students complete Problems 1–4, referring to the Worked Example as needed. Students should copy the problems into their Math Notebook as necessary and solve them there.

Objectives

- Given the perimeter of an everyday object in a story problem, find the whole-number length of an unknown side.

Tips

Rectangles always have two pairs of sides with equal lengths.

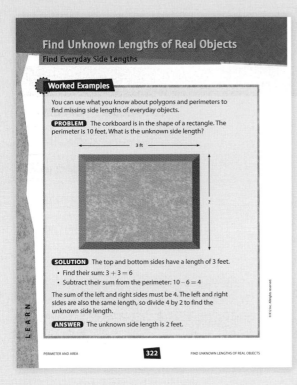

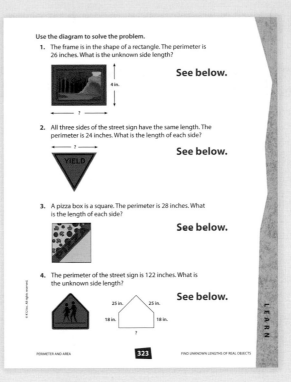

Answers

1. Add the known sides: $4 + 4 = 8$
    Subtract from the perimeter: $26 - 8 = 18$
    Divide to find the missing side length: $18 \div 2 = 9$
    The unknown side length is 9 in.

2. $24 \div 3 = 8$
    The length of each side is 8 in.

3. $28 \div 4 = 7$
    The length of each side is 7 in.

4. Add the known sides: $18 + 25 + 25 + 18 = 86$
    Subtract from the perimeter: $122 - 86 = 36$
    The length is 36 in.

Rectangular Area

GET READY Perimeter and the Area Model	10 minutes	OFFLINE
LEARN Geoboard Shapes and Area	20 minutes	ONLINE
LEARN Grid-Paper Story Problems	10 minutes	OFFLINE
TRY IT Area Story Problems	10 minutes	OFFLINE
CHECKPOINT	10 minutes	ONLINE

▶ Lesson Objectives

Use multiplication or division to solve a story problem involving rectangular area.

▶ Prerequisite Skills

Use an area model to explain multiplication.

▶ Content Background

Students will learn that area is the measure of the space inside two-dimensional figures. They'll learn that area is measured in square units. They will will use multiplication or division to solve story problems involving rectangular area.

Students will explore the area of rectangular shapes. They will see that the units of measure used to determine the length of a side of a rectangle can be used to create square units. They will also see that the area of a rectangle can be described by counting the square units. After counting units, students should recognize that it's easier to count the number of rows and the number of squares in each row and multiply those values. Students will not use a particular rule or formula to find area. Instead they will use their mathematical understanding to create their own strategy. Be sure they understand that area is measured in square units. Students need to understand that saying "the rectangle has an area of 20" has no meaning unless the units are identified, such as 20 square miles, 20 square inches, or 20 of another square unit.

▶ Common Errors and Misconceptions

- Students might think of all measurements as length. For example, they might perceive area as a distance—something that they can measure with a ruler. Consequently, they often measure the perimeter (the path around the figure).
- Students might believe that although the units of measure should be identical, it doesn't matter if they do not completely cover a region. As a result, they may overcount square units.

Materials to Gather

SUPPLIED

blocks – E (all)

Inch Grid Paper (printout)

Grid-Paper Story Problems activity page

Area Story Problems activity page

ALSO NEEDED

index card – 3 in. by 5 in.

▶ Advance Preparation

Print the Inch Grid Paper.

For the Get Ready: Perimeter and the Area Model activity, gather a 3 in. by 5 in. index card. The size is important because the card will be covered by an exact number of blocks.

GET READY Perimeter and the Area Model

OFFLINE 10 min

Students will review the concept of area that they learned with the area model of multiplication and will identify the difference between area and perimeter.
Gather the index card and the blocks.

1. Tell students that they have determined the perimeter of an object and now they are going to study area.

2. Give students the index card. Ask them to trace the perimeter of the card with their finger. They should run their finger around the rim of the card. Remind students that *perimeter* has the word *rim* in it.

3. Explain that the space on the surface of the card is called the *area*. Have students flatten their hand and rub it over the surface of the card. Have them write **area** on the card and then lightly shade the card with a pencil.

4. Have students look at a table and identify its perimeter by tracing their finger around the edge. Have them rub their hands across the surface of the table to identify the area.

5. Choose another flat surface that has a different area from the table. Have students use their finger to go around the perimeter of the second surface and use their hands to go over the area. Ask them which surface has a greater area and how they know. Students will probably say that there is more space on one surface than the other.

6. Remind students that they measure perimeter in straight units, called *linear units*. Tell them that inches and feet are examples of linear units. Explain that they need a way to measure area so they can describe the flat surface of an object.

   Say: You can't measure area in inches or units because that will only tell how long or wide something is. Instead, you need to use square units to measure area.

7. Have students use their square blocks to completely cover the index card. Guide students to fit the square blocks against each other so no part of the index card is showing.

   Ask: How many square blocks does it take to cover the index card?
   15 square blocks

8. Have students look at the square blocks covering the card. Ask them to explain what multiplication sentence is shown by the square blocks.
   Students should recognize that the square blocks show 3 rows of 5 or $3 \times 5 = 15$ (or 5 rows of 3 or $5 \times 3 = 15$).

   Say: Since each square block has a length and width of 1 inch, you say that each square is 1 square inch. You can use square inches as a unit of measure and say that the area of the card is 15 square inches. You can write 15 sq in. as an abbreviation.

   Have students write **15 square inches** on one side of the card and **15 sq in.** on the other.

Objectives

- Use an area model to explain multiplication.

Tips

Write the two multiplication sentences and have students explain how each matches the arrangement of squares covering the index card.

LEARN Geoboard Shapes and Area

Students will use the Geoboard Learning Tool to explore the area of rectangular shapes. They will recognize that area is measured in square units. They'll also explore the perimeter of rectangular shapes.

DIRECTIONS FOR USING THE GEOBOARD LEARNING TOOL

1. Click Lesson Mode. If necessary, click Menu and Help to review the instructions for the learning tool.

2. Have students use the Geoboard to create the smallest possible square, as shown here. Ask them to identify the perimeter of the square. 4 units

    Explain that area is a measure of the number of square units inside a shape or an object. Point out that the rubber band surrounds one square, so the area of the square is 1 square unit. Explain that on the Geoboard, the rubber bands show the perimeter and the squares inside show the area.

    Say: This square has a perimeter of 4 units and an area of 1 square unit.

3. Explain to students that for this activity, they will be working with shapes that have only lines that go up and down or sideways (vertical or horizontal lines). They will not create shapes with diagonal lines. Ask students to make a rectangle with an area of 3 square units. Guide them to use additional rubber bands to outline each square and show that the area is exactly 3 square units.

4. Have students make rectangular shapes with the following areas:
    - 8 square units
    - 12 square units

    Students should outline the square units in each figure and count to find the area.

5. Have students make larger rectangular shapes with the following areas:
    - 15 square units
    - 18 square units

    This time, encourage students to outline groups of squares, such as rows or columns. For example, they might show an area of 18 as a 3 by 6 rectangle. They could then use additional rubber bands to show 3 rows of 6, proving that there are 18 square units in the shape.

6. Have students explain the area and perimeter of one of their shapes. Encourage them to use their finger to go around the perimeter and their hand to move over the surface to show area.

7. Present the following story problem:
    - Winnie has 18 tiles. Show two different shapes that Winnie can make with the 18 tiles.

    Have students find both the area and perimeter of each shape. Help them recognize that 18 tiles will always have an area of 18, but the perimeter can change, depending on how the tiles are arranged.

Objectives

- Use multiplication or division to solve a story problem involving rectangular area.

Tips

If students have difficulty working with the Geoboard Learning Tool, have them draw the shapes on grid paper, shading squares as they count to find the area.

8. Have students create a complex shape. Guide them to use only vertical and horizontal lines, not diagonal lines. Tell students that their shape is the floor plan of a room that needs to be tiled. Have them use additional rubber bands to break the shape into rectangles to find the area. Students may shade areas by clicking a rubber band and then clicking a color.

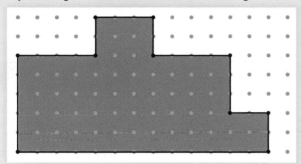

Encourage students to share any shortcuts they may have discovered for finding area. Students should begin to realize that they can count the number of squares in a row and then multiply by the number of rows to more quickly find the area of a rectangular section of a shape.

9. Have students follow these steps to check the area and perimeter they recorded:

- Click the rubber band that goes entirely around the figure.
- Click the yellow ruler button to see the lengths of the sides.
- Add all the lengths.
- Click Show Info to confirm their calculations and get more information on the shape.

10. Click Hide Info and turn off the yellow ruler. Have students find the area and perimeter of the entire Geoboard. Discuss with students how they might use shortcuts of repeated addition or multiplication to find the area. Have them count or calculate first and then check, using the Show Info button.

11. Have students use the Geoboard to solve the following problem:

- Alexander has some big tiles to make a giant game board. He has 63 tiles, and he wants his game board to be a rectangle that is 9 tiles wide. How long can he make his board? 7 tiles long

Ask students how they found their answer. Some will have counted by 9s, extending their rectangle until it had 63 squares. Some will have thought, "9 times what number equals 63?" or "63 divided by 9 equals what number?" Both of these methods work, but as the numbers in problems become greater, it is important for students to understand that they can divide the area by one dimension to get the other dimension.

12. Have students solve the following problem and explain how they found their answer:

- Serena has 45 squares of carpet for the hallway of a dollhouse. If she places the squares 3 across, how many squares long will the carpeting be? 15 squares long

LEARN Grid-Paper Story Problems

Students will use multiplication or division to solve story problems involving rectangular area. Gather the Inch Grid Paper and the blocks. View or print the Grid-Paper Story Problems activity page and read the directions with students.

Students should copy the problems from the Activity Book into their Math Notebook as necessary and solve them there.

1. Direct students' attention to the Worked Example. Go through each step together.

2. Have students read the story problem for Problems 1–3. Explain that each square on the grid represents 1 foot by 1 foot, which is 1 square foot.

3. Have students answer Problems 1 and 2. Point out the length and width labels next to the grid. Students can confirm the dimensions by counting the number of squares. Remind them that the grid is similar to an area model used for multiplication.

4. Discuss how finding the area of the tree house floor will help students determine how many square feet of carpet Megan needs. Have students describe different ways they might find the area. Guide them to use multiplication to find the area of the rectangle. Tell them that they should express their answer in square feet because area is measured in square units.

5. Have students read the story problem for Problems 4 and 5. Ask them how they can solve the problem. Guide them to see that finding the area of the wall decoration will tell them how many tiles are needed because each tile is 1 square inch.

6. Talk with students about how the grid can be divided into more than one rectangle. Have them use the given dimensions to find the area of the different rectangles. Encourage them to divide the grid in whatever way they find easiest. Then guide them to add the areas to determine the total area of the wall decoration. Tell students that no matter how the area was divided into rectangles, the total area will always be 54 square inches. Have students answer Problems 4 and 5.

7. Have students read Problem 6. Compare this problem to the Worked Example. Tell students that they need to find the area of the couch shown by the shaded L shape. Guide them to divide the L shape into two different rectangles, find the area of each rectangle, and then find the total area.

8. Have students read Problem 7. Have them use the grid paper and the square blocks to solve this problem. Guide them to choose 32 squares and arrange 4 in a row on the grid paper. Students can place the remaining squares in rows of 4 to determine how many concrete tiles in length the walkway will be.

9. Discuss with students how they can solve Problem 7 using division. Guide them to see that 32 divided by 4 equals 8.

10. Have students solve Problem 8 using division. They can use the squares to check their answer.

• Use multiplication or division to solve a story problem involving rectangular area.

Tips

By default, many printers scale documents to fit to a printable area. Be sure to turn off page scaling so that documents print at 100% of their intended size.

Rectangular Area
Grid-Paper Story Problems

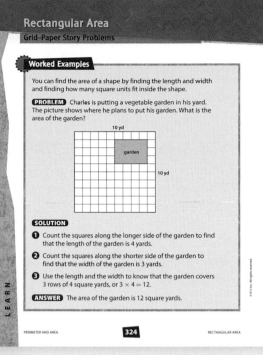

Worked Examples

You can find the area of a shape by finding the length and width and finding how many square units fit inside the shape.

PROBLEM Charles is putting a vegetable garden in his yard. The picture shows where he plans to put his garden. What is the area of the garden?

10 yd

garden

10 yd

SOLUTION

❶ Count the squares along the longer side of the garden to find that the length of the garden is 4 yards.

❷ Count the squares along the shorter side of the garden to find that the width of the garden is 3 yards.

❸ Use the length and the width to know that the garden covers 3 rows of 4 square yards, or 3 × 4 = 12.

ANSWER The area of the garden is 12 square yards.

PERIMETER AND AREA   **324**   RECTANGULAR AREA

Use this story problem to solve Problems 1–3.

Megan wants to carpet the floor of her tree house. The size of the floor is shown in the grid.

5 ft

length   7 ft

width

1. How many feet wide is the floor? **5 ft**

2. How many feet long is the floor? **7 ft**

3. How many square feet of carpet will Megan need? **35 sq ft**

Use this story problem to solve Problems 4 and 5.

Mrs. Parker wants to decorate part of a wall with tiles. The tiles are each 1 inch square. The grid shows the size of the area to be covered.

3 in.

4 in.

4. What is the area of each of the different rectangles?
   Sample answer: 42 sq in.; 12 sq in.

5. How many tiles will Mrs. Parker need? **54**

PERIMETER AND AREA   **325**   RECTANGULAR AREA

Solve.

6. This picture shows where the couch is in Johnny's living room.

   What is the area of the couch?
   24 sq ft

   15 ft

   couch

   10 ft

7. Patrick has 32 concrete blocks to make a walkway. If he makes the walkway 4 blocks wide, how long can he make the walkway? **8 blocks long**

8. Quinn has 27 tiles to use on the wall behind her sink. She wants to put 9 tiles in each row. How many rows of tiles can she make? **3**

PERIMETER AND AREA   **326**   RECTANGULAR AREA

TRY IT Area Story Problems

Objectives

- Use multiplication or division to solve a story problem involving rectangular area.

Students will practice using multiplication or division to solve story problems involving rectangular area. View or print the Area Story Problems activity page and read the directions with students.

Students should copy the problems from the Activity Book into their Math Notebook as necessary and solve them there.

Tips Allow students to use grid paper and squares to solve Problems 5, 7, and 8.

Rectangular Area
Area Story Problems

Use this story problem to solve Problems 1–3.

Mr. Jacoby wants to cover the playground shown here with rubber tiles. The rubber tiles are each 1 foot square.

15 ft

8 ft

Mr. Jacoby's playground

1. How many squares wide is the playground? (The shorter side is the width.) **8**

2. How many squares long is the playground? (The longer side is the length.) **15**

3. How many tiles will Mr. Jacoby need? **120**

Solve.

4. Ron put a desk in his bedroom. The picture shows where he put the desk.

What is the area of the desk? **16 sq ft**

10 ft Ron's desk

8 ft

TRY IT

Solve.

5. Gloria has 24 cork squares to make into a rectangular-shaped tack board. If she makes the board 6 squares long, how wide will the board be? **4 squares wide**

6. Seth used square patio blocks to make his patio. Each block was 1 foot long and 1 foot wide.

What is the area of Seth's patio?

22 sq ft

7. Aaron is making a rectangular patio in his yard. He has 36 square patio stones. Each stone is 1 foot by 1 foot. He wants to make his patio 9 feet long (or 9 stones long).

How wide will the patio be if Aaron uses all the stones? **4 ft**

9 ft

8. Kenta wants to arrange 20 stickers into a rectangular shape. Each sticker is 1 inch long and 1 inch wide. He wants to put 5 stickers in each row so the rectangle will be 5 inches long.

How wide will Kenta's rectangle be? **4 in.**

TRY IT

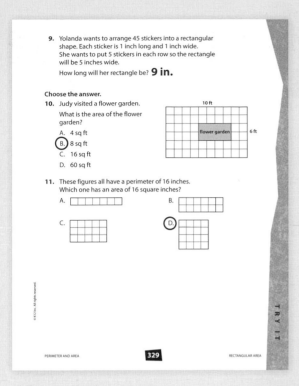

9. Yolanda wants to arrange 45 stickers into a rectangular shape. Each sticker is 1 inch long and 1 inch wide. She wants to put 5 stickers in each row so the rectangle will be 5 inches wide.

   How long will her rectangle be? **9 in.**

Choose the answer.

10. Judy visited a flower garden. What is the area of the flower garden?
    A. 4 sq ft
    B. 8 sq ft
    C. 16 sq ft
    D. 60 sq ft

    10 ft
    flower garden   6 ft

11. These figures all have a perimeter of 16 inches. Which one has an area of 16 square inches?
    A. [figure]
    B. [figure]
    C. [figure]
    D. [figure]

TRY IT

ONLINE
10min

CHECKPOINT

Objectives

Students will complete an online Checkpoint. If necessary, read the directions, problems, and answer choices to students and help them with keyboard or mouse operations.

- Use multiplication or division to solve a story problem involving rectangular area.

Combine and Take Apart Areas

Lesson Overview

GET READY Home Improvement Problems	10 minutes	**ONLINE**
LEARN Find Areas of Complex Figures	20 minutes	**ONLINE**
TRY IT Find the Area	20 minutes	**OFFLINE**
CHECKPOINT	10 minutes	**ONLINE**

▶ Lesson Objectives

- Decompose composite figures formed by rectangles into non-overlapping rectangles to determine the area of the original figure using the additive property of area.
- Define and demonstrate understanding of the area of any plane figure.

▶ Prerequisite Skills

Use multiplication or division to solve a story problem involving rectangular area.

▶ Content Background

Students will use the additive property of area to find the area of a complex figure that can be divided into two or more rectangles or squares.

Students have gained an understanding that area is measured in square units unlike perimeter, which is measured in units of length, or linear units. Students have also learned that simply saying a figure has an "area of 18" is meaningless unless the units are identified, such as 18 square inches (18 square in.), 18 square centimeters (18 square cm), or some other square unit.

When students are introduced to using multiplication to find the area of a rectangle or square, it is helpful if they are able to explain why multiplying the length by the width works. For example, multiplying the number or rows by the number of square units in each row gives the total number of square units. Although this process may seem repetitious, it will help students remember how to use multiplication to determine area because they understand how it is derived.

As students work through this lesson, they will learn how to break apart, or decompose, a complex figure into two or more simpler rectangles or squares. By finding the area of each simpler figure and then finding the sum of those areas, they can determine the area of the original figure. A complex figure often can be broken apart in more than one way, providing different paths for determining the area. Encourage students to look for alternative ways of breaking apart complex figures. Point out that calculating the area of a complex figure in more than one way is a good way to check their answers.

GET READY Home Improvement Problems

ONLINE 10 min

Students will solve story problems involving rectangular area.

Objectives

- Use multiplication or division to solve a story problem involving rectangular area.

LEARN Find Areas of Complex Figures

ONLINE 20 min

Students will use the additive property of area to find the area of a complex figure that can be subdivided into rectangles or squares.

Objectives

- Decompose composite figures formed by rectangles into non-overlapping rectangles to determine the area of the original figure using the additive property of area.
- Define and demonstrate understanding of the area of any plane figure.

TRY IT Find the Area

OFFLINE 20 min

Students will use the additive property of area to find the area of a figure that can be separated into rectangles or squares. View or print the Find the Area activity page. Students should copy the problems into their Math Notebook and solve them there.

Objectives

- Decompose composite figures formed by rectangles into non-overlapping rectangles to determine the area of the original figure using the additive property of area.
- Define and demonstrate understanding of the area of any plane figure.

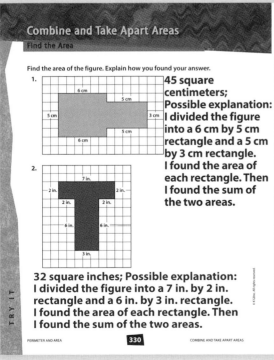

Combine and Take Apart Areas
Find the Area

Find the area of the figure. Explain how you found your answer.

1. **45 square centimeters; Possible explanation: I divided the figure into a 6 cm by 5 cm rectangle and a 5 cm by 3 cm rectangle. I found the area of each rectangle. Then I found the sum of the two areas.**

2. **32 square inches; Possible explanation: I divided the figure into a 7 in. by 2 in. rectangle and a 6 in. by 3 in. rectangle. I found the area of each rectangle. Then I found the sum of the two areas.**

PERIMETER AND AREA 330 COMBINE AND TAKE APART AREAS

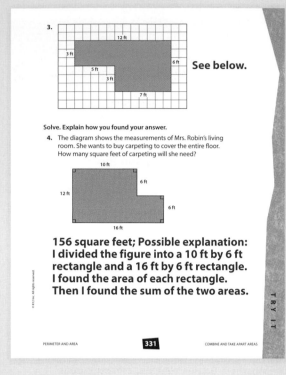

3.

12 ft

3 ft

5 ft

6 ft

3 ft

7 ft

See below.

Solve. Explain how you found your answer.

4. The diagram shows the measurements of Mrs. Robin's living room. She wants to buy carpeting to cover the entire floor. How many square feet of carpeting will she need?

10 ft

6 ft

12 ft

6 ft

16 ft

156 square feet; Possible explanation: I divided the figure into a 10 ft by 6 ft rectangle and a 16 ft by 6 ft rectangle. I found the area of each rectangle. Then I found the sum of the two areas.

T R Y I T

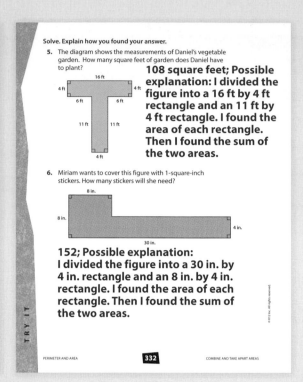

Solve. Explain how you found your answer.

5. The diagram shows the measurements of Daniel's vegetable garden. How many square feet of garden does Daniel have to plant?

16 ft

4 ft

4 ft

6 ft

6 ft

11 ft

11 ft

4 ft

108 square feet; Possible explanation: I divided the figure into a 16 ft by 4 ft rectangle and an 11 ft by 4 ft rectangle. I found the area of each rectangle. Then I found the sum of the two areas.

6. Miriam wants to cover this figure with 1-square-inch stickers. How many stickers will she need?

8 in.

8 in.

4 in.

30 in.

152; Possible explanation: I divided the figure into a 30 in. by 4 in. rectangle and an 8 in. by 4 in. rectangle. I found the area of each rectangle. Then I found the sum of the two areas.

T R Y I T

Additional Answer

3. 57 square feet; **Possible explanation:** I divided the figure into a 12 ft by 3 ft rectangle and a 7 ft by 3 ft rectangle. I found the area of each rectangle. Then I found the sum of the two areas. **Alternative explanation:** I divided the figure into a 7 ft by 6 ft rectangle and a 5 ft by 3 ft rectangle. I found the area of each rectangle. Then I found the sum of the two areas.

ONLINE

10min

CHECKPOINT

Objectives

Students will complete an online Checkpoint. If necessary, read the directions, problems, and answer choices to students and help them with keyboard or mouse operations

- Decompose composite figures formed by rectangles into non-overlapping rectangles to determine the area of the original figure using the additive property of area.

Core Focus
Area and Perimeter Comparisons

Lesson Overview

GET READY Find Area on a Geoboard	5 minutes	ONLINE
LEARN Same Perimeter, Different Areas	15 minutes	OFFLINE
LEARN Same Area, Different Perimeters	15 minutes	OFFLINE
TRY IT Area and Perimeter Problems	15 minutes	OFFLINE
CHECKPOINT	10 minutes	ONLINE

▶ Lesson Objectives

- Demonstrate understanding that rectangles that have the same area can have different perimeters.
- Demonstrate understanding that rectangles that have the same perimeter can have different areas.

▶ Prerequisite Skills

- Determine the perimeter of a polygon with whole-number side lengths.
- Define and demonstrate understanding of the area of any plane figure.
- Use multiplication or division to solve a story problem involving rectangular area.

▶ Content Background

Students will learn that rectangles that have the same area can have different perimeters and that rectangles that have the same perimeter can have different areas.

Students have developed strategies to help them find the perimeter or area of a rectangle or square whose dimensions are known. They have discovered that there is more than one way to find the perimeter or area of a rectangle. The way that students literally see perimeter or area, when given a shape, suggests which method or strategy will make the most sense to them. When they become adept at finding perimeter and area, they will discover that rectangles and squares with the same area can have different perimeters. For example, the four rectangles listed in the table all have the same area (48 square inches), but they have different perimeters.

Materials to Gather

SUPPLIED

color tiles – 50

Inch Grid Paper (printout)

Same Perimeter, Different Areas activity page

Same Area, Different Perimeters activity page

Area and Perimeter Problems activity page

ALSO NEEDED

ruler, inch

RECTANGLES: SAME AREA, DIFFERENT PERIMETERS

Length	Width	Perimeter	Area
48 in.	1 in.	98 in.	48 sq in.
24 in.	2 in.	52 in.	48 sq in.
12 in.	4 in.	32 in.	48 sq in.
8 in.	6 in.	28 in.	48 sq in.

Students will also discover that rectangles and squares with the same perimeter can have different areas. For example, the six rectangles listed in the table have the same perimeter (26 inches), but they all have different areas.

RECTANGLES: SAME PERIMETER, DIFFERENT AREAS

Length	Width	Area	Perimeter
12 in.	1 in.	12 sq in.	26 in.
11 in.	2 in.	22 sq in.	26 in.
10 in.	3 in.	30 sq in.	26 in.
9 in.	4 in.	36 sq in.	26 in.
8 in.	5 in.	40 sq in.	26 in.
7 in.	6 in.	42 sq in.	26 in.

Continue to emphasize that square units are the units for area and linear units are the units for perimeter.

▶ Common Errors and Misconceptions

- Students might think that all rectangles with the same area have the same perimeter.
- Students might think that all rectangles with the same perimeter have the same area.
- Students might think of all measurements as length. For example, they might perceive area as a distance—something that they can measure with a ruler. Consequently, they often measure the perimeter (the path around the figure) instead of multiplying to find the area.
- Students might believe that although the units of measure should be identical, it doesn't matter if they do not completely cover a region.

▶ Advance Preparation

Print several copies of the Inch Grid Paper.

GET READY Find Area on a Geoboard

ONLINE
5min

Objectives

Students will use the online Geoboard Learning Tool to construct a given shape and find the perimeter and area of the shape.

DIRECTIONS FOR USING THE GEOBOARD LEARNING TOOL

1. Click Lesson Mode.
   - Be sure that the ruler and Show info are not clicked.
2. Present the following story problem:
   - Ron cut out a rectangle that is 8 units long and 6 units wide. What is the perimeter of Ron's rectangle?
3. Have students use a rubber band to make the described rectangle on the Geoboard Learning Tool. Guide them to count the space between dots as 1 unit.
4. Have students find the perimeter of the shape by counting the number of linear units around the figure. 28 units

- Determine the perimeter of a polylgon with whole-number side lengths.
- Define and demonstrate understanding of the area of any plane figure.
- Use multiplication or division to solve a story problem involving rectangular area.

Say: The number of units around the shape is the perimeter of the shape. Then have students discuss other strategies they might use to find the perimeter. Add the lengths of the sides. Add the length and width and multiply the sum by 2.

5. Have student find the area of the shape by counting the number of squares inside the figure. 48 square units

    Say: The number of square units inside the shape is the area of the shape.

    Then have students discuss other strategies they might use to find the area. Multiply the number of squares in a row by the number of rows. Multiply the length by the width.

6. Have students use an additional rubber band to make a shape with an area of 36 square units. Remind them that the perimeter measurements are expressed as units and the area measurements are expressed as square units. Students should click Show Info to check their measurements.

7. Click Hide Info and present the following story problem:

    - Ron has a square with sides that are 5 units long. What are the perimeter and area of Ron's square?

8. Have students use the Geoboard Learning Tool to make the described shape and count the units around the shape to find the perimeter. They should find a perimeter of 20 units. Then have students count the squares within the shape to find the area. They should find an area of 25 square units. Students can click Show Info to check their measurements.

LEARN Same Perimeter, Different Areas

Objectives

- Demonstrate understanding that rectangles that have the same perimeter can have different areas.

Students will use 1-inch tiles to make different rectangles or squares with a given perimeter. They may also use 1-inch grid paper to draw the shapes. Students will discover that the rectangles have the same perimeter, but different areas.

Gather the grid paper and color tiles. View or print the Same Perimeter, Different Areas activity page and read the directions with students.

Students should copy the problems from the Activity Book into their Math Notebook as necessary and solve them there.

1. Tell students that the measure of each side of the tile is 1 inch. Ask students to tell you the area of one color tile. 1 square inch

2. Have students look at the Worked Examples. Instruct them to build as many rectangles or squares as possible with a perimeter of 14 inches by counting the 1-inch lengths that form the border.

3. As they build a rectangle with the given perimeter, students should count the number of 1-inch square tiles they used and record this number, or area, in the table. Remind them to record each rectangle one time only. For example, a 4-inch by 3-inch rectangle and a 3-inch by 4-inch rectangle are the same and should be recorded only once.

4. Ask students what generalization they can make about the areas of rectangles and squares that have the same perimeter. Squares and rectangles with the same perimeter can have different areas.

5. Have students complete Problems 1–6. Be available to help them build or draw the shapes and record the data in a table. Allow students to use the Geoboard Learning Tool, square tiles, or grid paper to find perimeters or areas.

Area and Perimeter Comparisons
Same Perimeter, Different Areas

Worked Examples

You can use 1-inch square tiles to build rectangles or squares with the same perimeter but different areas. You can also use 1-inch grid paper to draw rectangles or squares with the same perimeter but different areas. Then you can enter your data in a table to compare the areas of these shapes.

PROBLEM Build or draw rectangles or squares, each with a perimeter of 14 inches. Use the table to help you write the dimensions of each shape. Then write the area of each shape.

Same Perimeter, Different Areas				
Name of shape	Length	Width	Area	Perimeter
Shape 1	? in.	? in.	? sq in.	14 in.
Shape 2	? in.	? in.	? sq in.	14 in.
Shape 3	? in.	? in.	? sq in.	14 in.

SOLUTION

❶ Use the guess-and-test method of problem solving. Estimate how many tiles it will take to build a rectangle or square that has a perimeter of 14 inches. Count out the tiles and build a rectangle or square. You can also draw a rectangle or square on grid paper.

❷ Starting at one corner of your shape, count the 1-inch lengths that form a border completely around the shape, or the perimeter of the shape.

---

❸ If the perimeter of your shape is less than 14 inches, add 1 or more tiles. If the perimeter of your shape is greater than 14 inches, take away 1 or more tiles. Continue this process until you build a rectangle or square with a perimeter of 14 inches.

❹ Record the dimensions of your first shape.

❺ Count the 1-inch square tiles that make up the shape, or the area of the shape. You may also multiply the number of tiles in each row by the number of rows. Record the area of the shape.

❻ Continue to build rectangles that each have a 14-inch perimeter. The dimensions must be different for each shape.

❼ Record the dimensions and areas of each new shape, but do not record a shape twice. For example, a 5-inch by 2-inch rectangle should not also be recorded as a 2-inch by 5-inch rectangle.

ANSWER

Same Perimeter, Different Areas				
Name of shape	Length	Width	Area	Perimeter
Shape 1	6 in.	1 in.	6 sq in.	14 in.
Shape 2	5 in.	2 in.	10 sq in.	14 in.
Shape 3	4 in.	3 in.	12 sq in.	14 in.

Use 1-inch square tiles or 1-inch grid paper to solve the problem.

1. Build or draw rectangles or squares, each with a perimeter of 16 inches. Use the table to record the dimensions of each shape. Then record the area of each shape.

Same Perimeter, Different Areas				
Name of shape	Length	Width	Area	Perimeter
Shape 1	? in.	? in.	? sq in.	16 in.
Shape 2	? in.	? in.	? sq in.	16 in.
Shape 3	? in.	? in.	? sq in.	16 in.
Shape 4	? in.	? in.	? sq in.	16 in.

See next page.

2. Build or draw rectangles or squares, each with a perimeter of 8 inches. Use the table to record the dimensions of each shape. Then record the area of each shape.

Same Perimeter, Different Areas				
Name of shape	Length	Width	Area	Perimeter
Shape 1	? in.	? in.	? sq in.	8 in.
Shape 2	? in.	? in.	? sq in.	8 in.

See next page.

Use this table to answer Problems 3 and 4.

Rectangles: Same Perimeter, Different Areas			
Name of shape	Length	Width	Perimeter
Shape 1	9 in.	1 in.	20 in.
Shape 2	8 in.	2 in.	20 in.
Shape 3	7 in.	3 in.	20 in.
Shape 4	6 in.	4 in.	20 in.
Shape 5	5 in.	5 in.	20 in.

3. Which shape has an area of 24 square inches? Explain your answer. **See next page.**

4. The table shows the dimensions of four rectangles and one square that each have a perimeter of 20 inches. Could you use 1-inch square tiles to build a square with a perimeter of 18 inches? Explain your answer.

See next page.

Solve.

5. A 3-centimeter by 8-centimeter mailing label has a perimeter of 22 centimeters and an area of 24 square centimeters. What are the dimensions of another label that has the same perimeter but a different area? **See next page.**

6. Mr. Liska decides to buy one of the banners listed in the table. Each has a perimeter of 18 feet. Which banner should Mr. Liska choose if he wants one with the greatest area? Explain your answer.

Color of banner	Length	Width	Perimeter
yellow	7 ft	2 ft	18 ft
purple	5 ft	4 ft	18 ft
orange	8 ft	1 ft	18 ft
pink	6 ft	3 ft	18 ft

See next page.

Answers

1. The order of the shapes may vary.

Same Perimeter, Different Areas				
Name of shape	Length	Width	Area	Perimeter
Shape 1	7 in.	1 in.	7 sq in.	**16 in.**
Shape 2	6 in.	2 in.	12. sq in.	**16 in.**
Shape 3	5 in.	3 in.	15 sq in.	**16 in.**
Shape 4	4 in.	4 in.	16 sq in.	**16 in.**

2.

Same Perimeter, Different Areas				
Name of shape	Length	Width	Area	Perimeter
Shape 1	3 in.	1 in.	3 sq in.	**8 in.**
Shape 2	2 in.	2 in.	4 sq in.	**8 in.**

3. Shape 4 has an area of 24 sq in. **Possible explanations:** I multiplied the two lengths to find the area. I used square tiles to make the shapes and then I counted the tiles. Shape 1 has an area of 9 sq in. Shape 2 has an area of 16 sq in. Shape 3 has an area of 21 sq in. Shape 4 has an area of 24 sq in. Shape 5 has an area of 25 sq in.

4. No. The side of each tile represents a whole number length of 1 inch. Since a square has all 4 sides the same length, the perimeter must be divisible by 4.

5. **Sample answers:** 1 cm by 10 cm; 2 cm by 9 cm; 4 cm by 7 cm; 5 cm by 6 cm

6. the purple banner; I multiplied the two measurements to find the areas of each shape. The yellow banner has an area of 14 sq ft. The purple banner has an area of 20 sq ft. The orange banner has an area of 8 sq ft. The pink banner has an area of 18 sq ft. Since 20 > 18 > 14 > 8, Mr. Liska should choose the purple banner.

OFFLINE
15 min

LEARN Same Area, Different Perimeters

Objectives

- Demonstrate understanding that rectangles that have the same area can have different perimeters.

Students will use a specified number of 1-inch square tiles to make different rectangles. They may also use 1-inch grid paper to draw the shapes. Students will discover that the rectangles can have the same area but different perimeters.

Gather the ruler, grid paper, and color tiles. View or print the Same Area, Different Perimeters activity page and read the directions with students. They should copy the problems from the Activity Book into their Math Notebook as necessary and solve them there.

1. Give students one tile and the ruler. Have them measure each side of the tile.

   Ask: How long is each side? 1 inch

   Ask: What unit does the tile represent? 1 square inch

2. Tell students they will build or draw rectangles and squares. Have students look at the Worked Examples. Instruct them to gather the number of tiles listed in the table as the area. Have students build as many rectangles and squares as possible with an area of 16 square inches and then record the lengths of the sides.

3. After students record the lengths of the sides, they should find the perimeter of each shape by counting the 1-inch lengths that form its border. Then they should record the perimeter in the table. Tell them that an 8-inch by 2-inch rectangle and a 2-inch by 8-inch rectangle should be recorded only once.

4. Ask students what generalization they can make about the perimeters of rectangles and squares that have the same area. Squares and rectangles with the same areas can have different perimeters.

5. Have students complete Problems 1–6. Be available to help them build or draw the shapes and record the data in a table. Allow students to use the Geoboard Learning Tool, square tiles, or grid paper to find perimeters or areas.

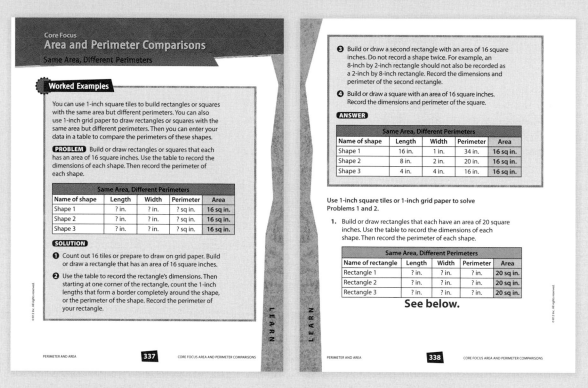

Additional Answers

1. The order of the shapes may vary.

Same Area, Different Perimeters				
Name of rectangle	Length	Width	Perimeter	Area
Rectangle 1	20 in.	1 in.	42 in.	20 sq in.
Rectangle 2	10 in.	2 in.	24 in.	20 sq in.
Rectangle 3	5 in.	4 in.	18 in.	20 sq in.

2. Build or draw a rectangle and a square that each have an area of 25 square inches. Use the table to record the dimensions of each shape. Then record the perimeter of each shape.

Same Area, Different Perimeters				
Name of shape	Length	Width	Perimeter	Area
Shape 1	? in.	? in.	? in.	25 sq in.
Shape 2	? in.	? in.	? in.	25 sq in.

See below.

Use this table to answer Problems 3 and 4.

Rectangles: Same Area, Different Perimeters			
Name of rectangle	Length	Width	Area
Rectangle 1	8 in.	6 in.	48 sq in.
Rectangle 2	12 in.	4 in.	48 sq in.
Rectangle 3	24 in.	2 in.	48 sq in.
Rectangle 4	48 in.	1 in.	48 sq in.

3. Which rectangle has a perimeter of 52 inches? Explain your answer. **See below.**

4. Which rectangle has the greatest perimeter? Explain your answer. **See below.**

Solve.

5. Alexander has a garden that is 5 yards by 6 yards. He wants to make another garden with the same area but different dimensions. Should he make a garden that is 10 yards by 3 yards, or one that is 4 yards by 6 yards? **See below.**

Solve.

6. Rosa has two rectangular rugs in her house. The two rugs have the same area but different perimeters. Which of the following rugs could belong to Rosa? Explain your answer.

Color of rug	Length	Width
blue	5 ft	4 ft
red	9 ft	2 ft
green	8 ft	2 ft
black	6 ft	3 ft

The red rug and the black rug; I found the areas of the rugs by multiplying the measurements of the two sides. I found the perimeters of the rugs by adding the lengths of all 4 sides. The red rug has an area of 18 sq ft and a perimeter of 22 ft. The black rug has an area of 18 sq ft and a perimeter of 18 ft. Both the red rug and the black rug could belong to Rosa.

Additional Answers

2.

Same Area, Different Perimeters				
Name of shape	Length	Width	Perimeter	Area
Shape 1	25 in.	1 in.	52 in.	25 sq in.
Shape 2	5 in.	5 in.	20 in.	25 sq in.

3. Rectangle 3; I added the lengths of all 4 sides of each rectangle to find their perimeters. Below I have shown how I know that Rectangle 3 has a 52-inch perimeter.

length = 24 and width = 2

24 + 24 + 2 + 2 = 52

Rectangle 3 has a perimeter of 52 inches.

4. Rectangle 4; I added the lengths of all 4 sides of each rectangle to find their perimeters. Rectangle 1 had a 28-inch perimeter. Rectangle 2 had a 32-inch perimeter. Rectangle 3 had a 52-inch perimeter. Rectangle 4 had a 98-inch perimeter. Since 98 > 52 > 32 > 28, Rectangle 4 has the greatest perimeter.

5. a garden that is 10 yards by 3 yards; A garden 10 yards by 3 yards has the same area as a garden 5 yards by 6 yards, but a garden 4 yards by 6 yards does not have the same area.

TRY IT Area and Perimeter Problems

OFFLINE
15 min

Objectives

Students will practice identifying similarities and differences in area and perimeter of various rectangles and squares. Gather the grid paper. View or print the Area and Perimeter Problems activity page and read the directions with students.

Students should copy the problems from the Activity Book into their Math Notebook as necessary and solve them there.

Tips If students have difficulty drawing rectangles on grid paper, allow them to build the rectangles with color tiles.

- Demonstrate understanding that rectangles that have the same area can have different perimeters.
- Demonstrate understanding that rectangles that have the same perimeter can have different areas.

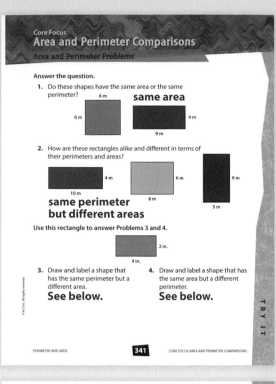

Area and Perimeter Comparisons
Area and Perimeter Problems

Answer the question.

1. Do these shapes have the same area or the same perimeter?

same area

6 m · 6 m | 4 m · 9 m

2. How are these rectangles alike and different in terms of their perimeters and areas?

4 m · 10 m | 6 m · 8 m | 9 m · 5 m

same perimeter but different areas

Use this rectangle to answer Problems 3 and 4.

2 in. · 4 in.

3. Draw and label a shape that has the same perimeter but a different area.
See below.

4. Draw and label a shape that has the same area but a different perimeter.
See below.

TRY IT

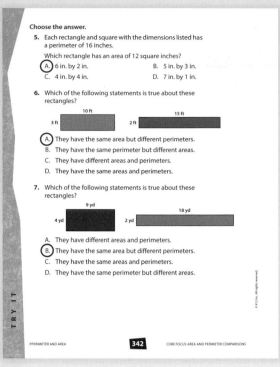

Choose the answer.

5. Each rectangle and square with the dimensions listed has a perimeter of 16 inches.

Which rectangle has an area of 12 square inches?
- (A.) 6 in. by 2 in.
- B. 5 in. by 3 in.
- C. 4 in. by 4 in.
- D. 7 in. by 1 in.

6. Which of the following statements is true about these rectangles?

3 ft · 10 ft | 2 ft · 15 ft

- (A.) They have the same area but different perimeters.
- B. They have the same perimeter but different areas.
- C. They have different areas and perimeters.
- D. They have the same areas and perimeters.

7. Which of the following statements is true about these rectangles?

4 yd · 9 yd | 2 yd · 18 yd

- A. They have different areas and perimeters.
- (B.) They have the same area but different perimeters.
- C. They have the same areas and perimeters.
- D. They have the same perimeter but different areas.

TRY IT

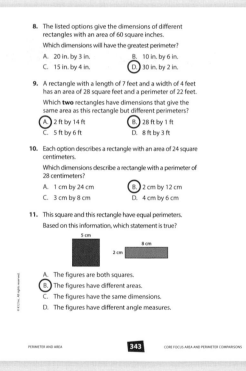

8. The listed options give the dimensions of different rectangles with an area of 60 square inches.

Which dimensions will have the greatest perimeter?
- A. 20 in. by 3 in.
- B. 10 in. by 6 in.
- C. 15 in. by 4 in.
- (D.) 30 in. by 2 in.

9. A rectangle with a length of 7 feet and a width of 4 feet has an area of 28 square feet and a perimeter of 22 feet.

Which **two** rectangles have dimensions that give the same area as this rectangle but different perimeters?
- (A.) 2 ft by 14 ft
- (B.) 28 ft by 1 ft
- C. 5 ft by 6 ft
- D. 8 ft by 3 ft

10. Each option describes a rectangle with an area of 24 square centimeters.

Which dimensions describe a rectangle with a perimeter of 28 centimeters?
- A. 1 cm by 24 cm
- (B.) 2 cm by 12 cm
- C. 3 cm by 8 cm
- D. 4 cm by 6 cm

11. This square and this rectangle have equal perimeters.

Based on this information, which statement is true?

5 cm | 8 cm · 2 cm

- A. The figures are both squares.
- (B.) The figures have different areas.
- C. The figures have the same dimensions.
- D. The figures have different angle measures.

TRY IT

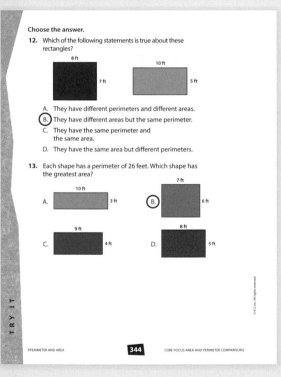

Choose the answer.

12. Which of the following statements is true about these rectangles?

8 ft · 7 ft | 10 ft · 5 ft

- A. They have different perimeters and different areas.
- (B.) They have different areas but the same perimeter.
- C. They have the same perimeter and the same area.
- D. They have the same area but different perimeters.

13. Each shape has a perimeter of 26 feet. Which shape has the greatest area?

- A. 10 ft · 3 ft
- (B.) 7 ft · 6 ft
- C. 9 ft · 4 ft
- D. 8 ft · 5 ft

TRY IT

Additional Answers
3. Shapes will vary. **Sample answer:**

1 in. · 5 in.

4. Shapes will vary. **Sample answer:**

1 in. · 8 in.

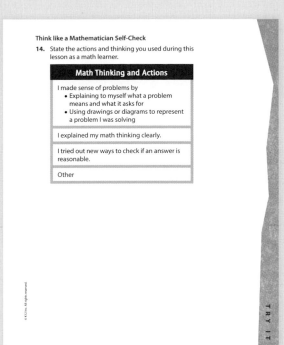

CHECKPOINT

ONLINE
10min

Students will complete an online Checkpoint. If necessary, read the directions, problems, and answer choices to students and help them with keyboard or mouse operations.

Objectives

• Demonstrate understanding that rectangles that have the same area can have different perimeters.

• Demonstrate understanding that rectangles that have the same perimeter can have different areas.

Unit Review

Lesson Overview

UNIT REVIEW Look Back	10 minutes	**ONLINE**
UNIT REVIEW Checkpoint Practice	50 minutes	**ONLINE**
⏩ **UNIT REVIEW** Prepare for the Checkpoint		

▶ Unit Objectives:

- Determine the perimeter of a polygon with whole-number side lengths.
- Given the whole-number perimeter of a polygon, students will find the whole-number length of an unknown side.
- Given the perimeter of an everyday object in a story problem, find the whole-number length of an unknown side.
- Decompose composite figures formed by rectangles into non-overlapping rectangles to determine the area of the original figure using the additive property of area.
- Use multiplication or division to solve a story problem involving rectangular area.
- Define and demonstrate understanding of the area of any plane figure.
- Demonstrate understanding that rectangles that have the same area can have different perimeters.
- Demonstrate understanding that rectangles that have the same perimeter can have different areas.

▶ Advance Preparation

In this lesson, students will have an opportunity to review previous activities in the Perimeter and Area unit. Look at the suggested activities in Unit Review: Prepare for the Checkpoint online and gather any needed materials.

Materials to Gather

There are no materials to gather for this lesson.

ONLINE

10min

UNIT REVIEW Look Back

Students will review key concepts from the unit to prepare for the Unit Checkpoint.

Objectives

- Review unit objectives.

ONLINE

50min

- Review unit objectives.

Students will complete an online Checkpoint Practice to prepare for the Unit Checkpoint. If necessary, read the directions, problems, and answer choices to students. Have students answer the problems on their own. Review any missed problems with students.

⤏ UNIT REVIEW Prepare for the Checkpoint

What you do next depends on how students performed in the previous activity, Unit Review: Checkpoint Practice. If students had difficulty with any of the problems, complete the appropriate review activity listed in the table online.

Unit Checkpoint

UNIT CHECKPOINT   60 minutes   **ONLINE**

▶ Unit Objectives

- Determine the perimeter of a polygon with whole-number side lengths.
- Given the whole-number perimeter of a polygon, students will find the whole-number length of an unknown side.
- Given the perimeter of an everyday object in a story problem, find the whole-number length of an unknown side.
- Decompose composite figures formed by rectangles into non-overlapping rectangles to determine the area of the original figure using the additive property of area.
- Use multiplication or division to solve a story problem involving rectangular area.
- Define and demonstrate understanding of the area of any plane figure.
- Demonstrate understanding that rectangles that have the same area can have different perimeters.
- Demonstrate understanding that rectangles that have the same perimeter can have different areas.

Materials to Gather

There are no materials to gather for this lesson.

ONLINE
60min

UNIT CHECKPOINT

Objectives

- Assess unit objectives.

Students will complete the Unit Checkpoint online. If necessary, read the directions, problems, and answer choices to students and help them with keyboard or mouse operations.

Extended Problems: Real-World Application

GRADED ASSIGNMENT   60 minutes   **OFFLINE**

▶ Lesson Objectives

- Determine the perimeter of a polygon with whole-number side lengths.
- Estimate or determine the number of squares required to cover the area of a solid figure.
- Given the whole-number perimeter of a polygon, students will find the whole-number length of an unknown side.
- Recognize or generate simple equivalent fractions; limited to fractions with denominators 2, 3, 4, 6, and 8.
- Divide shapes into parts with equal areas.
- Identify rectangles with the same perimeter and different areas.
- Determine the area of irregular figures by finding the area of each rectangle and adding them together.
- Apply mathematical knowledge and skills to evaluate and analyze real-world situations.

Materials to Gather

SUPPLIED

Extended Problems: Real-World Application (printout)

OFFLINE

60min

GRADED ASSIGNMENT

Open the Extended Problems: Real-World Application. Read the directions, problems, and answer choices to students, if necessary.
 You will grade this assignment.

- Students should complete the assignment on their own.
- Students should submit the completed assignment to you.
- Enter the results online.

Objectives

- Apply mathematical knowledge and skills to evaluate and analyze real-world situations.

Semester Review

Lesson Overview

SEMESTER REVIEW Look Back	30 minutes	**ONLINE**
SEMESTER REVIEW Checkpoint Practice	30 minutes	**ONLINE**
➔ **SEMESTER REVIEW** Prepare for the Checkpoint		

▶ Semester Objectives

- Compare and order unit fractions, such as $\frac{1}{4}$, and fractions with like denominators, such as $\frac{2}{6}$ and $\frac{4}{6}$, by using objects or sketches.
- Explain that a fraction can be used to represent the relationship of a part to a whole and a rational number on the number line.
- Write the fraction represented by a drawing that shows parts of a whole or a rational number on the number line.
- Recognize that the comparison of two fractions is only valid if the wholes are identical.
- Determine the answer to a story problem to a specific degree of accuracy, such as hundreds or tens.
- Demonstrate how fractions and whole numbers can be plotted on a number line.
- Solve a unit-conversion story problem by using multiplication or division.
- Determine whether addition, subtraction, multiplication, or division is the appropriate operation to use to solve a story problem and solve the problem.
- Solve a story problem involving two or more operations.
- Use a sketch to represent a fraction.
- Identify whether specific events are certain, likely, unlikely, or impossible.
- Identify and systematically record the possible outcomes for a simple event.
- Summarize and display the results of a probability experiment in a clear and organized way.
- Use the results of a probability experiment to predict future events.
- Identify the appropriate tools for measuring the length of an object.
- Identify the appropriate metric or English units for measuring the length of an object.
- Estimate and measure the length of an object to the nearest centimeter.
- Estimate the length of an object to the nearest $\frac{1}{2}$ inch and measure the length to the nearest $\frac{1}{4}$ inch.
- Tell time to the nearest minute.
- Determine elapsed time to the nearest minute.
- Identify the appropriate tools for measuring liquid volume.
- Identify the appropriate metric and English units for measuring liquid volume.
- Estimate and measure liquid volume to the nearest liter.

Materials to Gather

There are no materials to gather for this lesson.

- Estimate and measure liquid volume to the nearest cup.
- Identify the appropriate tools for measuring the weight or mass of an object.
- Identify the appropriate metric and English units for measuring the weight or mass of an object.
- Estimate and measure the mass of an object to the nearest gram.
- Estimate and measure the weight of an object to the nearest ounce.
- Write a simple unit conversion, such as inches to feet, as an expression or an equation.
- Use a simple unit conversion, such as centimeters to meters, to solve a problem.
- Analyze a story problem by identifying the question, recognizing relevant information, and developing a solution strategy.
- Demonstrate when and how to break a multistep story problem into simpler steps.
- Apply strategies and results from a simpler story problem to either a more complex problem or to a similar problem.
- Explain mathematical reasoning in a story problem by using words, numbers, symbols, charts, graphs, tables, diagrams, or models.
- Explain the advantages of exact answers and approximate answers to story problems.
- Check the accuracy of a calculation in a story problem.
- Determine the perimeter of a polygon with whole-number side lengths.
- Use multiplication or division to solve a story problem involving rectangular area.
- Explain why $\frac{a}{a} = 1$.
- Recognize and determine equivalent fractions.
- Define and demonstrate understanding of the area of any plane figure.
- Demonstrate understanding that rectangles that have the same area can have different perimeters.
- Demonstrate understanding that rectangles that have the same perimeter can have different areas.
- Draw a scaled picture graph to represent a data set with several categories.
- Draw a scaled bar graph to represent a data set with several categories.
- Solve one- and two-step "how many more" and "how many fewer" problems using information presented in scaled bar graphs.
- Collect measurement data and display the data in a line plot.
- Solve word problems involving addition and subtraction of time intervals in minutes.
- Represent problems involving time intervals in minutes on a number-line diagram.
- Given the whole-number perimeter of a polygon, students will find the whole-number length of an unknown side.
- Given the perimeter of an everyday object in a story problem, find the whole-number length of an unknown side.
- Decompose composite figures formed by rectangles into non-overlapping rectangles to determine the area of the original figure using the additive property of area.

▶ Advance Preparation

In this lesson, students will have an opportunity to review previous activities from the semester. Look at the suggested activities in Semester Review: Prepare for the Checkpoint online and be prepared to gather any needed materials.

SEMESTER REVIEW Look Back	ONLINE 30min	Objectives

- Review semester objectives.

As students prepare to complete the semester, they should refresh their knowledge of the math they have learned thus far. You may notice that some of the objectives in the Semester Review are not necessarily included in the Semester Checkpoint. Some of these concepts are particularly important to review in order to be successful with the upcoming topics students will encounter, and others contribute to a greater understanding of the concepts that are being assessed. Therefore, a complete review of the objectives in this lesson is recommended.

To review, students will play a Super Genius game. If students answer a problem incorrectly, the correct answer will display. Be sure to help students understand why the answer is correct before they move on to the next problem. If they miss several problems, have students play the game again.

SEMESTER REVIEW Checkpoint Practice	ONLINE 30min	Objectives

- Review semester objectives.

Students will complete an online Checkpoint Practice to prepare for the Semester Checkpoint. If necessary, read the directions, questions, and answer choices to students. Have students answer the problems on their own. Review any missed problems with students.

⤳ SEMESTER REVIEW Prepare for the Checkpoint

What you do next depends on how students performed in the previous activity, Semester Review: Checkpoint Practice. If students had difficulty with any of the problems, complete the appropriate review activity listed in the table online.

Because there are many concepts to review, consider using the Your Choice day to continue preparing for the Semester Checkpoint.

Semester Checkpoint 1

SEMESTER CHECKPOINT Online   60 minutes   **ONLINE**

▶ Semester Objectives

- Use the order of operations to evaluate an expression.
- Compare and order unit fractions, such as $\frac{1}{4}$, and fractions with like denominators, such as $\frac{2}{6}$ and $\frac{4}{6}$, by using objects or sketches.
- Explain that a fraction can be used to represent the relationship of a part to a whole and a rational number on the number line.
- Write the fraction represented by a drawing that shows parts of a whole or a rational number on the number line.
- Recognize that the comparison of two fractions is only valid if the wholes are identical.
- Determine the answer to a story problem to a specific degree of accuracy, such as hundreds or tens.
- Demonstrate how fractions and whole numbers can be plotted on a number line.
- Solve a unit-conversion story problem by using multiplication or division.
- Create a story problem that can be represented by a division number sentence.
- Determine whether addition, subtraction, multiplication, or division is the appropriate operation to use to solve a story problem and solve the problem.
- Solve a story problem involving two or more operations.
- Use a sketch to represent a fraction.
- Identify whether specific events are certain, likely, unlikely, or impossible.
- Identify and systematically record the possible outcomes for a simple event.
- Summarize and display the results of a probability experiment in a clear and organized way.
- Use the results of a probability experiment to predict future events.
- Identify the appropriate tools for measuring the length of an object.
- Identify the appropriate metric or English units for measuring the length of an object.
- Estimate and measure the length of an object to the nearest centimeter.
- Estimate the length of an object to the nearest $\frac{1}{2}$ inch and measure the length to the nearest $\frac{1}{4}$ inch.
- Tell time to the nearest minute.
- Determine elapsed time to the nearest minute.
- Identify the appropriate tools for measuring liquid volume.
- Identify the appropriate metric and English units for measuring liquid volume.
- Estimate and measure liquid volume to the nearest liter.
- Estimate and measure liquid volume to the nearest cup.

Materials to Gather

There are no materials to gather for this lesson.

- Identify the appropriate tools for measuring the weight or mass of an object.
- Identify the appropriate metric and English units for measuring the weight or mass of an object.
- Estimate and measure the mass of an object to the nearest gram.
- Estimate and measure the weight of an object to the nearest ounce.
- Write a simple unit conversion, such as inches to feet, as an expression or an equation.
- Use a simple unit conversion, such as centimeters to meters, to solve a problem.
- Analyze a story problem by identifying the question, recognizing relevant information, and developing a solution strategy.
- Demonstrate when and how to break a multistep story problem into simpler steps.
- Apply strategies and results from a simpler story problem to either a more complex problem or to a similar problem.
- Explain mathematical reasoning in a story problem by using words, numbers, symbols, charts, graphs, tables, diagrams, or models.
- Explain the advantages of exact answers and approximate answers to story problems.
- Check the accuracy of a calculation in a story problem.
- Determine the perimeter of a polygon with whole-number side lengths.
- Use multiplication or division to solve a story problem involving rectangular area.
- Explain why $\frac{a}{a} = 1$.
- Recognize and determine equivalent fractions.
- Divide a whole number by a fraction to solve a story problem.
- Define and demonstrate understanding of the area of any plane figure.
- Demonstrate understanding that rectangles that have the same area can have different perimeters.
- Demonstrate understanding that rectangles that have the same perimeter can have different areas.
- Draw a scaled picture graph to represent a data set with several categories.
- Draw a scaled bar graph to represent a data set with several categories.
- Solve one- and two-step "how many more" and "how many fewer" problems using information presented in scaled bar graphs.
- Collect measurement data and display the data in a line plot.
- Solve word problems involving addition and subtraction of time intervals in minutes.
- Represent problems involving time intervals in minutes on a number-line diagram.
- Given the whole-number perimeter of a polygon, students will find the whole-number length of an unknown side.
- Given the perimeter of an everyday object in a story problem, find the whole-number length of an unknown side.
- Decompose composite figures formed by rectangles into non-overlapping rectangles to determine the area of the original figure using the additive property of area.

SEMESTER CHECKPOINT Online

Students will complete this part of the Semester Checkpoint online. If necessary, read the directions, problems, and answer choices to students and help them with keyboard or mouse operations.

- Assess semester objectives.

Semester Checkpoint 2

SEMESTER CHECKPOINT Offline | 60 minutes | **OFFLINE**

▶ Semester Objectives

- Determine whether addition, subtraction, multiplication, or division is the appropriate operation to use to solve a story problem and solve the problem.
- Solve a story problem involving two or more operations.
- Explain mathematical reasoning in a story problem by using words, numbers, symbols, charts, graphs, tables, diagrams, or models.
- Compare and order unit fractions, such as $\frac{1}{4}$, and fractions with like denominators, such as $\frac{2}{6}$ and $\frac{4}{6}$, by using objects or sketches.
- Write the fraction represented by a drawing that shows parts of a whole or a rational number on the number line.
- Demonstrate how fractions and whole numbers can be plotted on a number line.
- Draw a scaled bar graph to represent a data set with several categories.
- Solve one- and two-step "how many more" and "how many fewer" problems using information presented in scaled bar graphs.

Materials to Gather

Semester Checkpoint 2 (printout)
Semester Checkpoint 2 Answer Key (printout)

SEMESTER CHECKPOINT Offline

OFFLINE 60 min

Objectives

- Assess semester objectives.

This part of the Semester Checkpoint and its answer key are located in the Resources section for this unit in the Online Book Menu of *Math+ Purple Lesson Guide*. Give students the Semester Checkpoint 2. Have students complete the Semester Checkpoint 2 on their own. Use the answer key to score the Semester Checkpoint 2, and then enter the results online.

Glossary

addend — one of the two or more numbers that are added to find a sum

addition — the process of combining, or putting together, groups of objects or numbers; a mathematical operation

additive property of area — a rule stating that the area of two or more shapes that do not overlap equals the sum of the individual areas of the shapes

algorithm — a step-by-step way to solve a problem

angle — a figure formed by two rays that share the same endpoint; The rays are called the sides of the angle.

angle measure — the measure of degrees that one ray rotates from the other in an angle

approximate (v.) — to estimate an amount or total; to give an approximation or say that an amount is approximately some value

area — the amount of space on a flat surface, most often measured in square units

area model — a model for multiplication that shows the product of two factors as the total number of squares on a rectangular grid; One factor is the number of rows, and the other factor is the number of columns.

array — a pattern of objects or numbers placed in a rectangular formation of rows and columns

associative property — a rule that says no matter how you group three numbers to add them two at a time (or three numbers to multiply), the answer will not change

associative property of multiplication — a rule that says no matter how you group factors to multiply, the product will not change

attributes — characteristics of an object, such as number of sides or types of angles

base — the bottom side or face of a geometric figure

boundary number — the upper or lower limit that is used to round a number to a given place value

capacity — a measure indicating an amount a container can hold

centimeter (cm) — a metric unit used to measure length; $1 \text{ cm} = \frac{1}{100} \text{ m}$

commutative property — a rule that says no matter what order you use to add two numbers (or multiply two numbers), the answer will not change

commutative property of multiplication — a rule that says no matter what order you use to multiply two factors, the product will not change

compare — to determine whether a number is less than, greater than, or equal to another number

cone — a solid figure with a circular base and a curved surface that forms a point, or vertex, at the top

cube — a solid figure with 6 square faces, 8 vertices, and 12 edges

cup (c) — the English, or customary, unit of liquid measure that equals 8 fl oz

cylinder — a solid figure with 2 circular faces that are the same size and have a curved surface between them

data — numerical information that has been gathered

decimal — a number written with a decimal point; sometimes called a decimal fraction

degree — a unit used to measure angles

degree of accuracy — the place value that is to be used to report an answer, such as tens or hundredths

denominator — the number in a fraction that is below the fraction bar

difference — the answer to a subtraction problem

digit — any one of the numerals 0, 1, 2, 3, 4, 5, 6, 7, 8, or 9

distributive property — a rule that says that multiplying a number by a sum gives the same answer as multiplying the number by each addend of the sum and then adding the products

divide — to share equally or group an amount into equal parts

dividend — the number to be divided; The dividend divided by the divisor equals the quotient.

division — an operation to share equally or group an amount into equal parts

division by 1 — the process of dividing a number by 1; The quotient equals the original number.

division symbol (÷) — the symbol that signals division, which is the process of sharing equally or grouping an amount into equal parts

divisor — the number that divides the dividend; The dividend divided by the divisor equals the quotient.

edge — a line segment or curve where two surfaces of a solid figure meet

elapsed time — the amount of time between a beginning time and an ending time

English system of measurement — a system of measurement using such units as inches, feet, and miles for length; quarts and gallons for capacity; and ounces and pounds for weight; This system is sometimes referred to as the customary system.

equal groups — a type of multiplication or division problem that includes groups that each have the same amount or value

equal measures — a type of multiplication or division problem that uses the same measurement, such as centimeters, over and over

equal sharing — a type of division problem that shares among equal groups or creates equal groups; same as equal groups

equals symbol (=) — a symbol between two values that says the values show exactly the same amount

equation — a number sentence; two expressions that are shown as equal to one another

equilateral — having equal sides, such as an equilateral triangle or equilateral pentagon

equilateral triangle — a triangle that has all sides equal in length

equivalent fractions — fractions that name the same amount, such as $\frac{1}{2}$ and $\frac{3}{6}$

equivalent measures — measures that are equal, such as 12 in. and 1 ft

estimate (n.) — a very good guess or rough calculation of an answer when the exact answer is not necessary

estimate (v.) — to make a very good guess or rough calculation of an answer when the exact answer is not necessary

even number — any whole number that has 0, 2, 4, 6, or 8 in the ones place

expanded form — a way to write a number that shows the place value of each of its digits; for example, 543 = 500 + 40 + 3, or 5 hundreds + 4 tens + 3 ones

expression — one or more numbers and symbols that show a certain value, such as 2 + 3, or 3 × ?, or 10 − 4 + 1

face — a flat surface of a solid figure

factor — one of two or more numbers that are multiplied

fluid ounce (fl oz) — the English, or customary, unit of liquid measure that equals $\frac{1}{8}$ c

foot (ft) — the English, or customary, unit for measuring length that equals 12 in.

fraction — a number that shows part of a set, a point on a number line, a part of a whole, a quotient, or a ratio

fraction bar — the line between the numerator and denominator of a fraction that can be read as "divided by"

fractions with like denominators — fractions that have the same denominator

fractions with unlike denominators — fractions that have different denominators

frequency table — a table that shows the number of times pieces of data occur

function — a rule that changes an input number to an output number; For example, the rule "add 3" would change an input of 5 into an output of 8.

gallon (gal) — the English, or customary, unit for measuring capacity that equals 128 fl oz or 4 qt

gram (g) — the basic metric unit of mass

greater-than symbol (>) — a symbol that shows that one amount is greater than another

grid — an arrangement of squares in rows and columns

histogram — a graph with adjoining bars; used to show the frequency of data or data groups

identity property of multiplication — a rule that says that the product of a number and 1 is always the original number

improper fraction — a fraction whose numerator is greater than or equal to its denominator

inch (in.) — the basic English, or customary, unit for measuring length

intersecting lines — lines that cross at one point

inverse operations — opposite operations that undo each other; Subtraction and addition are inverse operations; division and multiplication are inverse operations.

inverse relationship — the relationship between operations that reverse or undo each other; Addition and subtraction have an inverse relationship; multiplication and division have an inverse relationship.

isosceles triangle — a triangle that has at least 2 sides equal in length; An equilateral triangle is a special type of isosceles triangle.

kilogram (kg) — the metric unit for measuring mass that equals 1,000 g

kilometer (km) — the metric unit for measuring distance that equals 1,000 m

less-than symbol (<) — a symbol that shows that one amount is less than another

line — a straight path of points that goes on forever in both directions

linear pattern — a pattern of numbers in which the value of the next number goes up or down by adding or subtracting the same amount each time, such as 3, 6, 9, 12, … or 10, 8, 6, 4, …

line segment — a straight path of points that has endpoints at both ends; also called a segment

liquid volume — the amount of liquid a container will hold; the measure of liquid capacity

liter (L) — the basic metric unit for measuring capacity

mass — the amount of matter in an object; The amount of mass remains the same no matter where the object is, but the weight of an object can change depending on the pull of gravity on the object.

measurement — the use of units to find out a size or quantity

meter (m) — the basic metric unit for measuring length

metric system of measurement — a measurement system with units based on powers of 10

mile (mi) — the English, or customary, unit for measuring distance that equals 5,280 ft

milliliter (mL) — the metric unit for measuring capacity that equal $\frac{1}{1,000}$ L

mixed number — a whole number and a proper fraction that show a single amount

multiple — the product of a given number and any whole number

multiplication — an operation that is a shortcut for adding the same number over and over a certain number of times

multiplication fact family — a set of four related multiplication and division facts that use the same set of three numbers

multiplication facts — the set of multiplication problems with factors of 1 through 10; These problems should be memorized for easy computation.

multiplication symbol (×) — a symbol indicating that factors will be multiplied, as in $4 \times 3 = 12$

multiply — to use the shortcut for adding the same number over and over a certain number of times

number sentence — a math sentence that shows that two expressions are less than, greater than, or equal to one another

numerator — the number in a fraction that is above the fraction bar

odd number — any whole number that has 1, 3, 5, 7, or 9 in the ones place

operation — the process of addition, subtraction, multiplication, or division; More operations will be taught later in math.

order of operations — a set of rules that tells the correct order to use to solve a problem that has more than one operation

ounce (oz) — the basic English, or customary, unit for measuring weight as $\frac{1}{16}$ lb and capacity as $\frac{1}{8}$ c

outcomes — the results that are possible in a probability experiment

parallel — lying in the same flat surface but not intersecting

parallel lines — lines in the same flat surface that never intersect

parallelogram — a quadrilateral with two pairs of parallel sides

parenthesis — a type of grouping symbol used in expressions and equations

partial product — the product of each place value when a multidigit factor is multiplied by a single-digit or multidigit factor; The sum of the partial products is the final product for the problem.

perimeter — the distance around the edge of a shape

pictograph — a picture graph that shows information using picture symbols; The pictograph uses pictures of colored jelly beans to show the number of beans of each color.

pint (pt) — the English, or customary, unit for measuring capacity that equals 16 fl oz or 2 c

place value — the value of a digit depending on its position, or place, in a number

place-value chart — a chart that shows the value of each digit in a number

place-value mat — a mat with columns showing place values (ones, tens…); used with corresponding base-10 blocks

place-value period — a grouping of three digits separated by commas in numbers greater than 999; For example, the number 234,567 has two place-value periods shown.

plane figure — a flat shape with only two dimensions: length and width

polygon — a plane shape made of 3 or more straight sides that separate the inside of the shape from the outside

pound (lb) — the English, or customary, unit for measuring weight that equals 16 oz

predict an outcome — to observe a pattern of events to help determine future events

prism — a solid figure that has two congruent, polygon-shaped bases and other faces that are all rectangles

probability — the branch of mathematics that measures the chances of events happening

product — the answer to a multiplication problem

quadrilateral — a polygon with 4 sides

quart (qt) — the English, or customary, unit for measuring capacity that equals 32 fl oz or 2 pt

quotient — the answer to a division problem; The dividend divided by the divisor equals the quotient.

ray — a straight path of points that has an endpoint at one end and goes on forever from that endpoint

reasonableness — the sense that an answer is correct, given the facts

reasoning — the series of thoughts and steps used to understand a problem, to create a plan of solution, to solve a problem, and to accurately explain the results

rectangle — a parallelogram with four 90° angles; A square is a special type of rectangle.

rectangular prism — a solid figure with 6 faces that are rectangles

rectangular pyramid — a solid figure with a rectangle for a base and triangular side faces that meet in a point, or vertex

regrouping — renaming numbers from one place value to another, such as 1 ten and 3 ones = 13 ones

repeated addition — to add the same addend over and over again

repeated subtraction — a method of dividing by repeatedly subtracting the divisor from the dividend until a value less than the divisor remains

rhombus (plural: rhombuses) — a parallelogram that has all sides equal in length; A square is a special type of rhombus.

right angle — an angle that measures exactly 90°

rotate — to turn a certain number of degrees

round (v.) — to change a number to the nearest place value asked in a problem; For example, rounding 532 to the nearest ten would be 530.

scalene triangle — a triangle that has no sides equal in length

side — one of the line segments of a polygon

side of a polygon — one of the line segments that are the boundaries of a polygon

simplify — to create a value that is equal to the expression but more simple to understand; For example, when you simplify 2×5, you get 10.

skip count — to count by a number other than 1

solid figure — a figure with three dimensions: length, width, and height or depth

sphere — a solid figure that is perfectly round, like a ball

square — a parallelogram that has all sides equal in length and four 90° angles

square unit — a square with sides of a particular side length, such as a square meter, used to measure area

standard form — the usual way of writing a number by using digits

standard unit — a unit that is typically used in measurement, such as inches, centimeters, or kilograms

strategy — a technique used to solve a problem, such as working backward or drawing a diagram

subtraction — the process of taking away objects from a group or finding the difference between two groups; a mathematical operation

sum — the answer to an addition problem

survey — a strategy for collecting data by asking questions of a group of people

symbol — a figure that is used to represent something else, such as $+$ represents plus or addition, or $=$ represents equals

tablespoon (T) — the English, or customary, unit for measuring capacity that equals 3 t, $\frac{1}{2}$ fl oz, or $\frac{1}{16}$ c

teaspoon (t) — the English, or customary, unit for measuring capacity that equals $\frac{1}{3}$ T, $\frac{1}{6}$ fl oz, or $\frac{1}{48}$ c

target number — a number to be rounded to a certain place value

trapezoid — a quadrilateral with exactly one pair of parallel sides

triangular prism — a solid figure with a pair of identical parallel triangular bases joined by rectangular faces

triangular pyramid — a solid figure with a triangle for a base and triangular side faces that meet in a point, or vertex

vertex (plural: vertices) — the common endpoint of the two rays or segments that form an angle less than 180°; The vertex of a 180° angle is any point along the line.

weight — the measure of how heavy an object is, such as 10 lb

whole numbers — zero and the counting numbers (0, 1, 2, 3, 4, 5, 6, and so on)

yard (yd) — the English, or customary, unit for measuring length that equals 36 in. or 3 ft

zero property of multiplication — a rule that says that the product of a number and zero is always zero